marketing
management

THIRD EDITION

Geoff Lancaster / Lester Massingham

McGraw-Hill Publishing Company

ndon · New York · St Louis · San Francisco · Auckland · Bogatá · Caracas · Lisbon · Madrid · Mexico
ontreal · New Delhi · Panama · Paris · San Juan · São Paulo · Singapore · Sidney · Tokyo · Toronto

Published by
McGraw-Hill Publishing Company
Shoppenhangers Road, Maidenhead, Berkshire, SL6 2QL, England
Telephone: 01628 502500
Fax: 01628 770224
Website: www.mcgraw-hill.co.uk

British Library Cataloguing in Publication Data
A catalogue record for this book is available from the British Library

Library of Congress Cataloguing in Publication Data
The LOC data for this book has been applied for and may be obtained from
the Library of Congress, Washington, DC.

Sponsoring Editor	Tim Page
Editorial Assistant	Nicola Wimpory
Marketing Manager	Petra Skytte
Production Editorial Manager	Penny Grose
Desk Editor	Alastair Lindsay

Third Edition   2001

McGraw-Hill
A Division of The **McGraw-Hill** Companies

Cover and text design by Barker/Hilsdon, Dorset, DT7 3TT

Typeset by Mackreth Media Services, Hemel Hempstead
Printed and bound in Great Britain by Bell & Bain Ltd, Glasgow

ISBN 007 709752 1

Brief contents

Detailed contents

Preface and Guided Tour

Now in its third edition, *Marketing Management* has been thoroughly revised and updated so as to continue to meet the needs of undergraduate, postgraduate and MBA students undertaking Marketing Management or Marketing Strategy modules at intermediate or advanced levels.

Retaining the themes of the two previous editions, this text covers the subject of marketing at a strategic level and is very much about managerial decision making in marketing. This edition continues to bring together the most modern thinking in the area of strategic application such as to help marketing decision making to become more systematic. Contemporary thinking and recent developments in the area of strategic application are used in the development of practical strategic marketing plans. New coverage of the Internet and e-marketing has been integrated into the text, and a new chapter on services marketing, together with relationship marketing, has been added.

Pedagogically strengthened, this third edition now includes chapter-opening learning objectives, highlighted key terms, a glossary of key terms with definitions, chapter summaries, and chapter-end review questions.

The examples and illustrations used throughout the text have been chosen for their practical relevance, and include well-known companies such as British Airways, Philips, and Marks & Spencer to name but a few.

Case studies

Completing each chapter is a new mini case study designed to illustrate the practical application of the concepts covered in the chapter. Each study is followed by a question to encourage you to review and apply your knowledge.

Two comprehensive case studies are positioned at the end of the text in an appendix, and are preceded by a section that describes how you should approach and analyse case material. These cases highlight a diverse range of marketing management problems and solutions, illustrating how the key concepts in marketing management can be applied in helping you prepare for examinations based on the case study approach.

Changes to this edition

Here is a summary of the key changes to this edition of the text:

- New chapter on Services Marketing and Relationship marketing
- New integrated coverage of Internet and e-marketing concepts and its rapid growth in marketing management and strategy

- Strengthened pedagogical features, including chapter-opening learning objectives, highlighted key terms, chapter summaries, glossary of key terms with definitions, and references
- New boxed illustrative examples to highlight real-world concepts and techniques
- New mini case studies with questions at the end of each chapter
- New end-of-chapter questions to test your understanding of the main topics
- Specimen answers for the two comprehensive case studies have been made available to lecturers, via the website.

Finally, the text has been re-designed to provide a more open layout, with improved signposting and navigation through each chapter.

To familiarize yourself with the main features of the text, please turn to the Guided Tour on pages xiv-xv.

Teaching and learning resources – new to this edition

For this new edition we have provided a new range of password-protected on-line resources to support lecturers in their teaching, including case teaching notes and PowerPoint slides. Please visit the text's website at http://www.mcgraw-hill.co.uk/textbooks/lancaster.

Acknowledgements

We would like to thank the following academics who took part in the market research and reviewing for this project. They have added enormously to the development of this text.

Aileen Harrison, Oxford Brookes University
Dr G. Fahed, Middlesex University
Mike Flynn, Cheltenham and Gloucester University College
Gill Ross, University of Teesside
Lloyd Harris, Cardiff University

Guided Tour

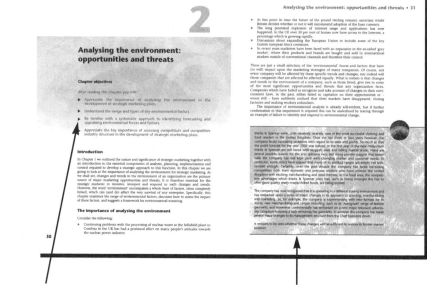

Learning objectives identify the primary topics in terms of the learning outcomes you should achieve after studying each chapter.

Boxed examples provide additional illustrative examples to highlight the practical application of marketing management and to encourage discussion and analysis. These are highlighted with an icon in the margin.

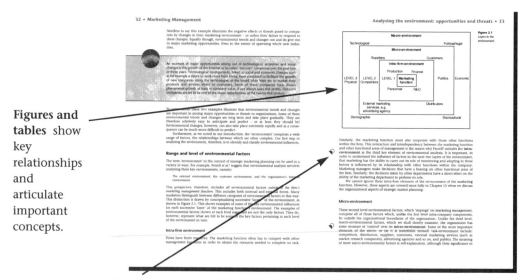

Figures and tables show key relationships and articulate important concepts.

Key terms are highlighted and marked with an icon throughout each chapter, alerting you to a core concept or technique. These are collected and defined in the glossary at the end of the book.

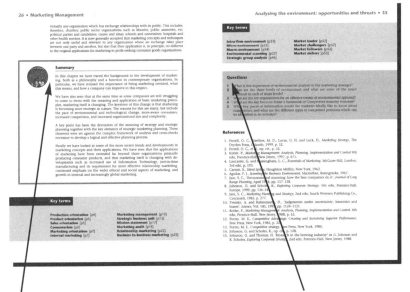

Chapter summaries briefly review and reinforce the main topics covered in each chapter.

Chapter end questions encourage you to test your understanding of the main topics in each chapter and reinforce your knowledge.

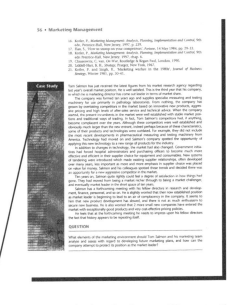

Case studies at the end of each chapter illustrate the relevant issues in each chapter with real world examples.

The development of a strategic approach to marketing

Chapter objectives

After reading this chapter you will:

► Understand the meaning, importance, and the evolution of the marketing concept.

► Appreciate the factors which have given rise to the need for a more strategic approach to marketing management.

► Be familiar with the steps in strategic marketing planning.

► Appreciate some of the contemporary developments in our understanding and application of marketing ideas and their implications for strategic marketing.

Introduction

Very few managers, students of business, shop-floor workers, or increasingly the consuming public itself – in short, anyone involved in one way or another with business and commerce – will have failed to notice the increased attention on, and importance attached to, the subject and practice of marketing. Both academics and practitioners have, over the last 30 years, witnessed at first a gradual and then an increasingly rapid recognition that effective marketing is one of the keystones of organizational success. Having said this, for many companies this recognition has come late – and for some too late! For yet others, its meaning and implications have, even now, not been sufficiently grasped or accepted. Perhaps more importantly is the fact that at the same time as some companies are still struggling to come to terms with the basic concepts and meaning of marketing, markets (and indeed marketing itself) are evolving and changing. With respect to the practice of marketing, the most significant of these changes is that, increasingly, marketing is becoming more strategic in nature.

The significance, meaning and implication of this shift towards a more strategic approach to marketing, together with the concepts, tools and frameworks needed to achieve such an approach, are the subject matter of this text.

In this chapter we aim to outline the background to the need for a newer strategic approach to marketing planning. We also offer an overview of what this entails and some of the key steps and analysis required to develop a strategic marketing approach. Much of this overview is then extended and developed in the chapters which follow.

We have also included a brief discussion of some of the more recent developments in marketing thinking and application together with some of the potential implications of these developments for the marketing manager. Again, many of these recent developments are considered in more detail in later chapters. So, for example, developments in Information Technology and particularly the growth of e-commerce and Internet technologies and applications are considered throughout the text.

We start by tracing the origin, development and meaning of marketing. Many of you may already be familiar with the issues introduced here, but for those who are not familiar with the background to and the meaning of marketing, this section is essential to understanding the second part of the chapter; namely, the factors which have given rise to the growth of strategic marketing.

The origin and development of marketing

As you might expect from a subject and management function which has attracted so much research, so much critical comment, and so much time and effort from those charged with the professional responsibility of managing it, we now have a substantial body of knowledge relating to both the theory and practice of marketing.

Attempting to pinpoint the exact origins of marketing as a business function is virtually impossible, as there is no single, universally agreed definition. The confusion over the exact meaning is demonstrated in the following passage, written by a number of American marketing scholars.

> It has been described by one person or another as a business activity; as a group of related business activities; as a trade phenomenon; as a frame of mind; as a co-ordinative, integrative function in policy making: as a sense of business purpose; as an economic process; as a structure of institutions; as the process of exchanging or transferring ownership of products; as a process of concentration, equalization and dispersion; as the creation of time, place and possession utilities; as a process of demand-supply adjustment; and as many other things.[1]

Marketing, then, tends to mean whatever the user wants it to mean and has, over the years, been the subject of numerous attempts at definition, including the very brief and succinct:

> The function of marketing is the establishment of contact.[2]
> Marketing is the delivery of a standard of living to society.[3]
> ... selling goods that don't come back to the people who do.[4]

A widely accepted UK definition is the one used by the Chartered Institute of Marketing:

> Marketing is the management process which identifies, anticipates and supplies customer requirements efficiently and profitably.

Another definition which captures the essence of what many would agree are the key elements of contemporary marketing thinking and practice is that proposed by Kotler[5], who defines marketing as:

> A social and managerial process by which individuals and groups obtain what they need and want through creating, offering, and exchanging products of value with others.

As has been previously mentioned, the plethora of meanings makes it very difficult to say where and when marketing first began. In its most basic form, i.e. people exchanging goods or services in a reciprocal manner, it has existed for many, many centuries. In fact, Thorelli[6] argues that it began with Adam and Eve. They each concentrated on the tasks of day-to-day living that they performed best, which led to intrahousehold marketing transactions. These, he argues, are analogous to sales and purchases between business units in a modern company. Adam and Eve were the first producers and the first consumers. However, the more sophisticated theories of marketing, such as the marketing concept, are still not fully understood or employed by many of today's less dynamic businesses.

The rudiments of contemporary marketing were discussed as far back as the eighteenth and nineteenth centuries by the theorists such as Adam Smith,[7] known as the father of modern economics, who wrote:

> Consumption is the sole end and purpose of all production and the interests of the producer ought to be attended to, only so far as it may be necessary for promoting that of the consumer.

This statement is very close to the basis of the modern marketing concept, which postulates that the needs and wants of the consumer should be the manufacturers' main concern and that they should only produce what can be sold.

Other early economists who were also aware of the overall function of marketing include Torrens, McCullough, Malthus, James Mill, Ricardo and, later, J. S. Mill, Marshall, Edgworth, and Pigou.

Over the years, marketing can be said to have developed in an evolutionary rather than revolutionary manner, alongside and at the same pace as our economy.

Many centuries ago, when economies were agrarian, the people were mostly self-sufficient. In such economies they grew or caught their own food, built their own houses and tools, and made their own clothes. As time passed, it became evident that some people excelled at certain activities and the concept of the *division of labour* began to emerge. Individuals concentrated on the products they were best at producing which, inevitably, resulted in them making more than they needed for themselves and their families. This laid the foundation for trade. Exchange then began to develop on a simple basis: usually one-to-one trading of products. Trade is at the very heart of marketing. Smith postulated that from the *division of labour* stem the benefits of specialization and the need for more effective means of exchange.

The next step in historical marketing sees small producers making relatively large amounts of goods in anticipation of future demand. This development produces another type of business person – the so-called 'middleman' or agent, who acts as an intermediary between producer and consumer. This go-between is of the utmost importance in a commercial society, as without such a person the right goods cannot be sold to the right people in the right place at the right time. Torrens[8] anticipated this philosophy by more than a century when he wrote:

> Activities designed to make commodities available at either times or places where they are more in demand than at times and places at which they are available at the outset creates wealth or utility just as much as activities designed to change their physical composition.

Torrens thus provided an economic justification for the existence of marketing intermediaries.

McCullough,[9] developing this argument, explained:

> Merchants, or dealers, collect goods in different places in the least expensive manner, and by carrying them in large quantities at a time, they can afford to supply their respective

customers at a cheaper rate than they can supply themselves. ... They also promote the convenience of everyone, and reduce the cost of merchandising to the lowest limit.

The parties involved, i.e. manufacturer, intermediary and buyer, tend to gather together geographically, and thus the trading centres of the world are formed.

As an economy becomes more advanced and sophisticated, so too does its marketing. It can be said therefore that marketing is adopted by a country's business and non-business organizations, depending upon the stage of development of its economy.

According to Stanton,[10] marketing in the USA began with the Industrial Revolution and, consequently, migration to urban centres. As the number of factory workers grew, so too did the service industries to meet their growing needs and those of their families. Marketing was a very basic business activity until the late 1920s, when emphasis was on the growth of manufacturing firms, because demand was, typically, far greater than supply.

Modern marketing in the US began after World War One when 'overproduction' and 'surplus' became commonplace words. Since the late 1920s (with the exception of war and immediate post-war periods) a strong buyer's market has existed in America. There was no difficulty in producing the goods; the problem lay in marketing them.

In tracing the development of marketing within the framework of business practice there are four distinct stages that can be identified:

1 Production orientation.
2 Product orientation.
3 Sales orientation.
4 Marketing orientation.

Brassington and Pettitt[11] summarized the key characteristics and nature of each type of business orientation.

Production orientation

1 Concentrate on increasing production.
2 Anything that can be produced can be sold.
3 Control and reduce costs.
4 Make profit through volume.

The era of **production orientation** occurred in the US from the mid nineteenth century up to the 1940s[12] and was characterized by focussing efforts on producing goods or services. Management efforts were devoted to achieving high production efficiency (mostly by mass production of standard items) thus denying the customer (much) choice.

The production department was the central core of the entire business, with other functions (such as finance, personnel and sales) being of secondary importance. The main philosophy by which production orientated firms operated was that customers would buy whatever goods were available if the price was low enough.

This era is best epitomized by Henry Ford's immortal statement that his customers could have 'any color they wanted as long as it was black'. This old mass production mentality called for producing one car and attempting to adjust everyone's desires and tastes toward wanting the 'Model T' Ford. Henry Ford saw the objective as changing consumer attitudes rather than making what the public wanted in the first place.

Absurd though it may seem, at the time (the US in the 1920s) Ford was correct: there was a demand for cheap private transport and his products were successful. A production orientation to business was suited to an economic climate where the potential demand was greater than the supply.

Product orientation

1 Good quality products 'sell themselves'.
2 Concentrate on improving/controlling quality.
3 More profit through increase in sales due to 'quality products'.

Product orientation, with its emphasis on quality and engineering was predominant in both the US and Western Europe through the 1950s and 1960s. In Britain in particular during this period, the predominant attitude amongst many manufacturing companies was that designing and engineering the 'best' products was all that mattered and that 'sensible' customers would buy those products which had the best engineering. This attitude underpinning the product oriented company proved, for many companies, and indeed in some cases whole industries, to be an unmitigated disaster.

In the late 1950s and early 1960s the once dominant UK motor cycle industry began to lose its share of home and export markets. The challengers were Japanese companies such as Honda and Suzuki. A major reason for the UK marques losing out to these new challengers was that the Japanese products were not taken seriously by the UK producers. The new Japanese machines were considered to be much inferior by British manufacturers with regard to their basic engineering and design. Indeed, it was true that the early Japanese export machines were of much poorer quality and engineering than their British counterparts. However, partly because of this 'inferior' specification, the Japanese machines were much cheaper to buy and run. In addition, they were easier to maintain and came with all sorts of back-up services. The Japanese products also came with features such as electric, rather than kick starts; fairings for protecting the rider from dirt; and innovations such as panniers for carrying shopping – all features which were initially scorned by British motor cycle engineers and designers.

We all now know, however, that from a marketing point of view, the Japanese had got it right. The combination of a much lower engineering specification with its attendant decrease in costs and prices, together with the customer-friendly product design and features meant that customers quickly warmed to the new machines. Within a few years the UK motor cycle industry was decimated. Quite simply, UK manufacturers suffered from being product oriented. Even now there are those who at the time were closely involved in the industry who look back and wonder how such 'inferior' products as the Japanese motor bike could ever have been so successful.

In using the example of motor cycles we are not denying the importance of good design and product engineering backed up by stringent quality assurance and control procedures. In fact, if anything, today's customers are even more interested in quality. However, a problem with the product oriented approach is that not all customers want, or can afford the best quality. More importantly, this orientation leads to a myopic view of the business with a concentration on product engineering rather than on the customers' real needs and the benefits they are seeking.

Sales orientation

1 Emphasis on disposal of stock.
2 Aggressive sales and promotion.
3 Profit through quick sales and volume.[13]

With the emergence of mass production techniques on a large scale in the US and Western Europe, the late 1920s and 1930s saw a shortage of customers rather than of goods. This fall-off in demand led to increased competition and to a number of firms adopting **sales orientation**. Dibb *et al.*[14] describe this particular kind of firm as one where:

the most important marketing activities were personal selling and advertising.

A key issue to management in these circumstances was high levels of output. Here the underlying philosophy was that customers are reluctant and need to be coerced into buying. However, even if the consumers were willing to buy there were now so many potential suppliers that firms had the problem of stiff competition to overcome.

This was the situation in many developed economies in the 1930s: overcapacity accompanied by a fall in demand due to the Depression. It was at this time that many of the 'hard sell' techniques were practised, a great number of which were both dishonest and unethical and which in no small way contributed to the tainted image of salesmen that still exists in the minds of many people today.

Although some firms still practise sales orientation the consumer is protected by law from the more dubious selling techniques. This is largely due to the consumer movement.

Consumerism

The transition from sales to marketing orientation was brought about partly by the advent of consumerism, which forced companies to become more aware of the needs and wants of their customers. **Consumerism** involves the efforts of the public, government and organizational bodies to try to protect the consumer from unscrupulous business practices.

The consumer movement first began in the late 1950s in the US with writers such as Vance Packard challenging the advertising industry; Rachel Carson criticising the business community for its pollution of the environment; and, most famous of all, Ralph Nader's attack on General Motors, whose dubious practices were uncovered and which shocked the public at large.

The role of the US government in consumerism was first set forth in President John F. Kennedy's famous 'Rights' speech:[15]

Additional legislative and administrative action is required, however, if the federal government is to meet its responsibility to consumers in the exercise of their rights. These rights include:

1. The right to safety;
2. The right to be informed;
3. The right to choose; and
4. The right to be heard.

The consumer movement gained popularity somewhat more slowly in the United Kingdom than it had in America. The publication of *Which?* Magazine first brought consumerism to the attention of the British public, with a completely new way of thinking: the consumer did not necessarily have to accept whatever manufacturers produced without question or argument. In the past 20 years or so many governments have shown an increasing concern for consumer affairs, which is reflected in the number of statutes introduced.

It is no coincidence that at consumerism's most powerful and popular time a growing number of companies began to adopt the marketing concept as a way of orientating their businesses.

Marketing orientation

As with the definition of marketing, there are almost as many interpretations of what is meant by our fourth stage in the development of business practices, namely, a **marketing orientation**, as there are writers on the subject. The following represents a small selection of these interpretations.

Michael Baker[16] suggests that one of the distinguishing features of a marketing orientation is, perhaps not surprisingly, its focus on the market place. In the marketing oriented company planning and decision making centre on customers and their needs – albeit that competitors and distributors must also be considered. This reflects the view of most marketing practitioners and experts including Adcock[17], who includes the following as being key indicators of a marketing orientation:

1 Customer is central.
2 Businesses will succeed through satisfying customer needs.
3 The activity of competitors must also be considered.

It is also important to recognize that in the marketing oriented company it is vital to satisfy customer needs through a co-ordinated set of activities, as Ferrell[18] states:

> One of the key aspects of the marketing concept is the coordination of activities.

'Activities' for Aaker refers to the actions and functions of all the employees of the organization, irrespective of the area of the business in which they work. In other words, a marketing orientation requires everyone in an organisation to become customer oriented and not just the marketers. An increasing awareness of this need to co-ordinate and integrate all the various functional areas of a business in delivering customer satisfaction has led to the growth of what is referred to as **internal marketing** in organizations. We shall be considering the nature and importance of internal marketing later in this chapter and again in Chapter 15 when we consider the implementation of strategic marketing.

Finally, Lancaster and Massingham[19] identify the marketing oriented firm as follows:

> A marketing oriented firm produces goods and services that consumers want to buy rather than what the firm wants to make.

When any company moves from a sales to a marketing approach it is not just a case of re-titling the Sales Director as Marketing Director and doubling the advertising budget; it requires a revolution in how a company practises its business activities[17]. When shown in diagrammatic form, as in Figure 1.1 from Lancaster and Jobber,[20] this fact is clarified. This also illustrates the importance of the consumer movement in the transition from a sales to a marketing approach in that marketing orientation stems from customer needs.

In order for a business to be successful, consumers and their needs must be placed at the very centre of business planning.

There is some confusion as to the difference between selling and marketing and they are sometimes thought to be similar. This is a fallacy. Theodore Levitt[21] sums up this distinction between selling and marketing orientation:

Selling focuses on the needs of the seller, marketing on the needs of the buyer. Selling is preoccupied with the seller's need to convert his product into cash; marketing with the idea of satisfying the needs of the customer. ...

Subscribing to a philosophy of marketing, even though an important first step, is not the same as putting that philosophy into practice. Once the framework of the marketing concept has been established the organization must then implement it.

Doubt has been expressed by many marketing authorities as to the extent to which the philosophy underlying the marketing concept has been adequately implemented – the extent to which marketing orientation really exists. The practical manifestations of marketing orientation are not well known and this prompts the question: how can marketing orientation be recognized?

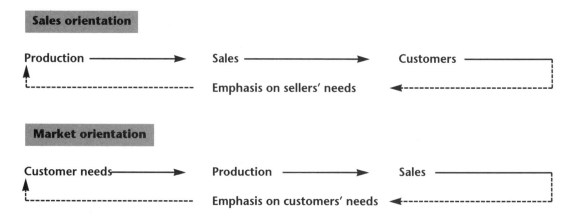

Figure 1.1
The distinction between sales and market orientations.
Source: Jobber, D. and Lancaster, G. A., *Selling and Sales Management,* Pitman, 2000, p. 13.

While it should not be assumed that the following items are in the order of priority, it is intended that they should be seen as constituting a comprehensive list of the requirements that must be met if a move towards marketing orientation within an organization is to be effective.

● Is there a good understanding of the needs, wants and behaviour patterns of targeted customers?
● Is the enterprise profit directed rather than volume driven?
● Does the chief executive see him or herself as the marketing strategist or marketing champion?
● Does the enterprise have a market driven mission?
● Do strategies reflect the realities of the marketplace (including the competitive situation)?
● Is marketing seen as being more important by managers than other functions and orientations?
● Is the enterprise organized in such a way that it can be more responsive to marketing opportunities and threats than its competitors?
● Does it have a well-designed marketing information system?
● Do managers make full use of marketing research inputs in their decision making?
● Are marketing costs and revenues systematically analysed in relation to marketing activities to ensure that the latter are being carried out effectively?
● Is there a strong link between the marketing function and the development of new products and services?
● Does the enterprise employ staff in the marketing area who are marketing professionals (rather than, say, sales orientated in their approach)?

- Is it understood that marketing is the responsibility of the entire organization?
- Are decisions with marketing implications made in a well co-ordinated way and executed in an integrated manner?

Developing marketing orientation is a long-term process and needs to be thought of as a form of investment. To a large extent this investment is in changing the organization's culture so that common values relating to the need to highlight service to customers, a concern for quality in all activities, and so forth, are shared throughout the organization. This is not an appropriate target for the 'quick fix'.

A variety of steps can be taken to enhance the degree of marketing orientation of an enterprise.

- The first step is to secure *top management support*. A bottom-up approach would be doomed from the outset given the company-wide implications of marketing orientation.
- There also needs to be a *specified mission* relating to the development of marketing orientation. This should have a plan associated with it, and the necessary allocation of resources to enable it to be executed.
- A *task force* should be set up as part of the plan to bring together managers from across the company (and consultants, who can help considerably) to carry out tasks such as identifying the current orientation of the company; carrying out a needs analysis as a basis for a management development programme to change the company's culture in a desired way; advising on structural change within the company to support marketing activities; and ensuring commitment to change via the system of rewards (such as bonuses and promotion) that will apply to facilitate change.
- The momentum of change can be maintained by continuously *monitoring marketing performance* to ensure that inertia does not set in. Progress towards improved marketing orientation can be measured by regularly asking questions: 'Are we easy to do business with?'; 'Do we keep our promises?'; 'Do we meet the standards we set?'; and 'Do we work together?'.
- Developing marketing orientation requires *a focus on customers, competitors, the changing environment, and company culture*. Achieving it is an expensive and time-consuming endeavour. However, those companies that really make the effort are likely to have a higher level of marketing effectiveness and greater organizational effectiveness than their competitors. The results may be extremely important amid the greater competitiveness of the new millennium.

Thankfully most companies now understand the meaning and importance of being marketing oriented. However, this understanding is still not the same as actually being marketing oriented. Even companies that recognize the importance of being marketing oriented sometimes forget or find it difficult to consistently keep customers at the centre of their decision making and activities.

Standard Life, a major financial services organization in the UK, has recently been the target of an attempt to demutualize the company. After a long and at times bitter campaign, the management of the company secured victory in their attempt to persuade policyholders to reject the demutualization proposal. In the course of fighting this campaign, however, Standard Life realized that one of the reasons many investors were considering voting for demutualization was partly because over time the company had through sheer inertia begun to lose contact with its customers, for example often only communicating with members when policies matured.

The challenge of the demutualizers has alerted an otherwise excellent company of the need to pay more than lip service to the needs of its customers and for this to be a company-wide effort backed by senior management commitment and resources.

Marketing management

Developing a marketing orientation, difficult though this can be in many organizations, is only one side of the coin of improving the marketing effectiveness of an organization. If becoming marketing oriented is the first step in this process, the second step is the development of **marketing management** skills. Put simply, marketing is not only a philosophy or approach to doing business but is also a management function.

As a management function marketing involves the process of analysis, planning, implementation and control.

Analysis An all encompassing term, perhaps, but effective marketing management requires the analysis of all those factors that can affect marketing success and failure for a company. Analysis is the prelude to planning and decision making, and includes, for example, analysis of the following factors:

- Market analysis – market size, trends etc
- Competitor analysis
- Customer analysis
- Company analysis – market share, portfolio analysis, profitability analysis, etc.

In turn, analysis presupposes, or rather requires, effective marketing research and intelligence, control of information, and forecasting systems.

Because of the importance of analysis to marketing effectiveness, many of the subsequent chapters of this book centre on the key areas and tools of analysis.

Planning As we shall see, analysis is only a means to an end. The analysis forms the basis of marketing plans. Plans, in turn, denote decision making. Much of this book centres on the elements of marketing decision making.

Among the major marketing decisions to be made by marketing managers are the following:

- Marketing objectives
- Product/market scope, segments, targets, etc
- Company targets
- Marketing strategies
- Marketing mix decisions – product, price, place, and promotion.

At this stage, do not worry if many of these terms and their meanings are unfamiliar to you. Again, we shall be addressing these, and other planning decisions, in the chapters which follow.

Implementation Having made marketing plans, the next step is to ensure they are implemented. In turn, implementation requires that staff and financial resources be allocated together with time-scales for action, responsibilities and any necessary authority. In addition, the organizational structure may need to be changed to enable effective implementation to take place. Again, these and other issues of implementation form the focus of subsequent chapters.

Control   The final element of the management tasks of marketing is monitoring and controlling marketing activities. Control, often a neglected area in organizations, is the subject of Chapter 16, but in essence the control element completes the cycle of management tasks in as much as control and measurement feeds back into the analysis and planning stages of marketing management to start the cycle again.

To summarize, the following are seen as capturing the essence of what marketing is about – the basic principles, if you like.

- The marketing concept is founded on the belief that profitable sales and satisfactory returns on investment can best be achieved by identifying, anticipating and satisfying customer needs and wants.
- Marketing is both a philosophy of business – an 'orientation' some would say – and a management function.
- As a business philosophy, marketing involves the adoption by a company of the marketing concept.
- A company which has adopted this 'concept' places the customers at the centre of *all* business decisions, i.e. the customers' needs permeate all levels and functions in the organization.
- As a management function, marketing involves analysis, planning, implementation and control.

These then are the basic principles of marketing but, as we remarked earlier, just as some companies are beginning to grasp and, with varying degrees of success, accept and implement these, so marketing itself is changing – perhaps not the basic concept or philosophy which we have outlined here, but rather the perspective and operation of marketing management. Earlier we suggested that the essence of this changing face of marketing is the shift towards a much more strategic approach to marketing; hence the focus of this book. So what does this more strategic approach consist of and what forces and factors have contributed to this change?

The need for a strategic approach to marketing

Ever since business began, many companies have followed some sort of planning framework. However, all too often this 'planning' is short-term, *ad hoc* and based on intuition and hunch. It is suggested that it no longer makes commercial sense to rely on 'gut feelings' and primitive planning tools. The need is for a more strategic approach; but before we consider what is meant by 'a more strategic approach' to marketing it is necessary to consider just why it is suggested that a strategic approach is required. Below are some of the key reasons why marketing needs to be more strategic.

The pace of change and environmental complexity

Philip Kotler[22] has suggested that the pace of environmental change is not only increasingly rapid, but that these changes are now often discontinuous in nature. We shall be looking at the importance of environmental factors in strategic marketing planning in

Chapter 2, but at this stage let us just consider a small sample of environmental changes with which organizations have had to cope in recent years.

- As we have already noted, consumers and legislative bodies have become increasingly concerned about the natural environment and about the ecological and/or health risks associated with some products.
- The last decade of the twentieth century witnessed the birth of a host of new products based on new technology. Developments in information technology, cryogenics and biotechnology are just some examples of these facilitating technologies.
- Divorce rates, crime rates and (in some countries) birth rates have continued to surge ahead.
- There have been substantial changes in patterns of world trade including the emergence of new trading relationships and regulations.

Healthy and particularly organic foods have been amongst the fastest growing markets in the UK. Once a minority market, appealing only to a relatively few health food 'fanatics', this sector now represents a huge and growing market. Some research indicates that nearly 300 food products were launched under the 'healthy' label in the UK in the second half of 1999 and the first half of 2000. In addition, sales of organic foods in the UK during 1999 topped £400 million, a figure which is expected to treble by 2004.

Brands such as ASDA's 'Healthy Choice', the Aviva range from Novatis and Johnson & Johnson's Benecol are all examples of brands which have flourished with the trend towards healthy eating.

Changes in attitude towards health, and healthy eating will continue to give rise to marketing opportunities and challenges for the marketer in the future.

No doubt you can think of many other examples of environmental change, but the real significance of this change is its increased magnitude and pace. Moreover, the increased interrelationships between environmental factors have added to the complexity of the environment facing organizations.

Increasing organization size and complexity

A second major reason why marketing needs a more strategic approach is the fact that organizations themselves have become increasingly large and complex. In fact, the need for strategic market planning has gone hand in hand with the move from functionally organized companies, with relatively narrow product lines, to large diversified companies producing many different products for many different markets. In turn, this has meant that planning processes which were appropriate for the 1980s and 1990s are no longer so. Increasingly complex organizations require increasingly sophisticated tools of planning.

An example of the strategic planning implications of increased organizational size and complexity is the concept of viewing the multi-product multi-market organization as a number of sub-units or '**strategic business units**' (SBU) as they are often called, which need to be viewed and managed as a portfolio of businesses that may each contribute, in different ways and to a different extent, to overall corporate objectives. Lynch[23] has suggested that, particularly in larger organizations the strategic business unit is very often the basic organizational unit for the development of strategic marketing plans. Certainly organizing around SBUs is very prevalent in today's multi-product/multi-market organizations. The concept of strategic business units is therefore outlined in more detail below.

The concept of strategic business units

As we have just suggested, increasingly the contemporary organization is often large and complex encompassing potentially many product lines sold in diverse markets to different customer groups. Because of this, the different parts of a business will each need a strategic marketing plan reflecting the different requirements of each product market. The American company General Electric is generally acknowledged to be the first company to have dealt with this requirement for individual strategic marketing plans in the large diversified company by organizing the business into separate SBUs. The focus for strategic analysis and ensuing strategic marketing plans for a business are individual SBUs. Having said this, this means that at the corporate level of planning, decisions must be made regarding the balance between the different individual SBUs in the business, and in particular, the allocation of resources between them. However, strategic marketing plans in the multi-product/multi-market business can only be developed at the level of each SBU. The SBU concept therefore, is crucial to the strategic marketing planner and it is essential to organize the business into identifiable SBUs.

In practice, identifying and delineating a business into SBUs is a complex task and the precise ways in which this will be achieved will depend on several factors which are individual to each organization. For example, the size of each product market in the business, and the extent of commonalties between the different product markets. Ideally, however, an SBU should meet the following criteria:

● It should have its own customers and competitors.
● It should, in theory, be able to be operated as a separate individual business.
● It should have its own resources and also its own identifiable costs and revenues.
● It should have a manager in charge who is responsible for the profitability of the business.

The Swiss multi-national company Nestlé organizes its worldwide operations around a series of SBUs. Each SBU has full responsibility for the development of its own strategic marketing plans. The SBUs are based on the different product areas within Nestlé. So, for example, there is an SBU covering confectionery and ice cream products throughout the world, another one for milk products, and so on.

Although increased organizational size and complexity has served as a distinct spur to strategic approaches to marketing, you should note that it is not being suggested that such an approach is confined to or only appropriate for the larger diversified company. Small companies too need a strategic approach, especially as they often are faced with a far less certain macro-environment than large companies.

Increased competition

Apart from one or two exceptions such as state-protected or 'natural' monopolies, most organizations throughout the history of commerce and trade have always faced competition, both existing and potential. However, as with environmental change, recent years have witnessed an intensifying of competition in many markets. Many factors have contributed to this, but amongst some of the more significant are the following:

- A growth of global competition as barriers to trade have been lowered and global communications improved.
- Linked to the above, the role of the multinational conglomerate which ignores geographical and other boundaries and looks for profit opportunities on a global scale.
- In some economies, including the UK, legislation and political ideologies have aimed at fostering entrepreneurial and 'free market' values.
- Continual technological innovation, giving rise to new sources of competition for established products and markets.

The importance of competition and hence competitor analysis in contemporary strategic marketing cannot be overemphasized. Indeed, because of this we shall be looking at this aspect in more depth in later chapters. This importance is now widely accepted amongst both marketing academics and practitioners. Adcock[24] suggests that successful marketing in a competitive economy is about competitive success and that in addition to a customer focus a true marketing orientation also combines competitive positioning.

HMV, the music store chain has long recognized the need to focus its strategies around both customers and competitors. It was one of the first music retailers to introduce new systems of display and mechandizing in the UK. More recently, recognizing the growing threat from new technology, it was the first music retailer to launch a transactional website in the UK. HMV is actively promoting the use of the Internet to promote music. This is a company which believes in staying ahead of the competition.

These are some of the key reasons why a strategic perspective on marketing has become so important. But what is meant by a 'strategic' approach and what elements does a strategic approach to marketing contain? It is to these questions that we must now turn our attention. We begin by examining the nature of strategy and strategic management.

Strategic marketing planning

Again, when it comes to defining strategy and/or strategic management, we encounter a plethora of different definitions. In fact, 'strategy' and 'strategic' are probably two of the most over-used words in the planning vocabulary. However, below are three definitions which move us from the concept of a *strategy* through to the notion of *strategic planning* and finally to the focus of this text, *strategic marketing*. Michael Baker[25] proposes this definition of strategy, illustrating both its directional nature and its military antecedents:

> A strategy is the achievement of a stated purpose through the utilization of available resources.

Strategies, however, are the outcome of the strategic planning process. Kotler[26] defines this process as follows:

> Market-oriented strategic planning is the managerial process of developing and maintaining a viable fit between the organization's objectives, skills, and resources and its changing market opportunities. The aim of strategic planning is to shape and re-shape the company's businesses and products so that they yield target profits and growth.

And finally, *strategic marketing* as defined by Cravens[27]:

> *Strategic marketing* is a process of: strategically analyzing environmental, competitive, and business factors affecting business units and forecasting future trends in business areas of interest to the enterprise. Participating in setting objectives and formulating corporate and business unit strategy. Selecting target market strategies for the product markets in each business unit, establishing marketing objectives, and developing, implementing, and managing program positioning strategies for meeting target market needs.

Cravens' early definition still encapsulates virtually all of the key elements or steps in strategic marketing, and is therefore felt to be a useful shorthand way of grouping the essentials. We now need to expand in these key steps as a prelude to looking at some of these in more detail in the rest of the text.

The setting for marketing plans: key considerations

Marketing plans may take a variety of forms, ranging from verbal intentions or a set of budgets for achievement, through to formalized structures and procedures used as part of the corporate planning process. This section seeks to provide a simple framework through which we can structure the key steps and inputs to a strategic marketing plan. In this way marketing can become a better organized function and make a more substantial contribution to organizational performance in areas which marketing orientation is needed but has yet to be achieved.

As in any planning system, the contributors must be clear on the intended use and the contribution desired from them. Therefore, certain key questions must be asked.

1 Do we have the ability to match our ambitions? Often the ambition to achieve a marketing planning system reaches beyond the realities of ability.
2 Have we considered the planning horizons in terms of time?
3 Have we defined the boundaries of the system clearly?
4 What purposes are to be served by the marketing planning system? (This will help later to determine objectives.)
5 What structure should exist to enable the plan to be implemented, planned and achieved?
6 What do we require to achieve the purpose we have now identified?
7 What constraints currently limit our ability, and can these be overcome?
8 What contributions are we seeking to organizational and financial performance from the plan?

Like all planning, marketing planning concerns the future. It is the approach to the future which is important. The future involves a time dimension which needs to be clearly specified and depends on a clear understanding of organizational and market needs.

The avoidance strategy of 'do nothing' achieves little. Therefore a planned approach to the future depends upon the ability to predict, anticipate, prepare, and adapt. Marketing planning means *change*. It is a process that involves deciding currently what to do in the future with a full appreciation of the resource position; the need to set clear, communicable, measurable objectives; the development of alternative courses of action; and a means of assessing the best route towards the achievement of specified objectives. Marketing planning is designed to assist the process of marketing decision making under prevailing conditions of risk and uncertainty.

Above all the *process* of marketing planning has a number of benefits. The marketing planning process:

- Motivates staff
- Secures participation and involvement
- Achieves commitment
- Leads ultimately to better decision making
- Requires management staff collectively to make clear judgemental statements about assumptions – the very basis upon which the future depends
- Ensures a systematic approach to the future has been taken
- Prevents 'short-termism's the tendency to place all effort on the 'here and now'
- Creates a climate in which change can be made and in which standards for performance can be established
- Enables a control system to be designed and established whereby performance can be assessed against predetermined criteria.

Marketing plans can be both strategic and tactical, the latter operating within the framework imposed by the former. It is this strategic framework that we are concerned with here.

Whether tactical or strategic, marketing planning requires the laying down of policies for the acquisition, use and disposal of resources.

Marketing planning as a functional activity can only work within a corporate planning framework. The marketing planner must not lose sight of the need to achieve corporate level objectives by means of exploiting product and market combinations. There is an underlying requirement for any organization adopting marketing planning systems to set a clearly defined business mission as the basis from which the organizational direction can develop.

An overview of the steps and inputs to developing the strategic marketing plan

The final part of this chapter provides an overview of the key steps and considerations in developing a strategic marketing plan. It is important that you spend some time familiarizing yourself with this framework, as in the following chapters we shall be looking at some of these steps in more detail. However, it is easy to lose sight of how the individual steps fit together. From time to time, therefore, you will need to return to this framework, especially for the case studies which we will consider later in the text.

1   The corporate plan remit

The corporate mission   The corporate **mission statement** needs detailed consideration by top management to establish the business the company is really in and to relate
this consideration to future business intentions. It is a general statement that provides
an integrating function for the business, from which a clear sense of business definition
and direction can be achieved.

This stage is often overlooked in marketing planning, and yet without it the plan
will lack a sense of contribution to the development of the total business. By deriving a
clear mission statement, boundaries for the 'corporate entity' can be conceived in the
context of environmental trends that influence the business.

It is helpful to establish the areas of distinctive competence for the organization
and, in so doing, to focus upon what customers are buying rather than upon what the
company is selling. This will assist in the development of a more marketing oriented
mission statement; it therefore takes into account trends in market consumption
patterns. A clear mission statement should include the customer groups to be served,
the customer needs to be served and the technologies to be utilized.

The corporate objectives of the organization are time dependent and determined to
achieve shareholder expectations. These should be derived from the mission statement
to ensure integration within a corporate and marketing planning system.

Corporate objectives   The time horizon for the achievement of corporate objectives
will vary from organization to organization, from market to market and from country
to country, with time-scales stretching from one to five – or even to 20 – years.

From a practical viewpoint both quantitative and qualitative objectives are
required to provide the foundation upon which measurable marketing activities can be
planned for. In particular, quantitative corporate objectives concerned with rates of
return on capital employed and invested, return on shareholder funds etc., are inextri-
cably linked to the company's financial year, where these key ratios are used as
indicators of annual financial performance.

Qualitative corporate objectives may relate to image, stance, positioning, projection, appeal, identity, recognition, and so on.

Essentially objectives are statements of *what* is to be achieved and hence provide
the stimulus for strategy, i.e. the means by which the objectives will be achieved.
Because these objectives are corporate and have company-wide parameters, balance is
needed for the attainment of integration in the organization as a whole.

Areas to consider when setting up corporate level objectives include: market standing; innovation; productivity; physical and financial resources; staff performance,
development and attitude; public responsibility; and profitability and financial health

Corporate constraints   Although not part of the marketing plan as such, corporate
constraints are an important consideration. It is the matching of ambition to ability to
maximize performance that is the perennial task which besets senior management of
most organizations. Corporate constraints, therefore, are the limiting factors which
govern corporate capability. As the process of planning is iterative, a clearer understanding of these constraints may arise at subsequent stages in the planning process.

A full appreciation of corporate capability at this stage will affect more realistic
resource deployment at later stages in the marketing plan and also assist the cross-functional plans which collectively are designed to achieve corporate level objectives.

2   The marketing audit

In most business enterprises, periodic financial reviews are mandatory and systems are established to ensure that these occur within the deadlines set. This should be the case with marketing, but rarely is it so formalized.

Essentially the **marketing audit** is a systematic internal and external environmental review of the company's marketing performance for a given period of time. This review provides the basis for subsequent SWOT analysis (i.e. a review of company Strengths, Weaknesses, Opportunities and Threats).

The purpose of auditing the external and internal environment of the organization is to separate controllable from uncontrollable variables which have a significant impact on corporate performance. Companies should develop a customized checklist of factors for examination which can then be reviewed systematically and periodically.

The external audit will examine the PEST factors – Political, Economic, Socio-cultural and Technological – in the general business environment, and consider the fiscal and legal impact of these on company operations. Recent thinking adds Legal and Environmental to this classification which makes the acronym 'PESTLE'. Even later, Ecological has now made the acronym 'STEEPLE'. In addition, a comprehensive market profile is required with a detailed understanding of market movements so that forecasts can be developed for market performance and changes thereto. To support this market profile, the company must place itself in the context of a competitive market environment and a comprehensive profile of competition must be obtained, together with an examination of competitive product offerings.

Internally, a thorough examination of the company's marketing performance is vital. Detailed sales analysis, market shares and profit contribution analysis must be undertaken, together with an assessment of the efficiency of the company's marketing mix and marketing control plans and procedures.

The process of auditing will raise a series of questions and will produce a series of discoveries. These will need to be compiled into an acceptable format for presentation, a format from which later stages of the plan can be developed. This format is known as 'SWOT analysis'.

3   SWOT analysis

This acronym classifies the results of the audit into internal current strengths and weaknesses (which largely concern controllable variables) and external future opportunities and threats (which concern largely uncontrollable variables).

It should be emphasized that the SWOT analysis used for presentation should be a succinct summary of the audit which concentrates upon main issues for resolution and for which objectives, strategies and tactics could be set if so required.

4   Assumptions

In order to move forward from analysis to planning, a conceptual transition is required, because something now has to be achieved from that which has been assessed, discovered and recorded.

The environmental scanning of the market, the analysis of the competitive and market situations, lead naturally to the statement of assumptions for a future planning time horizon. In order to avoid the need to state assumptions, we would have to have perfect knowledge; this is rare. It is upon the statement of assumptions that progress can now be made to the planning stage. Assumptions can be classified as internal and external, quantitative and qualitative, in the same format as previously prescribed for corporate constraints.

5 Time-scales

It is normal practice to design at least an annual marketing plan which coordinates with the fiscal year of the organization and hence integrates with the budgetary control and associated management information and control systems. Some companies then extend the planning horizon to a separate plan for five years, or incrementally to five years on a rolling planning basis. It is wise to apply a rolling planning principle so that plans are always at least one year ahead, although revised and updated quarterly.

6 Marketing objectives

To restate a point made earlier, objectives are statements of *what* is to be achieved, and strategies are the *means* of achieving objectives. The two should not be confused.

It is of considerable importance to realize that marketing objectives should be derived directly from corporate level objectives and, in turn, reflect both quantitative and qualitative areas.

Concentration should be focused on setting objectives for products and markets because corporate level objectives reflect product/market combinations. Marketing mix objectives can be separated out at a later stage.

This simplifies the process of setting marketing objectives, but remember that they must be actionable, achievable and measurable – otherwise the accomplishment of marketing strategies cannot be accurately assessed in the prescribed time-scale of the plan.

7 Marketing strategies

Strategy is the means by which objectives are achieved. If objectives specify *what* is to be done, then strategy lays down *how* it is to be done.

Determined strategy then leads to a series of action statements which are a clear set of steps to be followed to achieve the determined strategy. These actions are known as tactics.

Effective marketing strategy is critical to the success of the plan. It must exploit the strengths and opportunities, overcome weaknesses and avoid threats identified in the SWOT analysis.

A strategic marketing programme depends upon an incisive SWOT analysis and, arising from that clear market definition of planned marketing activity, company success is governed by marketing strategy. A company's marketing strategy is the basis upon which operational decisions are made and corporate and marketing objectives achieved within the time periods specified for the plan. The time period for the tactical plan is usually one year – the current operating year. It is through the tactical plan that marketing strategy is achieved in practice.

Commonly, the strategic element of the marketing plan concentrates upon the selection of target markets, positioning strategies and the planning and implementation of the elements of the marketing mix including product, price, promotion and place, and in the case of service products/markets, the extended marketing mix elements of people, physical evidence and process.

Marketing research should not be overlooked, since this information provides a vital strategic contribution to the plan.

A key part of the strategic elements of the marketing plan, again often overlooked, is the policy statement, which provides the guidelines by which the marketing strategy can be accomplished within the determined time planning horizons.

As part of strategic determination, it is common practice to identify alternative means by which specified marketing objectives can be achieved. Criteria for evaluation are then set, applied to the stated alternatives and the best course of action selected.

The intention of marketing mix strategy is to achieve marketing positioning for product/market combinations specified in the corporate and marketing objectives sectors above. Therefore market definition, market segmentation and market targeting are the prerequisites within which positioning must be achieved.

8 Detailed marketing programmes

The level of marketing strategy will vary from plan to plan and company to company, but the final intention is to put the plan into action. It is now time to construct a set of detailed action programmes to achieve the previously stated marketing strategy. This part of the plan is concerned with who should do what, where, when, how and why. In this way responsibility, accountability and action over a specified time-scale can be planned, scheduled, implemented and reviewed.

9 Selling and sales management

In many companies, the sales plan will be separated from the marketing plan or, indeed, will replace the marketing plan in a sales oriented situation.

However, if we adopt marketing as a business philosophy then sales must be included within the marketing plan – it is the means by which many of the plan's objectives will be achieved. Sales forecasts and budgets will provide the means for quantitative achievement and control.

Selling and sales management strategy and tactics should be designed to complement, support and integrate with the marketing mix components of marketing strategy – in particular promotion and distribution.

10 Staffing the plan

Objectives and strategy can only be achieved through people, structures, systems and methods. In the tactical section of the plan, responsibility and authority for operations should be designated. However, a total consideration is required for organizational and staff development – to bring about the changes required to meet the plan's objectives.

Training and development, career development programmes, remuneration systems, headcounts, etc. need to be considered and, usually, will require liaison with the human resource function.

11 Contingency measures

Despite planning ahead for change, environmental factors sometimes force us to change our course of action – often these factors are unforeseeable and frustrating. The time taken to adjust may be less rapid than we would like in order to avoid higher costs and incurring losses. Under such conditions, response to contingency situations becomes reactive. To minimize the impact of changed environmental circumstances, companies can be proactive by using contingency thinking to anticipate likely events which may occur, and then make plans to reconcile the changed position in which the company may then be placed.

For each element of marketing mix and sales strategy, the marketing planner should ask the question 'What if?' In so doing, a change scenario will be formulated, a scenario to which the company can choose to respond. By planning ahead, the impact of changes will be reduced. Such thinking, when used in marketing planning, also encourages control and may prevent the cost of expensive mistakes.

Refer back to the assumptions set previously and consider the impact on the plan if these are unfulfilled.

12 Budgets reviews and controls

A marketing plan cannot be operated without a control environment to monitor and measure progress.

A system of controls should be laid down whereby the plan is reviewed on a regular and systematic basis, and then updated to extend the horizon to the prescribed time-scale. Controls are needed to assess tactics and strategy in the progress towards the achievement of quantitative and qualitative objectives. Therefore, controls should be seen as both quantitative and qualitative in design.

The marketing information system and in turn the management information system provide essential inputs to the control system, but the organization depends on people to work the system through regular appraisal.

Comparison of performance against target and the coincident variance analysis will enable corrective action to be taken to further exploit marketing and market opportunities and threats. Again, contingency planning is a form of control that can and should be used, particularly where markets are volatile.

To some marketing personnel, marketing budgets alone are marketing plans, in that they forecast projected income and expenditure for a given period of time, but for companies using a formalized system of marketing planning, the budget is the means by which the entire plan is coordinated financially.

Each area of marketing activity should be costed and then allocated to centres of responsibility. Indeed, as a key functional area of business the marketing budget is one of the key budgets to contribute towards the total budgetary control system of the organization.

In many organizations, budgeting is the transitional step between planning and implementation, because the budget, and allocated centres within it, will project the cost of each activity over the specified period of time, and also act as a guide for implementation and control.

This overview of the strategic marketing planning framework has been kept deliberately brief. In practice, developing strategic marketing plans is complex and multi-faceted. This complexity is heightened by the fact that the process is essentially an iterative one, with the planner constantly having to return to earlier stages in the analysis and planning as final plans begin to emerge. In addition, the various elements of the marketing plan need to be consistent, one with another. For example, the marketing mix elements of product, price, place and promotion need to blend together into one coherent package. In addition, the mix elements must also be consistent with overall corporate and marketing objectives, and in particular with segmentation, targeting and positioning strategies. The whole process therefore is one of constant checking and re-checking, not only in the preparation of the plan, but throughout its operation.

Figure 1.2 represents an attempt to set out previously discussed steps in marketing planning into this wider framework, together with the key elements of the analysis which feed into the decision-making steps. In addition, the interrelationships and iterative steps in the process are also shown. At first glance it looks complex, but it represents a logical and ordered approach to the process of strategic marketing planning.

The key steps shown in this framework are essentially universal inasmuch as they remain essentially the same irrespective of the nature of a company, e.g. its size, nature of product markets, geographical dispersion etc, and therefore may be followed by any marketing manager preparing a strategic marketing plan for the individual Strategic Business Unit. Although strategic planning frameworks do differ between both academics and practitioners, the essentials, together with the sequencing of these, are now more or less generally agreed. However, where marketing extends beyond domestic boundaries to include international markets a number of additional complexities and considerations and steps therefore which international marketing gives rise to are the subject of Chapter 17 in the text. In addition, as we shall see throughout this text, markets and marketing are nothing if not dynamic. Marketing concepts and techniques are constantly evolving and changing as markets themselves change and the tools and techniques for marketing are improved. Because of this, although the basic elements shown in our framework for strategic planning remain essentially the same, it would be useful to conclude this chapter by briefly outlining some of the more recent developments and trends in marketing thinking and application, together with some of the more important potential implications of these for marketing management.

Some recent trends and developments in marketing concepts and applications

As we have already seen marketing and marketers operate in an increasingly dynamic environment. Not only must marketers and strategic marketing planning reflect this, but as a result, marketing concepts and applications are constantly evolving and changing.

It is neither possible nor appropriate to examine all of the recent trends and developments in the concept and application of marketing. However, some of these trends and developments are so important that it is essential for the strategic marketing planner to be aware of them. We have selected what we consider to be some of these most important trends and developments for us to consider. These are introduced below.

An evolving marketing concept: relationship marketing

The first major change concerns the evolving nature of the concept of marketing itself, and in particular the trend towards a concept of marketing based upon developing and maintaining relationships with customers. For perhaps obvious reasons this is referred to as **relationship marketing** and for many represents a paradigm shift in the nature of marketing itself.

You will recall that the conventional marketing concept centres on the notion of understanding customer needs so that the marketer can develop a marketing strategy better to meet these needs. As a consequence of course, the organization achieves its aims. The process of dealing with customers, however, is viewed as essentially a one-off transaction where the customer receives satisfaction and the company achieves its objectives, whether these be for profits or some other organizational objective. As

Baker[28] suggests, this transaction view of conventional marketing essentially is concerned with what marketing can do 'to' buyers. He contrasts this with the emerging notion of relationship marketing, which he describes as follows:

> Relationship marketing is built upon the creation and maintenance of mutually satisfying exchange relationships. It enjoys a win–win perspective and sees the role of a producer as doing things 'for' customers.

At first glance this appears to be only a slightly different perspective from the traditional transactional view of marketing. In fact it is a fundamentally different perspective on the marketing concept and gives rise to potentially very different approaches to developing marketing strategies, in fact very much the paradigm shift referred to earlier. Adopting a relationship marketing approach has implications for example about how we promote products and services, how we deal with customers and customer service functions, and how we develop and use information about customers for targeting and other purposes. The growth of relationship marketing is so important that we need to consider its nature and implications in more detail, which we shall do therefore later in Chapter 17.

Many of the customer loyalty programmes which have been such a feature, particularly of retail marketing, during the 1990s are in part at least based on the concepts and ideas of relationship marketing. Programmes such as Tesco Clubcard and Thomson Founders Club are based on the notion of developing relationships with customers in order to create customer loyalty. The essence of effective loyalty programmes is building communication and trust between the marketer and customers. Other companies such as Waitrose, the grocery retailer, and B&Q in the home improvement market, have both successfully built relationships with customers based on high levels of customer service.

Services marketing

A second major trend and development in marketing has been the growth of services marketing. Service industries have been the major growth area in many, if not most developed economies. Industries such as banking and finance, insurance, healthcare, tourism and leisure, etc. are all examples of industries which need and use the tools and concepts of marketing. Although, as we shall see in later chapters, there are differences in some of the applications the basic principles of marketing management, including our strategic planning framework, apply to service industries and markets. A key difference perhaps in the application of this framework is in the need to consider the elements of the marketing mix from a slightly different perspective. The characteristics of service products have led to the notion of an extended marketing mix for service marketers. In addition to the conventional 'four Ps' of product, price, place, and promotion it is suggested that a fifth 'P' at least should be added to this mix, namely the 'people' element. In addition, two further 'Ps', namely 'physical evidence' and 'process', may be added. Certainly, there is no doubt that the 'people' element is crucial in the marketing of services and therefore needs to be considered and planned for by the service marketer – and some would argue, by all marketers. We shall therefore be examining the issues which services marketing gives rise to and the extended marketing mix elements associated with services marketing in more detail in Chapter 17, together with the previously described relationship marketing.

New technology: e-commerce and the Internet

A third major development affecting virtually every facet of organizational functioning, but in particular the marketing function, has been the increasing impact and importance of new technology on marketing. A problem here is that there are so many ways in which new technology is affecting marketing, ranging from the developments in IT and communication technology through to technologies of transportation and distribution, and underpinning product technologies such as for example genetic engineering. Perhaps one of the most significant developments for the marketer, however, both currently and in the future, is the growth of so-called e-commerce and of course the now ubiquitous Internet.

Virtually every aspect of marketing management and the development of strategic marketing plans is now actually or potentially affected by developments in e-commerce and the Internet. So much so that every marketing manager now needs to be conversant with developments in this area. Because of this, and because the impact of e-commerce and the Internet is so ubiquitous in marketing, affecting virtually every element of the process, we shall be discussing the impact and implications of these facets as appropriate throughout the subsequent chapters.

International/global marketing

Another major development and trend in marketing has been the increasingly international and global approach to marketing. Marketers are now extending their activities into international and global markets. International marketing has been one of the fastest growing areas of trade and commerce. Factors such as the continued liberalization of international trade, more cosmopolitan customers and the potential for profit opportunities have led to the growth of global companies increasingly marketing global brands. Once again, the basic concepts and techniques of strategic marketing apply irrespective of whether we are marketing in purely domestic markets or across several international frontiers. However, as with services marketing, the extra considerations caused by the sheer complexity of marketing on an international or global scale means that there are a number of special issues for the marketing manager which do not arise when marketing on a purely domestic basis. International and global aspects of marketing are considered in more detail in Chapter 18.

Internal marketing

You will recall that earlier in this chapter when discussing the marketing oriented company it was suggested that it is essential for everyone in an organization to become customer oriented and not just the marketers. This in turn has led to the growth of the notion of internal marketing. The idea of internal marketing centres on the notion of 'marketing' the importance of customers and of customer orientation to everyone in the organization. The idea is that employees of the organization can usefully be looked at and dealt with in the same way as external customers. So, for example, production staff are urged to consider, say, the sales force who have to sell the products as internal customers. At the same time the sales force should look at the production staff as one of their internal customers. There are several suggested reasons and advantages for looking at other parts of the organization as customers in this way. Amongst the most important of these advantages is the fact that it encourages functions which do not have a direct contact with the external customers to appreciate the ideas of marketing and customers and also to understand how their activities can affect external customers with regard to customer satisfaction and service, etc. Again as mentioned earlier, internal marketing has important implications for the implementation of strategic marketing and in particular the development of a marketing orientation throughout the company. Internal marketing therefore is considered in more detail again in Chapter 15.

Ethical and social aspects of marketing

Over the years, there is no doubt that marketing and marketers have, sometimes with justification, sometimes without, generated antagonism and criticism regarding some of the ethical and social implications associated with their marketing activities. On occasion this antagonism and criticism has been generalized in nature, for example, attacking notions such as the 'consumer society', or the 'money wasted' on advertising and packaging. At other times, the antagonism and criticism has been focused on a particular company and/or incident such as the controversy when Green Peace criticised the Shell company for their plans to sink the Brent Spar oil platform. Overall, consumers are much more aware of their rights and the responsibilities of marketers. Similarly, more and more consumers are concerned about protecting the environment and indeed their own health from the worst excesses of the marketer. The so-called 'green consumer' is here to stay in many economies. Increasingly, as we shall see, marketers must plan within a complex and tough regulatory environment, but even where there are few or lax regulations marketers are learning the value of imposing self-regulation on some of their activities. Because of these developments there is no doubt that the marketing manager of today and tomorrow needs to be aware of, take account of, and plan for, the social and ethical implications of his marketing strategies. Again, where ethical and social aspects are felt to be important/relevant to our discussion in later chapters, we shall include them.

One of the most controversial areas of marketing with regard to ethical and social aspects in recent years has concerned marketing to children. As an example of just one issue in this area has been the considerable criticism from some quarters regarding the marketing of what some have suggested are unhealthy children's food products. Needless to say, some marketers have responded positively to these criticisms.

The Co-op for example has undertaken to use its advertising in the future to promote healthy diets to children. It is has also banned the use of characters and cartoons on products which are judged to be high in fat, sugar or salt.

Extended applications for marketing

Our final example of recent trends and developments concerns the increasingly varied applications for marketing. Originally, and for many years, marketing concepts and techniques were primarily associated with, and applied to, the marketing of consumer products. These applications then spread into so-called **business-to-business marketing** (B2B), such as component suppliers, industrial equipment suppliers and so on. Increasingly, however, marketing concepts and techniques are being utilized by virtually any organization which has exchange relationships with its public. This includes, therefore, charities; public sector organizations such as libraries, public amenities, etc; political parties and candidates; causes and ideas; schools and universities; hospitals and other health services. It is now generally accepted that marketing concepts and techniques are not only useful and relevant to any organization where an exchange takes place between one party and another, but also that their application is, in principle, no different to the original applications for marketing in profit-seeking consumer goods organizations.

Summary

In this chapter we have traced the background to the development of marketing, both as a philosophy and a function in contemporary organizations. In particular, we have stressed the importance of being marketing oriented, what this means, and how a company can improve in this respect.

We have also seen that at the same time as some companies are still struggling to come to terms with the meaning and application of basic marketing principles, marketing itself is changing. The keystone of this change is that marketing is becoming more strategic in nature. The reasons for this are many, but include the pace of environmental and technological change, more-aware consumers, increased competition, and increased organizational size and complexity.

A key point has been the discussion of the meaning of strategy and strategic planning together with the key elements of strategic marketing planning. These elements were set against the complex framework of analysis and cross-checks necessary to develop a logical and effective planning process.

Finally we have looked at some of the more recent trends and developments in marketing concepts and their applications. We have seen that the applications of marketing have been extended far beyond those organizations primarily producing consumer products, and that marketing itself is changing with developments such as increased use of Information Technology, just-in-time manufacturing and its requirement for more effective relationship marketing, continued emphasis on the wider ethical and social aspects of marketing, and growth in internal and increasingly global marketing.

Key terms

Production orientation [p4]
Product orientation [p5]
Sales orientation [p5]
Consumerism [p6]
Marketing orientation [p7]
Internal marketing [p7]

Marketing management [p10]
Strategic business unit [p13]
Mission statement [p17]
Marketing audit [p18]
Relationship marketing [p22]
Business-to-business marketing [p25]

Questions

1 What factors have given rise to the need for a strategic approach to marketing?
2 What are the key benefits that derive from the process of marketing planning?
3 Describe what you consider to be the most important corporate considerations and inputs to the marketing planning process.
4 Distinguish between marketing objectives, marketing strategies and marketing programmes.
5 What are some of the most recent trends and developments in marketing concepts and applications?

References

1. Lamb, J. (ed.), Marketing Staff at Ohio State University, 'A statement of marketing philosophy', *Journal of Marketing*, Jan. 1965, p. 43.
2. Cherington, P. T., *The Elements of Marketing*, Black and East, New York, 1920.
3. Mazur, P., 'Does distribution cost enough?', *Fortune*, Nov. 1947, p. 138.
4. Baker, M. J., *Macmillan Dictionary of Marketing and Advertising*, The Macmillan Press Ltd, London and Basingstoke, 1984.
5. Kotler, P., *Marketing Management: Analysis, Planning, Implementation and Control*, 9th edn., Prentice-Hall, New Jersey, 1997.
6. Thorelli, H. B., 'Concepts of marketing: a review, preview and paradigm' in: *The Marketing Concept: Perspectives and Viewpoints*, P. Varadarayan (ed.), A & M University, College Station, Texas, 1983, p. 5.
7. Smith, A., *Inquiry into the Nature and Causes of the Wealth of Nations*, W. Campbell, P. Skinner and S. Todd (eds), Oxford University Press, London, 1976.
8. Torrens, R., *The Economist Refuted*, Oddy, 1805, p. 13, quoted by L. N. Rodger in *Marketing in a Competitive Economy*, 3rd revised edn., Associated Business Programmes, London, 1971, p. 24.
9. McCullough, J. R., *A Treatise on the Principles, Practice and History of Commerce*, Society for the Diffusion of Useful Knowledge, Baldwin and Cradock, London, 1833, p. 2.
10. Stanton, W. J., *Fundamentals of Marketing*, 8th edn., McGraw-Hill, London, 1998, p. 8.
11. Brassington, F., and Pettitt, S., *Principles of Marketing*, 2nd edn., Pearson Education, England, 2000, p. 13.
12. Brassington, F., and Pettitt, S., op.cit., p. 13.
13. Brassington, F., and Pettitt, S., op.cit., p. 13.
14. Dibb, S., Simkin, L., Pride W. M. and Ferrel, O.C., *Marketing Concepts and Strategies*, third European edn, Houghton Mifflin, Boston, p. 16.
15. 'Consumer Advisory Council, First Report', Executive Office of the President, Washington DC, US Government Printing Office, October 1963, pp. 5–8.
16. Baker, M., *Marketing Strategy and Management*, third edn., Macmillan, Hampshire, 2000, p. 462.
17. Adcock, D., *Marketing Strategies for Competitive Advantage*, Wiley, Chichester, 2000, p. 328.
18. Ferrel, O. C., Hartline, M. D., Lucas, G. H. (Jr) and Luck, D., *Marketing Strategy*, Harcourt Brace & Co, Orlando, 1999, p. 8.
19. Lancaster, G. A. and Massingham, L. C., *Essentials of Marketing*, 3rd edn, McGraw-Hill, London, 1999, p. 13.
20. Jobber, D. and Lancaster, G. A., *Selling and Sales Management*, 4th edn, Pitman, London, 1999, p. 13.

21. Levitt, T., 'Market myopia', *Harvard Business Review*, July–August 1960, pp. 45–6.
22. Kotler, P., op.cit., p. 63.
23. Lynch, R., *Corporate Strategy*, 2nd edn, Pearson Education, Harlow, 2000, p. 537.
24. Adcock, D., op.cit., p. 10.
25. Baker, M., op.cit., p. 76.
26. Kotler, P., op.cit., p. 63.
27. Cravens, D. W., *Strategic Marketing*, 5th edn, Irwin, 1999, p. 20.
28. Baker, M., op.cit., p. 20.

Case Study

John Dorey loves vegetables, so much so that he has given up his full-time job as a production engineer to concentrate on growing and marketing organic vegetables. He started growing vegetables 20 years ago in his back garden and eventually became fully self-sufficient in supplying vegetables for the family. Partly bored with his production engineers job and tempted by an attractive redundancy package, John decided he would try to establish his own vegetable supply business. Eighteen months ago, therefore, he looked around for a couple of fields to lease in which he could grow organic vegetables.

Organic products including organically grown vegetables, is a growth market in the UK. Increasing awareness of the problems associated with many pesticides and fertilizers, coupled with an increased interest in healthy eating habits and 'wholesome' food, has meant that many consumers are now either purchasing or interested in purchasing organic vegetables. This is true not only of the household customer but in addition many restaurants are using the lure of organic produce to give them a distinctive edge in the market place. All this has meant that many of the larger supermarkets in the UK have begun to stock more and more organic produce from what was a relatively specialised market in the early 1990s, the market has grown to where overall organic produce accounts for some 6% of the total UK grocery market. The market for organic vegetables has grown even more rapidly than other organic product markets and it is estimated that by 2010 some 15% of all vegetables marketed in the UK will be organic.

Organic vegetables offer several advantages over their non-organic counterparts:

- They are generally tastier and because they are not treated in the same way, are usually fresher than non-organic products.
- They are good for a healthy lifestyle because they contain no pesticides and chemicals.
- The fact that no pesticides or herbicides are used in their production means that they are much 'greener'. For example, they help to reduce the problems associated with nitrates in the soil and water supplies.
- On the downside organic vegetables are generally less uniform, and as far as some consumers are concerned, therefore less attractive in appearance. This lack of uniformity has also been a problem in the past with supermarket buyers who have traditionally been taught to look for uniformity in fresh products to aid their merchandising and marketing in the retail outlet.
- Finally, although prices are falling, generally speaking organic vegetables are more expensive than their non-organic counterparts. Currently, on average they are somewhere in the region of 50% more expensive.

In the UK, anyone wishing to claim that their produce is organic and market it in this way generally needs to obtain the approval of the Soil Association, which checks the organic credentials of a supplier. For example in this case, they check the conditions under which the produce is grown, the seeds used, etc.

Two interesting developments are taking place in the organic produce market. One is the growth of home supplies. This is where the producer supplies direct to the householder. There are a variety of ways of doing this. Some smaller growers use mail-shots and leafleting to build up a client base. They then deliver locally to customers who order from a list. Very often the supplier will simply make up a box of a pre-determined value or weight containing a selection of vegetables which are in season and ready for picking. Other suppliers are using a similar system but taking orders via the Internet. This is particularly suitable for this type of product as the customer can check on a regular basis what is available and order from home. As before the produce is then delivered at a pre-arranged time and place.

The second development in the organic produce market is the growth of the so-called farmers' markets. These markets are usually run by local authorities, often on Saturdays or Sundays. Local and other producers attend these markets, paying a small fee for a stall and then sell their produce direct to the consumer. These farmers' markets partly came about as a result of the frustration felt by many farmers and growers at the way they were being treated by retailers and at the margins they were receiving. In addition, such farmers' markets have been successful because consumers feel they are getting fresher produce, at lower prices than they might be able to obtain through supermarkets.

Despite the growth in the market for organic vegetables, however, after 18 months in his business John is worried. Quite simply, his business has not been as successful as he envisaged it would be and as a result he is not earning enough to make a living. The real worry is that he is not sure why. His produce, he believes, is as good as anything in the business. He is a very good grower and the land he has leased is perfect for the range of produce he wishes to grow. Starting with organic potatoes he now produces a range of organic vegetables including, for example, beans, sprouts, carrots, lettuce and his latest venture organic tomatoes and corn grown in poly-tunnels. Although the customers he currently supplies are very loyal to John, indeed many of them are friends and acquaintances he has known over the years when he grew vegetables in his back garden, there are simply not enough of them. As a result, his turnover which increased rapidly over the first year of the business has for the last six months stagnated. He mainly supplies locally and has tried to increase his customer base by taking leaflets out and posting them through letterboxes in the area. He has done this by dividing up the housing areas in a ten mile radius around his growing area and dropping leaflets throughout the area to as many houses as he can cover on a systematic basis. Only some 2% of customers have responded with an order, usually contacting by telephone. For some reason these customers all seem to come from the more middle class areas. He has considered taking a stall at one of the farmers' markets, the nearest of which is some 80 miles away and operates one day per month, but he realises this would not be enough to reach the turnover levels he requires. He has in the past supplied one or two local restaurants and hotels but usually only when they have contacted him because they have had a problem with their existing supplier. He has never followed these up. His growing area is currently too small to supply a major retailer, although he has been approached on an informal basis by the buyer of a voluntary chain of local grocers representing some 60 outlets in the county.

John is wondering where he goes from here then. He simply cannot understand why his superior products are not selling like hot cakes. The marketing director at his old company has suggested that John needs a more strategic approach to his marketing. John is not convinced however. He feels that his business is far too small to warrant any kind of marketing, never mind strategic marketing, and he has always felt anyway that a good product should sell itself. He is, however, anxious to grow the business and become a leading organic vegetable supplier.

QUESTION

What advice would you give to John about developing his business through more effective strategic marketing?

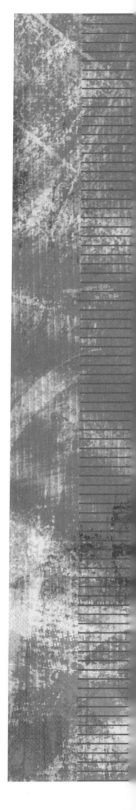

Analysing the environment: opportunities and threats

Chapter objectives

After reading this chapter you will:

▶ Appreciate the importance of analysing the environment in the development of strategic marketing plans.

▶ Understand the range and types of key environmental factors.

▶ Be familiar with a systematic approach to identifying forecasting and appraising environmental forces and factors.

▶ Appreciate the key importance of assessing competitors and competitive industry structure in the development of strategic marketing plans.

Introduction

In Chapter 1 we outlined the nature and significance of strategic marketing together with an introduction to the essential components of analysis, planning, implementation and control required to develop a strategic approach to this function. In this chapter we are going to look at the importance of analysing the environment for strategic marketing. As we shall see, changes and trends in the environment of an organization are the primary source of major marketing opportunities and threats. It is therefore essential for the strategic marketer to monitor, interpret and respond to such changes and trends. However, the word 'environment' encompasses a whole host of factors, often complexly linked, which can (and do) affect the very survival of any enterprise. Specifically, this chapter examines the range of environmental factors, discusses how to assess the impact of these factors, and suggests a framework for environmental scanning.

The importance of analysing the environment

Consider the following:

● Continuing problems with the processing of nuclear waste at the Sellafield plant in Cumbria in the UK has had a profound effect on many people's attitudes towards the nuclear power industry.

- At this point in time the future of the pound sterling remains uncertain whilst Britain decides whether or not it will recommend adoption of the Euro currency.
- The long promised explosion of Internet usage and applications has now happened. In the UK over 30 per cent of homes now have access to the Internet, a percentage which is growing rapidly.
- Discussions about expanding the European Union to include some of the key Eastern European blocs continues.
- In recent years marketers have been faced with an expansion in the so-called 'grey market', where their products and brands are bought and sold in international markets outside of conventional channels and therefore their control.

These are just a small selection of the 'environmental' forces and factors that have (or will) impact upon the marketing strategies of many companies. Of course, not every company will be affected by these specific trends and changes, nor indeed will those companies that are affected be affected equally. What is certain is that changes and trends in the environment of a company, such as those listed, give rise to some of the most significant opportunities and threats that any organization faces. Companies which have failed to recognize and take account of changes in their environment have, in the past, either failed to capitalize on their opportunities or – worse still – have suddenly realized that their markets have disappeared, closing factories and making workers redundant.

The importance of environmental analysis is already self-evident, but if further confirmation of this importance is required this can be underlined by tracing through an example of failure to identify and respond to environmental change.

Marks & Spencer were, until relatively recently, one of the most successful clothing and food retailers in the United Kingdom. Over the last three or four years however, the company faced increasing problems with regard to its sales and profits. So much so that the profit forecast for the year 2000 was halved. In the first year of the new millennium Marks & Spencer are still faced with sluggish sales and falling market share. There are several possible reasons for this and opinions vary, but many pundits suggest that essentially the company has not kept pace with changing market and customer needs. In particular, some critics have argued that many of its product ranges are simply not fashionable enough. Certainly, over the past decade the company has faced increasing competition both from domestic and overseas retailers who have entered the United Kingdom with exciting merchandising and retail formats. In the food area, the competitive advantages which Marks & Spencer once had, such as being amongst the first to offer good quality ready-made/chilled foods, are being eroded.

The company has now recognized that it is operating in a different trading environment and has embarked upon a series of major changes in its approach to sourcing, merchandising and marketing. So, for example, the company is experimenting with new formats for its stores, new merchandising and ranges including, such as its 'Autograph' range of fashion garments, and somewhat controversially has embarked on a new major television advertising campaign featuring a lady removing her garments. In addition the company has made several major changes to its management structure from the Chief Executive down.

It remains to be seen whether these changes will be sufficient to restore its former market position.

Needless to say this example illustrates the negative effects or threats posed to companies by changes in their marketing environment – or rather their failure to respond to these changes. Equally though, environmental trends and changes can and do give rise to major marketing opportunities. Even to the extent of spawning whole new industries.

An example of major opportunities arising out of technological, economic and social changes is the growth of the Internet or so-called 'dot-com' companies over the past two or three years. Technological developments, linked to social and economic changes such as for example a desire to work more from home, have combined to facilitate the growth of new companies using the technologies of the World Wide Web etc to market their products and services direct to customers. Some of these companies have shown phenomenal growth at least in company value, if not always sales and profits. Dot-com companies are set to be one of the major opportunities of the twenty-first century.

To some extent these two examples illustrate that environmental trends and changes are important in posing major opportunities or threats to organizations. Some of these environmental trends and changes are long term and take place gradually. They are therefore relatively easy to anticipate and predict – or at least they should be! Environmental changes, however, can also take place extremely rapidly and as a consequence can be much more difficult to predict.

Furthermore, as we noted in our introduction, the 'environment' comprises a wide range of factors, the relationships between which are often complex. Our first step in analysing the environment, therefore, is to identify and classify environmental influences.

Range and level of environmental factors

The term 'environment' in the context of strategic marketing planning can be used in a variety of ways. For example. Ferrell *et al.*[1] suggest that environmental analysis involves analysing three key environments, namely:

> The external environment, the customer environment, and the organization's internal environment.

This perspective, therefore, includes *all* environmental factors *outside of the firm's marketing management function*. This includes both internal and external forces. Many marketers distinguish between different categories of environmental factors in this way. This distinction is drawn by conceptualizing successive 'layers ' of the environment, as shown in Figure 2.1. This shows examples of some of the key environmental influences for each successive 'layer' of the marketing function's environment. The examples of environmental factors shown at each level suggested are not the only factors. They do, however, represent what are felt to be some of the key factors pertaining to each level of the environment in turn.

Intra-firm environment

Firms have finite resources. The marketing function often has to compete with other management functions in order to obtain the resources needed to complete its task.

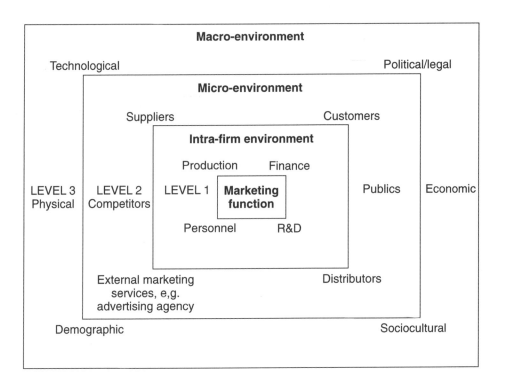

Figure 2.1
Layers in the
environment.

Similarly, the marketing function must also cooperate with those other functions within the firm. This interaction and interdependency between the marketing function and other functional areas of management is the reason why Ferrell[2] includes the **intra-firm environment** as the third key element of environmental analysis. It is important, in order to understand the influence of factors in the next two layers of the environment, that marketing has the ability to carry out its role of monitoring and adapting to these factors is influenced by its relationship with other functions within the company. Marketing managers make decisions that have a bearing on other functional areas of the firm. Similarly, the decisions taken by other departments have a direct effect on the ability of the marketing department to perform its role.

We cannot ignore these intra-firm elements of the environment of the marketing function. However, these aspects are covered more fully in Chapter 15 when we discuss the organizational aspects of strategic market planning.

Micro-environment

These second level environmental factors, which 'impinge' on marketing management, comprise all of those factors which, unlike the first level intra-company components, lie outside the organizational boundaries of the organization. Unlike the third level, macro-environmental factors, which we shall shortly examine, the organization has some measure of 'control' over its **micro-environment**. Some of the more important elements of the micro- or (as it is sometimes termed) task-environment include: competitors, distributors, suppliers, customers, external marketing services (such as market research companies), advertising agencies and so on, and publics. The meaning of most micro-environmental factors is self-explanatory, although their significance to strategy formulation is such that many of them, including competitor, customer and distributor analysis, are considered in more detail in this and later chapters. However, perhaps the micro-environmental factor 'publics' needs further explanation at this stage.

Kotler[3] defines a 'public' as follows:

> A public is any group that has an actual or potential interest in, or impact on, a company's ability to achieve its objectives.

As you would expect from such a broad definition, a company's 'public(s)' are very diverse and include groups such as the local community, the general public, shareholders, the financial community in general and governments.

The key points for the marketing strategist are first to acknowledge the importance of such publics to the process of planning and then to ensure that relationships with significant publics are effectively managed. Traditionally these relationships have been the concern and responsibility of the public relations function in companies, but many now subscribe to the view that this is too narrow a view and that everyone in a company can, and does, contribute to effective (or ineffective) relationships with an organization's public(s).

A good example of the importance of a company's public(s) in developing strategic marketing plans is the increased influence and power which company shareholders are having in this area. At one time the interest of shareholders was restricted mainly to the level of financial return and profits which they were receiving from their investment. Increasingly though shareholders are taking in increased interest in how companies are managed, including their marketing strategies. Our earlier example of the Standard Life company and attempts by some of its shareholders to demutualize the company illustrate that shareholders can, and do, get companies to change their marketing actions and policies so as to be more in line with shareholders' requirements and expectations.

Macro-environment

Up to now we have considered those environmental forces and factors that are either within the marketing function's own organizational boundaries or, alternatively, in its immediate task environment. The third level of environmental factors comprises broader factors in the wider **macro-environment** of the organization over which the individual company has little or no control. It is from changes and trends in these macro-environmental factors that perhaps some of the most significant and far-reaching marketing opportunities and threats for the organization will stem. They are now discussed in more detail.

Sociocultural environment Changes and trends in the sociocultural environment present significant challenges to the strategic marketing planner. People's basic beliefs, attitudes and values are shaped and conditioned by the society in which they grow up. Their general behaviour, including of course their purchasing behaviour, is profoundly influenced by societal and cultural norms.

Core cultural and social values are firmly established within a society and are generally difficult to change. If and when they do change, they do so only slowly. In the short term, therefore, they should be treated as parameters within which marketing strategies need to be formulated. However, over a period of say 20 to 30 years, we can expect some social and cultural values to have changed dramatically. Detailed examples of some of these changes in the UK are outlined in Lancaster and Massingham[4] and include, for example, changes in attitudes towards credit, an increasing awareness of and interest in healthy lifestyles, changes in attitudes towards women in society and so on.

It is important to note that although core cultural and social values change relatively slowly, changes in this area are now taking place increasingly rapidly. Some societies at least are witnessing the most rapid social and cultural changes they have ever experienced in many of the developed Western economies. In particular social and cultural change has been very rapid in some areas including, for example: attitudes towards work and leisure, women in the home and at work, bringing up and disciplining children, sexual attitudes and behaviour, etc. Having said this, in some other societies political, religious and economic forces and factors still combine to limit the nature and speed at which social and cultural changes take place.

In the UK, Channel 4's 'Big Brother' programme has experienced phenomenal success. The programme, which centred on continuously observing a group of selected people living together in a house, with each week a member of the group being nominated for expulsion by the others, attracted regular viewing audiences of 4 million plus, whilst at the same time making its participants overnight celebrities even, and indeed especially, when they were expelled.

The format of this programme and its content would probably never have been envisaged, and almost certainly would not have been as successful, even as little as three or four years ago. Essentially, the participants in the programme had no privacy whatsoever. The camera observed and recorded them 24 hours a day, 7 days a week. This observation extended into the most private activities of the group, and in some ways many would argue is an invasion of privacy and/or distasteful involving as it does nudity, strong language and so on.

The surprising success of the programme was in part due, no doubt, to the fact that it was a product of its time. There is a demand for this sort of voyeuristic entertainment. The somewhat ruthless nature of the expulsions satisfies at least some of the viewing public with regard to perhaps a more aggressive and individualistic approach in society.

Political/legal environment The political/legal environment is the starting point from which many other macro-environmental forces originate. The outcome of political decisions can often be seen in the economic and legislative policies of governments. In the UK, major marketing opportunities and threats in recent years have stemmed from the political policies and legislation of successive governments irrespective of their political hue. For example, John Major's Conservative government with its continued belief in the free market mechanism created significant marketing opportunities for many companies and threats for others through its policies of privatization. The Labour government of Tony Blair which replaced it has similarly created marketing opportunities through its policies regarding public–private co-operation and funding in many sectors of the economy. For the marketing strategist, what matters in a planning context is not whether these and other policies and the legislation which has accompanied them have been 'right', but more the implications for marketing strategy. Not only must strategies be planned to take account of existing policies and legislation, but account must also be taken of likely future changes. The important thing to realize is that the political and associated legislative environment is of great significance to the marketer and is likely to have a direct bearing on the formulation of marketing strategy.

We need also to remember that it is not simply domestic politics which will impact on marketing strategy, but increasingly, international politics. Nowhere is this more evident than in the former 'Eastern bloc' countries.

Economic environment Closely related to, and intertwined with, the political/legal environment is the economic environment. The marketing strategist must understand the variety of economic variables that will shape marketing plans.

Factors such as rates of inflation, interest rates, exchange rates, industrial output, levels of disposable income and the balance of payments are just some of the factors of potentially major concern to marketing management because they, in turn, influence costs, prices and demand.

Once again, not just domestic but international economic developments and trends must increasingly be considered. Consequently, marketing strategy needs to take account of the 'ebb and flow' of economic factors in a global setting.

The Euro issue continues to dominate much of economic debate in the UK. There is still broadly a commitment to enter the single currency provided certain economic conditions are met. The current Labour government has promised a referendum regarding adopting the single currency after the next election. In the meantime this aspect of the economic environment continues to be a major subject of debate and an area of uncertainty for companies with regard to their future planning.

Technological environment Technology is a major environmental influence upon marketing strategy. This influence is manifested in a variety of ways. For example, developments and breakthroughs in technology are the basis for new products and sometimes new industries. Home computers, compact disc players, video recorders and instant cameras are just a few of the products which have emerged in recent years. Biotechnology, information technology and energy conservation are just a few of the new industries.

Equally important is the fact that technology also affects the way marketing is practised. For example, in the marketing research area it is now possible to design and administer questionnaires directly via computer terminals. The development of computers and information technology in general has enabled the use of sophisticated forecasting techniques. In the retailing sector of distribution, electronic point of sale (EPOS) data capture is now in use by many major retailers together with 'laser checkouts' and direct transfer of funds.

Technological changes affect the way products are produced. Robotics, flexible manufacturing systems and fully automated factories are just some examples of the ways in which the basis for competitive advantage can be changed.

As already mentioned, perhaps one of the most significant and far-reaching technological developments in recent years has been the growth of e-commerce, in particular the development of the World Wide Web and of course the Internet. So ubiquitous and potentially far-reaching have been these technological developments that virtually every area and aspect of marketing is affected. Because of this we shall return to this technological development throughout this text. At this stage, however, it is sufficient to note that the marketer of today and the future must be aware of trends and changes in this area together with the implications for their businesses.

The physical environment   Sometimes referred to as the 'natural' environment, this element of an organization's environment was, until comparatively recently, felt by many strategic planners to be of little direct relevance to the formulation of future strategies. This was primarily because it was assumed that it had little direct effect upon organizations. Recent trends and events have shown this assumption to be ill founded and myopic.

In fact, as long ago as 1962 authors such as Rachel Carson[5] were warning of the dangers to the physical environment from industrial and commercial activities. All too frequently such warnings were dismissed on the grounds that they represented the views of a relatively small number of 'environmentalists' who were at best misguided or overly pessimistic, and at worst scurrilous and subversive. In fact, this 'small' number of critics proved to be in the vanguard of what has now become a popular, powerful and global movement concerned to protect the natural environment in which we all live.

Clearly, and quite rightly, we each have our own views on issues such as the use of the world's natural resources of minerals, forests and water. Similarly, you may be aware of some of the most fervently contested contemporary issues regarding phenomena such as the so-called 'greenhouse' effect, acid rain and the depletion of the ozone layer. Regardless of personal views and attitudes on these matters, there is absolutely no doubt that they have become issues for the strategic marketing planner. For example, in Europe and America we have seen a proliferation of adapted aerosol products which are now 'ozone friendly'; increasingly, products and technologies are designed to be energy efficient; degradable plastic packaging is now widely available, as is recyclable packing. More car manufacturers are working towards completely recyclable vehicles. Whatever your views are as an individual on these issues, concern for the physical or natural environment is here to stay and the process of strategic market planning must reflect this.

A system of environmental scanning identifying, forecasting and appraising environmental factors

Our discussion so far has concentrated upon reviewing the significance of environmental factors. Secondly, we proposed a format for classifying different levels of environmental factors together with a description of the sorts of factors associated with each level. Thirdly, at any time particular environmental factors may impact on different industries in different ways and to a different extent. Fourthly, we have suggested that a given trend or change in the environment may affect an organization and its strategic marketing planning in a different way from other organizations in the industry. Fifthly, our discussion so far shows that it is trends and changes in the environment which give rise to marketing opportunities and threats.

 These observations point the way towards suggesting the requirements for an effective **environmental scanning** system: effective, that is, in the sense of improving the process of strategic marketing planning. These requirements, we suggest, are as follows:

1   The ability to identify which of the environmental forces and factors at any one point in time are of particular significance to the particular organization, i.e. which

of the environmental forces are likely to pose the most significant opportunities and threats to the company.

2 The ability both to monitor and forecast *future* trends and changes in these factors.

3 The ability to interpret the significance of these environmental trends and changes, i.e. their implications for future marketing strategies.

4 The ability to develop and implement marketing strategies to respond to environmental trends and changes.

Perhaps the last of these requirements, it could be argued, is not only a requirement of an effective environmental scanning system, but also part of a broader set of issues involving the ability of the organization to cope with environmental change, encompassing organizational resources, flexibility and the quality of management. We have included this final element because it illustrates the important point that the sole purpose of a system of environmental scanning is that it should improve strategic marketing plans in the sense of improving the *opportunity* of organizational success. Having emphasized this, we can now focus upon some of our requirements for an effective environmental scanning system.

Organizational practice and environmental scanning

Evidence suggests that systematic environmental scanning has only recently begun to be developed in companies as part of their strategic marketing planning process.

One of the earliest studies on environmental scanning in organizations was that conducted by Francis Aguilar and published in 1967.[6] Based on a sample of selected chemical companies in Europe and America, Aguilar identified four basic patterns for scanning information about the environment:

1 *Undirected viewing*
This represented the most unsystematic approach to environmental scanning and was largely composed of 'exposure without a specific purpose'.

2 *Conditioned viewing*
This approach was adopted by those companies who were aware of some of the key factors and trends in their environment, but who did not undertake any active search.

3 *Informal search*
Some companies actively collected information on their environment for specific planning and decision-making processes, but did so in a largely informal and *ad hoc* manner.

4 *Formal search*
This represents the most highly developed environmental scanning practices. Aguilar found that some companies had a structured process for the collection of specific information for a specific purpose.

In fact, Aguilar's study showed that there was a distinct lack of a systematic approach to environmental scanning in the companies, studies, with comparatively few conducting formal searches.

However, over time, more and more companies have come to develop formal scanning systems. By the mid 1980s Jain's[7] study suggested that although still evolving, more and more companies were beginning to develop formalized environmental scanning procedures. Jain identified four distinct phases in this evolution, namely:

Phase 1: Primitive
Information noted, but no purpose and effort to scanning; little or no discrimination used to distinguish between strategic and non-strategic information.

Phase 2: Ad hoc
No formally planned scanning as such, but increased sensitivity to information on certain issues or events which may be explored further.

Phase 3: Reactive
Scanning still unstructured and random, but often specific information collected with a view to making appropriate responses to markets and competition.

Phase 4: Proactive
Scanning structured and deliberate, using pre-established methodologies with a view to predicting the environment for a desired future.

Perhaps the overriding reason for the slow development of formal environmental scanning and appraisal systems is that it is difficult to achieve. However, more and more companies are beginning to develop skills in this area. In addition, although it was once a neglected area in the planning literature, Johnson and Scholes[8] illustrate how environmental appraisal is now the subject of more research as its importance to strategic planning has become appreciated. In order to develop more 'proactive' appraisal systems requires the establishment of systematic procedures designed specifically to input into strategic marketing decisions. We consider one such system below.

A framework for appraisal

A number of frameworks for environmental appraisal have been developed. In our view, one of the most useful of these is that proposed by Jain[9] and shown in Figure 2.2.
The six key steps in Jain's appraisal system are as follows:

1 Seek to maintain an awareness of broad trends in each of the key environmental factors outlined earlier. At this stage, scanning need not be detailed so long as trends are monitored.
2 Delineate those trends which are deemed most relevant – i.e. to have potential significance to the company – for further, more detailed investigation.
3 Undertake an in-depth analysis on the possible impact of these selected trends on the company's current product or markets. In particular, this analysis should delineate the extent to which the trend is an opportunity or a threat and the potential magnitude of its impact. In addition, an analysis should be made of the extent to which the trends isolated open up new opportunities.
4 Forecast the future direction of the trends isolated.
5 Further analyse the possible effects of the forecasted trends on future product or market momentum: (a) on the assumption of no action, (b) on the assumption that trends are responded to.
6 The final step in the procedure is to assess the implication of the preceding analysis for overall strategic decision making.

We can see that this framework for environmental appraisal represents a structured and logical approach to this procedure. Moreover, it fulfils many of the requirements outlined earlier in this chapter for an effective appraisal system. However, there are still practical problems in this appraisal process which we need to consider further.

Figure 2.2
A systematic
approach to
environment
appraisal and
strategic planning.
Source: adapted from
Jain, S.C., *Marketing
Planning and Strategy,*
2nd edn, South Western
Publishing Co.,
Cincinatti, 1985, p. 277.

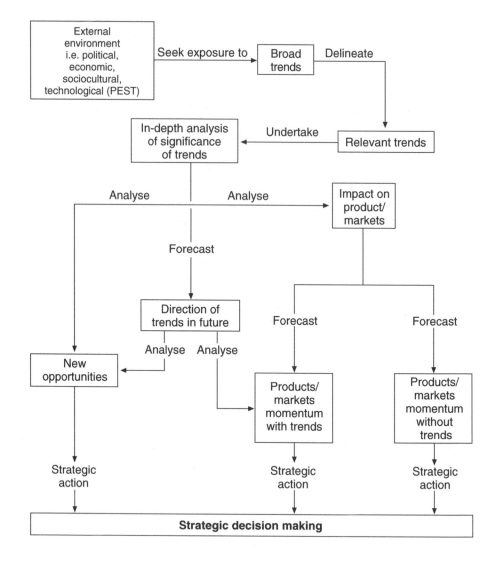

Identifying the most significant trends for detailed analysis

We have seen that by definition the 'environment' encompasses all events and trends outside the boundaries of the marketing function. As we know, a key problem in environmental appraisal is the identification of the most significant of these trends for further analysis. Jain suggests that there are no 'hard and fast rules' for distinguishing between what is relevant and irrelevant.

A useful approach to identifying what to scan and which environmental trends and changes are relevant is the business definition for a strategic business unit.

So, for example, imagine that a strategic business unit of a large insurance company has defined its part of the business as being:

the provision of peace of mind insurance solutions to the private motor car owner.

The following might be some of the more important environmental trends and changes for the strategic business unit to monitor:

- Trends and changes in levels and types of private car ownership together with the factors affecting these
- Trends and changes in car usage levels and patterns together with the factors affecting these
- Strategies of major competitors
- Potential new entrants to the market
- Changes in legislation that might affect the types of insurance cover legally required
- Technological developments which might affect the way in which, say, customers purchase private car insurance

Obviously these are just a few examples but they do illustrate the potential range and complexity required in environmental scanning.

Although business definition provides the key to isolating relevant trends – for example, any one of the environmental factors just described would give rise to major environmental opportunities and threats – identifying relevant areas does require a considerable degree of creativity and foresightedness. Although some trends or changes are very obviously significant – e.g. the emergence of a new and potentially strong competitor – often the environmental scanning process requires considerable judgement and experience in spotting opportunities and threats. Often a seemingly unrelated trend or change can be highly significant in the long run.[10]

Who would have thought that one of the most significant threats to the publishers and distributors of books would have come from the Internet? After all, traditionally the book-buying public has selected and purchased books by browsing through them on the booksellers' shelves. From nothing in this market, the Internet bookseller Amazon has taken a substantial market share in next to no time. Initially, probably considered as simply an upstart in the industry by the large publishing and book distributing organizations, Amazon has, through its success, forced these more traditional companies in the market to consider them as a powerful competitive force.

This example not only shows the need for constant vigilance in environmental scanning, but in addition illustrates the need to think creatively about what is relevant.

Forecasting the future

Remember that strategic market planning is concerned with plotting the future of a company. In addition, as you would expect, it is not enough to wait until a major environmental threat has emerged before taking action. The company will require not only the *identification* of environmental trends but the forecasting of both the magnitude and direction of these trends in the future. But forecasting the future – especially with regard to complex and often interrelated trends in the environment – is not easy, and may require both specialist techniques and personnel.

We shall be looking at some of these techniques – and in particular the specialist techniques of technological forecasting – in later chapters, but at the very least the strategic market planner needs to make some estimate of the likely sources of future threats and opportunities.

Assessing the impact of environmental trends

In addition to identifying and forecasting environmental trends and the opportunities and threats to which they give rise, the strategic market planner must also try to assess their likely impact on the organization: after all, there is no other reason for appraising the environment! Kotler[11] suggests that the planner can begin to make this assessment using opportunity and threat matrices, as illustrated in Figures 2.3 and 2.4. The opportunity matrix is based on the planner assessing the relative attractiveness of an environmental *opportunity* and the probability of success should the company decide to act upon it. In turn, this assessment requires an assessment of the strengths and weaknesses of the company, which we look at in Chapter 3.

In the same way, the planner should assess the likely impact of any possible *threats* to which trends in the environment give rise. Here we need to assess both the probability of the threat occurring and its seriousness for the activities of the organization.

Clearly, these matrices are an oversimplification of the analysis required to assess the impact of environmental changes on an organization. Not uncommonly, two or more trends – each of which on its own would not represent significant opportunities or threats – can, in combination, be highly significant. This means that several trends may need to be evaluated together to assess their cross-impact.

Despite the problems of determining the impact of trends it is essential to do so. In fact, one of the benefits of doing so is the fact that even if the precise effects are difficult to predict, the very process of assessment and the necessary cross-functional discussion to which this should give rise can help the company in becoming prepared for the future.

Figure 2.3
Opportunity matrix.
Source: adapted from Kotler, P., *Marketing Management: Analysis, Planning, Implementation and Control.* Prentice-Hall, New Jersey, 1988, p. 52.

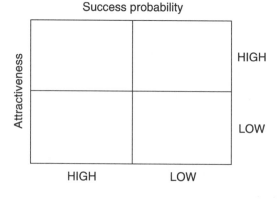

Figure 2.4
Threat matrix.
Source: adapted from Kotler, P., *Marketing Management: Analysis, planning, Implementation and Control.* Prentice-Hall, New Jersey, 1988, p. 52.

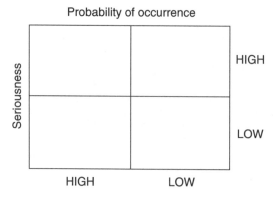

Competitor analysis

In later chapters we will consider in more detail some of the key factors in the micro- or task-environment of organizations and, in particular, customers and distributors. It is now increasingly recognized that in today's environment, effective strategic marketing plans are as much about being *competitor*-oriented as customer-oriented, as evidenced in the following quote from Porter:[12]

> Competition is at the core of the success or failure of firms. Competition determines the appropriateness of a firm's activities that can contribute to its performance, such as innovations, a cohesive culture, or good implementation. Competitive advantage is the benefit derived through competitive strategy aimed at establishing a profitable and sustainable position against the forces that determine industry competition.

Hence the remainder of this chapter is devoted to examining the nature and significance of competitor appraisal in strategic market planning.

Elements of competitor analysis: competitive industry structure

Business nowadays can be compared to running a competitive race, with all the awards going to the winners. It thus behoves the marketing manager to make a careful analysis of the company's competitors before devoting resources to marketing strategies.

Competitor analysis involves the examination of competitors in order that the planner can develop and sustain superior competitive performance for the organization. This deceptively simple statement belies the fact that in order to do this we must first establish from where the competition currently stems and from where it might stem in the future. We also have to consider and appraise competitors' present (and likely future) objectives and strategies. Finally, we have to consider competitors' likely reactions to the competitive moves which we might make.

The marketing strategist must also widen the focus to include in the analysis not only 'competition' in the more traditional sense, but also the competitive structure of the industry. This includes the assessment of factors such as barriers to entry and exit and hence, for example, the threat of new entrants; the assessment of potential substitute products or services; the bargaining power of suppliers; the bargaining power of buyers; and so on. In short, once again, competitor analysis is complex and multifaceted. Let us now look at how we might seek to conceptualize the competitive structure of an industry, starting first with the more traditional approach based on the number of sellers (competitors) and degree of product differentiation in a market.

Traditional view of competitive industry structures

Figure 2.5 shows the traditional view of competitive industry structures preferred by economists. Different types of industry structure are based upon the two key dimensions of 'number of sellers' (competitors) and the degree of product differentiation in the market. This results in five distinct types of competitive industry structure, ranging on the one hand from 'pure monopoly', which is characterized by there being only one supplier and hence no competition, to, on the other hand, 'perfect competition', this market structure being characterized by many sellers (competitors) and undifferentiated products.

Certainly both numbers of competitors and degree of product differentiation are important facts of competitive industry structure. Useful though this framework is, it is

Figure 2.5
The traditional view
of competitive
industry structure.

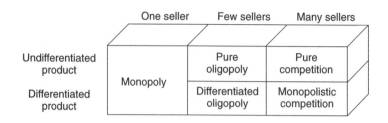

now generally recognized that it yields only a partial view of the competitive forces at work in an industry. Hence the planner needs to look to some of the more comprehensive frameworks of industry analysis.

The Porter framework of competitive industry structure

One of the most useful frameworks for analysing the competitive structure is that developed by Michael E. Porter.[13] Porter suggests that competition in an industry is rooted in its underlying economic structure and goes beyond the behaviour of current competitors. The state of competition depends upon five basic competitive forces, as shown in Figure 2.6. Together, these factors determine the ultimate profit potential in an industry where profit potential is measured in terms of long-run return on invested capital. Not all industries have the same potential. Forces range from intense – tyres, paper, steel – with no spectacular returns available, to mild – cosmetics, toiletries, soft drinks – with high returns being common.

The goal of competitive strategy is to find a position in the industry where the company can best defend itself against these forces, or can influence them in its favour. Knowledge of these underlying pressures highlights the critical strengths and weaknesses of the company, shows the position in the industry, clarifies areas where strategy changes yield the greatest pay-off, and highlights areas where industry trends hold greatest significance as opportunities or threats. Structure analysis is fundamental for formulating competitive strategy.

The five competitive forces in Porter's model

As suggested earlier, the five competitive forces suggested by Porter jointly determine the intensity of industry competition and hence profitability. As Figure 2.6 shows, each of the five major forces in turn comprises a number of elements which together combine to determine the strength of each factor and hence its effect on competitiveness. Some of these are now outlined.

1 *New entrants*
   New entrants can potentially serve to increase the degree of competition in an industry. In turn, the threat of new entrants is largely a function of the extent to which barriers to entry exist in the market. Some of the key factors affecting these entry barriers include:

   • Economies of scale
   • Product differentiation and brand identity
   • Capital requirements
   • Switching costs
   • Government policy
   • Access to distribution.

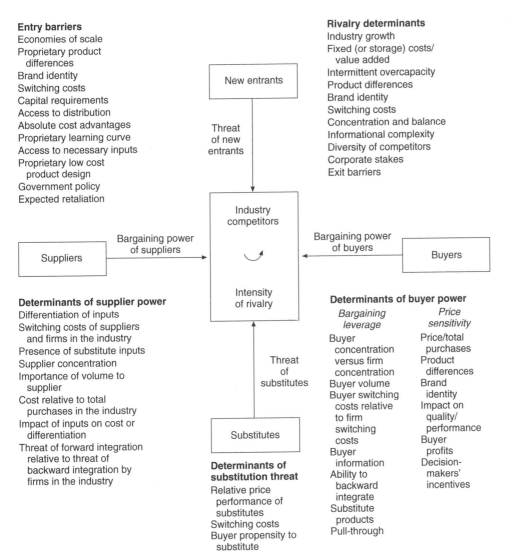

Figure 2.6
The Porter model of competitive industry structure.
Source: Porter, M.E., *Competitive Strategy,* Free Press, 1980, p. 4.

Because high barriers to entry can make even a potentially lucrative market unattractive (or even impossible) to enter for new competitors, the marketing planner should not take a passive approach but should actively pursue ways of raising barriers to new competitors.

2 *Suppliers*

The bargaining power of suppliers is greater when, for example:

- Supply is dominated by a few companies and they are more concentrated than the industry they sell to
- Their products are unique or differentiated, or if they have built up switching costs
- They are not obliged to contend with other products for sale to the industry
- They pose a credible threat of integrating forward into the industry's business
- The industry is not an important customer to the supplier group.

3   *Buyers*
    The bargaining power of buyers is greater when, for example:

- They are concentrated or purchase in large volumes
- The products they purchase are standard or undifferentiated
- The products they purchase from the industry form a component of the product and represent a significant fraction of the cost
- They earn low profits which create a great incentive to lower purchasing costs
- The industry's product is unimportant to the quality of the buyer's products
- The industry's product does not save the buyer money
- The buyers pose a credible threat of integrating backwards to manufacture the industry's product.

A company can improve its strategic posture by finding suppliers or buyers who possess the least power to influence it adversely.

4   *Substitute products*
    Substitute products can limit the potential of an industry by placing a ceiling on prices it can charge. If the industry is successful and earning high profits then it is more likely that competitors will enter the market via substitute products in order to obtain a share of the potential profits available.

5   *Industry competitors*
    The intensity of rivalry between industry competitors depends upon, for example.

- The concentration of the industry (numerous competitors or equal size will lead to more intense rivalry)
- Rate of industry growth (slow growth will tend towards greater rivalry)
- Value of fixed costs (high fixed costs might be a temptation to cut prices)
- Whether the product is a commodity dependent upon price and service
- The similarity of competitor strategies (if they have different ideas of how to compete they will run into each other continuously)
- Whether the firm has high stakes in achieving success
- Whether the industry exhibits high exit barriers (if yes, then firms will tend to remain in the industry even if they are making low or negative returns).

There is little doubt that the Porter framework has added considerably to our knowledge of how to appraise the elements of competitive industry structure. A third approach, however, is the concept of *strategic group analysis*. Porter has also contributed to the useful notion of 'strategic' group analysis.

Strategic group analysis

The idea of **strategic group analysis** is based on the notion that groups of companies with similar strategic characteristics within an industry are, in fact, in more direct competition with one another than other groups of companies in the same industry with dissimilar strategic characteristics. The strategic characteristics appropriate to form strategic groupings differ from industry to industry, but Johnson and Scholes[14] include, for example, the following:

- Extent of geographic coverage
- Distribution channels used
- Size of organization
- Number of market segments served
- Pricing policy

- Marketing mix
- Cost position
- Utilization of capacity.

An example of strategic groupings for the UK brewing industry produced by Johnson and Thomas[15] is shown in Figure 2.7 to illustrate how this concept works. The figure shows that there were four distinct strategic groupings in the UK brewing industry when this analysis was conducted. In this particular example, the strategic groupings (which, remember, show companies with similar strategic characteristics and/or following similar strategies and/or competing on a similar basis) have been arrived at on the basis of the extent to which the companies are national or local, and the extent to

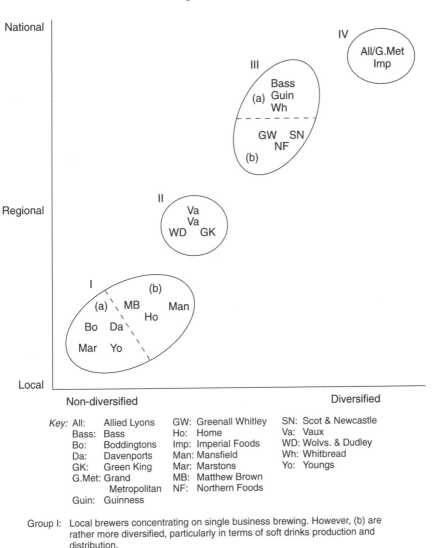

Figure 2.7
Strategic groups in the UK brewing industry.
Source: 'Research in the brewing industry' by Johnson, G. and Thomas, H. in Johnson, G. and Scholes, K., *Exploring Corporate Strategy*, 2nd edn, New Jersey, 1988, p. 74.

Key:

All:	Allied Lyons	GW:	Greenall Whitley	SN:	Scot & Newcastle
Bass:	Bass	Ho:	Home	Va:	Vaux
Bo:	Boddingtons	Imp:	Imperial Foods	WD:	Wolvs. & Dudley
Da:	Davenports	Man:	Mansfield	Wh:	Whitbread
GK:	Green King	Mar:	Marstons	Yo:	Youngs
G.Met:	Grand Metropolitan	MB:	Matthew Brown		
Guin:	Guinness	NF:	Northern Foods		

Group I: Local brewers concentrating on single business brewing. However, (b) are rather more diversified, particularly in terms of soft drinks production and distribution.

Group II: More geographically extended regional brewers.

Group III: National (a) or semi-national (b) brewers who have grown and diversified from a brewing base.

Group IV: Diversified conglomerates with interest in brewing.

which they have diversified into non-brewing activities. Perhaps not surprisingly these two characteristics also appear to be linked to the size of the organization, with the smaller companies being less diversified and more local.

Competitors' objectives and strategies

As the strategic group analysis approach to analysing competitive industry structure indicates, in addition to structural characteristics of an industry, it is also important to assess how a company's competitors compete (their strategies) and to what purpose (their objectives).

If a company were contemplating entering a new market in which there were existing competitors, it would be important to analyse the ways in which these competitors compete. For example, competition in the market may be based primarily on price, or it might alternatively be on delivery and quality. Whatever the basis, it is important to assess the extent to which either your company can compete successfully on the same basis, or the extent to which a different basis for competing might be more appropriate or feasible.

In markets where competitors compete on a similar basis – i.e. where their competitive strategies are similar – competition tends to be fiercer. Markets where there are a variety of strategies for competing tend to offer more scope for establishing a competitive advantage for a company and are usually more attractive.

Competitor objectives, too, should be considered in this part of the appraisal. In many organizations the overall objective may be to maximize profits, but objectives are rarely as simple as this. In any event, many companies that operate in the non-profit making business arena still have fierce competition.

As an example of the importance of establishing competitor objectives, consider the case where a company establishes that its major competitor has the objective of increasing market share with a long-term view to securing market leadership. Knowing this would not only indicate what the major thrusts of this competitor are likely to be, but in addition, the company would also begin to delineate what its defensive *reaction* should be.

Similarly, if our competitors are part of larger companies it is extremely useful to know how they figure in the overall operation and plans of these parent companies.

Competitors' strengths and weaknesses

Having identified our competitors, assessed the competitive structure of the industry, and assessed our competitors' present and future objectives and strategies, the next stage is to assess their relative strengths and weaknesses.

It is not too difficult to appreciate the importance of this part of competitive analysis. A football team manager assesses the relative strengths and weaknesses of the opponents before deciding how to take them. If our major competitors are aggressive, cash rich and have lower operating costs than we have, it would hardly make sense to attack them on price. Similarly, if our competitors are much larger than ourselves (and consequently more powerful), it would probably make more sense to avoid head-on confrontation and instead pursue flanking or niche strategies in the market. We shall examine the range of competitive strategies in later chapters; at this stage we need to consider the sort of factors that should be included in an analysis of their strengths and weaknesses.

Below are listed some of the possible factors that might form part of a detailed competitor strengths and weaknesses assessment:

Financial
- Liquidity ratio
- Profits
- Turnover
- Breakeven points
- Return on investment.

Personnel
- Labour supply
- Qualifications
- Experience
- Aggressiveness
- Style.

Production
- Capacity
- Size of plant
- Productivity
- Plant location
- Quality control.

Market
- Market share
- Customer service
- Price competitiveness
- Distribution channels

Clearly there are many factors against which we might assess the relative strengths and weaknesses of our identified competitors and, in addition, some of them would not be easy to assess. In order to help in this process of assessment it helps to proceed in a systematic and objective way using rating scales. One possible approach is as follows:

1 *Identify key factors for success (KFS) in the industry*
For example, if product quality, price and delivery are essential to competitive success in the industry, it makes sense to appraise your own company and competitors against these factors.

2 *Rank both your own company and competitors against these factors using an appropriate rating scale*
For example, you might assign a score to your own company and competitors against each criterion on the following basis:

Score	Evaluation
0	Very poor/dismal
1	Poor
2	Below average
3	Average
4	Above average
5	Good
6	Excellent

Better still, where appropriate get your customers to make the evaluation; after all it is their perceptions which count.

3 *Assess implications for future competitive strategies*
Having completed the evaluation, a company is then in a position to assess what

its future competitive strategies need to be, so that account can be taken of the relative strengths and weaknesses identified.

You will note that we have included in this assessment the assessing company itself: this is important. Remember, we are assessing *relative* strengths and weaknesses. The fact that your competition is strong, but you are stronger, would result in a very different competitive strategy from where the assessment shows that you are strong, but your competitors are stronger! Similarly, an assessment which showed your competitors to be weak, but your company weaker would result in very different strategies from where the assessment showed your company to be weak but your competitors weaker. This sort of analysis can be particularly useful in determining which competitors to attack (if any) and which to avoid.

You should also note that it is impossible to be definitive about the criteria for assessment. After all, the key factors for success will vary from industry to industry, and even from one customer group to another. Certainly, financial and market strengths and weaknesses are likely to figure in most assessments, but it is for the marketing planner to determine the assessment criteria most appropriate to the circumstances.

Owing to the importance of assessing 'relative' strengths and weaknesses we shall return to this important aspect in Chapter 3 when we look at the assessment of internal strengths and weaknesses.

Assessing and anticipating competitors' reactions

A crucial stage in competitor analysis is to try to gauge how your competitors will react in the marketplace, and in particular to assess how they might respond to your own competitive moves. In a sense this is similar to an army general trying to assess how his counterpart might respond in battle, and is just as difficult!

Studying competitors can tell us a lot about their likely moves and reactions to such things as promotional campaigns, price cuts or new product launches. However, different competitors will react in different ways to different forms of competition. Kotler[16] outlines four common 'reaction profiles' among competitors:

- The *laid-back competitor:* little or no response to competitive moves
- The *selective competitor:* is sensitive to some strategies (e.g. price cutting) but not to others
- The *tiger competitor:* will respond quickly and aggressively to any competitor move
- The *stochastic competitor:* responds in an unpredictable manner

Likely competitor actions are perhaps the most difficult aspect of a competitor's behaviour to assess. Even the most predictable of competitors can sometimes act or react in an unpredictable way. Just as it would be unwise for the army general not even to attempt to gauge his enemies' possible responses, so too must the strategic market planner attempt to gauge competitors' reactions.

Competitor intelligence: collecting information on competitors

Clearly, competitor analysis requires an efficient and effective competitor intelligence system. One of the problems here is that, understandably, competitors are not knowingly willing to volunteer the information required for the analysis we have just covered. Indeed, this information can be amongst the most difficult and sensitive of market information to obtain. Some sort of competitor intelligence gathering goes on in most organizations; the essentials of an effective system are now outlined.

A competitor intelligence system should address the following considerations:

1   Nature and type of information required
2   Frequency of information gathering and reporting
3   Responsibility for information gathering
4   Methods of data collection and sources
5   Information analysis and dissemination procedures

There is probably a fine dividing line between what could properly be termed 'legitimate' intelligence gathering activities on competitors and what might more rightly be termed 'snooping'. At the extreme, of course, some intelligence gathering activities fall into the category of industrial espionage, which may bring with it legal ramifications. Having said this, competitor intelligence gathering is becoming more and more intense. The extent to which some companies will now go to in order to collect this information is evidenced by Flax[17] who lists at least 20 techniques for 'snooping' on competitors.

In addition to the more conventional sources, such as competitors' publications, balance sheets and past employees, Flax also includes more radical approaches such as 'collecting competitors' garbage' and aerial photography.

Marketing strategies for different competitive positions in an industry: marketing warfare

In recent years it has been suggested that a company's competitive position in an industry will be one of the most important determinants of marketing strategies. Some of the most significant contributions to thinking in this area have stemmed from the work of the A. D. Little Consultancy Company. They have suggested the following alternative categories of possible competitive position for a company in an industry. Associated with each category of alternative competitive position we have given a brief indication of some of the possible implications for strategic marketing.

- *Dominant:* As the term suggests, the dominant competitor in an industry is the company which overtly or tacitly controls all of the competitors. Dominance may stem from a number of factors such as size/resources, control of raw materials, control of distribution channels, control of technologies etc. Needless to say the dominant company is in a very strong position as it can exercise considerable choice over strategies such as pricing.
- *Strong:* Although these companies do not dominate the market, their size and strength enables them to exercise considerable discretion over their marketing strategies. Although other competitors cannot be ignored, strong competitors are understandably treated with caution by other companies.
- *Favourable:* These competitors in a market have particular strengths which enable them to compete effectively even though they may not be amongst the largest and strongest companies. Often their favourable position derives from a particular aspect of their marketing such as a strong brand name, a reputation for technological innovation etc. Often these strengths may be used to lever a stronger position within a market and companies in this position can in the long run, become strong or even dominant in a market.
- *Tenable:* Although these competitors can make profits and survive, they are often at the mercy of the dominant, strong, and favourable competitors. Companies in this

position have no particular significant differential advantages over their competitors and therefore must follow the market leaders in much of their elements of marketing strategy.

- *Weak:* These competitors are at a considerable disadvantage in the market. Their weakness may stem from many factors, e.g. small size, weak brands, poor quality, etc. Weak competitors must either improve in those areas where their weaknesses are significant or they would be driven out of the market.
- *Non-viable:* As the term implies these competitors should not be in the market as they are in no position to compete. Nor do they have any avenues left which will enable them to improve their position, and therefore should leave the industry before they are forced out of it.

An alternative perspective on competitor position and marketing strategies is that proposed by Kotler[18]. He distinguishes between the strategies available to the following types of competitors in an industry:

- *Market Leaders:* **The market leader** is the company with the largest market share. This competitive market position often gives a company significant cost and power advantages. There is strong evidence that market leaders invariably have the highest rates of return on capital employed. Market leaders may also shape prices, industry standards, and methods of competing in a market. Market leaders are often the target for other companies and therefore need to make every effort to maintain their leadership position. A number of strategies may be used in an effort to maintain market leadership. First of all, the market leader may attempt to expand the total market through, e.g. new uses or more frequent usage. Market leaders tend to benefit disproportionately from any increases in overall market size and hence this strengthens their market share position. Secondly, the market leader must also do everything in its power to defend its market share against market challenges. This means that market leaders must not become complacent and must seek to constantly innovate and move to protect any weaknesses.
- *Market Challengers:* **Market challengers** are the companies in particular that market leaders need to defend their position against. They can be second in market share terms or lower, but they are distinguished by their desire to become market leaders. Market challengers often take advantage of the potential for complacency by market leaders referred to earlier. Many companies have risen from relatively low market shares to become dominant market leaders. Many of the Japanese companies in particular have risen in this way. Market challengers must seek to outperform the market leader in some way. This may involve finding new ways to attract customers in a market and/or attacking the weaknesses of the market leader.
- *Market Followers:* **Market followers** are companies that do not want to challenge for market leadership, but for a variety of reasons prefer instead to follow the strategies of the market leader. This does not necessarily mean that they will do exactly what the market leader does with respect to, e.g. prices, etc, but it does mean that their strategies are primarily shaped by the market leader. There are disadvantages to being a market follower but many companies have found that this is a viable and profitable strategy, particularly where they have no significant advantages compared to the market leader.
- *Market-nichers:* A very successful strategy for many companies has been to concentrate on specialist parts of the market which the larger companies have either consciously or unconsciously ignored. This strategy is particularly useful for the smaller company. Essentially, **market niching** is a target marketing strategy and hence is also discussed in Chapter 6 where we refer to this targeting strategy as 'Concentrated marketing'.

An interesting development in the formulation of marketing strategies in recent years has taken these notions of competitive market positions and the importance of building strategies around these and relative competitor strengths and linked them to some of the concepts and techniques developed by military strategists when considering techniques of warfare. In part, this in itself is a recognition of the extreme competition in many markets now faced by competitors and, the notion that companies must either 'kill' or be 'killed' by their competitors. Important indirect or direct contributors to this notion of marketing as a 'war' include both the conventional military strategists and thinkers such as Carl von Clauserwitz[19] and B. Liddell-Hart[20] and, more recently, marketing writers such as Kotler and Singh[21]. Although some do not like the idea of applying the principles of warfare to markets and marketing and others believe that some of the analogies made between markets and battlefields are not particularly useful, there is no doubt that this concept of marketing as warfare and hence the application of some of the principles of battlefield command is becoming increasingly popular amongst some marketing academics and practitioners.

Data for analysing the environment

The scope and complexity of environmental analysis mean that the marketer can be involved in extensive data collection. As we have seen, not all of this data is readily and easily available. For example, information for analysing competitors is perhaps understandably sometimes difficult to acquire. Moreover, the amount of data which can be required for environmental analysis means that the marketer must be careful to avoid the potential problem of information overload. The marketer therefore must discriminate between essential and non-essential data for the analysis. Data can come from a variety of sources: internal data, for example, can come from sales, accounts, customer service, research and development and so on, whereas external data can come from both secondary sources such as, say, government publications, industry statistics and so on, and primary sources such as customer questionnaires, focus groups and so on.

Increasingly information for environmental analysis is collected and analysed via computer-based information systems, and increasingly this information is on-line and therefore real time information. In particular, in recent years we have seen the growth of databases which allow constant and instant access to-up-to date information on a company's environment. These, and other aspects of information provision for marketing analysis and decision making are considered further in subsequent chapters but particularly in Chapter 13.

Summary

In this chapter we have looked at the nature and importance of environmental analysis in strategic market planning. This appraisal is crucial because it is from trends and changes in the environment that marketing opportunities and threats arise.

The importance of environmental trends and changes means that it is important for the planner to appraise or 'scan' the environment. We have also seen the development of formal systematic scanning systems, but this has not perhaps kept pace with the development of strategic approaches to planning.

Summary – continued

The 'environment' of the marketing planner and organization includes all those factors outside the marketing management function of the firm; it encompasses the intra-firm environment, the micro-environment and the macro-environment. In this chapter we have concentrated principally on the key elements of the wider macro-environment and the competitive element of the micro-environment.

Effective environmental appraisal requires, first and foremost, the use of a systematic framework in an organization; although, as we have seen, according to the marketing literature such frameworks are few and far between.

Even using a systematic framework, environmental appraisal is made more difficult by the problems of:

1   Identifying 'relevant' trends.
2   Forecasting the future.
3   Assessing the impact of environmental trends and changes.

Again, it is important to remember that the prime purpose of the assessment of environmental factors is to identify marketing opportunities and threats.

We have also seen that a key element of environmental appraisal for planning purposes is the analysis of the competitive environment. The marketing planner must identify competitors in existing and proposed markets and in particular should understand the competitive *structure* of relevant industries.

In addition to the identification of competitors and industry structure analysis, the strategic marketing planner must also appraise and understand competitor objectives and strategies; their relative strengths and weaknesses; and their likely reactions to competitive moves. All of this requires an effective system of competitor intelligence gathering activities.

The extent of competition in many markets has prompted considerable research regarding the relationship between a company's competitive position in an industry and the choice of strategies. We have seen that strategies will differ according to a company's competitive market position. On the one hand a company's competitive position may be designated along a continuum ranging between 'dominant' to 'untenable'. An alternative perspective on competitive position is that of market leadership, challenger, follower or nicher. Both perspectives provide useful insights into possible marketing strategies. Finally, with respect to the competitor element of the environment, we have seen that increasingly marketers are drawing upon the concepts and principles developed for the 'battlefield' in developing suitable marketing strategies.

Important and essential though the appraisal of environmental factors is, in fact, it represents only one half of a SWOT analysis. Clearly, as already mentioned, it is the environment that gives rise to the opportunities and threats side of the SWOT analysis. The other half of our SWOT analysis concerns the assessment of the organization's strengths and weaknesses. It is to this part of the analysis that we now turn our attention in Chapter 3.

Key terms

Intra-firm environment [p33]
Micro-environment [p33]
Macro-environment [p34]
Environmental scanning [p37]
Strategic group analysis [p46]

Market leader [p52]
Market challengers [p52]
Market followers [p52]
Market nichers [p52]

Questions

1 What is the importance of environmental analysis to the marketing manager?
2 What are the three levels of environment and what are some of the major elements in each of these levels?
3 What are the key requirements for an effective system of environmental appraisal?
4 What are the key forces in Porter's framework of Competitive Industry Structure?
5 What key pieces of information would the marketer ideally like to know about competitors, and what are the different types of competitor positions which can be identified in an industry?

References

1. Ferrell, O. C., Hartline, M. D., Lucas, G. H. and Luck, D., *Marketing Strategy*, The Dryden Press, Orlando, 1999, p. 32.
2. Ferrell, O. C., *et al.*, op. cit., p. 32.
3. Kotler, P., *Marketing Management: Analysis, Planning, Implementation and Control* 9th edn, Prentice-Hall, New Jersey, 1997, p. 671.
4. Lancaster, G. and Massingham, L. C., *Essentials of Marketing*, McGraw-Hill, London, 3rd edn, p. 193.
5. Carson, R., *Silent Spring*, Houghton Mifflin, New York, 1962.
6. Aguilar, F. J., *Scanning the Business Environment*. Macmillan, Basingstoke, 1967.
7. Jain, S. C., 'Environmental scanning: how the best companies do it', *Journal of Long Range Planning*, April 1984, pp. 117–128.
8. Johnson, G. and Scholes, K., *Exploring Corporate Strategy*, 5th edn, Prentice-Hall, Europe, 1999, pp. 136–141.
9. Jain, S. C., *Marketing Planning and Strategy*, 2nd edn, South Western Publishing Co., Cincinatti, 1985, p. 277.
10. Tversky, A. and Kahnemann, D., 'Judgements under uncertainty, heuristics and biases', *Science*, Vol. 185, 1995, pp. 1124–1131.
11. Kotler, P., *Marketing Management: Analysis, Planning, Implementation and Control*, 6th edn, Prentice-Hall, New Jersey, 1988, p. 52.
12. Porter, M. E., *Competitive Advantage: Creating and Sustaining Superior Performance*, Free Press, New York, 1985, p. 32.
13. Porter, M. E., *Competitive strategy*, Free Press, New York, 1980.
14. Johnson, G. and Scholes, K., op. cit., p. 128.
15. Johnson, G. and Thomas, H. 'Research in the brewing industry' in G. Johnson and K. Scholes, *Exploring Corporate Strategy*, 2nd edn, Prentice-Hall, New Jersey, 1988.

16. Kotler, P., *Marketing Management: Analysis, Planning, Implementation and Control*, 9th edn, Prentice-Hall, New Jersey, 1997, p. 239.
17. Flax, S., 'How to snoop on your competitors', *Fortune*, 14 May 1984, pp. 29–33.
18. Kotler, P., *Marketing Management: Analysis, Planning, Implementation and Control*, 9th edn Prentice-Hall, New Jersey, 1997, chap. 6.
19. Clauserwitz, C. van, *On War*, Routledge & Kegan Paul, London, 1990.
20. Liddell-Hart, B. H., *Strategy*, Praeger, New York, 1967.
21. Kotler, P. and Singh, R., 'Marketing warfare in the 1980s', *Journal of Business Strategy*, Winter 1981, pp. 30–41.

Case Study

Tom Salmon has just received the latest figures from his market research agency regarding last year's overall market position. He is well satisfied. This is the third year that his company, in which he is marketing director has come out leader in terms of market share.

The company was formed ten years ago and supplies specialist measuring and testing machinery for use primarily in pathology laboratories. From nothing, the company has grown by overtaking competitors in the market based on innovative new products, aggressive pricing and high levels of after-sales service and technical advice. When the company started, the present incumbents in the market were well established with stable market positions and traditional ways of trading. In fact, Tom Salmon's competitors had, if anything, become complacent over the years. Although these competitors were well established and obviously much larger than the new entrant, indeed perhaps because of these characteristics, some of their products and technologies were outdated. For example, they did not include the most recent developments in pharmaceutical measuring and testing machinery from America. Technology had moved on and Salmon's company spotted the opportunity of applying this new technology to a new range of products for the industry.

In addition to changes in technology, the market had also changed. Government initiatives had forced hospital administrators and purchasing officers to become much more effective and efficient in their supplier choice for equipment and consumables. New systems of tendering were introduced which made existing supplier relationships, often developed over many years, less important as more and more emphasis in supplier choice was placed on value for money. Salmon and his colleagues spotted these trends and decided there was an opportunity for a new aggressive competitor in the market.

Ten years on, Salmon quite rightly could feel a degree of satisfaction in how things had gone. They had moved from being a market nicher through to being a market challenger, and eventually market leader in the short space of ten years.

Salmon has a forthcoming meeting with his fellow directors in research and development, finance, personnel, and so on. He is slightly worried that their now established position as market leader is beginning to lead to an air of complacency in the company. It seems to him that new product development has slowed, and there is not as much enthusiasm to secure new business. He is also worried that 2 more small new companies have entered the market with exceptionally good products and very cost-effective pricing policies.

He feels that at the forthcoming meeting he needs to impress upon his fellow directors the fact that history appears to be repeating itself.

QUESTION

What elements of the marketing environment should Tom Salmon and his marketing team analyse and assess with regard to developing future marketing plans, and how can the company attempt to protect its position as the market leader?

3

Appraising resources: strengths and weaknesses

Chapter objectives

After reading this chapter you will:

▶ Appreciate the importance of appraising the resources of a company.

▶ Understand how this appraisal should be organized and conducted.

▶ Understand how to translate the internal appraisal into an assessment of the Opportunities and Threats elements of the SWOT analysis.

▶ Be familiar with how the Strengths and Weaknesses assessment feeds into and affects the process of strategic market planning.

Introduction

In Chapter 2 we looked at the appraisal of environmental factors in strategic marketing planning. The significance of environmental appraisal, it was suggested, is that environmental trends and changes can, and do, give rise to major marketing opportunities and threats. We have also noted that the identification of these opportunities and threats represents one half of our SWOT (or TOWS) analysis. The other half of our SWOT analysis entails the appraisal of organizational resources in order to ascertain strengths and weaknesses. The important point to reiterate here is that, as shown in Chapter 1, the assessment of possible opportunities and threats and the appraisal of strengths and weaknesses only makes sense if we consider both internal and external factors together. Lancaster and Massingham[1] provide the following example to illustrate this point:

> Long-term forecasts of world oil reserves suggest major profit opportunities for those organizations with the necessary resources to develop, say, alternative forms of energy, and a major threat to those who, for one reason or another, do not have the skills, resources or wisdom to develop these alternative sources of supply.

As a practical illustration of how both strengths and weaknesses and opportunities and threats go together, and continuing our oil example, we can consider the recent worldwide increases in the price of oil.

Continued high demand due to high levels of economic activity in many of the developed economies of the world coupled with restrictions on production by the OPEC countries have combined rapidly to increase oil prices at the start of the new millennium. In the UK over a period of 12 months during the year 2000, prices have increased by over 30%. For some companies these increases represent major threats to their business. Obviously those companies that rely heavily on oil or oil-derivative products either for producing their own products or in, say, delivering their products to customers, are particularly threatened by these trends in oil prices. So, for example, companies producing plastic and synthetic products such as textile fibres, some of which are almost exclusively derived from oil products, are either having to increase their prices and/or reduce their costs in other areas. In contrast, other companies and industries are finding that the increases in oil prices are leading to major marketing opportunities. For example, producers of alternative energy forms and/or alternative powered vehicles in the motor industry car such as, say, battery-powered cars, are experiencing much greater levels of interest and demand. Within these broad patterns of opportunities and threats, however, some companies are more or less threatened than others according to their profile of strengths and weaknesses. In the car industry, for example, both Volkswagen and Honda have developed strengths in the area of energy-saving vehicles, including ones powered by solar and battery power. This, therefore, places them in a much stronger position than many of their competitors who through lack of investment are weak in these new products and technologies.

To reiterate this point, we can see that it is impossible for the individual company to assess the strategic implications of environmental trends and changes, and specifically the extent to which they will pose opportunities or threats, without considering these trends and changes in the context of organizational resources. In addition, selection and implementation of strategies are also dependent on organizational strengths and weaknesses. In short, then, resource analysis and the assessment of organizational strengths and weaknesses which stem from this analysis are a key task of strategic marketing management. As we shall see, important though this task may be, it is one which is fraught with the problems of complexity.

Problems and issues in assessing strengths and weaknesses

The assessment of strengths and weaknesses is, as we have seen, central to the development of strategic marketing plans. Indeed, in most case-based marketing courses and texts, this analysis is often suggested as being the starting point for students. Notwithstanding this, resource analysis, and in particular, interpreting what this analysis implies in terms of strengths and weaknesses, is often misunderstood and therefore performed poorly by academic analysts and marketing practitioners alike. Underpinning this misunderstanding are two basic factors.

Firstly, the assessment of strengths and weaknesses is complex and multi-faceted. Furthermore, and related to this, is the need to exercise creativity, judgement and substantial managerial expertise in the assessment process. In short, the assessment of strengths and weaknesses involves more than just a straightforward 'mechanical' listing of organizational resources (although, unfortunately, such a 'listing' commonly occurs in practice).

Secondly, and relatedly (albeit somewhat surprisingly), it has to be admitted that until relatively recently, the development of both conceptual frameworks and systematic methods to help the marketing planner assess strengths and weaknesses have been poor. Subash Jain[2] brings this point home forcibly:

A systematic scheme for analysing strengths and weaknesses is still in its embryonic form. One hardly finds any scholarly work on the subject of strengths and weaknesses . . .

Notwithstanding these problems, again we need to stress the importance of developing an assessment of strengths and weaknesses. Indeed, we first need to recognize and deal with the practical problems and issues which confront the strategic marketing planner in this area. Specifically, it is essential to address the following questions:

- What attributes and activities should be included in an appraisal of strengths and weaknesses?
- How can we evaluate what are 'strengths' and what are 'weaknesses'?
- How should we organize and conduct the appraisal procedure?
- How can we interpret and use the output of our strengths and weaknesses appraisal?

We can now turn our attention to each of these questions in turn.

What attributes and activities should be included in the appraisal?

The first step in conducting an appraisal of strengths and weaknesses is to determine the attributes to assess, i.e. what activities and/or resources of an organization should form the basis of the analysis?

According to what we assess in our strengths and weaknesses analysis, we will arrive at very different conclusions and, thus, very different strategy formulations. Determination of the 'right' attributes to measure is not easy and may require considerable analysis and creativity.

The most common approach to analysing strengths and weaknesses is to use a checklist for the delineation of resources and/or activities to be assessed. For example, it is often suggested that one should start by listing all the functional areas in the organization and then proceed to produce a list of all the attributes in each functional area which might conceivably be assessed for strengths and weaknesses. An example of this type of approach is:

Marketing, e.g.
- Brand names
- Corporate image
- Distribution
- Product range
- Prices
- Sales force
- Marketing systems.

Financial, e.g.
- Cost of capital
- Liquidity
- Profitability
- Asset structure
- Price/earnings ratio.

Manufacturing, e.g.
- Capacity usage

- Age profile of plant
- Manufacturing systems
- Quality control
- Flexibility
- Economies of scale.

Personnel, e.g.
- Skill levels
- Adaptability
- Manpower planning
- Industrial relations
- Working conditions.

Many texts on strategic management and marketing offer 'standardized' checklists for the appraisal of strengths and weaknesses, including, for example, Kotler,[3] Lynch[4] and McDonald.[5] Our intention is not to criticize the use of such checklists; indeed, they are particularly helpful in enabling the market planner to think more broadly about the range of factors which might usefully be assessed. However, there are three particular problems with the use of checklists and especially the use of 'textbook' checklists, as follows:

1   *Number of attributes*
First, there are literally dozens of possible attributes which could conceivably be appraised. Analysis of all of them is likely to be extremely time-consuming and costly. More importantly, however, not all company resources and activities are strategically significant. This brings us to the second problem, which is associated with using 'standardized' checklists.

2   *Which attributes?*

As has been suggested, a particular company's resources and activities are strategically important. Which ones are vital to assess from a strengths and weaknesses perspective are specific to that company and the product/market combinations in which it operates. It is crucial to assess the resources and activities which are **key factors for success** in the markets in which the company competes, or intends to compete. The Japanese strategist Ohmae[6] has referred to these as 'key factors for success' and it is, therefore, those resources and activities which underpin these key factors which should be assessed. This point cannot be more strongly emphasized. This, in turn, means that each company must establish its *own list of attributes* for assessment according to its existing and/or proposed product/market strategy. It also means that if a company does not know what these critical success factors are, it must then establish them. It is important that the process of establishing these key attributes be carried out as systematically and objectively as possible and not based, for example, on guesswork or on the basis of what management 'feels' the key attributes should be; nor, indeed should it be based on an uncritical use of standard checklists.

In most industries and in most companies the critical attributes against which to assess strengths and weaknesses will be 'known' to experienced market managers. For example, in the confectionery industry, both brand reputation and strong distribution are critical factors to competitive success and these will need to be appraised in any analysis of strengths and weaknesses. Similarly, for most companies, assessment of, say, financial strengths and weaknesses will be critical in delineating and selecting between alternative marketing strategies. Indeed, it is often the case that only relatively few factors will be critical to success or failure in a market.

Most industry pundits agree that the key factors for success in the UK fashion jeans market are the following:

- Strong and effective branding.
- Distribution effectiveness.
- Quality.
- Innovation and new product development.

A company which has all of these attributes and therefore remains a leader in this market, despite extensive competition, is the Levi Strauss Company. Building on its strong brand presence in his market, combined with a reputation for quality, Levi Strauss continues to innovate. Its latest brand of denim products, the 'Engineered' range, looks set to take the market by storm. Levis has continued to focus on the quality end of the market with this product and its strong distribution channels give it a competitive edge in the market.

A key attribute for strengths and weaknesses assessment is *how and why customers choose,* and in particular *what they consider to be of value.* In fact, customer needs assessment is crucial in answering our second question, namely: 'How can we evaluate what are strengths and what are weaknesses?' A customer-oriented focus is vital.

Before we turn our attention to this second question we must first consider the third problem in the checklist approach to assessing strengths and weaknesses, namely, the problem of the interrelationships between the various organizational resources and activities.

3   *Interrelationships between attributes, synergy and balance*
Even if we have identified the key attributes for our strengths and weaknesses assessment, it is important to recognize that invariably the individual attributes will be interlinked. A simple checklist approach, even if this is based on an objective, customer-based assessment of key attributes, fails to recognize this. For example, a company may be only moderately strong in, say, selling and sales management, branding and promotion, and product range when these are assessed independently. Looked at in combination, those 'moderate strengths' may be such as to render the company extremely competitive and a real force to be reckoned with in the marketplace. You may recognize this concept of the combined effect of parts being greater than the sum of their individual effects as the concept of *synergy*, first popularized in planning circles by Ansoff.[7] Needless to say, synergy can be both positive or negative in its effect. What is important is the need to recognize that the checklist approach tends to underestimate the importance of assessing the extent to which the various activities and resources of an organization complement, or do not complement, each other. Very often it is the *balance* of organizational resources and activities which is important. Although this makes the assessment of strengths and weaknesses more problematical, it is a vital consideration. The question of 'balance' is increasingly being recognized as an important facet of a strengths and weaknesses appraisal and some of the more recent techniques and tasks of strategic appraisal, such as portfolio analysis, which we shall consider in the next chapter, are particularly useful in this respect.

How can we evaluate what are strengths and what are weaknesses?

Our second practical problem for the strategic marketing planner relates to the seemingly straightforward issue of what constitutes a strength or weakness, i.e. what is involved in evaluating strengths and weaknesses. This is not perhaps straightforward at all. To illustrate the issues in this area we will consider first the question of what is a strength and the significance of **distinctive competencies**. Secondly, we shall look at customer needs and the notion of *value chains*. Thirdly, we shall examine, once again, the importance of *evaluating competition*. Finally, we will look at the use of *profiles* in assessing strengths and weaknesses.

In order to illustrate some of these key issues in evaluating organizational strengths, let us imagine that a company has recently completed an analysis of its strengths and weaknesses and that this analysis suggests that the company has the following 'strengths':

- A reputation for high quality
- Good after-sales service
- Distinctive brands and packaging
- Efficient production
- Spare capacity
- A well trained and effective sales force

Certainly, any company which possessed these attributes would, at first glance, seem to have a number of significant strengths. The key questions for our hypothetical company are the extent to which these are truly strengths, and how it has arrived at the conclusion that they indeed are. Here are some of the important considerations in answering these questions.

First, how strong is 'strong'? One of the considerations for our company is to assess precisely how strong the company is in each of the areas listed above. For example, the company feels it has a strength in the areas of after-sales service – but does this mean that it is 'very strong' in this area, or is it rather only 'moderately strong', or is it simply 'not weak'? At first glance, these distinctions may appear to be somewhat pedantic. Nevertheless, in strategic terms the *degree* of strength is crucial. Being 'satisfactory' or even 'moderately strong' along some dimension is very different from having a major strength.

Where a company has a major strength with respect to some factor, we refer to it as having a *distinctive competence*.

Hamel and Prahalad[8] clarify for us the importance of being distinctively competent as opposed to merely competent:

> Differentiation must be unique. If every company in the industry has the skill, then it is not a basis for differentiation unless the organization's skills in the area are really special.

There are plenty of examples of companies going out of business because they have failed to identify new real strengths, i.e. their distinctive competence as opposed to what they merely 'can do'. Similarly, many companies fail to capitalize on the marketing opportunities to which an identification of their true strengths might give rise.

Next, are these the factors which are relevant to competitive success? A second consideration in assessing a company's strengths is to relate distinctive competence to customer needs. Let us assume that after-sales service in our company is a distinctive competence. We must then ask whether or not after-sales service is an important factor to its customers. Put another way, the company has to determine the extent to which after-sales service is important in business success. The point here is that a company can be extremely strong in areas which are unrelated to business success, either in existing, or future/envisaged business areas. Such 'strengths' then are not strengths at all, and they can in fact constitute a major source of weakness if a company attempts to use these to compete strategically.

You will have recognized that this consideration is, in fact, related to our first problem of which attributes to include in our assessment of strengths and weaknesses. You will recall that it was suggested that the key attributes for a strengths and weaknesses assessment are those which underpin customer choice and in particular what they consider to be of value. It was also suggested that most experienced marketing managers in an industry will have a good 'feel' for what these key success factors are for their own product/market combinations and that often there are relatively few key factors. Nevertheless, both in the selection of attributes for assessment and in the assessment process itself it is vital to ensure that we understand what the customer considers value to be and the activities of the company which either add to or detract from this value. A useful concept in this respect is the concept of 'value chains'.

The concept of value chains

Developed by Porter,[9] **value chain analysis** is aimed at identifying potential competitive advantages. Porter suggested that the activities of a company can be broken down into nine 'value activities', five primary and four secondary. These value activities collectively comprise all those activities involved in designing, manufacturing, marketing and delivering the organization's products and services. Figure 3.1 illustrates the nine major groupings of activities in the value chain.

Primary activities comprise those activities associated with the input, throughput and output of goods and services in the organization, and include the following:

1 Inbound logistics: examples of activities in this area would include materials handling, stock control and delivery inwards.
2 Operations: examples of activities here would include packaging, assembly, equipment maintenance and testing.
3 Outbound logistics: for example, finished goods warehousing, materials handling, order processing and delivery outwards.
4 Marketing and sales: for example, advertising, promotion, sales force, pricing and channels.
5 Service: for example, installation, repairs and parts supply.

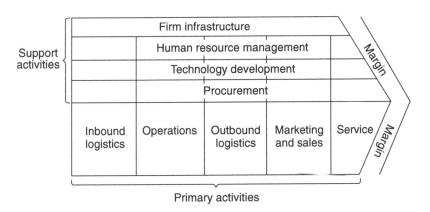

Figure 3.1
The value chain.
Source: Porter, M.E.,
Competitive Advantage: Creating and Sustaining Superior Performance, Free Press, New York, 1985, p. 37.

Support activities comprise those activities which facilitate primary activities in the physical creation of the product and its sale and transfer to the buyer and include the following:

6 Procurement: here, procurement refers to the *function* of purchasing inputs used in the organization's value chain and not to the purchased inputs themselves. Examples of activities here would include purchasing procedures, techniques of vendor analysis, information systems and so on. In addition, procurement activities may also include the procurement of more than simply, say, raw materials and components. An organization also 'procures' market research or accountancy expertise; hence activities concerned with procuring these services would also be included.

7 Technology development: these are support activities which improve the product and the process. The obvious areas of support activities here are those which are carried out in the research and development function, but they also include, for example, technology support activities for, say, office automation, communicating with customers, measuring quality and so on.

8 Human resource management: activities here would include, for example, recruitment, selection, training and development.

9 Firm infrastructure: examples of support activities in this category would include systems of quality control, financial systems and marketing planning.

Clearly, although the broad categories of value activities, both primary and secondary, are common to most organizations, individual components of value activities will tend to be company specific. The basic idea of the value chain concept is that each activity can be categorized and analysed with a view to securing competitive advantage. Specifically, Porter suggests that a company should analyse all its activities with a view to determining how these contribute to the value which the customer receives. They should also be analysed with respect to cost; the competitors' 'margin' shown in Figure 3.1 is the difference between total value and the cost of performing all the value activities. In simple terms, by looking at both value activities and the cost of performing them compared to the competition, it is suggested that an organization can look for competitive advantage either by cutting the costs of performing the value activities, whilst at the same time maintaining the value, or by increasing the value of the activities to the customer. Two further points about value chain analysis are also worthy of note.

1 First of all, value chains extend outside the organization itself to include, on the one hand, suppliers and, on the other, distributors. For example, a supplier may, through its own quality control activities, enhance the inbound logistics and operations activities of its customers, thereby adding value to its customers' customers. Similarly, distributors too can influence value. For example, a distributor may undertake to offer after-sales service for the manufacturers' brands which it supplies, thereby potentially adding value to these brands for the customer. Porter[9] refers to these as 'vertical linkages'.

2 Secondly, it is important to recognize that the value chain is not a set of independent activities. Each of the primary and secondary activities is potentially and actually interdependent. These are what Porter[9] calls '**horizontal linkages**' and it is often these linkages which form the basis of competitive advantage. For example, improved quality management (a 'firm infrastructure' activity) can enhance both manufacturing (an 'operations' activity) and marketing and service activities. In other words, all the value activity areas must be looked at together to achieve optimization and coordination.

This is necessarily a relatively brief introduction to the powerful concept of value chains. In fact, the uses of value chain analyses are complex and multi-faceted. Porter has developed the concept and techniques of value chain analysis in some depth in order to enable the company to look for ways of securing competitive advantage. In the context of assessing strengths and weaknesses, however, value chain analysis has four distinct benefits:

1   First of all, it provides a framework for addressing our earlier problem of which attributes (or activities) to assess in our strengths and weaknesses analyses.
2   Secondly, by using the concept of 'value' it forces the analysis of strengths and weaknesses to be more in relation both to how the customer views them and in relation to competition. Johnson and Scholes[10] have captured this use of the value chain well, as can be seen from the following extract from their text on corporate strategy:

> Value chain analysis describes the activities within and around an organization and relates them to an analysis of the competitive strengths of the organization or its ability to provide 'value for money' products or services.

> The analysis of value chain activities enables us to assess what are truly 'strengths' and what are truly 'weaknesses'.

3   Thirdly, the concept of horizontal linkages in value chain analysis reinforces our earlier point about the importance of looking at the interrelationships between resources and the related concepts of synergy and balance.

4   Finally, the concept of **vertical linkages** in value chain analysis forces us to think more broadly of possible strengths and weaknesses that derive from linkages with suppliers and distributors and which, in turn, stem from their strengths and weaknesses in relation to ours.

From its highly successful American base, the US retailer Walmart is now expanding into Europe. The company recently acquired the ASDA group of supermarkets in the UK and is threatening to turn the competitive structure of the industry inside out. Walmart has built its strategy for success around offering extremely good value products with low prices, whilst maintaining good quality. This strategy is built upon very effective value chain management and in particular the effective use of vertical links with suppliers. Perhaps more than any other company in the industry, Walmart has been able to reduce its costs thoughout the supply chain, thereby being able to pass these cost savings onto its customers. In order to compete successfully against this, Walmart's competitors will need to secure and manage their own vertical links in the value chain as effectively and efficiently as Walmart have done.

Next, are our competitors stronger or weaker than ourselves? The third consideration in evaluating what are strengths and weaknesses takes us back again to the importance of competitor analysis.

We saw in Chapter 2 that part of our competitor analysis is the assessment of *their* strengths and weaknesses. Once we have identified what are key strengths and weaknesses, and where our distinctive competences lie, we need also to assess the extent to which we have a *competitive advantage* with respect to these competences.

In the same way that we cannot make sense of what constitutes a 'strength' or a 'weakness' without assessing the extent to which the customer values these competences, so too we should not proceed to develop marketing strategies and plans based on these competences without also assessing how strong or weak our competitors are in these areas. Put concisely, strengths and weaknesses are always relative: relative to customer needs, and relative to competition. Therefore, the perspective to be taken is from the market to the company, and not from the company to the market – the essence again of marketing orientation.

The importance of assessing strengths and weaknesses in relation to competition (as well as customer needs) stems from the fact that a key reason for the assessment of strengths and weaknesses is, as we have seen, to help in the delineation and selection of competitive marketing strategies. So, for example, our company might have distinctive strengths in the areas of quality and after-sales service, and furthermore these might be strengths which the customer values and hence are key factors for success in the market. However, it might also be the case that our competitors are even stronger in these areas. Stronger, weaker or equal, it simply does not make sense to evaluate our strengths and weaknesses without comparing ourselves to the competition.

We can see from our discussion of the issues which arise in the process of evaluating strengths and weaknesses that these issues are complex. In some ways it might be said that weaknesses are easier to understand than strengths. Essentially weaknesses are constraints, but again, as with strengths, we need to assess weaknesses in the context of both customer and market needs and of the competition. A weakness in terms of after-sales service would matter less, and may not matter at all, if this factor were unimportant to business success and if our competitors were even weaker. Again, as with strengths, we also need to assess if our weaknesses are major or minor.

A particularly useful approach to the evaluation of both strengths and weaknesses relative to the competition is the use of a strengths and weaknesses profile.

Profiling systems in evaluating strengths and weaknesses

We have seen that the first two issues in appraising resources for strategic marketing planning relate to the important areas of attribute selection and the evaluation of those attributes with respect to the extent to which they are truly strengths or weaknesses. We have also seen that the second of these, i.e. the evaluation of strengths and weaknesses, involves both the identification of distinctive competences and the assessment of competitor strengths and weaknesses in the same areas. Simple profiling systems may be used to address both these issues, and is now described.

Having identified key resources or attributes for our strengths and weaknesses evaluation, we can then score our company with respect to these key attributes or resources using a simple numeric scale, as shown in Figure 3.2. Once this is completed for each attribute we can then repeat the process for each of our key competitors. Admittedly, this second part of the process is not easy, but it is extremely useful. In this way we can build up a series of 'profiles' of our own and competitor strengths and weaknesses, as shown in Table 3.1, which in turn can be used to delineate and select future strategies. Although such profiling enables a systematic approach to be made when evaluating strengths and weaknesses, inevitably the resultant profiles will depend on who is carrying out the evaluation. For example, the marketing manager may have a very different view of, say, product quality from the production manager. This brings us to the question of how we might organize and conduct the appraisal procedure.

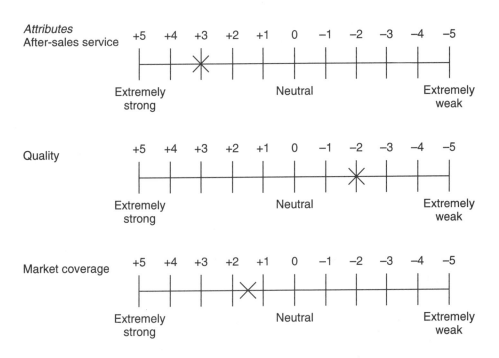

Figure 3.2
Key attributes scale.

Table 3.1 Strengths and weaknesses: company and competitor profiles				
	Assessment of relative strengths			
Attributes	Own company	Competitor A	Competitor B	Competitor C
Range of products	+5	−1	+5	+2
Terms of trade	+3	+2	+4	−1
Low cost production	−2	+2	+3	−1
After sales service	+4	+2	−1	−3
Quality of products	+5	−3	+4	+1
Market coverage	+3	+5	+5	+1

How should we organize and conduct the appraisal?

Even though a company's approach to evaluating strengths and weaknesses may be systematic, it may not always be objective. Perhaps inevitably the evaluation is likely to be essentially subjective, especially when it is carried out by the managers of that company. After all, everyone to some extent finds it difficult to be objectively self-critical.

For this reason, whenever possible, it is preferable to use an inter-functional team approach to internally based assessment systems. Where a company can call in external consultants to make the assessment, this is better still. Perhaps the best of all, however, as we saw in Chapter 2 with competitor analysis, is where the evaluation is at least partially based on a customer assessment of strengths and weaknesses. Not only are customers likely to be more objective and thorough, but it is the customers' perception of our strengths and weaknesses which is critical. The customer will not necessarily be in a position to make a full assessment – e.g. on finance and production. The customer is, however, capable of appraising perceived marketing strengths and weaknesses.

A related problem with company staff being involved in strengths and weaknesses assessment is that the process is often seen as being threatening: a fact that can severely detract from the objectivity, and hence usefulness, of the exercise.

In fact, Ferrell *et al.*[11] suggest that properly administered, the effective use of a SWOT analysis delivers several key benefits over and above its obvious input to the marketing plan. In particular, they suggest that the SWOT analysis helps to foster collaboration and information exchange between the different functional areas of the business. In turn, this can help create an environment of creativity and innovation. In order to achieve this benefit, however, the SWOT analysis process should be approached positively. In particular, it must not be used to punish or even criticize functions and/or individuals in the organization whenever weaknesses are identified.

How can we interpret and use the outcome of our strengths and weaknesses assessment?

The assessment of a company's strengths and weaknesses is not, of course, an end in itself. This assessment should feed into, and affect, the process of strategic market planning. Some of the major uses of the outcome of a strengths and weaknesses assessment, together with some of the major strategic planning concepts which accompany this use, are now described.

Matching strengths and weaknesses to opportunities and threats: the concept of 'strategic' fit

Environmental monitoring is important in order to assess the opportunities and threats which might face an organization. Once a company has assessed its own strengths and weaknesses, only then is it in an objective position to evaluate what constitutes a company marketing opportunity or threat. By carefully matching environmental trends and changes to its own particular blend of distinctive competences the strategic market planner is able to devise strategies which build on the company's strengths, whilst at the same time minimizing its weaknesses. By so doing, the planner aims to achieve what is termed a **'strategic fit'**.

Responding to environmental changes and trends: the concept of 'strategic windows'

A key feature of the environment is that it is constantly changing. Because of this, both the opportunities and threats assessment and the assessment of company strengths and weaknesses (SWOT analysis) should be carried out at regular intervals. If a company does not do this, then over time it is likely to find that its previously good 'strategic fit' has changed.

We should also not forget the fact that in a changing environment there are often only limited periods when the fit between the distinctive competences of a company and the opportunities presented by the environment are at optimum positions. Abell[12] has referred to such periods as 'strategic windows'; unless the organization acts quickly (which requires an effective system of SWOT analysis) then these windows will close.

Abell[12] suggests that the 'strategic window' concept can be used both by companies already in a market and by would-be entrants. For the incumbents, the concept enables the assessment of future strategies to take account of changes in the environment, and in particular for assessing the allocation of resources to existing activities. For the would-be entrant, the concept provides a framework for assessing possible diversification and new market entry opportunities based on matching these to organizational strengths.

The 1990s saw a huge increase in the number of people living alone. This group comprises several segments including, for example, young people leaving home for the first time, newly divorced individuals, new widows and widowers. It is primarily the first two of these groups which account for the increase in the demand for small, one-person dwellings that are easily managed and affordable. This trend is forecast to continue at least during the first part of the new millennium. The builder and developer, Barratts, were one of the first companies to spot this trend and to develop products and marketing programmes to fill this need. Certainly other companies are following and will move into this market, but Barratts developed a competitive edge by being amongst the first to spot this strategic window of opportunity.

Relationship to other areas of strategic market planning

We have seen that the assessment of an organization's strengths and weaknesses, together with the analysis of environmental trends and changes, is a key input to the identification of strategic windows and the development of a strategic fit. It is important to recognize that in achieving this, the appraisal of strengths and weaknesses is an essential input to the whole of the strategic marketing process, including for example:

● Business definition and objective setting
● The selection of appropriate target markets
● The formulation and implementation of marketing mix strategies

In particular, we must also remember that our strengths and weaknesses assessment enables the planner to determine what might be wanted or needed to change the company's profile of strengths and weaknesses. In contrast to environmental opportunities and threats, over which the company may have little or no control, with strengths and weaknesses it can implement action programmes to alter its profile.

For example, if an assessment indicates areas of relative weakness which are important to competitive success in the markets in which a company operates, then steps can be taken to correct these weaknesses. Similarly, a company need not limit itself to future strategies and opportunities which make use only of its existing strengths. If the opportunity is potentially substantial then a company can seek to develop or acquire the strengths required to take advantage of the situation.

Assessing core competencies

Closely related to the notion of distinctive competencies and key factors for success discussed earlier, Prahalad and Hamel[13] have suggested that a sustainable competitive advantage for a company is often based on a set of central strengths which, together form what they term a '**core competence**'. This core competence is what can be used to develop successful strategies against competitors. So, for example it is suggested that 3Ms core competence is based on their knowledge and applications of sticky-tape technology. Canon, on the other hand, has core competencies in precision mechanics, optical technologies and micro-electronics. The Black and Decker company has core competencies in the design and manufacture of small motors. Central to Prahalad and Hamel's notion of core competencies is the fact that the competencies underpin the company as a whole and can be used to support a number of different markets and businesses in the organization. For this reason they liken core competencies to the root system of a tree which supports the rest of the structure, the core products of the company which stem from the core competencies represent the trunk of a tree and its major limbs, whereas the smaller branches are business units and the leaves and flowers, specific end products. A company must therefore identify the core competencies around which its current and possibly future success will be built and seek to ensure that these core competencies are nurtured, protected, and enhanced. Nevertheless, as with all strengths, core competencies can only be used to develop a sustainable competitive advantage where they can be used to generate customer value and where the competencies are superior to competitors and defendable.

The notion of marketing assets

First used by Davidson in a series of articles in *Marketing* magazine,[14-16] the notion of **marketing assets** is perhaps one of the most valuable contributions to our knowledge of how to actually utilize an internal appraisal of strengths and weaknesses in competitive marketing. Essentially, marketing assets are for Davidson, strengths that can be used to advantage in the marketplace which is after all the reason for assessing a company's strengths and weaknesses in the first place. Davidson contrasts asset based marketing with a more traditional market based marketing. Market based marketing is the notion of identifying customer needs and then seeking ways to satisfy these needs profitability. Asset based marketing, somewhat controversially starts with a company and its assets and asks how the company can use these assets more effectively in the marketplace. It involves considering for example, how any identified skills and resources from an internal appraisal can be converted into better value for the customer. In practice of course there needs to be a combination of both market based and asset based marketing. This makes sense because strategic market plans are essentially matching company resources and strengths to the needs of the environment and the marketplace.

The start point of developing an asset based approach to marketing is essentially the same as in a conventional strengths and weaknesses assessment in as much as it commences with the identification and appraisal of all the resources, skills and assets of a company. Davidson in fact suggests our old friend the checklist to identify key areas of assets. The checklist encompasses the following examples of asset types: people; working capital; capital equipment; customer franchises such as brand names, unique products or processes, patents, superior service skills, access to third party resources such as joint ventures or agreements; sales distribution and service networks; scale advantages due to, e.g. market share, size etc.

Having established an inventory of assets, the marketing manager should then establish which are the key exploitable assets for future strategy. This will involve asking a number of key questions about the identified assets such as for example 'How can the brand name be exploited further, and how far can the brand be stretched without weakening the franchise.' Overall, we are seeking to establish how the assets of the company can be exploited more effectively in marketing terms. It is important to note that throughout the exercise assets are examined from a marketer's point of view and not from an accountant's. An example of how this can lead to more effective marketing which exemplifies this notion of asset based marketing is the strategy of brand extension. Davidson gives the example of Johnson & Johnson's baby shampoo which until the early 1970s was positioned exclusively for babies. Research showed that it was also being used by mothers and the company decided that by repositioning the brand to extend product usage much more effective use could be made of the powerful asset of the brand name. A similar example is the move by many of the food companies to extend their brand franchises. For example, Mars have extended the brand to include ice cream and food products.

There is no doubt that Davidson's notion of marketing assets has proved to be a useful perspective on the assessment and uses of an analysis of strengths and weaknesses. However, both market based and asset based marketing are probably both necessary in order to achieve a balance between satisfying consumers and the effective utilization of a company's resources.

Summary

In this chapter we have seen that the assessment of an organization's strengths and weaknesses is the second key strand in the process of conducting a SWOT analysis. At first sight this seems to be deceptively straightforward. In fact, the analysis of strengths and weaknesses is complex and multi-faceted. In particular, we have seen that the planner must think beyond simply listing resources, though the use of checklists can be helpful. It is important to establish the attributes to be assessed, with the key ones deriving from the key factors for competitive success in an industry which, in turn, are linked to how customers choose and what they consider to be 'good value'. Related to this, it is vitally important to understand precisely what constitutes a 'strength' or a 'weakness', in order to establish the magnitude of these in the organization and to assess these in relation to competition.

We have also seen that there are distinct advantages to having outside consultants conduct a strengths and weaknesses assessment, although with careful organization and cross-functional teamwork the problems of using company personnel to perform the analysis can be minimized. Valuable insights into organizational strengths and weaknesses can be gleaned from customers' perceptions of a company and its competitors and the use of profiling systems.

We need to remember that the SWOT analysis is an essential but preliminary step in the delineation and selection of marketing strategies. A strengths and weaknesses assessment provides a key input into defining the business, objective setting, and strategy selection and implementation. Finally we have looked at the notions of relating the analysis of strengths and weaknesses to the concept of 'core competencies' and 'marketing assets'.

Questions

1 What is the importance of a strengths and weaknesses analysis to the marketing manager?
2 What are the problems associated with the use of checklists in an appraisal of strengths and weaknesses?
3 Why is the concept of value so important in the appraisal of company resources, and what are the major groupings of activities in Porter's value chain?
4 What are 'horizontal' and 'vertical' linkages in an organization's value chain, and why can they be important in developing competitive strategies?
5 What do you understand by each of the following terms in the context of appraising company resources?

(a) strategic fit.
(b) core competencies.
(c) marketing assets.

References

1. Lancaster, G. and Massingham, L. C., *Essentials of Marketing*, 3rd edn, McGraw-Hill, London.
2. Jain, S., *Marketing Strategy and Planning*, 2nd edn, South Western Publishing Co., Cincinnati, 1985, p. 311.
3. Kotler, P., *Marketing Management: Analysis, Planning, Implementation and Control*, 9th edn, Prentice-Hall, New Jersey, 1997.
4. Lynch, R., *Corporate Strategy*, 2nd edn, Prentice-Hall, Harlow, 2000, p. 562.
5. McDonald, M. H. B., *Marketing Plans*, 2nd edn, Heinemann, London, 1990.
6. Ohmae, K., *The Mind of the Strategist*, Penguin, Harmondsworth, 1983, chapter 3.
7. Ansoff, H. I., *Corporate Strategy*, McGraw-Hill, New York, 1965.
8. Hamel, G. and Prahalad, C. K., 'Strategic Intent', *Harvard Business Review,* **67**, No. 3, 1989, pp. 63–76.
9. Porter, M. E., *Competitive Advantage: Creating and Sustaining Superior Performance*, Free Press, New York, 1985.
10. Johnson, G. and Scholes, K., *Exploring Corporate Strategy*, 5th edn., Prentice-Hall, London, 1999, p. 156.
11. Ferrell, O. C., Hartline, M. D., Lucas, G. H. and Luck, D., *Marketing Strategy*, The Dryden Press, 1999, pp. 56–9.
12. Abell, D. F., 'Strategic windows', *Journal of Marketing*, July, 1978.

13. Prahalad, C. K. and Hamel, G., 'The core competence of the Corporation', *Harvard Business Review*, May–June 1990, pp. 79–91.
14. Davidson, H., 'Putting assets first', *Marketing*, Haymarket Business Publications, 17th Nov. 1983.
15. Davidson, H., 'Building on a winner', *Marketing*, Haymarket Business Publications, 24th Nov. 1983, pp. 32–6.
16. Davidson, H., 'Making an entrance', *Marketing*, Haymarket Business Publications, 1st Dec. 1983, pp. 38–41.

Case Study

The Herring company produces and markets computer games software. The company has been trading for five years and is reasonably successful. It is now looking to diversify into producing business software such as, for example, financial accountancy, forecasting, statistical packages, etc. In assessing its diversification opportunities in this new market to the company, it is currently undertaking an assessment of its strengths and weaknesses.

Two months ago, the marketing director asked each functional area of the business to prepare a critical and objective appraisal of what it felt its strengths and weaknesses were. As a result, the director now has a list of these strengths and weaknesses and has distilled them to identify those which are felt to be particularly relevant to the development of future marketing strategies. The following represent some of the key strengths the company:

- Strong financial structure, ie low gearing.
- State of the art design facilities.
- Excellent quality control.
- Strong reputation in computer games software industry.
- Comparatively young workforce.
- Strong links with some of leading computer hardware manufacturers.

The following represent some of the key weaknesses in the company:

- Little or no experience of markets other than computer games market.
- Weak distribution channels, for instance no access to major computer hard ware and software retailers.
- Comparatively inexperienced salesforce.
- Weak systems of marketing planning.
- Lack of experience in procurement function.

QUESTION

1. How can the company assess the extent to which its strengths and weaknesses are relevant and important to its proposed diversification plans?
2. How might the concept of value chains be used to appraise this company's resources?
3. What are the weaknesses of the approach adopted to assessing strengths and weaknesses in this company?

4

Strategic marketing planning tools

Chapter objectives

After reading this chapter you will:

▶ Appreciate the evolution and uses of strategic marketing planning tools.

▶ Understand how these tools have become increasingly sophisticated and complex.

▶ Be familiar with the applications and limitations of the most frequently used strategic marketing planning tools.

▶ Appreciate the ways in which our knowledge of these tools of planning is constantly evolving and improving.

Introduction

In Chapter 1 we examined the background to the increasingly strategic flavour of marketing management. Accompanying this interest in the need for a more strategic approach has been a growth in the development of what we have termed here 'strategic marketing planning tools'. Perhaps it would be useful first to remind ourselves of the background to the development of more strategic marketing and the relevance of this to the growth and techniques of strategic market planning.

We live in an age which is increasingly characterized by uncertainty and complexity. Decisions made now in companies can commit resources for many years into the future and often involve high risk and high cost. Furthermore, as we saw in Chapter 1, competition for customers is now intense and increasingly global in nature. Last, but very importantly, companies have grown in size and often complexity by extending product ranges, entering new markets and acquiring new businesses. It is because of this environmental background that the strategic market planner must be equipped with every managerial tool which might make the task of analysis and decision making that much easier.

It is only relatively recently that the marketing planner has had access to sufficiently rigorous and well developed frameworks of analysis for them to be useful. Even now these frameworks are not without their limitations, and need to be used with caution.

Initially, the tools of strategic market planning tended to be partial (i.e. addressing only single aspects of marketing decision making) or rather simplistic (such as checklists for the decision maker). The tools of analysis discussed in the first part of this chapter represent some of these first developed tools of market analysis. As you would expect, the more useful of these earlier analytical tools of market analysis have withstood the test of time and are still potent weapons for the strategic marketer to use.

Increasingly, as research effort and knowledge have developed in marketing, the tools of strategic analysis have developed too, becoming increasingly sophisticated and powerful. We shall examine some of these more powerful tools in the second part of the chapter. Before doing this it is necessary to understand and appreciate the intellectual forebears upon which some of the more developed techniques are based and which still have relevance to the strategic marketing planner.

In this chapter, therefore, we shall start by examining product life cycle analysis, together with criticisms and refinements to the basic concept, including the concept of industry/market evolution. We shall then turn our attention to the concept of experience curve effects and how these can be used in strategic market planning. Potentially useful though these concepts are, they represent only partial frameworks for analysis. In the second part of the chapter, then, we shall introduce some of the more recently developed (and some would argue more comprehensive and powerful) tools of analysis, including the portfolio planning tools and the Strategic Planning Institute's PIMS service.

The product life cycle concept

The **product life cycle** concept is such a ubiquitous marketing concept that you are most probably familiar with it. However, before we examine the uses and limitations of this concept in strategic market planning, we shall remind ourselves of the essentials of the concept.

The concept of the product life cycle proposes that, like all life forms, products too have finite lives. Hence, once a product or service is introduced to the market it enters a 'life cycle' and will eventually fade from the market. In addition, the concept proposes that during its life cycle a product will pass through a number of different stages, where each stage has characteristic phenomena which, in turn, suggest specific and different marketing strategies. This notion, together with the suggest shape and stages of the 'typical' product life cycle, are shown in Figure 4.1. The characteristics of each stage are as follows:

1   *Introduction*
    At this stage the product or service is new to the market. The risk of failure is high and any initial sales are likely to be slow. Purchasers at this stage are likely to be innovators who are willing and able to take risks. Profit margins are likely to be small or non-existent due to the low volume of sales and high initial launch and marketing costs.

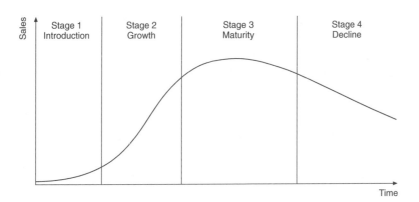

Figure 4.1
The product life cycle concept.

2   *Growth*

Provided the product or service meets customer needs and there is a favourable market reaction, sales will begin to accelerate as news of the product permeates the market. Customers who like to take fewer risks than the initial innovator purchasers, but who welcome novelty, will begin to purchase the product. Attracted by the sales growth and potential profit, new competitors will enter the market, often offering variations on the original product in order to attract brand loyalty and/or to avoid patent infringement.

3   *Maturity*

Eventually, although still increasing, the rate of sales growth will begin to slow down and eventually cease. A number of factors may contribute to this process; for example:

- *Approaching market saturation:* Quite simply, there remain fewer and fewer potential customers left still to purchase the product as the product is diffused through the market. Eventually, only replacement sales are being made with comparatively few new customers left to purchase.
- *Customer boredom/desire for novelty:* Customers are notoriously fickle when it comes to their appetite for new products. Customers who initially purchased the new product or service may eventually become bored and switch to other products or brands.
- *New products/technological change:* Successful new products carry within them the seeds of their own destruction. As sales and profits grow then competitors will be attracted to the market. Often they can only gain entry and market share by developing new or improved versions of the original product. If successful, new products and changes in technology begin to supersede the old and sales begin to slow.

4   *Decline*

Eventually, the forces and factors which contribute to the onset of maturity will erode the market for a product to such an extent that sales begin to diminish. The rate at which this will occur, and hence the length of time which the old product will remain viable in the market, varies enormously. Sometimes decline is extremely rapid, as in fashion markets, or when a major technological break-through occurs. In contrast, the rate of decline may take many years with, for example, a hard core of loyal customers who refuse, or cannot bring themselves, to switch brands.

The product life cycle concept has attracted much attention and criticism as a tool of strategic market planning. As a result of this attention, the basic notion of the concept which has been described here has been developed and refined to include, for example, the notion of different levels of life cycle, i.e. life cycle analysis for brands, product forms and product classes and the notion of variations on the classic S-shaped curve. We shall examine some of these refinements and their relevance to the use of the concept in strategic market planning shortly, but first we need to look at some of the suggested uses of the basic concept in strategic decision making.

Suggested uses of the product life cycle concept in strategic marketing planning

The basic product life cycle concept brings with it a number of suggested implications for strategic market planning. Here are two of the more important ones.

Different objectives and strategies for each stage

One of the major suggested uses of the product life cycle concept in strategic market planning is based on the notion that the characteristics of each stage of the life cycle lend themselves to particular objectives and strategies, especially with regard to the use of the elements of the marketing mix. We shall examine this notion by tracing through each of the life cycle stages in turn.

Introductory stage   At this stage, awareness of the new product is initially low, and competition is small or non-existent. Considerable effort may have to be made to bring the product to the attention of both distributors and consumers. Marketing efforts are likely to be focused on the promotional and distribution elements of the marketing mix and will be targeted at innovator categories. Pricing strategies can be aimed either at 'skimming' the market through high prices, or at 'market penetration', aiming to achieve high levels of market share quickly through low prices. Distribution will tend to be exclusive or selective, and advertising will be aimed at building awareness.

Growth stage   If the new product is successful, we can expect a rapid growth in sales. During this stage new competitors can be expected to enter the market and marketing strategies will need to be focused on combating these new entrants. Although price wars are unlikely to develop at this early stage, considerable effort may be required to establish the intensive distribution required for ultimate mass market demand. Communications will be aimed at creating brand image.

Maturity stage   In the maturity stage of the life cycle, competition is at its peak. Market share needs defending, whilst at the same time preserving profit levels. Brand preferences and loyalties are likely to be already established by this stage, but there is likely to be considerable emphasis on trying to encourage brand switching through sales promotion. In addition, distribution efforts will be aimed at maintaining dealer relationships.

Decline stage   Sales promotion may be reduced to a minimum as the market shrinks. Price competition and price cutting are likely to be intense at this stage. As will be seen, emphasis is likely to switch either to looking for ways to extend the product life cycle or to new products, with the old product being 'milked' for profits.

As we can see, even from this relatively brief outline of strategies, within very broad limits the suggestion is that by identifying the life cycle stage of a product we can develop appropriate marketing mix strategies for each stage. If this suggestion is correct we can see how the concept would be of assistance to the strategic market planner.

Needless to say, these suggested emphases in marketing mix strategies for each stage of the life cycle can only serve as guidelines. John O'Shaughnessy[1] describes these suggested strategies as follows:

> In no case can these suggestions be taken too seriously. It is always possible to think of circumstances where the very opposite advice would be better.

The issue here is that if these suggestions cannot be taken too seriously then what, if anything, is the use of them in strategic market planning? Indeed, one could argue (and some have) that at the very least there is a distinct danger of allowing the life cycle concept to dull the planner's management judgement and expertise by over-relying on 'recipe marketing'. At the worst, and again as we shall see when we look later at criticisms of the life cycle concept, there may be a danger of selecting entirely inappropriate strategies for a particular stage of the life cycle of a product because of the unique circumstances which pertain to that particular product.

We can see, therefore, that this first suggested use of the product life cycle concept is one which raises considerable uncertainty (and considerable debate) as to its usefulness or otherwise in strategic market planning. The position taken here with respect to this uncertainty and debate, and hence with regard to this use of the life cycle concept, is once again well summarized by O'Shaughnessy,[1] with whose views we are in accord.

> Such market life stage conditions set semi-constraints on the strategy adopted (in the sense that any strategy must take them into account), but they are just one input into our thinking about appropriate strategies. There is no one-to-one relationship between life cycle stage and the marketing strategy to be adopted, although life cycle stage gives us a few ideas to start us off.

Managing the product line: new product development, product life cycle extension strategies

This second suggested major use of the product life cycle concept in strategic marketing is that of managing the product line and in particular identifying the need for, nature and timing of product development plans.

The basic premise of this use of the concept is underpinned by the very term 'life cycle'. Specifically, in the absence of suitable strategies, and particularly if a company does not take any steps to prevent it, the dynamics of the life cycle are such that over time, sales and profits will be eroded and probably disappear. What is required is a constant programme of carefully planned strategies to ensure that long-run profit and sales objectives are met. In particular, the planner must consciously seek to develop a 'portfolio' of products to maintain long-run success. Using the concept in this way means that the planner must undertake four steps:

Step One: Identification of the current positions of the company's different products in their product life cycles
The first task of the marketing planner is to locate the position in their life cycles of the various products or services that the organization markets. This is not easy. Jain[2] suggests that the following should be analysed for each product:

- Sales growth pattern since introduction
- Any design and technical problems that need to be sorted out
- Sales and profit history of allied products
- Number of years the product has been on the market
- Casualty history of similar products in the past
- Extent to which customers are becoming more demanding *vis-à-vis* price, service etc.
- Extent to which additional sales efforts are necessary
- Ease or difficulty of acquiring dealers and distributors

Based on this analysis, Jain[2] suggests it is possible to relate the information to the known characteristics of each stage of the cycle and thereby pinpoint the position of each product in its life cycle curve.

In fact, pinpointing the position of products in their life cycles is extremely difficult: a dip in company sales and profits may be simply a result of poor marketing effort rather than a sign that the life cycle curve has peaked. The next step in the process, however, is more difficult still.

Step Two: Analysis of the future sales and profit position of the products in their life cycles
In addition to pinpointing the current position of products in their life cycle the planner must attempt to forecast the future shape of the life cycle curve. We shall be looking at forecasting techniques in a later chapter, but many critics have suggested that forecasting the life cycle curve is dangerous as the stages can vary enormously in their duration and there are several possible shapes for the life cycle curve itself.

The view taken here is to concur with the suggestions that forecasting life cycle curves is difficult but that this should not deter the planner from making some attempt to forecast. After all, planning decisions must (and do) reflect some view of the future: it is far better to make at least some systematic attempt to predict what this future might be.

Not only must the planner attempt to forecast the future sales curves of products, but it is also important to forecast the associated profit curves for products. The generated relationship between product life cycle sales curves and product life cycle profit curves is shown in Figure 4.2. As we can see, 'typically' the profit life cycle lags the sales life cycle of a product, for reasons we have discussed earlier. For example, in the introductory stage of the life cycle, losses and not profits are likely to occur, due to previous research and design, initial launch costs etc. In addition, as we can see, profits are also likely to peak around the peak of the growth phase in sales as competition becomes fiercer.

Step Three: Analysis of implications of current and future forecast sales and profits curves: 'gap analysis'
Once the present and forecast future sales and profits curves have been established, the results of this analysis can then be compared with future corporate objectives for sales and for profits. In particular, we are concerned to identify any discrepancies between forecast and required sales or profit levels. This **'gap analysis'**, as it is not surprisingly called, is illustrated in Figure 4.3 for future desired and forecast profit levels. As we can see, based on current and forecast profit life cycles compared to objectives for future profits, there exists a gap between what is required and what we forecast will be achieved. Furthermore, in our example, in the absence of any action to prevent it, our projections of future sales and profit life cycles suggest that this gap will grow. Of

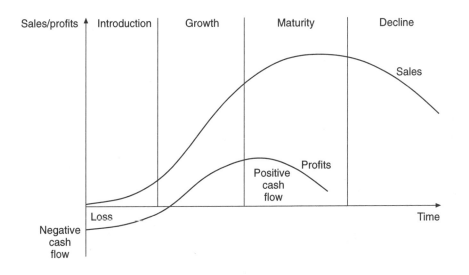

Figure 4.2
Sales/profit cycles.

Figure 4.3
Gap analysis.

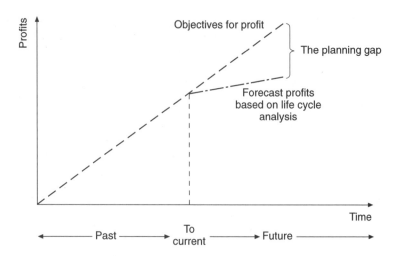

course, many other factors may give rise to such 'planning gaps' in companies, including, for example, adverse economic and other environmental trends, increased costs and so on. However, product life cycle analysis will at least enable the planner to assess how much of this gap is attributable to life cycle forces and hence the 'balance' within the product range. Our example would tend to suggest a company which, in terms of its current product mix, Philip Kotler[3] would classify as being 'long on yesterday's breadwinners'. In other words, it has too many of its products approaching, or at, the maturity and decline stages.

Step Four: Developing innovation and/or extension strategies
The final step in this use of the product life cycle concept is the delineation and assessment of possible strategies to counter the underlying life cycle dynamics for the product range. In other words, we must determine how any gaps, if forecast, are to be filled.

Of course, forecasted sales and profit gaps can be filled in many ways. For example, we might determine that at least part of a profit gap can best be filled by, say, reducing manufacturing costs. Alternatively, or additionally, we may decide to 'plug a gap' by diversification or by exporting.

Which of the many strategies are likely to be available when we eventually choose is dependent on a wide set of complex factors, including, for example:

● Our competitive strengths and weaknesses
● The nature of the environment
● Managerial attitudes towards risk

However, remembering that at least part of the reason for such gaps emerging in the first place is the product life cycle, then we might look to the area of product management to fill these. Specifically, we might need to consider both ways of extending the life cycle of those products in a range which are beginning to mature or decline and/or the need to innovate and introduce new products. The second of these, new product development and innovation, is the subject of Chapter 7, so we shall conclude our discussion of this use of the product life cycle concept by considering product life cycle extension strategies.

The concept, and hoped for results of product life extension strategies, is shown in Figure 4.4. As can be seen from the diagram, and indeed as the term implies, product

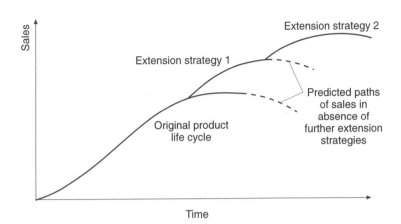

Figure 4.4
Extending product
life cycles.

Table 4.1   Extending the product life cycle

Broad thrust of strategy	Examples of means of achieving it
Expand number of brand users	● Convert non-users ● Enter new market segments ● Win competitors' customers
Increase usage of the brand by current brand users	● More frequent use ● More usage per occasion ● New and more varied usage
Product modification to attract new users/more frequent usage	● Quality improvement ● Style improvement ● Feature improvement
Marketing mix modification	● Reduced prices/special offers ● Improved penetration of distribution channels ● Improved/more intensive advertising/personal selling ● Better/improved service

---

life cycle extension strategies are aimed at not simply delaying the seemingly 'inevitable' onset of terminal decline, but actually initiating a period of further sales growth. As can also be seen, this process can be repeated a number of times, giving a series of enveloping curves, each one extending sales further.

A number of strategies can be used to extend the product life cycle. Kotler,[3] for example, suggests some of the possible ways of extending the life cycle (Table 4.1).

So far we have looked at the basic concept of the product life cycle, together with some of its suggested major uses in strategic market planning. Earlier in the chapter we suggested that the concept has attracted its fair share of criticism with regard to its usefulness in this respect – criticism which has, at least in part, been responsible for a number of refinements to the basic concept which we have so far discussed. We shall now turn our attention to some of these criticisms and refinements.

One of the latest electronic 'consumer goodies' to hit the market has been the DVD (digital video data) recorder. This is a good example of how the product life cycle for a product/technology can be extended.

Video recording machines were first launched in the 1970s. Since then, in many countries they have penetrated most households which own a television set. Other than replacement sales then, the market was virtually saturated by the mid-1990s with comparatively few late adopters and laggards still remaining to come to the market. In an effort to revitalize sales, many of the manufacturers in this market, including companies such as Sony, Panasonic and Philips, have looked to new technology to extend the life of their products. DVD is the replacement technology for the VHS video.

Launched in the late 1990s DVD recorder has already moved past the introduction stage of its life cycle and is set to grow considerably over the next four to five years. The new technology is claimed to be superior and offers several consumer benefits over its predecessor technology. Perhaps most important of all in the growth of this new technology, however, will be the desire by many customers to appear to be up to date and fashionable by having the latest electronic technology in their home. No doubt as the DVD recorder reaches maturity a successor technology and range of products will be developed to replace it.

Criticisms and refinements of the basic product life cycle concept

In this chapter we have already pointed to some of the problems and limitations of the basic product life cycle (PLC) concept. Some of the critics of this concept have gone further in their assessment of the limitations of the conventional life cycle in strategic market planning. Essentially, these criticisms are based on the extent to which the concept is, at best, irrelevant and, at worst, misleading and dangerous.

The most fundamental, and hence most important, of the criticisms of the product life cycle concept is that there is little or no consistent empirical evidence to support the notion of products following a natural and preordained life cycle with the distinct stages that we have outlined here. In short, the product life cycle simply does not exist.

Amongst the most cogent of these critics have been Dhalla and Yuspeh,[4] who have challenged the whole concept of the product life cycle. Indeed, in their influential article we are counselled to forget the concept, the use of which, they suggest, can lead to costly and potentially irrevocable mistakes in strategy. Levitt,[5] has made similar criticisms about the use of the concept, likening the status of our useful knowledge about it to that which existed over 450 years ago with respect to the Copernican view of the universe.

Of course, doubt about the existence or otherwise of both the S-shaped life cycle and the distinct stages of which it is suggested to comprise, can only be resolved by an appeal to the facts. Needless to say, with such a long-standing piece of marketing theory, numerous empirical studies have been undertaken over the years designed to confirm or refute the PLC concept, early studies include those of Cox,[6] Polli and Cook,[7] Cunningham[8] and Day.[9] More recently, Baker[10] has provided further evidence regarding the validity, or otherwise, of the PLC concept.

Overall, the evidence from these and other studies suggests that the classic S-shaped life cycle does indeed exist, but not for all products or for similar products on all occasions. In other words, we cannot (indeed should not) consider the traditional PLC concept as a universal law or fact. But if this is the case, then where does this leave the strategic marketing planner with respect to the use of the concept, and particularly with regard to the suggested application of the concepts which were outlined earlier in this chapter? You will recall that we have already counselled the use of judgement and experience in interpreting the concept for marketing strategy, but does not the evidence of the lack of universality of the concept tend to undermine the wisdom of using the concept at all? Clearly this is the Dhalla and Yuspeh[4] view. However, the view taken here is that critics and researchers of the concept, and particularly those who have not supported the classic S-shaped PLC have added to, rather than detracted from, the usefulness of the concept to strategic marketing planning.

The reason for this seemingly contradictory statement derives from our assertion that much of this criticism, coupled with empirical research, has helped develop and refine our knowledge of the basic concept. The following are seen as being particularly useful additions to our stock of knowledge about the PLC concept.

Different PLC patterns

In addition to the S-shaped life cycle, a number of other variations on this pattern have been observed. Some of these are shown in Figure 4.5. As this illustrates, the product life cycle can exhibit very different patterns from that epitomized by the traditional notion of an S-shaped curve. Moreover, there is some evidence to suggest that the 'typical' shape of the pattern may be associated with the type of product/market under consideration.

For example, life cycle (a) is suggested as being frequently found in the market for many small household appliances. Initial sales growth after a new product launch is rapid, followed by a quite severe drop in sales as the novelty wears off. Eventually,

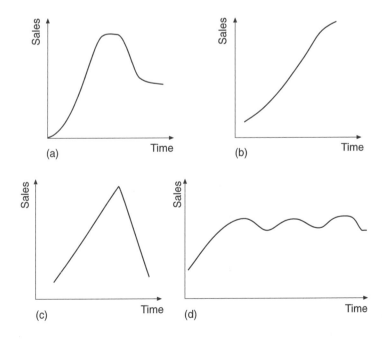

Figure 4.5
Alternative product life cycle patterns.

however, the decline in sales will stop and the product will enter a relatively long period of stability in sales as late adopters purchase the product and early buyers purchase again to become replacement purchasers.

The pattern shown in Figure 4.5(b) represents a 'truncated' pattern. The shape of this pattern illustrates that there is no introductory period. Sales grow rapidly right from product launch. This type of PLC curve may be associated with new products where there is a substantial market appeal and where little learning is required or risk perceived.

Pattern (c) in Figure 4.5 illustrates a rapid growth in sales, again with no introductory stage, followed by an equally rapid decline with no maturity stage. Products that exhibit this shape of life cycle are typical novelty products or fads, such as many children's toys.

Finally, pattern (d) illustrates a succession of product life cycle curves with a relatively short introductory period, rapid sales growth, a short maturity, followed by rapid decline. After this, the process is repeated. This pattern is frequently associated with fashion type products, such as clothing or records.

Different categories (levels) of life cycle

Related to the possibility of different life cycle patterns is the important and equally useful notion of different categories or levels of life cycle. According to Kotler,[3] the same 'product' market may be examined at a number of different levels, giving rise to different categories of life cycle as follows:

1 *Product category life cycles*
   Examples of this category would be the life cycle for washing powders, cars and cigarettes; i.e. the generic product. Product category life cycles may extend over considerable periods of time and may not exhibit any sign of decline at all, e.g. shoes.
2 *Product form life cycles*
   Examples of this category would include liquid detergent wash or powder detergent wash, petrol-driven cars, untipped cigarettes or leather shoes. Product form life cycles exhibit shorter life cycles than those found at the product category level. There is some evidence that the S-shaped curve is most prevalent at this level.
3 *Brand life cycles*
   Examples include Procter & Gamble's Ariel 'Ultra' washing powder, Ford 'Ka' cars, Gallagher's 'Park Drive' untipped cigarettes, and Clark's 'big gripper' shoes. Brand life cycles are normally the shortest of the three life cycle categories.

Clearly, in using the product life cycle for marketing decision making, the marketing manager must be careful to distinguish between these different levels.

As we can see, partly owing to criticisms of the basic product life cycle concept, and based on empirical research, our knowledge about the concept and how to use and interpret it in strategic market planning has improved. Certainly, there is still controversy surrounding the utility of the product life cycle, but most marketers are agreed that used with care, and tempered by managerial judgement, the concept is of value as a tool of strategic market planning.

Perhaps the concept is most usefully viewed as being what O'Shaughnessy[1] has referred to as an 'ideal type':

> An 'ideal type' is an abstraction that may or may not correspond too closely with the real world. Pure competition as defined by economists and bureaucracy as defined by sociologist Max Weber are ideal types since concrete cases can be expected to deviate somewhat from the

'ideal'. An ideal type is used to compare with real examples to explain why the ideal type did not occur. The PLC as an ideal type is a standard against which to compare or predict real life cases. It can be viewed as a heuristic device for explaining particular patterns of sales…

In fact, the product life cycle concept has spawned and underpins many of the more recently developed tools of strategic market analysis, including some of the so-called 'portfolio' planning tools. One of the most direct descendants of the PLC concept, however, is the concept of industry/market evolution.

The concept of industry/market evolution

An interesting development in life cycle analysis, and at least in part as a direct result of criticisms of the original concept, has been the development of strategic market planning concepts related to the life cycle (or evaluation) of industries rather than products. Examples of this approach are those developed by the management consultancy firm, Arthur D. Little[11] and Michael Porter.[12]

Rather than focusing on the shape and stages of the sales curve for products, the industry/market evolution model focuses on the stages of industry/market development, tracing the characteristics of successive stages as an industry/market evolves. Each of these stages is examined with respect to structural characteristics, the nature of competition, purchasing patterns, relative attractiveness and so on (according to the conceptual framework of industry evolution being used) and the implications for marketing strategy are then assessed.

Porter's model of industry/market evolution

As an example, Porter[12] distinguishes between the following three broad stages in the evolution of an industry/market:

- Emerging industry
- Transition to maturity
- Decline.

According to Porter, each of these stages has its own particular characteristics, some of the more important of which are shown for each stage.

Emerging industry:
    Uncertainty among buyers over:
        product performance
        potential applications
        likelihood of obsolescence
    Uncertainty among sellers over:
        customer needs
        demand levels
        technological developments.

Transition to maturity:
    Falling industry profits
    Slow down in growth
    Customers knowledgeable about products and competitive offerings
    Less product innovation
    Competition in non-product aspects.

Decline:
   Competition from substitutes
   Changing customers needs
   Demographic and other macro-environmental forces and factors affecting markets.

Porter then uses the characteristics of each stage to suggest the following strategies as being appropriate to each:

Emerging industry:
   Strategies developed to take account of industry competitive structure characteristics, i.e.

*   Threat of entry
*   Rivalry among competitors
*   Pressure of substitutes
*   Bargaining power of buyers and suppliers.

Transition to maturity:
   Strategies focused on:

*   Developing new market segments
*   Focus strategies for specific segments
*   More efficient organization.

Decline:

*   Seek pockets of enduring demand
    or
*   Divest.

Clearly this approach is similar to the conventional concept of product life cycle analysis in identifying the stage; specifying the characteristics of each stage; and suggesting appropriate strategies for the stages. Porter has developed the notion of industry life cycle further by linking it to the 'strategic position' of the individual organization. Strategic position is categorized in terms of whether the individual organization is a leader or a follower. This approach is shown in Figure 4.6.

Genetic engineering and biotechnology are good examples of what Porter would classify as 'emerging' industries. At the moment in these industries there is substantial jockeying for position amongst the incumbents. Some organizations, however, are already emerging as leaders. For example, in genetic engineering, particularly in the area of food production, the Monsanto company is probably ahead of the field.

A good example of an industry in Porter's stage of 'transition to maturity' is the market for cars in the Western world. For example, companies such as Mercedes and Volkswagen have recently been putting much more attention on developing new market segments.

Finally, and in some ways unfortunately, it is not too difficult to find examples of industries in Porter's 'decline' stage. The textile industry in the UK is probably a good example of this. Coates Viyella, a once major employer in the UK textile industry, is now pursuing strategies of divestment whilst at the same time seeking pockets of enduring demand – just as Porter predicts.

Stage of industry development

		Growth	Maturity	Decline
Strategic position of organization	Leader	• Keep ahead of the field	• Cost leadership • Raise barriers • Deter competitors	• Redefine scope • Divest peripherals • Encourage departures
	Follower	• Imitation at lower cost • Joint ventures	• Differentiation • Focus	• Differentiation • New opportunities

Figure 4.6
Industry life cycle and strategic position.
Source: Porter, M.E.,
Competitive Advantage: Creating and Sustaining Superior Performance,
Free Press, 1995, p. 192.

Arthur D. Little's industry maturity/competitive position matrix

A similar approach to that developed by Porter is that used by the business consultants, Arthur D. Little. A summary of this approach is shown in Figure 4.7. As can be seen, the two axes of the matrix comprise 'stage of industry maturity' on the horizontal axis and 'competitive position' on the vertical axis.

Stage of industry maturity is broken down into four categories as follows:

- Embryonic
- Growth
- Maturity
- Ageing.

Classification of which of these four the industry is in is determined by assessing eight key descriptions, as follows:

- Rate of market growth
- Industry potential
- Product line
- Number of competitors
- Market share stability
- Purchasing patterns
- Ease of entry
- Technology.

A 'mature' industry, for instance, is characterized by slow or negligible rates of growth; little or no further growth potential; few changes in breadth of product lines; stable or declining numbers of competitors; stable market share positions; established buying patterns; high barriers to entry; and process and materials innovation in technology.

Company's competitive position	Stage of industry maturity			
	Embryonic	Growth	Maturity	Ageing
Dominant				
Strong				
Favourable				
Tentative				
Weak				

Figure 4.7
The A. D. Little competitive position/industry maturity matrix.

In both Porter's and the Arthur D. Little approach we can see a strong flavour of their intellectual forebear, the basic product life cycle. This, in itself, is a measure of the enduring impact which the PLC concept continues to have in strategic market planning.

We shall now turn our attention to another early tool of strategic marketing planning, namely, the 'experience curve' effect.

The experience curve effect in strategic marketing planning

In 1925, the commander of the Wright Patterson Air Force Base in the USA observed that the number of direct labour hours required to build an aeroplane decreased as the number of aircraft previously assembled increased. Eventually this phenomenon was explored across a wide range of industries and was found to be present in most of them. The phenomenon eventually came to be termed the **'experience curve effect'** (or, as it is sometimes called, the 'learning curve'). It has significant implications for the determination of marketing objectives and strategy.

Basis and definition

The basis and meaning of the experience curve effect are relatively easy to understand, and are encapsulated in the name of the phenomenon itself. Put simply, experience curve effects are derived from the fact that the more times we repeat an activity the more proficient we become: in other words 'practice makes perfect'. In the case of the Wright Patterson Air Force Base, the commander noticed that this led to a reduction in the time it took to assemble an aircraft as cumulative production increased. The assembly workers simply became more adept at assembling an aircraft because over time they had assembled increasing numbers.

In the 1960s, the Boston Consulting Group,[13] whose work we shall be looking at in more detail later in this chapter, observed that the experience curve effect was not confined only to assembly operations, or even simply to direct labour costs, but rather it encompassed almost all cost areas of a business:

> The experience curve effect is observed to encompass all costs – capital, administrative, research and marketing – and to have transferred impact from technological displacements and product evolution.

Furthermore, not only was the experience curve effect found to encompass more than just production, even more important, the effect was found to be predictable:[14]

> Personnel from the Boston Consulting Group and others showed that each time cumulative volume of a product doubled, total value-added costs ... fell by a constant and predictable percentage.

It is this predictable relationship between costs and experience that constitutes the experience curve effect.

Specific sources of experience curve effects

We have already observed that experience curve effects are based on the old adage 'practice makes perfect'. We can now isolate five specific major sources:

1 Increased labour efficiency, e.g. the learning of short cuts, improved dexterity, greater familiarity with systems/procedures.
2 Greater specialization/redesign of working methods.
3 Process and production improvements, e.g. design of more effective plant, increased automation.

4 Changes in the resources mix, e.g. substitution of initially highly qualified labour for less qualified personnel.
5 Product standardization and product redesign.

The important point to note about these sources of experience curve effects is that many of them are not 'automatic', i.e. in order to achieve experience curve effects, management must undertake the necessary steps and exercise initiative.

Experience effects provide the opportunities to lower costs, but appropriate strategies are required to grasp them.

Calculating experience curve effects

Understandably, experience curve effects differ between industries and between companies. The basic formula for the experience curve is

$$Cq = Cn \left(\frac{q}{n}\right)^{-b}$$

where:

  q = the experience (cumulative production) to date
  n = the experience (cumulative production) at an earlier date
Cq = the cost of a unit q (adjusted for inflation)
Cn = the cost of a unit n (adjusted for inflation)
  b = a constant depending on the learning rate.

Experience curves are normally expressed in percentage terms, e.g. an '85 per cent' experience curve or a '70 per cent' experience curve. Expressing the experience curve in this way tells us the expected reduction in costs for each doubling of cumulative production. An '85 per cent' curve means that the unit cost of producing (say) 2000 cumulative units of production will be only 85 per cent of the unit cost when cumulative production had reached only 1000 units. It is important to note that the evidence shows that this percentage impact in costs is the same across the whole range of cumulative experience, i.e. doubling experience from four million to eight million units results in exactly the same percentage cost reduction as doubling experience from 100 to 200 units in the company. This, too, has important strategic implications.

A typical experience curve is shown in Figure 4.8. Note how the curve shows that at higher levels of cumulative production (experience) larger and larger amounts of cumulative production are required to achieve any given percentage reduction in unit costs.

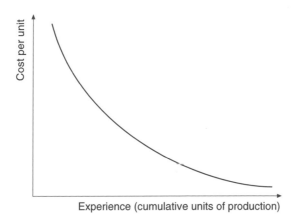

Figure 4.8
A typical experience curve.

Strategic implications of the experience curve effect

In industries where experience curve effects are present (and this is in most industries), and particularly where these are substantial, a significant competitive edge can be gained by adopting a strategy aimed at moving down the experience curve more rapidly than competitors.

In effect, this means being the dominant firm in an industry, with strategies aimed at being the early leader and capturing market share. Remember that the experience curve effect is based on cumulative production and not scale of production. *This means that in the early stages it is simple to, say, double market share at relatively low volumes.* Early leadership can thus ensure that the leaders' costs can be reduced relatively quickly and often before competitors have time to enter the market. By the time these competitors are able to do so, the early market leader has established an unassailable cost advantage and competes on price leadership. Owing to the experience curve effect, high market share thus undoubtedly becomes a prime objective in marketing strategies. When considering this strategy the following points need to be borne in mind:

- Achieving high market shares can be expensive. In the short term we need to consider if we can finance the capture of market shares.
- Market share – and hence cumulative volume – is easier to achieve in high growth markets where experience can be gained by taking a disproportionate share of new sales.
- The pursuit of market share in order to lower costs – and hence competing through price leadership – assumes that the market is price sensitive. Not all markets are; it often makes more sense to compete on superior products or service rather than price.

Experience curve effects are much greater and therefore more relevant in industries such as Aerospace than they are in many service product industries. This explains why the European Consortium which has produced the so-called 'Eurofighter' aeroplane is reliant on securing market share. Only major orders from the Defence departments of different governments will enable the venture to succeed.

In short, the pursuit of competitive advantage based on experience curves is not a certain solution for success in an industry. The experience curve concept is a useful adjunct to the strategic market planner's portfolio of ideas and is particularly useful for market share and pricing decisions. Like the PLC concept it has in part provided the impetus to the development of more comprehensive planning tools. The first of these we shall look at is the Boston Consulting Group's growth/share matrix, but before this we need to consider the nature of these more recently developed tools of strategic marketing planning.

More comprehensive tools of strategic marketing planning

In the first part of this chapter we have looked at some of the earlier tools of analysis available to the marketing planner for analysing strategic alternatives and choices. We have seen that, useful though these tools are, they represent only partial frameworks for analysis and decision making. In recent years substantial progress has been made towards developing more comprehensive tools of strategic analysis.

Different though the various tools may be, they are all primarily directed towards two essential activities:

1 Diagnosis of the current position of the company
2 Prescription of strategies for the future aimed at maintaining – or improving – performance.

A particular problem for the marketing planner in the large multi-product/multi-market company is that decisions must be made as to what priority to place on each of several business areas, each competing for scarce resources. For future success in business, it is vital that these conflicting demands for resources are balanced so as to offer the greater chance of meeting overall corporate objectives. The partial perspectives offered by the tools of analysis examined earlier are particularly inappropriate for this need; hence the development of more comprehensive approaches.

Before we begin to look at some of these more comprehensive tools of strategic market planning, we must emphasize that none of the tools available provides a fail-safe panacea for diagnosis and decision. Each requires managerial judgement and experience in its application and interpretation. If we think of them as being aids to marketing management rather than a replacement for judgement, we have gone some way towards using these more powerful tools wisely.

Several of the modern tools of strategic market analysis fall into the category of 'portfolio analysis models'. Sometimes referred to as 'product market grids', these models are essentially based on positioning each business unit, or specific product market, on a grid according to the attractiveness of the market and the company's competitive position.

One of the earliest and most influential of the product/market portfolio techniques is that developed by the Boston Consulting Group. We will now examine this strategic tool in some detail, and examine its uses and limitations.

The Boston Consulting Group's (BCG) growth/share matrix

In the mid 1960s the Boston Consulting Group (BCG) was founded to provide advice to strategic marketing planners. Building on their previous work and evidence relating to the experience curve effect, which we discussed earlier, BCG developed a simple, but potentially powerful, framework for analysing an organization's business with a view to providing strategic guidelines. The essentials of **BCG's growth/share matrix** are illustrated in Figure 4.9.

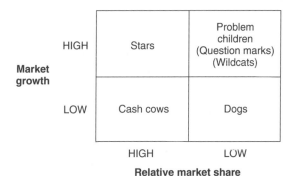

Figure 4.9
BCG's growth/share matrix.

Compiling the BCG matrix

The completion of the matrix is very straightforward. The four steps are:

1 For each strategic business unit (SBU) or product determine annual growth rate in the market.
2 According to this growth rate, next determine the extent to which growth rate is 'high' or 'low'. Normally growth rates of 10 per cent or more are considered 'high'.
3 For each SBU or product then determine relative market share. Normally this is calculated on the basis of market share compared to that of the largest competitor.
4 According to relative market share, then determine the extent to which this is 'high' or 'low'. Normally a relative market share of 10 per cent or above is required to fall into the 'high' category.

We now have all the information we need to position our SBUs or products in the matrix. We can also calculate the value of the turnover of each business or product and denote this by using circles for either, where the area of the circle is proportionate to this turnover.

Interpreting and using the matrix

An illustration of a completed growth/share matrix is shown in Figure 4.10. Having completed the growth/share matrix, each SBU may be classified as follows:

● *Low growth/high share: 'cash cows'*
As the term implies, these products or SBUs generate more cash than they use and can be used for funding other products or SBUs.
● *Low growth/low share: 'dogs'*
These products or SBUs tend to be loss makers but might provide small amounts of cash; long-term their potential is usually weak.
● *High growth/low share: 'problem children' (sometimes called 'question marks' or 'wildcats')*
These are products with possible long-term potential, but they do tend to use large amounts of cash. This is so if (as they must if they are to survive in the long run) they increase their market share.
● *High growth/high share: 'stars'*
Managed well, these SBUs or products have the potential to become the cash cows of the future. This means that the company must maintain their market share, usually in the face of strong competition, until market growth subsides. This means that these products or SBUs tend to be heavy users of cash arising from high promotional expenditures.

Figure 4.10
Example of a
completed BCG matrix.

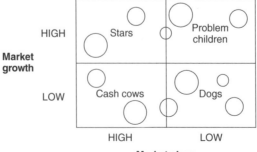

The concept of building a balanced portfolio

Once strategic business units have been analysed in this way, a key feature of the BCG approach is its stress on the need to build a balanced portfolio of businesses or products. This notion is captured in the following quote from Lancaster and Massingham:[15]

> A balanced portfolio would ideally contain few or no dogs, some problem children, some stars and some cash cows. The balance between problem children, stars and cash cows should be such as to ensure that the company has sufficient net positive cash flow from its cash cows to fund its stars and turn them eventually into cash cows. Funds from cash cows are also used to turn products which are currently problem children . . . into stars. Not all problem children can be moved in this way and eventually some of them will . . . become dogs. In the long run all dogs are potential candidates for elimination from the product range.

A balanced portfolio is thus intended to ensure sufficient positive net cash flow (NCF) to ensure long run success for the company as a whole. In order to achieve this, each SBU or product must be analysed and a decision made as to which of the following strategies is to be applied in order to maintain the balanced portfolio:

- *Build:* As the term implies, this means increasing the product or SBU's market share, usually implying a net input of cash or resources.
- *Hold:* This strategy is aimed at maintaining market share and is therefore appropriate for strong cash cows.
- *Harvest:* Here a decision is made to generate as much short-term cash flow from the SBU or product as is possible and it is, therefore, appropriate to weak cash cows.
- *Divest:* A divest strategy means either selling or liquidating the SBU. This strategy is appropriate for weaker problem children and for most dogs. It should be noted, however, that sometimes dogs may be retained for other strategic reasons such as maintaining a full product portfolio.

The BCG approach seems to offer both a simple method of analysing and evaluating current businesses and a relatively straightforward way of arriving at future strategies for them. There are, however, a number of problems with the use of the BCG growth/share matrix.

Criticisms and limitations of the BCG approach

Among the major criticisms and limitations of this particular portfolio technique we can include:

- *Over-simplification:* The matrix uses only the factors of market growth and relative market share to assign products of SBUs to the various cells of the matrix. This is based on strong empirical evidence showing that cash flow is related to these two factors. There are usually many more factors that can, and do, affect net cash flow in a company.
- *Cash flow as the performance criterion:* There are those who doubt the use of cash flow as being the most appropriate objective in a company, arguing instead that return on investment (ROI) is more appropriate.
- *Ambiguity in classifications:* The analysis in BCG's product portfolio matrix can be undertaken either at the SBU level, or for each product/market. It is, however, often difficult in practice to separate these. There is also considerable controversy over what constitutes a 'high' versus a 'low' market growth rate and also what constitutes a 'high' versus a 'low' market share.

- The technique does not deal with the issues surrounding new products, or markets with negative rates of growth.

Partly because of these criticisms, a number of other techniques have been developed which go some way to countering these problems. The techniques we shall now look at are some of the better known examples of these, i.e. the McKinsey/General Electric business screen, the Shell International directional policy matrix, and the product life cycle portfolio matrix. We start with the McKinsey/General Electric model.

The McKinsey/General Electric business screen

As mentioned already, a major criticism of the BCG growth share matrix is its reliance on only two factors to position strategic business units in the matrix. A number of strategic planning portfolio techniques have been developed which use several factors to analyse strategic business units, instead of only the two found in BCG's approach. Working in conjunction with McKinsey & Co. (a management consultancy firm), General Electric (GE) have developed one of the more popular of these **multi-factor portfolio matrices**.

In the GE matrix, SBUs are evaluated using the two dimensions of 'market attractiveness' and 'business position'. In contrast to the BCG approach, each of these two dimensions is, in turn, further analysed into a number of factors which underpin each dimension. In order to use this technique, the strategic planner must first determine these various factors contributing to market attractiveness and business position.

Cravens[16] gives some good examples of the possible factors associated with market attractiveness and business position, and the relationship between them. Table 4.2 lists some of these.

Table 4.2 Cravens' factor analysis

Attractiveness of market	Status position of business
Market factors	
• Size (volume/value, both)	• Market share
• Growth rate per year	• Company's annual growth rate
• Sensitivity to price	• Your influence on market
• Cyclicality, etc.	• Lags or leads in sales
Competition	
• Types of competitor	
• Degree of concentration	• Comparison in terms of products, markets, capabilities
• Changes in share	• Relative share change
• Degrees and types of integration	• Company's level of integration
Financial and economic factors	
• Contribution margins	• Company's margins
• Barriers to entry/exit	• Barriers to company's entry or exit
• Capacity utilization	• Company's capacity utilization
Technical factors	
• Maturity and volatility	• Company's ability to cope with change
• Patents and copyright	• Degree of patent protection
• Complexity	• Depth of company skills

GE's product/market attractiveness factors

The original GE matrix used certain factors to assess product/market attractiveness:

- Size
- Growth rates
- Competitive diversity and structure
- Profitability
- Technological impacts
- Social impacts
- Environmental impacts
- Legal impacts
- Human impacts.

GE's business strength factors

For assessing business strength, the GE matrix uses ten factors:

- Size
- Growth rate
- Market share
- Profitability
- Margins
- Technology position
- Strengths and weaknesses
- Image
- Environmental impact
- Management.

GE believe that these are the key factors for their business, which taken together influence return on investment (note that the BCG approach uses cash flow). This list of GE factors can be modified for each company according to its own particular circumstances, and indeed many of the alternative multiple factor matrices simply use a different checklist of attributes.

Constructing the GE matrix

The five steps in compiling the GE matrix are:

1 Identify strategic business units
2 Determine factors contributing to market attractiveness
3 Determine factors contributing to business position
4 Establish ways of measuring market attractiveness and business position
5 Rank each SBU according to whether it is:

- High, medium or low on business strength
- High, medium or low on market attractiveness.

The final two factors (measuring and ranking) require that some numerical rating be given to both the relative importance of each factor used to assess market attractiveness (assuming they are not all equally important) and to assess business strength.

Multiplying these together and totalling them for each strategic business unit then gives an overall composite score which, in turn, enables the compilation of the matrix. In addition, the total market size for each SBU can be represented by the area of a circle, with the share of the company's SBUs in each product market being indicated by a segment in the circle.

The approach typically results in a portfolio similar to the one shown in Figure 4.11. As with BCG's matrix, the visual presentation enables a considerable amount of complex information to be presented in an easily digestible form.

Interpreting and using the GE matrix

Having completed the matrix, as with the BCG approach, the marketing planner can then assess the balance of SBUs in the organization and determine appropriate future strategies for each.

Strategy guidelines Of itself, the GE matrix does not purport to establish detailed strategies for each SBU. This is a task for the management of the company and will require consideration of many factors. However, according to an SBU's position in the matrix we can distinguish between three broad strategic guidelines. These are indicated in Figure 4.12.

Strategy guidelines in action Clearly, those SBUs which score high/strong or medium/strong or average/high on competitive position and market attractiveness are SBUs where a company should seek at least to maintain investment, and preferably grow.

Figure 4.11
Illustrative
presentation of a
GE matrix.

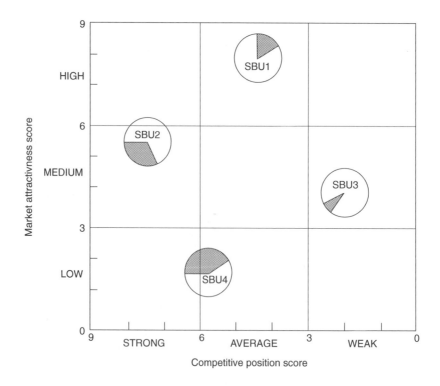

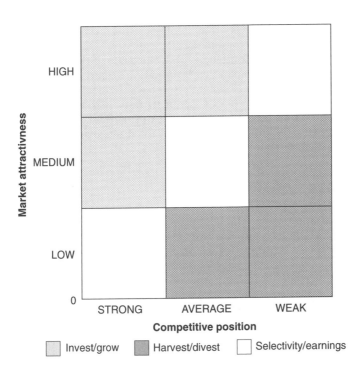

Figure 4.12
Strategy guidelines
from the GE matrix.

SBUs which score a combination of low/weak or low/average or medium/weak or competitive position and market attractiveness are candidates for which, at the very least, no more investment can be warranted. Wherever possible, as much cash should be harvested from them as is feasible.

SBUs scoring either high/weak or medium/average or low/strong combinations on competitive position/market market attractiveness should be examined to see if some degree of selective investment to maintain or increase earnings would be appropriate.

Criticisms and limitations of the GE matrix

Wind and Mahajam[17] criticized obtaining composite scores on position and attractiveness. They pointed out that identical scores can hide key differences between products, and suggest there are limitations to the simple weighting system that is used. They suggested more custom-built approaches. Each cell will contain several SBUs, so it is argued that because a number of different criteria have placed each SBU in the cell that a simple singular investment strategy is insufficient.

Abell and Hammond[18] suggested three very distinct problems in making assessments of either industry attractiveness or business position:

1   The relevant list of contributing factors in any given situation has to be identified.
2   The direction and form of the relationships have to be determined.
3   Each of the contributing factors has to be weighted in any composite measure of 'attractiveness' or 'position', depending on its relative importance.

Porter[19] suggested that the company position/industry attractiveness screen is less easily measured than the growth/share approach, requiring subjective judgements about where a particular business unit should be placed. This is far more likely to be open to misjudgement. He suggests that it offers little more than a basic check in formulating competitive strategy for a particular industry.

Johnson and Scholes[20] have pointed out that the value of the GE matrix very much depends on having access to comparative information regarding competitors – access which, as we have already seen in Chapter 2, is not always readily or easily available.

We can see then that the GE matrix is not without its limitations and problems. Nevertheless we should not discount the fact that this particular matrix was instrumental in spawning several later multi-factor matrices for strategic market planning. One of these is Shell's so-called 'directional policy matrix'.

The Shell directional policy matrix

A somewhat similar approach to the GE business screen is the Shell directional policy matrix (DPM).[21] This approach also has two dimensions – company's competitive capabilities (vertical axis) and prospects for sector profitability (horizontal axis) as shown in Figure 4.13.

The firm's products are plotted into one of the nine cells in Figure 4.13 and subsequently there is a suggested strategy for each of the nine cells. There follows a brief description of how to complete the matrix and what each of the horizontal and vertical axes in the model mean.

The horizontal axis: sector profitability

This includes the criteria of market growth rate, market quality, industry situation and environmental considerations. On each of these factors a product is given from one to five stars. For instance, the factor of 'market quality' might be judged on the basis of several

Figure 4.13
The Shell directional policy matrix.
Source: Shell Chemicals UK, *The Directional Policy matrix: A New Aid to Corporate Planning,* November 1975.

Prospects for sector profitability

	UNATTRACTIVE	AVERAGE	ATTRACTIVE
WEAK	Disinvest	Phased withdrawal Custodial	Double or quit
AVERAGE	Phased withdrawal	Custodial Growth	Try harder
STRONG	Cash generation	Growth Leader	Leader

Company's competitive capabilities

criteria such as pricing behaviour, past stability in the profitability of that sector. The qualitative or quantitative evaluation of market quality is then converted into a rating from nought to four. The same procedure is followed for each of the other three factors, so the overall score on sector profitability is the total of the ratings on all four factors.

The vertical axis: competitive capabilities

The same approach is used here, except that the company's capabilities are assessed on the basis of market position, product research and development, and production capability. These are further divided into sub-factors applicable to any particular industry.

The strategy recommendations contained in the nine cells of the matrix are shown in Figure 4.13. Shell emphasize that whatever strategy is eventually selected, the aim is that it should be 'resilient', i.e. viable in a diverse range of potential futures. Hence, each strategy ideally should be evaluated against all future possible scenarios. The results in all of these should be acceptable and no potential 'disasters' should result.

The limitations of the directional policy matrix

The directional policy matrix has been criticized on the grounds that, like the BCG approach, it assumes that the same set of factors is universally applicable for assessing the prospects of any product or business. Many critics believe that the relevant factors and their relative importance will vary both according to the firm's products and the individual characteristics of each company.

In addition, the matrix does not provide any guidelines on how to implement the strategies suggested in each cell of the matrix.

The product life cycle portfolio matrix

Developed by Barksdale and Harris[22] the product life cycle portfolio matrix is specifically designed to deal with the criticisms that the BCG matrix (a) ignores products that are new, and (b) overlooks markets with a negative growth rate, i.e. markets that are in decline. Because of this, the product life cycle portfolio matrix includes a specific focus on the growth and maturity stages of the product life cycle in developing the portfolio technique.

However, the same assumptions that underlie both the conventional product life cycle experience curves and the BCG growth/share matrix are also built into the model. These assumptions, which we have already witnessed earlier in this chapter, are now repeated:

- Products have finite life spans. They enter the market, pass through a period of growth, reach a stage of maturity, subsequently move into a period of decline and finally disappear.
- Strategic objectives and marketing strategy should match the market growth rate changes so as to take advantage of the challenges and opportunities as the product goes through the different stages.
- For most mass produced products, costs of production are closely linked to experience (volume). Hence, for most types of products, the unit cost goes down as volume increases.
- Expenditures – investment in plant and equipment and marketing expenses are

directly related to rate of growth. Consequently, products in growth markets will use more resources than products in mature markets.

- Margins and the cash generated are positively related to share of the market. Products with high relative share of the market will be more profitable than products with low shares.
- When the maturity stage is reached, products with high market share generate a stream of cash greater than that needed to support them in the market. This cash is available for investment in other products or in research and development to create new products.

Building on these assumptions, Barksdale and Harris also highlight the additional issues which arise out of pioneering new products, which they label *infants*, and products in declining markets which they label as either *warhorses* (high share products in declining markets) or *dodos* (low share products in declining markets). The result is a combined PLC/product portfolio model as shown in Figure 4.14.

This approach is based on the notions that both the initial and decline stages of the life cycle are important and, more specifically, recognizes that product innovations as well as products with negative growth rates are important and should not be ignored in strategic analysis. The result is an expanded (2 × 4) portfolio matrix, as shown in Figure 4.15. The eight-cell matrix is composed of the usual four BCG categories plus the new categories as outlined.

Warhorses

When a market begins to exhibit negative growth, cash cows become warhorses. These products still have high market share and hence can still be substantial cash generators. This might require reduced marketing expenditure or it may take the form of selective withdrawal from market segments or elimination of certain models.

Dodos

These are products that have low shares of declining markets with little opportunity for growth or cash generation. The appropriate strategy is to remove them from the portfolio, but if competitors have already removed themselves from the market it may still be profitable to remain. Timing is thus crucial.

Figure 4.14
Combined
PLC/product
portfolio concepts.
Source: Barksdal, H.C.
and Harris, C.E.,
'Portfolio analysis and
the product life cycle',
*Journal of Long Range
Planning,* **15**, 6, 1982,
p. 42.

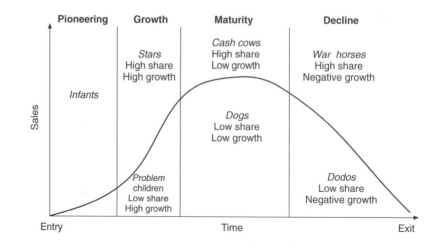

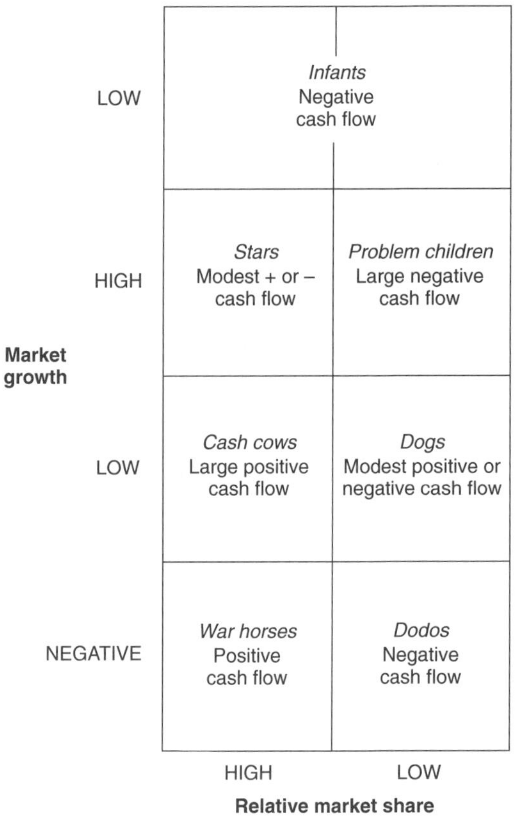

LOW	*Infants* Negative cash flow	
HIGH	*Stars* Modest + or − cash flow	*Problem children* Large negative cash flow
LOW	*Cash cows* Large positive cash flow	*Dogs* Modest positive or negative cash flow
NEGATIVE	*War horses* Positive cash flow	*Dodos* Negative cash flow

Market growth (vertical axis)

HIGH   LOW
Relative market share

Figure 4.15
Product life cycle portfolio matrix.
Source: Barksdale, H.C. and Harris, C.E., 'Portfolio analysis and the product life cycle', *Journal of Long Range Planning,* **15**, 6, 1982, p. 48.

Infants

These are pioneering products that possess a high degree of risk. They do not immediately earn profits and consume substantial cash resources. The length of the innovative can vary from a short time with consumer packaged goods to an extended period with a product that is innovative enough to require a shift in buying habits.

Uses and limitations of the product life cycle portfolio matrix

Barksdale and Harris, the developers of the matrix, claim that it is more comprehensive. Regardless of the level of analysis – corporate, business division or product/market categories – they suggest that the expanded model provides an improved system for classifying and analysing the full range of market situations. Classification of products according to this expanded model is meant to reveal the relative competitive position of products, indicate the rate of market growth and enable the configuration of strategic alternatives in a general sense if not in specific terms.

The key here is that it is only 'general'. Barksdale and Harris admit that the new matrix does not eliminate the problems involved in defining, say, products and markets, or the problems in defining rates of growth. As with the other strategic planning tools, the benefits a company can achieve are only as good as the inputs upon which they are based.

It is claimed, however, that it does provide an improved framework that identifies the cash flow potential and the investment opportunity for every product offered by an organization. In addition, it helps to conceptualize the strategic alternatives of all product/market categories of an organization.

Profit impact of marketing strategy (PIMS)

In the mid 1960s, Sidney Schoeffler and his colleagues at the Strategic Planning Institute in Cambridge, Massachusetts, began to collect and analyse data from a large number of companies, covering literally hundreds of different product markets. The intention was to provide participating companies with advice, based on empirical evidence, about the most suitable strategies to pursue in search of increased profitability. Essentially the analysis focused on comparing the effect of various business strategies on net cash flow and profitability and this came to be termed the **'profit impact of marketing strategies'** (PIMS).

The full PIMS service is available only to subscribing companies (i.e. clients). Each client is asked to subscribe more than 100 data items for each 'business', which is defined as an operating unit that:

- Sells a distinct set of products or services
- Sells to an identifiable set of customers
- Is in competition with a well-defined set of competitors.

Using a special data form, the client answers questions on factors such as:

- the market environment
- the state of competition
- strategy pursued by the business
- operating results
- assumptions as to the future, prices, sales, etc.

Information reports

Using the evidence built up in the database, the subscribing company then receives both diagnostic and prescriptive information contained in four main reports:

- *The 'Par' Report:* Specifying what return on investment is normal (or 'par') for that particular type of business.
- *The Strategy Analysis Report:* The likely outcome (on profit, sales, cash flow, etc.) of several possible 'broad' strategic moves, based on evidence of similar moves by similar businesses.
- *The Optimum Strategy Report:* Nominates the combination of strategic moves likely to give the client optimal results for the business.
- *Report on 'Look Alikes' (ROLA):* Provides information on likely successful tactics based on analysing the successful moves of strategically similar businesses.

The information is thus client- and business-specific but, in addition, the extensive analyses made by the Strategic Planning Institute have provided a number of general guidelines to strategy selection and implementation.

Thirty-seven basic strategic influences on profitability and cash flow have been identified by the Institute. Taken together, the Institute suggests that these account for

80 per cent of the determination of business success or failure. Of primary importance, however, are the following:

- *Investment intensity:* Higher investment intensity is associated with lower rates of return and cash flow.
- *Productivity:* High value is added for each employee in the businesses, making the company generally more profitable.
- *Market position:* Higher share of served markets leads to higher profits and cash flow.
- *Growth of served market:* 'Favourable to cash' measures of profit; no effect on percentage measures of profit; negative effect on cash flow.
- *Quality of products or services:* Favourable impact on all measures of financial performance.
- *Innovation/differentiation:* Usually positive effect on financial performance, but only if company has strong initial market position.
- *Vertical integration:* Positive effect in stable markets, negative in unstable ones.
- *Cost push:* Increases in salaries, raw material prices etc. have complex effects on performance according to specific nature of business or company.
- *Current strategic effort:* The existing direction of change of any of the preceding factors often affects financial performance in an inverse manner, e.g. having strong market share increases cash flow; achieving strong market share reduces it.

These and other profit impact marketing strategies (PIMS) findings can provide useful insights for the process of strategy development and implementation. A company can use PIMS data in a variety of ways to help in strategic market planning. Clearly, for the subscriber company the information provided is detailed and wide-ranging. In particular, PIMS data can be used for:

- Analysing business performance
- Formulating and selecting future strategies
- Analysing and focusing on problems and opportunities
- Assessing competitor performance.

Criticisms and limitations of PIMS

Although PIMS is useful, there is some criticism. The findings are given as conclusions from empirical research, but many of them are self-evident. O'Shaughnessy[23] believes that 'the findings cannot distinguish between causal factors and factors in a state of mere co-existence'. He goes on to say: 'without supporting explanations and appropriate tests, the findings can be misleading in tempting management to deal with symptoms rather than causes'.

Day[24] to some extent agrees with O'Shaughnessy when he states three basic limitations of PIMS:

1 Interpreting and utilizing PIMS findings: PIMS has been used to predict profitability. This should not be so because the model does not tell us about causality.
2 Specification problems: i.e. whether the regression models have omitted important variables and have been properly structured.
3 Measurement error: this happens because of eliminating outliners, standardized inputs etc.

More recent research by Doyle[25], although not specifically aimed at criticizing the PIMS system, has shown that perhaps the database does not give sufficient importance to certain facets of marketing strategy. In particular, Doyle's research illustrates the significant potential impact of the brand and its management on company profitability, an aspect which the PIMS data perhaps tends to understate.

Recent developments in portfolio analysis

Despite criticisms of the techniques of portfolio analysis in Strategic Marketing Planning, the techniques and applications of these sorts of analysis have continued to develop. One of the most recent developments in the application of portfolio analysis tools which illustrates how these tools are continuously evolving to meet the needs of the contemporary marketer is the combination of portfolio analysis and the contemporary issue of 'green' marketing. Developed by Ilinitch and Schaltegger[26] this notion of a 'green' business portfolio is shown in Figure 4.16.

The basic notion in this three-dimensional matrix is suggested by Ilinitch and Schaltegger as involving the following.

> . . . quantifying the environment impacts of business activities and comparing them with economic aspects of examined business.

The horizontal plane of the matrix consists of the traditional BCG matrix of growth against profitability with the quadrants retaining their respective metaphors. The size of the circle represents the size of the product or firm, in economic or environmental terms. The third, vertical dimension measures environmental impact. Recent developments in accounting mean this can be quantified at plant, SBU, or firm level. The pollution units are calculated by multiplying toxic discharges by regulation standards weighting coefficients. Products deemed to be ecologically sound are called *'green'* and their counterparts are called *'dirty'*. Thus we see the notion of the somewhat entertaining *'green cash cow'* and *'dirty dogs'*.

The authors suggest that 'dirty cash cows' are usually old, declining industries that

Figure 4.16
The 'Green' Business Portfolio.
Source: Ilinitch, A.Y. and Shaltegger, S.C., 'Developing a green business portfolio', *Journal of Long Range Planning,* **28**, 2, 1995.

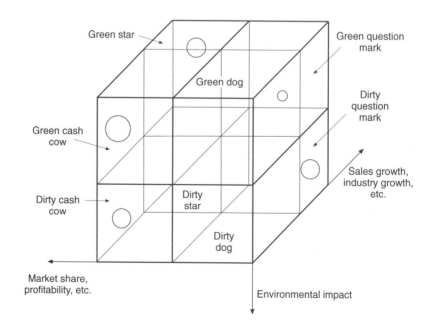

are in the short term very profitable to firms and communities. However, in the long term, the negative publicity and financial penalties make such industries risky in the long run. Alternatively, although the 'green dog' is financially unprofitable, the authors argue that the strategic challenge in fact is to make it viable. This, they suggest, can be done by creating a market for the product and/or capturing market share. Creating a market may in turn involve changing customer values and behaviour, whereas capturing market share may involve lowering production costs.

Battery-powered vehicles probably represent a good example of 'green dogs'. Many of these vehicles, both cars and motor bikes, are now at the stage where technologically, they represent a substitute for the conventional petrol- and diesel-engined alternatives. The most recently launched battery powered motorbike is capable of an average speed of 50 miles per hour and has an operating range of 150 miles between charges. The most striking advantages of the bike however, are its exceptionally low running costs and its 'green' credentials with virtually no noise or emission pollution. Technically proficient as such vehicles may be, the strategic challenge facing their marketers is as the green business portfolio suggests: that of creating a market. Quite simply, still not enough customers value the undoubtedly green benefits which electric vehicles clearly offer. The marketers of such vehicles therefore, including the new electric superbike face an uphill task in changing customer values and behaviour.

We have included this interesting 'green' portfolio technique not because there is any evidence of it being potentially more valuable to the development of strategic marketing than some of the other recent ideas on portfolio analysis, but rather that it illustrates that portfolio techniques are being constantly improved and have changed substantially since the early days of the original BCG portfolio. Chisnall[27] suggests that portfolio planning is here to stay because it can provide three essential core benefits to management, namely:

1 The generation of improved strategies because of the analysis involved in applying the portfolio techniques to a business.
2 At least a partial solution to the critical issue of more effective resource allocation and decisions for improving this through the analysis of trade-offs between the different parts of the business.
3 The techniques encourage a more 'professional' approach to the management process which, although not exactly scientific as such, at least is more rigorous and systematic than using intuition and hunch to make marketing decisions.

Mercer[28] perhaps captures best how to use the portfolio techniques when he suggests that the techniques are best thought of and used as the servant of the marketer rather than the master. The techniques, he suggests, are simply additional aids to the creative decision-making processes and should not be used as a substitute for them. Their role is to offer helpful insights rather than definitive answers.

Summary

The contemporary marketing planner needs the right tools if marketing strategies are to be effectively developed and implemented. Recent years have seen significant developments in analytical concepts and frameworks of marketing analyses and decision making.

Though only partial tools of analysis, and often severely criticized, some of the earlier frameworks of marketing planning, such as the product life cycle and the technique of experience curve analysis, despite their limitations, are still useful concepts.

More recently, more comprehensive tools of analysis and planning, including the so-called portfolio planning tools, have been developed, ranging from the two-dimensional growth/share matrix to the multi-factor matrices of which the General Electric and Shell directional policy matrix are prime examples.

We have also seen the emergence of empirically based comprehensive planning tools, of which PIMS is perhaps the best known. These are aimed at helping the strategic planner delineate and select between alternative strategies for achieving the highest return on investment.

Towards the end of the chapter we looked at some of the recent developments in portfolio analysis and in particular stressed the fact that these tools are continually being improved and updated as our empirical knowledge and experience regarding the uses and limitations of the portfolio techniques itself develops. In addition, we have seen that the tools are evolving to meet the needs of the contemporary marketing environment.

We should remember that the tools selected and discussed in this chapter represent only some of the planning tools now available to the strategic marketer. We should also remember that none of these tools was designed or is able to replace management judgement: nor should they.

Finally, as we have seen, each of the approaches and tools discussed in the chapter has its own advantages and limitations. Ideally, the various planning tools are best used in combination when developing marketing plans and strategies.

Key terms

Product life cycle [p75]
Gap analysis [p79]
Experience curve effect [p88]
BCG growth/share matrix [p91]

Multi-factor portfolio matrices [p94]
Profit impact of marketing strategies (PIMS) [p102]

References

1. O'Shaughnessy, J., *Competitive Marketing: A Strategic Approach*, 2nd edn, Unwin Hyman, London, 1988, p. 182.
2. Jain, S. C., *Marketing Planning and Strategy*, 2nd edn, South Western Publishing Co., Cincinatti, 1985, p. 473.
3. Kotler, P., *Marketing Management: Analysis, Planning, Implementation and Control*, 9th edn, Prentice-Hall, New Jersey, 1997, Chap. 12.
4. Dhalla, N. K. and Yuspeh, S., 'Forget the product life cycle concept', *Harvard Business Review*, January–February 1976, pp. 102–104.
5. Levitt, T., 'Exploit the product life cycle', *Harvard Business Review*, November–December, 1965, p. 81.
6. Cox, W. E., 'Product life cycles as marketing models', *Journal of Business*, October 1967, **40**, 4, pp. 375–384.
7. Polli, R. and Cook, V., 'Validity of the product life cycle', *Journal of Business*, October 1969, **42**, pp. 385–400.
8. Cunningham, M. T., 'The application of product life cycles to corporate strategy: some research findings', *British Journal of Marketing*, 1969, **3** (Spring), pp. 32–34.
9. Day, G. S., 'The product life cycle: analysis and application issues', *Journal of Marketing*, Fall 1981, pp. 60–67.
10. Baker, M. J., *Marketing Strategy and Management*, 3rd edn, Macmillan, Basingstoke, 2000, p. 106.
11. Little, Arthur D., Concepts of market/industry evolution are contained in a series of booklets published by A. D. Little, Inc., New York.
12. Porter, M. E., *Competitive Advantage: Creating and Sustaining Superior Performance*, Free Press, New York, 1985.
13. The Boston Consulting Group, *Perspectives on Experience*, Boston, 1970.
14. Abell, D. F. and Hammond, J. S., *Strategic Market Planning*, Prentice-Hall, New Jersey, 1979.
15. Lancaster, G. A. and Massingham, L. C., *Essentials of Marketing*, McGraw-Hill, London, p. 69.
16. Cravens, D. W., *Strategic Marketing*, Irwin, Homewood, Illinois, 1982.
17. Wind, Y. and Mahajam, V., 'Designing product and business portfolios', *Harvard Business Review*, January–February 1981, pp. 37–63.
18. Abell, D. F. and Hammond, J. S., *Strategic Marketing Planning*, Prentice-Hall, New Jersey, 1979, pp. 112–113.
19. Porter, M. E., *Competitive Strategy: Techniques For Analysing Industries and Competitors*, Macmillan, New York, 1980, pp. 35–38.
20. Johnson, G. and Scholes, K., *Exploring Corporate Strategy*, 5th edn, Prentice-Hall Europe, Hertfordshire, 1999, p. 136.
21. Shell Chemicals UK, *The Directional Policy Matrix: A New Aid to Corporate Planning*, November 1975.
22. Barksdale, H. C. and Harris, C. E., 'Portfolio analysis and the product life cycle', *Journal of Long Range Planning*, **15**(6), 1982, pp. 35–64.
23. O'Shaughnessy, J., *Competitive Marketing: A Strategic Approach*, 2nd edn, Unwin Hyman, London, 1988, p. 44.
24. Day, G., 'Analytical approaches to strategic market planning', *Review of Marketing*, 1981, pp. 89–95.
25. Doyle, P., 'Branding', in Baker, J. (ed.), *The Marketing Book*, 4th edn, Butterworth-Heinemann, Oxford, 1999.
26. Ilinitch, A. Y. and Schaltegger, S. C., 'Developing a green business portfolio, *Journal of Long Range Planning*, **28**(2), 1995, pp. 29–58.

27. Chisnall, P. M., *Strategic Business Marketing*, 3rd edn, Prentice-Hall International, 1995, pp. 233–261.
28. Mercer, D., *Marketing,* Blackwell, Oxford, 1992, pp. 314–331.

Case Study

Breakwater Products PLC produce a range of leisure products for the UK market. Originally, the company was set up to produce rubber airbeds and swimming rings in the 1950s as swimming boomed as a leisure pursuit. From these humble beginnings the company now produces over 150 different products, all in some way connected with leisure pursuits.

The company is organized into for strategic business units (SBUs). This organization is based on the fact that the different business units supply different end-use markets and/or customers and in doing so are responsible for different product ranges. So we have the following strategic business units together with their latest market share and market growth rates for the previous year:

SBU1   Inflatable products: including the original airbeds and swimming rings (now in plastic) but also including fun items and inflatable dingys, etc.

Market share for this SBU 55 % (UK market)
Market growth rate 5 %

SBU2   Wheeled products: including skateboards, mountain bikes and scooters, including the most recent fashionable city scooters, etc.

Market share for this SBU 20 %
Market growth rate 15 %

SBU3   Outdoor products: including tents, climbing boots and clothing, accessories, etc.

Market share for this SBU 5 %
Market growth rate 3 %

SBU4   Fitness products: including fitness wear, rowing machines, exercise bikes, cross trainers, etc.

Market share for this SBU 8 %
Market growth rate 15 %

QUESTION

1.   How can Portfolio Analysis be used by Breakwater Products PLC?
2.   What further information would be required in order to conduct a Boston Consulting Group Analysis?

5

Markets and customers: buyer behaviour and marketing strategy

Chapter objectives

After reading this chapter you will:

▶ Appreciate the importance of understanding the behaviour of customers, both household and organizational.

▶ Understand some of the key questions which the marketer needs to address in connection with developing this understanding.

▶ Be familiar with a number of frameworks for analysing consumer and organizational buyers encompassing both the steps and stages involved in the buying process and the factors affecting the buyers at each stage.

▶ Appreciate some of the recent developments in thinking and research in this area.

▶ Understand some of the key strategy implications of buyer behaviour.

Introduction

In the previous chapters a range of factors have been discussed that need to be analysed before developing marketing strategies. In particular, environmental factors, company resources and competitive forces were identified as key inputs into strategic marketing decision making. However, as we have seen, irrespective of the particular definition of marketing we select, all the definitions stress customer orientation or market needs in both the concept and practice of marketing. A key element in strategic marketing planning is an understanding of the buyer behaviour of individuals or organizations in the market.

In this and the following chapter, we will consider markets and customers. In this chapter, we start by explaining some of the key issues associated with the understanding of buyer behaviour. In so doing, we consider in detail both consumer and organizational decision making. The focus of this chapter is primarily upon how individual consumers and organizations behave with regard to their purchase decisions. However, as we shall see, marketers are more often concerned with how groups of customers behave and which groups they can best serve. In addition to understanding individual purchasing behaviour, therefore, the marketer must also understand the seemingly simple, but in fact complex, concepts of how individual needs combine to form markets and market segments. These concepts and the related issues of market targeting and positioning, therefore, are the subject of Chapter 6. In this chapter, however, we will be investigating buyer behaviour and developing strategic marketing implications throughout the text. We will also be considering how to research buyer behaviour, and taking a detailed look at buyer behaviour in the strategic marketing process. First, it is worthwhile to take some time to look at the scope of buyer behaviour and to understand the complex nature of the subject area.

The scope and complexity of buyer behaviour

Before we proceed, first consider the following seemingly simple questions:

- 'What was the last product or service you purchased?'
- 'Why did you purchase the product or service?'
- 'How did you decide between competing brands and/or suppliers?'
- 'Who, if anybody, other than yourself, was involved in the purchasing decision?'

You will probably have had little difficulty answering these questions. You, the consumer, know the answers. Now think of these questions from the point of view of the supplier of the product or service in question. These apparently simple questions about your purchasing behaviour then become much more complex. Without the answers to them, though, it is difficult, it not impossible, to make effective strategic marketing decisions.

Most companies would be able to resolve these questions with straightforward 'factual' answers. However, unless they have some knowledge of buyer behaviour, they would be unaware of and unfamiliar with the complex range of behavioural factors which impinge upon purchasing behaviour. The truth is that, like much of human behaviour, purchase behaviour is complex and multi-faceted. We now know that even the 'simplest' of purchasing decisions is an amalgam of behavioural forces and factors of which even the purchaser may not be aware. For instance, the purchase of a lipstick is not simply to colour the lips. The purchaser may feel more attractive wearing lipstick, the colour may be purchased to match certain clothing or it may contain sunscreen or moisturizers that protect the lips. Partly arising from this complexity, researching and understanding consumer behaviour is a specialist area within marketing. Non-behaviourally trained marketers will often have to seek specialist advice. Certainly, in this chapter we would not profess to be able fully to discuss all the behavioural concepts and techniques relevant to understanding buyer behaviour. For a more detailed treatment of the subject area the reader is advised to consult one of the seminal texts, such as Engel, Blackwell and Miniard,[1] Louden and Della Bitta[2] or Schiffman and Kanuk.[3] However, even though consumer behaviour is a complex subject, marketing planners should at least have some understanding of their behaviour. For our purposes we are seeking to develop an appreciation of buyer behaviour in both consumer and organizational markets. Marketers are specifically interested in the behaviour associated with groups, or segments, of consumers as it would be impossible to serve the exact needs and wants of individuals in a market and remain profitable.

What then does the area of buyer behaviour cover? Kotler[4] categorizes buyer behaviour into the 'seven Os of the market place', namely:

Occupants	Who constitutes the market?
Objects	What does the market buy?
Occasions	When does the market buy?
Organization	Who participates in the buying
Objectives	Why does the market buy?
Operations	How does the market buy?
Outlets	Where does the market buy?

Answers to these questions will give a company an added advantage over less aware competitors. They will enable the company to fit their product offerings to the customer more closely and therefore satisfy customer needs more than competitors. Marketers will also need to know whether their controllable variables, e.g. marketing mix variables, will affect buying behaviour. There are many definitions of what exactly consumer behaviour is. One of the most popular is:[5]

> Those acts of individuals directly involved in obtaining, using and disposing of economic goods, and services, including the decision processes that precede and determine these acts.

It therefore not only encompasses the observable buying decisions but also the underlying, less measurable reasons for purchase decisions. This definition can also be applied to organizational buyer behaviour, although many decisions in this area are made by groups. Throughout this chapter we will be concentrating on buyer behaviour in the commercial sector. However, the concepts and implications associated with buyer behaviour can be applied also to non-profit organizations.

Social organizations should also understand consumer behaviour if they are to be successful. Charities suffering from 'donor fatigue' need to look at the motivation people feel to donate time and money, and respond to this. Political parties and government organizations also need to look at consumers of their services. Governments at local level need to match services to customer needs. Location of parks and public transport services need to be researched for consumer wants, needs and usage rates.

It can be seen that the study of buyer behaviour has broad application and the term 'buyer' can be applied to the numerous publics that organizations service. However, before looking further into details of consumer and organizational buyer behaviour it is worth reflecting upon models of buyer behaviour as they are often used in literature on the subject.

Most men who shave use either an electric razor or a bladed safety razor of some sort. In the case of the safety razor, one might be tempted to think that the choice and purchase process might be relatively straightforward. After all, for most men these are items that are used every day, are relatively inexpensive, and are purchased frequently, usually as part of the weekly grocery shop at the supermarket. Moreover, unlike clothing or a car the brand of razor and blades that we buy does not say much about us to the outside world. Buyer behaviour in this case then, can hardly be complex, can it?

The Gillette Company believe so.

In marketing their razors and razor blades the Gillette company invest considerable time and effort in researching consumers' needs and wants and how these are changing. In fact, the behavioural forces and factors which underpin the purchase and brand choice of these seemingly mundane items can be very complex indeed. For example, there is a considerable amount of reference group influence when it comes to how men shave and what products they choose. Razors are a particularly good example of where the user is different to the purchaser in as much as it is often women who actually purchase these products during the weekly shop. Fashions change in shaving in as much as it affects appearance. Ten years ago, 'clean shaven', was the fashionable look, but this then changed and 'designer stubble' became the look. At the moment the fashion is now changing again back towards clean shaven.

The point is that buyer behaviour is complex in this area of product purchase. Gillette spend millions on developing new and ever more sophisticated products for this market, as the recent 'triple blade' product launch demonstrates.

One approach to dealing with the potential complexity in buyer behaviour has been the development of buyer behaviour models.

Buyer behaviour models

The aim of buyer behaviour models is to take the complex interrelated variables involved in purchase decisions and to simplify them to be of use to the marketer. Chisnall[6] states that buyer behaviour models have two basic functions:

1 They describe, in simplified form, the parameters or characteristics affecting the purchase of certain types of goods and services.
2 They allow predictions to be made of the likely outcomes of specific marketing strategies.

Many buyer behaviour models have been developed from a 'black box' model. The information that is processed by the buyer is not explained by the model. Figure 5.1 shows a typical **black box model**.

This type of basic model has been developed into more complex models. In this model, the process and influences on the buyer's decision are not explained. **Multivariate models** try to explain in more detail what is going on in the buying decision. Most view the buyer as a 'problem solver' and concentrate on the influences upon behaviour and the process involved in purchase. Awareness of a problem arises from some stimuli, information is processed, environmental and individual influences are evaluated and there is an output of purchase or non-purchase. Models have been developed for consumer, family and organizational buying. Discussions of the most popular models can be found in Lancaster and Massingham[7] and Schiffman and Kanuk.[8] Criticisms have, however, been made regarding the practicality of these models because

Figure 5.1
A 'black box' model.

of the difficulty in testing them empirically. Tuck[9] criticized multivariate models because they are not operational. She says the approach takes the basic 'black box' and simply breaks it into numerous black boxes. Therefore the 'prediction' criterion for a good model (as outlined by Chisnall above) has not been fulfilled. However, although this criticism is valid, multivariate models do give valuable insights on the influences and process involved in buying decisions. They provide a framework marketers can use to evaluate important marketing opportunities in the buying process. Indeed, in this chapter, a simple model is used to discuss aspects of consumer behaviour. One of the main areas where models are of use is in investigating areas that merit specific research.

Researching buyer behaviour

Given that buying behaviour is complex and multifaceted, it is easy to assume that it is too difficult to research the area meaningfully. This would be denying the importance of good information on the behaviour of customers. The basis for research can start with Kotler's seven Os of the marketplace outlined earlier. Marketers can use a number of methods to research buying behaviour. The introspective method is where marketers think about their own probable behaviour. Customers can be interviewed after purchasing their goods and questioned, which is the retrospective method. Prospective customers can be asked about how they will purchase the product (prospective method). Customers could also be asked about their ideal way to purchase the goods. These methods would give insights into how the consumer goes through the process of buying. More difficult from a research point of view is information on the influences of buying behaviour. These are often not product-related and involve less measurable aspects of human behaviour, such as perception and attitudes.

Of particular use in trying to understand some of the more complex underpinning factors affecting behaviour are the techniques of so-called qualitative research. Much qualitative research has as its objective, the exploration of things such as underpinning attitudes, perceptions, and motives. As early as the '60s and '70s marketers began to use the techniques of so-called 'motivational research' which in turn were derived from the tools and techniques of the clinical psychologists and were very much rooted in the concepts and ideas of Freudian psychologists. In recent years, however, marketers have concentrated their qualitative marketing research into consumer behaviour using *focus group* discussions and/or *depth interviews*.

Focus groups

Focus groups involve a trained moderator guiding a group of selected customers or potential customers through a semi-structured interview. The moderator may have a psychology background and will of course be a skilled marketing researcher and interviewer. Normally a focus group will consist of between 6 to 10 selected individuals. The idea is to encourage the respondents to discuss factors which will reveal some of their innermost thoughts and feelings regarding a product or service in question. So, for example, if we were conducting research into consumer attitudes towards say, the purchase and wearing of ties, the moderator may encourage the group to talk informally about their purchasing in general and then gradually as the group begins to open up and discuss between themselves, focus the discussion towards the product market in question, in this case, ties. Great skill and expertise is required in order to elicit useful information about the product market in question without, at the same time, leading the group towards responses which are more in line with the ideas of the moderator than the individuals in the group. In other words, care must be taken not to bias the answers. A focus group interview will last anything between one to two and a half hours and therefore it will usually be taped for later analysis. It would be common practice, if say, we were using focus groups in the development and launch of a new product in the UK market to conduct anything up to 12 or more focus group interviews which would be designed to provide a representative sample. At a current average cost per focus group of anything between £1300 to £2500 each focus group interviewing is not cheap. It does however, provide potentially very rich information on which to base marketing decisions. Initially used primarily for exploratory research prior to conducting quantitative research, focus groups are now increasingly being used to explore further issues highlighted from initial quantitative research based on more traditional questionnaire research and analysis. Focus group interviewing is now felt to be so useful that it is being used by companies ranging from banks through to detergent manufacturers and political parties.

Although widely used in the US for a long time now, the use of focus groups to research consumer attitudes, potential voting patterns, and key issues amongst voters in the UK really came into its own in the run up to the 1997 General Election. The Labour Party in particular made use of this type of research. Partly as a result of their success in this election, and the role which focus groups were felt to have played in this, all the main political parties in the UK now use focus groups extensively on a regular basis as a way of gauging voter opinions. Although there is some concern about the extensive use of these groups, for example some argue that it tends to detract from developing and implementing policies, there is no doubt that in the political arena, focus groups are here to stay.

Depth interviews

Depth interviews are used less frequently to research buyer behaviour these days but can be useful when researching areas which are of a sensitive nature and therefore where a group discussion situation would not be ideal or even appropriate. The key difference therefore between depth interviews and focus groups is that the respondent talks on a one-to-one basis with the researcher. The interview may be semi-structured or unstructured depending on the purpose and nature of the research. In all other respects with regard to, e.g. the skills required on the part of the interviewer etc., the depth interview is very similar to the focus group. As with a focus group therefore, depth interviews can be used to explore what would normally be the more 'hidden' aspects of buyer behaviour and choice. Certain broad trends in society can be monitored more or less constantly. So the changing demographic structure of markets at both domestic and international levels can be tracked and threats can then be changed into opportunities. In Britain there is an ageing population, which means that there are going to be more opportunities for products aimed at older consumers, although suppliers of products made for the younger age groups may have to consolidate their positions and try to gain market share. Changing cultural factors, such as the attitude to women becoming the main wage earners, and men assuming roles traditionally deemed to belong to women, can also be monitored to enable the marketer to take situations into account in a strategic manner. Now we will look at the buying behaviour of consumers in greater depth.

Futures research

Although, as already mentioned, focus group research has become one of the most widely used techniques for researching buyer behaviour, it is not without its limitations and hence its critics. In particular, some researchers have begun to question its usefulness, particularly for **futures research** on needs and wants or in assessing attitudes to revolutionary and novel ideas for new products and services.

Critics of focus groups argue that all too often focus group members will knowingly, or subconsciously at least, simply tell the focus group leader what they feel he or she wants to hear. Similarly, some argue there is a danger that group members simply say what they think the rest of the group will want to hear. With regard to focus groups being particularly weak at uncovering future trends and needs, the argument is that more often than not, the focus group members will find it difficult to imagine or conjecture that product and brand usage will be any different in the future. In other words, there is a tendency for the focus group to think along conventional lines.

As a result of these criticisms some researchers have turned to alternative and often unconventional methods to try to gain insights into buying needs and wants, especially when trying to detect ideas and responses to new products and services for the future. Perhaps not surprisingly, these methods now increasingly being used in marketing research are often collectively referred to as 'futures research'.

Perhaps somewhat confusingly, futures research is not actually about forecasting the future. Rather it is the application of often innovative research techniques to gain insights into the possible future needs and wants of consumers and the implications of these for the marketer with regard to, for example, possible new products. As this is a comparatively new approach to research in consumer behaviour, there are no hard and fast rules about how to conduct this type of research and the techniques to use. However, futures research has already spawned several innovative and different research techniques to those conventionally used in focus groups.

One of the leading companies in the UK using futures research at the moment, Brand Futures, uses several innovative approaches to its group consumer behaviour research, albeit often coupled with traditional focus groups. Below are outlined some of the differences in this company's futures approach compared to traditional focus group methods:

- Instead of using 'representative' consumers, often the company will conduct interviews using panels of individuals who have previously been judged to be 'thinking ahead' in their particular field.
- Often the groups will deliberately include individuals with alternative views to the rest of the group. For example, a group assembled to investigate possible future meat-based food products might include a vegan.
- New techniques for uncovering attitudes and factors underpinning behaviour are used. One such technique is a technique known as 'deprivation'. With this technique panel members are asked to go without a particular good or service for a while and then interviewed to see what effect this has had on their behaviour. At the other extreme another technique is 'inflation', where group members are asked to consume a product in much greater quantities than normal, again with a view to gaining new insights into possible future consumer behaviour.

Using techniques such as this it is suggested enables the marketer to gain more insights into possible future needs, areas for new product development, brand extension strategies, and innovative and creative approaches to marketing existing products.

Consumer buyer behaviour

The distinguishing feature of consumer as opposed to organizational buyer behaviour is the fact that consumer buying behaviour consists of the activities involved in the buying and using of products or services for personal and household use. Organizational buyers, on the other hand, purchase primarily for organizational purposes. As we shall see, this seemingly obvious difference in fact gives rise to further major differences between the two types of buying. As stated earlier in this chapter, consumer behaviour is complex. In order to investigate it in detail it is advantageous to break down the purchase process into a model to simplify the process and factors influencing purchase behaviour. Figure 5.2 shows a simplified model of consumer behaviour. As can be seen, environmental influences that are external to the consumer have an effect on purchase behaviour. The consumer also has influences that are individually determined. Both these types of influence are carried, consciously or subconsciously, within the consumer's memory. The third box in the diagram shows the decision-making process an individual goes through when purchasing a product. The feedback lines show that at any stage, information can be fed back and the purchase process can be stopped and resumed at an earlier stage. The model will now be discussed in greater detail.

Figure 5.2
Simplified model of consumer-buying behaviour.

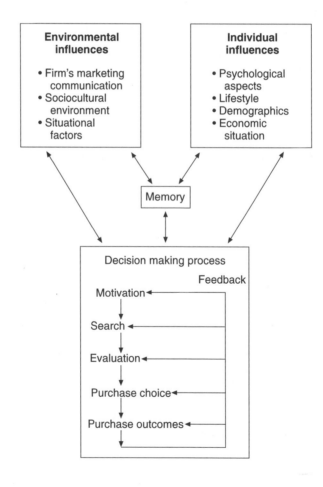

Environmental influences

Marketing communications from companies are always around us. Some of these are retained in memory, and we have an image of companies and the goods and services they provide. This may lead to a motivation to purchase the product or to be aware of the product and provide for future use. Recent television campaigns promoting personal pensions have stimulated a perceived need in this area.

Culture   Culture is the broadest environmental factor and is defined by Assad as:[10]

> Norms, beliefs and customs that are learned from society and lead to common patterns of behaviour.

So, as behaviour is learned, culture determines the broad values and attitudes an individual holds. Culture can be investigated by using an inventory of values. A child growing up in a certain culture learns its cultural values from the people with whom it socializes. So the family, school and friends have a large impact on the cultural values with which the child grows up. Some aspects of culture, for instance, freedom in the UK, have not changed over time. Some aspects of culture are, however, dynamic. For example, the role of women in some societies has changed dramatically over the years. So, even though culture is a basic foundation of society, in the strategic management process it has to be monitored for changes. In addition, culture is often assumed, and this has meant that many mistakes have been made when companies have tried to market their products abroad, where there are cultural barriers to entry. We shall explore these important international cross-cultural factors in more detail later on in Chapter 18 on International Marketing. Within an individual national culture, however, other aspects of the sociocultural environment include subculture, social class, and group and family influences.

Subculture refers to groups in society that have distinct cultural differences. This includes nationality groups such as Indian, West Indian, Italian or Irish, who may have individual lifestyles and values. Religious groups, such as Jews, Muslims, Christians and Hindus are another subculture within the larger cultural group. Blacks, whites and Asians are examples of broad racial groupings and geographical groups can include northerners, southerners or people living in Scotland as distinct groups. Subcultural groups can vary in the products they wish to buy, the outlets they buy from, prices paid and the media selected. In the UK, marketers are often criticized for ignoring subcultural groups in their market targeting.

Social class   Social class is the grouping together of individuals or families who have certain common social or economic characteristics. Members of the same social class are often felt to exhibit similar patterns of behaviour and hence similar views and interests. As we shall see in Chapter 6 social class is often used to separate markets and determine targeting strategies. Criteria used for this type of grouping can be occupation, education or income. People from the same social class are supposed to be more alike than people from differing classes. Social class is seen in terms of higher or lower classes (although individuals can move from one class to another), but this does depend upon the rigidity of the social system in the society in question. Social class is a major influence of buyer behaviour because classes show different product purchase behaviour in certain product categories. Examples include cars and holidays, where social class is a determining factor of the types of product purchased. The 'best' measures of social class have a number of factors included in them rather than just one, for example, income. Social class may not only determine the products people do choose to purchase but also the store type chosen. For example, a department store, market stall, mail order or independent retailer may be favoured by certain social classes.

Groups and family Group and family influences can also affect purchase decisions. *Reference groups* are all the groups that an individual is exposed to that have a direct or an indirect influence on behaviour and attitudes. *Primary groups* are ones with which the contact is continuous, and can include family, neighbours, friends and colleagues. *Secondary groups* are groups which have less contact with individual members, for example, a football team. People also have aspirations and may then be affected by group pressure from an *aspirational group*. For example, this is used quite often in the marketing of cosmetics, where advertisements show women from the aspirational group of beauty, wealth and desirability using the product. Reference groups affect individuals in three ways:

1 They influence self image and attitudes
2 They expose individuals to new behaviour
3 They create pressure to conform.

Of course, reference group importance will depend greatly upon the product in question. If group influences are strong it is worthwhile for the marketer to identify opinion leaders in the group. Opinion leaders have influence over members of their reference group. For instance, if a friend you know is interested in computers and you wish to purchase one, you may ask your friend for advice. Then the friend is an opinion leader. The family group also has an influence on purchase behaviour. Indeed, some purchases are made as a family group. Examples of such purchases include houses, holidays, cars and furniture. In family decision making, individual members may assume different roles. Depending on the purchase and individuals involved they may perform one or many roles. These are outlined below:

1 Information gatherer
2 Influencer
3 Decision maker
4 Purchaser
5 Consumer.

So for the purchase of a holiday a mother and daughter may go into a travel agent and pick up brochures; all the family will influence the decision. The final decision may be made by the father, but the mother books the holiday and is then the purchaser. All the family are consumers. Some products within family decision making are dominated by the husband or wife. Others are made jointly.

Recent research has indicated that on average, children in the UK spend approximately £2.50 pocket money each week. This adds up to a total spend by children in the UK in 2000 of approximately £1.5 billion a year. Clearly a market worth serving.

In addition to the amount spent by children, manufacturers and marketers of many brands have also recognized that consumption habits, including brand choice and patterns of product usage, are often established very early on in the consumer's life and once established they can in fact last a lifetime. Not surprisingly then, marketers are interested in 'catching their customers young'.

- Procter and Gamble's 'Sunny Delight' has been one of the most successful new brands to be launched in the UK in recent years. It appeals particularly to children, with this appeal being backed by a multi-million pound advertising budget.
- One of the biggest user groups on the Internet is children. Not surprisingly then, brands such as 'Slush Puppie' have been amongst the first to create websites on the Net.
- The retailer Tescos recently launched 'Computers for Schools' campaign is sponsored by the Pepsi, Tango and 7-Up brands.

Situational factors These may also determine a purchase or consumption situation, and may be a major aspect in purchase behaviour. If you were asked about your favourite food it would be quite acceptable to state that it depends upon the situation. At times you may prefer a snack, others a meal with the family and at other times a special meal, perhaps in a restaurant. The consumption situation will directly influence consumer brand perceptions and purchase behaviour; that is, where precisely the product is going to be consumed. The purchase situation is also important. Product availability, change in price and the existence of queues may have an effect on purchase behaviour.

Individual influences

In addition to the environmental factors that influence a consumer's purchase decisions there are other influences that are personal or individual to the consumer. Psychological factors (in Figure 5.2) include *perceptions, motivations, attitudes* and *personality*. Perception is the way in which people select, organize and interpret stimuli. This includes how a person sees and interprets a company and its products. When a message is perceived it is modified by the individual's interpretation. An individual selects (subconsciously) the exposure, attention, comprehension and retention of stimuli. This information is then organized so that it can be easily understood. This can be effected by placing information in categories or combining these into brand images. It is therefore important that marketers build up brand awareness so that a personality for the brand is developed in the minds of existing or potential buyers.

Attitudes are specific. An attitude is held about a certain good or supplier in the context of consumer behaviour. Attitudes are very difficult to change, so companies finding that certain products are associated with a poor attitude would, if at all possible, be better advised to change the product than to try to change consumer attitudes.

Demographic variables describe individuals according to age, sex, income, education and occupation. Demographic factors will have a bearing on the types of product individuals want, where they shop and how they evaluate possible purchases. For instance a teenage girl will want, in the main, different products from her mother. A concept similar to age is life cycle stage. Throughout life, people go through stages: single, married, married with children, children left home and retired. At each of these stages their product needs will be changing.

Lifestyle variables encompass an individual's activities, interests and opinions (indeed it is often called AIO research). A person's lifestyle is how a person interacts with his or her environment. This again will have consequences for purchase behaviour.

Lifestyle concepts and research have proved particularly useful to the contemporary marketer, especially with regard to market segmentation and targeting. We shall therefore explore lifestyle variables including some of the recent developments in this area in more detail in Chapter 6 which follows.

The economic situation an individual faces also greatly affects purchase decisions. Economic situation not only encompasses how much income individuals have but whether they have borrowing power and their attitude towards spending. Individual and environmental influences may then be stored in an individual's memory, which will be brought into play during the decision-making process.

Decision-making process

A further aspect of consumer decision making is the process involved in purchase. In Figure 5.2 on page 116 this is shown in the lower box and encompasses five stages. The first stage is when an individual feels a need that a product will satisfy and is motivated to evaluate the goods on offer. People have many varying needs. If a need is intense then they become motivated to purchase the good that will satisfy it. Maslow[11] described the different needs of human beings as being hierarchical. Figure 5.3 shows Maslow's hierarchy of needs. This shows, at the bottom of the pyramid, physiological needs. These are the most basic and important of human needs. So when needs are met lower in the pyramid, individuals move up the hierarchy to fulfil 'higher' needs. Motivation can be stimulated by marketing. For instance, when people see an advertisement for a burger they may then feel hunger and purchase one. Alternatively, they may search for alternatives to fulfil the need to satisfy hunger. They could, perhaps, go to a restaurant, have a pizza or a sandwich. This searching for alternatives may be *external*, that is, physically looking for alternatives or *internal*, searching the memory for what a person knows about products and suppliers. Marketers, then, need to research how they can stimulate need for their products and the types of information consumers want on their products.

An example of how Maslow's hierarchy of needs can be useful to the development of strategic marketing plans is contained in an interesting piece of research by Foreman and Ven Sviram[12]. In a study which looked at some of the recent developments in modern retailing, they explored the extent to which the shopping experience was

Figure 5.3
Maslow's hierarchy
of needs.

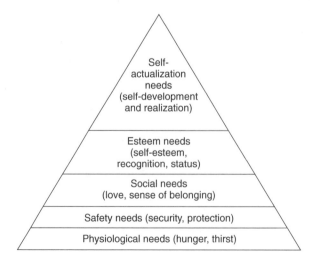

important in fulfilling the needs of individuals with respect to the social needs (love, sense of belonging) in Maslow's hierarchy. In particular, they looked at the differences in this respect with regard to what they classified respectively as 'lonely' versus 'non-lonely' consumers. The notion was that for many shoppers shopping isn't just a commercial transaction, but has a value as a surrogate social contact. This value, they hypothesized, would be greater for their category of lonely customers than for non-lonely customers. In turn, therefore, they further hypothesized that lonely consumers would perceive a greater depersonalization of the retail encounter due to such trends in modern retailing as self-service, than would be non-lonely customers. Because of this, the lonely consumers, they suggested, would increasingly experience shopping as unsatisfying and unenjoyable. Their research is particularly interesting in the context of the growth of internet shopping at home.

Their results broadly confirmed their ideas with the lonely consumers very much relying on the shopping experience to fulfil some of their social needs particularly with respect to belonginess. In turn, this category of consumers were found to be dissatisfied and disappointed with some of their shopping experiences. They suggested that for this particular category of customers, retailers should look to how they can 're-personalize' the shopping encounter to provide social experiences in order to fulfil social needs. Retailers, they suggested, should be sensitive to the desire of many customers for human contact and balance this with both a retailers' and customers' desire for speed and efficiency in the shopping process. Before retailers undertake steps which may further de-personalize the shopping experience such as many elements of increased automation, and certainly the move towards home shopping, they should carefully research the needs of at least some shoppers for more social interaction in the shopping process.

There are many sources of information on products. Friends and relatives can be used as information sources in addition to company information, e.g. advertising. There may be some public media sources of information, for example, press articles about product areas. Another source of information is the actual handling of the products. When information has been assimilated by the individual he or she can then make judgements about the brands that are available. Marketers then, as well as building awareness, need to make their products have **unique selling propositions (USPs)** so they stand out amongst competing brands.

When consumers have enough information they will evaluate the alternatives in the marketplace. The criteria on which products are evaluated vary depending on the products and how many brands are available. The evaluative criteria used will depend on what need is being fulfilled by the product. Most often discussed are the role of price and the brand image. Again it is imperative that marketers know on what basis their products are being judged. If there are common themes from consumers for the evaluation of alternative products and the ideal product offering, this has implications for marketing management. It means that products can be tailored to suit consumer needs and marketing communications can respond to the evaluating criteria they use. Evaluating products often coincides with searching for the products.

When products or brands have been evaluated, one product is selected for purchase. However, purchase intention can be affected by unforeseen factors; for example, the price may rise. Also, other people can have an effect on purchase choice even at this late stage. There may now be no purchase at all.

Purchase outcomes or *post-purchase behaviour* will be either satisfaction or dissatisfaction with the purchase choice. Again the product will be judged against the needs that were to be fulfilled by the product and by the criteria on which alternative brands were judged. Satisfaction occurs when expectations of the product are either met or exceeded. This is remembered the next time the product is purchased. Also, the consumer may tell friends about being satisfied with the product. If expectations have not been met the consumer experiences some *post-purchase dissonance*. There are many ways in which consumers try to reduce their post-purchase dissonance. They can find information to support their product choice, or avoid information that will not confirm their purchase. If dissonance is strong then the consumer may take action either to the company directly, perhaps asking for a refund, or indirectly; for example, telling friends about the problems with the product.

Marketers are increasingly aware of the importance of post-purchase feelings, and in particular the need to ensure that customers are satisfied with their purchase decisions. The more effective marketers these days, for example, will contact their customers after purchase to enquire if they are happy with their purchase and the way they have been dealt with. Clearly this cannot always be done on an individual personal basis but it is possible to communicate with customers in writing to demonstrate that we value their custom and are willing to respond to any dissatisfaction which they may be experiencing as a result of having purchased our products and services. Similarly, companies are increasingly using 'tracking' studies to assess levels of customer satisfaction or dissatisfaction over time. Most companies now realize that a dissatisfied customer will on average express this dissatisfaction to nine other actual or potential customers. As we have seen in our discussion of reference groups earlier in this chapter word-of-mouth is extremely important in influencing customer choice. In addition, marketers now appreciate that it is much more cost effective to retain existing customers than to attract new ones. Kotler[13] estimates that attracting a new customer costs approximately five times the cost of retaining an existing one. The importance of this initial cost difference is further underpinned by the lifetime value of loyal customers, which can give rise to substantial amounts of revenue and profit to a company. Because of this Kotler suggests that it is vital to assess levels of customer retention and causes of customer attrition and then to take steps to increase the former whilst reducing the latter. The recognition of the importance of keeping customers, and building their loyalty is one of the reasons for the growth of relationship marketing introduced in Chapter 1. Remember, this development in marketing is so far-reaching and important that we shall be returning to it in more detail in Chapter 17.

Of course, whether all these stages are experienced and the time spent at each of them depends on the individual and the product purchased. Some products require extensive problem solving where a great deal of information is required to make a decision. This type of product is usually expensive, complex to understand, and/or has not been bought previously; for example, a house, a personal computer or a car. Limited search and evaluation would be used when there is some knowledge of the products on offer: for example, a small item of furniture for the house or a car radio. When customers know a great deal about the products then there is little search and evaluation. The purchase may be habitual; for example, the repeat buying of the same brand of toothpaste or washing powder. This 'low involvement' decision making causes some problems for marketers. Should marketers try to make such decisions higher involvement? Are consumers being brand loyal to products in an active way or are they displaying inertia? What is the best way of promoting the product in a low involvement market? Ways in which marketers try to increase involvement of consumers include:

1   Link the product with an issue. A recent example here is the marketing of relatively mundane products being described as environmentally friendly or 'green'.
2   Use advertising that involves consumers, e.g. 'try the Pepsi challenge'.
3   Change product benefits. For example, Radion advertisements emphasized the 'new' benefit of clean smelling clothes.

A more extreme example, perhaps, of trying to increase the level of consumer involvement is the controversial approach to advertising used by the Benetton company. Their campaigns for their clothing products have included pictures of dying Aids patients, kissing nuns, and prisoners on 'death row'. Although the advertising campaigns are complex and multi-faceted, as much as anything they are probably designed to increase the customer's involvement with the product and brand by linking products with issues.

For a more detailed investigation of the marketing strategies that are successful for low, medium and high involvement purchasing see Assael.[14]

Using a model such as Figure 5.2 shows the marketer how to break down consumer behaviour into aspects that can be analysed for effective strategic marketing planning. It can be used as a framework for answering the questions asked earlier in the chapter. Many aspects of consumer behaviour can also be used to evaluate organizational buying behaviour and we now turn our attention to this.

Organizational buying behaviour

Consumer behaviour relates to the buying behaviour of individuals (or families) for products for their own use. Organizations buy to enable them to provide goods and services to the final customer. This has implications for marketing management as we shall see later. Organizational buying behaviour has many similarities to consumer behaviour. Both encompass the behaviour of human beings, whether individually or in groups. Organizational buyers do not necessarily act in a more rational manner than individual consumers.[15] Organizational buyers are affected by environmental and individual factors, as outlined in the previous section. One of the main differences from consumer buying is that organizational buying usually involves group decision making (known as the 'decision-making unit' (DMU) or sometimes referred to as the **buying centre**). In such a group individuals may have different roles in the purchase process. These can be categorized as:

1 *Users*
   The people in the organization who will be using the product. Sometimes they will also be involved in devising product specifications.
2 *Buyers*
   Buyers have the formal authority to purchase the product.
3 *Deciders*
   Deciders actually make the buying decision.
4 *Influencers*
   Influencers affect the buying decision in many different ways. For example, they might be technical personnel who have developed the product specifications.
5 *Gatekeepers*
   Gatekeepers control the flow of information to and from the DMU (or 'buying centre').

One person may play all the above roles in the purchase decision or each role may be represented by a number of personnel. The salesperson trying to sell to an organization should be aware of the roles people assume in the buying centre.

Another difference in organizational buying is that many products are more complex and require specialist knowledge to purchase. As many products are changed according to the specifications of the buyer there is more communication and negotiation between buyers and sellers. After-sales service is also very important in organizational buying and suppliers are often evaluated quite rigorously after purchase. In general, organizational markets have fewer, larger buyers who are geographically concentrated. Another aspect of organizational buying is the nature of **derived demand**. That is, demand for organizational (especially industrial) goods is derived from consumer markets. If demand for the end product consumer good falls then this has an effect along the production line to all the inputs. So, in organizational marketing the end consumers should not be ignored and trends should be monitored.

 Organizational buying decisions can be categorized into **buy classes** as to how complex they are, similar to the low–high involvement decision making in consumer markets:

1 *Straight re-buys*
These occur often, are relatively cheap and are usually a matter of routine. If the supplier is an 'in supplier', that is, they are on the company's approved list of suppliers, then they have to perform so they do not get taken off the list. If they are 'out suppliers' they have to try to get on to the approved list.

2 *Modified re-buy*
This situation requires some additional information or evaluation of suppliers. It is usually the case that specifications etc. have been modified since the last purchase.

 3 *New task*
A **new task** or new buy situation is the most complex purchase decision, when the company has not bought this product before. Search and evaluation procedures are extensive.

The process of organizational buying

The process involved in organizational buying has many similarities to consumer buying. Both go through a form of need recognition, search, evaluation, choice and post-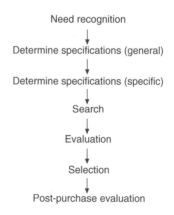purchase evaluation. Figure 5.4 shows the specific **buy phases** organizations go through when buying. Need recognition occurs when the company has a need that can be fulfilled by the purchase of a product. Need can be stimulated internally from within the organization or through external means (e.g. if a salesperson visits with a new product). The company will then draw up general specifications. This can be done in consultation with the prospective seller. Then more detailed specifications are assimilated. Value

Figure 5.4
Organizational
buying process.

Need recognition
↓
Determine specifications (general)
↓
Determine specifications (specific)
↓
Search
↓
Evaluation
↓
Selection
↓
Post-purchase evaluation

analysis can be used to reduce the costs of components in the production process by critically examining the function and specification of each part in every component and sub-component. In the search stage, buyers can use numerous sources of information. They may advertise for tenders for certain products, investigate trade journals or directories, speak to sales people, look at their own records or visit trade shows.

Marketing implications for suppliers include achieving a good reputation in the marketplace, attending trade shows, advertising and trying to identify prospective customers. By so doing the company can be considered early in the decision process and may even be involved in the formulation of specifications.

Evaluation may be systematic, involving some form of supplier evaluation technique. These can be very detailed, covering quality, price, delivery and after-sales service, for example. The buying centre will evaluate the proposals and alternative product offerings and decide upon the most suitable purchase choice. At this stage there may be further negotiations to alter the price on certain product specifications. The buying centre may choose to have a number of suppliers to protect it from being too dependent on one supplier. The selection stage may also incorporate some form of reordering system and the evaluation of the product after purchase is often formalized.

Again, the time spent, resources committed and, indeed, whether all the stages are passed through, depends on the type of product bought. A 'new task' product will mean that all the stages will probably be passed through. A straight re-buy situation will be a relatively quick process, missing a number of stages. Indeed, this type of purchasing is often accessed by computerized buying. For a discussion of *buy classes* (new task etc.) and their relationship to *buy phases* (the decision-making process) see Robinson, Faris and Wind.[16]

The people involved in the decision-making process can also change over time, although it is still very important for the marketer to be aware of the process and the ways in which he can develop marketing strategy around this. Cardozo[17] stated that it is very important to be involved in the buying process (from a seller's point of view) at an early stage.

Members of the buying centre (or DMU) are influenced by both rational and emotional factors in their decision making. Marketers should be aware of the different influences on the buying centre, although emotional factors are much more difficult to predict and interpret. Hutt and Speh[19] discuss the different types of motivation in the buying process listed below:

Rational motives	*Emotional motives*
Price	Status and rewards
Quality	Perceived risk
Service	Friendship
Continuity of supply	
Reciprocity	

These motivations for purchase are not the only influences on organizational buyers of which strategic marketers should be aware. We will now examine other factors that influence organizational buyer behaviour.

Influences on organizational buying

In consumer buying behaviour we discussed two main influences on purchase behaviour – environmental and individual factors. In organizational buying we have a more complex environment for buying decisions. Figure 5.5 shows the main influences in the purchase process.

Figure 5.5
Influences on
organizational
buying.
Source: adapted from
M. D. Hutt and Speh,
T.W., *Business Marketing
Management,* Dryden
Press, London, 1999.[18]

Environmental forces on buyer behaviour include economic, legal, political, cultural, physical and technological factors, so the general economic trends of the area where the buying organization is located are important, as are the economic trends of any areas in which it trades (due to derived demand). Increasingly, when evaluating economic trends, the marketer should take a global perspective as world trade increases. The political and legal environment, which includes government spending, taxation and import and export controls, should also be evaluated for their influence upon buying decisions. In the developing global markets for goods and services it is easy to disregard cultural differences. However, there are still many different cultural climates in the world and they do not appear to be diminishing in importance. Physical influences involve the geographical location of the organization. The changing technological environment also influences buying decisions.

Marketers must take account of group force purchasing influences:

1 Who is involved in the buying decision?
2 What influence does each member have?
3 How does each member of the buying centre evaluate alternative products?

The type of information that is needed on group forces is the type that only becomes available when close contact is maintained with the buyer. This reinforces the role of the sales person in the buying decision process. Members of the DMU or buying centre were outlined earlier in this chapter, as distinguishing the roles that individuals carried out.

Organizational forces, such as the organizational culture of the business, also have an effect on the buying decision. For instance, when marketing to an organization that has a highly centralized structure, including the buying function, this needs a different marketing approach to companies that have a decentralized structure.

It is easy to assume that organizational buying has little to do with individual factors. However, in any buying centre, individuals make buying decisions, not the organization. Different members of the buying centre may evaluate products using different criteria, which complicates the issue for the organizational marketer. Some of the motivations of individual buyers were outlined earlier in this chapter. Individuals will also try to reduce the level of risk they are exposed to in the purchase decision; for example, using multiple sources or making use of an extensive information search.

These factors have been developed into a comprehensive model of organizational buying behaviour by Webster and Wind.[20] There are a number of trends within organizational purchasing that have implications for marketing management:

1 Purchasing is more specialized and professional.
2 There is more centralized purchasing.
3 Computerized purchasing has increased.

4   There are new philosophies of purchasing, e.g. just-in-time, zero defects and ma-
    terials management.
5   More, and improved, supplier capability and performance analysis.
6   More and more use of e-commerce purchasing and supply.

These trends within organizational purchasing are important in the sense that they
have potentially significant implications for the development of marketing strategies
and plans. However, three of these trends in organizational purchasing are felt to have
been particularly important in this respect and are therefore considered in more detail
below.

Just in time purchasing

Originally devised in America, many manufacturing companies throughout the world,
but particularly the Japanese manufacturers, have moved towards a system of manufacturing based on having parts and components for production in stock and available
when, and only when, they are required by the production line or unit. For rather
obvious reasons this system of manufacturing and inventory control has come to be
termed **Just In Time (JIT)** although some writers now term this 'lean manufacturing'.
Used extensively in Japan for many years now it has also made major inroads into the
manufacturing of western economies. A definition of JIT by Dion *et al.*[21] explains the
meaning of JIT and captures its essential features and the thinking behind it.

> An inventory control system which delivers input to its production or distribution site only
> at the rate and time it is needed. Thus it reduces inventories whether it is used within the
> firm or as a mechanism regulating the flow of products between adjacent firms in the distri-
> bution system channel. It is a 'pull' system which replaces buffer inventories with channel
> member co-operation.

Companies have realized that holding stock, of any type, including stock for production or sale, is extremely costly. Not only is capital tied up, but in addition there are
potential costs in stock holding due to, e.g. pilferage, damage, changes in customer
demand or product specification which renders stock obsolete, etc. Because of this, a JIT
system aims to minimize stockholding, and hence stockholding costs by supplying
parts etc. for production, as already mentioned just at the time they are needed. The
consequence of a JIT manufacturing and purchasing system for the supplier is that the
supplier must be able to provide parts and components, raw materials etc. on a JIT basis
to customers who are operating JIT manufacturing and purchasing systems. In turn,
this means that there must be a close working relationship and exchange of information between customers and suppliers and to this end, as Lancaster[22] has pointed out,
close associations must be developed between marketer and customers. In fact, JIT
purchasing is another one of the main factors underpinning the growth of so-called
'relationship marketing' which we shall consider in more detail in Chapter 17. In addition to the need for very close working relationships between suppliers and customers
because of JIT purchasing, obviously, supplying on a JIT basis increases the importance
of effective distribution and especially logistical systems on the part of marketers. We
shall also consider some of the impacts of JIT therefore on this element of marketing in
our Chapter 11 on logistics. The introduction of JIT purchasing by a customer usually
means an initial reduction in total supplier numbers often with increasing numbers of
component parts being purchased from outside rather than being manufactured internally. In a properly synchronized JIT system customer demands can be met and profits

maintained or increased through a reduction in stockpiles and inventory levels. There are, however some reservations to JIT. An obvious one is the need for synchronization. According to Dion[23] suppliers can have commitments to other customers and so delays can be caused by this. A company's industrial relations must be excellent to operate a successful JIT system including provision for extremely flexible work routines and manning arrangements.

Zero defects

Very much related to JIT purchasing, and indeed necessary for JIT systems to work is the need for **zero defects**, very reliable quality on the part of the supplier. Because components and supplies are incorporated into the customer's manufacturing process almost immediately following delivery there is no time to test components or to inspect for defective supplies. In addition, all companies in recent years have become very aware of the insistence by many customers for good quality products and services. Finally, customers themselves in markets have begun to demand better and more consistent quality and this therefore has pushed the need for such quality levels back down the chain of manufacture and supply to involve all the different companies in the production and supply chain. So, for example, the Jaguar Motor Company in the 1970s, when experiencing substantial loss of market share and falling profits, particularly in export markets due to the supply of poor quality components turned the situation round by insisting on improved quality from their suppliers. Early recognition of the importance of quality, however, has now moved on with many companies now implementing and operating total quality management systems or TQM as it is often called. Lancaster[24] has shown that companies must focus on the total product quality of their goods to differentiate themselves from the opposition. JIT purchasing means that components and supplies must be 'right first time'. This has meant that suppliers must operate 'zero defects' policies and systems. In the '60s and '70s it was sufficient to ensure that defects were within controllable and acceptable levels when supplying customers. These days, however, customers insist that there must be no defects in supply. This has revolutionized manufacturing, quality control, design, and marketing/logistical systems.

Wherever a company is focusing on improving quality, however, it is important to remember that in business to business markets, customer satisfaction is an overall evaluation of the supplier based on the purchase and consumption experience over time and the customer is the ultimate judge of quality. Therefore the industrial marketer has to ascertain customer perceptions of quality and how they relate to customer satisfaction and firm performance. A study by Qualls and Rosa[25] investigated a framework for assessing industrial buyers' perception of quality and their relationship to customer satisfaction. It was found from the study that when integrating customer satisfaction into quality improver programmes, multiple measures of satisfaction and quality must be used. It appears that buyers employ different criteria when evaluating supplier performance. The dimensions of quality used by organizational buyers and their influence on customer satisfaction were also found to vary across organizational functions. Functional areas have different factors that determine their satisfaction with different suppliers. Engineers, for example, use different criteria with suppliers than purchasing or manufacturing personnel. In assessing the industrial buyers' perceptions of quality and satisfaction therefore, one has to look at the buying group and not just the purchasing function. Nevertheless, despite these possible differences in perceptions of what constitutes quality, the overall emphasis on quality and its importance in organizational supplier choice remains unaltered in today's marketing environmental. This importance is exemplified in the following statement by Nissan Motor Manufacturing (UK) regarding quality requirements for suppliers.[26]

> The Nissan quality philosophy is one of commitment to customer satisfaction through continuous improvement in quality, safety and reliability.
>
> The supplier has total responsibility for the delivery of zero-defect products and will establish quality systems accordingly. These systems will include the continual review and development of management, production design, material specification and manufacturing process.
>
> The development of mutual trust and co-operation will bring about quality and productivity improvements to the shared benefit of both supplier and Nissan.

E-commerce and organizational buying

Throughout this text so far we have suggested that one of the major developments affecting the marketer in recent years, and one which will continue to grow in importance, is the development of electronic commerce. Electronic commerce, or e-commerce/business as it is often referred to, is revolutionising our lives and therefore has major implications for the marketer and marketing practice.

The term 'e-commerce' embraces a huge range of techniques and procedures for conducting business electronically and is just as important to both consumer and business-to-business markets these days. In essence, e-commerce is the use of electronic technologies and systems to facilitate and enhance transactions between different parts of the value chain.

One of the first applications of e-commerce was in the area of business-to-business marketing. Over 20 years ago, companies began to use their computers in purchasing and supply. Eventually, this computerization developed into systems whereby suppliers and buyers could readily exchange information through their computer systems. This eventually developed into full **electronic data interchange** (EDI) systems. These systems offer many advantages to both parties in the transaction. For example, in the customer's company, when stocks reach a pre-ordained minimum level an automatic order is sent via the computer to the supplier's company whose computerized systems will in turn set in train the complete sequence of actions required to fulfil the customer's order. EDI systems are now so widely used in business-to-business markets that very often a supplier would simply not be selected by a buyer if they do not have or cannot acquire such systems.

> Most of the motor companies in the world now insist that their suppliers can supply on an EDI system basis. For example, the Ford Motor Company have all their suppliers on this system. Needless to say, the Japanese companies have been at the forefront of this practice.

Continuing the trend towards more and more electronically based systems, companies now have **Extranet** systems.

Lancaster *et al.*[27] illustrate that the Extranet goes further than linking just suppliers and buyers and seeks to link together all the companies in the value chain, including, therefore, the suppliers' suppliers and distributors and intermediaries. The Extranet allows much closer and sophisticated relationships to be developed between the members of the value chain. The Extranet requires access to and use of information between the members of the chain and therefore requires trust and commitment between these members. The Extranet is used in a growing number of organizations where such access to information is helping in planning sales and logistics throughout the supply chain.

We have discussed the main influences on, and the process of, buyer behaviour in consumer and organizational markets. We have also looked at some of the key trends and developments particularly regarding JIT purchasing, zero defects and the growth of e-commerce in business to business markets. However, as this text is based upon a strategic marketing outlook, it is worth taking some time to re-examine the application of the strategic marketing concept and assess the insights that understanding buyer behaviour can offer.

Strategic implications of buyer behaviour

As stated in the introduction to this chapter, whatever definition of marketing is selected, consumer orientation is central to it. Implicit in a marketing oriented company is the assumption that it wishes to satisfy customers. In this section we will look at aspects of the strategic marketing process and discuss applications of buyer behaviour at each stage, starting, of course, with the business mission.

Business mission

Production and sales orientated companies usually have 'company' based missions rather than 'customer' based missions. A customer based mission necessarily aligns the company with the marketing concept and affirms the importance of consumer behaviour to the firm.

SWOT analysis

Strengths and weaknesses that are internal to the organization are assessed to discover the capability and resources of the organization. Opportunities and threats are external to the organization and are assessed to discover the broad environmental and competitive trends that have an impact upon the organization. Companies that can diagnose threats and turn them into opportunities have an added advantage in the marketplace. This includes trends in consumer behaviour; for example, a change in lifestyle may have implications for the company. Over recent years more people have been concerned with healthy eating, so the food producer who monitored this trend and possibly *anticipated* these changes would be in a better position than competitors. It may have changed its product offerings or communicated existing healthy attributes about its products to consumers. Consumer behaviour can also be used in the strengths and weaknesses analysis to discover attitudes and awareness of brands.

Market opportunity analysis

From an analysis of consumer behaviour it can be seen how existing products are perceived in comparison to those of competitors. It can also be seen whether there are any gaps in the market that your company can meet profitably with new products. For example, the shampoo Empathy was launched to cater for the specific needs of older female consumers, a segment that was previously ignored. Although segmentation targeting and positioning will be dealt with in the next chapter, it has a strong link with the study of buyer behaviour. Markets can be segmented into relatively homogeneous groupings of consumers in a number of ways. Some of these ways are included in the earlier model of consumer behaviour; for example, demographics, lifestyle and social class. Therefore, consumer behaviour itself is often used as a segmentation variable. When groupings of consumers are identified, companies decide which ones to 'target' with their products. Their 'positioning' strategies will aim to take the product offering and 'position' it in the mind of consumers to reflect the consumer behaviour of the target customers.

Design of marketing strategies

The marketing strategies companies decide to implement should be consistent with the consumer behaviour associated with the product or service. Figure 5.6 shows how knowledge of consumer behaviour can aid the development of successful marketing strategies. Firstly, the variables affecting purchase behaviour are understood and analysed. This then allows for the prediction of behaviour using the most important variables. Strategies based on controllable variables, that is, marketing mix variables, are then designed and implemented. This should lead to influence over desired outcomes (i.e. purchase).

The controllable variable encompasses the marketing mix; that is the product, price, place and promotion. We now examine each of these in turn.

Product The study of consumer behaviour should indicate the type of product or service that will be successful. This can be extended into quite detailed product attributes and packaging decisions, including after-sales service. For example, a car manufacturer, to be successful, should look at consumer behaviour to see:

1 The preferred types of cars for certain groups of customers.
2 What product attributes/features are required, e.g. large boot, four doors, speed, etc.
3 The warranties that are required after sale.

In organizational markets we have already seen that with regard to the product, what is particularly crucial is control of the quality of the product or service being supplied and the need to look at quality and its attributes from the perspective of the decision-making unit of the customer.

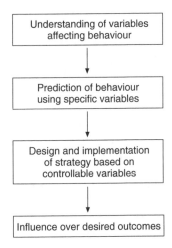

Figure 5.6
Knowledge of consumer behaviour facilitates development of successful marketing strategies.
Source: Schiffman and Kanuk.[28]

Price Research into the relationship between price and consumer behaviour is very important to the marketer. Consumers may not be aware of the prices of certain goods they purchase. This is especially true in fast-moving consumer goods (FMCG) markets. However, consumers may be sensitive to price differentials between competing brands. In this case the marketer will have to monitor competitors' pricing strategies and either compete on price or try to add value to the product in another way. For many products, there is a relationship between price and perceived quality. An appropriate marketing strategy should then take into account consumer attitudes towards price for the product category in question.

In marketing to organizational buyers it is important not to make the mistake of believing, and therefore acting upon the notion, that organizational buyers buy only on price and therefore will select the lowest priced supplier. In both consumer and organizational markets it is overall value which is most important. Again, many organizational buyers these days recognize that the lowest price supplier does not necessarily equate with the lowest cost solution, particularly where this means lower quality.

Place 'Place' decisions concern the channels of distribution from the producer to the consumer. Different consumer groups have preferences for different retail outlets for certain products. For example, in ladies' fashion, some consumers prefer to shop in department stores or in independent retail outlets, market stalls, mail order or chain stores. In addition to the type of outlet that is most suited to the target market, consumer behaviour research can indicate how many outlets there should be and where they should be located. The study of consumer behaviour can indicate to a company whether to provide out-of-town shopping facilities or to locate in a city centre. Where and how products are sold is also linked to store design. The layout of the shop is important as are 'atmospherics' within the store. Research has shown that consumers like the convenience of supermarket shopping but also want good quality fresh food. Fresh fruit and vegetables are usually displayed as a consumer enters a supermarket to indicate freshness and quality. In-store bakers are not simply there to provide fresh bread but also to provide the *smell* of baking bread. Consumer behaviour research can allow the marketer to make decisions to enhance the atmospherics of the retail outlet.

In organizational markets, as we have seen from our discussion of JIT purchasing, effective delivery and hence the design of distribution and logistics systems is crucial.

Promotion Different consumer groups will respond positively or negatively to firms' marketing communications. Research into consumer behaviour will indicate to which promotional tools the target market will respond favourably. This can be used for general media planning: for example, if you are marketing a skin cream to teenage girls, research may make you decide upon press advertising. Further research may then indicate more specific media, for example a teenage monthly magazine. Yet further research may indicate how often your advertisement should be inserted and the type of copy and images you should use. Promotion can be used to try to change a poor consumer image. In Britain, insurance companies have been attempting to change their images by positive promotional campaigns.

As with price, there are some misconceptions about the role and value of promotion when marketing to organizational buyers. In the past many companies appear to have held the belief that the 'rationality' and 'hard-headedness' of organizational buyers have meant that the promotional element of the mix is less effective and therefore less important in forming the attitudes of these buyers. However, as we have discussed in this chapter, organizational buyers are also individuals and in this context are just as likely to be swayed by effective advertising and imagery provided of course that the other elements of the marketing mix are deemed to be satisfactory. There is strong evidence to suggest that advertising in particular in organizational markets can help to substantially reduce the costs of selling.

Control of marketing effort

Observed consumer behaviour can be used to evaluate the success of marketing programmes. Marketing strategies can then be refined to fit customer needs more closely.

Summary

This chapter has sought to discuss buyer behaviour and the study of buyer behaviour from the point of view of the strategic marketer. It has been shown that there are many implications from a marketing point of view in the analysis of buyer behaviour. The concept of fulfilling consumer needs is central to successful marketing strategy. The study of buyer behaviour is a relatively new discipline and has become a specialist area of marketing, owing to its complexity. The area of buyer behaviour covers questions concerning who is in the market, what they buy, when they buy, how they buy and where. Marketing mix variables – price, product, place and promotion – have effects on buyer behaviour so the strategic marketer should be aware of the impact of these controllable variables.

Buying behaviour does not simply encompass the straightforward decision process, but also covers the underlying influences and motives for purchase. These are difficult to measure but are nonetheless very important in a thorough understanding of purchase behaviour. The principles of buyer behaviour theory can be applied to the commercial sector (both consumer and organizational), non-profit making institutions and service providers. A simple model has been used in this chapter to describe the factors that might influence purchase behaviour. Models range in complexity from simple 'black box' models to comprehensive multivariate models. They are useful in providing a framework for study. In the consumer model that was outlined, individual and environmental influences have an effect on the decision-making process of motivation, search, evaluation, choice and outcomes.

In organizational decision making, two additional influences are included. These are group influences and organizational factors. The actual decision-making process will depend on whether the purchase is a new task, a modified re-buy or a straight re-buy for the organization. The process involved is similar to the consumer decision-making process. Within organizational buying, motivation is not simply rational; emotional motives for purchase also play a part in the decision to purchase. Recent trends in organizational purchasing have implications for marketing management.

For example computerized purchasing and centralized purchasing have meant sales persons' roles and responsibilities have changed. In particular, though, the growth of JIT purchasing and its associated requirement for zero defects policies together with developments in e-commerce have had a particularly important impact on marketing in organizational markets.

The implications of researching buyer behaviour apply throughout the strategic marketing process. The next chapter takes the concept of consumer behaviour further into the field of market segmentation.

Key terms

Black box models [p112]
Multivariate models [p112]
Focus groups [p113]
Depth interview [p114]
Futures research [p115]
Unique selling propositions (USP)
[p121]
Decision-making unit (DMU) [p123]
Buying centre [p123]
Gatekeepers [p123]

Derived demand [p124]
Buy classes [p124]
New task [p124]
Buy phases [p124]
Just in time (JIT) [p127]
Zero defects [p128]
Electronic data interchange (EDI)
[p129]
Extranet [p129]

Questions

1   What are the key questions which the marketer must ask and answer about the buying behaviour of his customers?
2   What are the uses and limitations of focus group discussions in researching buyer behaviour?
3   What are the key steps and stages in consumer buyer behaviour and what are the main categories of forces and factors which affect these?
4   What are the key steps and stages in organizational buying behaviour and what are the main categories of forces and factors which affect these?
5   What do you understand by each of the following and what is their relevance to the organizational marketer?

    (a) Just in time purchasing.
    (b) Zero defects.
    (c) EDI systems and the Extranet.

References

1. Engel, J. F., Blackwell, F. D. and Miniard, P. W., *Consumer Behaviour*, 8th edn, Dryden Press, Hinsdale, Ill., 1998.
2. Louden, D. and Della Bitta, A. J., *Consumer Behaviour: Concepts and Application*, 5th edn, McGraw-Hill, London, 1998.
3. Schiffman, L. G. and Kanuk, L. L., *Consumer Behaviour*, 6th edn, Prentice-Hall, New Jersey, 1999.
4. Kotler, P., *Marketing Management: Analysis, Planning, Implementation and Control*, 9th edn, Prentice-Hall, New Jersey, 1997, p. 171.
5. Engel, J. F., Blackwell, F. R. and Miniard, P. W., *Consumer Behaviour*, 8th edn, Dryden Press, Hinsdale, Ill., 1998.
6. Chisnall, P. M., *Marketing: A Behavioural Analysis*, 3rd edn, McGraw-Hill, London, 1995.
7. Lancaster, G. A. and Massingham, L.C., *Essentials of Marketing*, 3rd edn, McGraw-Hill, London, 1993.

8. Schiffman, L. G. and Kanuk, L. L., *Consumer Behaviour*, 6th edn, Prentice-Hall, New Jersey, 1999.
9. Tuck, M., *How Do We Choose?*, Methuen, London, 1976.
10. Assael, H., *Consumer Behaviour and Marketing Action*, 5th edn, Kent Publishing Co., Boston, Mass., 1996.
11. Maslow, D., *Motivation and Personality*, Harper & Row, New York, 1954.
12. Foreman, A. M. and Ven Sriram, P. 'The depersonalization of retailing: its impact on the lonely customer', *Journal of Retailing*, **67**, 2, 1991.
13. Kotler, P., *Marketing Management: Analysis, Planning, Implementation and Control*, 9th edn, Prentice-Hall, New Jersey, 1997, pp. 46–48.
14. Assael, H., *Consumer Behaviour and Marketing Action*, 5th edn, Kent Publishing Co., Boston, Mass., 1996.
15. Thompson, K. and Mitchell, H., 'Organizational buying behaviour in changing times' *European Management Journal,* **16**, 6, December 1998, pp.698–705.
16. Robinson, P. J., Faris, C. W. and Wind, Y., *Industrial Buying and Creative Marketing*, Allyn & Bacon, Boston, 1967.
17. Cardozo, R. N., 'Modelling organisational buying as a sequence of decisions', *Industrial Marketing Management*, **12**, February 1993.
18. Hutt, M. D. and Speh, T. W., *Business Marketing Management*, 6th edn, Dryden Press, London, 1999.
19. Hutt, M. D. and Speh, T. W., *Business Marketing Management*, 6th edn, Dryden Press, London, 1999.
20. Webster, F. E. and Wind, Y., 'A general model for understanding buyer behaviour', *Journal of Marketing*, **36**, April 1972.
21. Dion, P. A., Banting, P. M. and Halsey, L. M., 'The impact of JIT on industrial marketers', *Industrial Marketing Management*, **19**, p. 42.
22. Lancaster, G., 'Marketing and Engineering: Can there ever be Synergy?' *Journal of Marketing Management*, 1993, **9**, pp. 141–153.
23. Dion, P. A., op. cit.
24. Lancaster, G. A., 'Marketing and engineering revisited', *Journal of Business and Industrial Marketing*, **10**, 1, 1995, pp. 6–15.
25. Qualls, W. J. and Rosa, J. A., 'Assessing industrial buyers perception of quality and their effects on satisfaction', *Industrial Marketing Management*, **24**, 1995, pp. 349–368.
26. Jones, A. K. V., 'Quality and its Application', unpublished MPhil. thesis, University of Newcastle, 1993.
27. Lancaster, G. A., Ashfield, R. and Withey, F., *Marketing Fundamentals*, Butterworth-Heinemann, Brighouse, 2000, p. 212.
28. Shiffman, L. G. and Kanuk, L. L., *Consumer Behaviour*, 4th edn, Prentice-Hall, New Jersey, 1992.

Case Study

Six to Seven is a telecommunications company marketing state of the art telecommunications equipment.

The company is currently in the process of developing what it hopes will be the fourth generation type of mobile phone. When developed, this phone will enable users not only to make standard telephone calls and connect to the Web, but will also have a small screen which will enable users to view the person at the other end of the line. Needless to say, the investment required to develop the technology and market the product is substantial.

As part of the development process the company is eager to find out more about the potential customer for this product. In particular, they are interested in finding out if there is a market for the product, how big this market might be, and how customers will respond to the concept. They are proposing hiring a specialist market research agency with skills in the area of researching buyer behaviour, particularly for new product concepts.

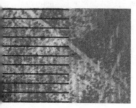

QUESTION

1. What areas of buyer behaviour should this proposed research encompass, and why?
2. What types of research techniques might be useful in researching these areas?

Markets and customers: market boundaries and target marketing

Chapter objectives

After reading this chapter you will:

▶ Understand the meaning and importance of the concept of market boundaries.

▶ Understand the relationship of market boundaries to the key process of target marketing.

▶ Be familiar with the steps in target marketing.

▶ Appreciate the different bases which may be used to segment both consumer and industrial markets, including some of the more recent developments in this area.

▶ Be aware of the main considerations in evaluating markets for targeting strategies.

▶ Be familiar with the concepts and techniques relating to product positioning.

Introduction

In Chapter 5 we explored some of the key questions pertaining to analysing and understanding buyer behaviour in both consumer and industrial markets. Although these questions were examined against a general framework for improving our understanding of how and why customers purchase, together with the broad range of behavioural forces and factors which impinge upon these decisions, the emphasis was on the behaviour of individuals, whether final consumers or organizations.

In this chapter we look at how individual customers aggregate to form market segments. We will also examine how these market segments form part of a larger market, the boundaries of which need to be clearly defined. The importance of understanding the notion of boundaries in markets is that it leads us on to the key strategic process in contemporary marketing management, normally referred to these days as target marketing. As we shall see, target marketing is essential to effective marketing and is therefore a key task of the marketing management function.

We start by examining the concept of a 'market' and the important, if problematical issue of defining market boundaries. We then move on to the key strategic and interrelated decisions of segmentation, targeting and positioning, which together comprise target marketing.

The concept of a market: defining market boundaries

Unless and until the strategic marketing planner has defined the market(s) the organization currently and potentially may operate in, then few, if any, effective strategic decisions can be taken. George Day and Allan Shocker[1] have highlighted this strategic significance of defining market boundaries:

> The problem of identifying competitive product-market boundaries pervades all levels of marketing decisions. Such strategic issues as the basic definition of a business: the assessment of opportunities presented by gaps in the market; the reaction to threats posed by competitive actions; and the decision on major resource allocations, are strongly influenced by the breadth or narrowness of the definition of competitive boundaries.

We can see from this reference that defining the market affects virtually every element of strategic marketing planning. As an example, consider a question which virtually every strategic marketing planner, at one stage or another in the planning process, will need to ask and answer, namely: 'What is our market share?'. The answer to this, and many other questions of importance to strategic marketing, depends on how we 'define' the market. Unfortunately, a market definition is not always easy.

Consider, for example, the 'holiday market'. A company considering the potential in this market, with a view to possible entry, could consider the 'holiday market' to comprise of the total number and value of all holidays taken in any one year. However, within this total market there are very many different types of holidays and indeed ways of classifying them. For example, we could distinguish between, say, Winter and Summer holidays, Package holidays and Self-catering holidays, Domestic and Overseas holidays, and so on. In other words, although they are all 'holidays', they differ significantly. If the company was to assess, for example, market size, requirements for competitive success, market growth or market profitability it would probably find that each of these various holiday markets would differ substantially.

The marketing planner, therefore, must be careful to define market(s) and in doing so must be aware of the different dimensions available. We shall now consider some of these dimensions, where appropriate, commenting upon their uses and limitations.

Product/industry-based definitions

Conventionally, many markets are defined, or at least thought of by those working in these 'markets', on the basis of products and/or industries. For example, we have:

- The confectionery market
- The cigar market
- The computer software market
- The over-the-counter pharmaceutical market
- The credit card market
- The industrial adhesive market
- The children's toy market
- The lead pencil market.

This basis of market definition centres on the nature of the product(s) or service(s) produced and marketed. As we can also see, even a product-based definition can lead to either very broad, generic product class definitions, which are akin to defining the market on an industry basis (e.g. the computer software market) or at the other extreme, a narrow product item-based definition, e.g. the lead pencil market.

Initially, this might seem a logical, and indeed simple, way to define a market, even if admittedly we still have the problem of how broad or narrow to pitch our product-based definitions. However, the problem with product-based definitions is that, although they accord with how many companies are in their existing and potential markets, they can be, and often are, misleading and hence dangerous for marketing planning purposes. In particular, product-based definitions neglect the fact that customers purchase benefits, not products, and even where generic product class or industry-based definitions, as opposed to product item definitions, are used there is a danger of defining the market too narrowly.

This danger of product based market definitions was recognized and highlighted in Levitt's[2] classic article on 'Marketing myopia' as long ago as 1960. He suggested that many companies were defining their businesses in product terms and hence too narrowly. This in turn, he also suggested, was leading at best to missed opportunities and, at worst, business failure.

For example, Levitt cites the case of the American railroad companies who appeared to define and operate their businesses on the assumption that they were in the 'railway market'. Arising from this, he claimed that many of these companies had subsequently either gone out of business or were struggling to survive. The reason was because they had failed to define their market accurately. In short, according to Levitt, product-based market definitions are indicative of a lack of customer orientation in a business and result in a narrow and shortsighted view of marketing opportunities and threats. In order to avoid these problems, Levitt suggests defining markets in terms of 'generic need'.

Surely these days there are no companies that are product as opposed to marketing oriented, are there?

There is no doubt that the so-called 'Smart Car' is a brilliant product.

Developed initially as a joint venture between Mercedes and the makers of Swatch watches, the car was officially launched in 1998. It is now marketed by Daimler Chrysler. The car is extremely innovative in concept. Exceptionally small and with two seats, the car is designed to be used primarily in cities where its size facilitates easy parking. It is also exceptionally low priced at approximately £6000 and very cheap to run.

From an engineering and design point of view the car is brilliant, but will consumers buy it in sufficient quantities to make it a success? Of course only time will tell, but it could be a case where the product concept is ahead of the market.

Generic need-based definitions

In suggesting a generic need-based definition of markets, Levitt argues that the market is better viewed from the point of view of 'that which the customer buys' rather than 'what the organization or industry makes'. Accordingly, the railroad business would have been better to define their market as 'transportation' rather than 'rail travel'. Similarly, a cosmetics company might define its market (generic need) as the 'beauty' market; an insurance company the 'peace of mind' market; and a camera company the 'memories' market.

Clearly, this is a more customer and hence marketing oriented method of defining markets. The specific advantages claimed for a generic need-based definition include the following:

- It forces an organization to look at its markets from a customer perspective
- It widens the perspective on what currently and potentially constitutes competition, i.e. it helps define competition
- It helps in identifying future opportunities and threats
- It helps identify key factors in competitive marketing success.

Again, drawing upon Levitt's article in order to illustrate some of these claimed advantages, we can consider the case of the film industry. Levitt suggested that planners in this industry defined their market, and hence structured their marketing plans, as being the movies market. The generic need they were supplying, however, was 'entertainment'. Therefore they failed to anticipate the threat to their markets from the new 'competitor', television. Consequently, they lost out to this newer form of entertainment and could only watch with deep concern as their customer base dwindled, attracted to a cheaper, more innovative and more convenient way of fulfilling its entertainment needs.

Thankfully, most companies now recognize the dangers of defining their markets and businesses too narrowly and have moved much more towards these generic need-based definitions.

Disney were once known as, and indeed thought of themselves as, an animated film company. Their portfolio of businesses suggests that they now think of themselves as being in the entertainment business. Their portfolio consists therefore, of businesses as diverse as theme parks, retail outlets, and conventional films and video.

Generic need-based definitions thus seem to offer several advantages over product-based areas. Useful though the concept of generic needs is in avoiding a myopic view of markets, in strategic marketing planning terms it also has a number of drawbacks.

First of all is the problem of precisely what is meant by 'generic needs' and, specifically, how broadly we define these. We have seen that with this approach to defining markets, the intention is deliberately to push back the narrower market boundaries to which product/industry-based definitions give rise. However, the danger with using generic needs to define markets is that we can end up with definitions which are so broad as to be meaningless, and worse, possibly misleading for marketing planning purposes.

To illustrate these problems consider the earlier example of the cosmetics' manufacturers being in the generic needs market of 'beauty'. Clearly, there are many ways in which this need can be filled by customers. For example, the customer can meet this need by visiting say a health farm or a plastic surgeon. Similarly, the customer could have an early night's sleep, or purchase a new outfit. Indeed, our customer might also fulfil this need by going on a diet. We could go on thinking of different ways in which an individual could meet a need to be more 'beautiful'. From the point of view of the cosmetics company it is helpful, and more realistic, to define its market in such wide generic terms as beauty? For example, is a cosmetics company really in competition with a manufacturer of clothing or a plastic surgeon? The answer, of course, is 'no'!

We can see that the concept of generic needs is useful in reminding us of the fact that we must think of competition from outside the industry boundaries. It helps to prevent a myopic view of our markets, customers and competition. For the most part it is far too broad to be of operational use in defining market boundaries and hence helping develop strategic marketing plans.

What we need, therefore, is an approach to defining markets which is neither too narrow nor too broad. One approach put forward by Derek Abell[3] is to define markets in terms of customer function, technology and customer group.

Customer functions, technology and customer group-based definitions

Customer functions We have already seen that customers purchase benefits when they buy. For example, when we purchase a car it fulfils the functions of transport, prestige, convenience and so on. When we purchase a watch we are purchasing time measurement, status and so on. But similar products often serve different use functions (benefits) and hence serve different markets. Products and services serving similar use functions are in similar market, and hence they are in competition. For example, let us consider computer software. Instead of defining the market in terms of generic needs, which might be 'rapid and accurate information processing', we might identify and define different markets according to the function(s) computer software serves or the ways in which it is used. For example, Function A might be 'Games and entertainment', while Function B could be 'Business problem analysis'. Clearly, each of these functions represents a very different market. We can see that the concept of functions served is very close to our previous generic needs basis of market definition, but as O'Shaughnessy[4] contends, generic needs is at 'one level of abstraction' from our function-based definitions. Different functions do, however, provide different customer benefits and represent more meaningful ways to define markets. We still have the decision to make as to how narrowly or widely to define functions (and hence markets). For example, the 'business problem analysis function' could be broken down further into sub-fractions as shown in Figure 6.1.

The question of how broadly or narrowly to define functions can only be resolved by reference to the strategic purpose of our definition. For example, if we are concerned to consider potential competition from outside the conventional industry boundaries, we need to think at a higher level of abstraction than if we were evaluating direct competitor threats. Again O'Shaughnessy[4] captures this notion succinctly:

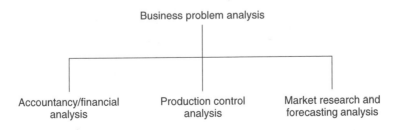

Figure 6.1

A 'business problem analysis function'.

The fact remains, the products that serve different use-functions serve different markets, and different use-functions attract different competitors. The more broadly we define the use-functions, the wider the market and the wider competition embraced. There comes a stage, of course, where the definition of use-function is so wide as to lose all utility.

Technology The second key dimension in Abell's bases for market definition is the type of technology(ies) used to fulfil a function. For example, the function of 'convenience meals' can be met by the technologies of canned foods, boil-in-the-bag or microwaving. Similarly, the function of 'packaging' can be fulfilled by the alternative technologies of plastic, metal or glass. In defining the market, the strategic marketing planner must determine the technological bases to be used.

Customer Groups As we shall see, most markets comprise sub-markets or segments, which are in turn smaller groups of customers. Each of these subgroups is homogeneous with regard to an important attribute, e.g. benefits sought, but heterogeneous when compared to other subgroups with respect to these dimensions. The market for clothing, for example, can broadly be broken down into male and female subgroups. In turn, each of these broad subgroups can be further divided into, say, different age groups and/or income groups or 'fashion conscious' vs. 'traditional' groups, and so on. The definition of 'market' should specify which of these customer groups is to be served.

Combining the factors to define market boundaries

Combining these three factors, we are now in a position to illustrate how they may be used to define existing and potential market boundaries. An illustration of how these three elements might be combined is contained in Figure 6.2 for a supplier of drugs for medical use. Market boundaries in Figure 6.2 are defined by any combination of the three axes:

Of course, there are different cells in the matrix of options, each representing what are essentially individual building blocks for market definition, Each cell in the matrix may be defined in terms of customer function, customer group, and technology.

From the point of view of the hypothetical drugs supplier, the current market boundary may be redefined using any one or combination of the basic dimensions. For example, new customer groups can be added, new functions served, or alternative tech-

Figure 6.2
Market boundary
definition.

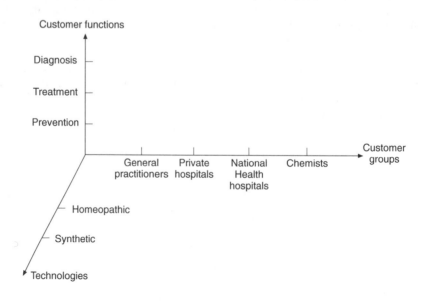

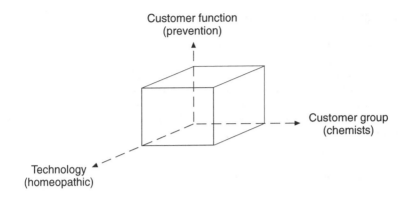

Figure 6.3
An illustrative market
cell.

nologies used. The market cell shown in Figure 6.3 might represent the current 'served' market for our company. The remaining cells represent *potential* markets.

Practical illustrations of the different market boundaries using the medical analogy are:

> *Homeopathic* drugs (technology) supplied to *chemists* (customer group) for the *prevention* (customer function) of disease (see Figure 6.3).
> *Synthetic* drugs (technology) supplied to *private hospitals* (customer) for the *treatment* (customer function) of disease.

In practice, the process of identifying and grouping market cells is complex. In particular, it requires both detailed and objective market analysis combined with substantial managerial experience and insight.

It is important to remember that ultimately market boundaries are determined by customers and their perceptions, needs and choice behaviour rather than by the marketer. So, for example, we can establish how a market is divided into sub-markets by asking customers, or potential customers, how they choose between different product offerings. An interesting insight into the way that customers, through their choice decisions, ultimately determine the boundaries of a market, and hence factors such as what constitutes competition within a market, is given by Day *et al.*[5] Day and his colleagues illustrate that by asking consumers to identify a list of products which they feel could be used in a particular context or application, it is possible to establish the different ways in which a market divides so far as customers are concerned. This approach is sometimes referred to as 'item by use analysis'. So, for example, within the total market for chocolate bars, some customers may see a particular bar as being most appropriate for snack occasions. So far as the customer is concerned, therefore, a key sub-division of the chocolate bar market is based on the primary need which a particular product fulfils, and in this case the sub-market is the 'snacks' market.

Despite the added complexities this more sophisticated approach to defining market boundaries offers significant advantages over both product/industry-based definitions, and definitions based on generic needs. In order to use this three-dimensional approach, we need to understand how and why markets divide into different customer groups and also the range of customer functions which may be represented in the market. Identifying alternative technologies is less problematic.

Increasingly powerful research techniques are enabling marketers to identify market boundaries more easily. Hooley and Saunders[6], for example, demonstrate how these techniques, particularly the techniques of **automatic interaction detection** (AID) and cluster analysis, are becoming increasingly widespread in this respect.

Understanding different customer groups and functions leads to what, for the purpose of strategic market planning, is a most important areas of marketing, namely *market segmentation*, together with the related decision areas of *targeting* and *positioning*.

Market segmentation, targeting and positioning

 In the example of the hypothetical supplier of medical drugs, the market served consisted of just one cell or segment. The total market, however, comprises several **market segments**. In other words, the market is not homogeneous, but rather is made up of separate cells of demand preferences. It is this heterogeneity of markets which gives rise to the need for effective segmentation, targeting and positioning; three distinct steps in the process of what is known collectively as *target marketing*. We shall start by examining the meaning and importance of target marketing.

The meaning and importance of target marketing

 The concept of **target marketing** is a logical interpretation of the basic philosophy of marketing. Essentially it comprises the identification of different needs for specific groups or segments of customers, deciding which of these groups the organization should target or serve (and on what basis) and then designing marketing mix programmes so that the needs of these targeted groups are then more closely met.

As mentioned earlier, target marketing derives from the fact that demand within markets is heterogeneous. In the 'total' market for a product or service different groups of customers will be looking for different clusters of benefits. In order to understand this better, you should reflect on the products and services which you purchase. Do you purchase exactly the same kind of products as your friends and neighbours? Are your specific requirements with respect to purchasing certain products and brands different? Perhaps your friends and neighbours have different tastes in clothes or in the type of holidays they take. Perhaps they purchase and drive different cars or use different brands of toothpaste or breakfast cereals. Market segmentation, targeting and positioning starts by recognizing that increasingly, within the total demand/market for a product, specific tastes and demand may, and often do, differ. We refer to a market which is characterized by differing specific preferences as being heterogeneous. Market segmentation is thus disaggregative in nature. It breaks down the total market for a product or service into distinct patterns or segments of customers who share similar demand preferences within each segment. This is illustrated in Figures 6.4(a) and (b).

In Figure 6.4(a) there is no market segmentation. Each and every customer in the total market is assumed to have similar demand preferences and wants, i.e. demand is *homogeneous*. In fact, demand in most markets is *heterogeneous* as we have already

Figure 6.4
The meaning of
market segments.

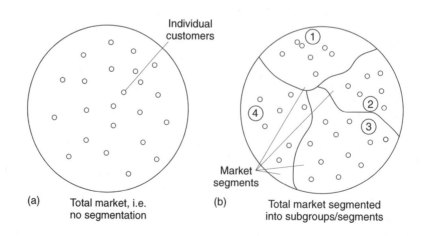

(a) Total market, i.e. no segmentation

(b) Total market segmented into subgroups/segments

explained. Hence, the total market can be broken down into segments of customers, as shown in Figure 6.4(b).

Effective segmentation is achieved when we group together customers who share similar patterns of demand and where we can differentiate each segment in the pattern of demand from other segments in the market. In other words, effective segmentation is achieved when the clustering gives rise to homogeneous demand within, and heterogeneous demand between, each segment. Most markets, both for consumer and industrial products, are capable of being segmented.

The fact that most markets are made up of heterogeneous demand clusters means that companies have to decide which of these clusters to serve. The majority of companies now recognize that they cannot effectively serve all the segments in a market. They must instead target their marketing efforts. An example will illustrate this.

Imagine that you are a part of the project team developing a new car. Should the proposed new model be a two, four or five seater model? Should it have a 1000, 2000 or 3000cc engine? Should it have leather or fabric seats?

In deciding these issues, the overriding factor is customer demand, i.e. what are the customers' needs? Some customers (segments) may want a five seater, 2000cc model with leather upholstery, whilst others may prefer a four seater with a 1000cc engine and fabric seats. One solution is to compromise and produce a four seater 1500cc model with leather seats and fabric trim. Clearly, such a model would go some way to meeting the requirements of both groups of buyers. The danger is that because the needs of neither market segment are precisely met and catered for, customers will prefer and purchase from those suppliers who meet their requirements exactly.

In short, the patterns of demand we referred to earlier in this section require that marketers develop specific marketing mixes (i.e. products, prices, promotional appeals and channels that are aimed or targeted at specific market segments). Many marketing textbooks compare this 'targeting' vs. 'mass marketing' approach to using a 'rifle approach' as opposed to using a 'shotgun approach' to achieve market impact.

Advantages of target marketing: criteria for effective segmentation

Specifically, Dibb *et al.*[7] point to the following advantages of target marketing:

- A better understanding of customers and their needs and wants.
- A better understanding of competition and the kind of competitive advantage to pursue.
- A more effective use of company resources.
- The development of more effective marketing plans.

In order to secure these advantages, the base(s) used for segmentation should fulfil the following criteria:

1 *Measurability/identifiability:* The base(s) used to segment a market should ideally lead to ease of identification (who is in each segment) and measurability (how large is each segment).
2 *Accessibility:* The base(s) used to segment a market should ideally lead to marketers being able to reach selected market targets with their marketing efforts.
3 *Substantiality:* The base(s) used to segment markets should ideally lead to segments which are sufficiently large to be worthwhile serving as distinct market targets.
4 *Meaningfulness:* The base(s) used to segment markets must lead to segments which have different preferences/needs and show clear variations in market behaviour/response to marketing efforts.

Of all the requirements for effective segmentation, this last one is the most important. It is, indeed, an essential prerequisite in identifying and selecting market targets.

We need to keep these criteria in mind for later in this chapter when we discuss the variety of bases which can be used to segment markets. But first it is necessary to examine further the steps in target marketing and how these steps work in practice.

Steps in target marketing

The following sequence represents the steps to be taken when conducting a segmentation, targeting and product positioning exercise for any given market:

1 Dividing the market into segments; selecting bases for segmentation.
2 Evaluating and appraising the market segments resulting from the above.
3 Selecting overall targeting strategy.
4 Selecting specific targets in line with the previous step.
5 Developing product positioning strategies for each target segment.
6 Developing an appropriate marketing mix for each target segment in order to support the positioning strategy.

We will now examine each of these steps in more detail in order to understand and appreciate further what target marketing means.

Dividing a market into segments

In segmentation, targeting and positioning, we are seeking to identify distinct subsets of customers in the total market for a product. Any subset might eventually be selected as a market target, and on that basis a distinctive marketing mix will be developed. For example, we might find that in the market for hi-fi equipment we can identify a number of distinct subsets (segments) of customers based upon income levels. This is shown in Figures 6.5(a) and (b).

Continuing our example, we may find that income segments can be broken down even further into a combination of income and age segments. This is illustrated in Figures 6.6(a) and (b).

Figure 6.5
Segmenting the
market for hi-fi by
income.

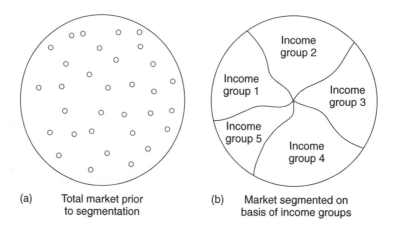

(a) Total market prior
to segmentation

(b) Market segmented on
basis of income groups

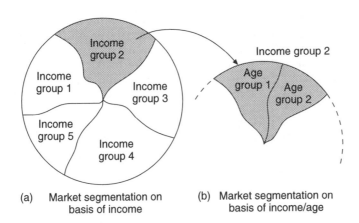

Figure 6.6
Further segmenta-
tion of each income
group based upon
age.

(a) Market segmentation on
basis of income

(b) Market segmentation on
basis of income/age

We need to recognize that in our example (Figure 6.6(b)) we assume that both income and age are associated with differences in buyers' behaviour towards the product, i.e. different age/income groups will have different needs/preferences with respect to hi-fi products and will tend to respond to a different marketing approach. If we are correct in our assumption, this means that the bases selected for segmentation (age/income) are *meaningful* ones upon which to segment the market. Remember that this is the most important criterion for effective segmentation. In addition, both these particular segmentation bases pose relatively few problems for the marketer in terms of identifying/measuring and reaching the segments to which they give rise. For example, in the UK we know what proportion of the total population falls into the discrete age groups (identifying/measuring). Furthermore, the media habits of the different age groups (e.g. television viewing, readership of magazines/newspapers) enable the marketer to direct marketing at selected target age groups (reachability). Note that these are 'ideal' criteria for effective segmentation and count for little if they are not associated with meaningfulness.

With regard to the criterion of 'substantiality', to which we referred earlier, the hi-fi example shows that a market may be segmented using a succession of different bases. This leads to the breaking down of the market into an increasing number of smaller and smaller segments. The ultimate to which this process can be taken is illustrated in Figure 6.7 where the market has been completely segmented into individual buyers, i.e. a fully customized market.

The extent to which it makes business sense to continue to subdivide markets in this way depends solely upon the extent to which the resulting segments are worthwhile serving as distinct market targets with a separate marketing mix. In

Figure 6.7
Complete market
segmentation.

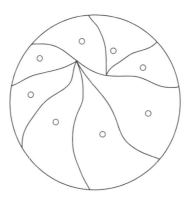

some product markets, complete segmentation (i.e. tailoring the marketing mix to individual customers) is not simply desirable, but essential. For example, in shipbuilding or the supply of aircraft, each customer may be treated as a separate market. For many consumer product markets, such 'customizing' of the marketing effort is unnecessary.

In the hi-fi example we used the bases of income and age in segmenting the market. In fact, there is no 'right' way to segment a market, and different bases and combinations of bases, particularly what Fifield[8] refers to as 'motivational' ones, should be sought by the marketer. Having said this, a number of relatively common bases are quite frequently used by marketers. We now look at some of these, starting first with bases that are typically used in consumer product markets, followed by those used in industrial product markets.

Bases for segmenting consumer markets

As mentioned already, a market may be segmented using a number of different bases. At the end of the day, the bases selected, for as we shall see later, they are often used in combination to segment markets, must fulfil the criteria outlined earlier for effective segmentation. Having said this, there are a number of bases in consumer markets which, in the past, have been widely used in segmenting these markets. What we shall do therefore is discuss some of these most frequently used bases. We shall start with some of the more traditional and conventional bases of segmentation in consumer markets such as geographic and demographic bases. We shall then look at some of the more recent developments in segmentation, and in particular the use of geodemographic, lifestyle, and combination bases. Finally, in this section on consumer market segmentation we shall examine what are often referred to as *behavioural segmentation bases* which use the behaviour of consumers themselves as the basis for identifying market segments.

Beginning first with two of the more conventional, and still widely used bases for segmenting consumer markets, we can identify Geographic and Demographic bases for segmentation.

Geographic segmentation

This consists of dividing a market on the basis of different geographical units. In international marketing, different countries may be deemed to constitute different market segments. Similarly, within a country a market may be segmented regionally into, for example, north versus south segments.

Geographic segmentation is still widely used, at least as one element in a combination of segmentation bases. Clearly, geographic segmentation is potentially at its most powerful and useful when considering international markets, and therefore is considered in more detail in Chapter 18.

Demographic segmentation

This approach comprises a wide variety of bases for subdividing markets and some of the more common bases used include:

Social class/occupation
Age
Sex
Income
Education

Family size
Nationality
Family life cycle.

Demographic bases have in the past, and to some extent even now, been probably the most popular for segmentation in consumer product markets. This is because they were felt to be most strongly associated with differences in consumer demand (i.e. they were meaningful). There are still many examples from consumer product markets where one or more of the bases in the list is likely to be useful. With the exception of family life cycle and social class/occupation, their meaning and potential application is self-evident. Brief explanations of these two exceptions therefore are given below.

Family life cycle

 This basis for **life cycle/stage segmentation** centres on the idea that consumers pass through a series of quite distinct phases in their lives, with each phase being associated with different purchasing patterns and needs.

The unmarried person living at home may have very different purchasing patterns from a chronological counterpart who has left home and recently married. It is also recognized that the purchasing pattern of adults often changes as they approach and move into retirement.

Recently in the UK, the Newspaper Society together with the Market Research Company, British Market Research Bureau (BMRB), have developed a variation on family life cycle segmentation which they call their 'life stage' classification system[9]. Based on detailed market research and analysis, this life stage classification identifies the following life stage segments for classifying consumer groups:

- Live with parents
- Left parents' home and live alone or in shared accommodation
- Live with partner only
- No children
- Children in household, majority pre-school age
- Children in household, majority beyond school age
- Children have all left home
- Live with partner or alone.

These life stages can be grouped into three major categories, namely:

- Pre-family stages
- People with children at home
- People with children who have left home.

The developers of this system claim that it has worked well in distinguishing between different customer groups with regard to their lifestyles, media habits, and perhaps in some ways most important of all, their purchasing patterns.

Occupation/social class

These are linked together because, in many developed economies, official socio-economic group (social class) categorizations are based upon occupation. In the UK, this occupation is that of the 'head of the household', because this is what is regarded as being the criterion that determines the social class of the household. It is thus a family classification unlike say, sex, which is an individual classification. Of all the various demographic bases for segmenting consumer product markets, social class is probably the most widely used.

Social class scores highly against the segmentation criteria of 'identifiability' and to a lesser extent 'accessibility'. It is a simple task to classify individuals on the basis of occupation and then to reach the different social classes so categorized, according to their different patterns of media usage and shopping habits. Table 6.1 shows what, until relatively recently, was the system of social class gradings used in the UK together with an indication of the types of occupations associated with each.

As occupation is the only factor in this system which is used to ascribe social class, it is obviously important that the codex used to classify occupations into the different social categories – six in this case – is valid. Of greatest importance in this validity aspect is that the different occupations used to designate social class actually discriminate and distinguish between different customer groups, and their purchasing habits and needs. In other words, it must meet our 'meaningful' criterion which was identified earlier. It is this aspect of the traditional social-class grading system which has been causing marketers, and many others who have traditionally used this social class designation, most concern in recent years.

Quite simply, although this long-established system of assigning social class is widely used in marketing, there is increasing doubt as to the extent to which social class is nowadays a 'meaningful' basis for segmenting some markets. In part this arises from the fact that they are no longer so strongly related to income groups. For example, it is often the case that the skilled manual group (C2) earn higher incomes than their lower or even intermediate management counterparts (C1 or B) in industry. Such groups are often in a position to purchase products and services which were once 'traditionally' the prerogative of the upper social grades.

This is an example of how some of the more conventional methods of segmenting markets, and in particular in this case, some of the more traditional demographic bases including social class, have become increasingly less meaningful and therefore less useful to marketers as bases for segmenting consumer markets. In fact, in the case of social class, there is clear evidence to suggest that this basis for segmentation may at best be a poor predictor of customer needs and behaviour, and possibly a very misleading and therefore ineffective basis on which to segment today's markets.

Because of this, efforts are being made to develop an updated social class system which more nearly reflects the social groupings of today. One such system is being developed for the UK office of National Statistics. This system, although still based on occupation, proposes eight new categories of socio-economic groups, as opposed to the

Table 6.1 Occupation and social class.	
Social class grading	*Occupation*
A	Higher managerial
B	Intermediate management
C1	Supervisory/lower management
C2	Skilled manual
D	Semi-skilled/unskilled
E	Lowest levels of subsistence, e.g. pensioners (with no supplementary income)

existing six. In this system gone is the familiar 'alphabet' of As, Bs, C1s, C2s and D/Es, to be replaced with a numerical system simply ranged from 1 to 8. Although this system of classification is still being researched, the interesting thing about it is the way in which some of the occupations of the former system of social grading have been re-assigned; for example, social workers, previously at maximum social grade B according to the precise nature of position in the old system is now classified in Group 1 under this system. We can expect further developments in this area and marketers will need to keep abreast of these with regard to their use of social class in marketing strategies. Certainly at this stage the newer methods of social-class grading look promising. However, there is still concern about the meaningfulness and therefore the predictive power of this and other conventional demographic bases.

This increasing concern regarding the poor predictive power of many of these more conventional demographic bases for segmenting consumer markets, coupled with improvements in data collection and analysis methods, has led to the development in recent years of newer and, some would suggest more powerful, bases for segmenting consumer markets. There have been many advancements in this area, but we may group these newer bases for segmenting consumer markets into three main types, namely, the so-called 'Geodemographic' bases, the so-called 'Lifestyle/Psychographic' bases, and the so-called 'Combination' bases. Each of these is discussed below together with specific examples of systems and approaches within each of these three categories of newer bases for segmentation, some of them developed by commercial organizations specializing in this important area of marketing.

Geodemographic bases

 As the term implies, **geodemographic segmentation** of consumer markets is based on a combination of demographic and geographic factors. It is perhaps easier to under-stand the ideas behind geodemographic segmentation if we look at one of the first, and widely used system of geodemographic segmentation used in the UK. Namely, the ACORN system (which is short for 'A Classification of Residual Neighbourhoods'). The ACORN system is produced by CACI Market Analysis, and like many of the Geodemographic systems of segmentation, both in the UK and in other parts of the world where such data is systematically collected, it is based on census data. In the UK this census data is collected on a ten-yearly cycle and consists of the collection and analysis of detailed information on every household concerning factors such as, e.g. household size, incomes, occupations, car ownership etc. In short, this is very detailed data covering, in this case, every household in the UK. This data is collected and analysed on the basis of 'census enumeration districts' which to all extents and purposes, effectively correspond to a postal code district. CACI established that these districts could be described on the basis of the type of property and householder predominantly prevalent in each census enumeration district. Furthermore, extensive research established that the different types of property and the neighbourhoods in which they were located, were strongly related to purchasing behaviour and patterns, so much so that in some cases it was possible from the type of neighbourhood and property alone, to predict things such as average wine consumption by households in the area, holiday preferences, incidence of frozen food purchase etc. The ACORN system has classified the approximately 125,000 census districts in the UK into one of six major ACORN categories, these six categories are further sub-divided into 17 groups which in turn are derived from a total of 54 specific neighbourhood types within the ACORN system. The six major categories, together with the different 17 groups related to them are shown in Table 6.2. As already mentioned, the ACORN system has been

Table 6.2 ACORN groups in the United Kingdom.

Major ACORN categories	Sub-groups within each category
A Thriving	1. Wealth achievers, suburban areas
	2. Affluent greys, rural communities
	3. Prosperous pensioners, retirement areas
B Expanding	4. Affluent executives, family areas
	5. Well-off workers, family areas
C Rising	6. Affluent urbanities, town and city areas
	7. Prosperous professionals, metropolitan areas
	8. Better-off executives, inner city areas
D Settling	9. Comfortable middle aged, mature home owning areas
	10. Skilled workers, home owning areas
E Aspiring	11. New home owners, mature communities
	12. White collar workers, better-off multi-ethnic areas
F Striving	13. Older people, less prosperous areas
	14. Council estate residents, better-off homes
	15. Council estate residents, high unemployment
	16. Council estate residents, greater hardship
	17. People in multi-ethnic, low income areas

Source:©CACI LIMITED (2000). ACORN is a registered trademark of CACI Limited. Reproduced with permission.

shown to be a good indicator of some patterns of purchasing – brand choice, average spend etc., and hence goes some way towards fulfilling the 'meaningfulness' criterion which we identified earlier.

Among some of the marketing applications where ACORN has proved to be useful are the following:

- Compilation of direct mailing lists
- Siting of new stores and distribution outlets
- Management of advertising campaigns, particularly in the local press
- Quantifying sales potential in any given area.

Another geodemographic system of segmentation is the MOSAIC system. This system classifies groups of homes on the full postcode. On average, 15 houses share a single postcode and each group shares a MOSAIC classification. According to the MOSAIC system (developed by a company called CCN Marketing) there are 58 types of residential area in the UK (an example being M12: 'lower income enclaves in high income suburbs'). The system is used largely for targeting direct mailshots according to MOSAIC category.

Geodemographic segmentation systems are now widely available throughout Europe and may potentially become much more important to marketers in future, particularly when considering marketing in the different countries of Europe. As with any basis for segmentation the ACORN and other systems of Geographic segmentation are not perfect. We know, for example, that in some census emuneration districts the types of neighbourhood and property can differ considerably even though they are grouped into, e.g. one ACORN category. We must be very careful therefore to establish that the geodemographic system being used is appropriate to our particular market and products. Systems such as ACORN are usually linked with market research survey systems such as the Target Group Index survey conducted in the UK by the British Market Research Bureau which can be used to assess the potential and effectiveness of any proposed geographic segmentation basis for a particular product market.

Lifestyle segmentation

A second, more contemporary basis for segmenting consumer markets, **lifestyle segmentation**, is often referred to as **'psychographics'**. It is based upon the fact that individuals have characteristic modes and patterns of living which may influence their motive to purchase selected products and brands. For example, some individuals may prefer a 'homely' lifestyle, whereas others may see themselves as living a 'sophisticated' lifestyle. Although there is much evidence to support the idea of this form of segmentation, in its earliest applications it proved to be disappointing in practice. However, more recent applications are proving that this form of segmentation now has much to commend it.

Two examples of Lifestyle/Psychographic segmentation techniques will serve to illustrate this approach to segmenting consumer markets, and the potential power and hence increasing use of these bases for segmentation into today's consumer markets.

1 *Young and Rubicam's '4 Cs'*
   The advertising agency Young and Rubicam developed a lifestyle segmentation system which analysed how consumers perceive themselves and in turn how these perceptions were reflected in their interests, values, and activities, and subsequently gave rise to different purchasing preferences, brand choices etc. Using extensive marketing research involving in-depth interviews, focus groups, and questionnaires, Young and Rubican identified three main lifestyle groups based on a Cross-Cultural Consumer Characterization (the 4 Cs). Each of these three main lifestyle groups contains a number of sub-groups as follows:

Lifestyle Group	Sub-groups
The Constrained	Resigned poor Struggling poor
The Middle Majority	Mainstreamers Aspirers Succeeders
The Innovators	Transitionals Reformers

As already mentioned, and indeed in all segmentation bases, this classification was based on the notion that each group and sub-group, in this case because of their lifestyle/personalities, had differing needs and would exhibit different purchasing patterns, brand choices etc. So, for example, in the '4 Cs' system, in the Middle Majority group, Mainstreamers were consumers who were conventional in their lifestyle patterns, values etc. Young and Rubican found that the Mainstreamers tended to prefer and purchase well-known brands. They tended not to purchase own-label brands. Similarly, the Mainstreamer tended to buy from domestic rather than overseas producers wherever possible. In contrast, the Aspirers, who were motivated to improve themselves in life tended to purchase the latest products and brands which in their view will bestow higher status on them. They tended to indulge in the latest activities and pastimes and purchase conspicuously. Young and Rubican therefore suggested that knowing a lifestyle group to which an individual belongs can be used in market segmentation and targeting, and in particular in the development of promotional campaigns to appeal to the various target groups.

Ten years ago the Jaguar Motor Company was struggling. Today it is experiencing as much success as it did in its hey-day. There are many reasons for this turn around, including vastly improved reliability, a successful product range, and of course the recent injection of capital from its new parent company, Ford. A key factor in this success, however, has been its advertising and promotional programmes. Quite simply, advertising for the Jaguar appeals to exactly the sort of lifestyle of their key target market, namely the 'Succeeders'. Its advertising tends to show individuals who are in control of their lives and are not willing to accept second best. Small wonder that their flagship S-type sells so well even at a price of approximately £40,000.

2   *The VALS System*

Originally developed by the Stanford Research Institute this approach to lifestyle/psychographic segmentation is based principally on information collected from self-administered questionnaires embracing respondents' Activities, Interests, and Opinions (AIO measures) together with motives, attitudes, and various other aspects such as values. The updated system of VALS (VALS 2) uses two key dimensions to classify customers into eight lifestyle types. These two dimensions are 'Self Orientation', and 'Resources Available to Sustain the Self Orientation'. For our purposes we need not concern ourselves with the details of precisely what is encompassed by these two dimensions but they are used to classify a customer into one of the following lifestyle categories:

> 'fulfilled'
> 'believer'
> 'actualizer'
> 'achiever'
> 'striver'
> 'struggler'
> 'experiencer'
> 'maker'.

So, for example, "experiencers" are action-oriented with regard to the self-orientation dimension and therefore a have lifestyle characterized by a high degree of physical and social activity coupled with variety seeking and risk taking behaviour. With regard to the resources available dimension, so they have the most resources of any of the eight lifestyle groups to sustain their self-orientation. Stanford Research Institute claim that this lifestyle group seek wealth, power and fame, and are substantial consumers of exercise and sports products, and tend to be non-conformist in their purchasing. In fact, the VALS 2 system is said to be the major lifestyle/psychographic system in the US and therefore readers who are particularly interested in this method of lifestyle segmentation are recommended to read a more extensive coverage of the ideas and concepts which underpin it such as that contained in O'Shaughnessy[10].

Like the '4 Cs' system, VALS 2 is used predominantly to develop promotional appeals and has been used extensively for this purpose in the US.

It is important to remember that these are just two of a large and increasing number of lifestyle systems for classifying consumers. In recent years, marketers have become increasingly interested in the potential of lifestyle segmentation for developing more effective marketing strategies. Although not without their problems, both with regard to underpinning concepts and particularly problems of data collection and analysis often associated with many of the lifestyle segmentation techniques, lifestyle segmentation has proved powerful for developing marketing and particularly promotional strategies. This usefulness of lifestyle segmentation bases for developing advertising and promotional strategies in part explains why many of the approaches and techniques of lifestyle segmentation have been developed as packages by some of the leading advertising and market research agencies.

The approaches to consumer market segmentation that have been described so far have all been *associative* segmentation. That is to say, they are used where we feel that differences in purchasing behaviour/customer needs may be associated with them. If, say, we use social class or lifestyle to segment a market we are assuming that purchasing behaviour is a function of social class or lifestyle. Most of the problems with using such associative bases tend to be related to the issue of the extent to which they are truly associated with, or are a reflection of, actual purchasing behaviour. Because of this, many marketers believe that it is more sensible to use *direct* bases for segmenting markets. As mentioned, such bases take actual consumer behaviour as the starting point for identifying different segments, and they are often referred to as *behavioural* segmentation bases.

Examples of some of the more frequently used behavioural bases in consumer markets include the following:

Occasions for purchase

Here, segments are identified on the basis of differences in the occasions for purchasing the product. For example, in the market for perfume, the occasions for purchase might include a Christmas gift, a birthday gift, a wedding anniversary present or simply the opportunity to try out a new perfume brand.

User/usage status

Here, the distinction may be made between 'heavy', 'light' and 'non-user' segments.

Benefits sought

This is a very meaningful way to segment a market. The total market for a product or service is broken down into segments distinguished by the principal benefits sought by each segment. For example, the market for hair shampoo includes the following benefit segments which can be clearly observed from manufacturers' advertisements:

Cleanliness
Protection from dandruff, greasiness, dryness etc.
Reasons of scalp medication
Reasons of 'well being'.

A 'benefits sought' basis for segmentation can provide useful insights into the nature and extent of competition and the possible existence of gaps in the market.

Loyalty status

This direct approach is based on the extent to which different customers are loyal to certain brands (brand loyalty) or possibly to certain retail outlets (store loyalty). Identifying segments with different degrees of loyalty enables a company to determine which of its customers or prospective customers may be brand- or store-loyal prone. Such a market segment is a very attractive one upon which to concentrate future marketing efforts. Once they are convinced of the relative merits of a brand or supplier, such customers are unlikely to transfer their allegiances.

Where existing brand loyalty is already strong in a market, the would-be new entrant is faced with a particularly difficult marketing problem. In such a situation, it may be necessary to identify and target the non brand-loyal segment.

Combination segmentation bases

As already mentioned, often individual segmentation bases are used in combination to segment markets and delineate target customers. So, for example the marketer may well determine that targets are best identified in a particular product market by using a combination of, e.g. gender, income, social class etc. Some approaches to segmentation however have been specifically developed to combine certain selected variables as the overall basis for segmenting a market. An example of this approach is SAGACITY developed by Research Services Ltd in the UK. This market segmentation technique is based on a combination of family lifecycle, occupation and income. These combinations are used to identify and describe some 12 consumer segments which Research Services Ltd suggest have differing purchasing needs and purchasing behaviour. The combination of individual segmentation bases in ways which are meaningful for a particular product market application probably represents one of the most useful and flexible ways to delineate market segments.

Developments in consumer segmentation techniques: databases, one-to-one marketing, and the Internet

Yet again, some of the most significant developments in this area of marketing stem from developments in information technology and particularly the Internet.

Effective segmentation and targeting, like so many areas of marketing, requires information and analysis of consumer data. The development of cheap and readily available computing power puts this information increasingly at the disposal of the marketer. Modern data collection, storage and analysis techniques enable the marketer to understand their customers, and their buying preferences and habits much better. This has reached the stage where it is now possible and economically viable to profile the buying patterns of individual customers and to access this information through a database. In fact, this development is moving closer and closer to the situation where instead of thinking of marketing to groups or segments of customers, the marketer is able to consider one-to-one marketing. This so-called fragmentation of marketing is increasingly prevalent and may in the future even become the norm. The Internet, too, is playing a significant role in this respect. Through the Internet the marketer can build an effective and detailed database on individual customers. Moreover, through the same mechanism, the marketer can also reach individual customers on the Internet with tailored marketing programs. In the not too distant future the notion of customer groups may well be thought of as extremely primitive marketing.

Bases for segmenting organizational/industrial markets

The basic approach to segmentation, targeting and positioning does not differ greatly between consumer and organizational markets. As one might expect, segmenting industrial product markets introduces a number of additional bases for segmentation, whilst precluding some of the more frequently used ones in consumer product markets.

The most commonly encountered bases for segmenting industrial markets include:

- Type of application/end use: e.g. fabric for curtains and fabric for fashion wear
- Geographical: e.g. north and south; the European Union; the US
- Customer type: e.g. heavy engineering and light engineering
- Product technology: e.g. glass tubing, metal tubing and plastic tubing
- Supplier loyalty status
- Customer size and usage rates
- Purchasing procedures: e.g. tender and non-tender; centralized and non-centralized buying
- Benefits sought.

Similar to consumer markets, industrial market segmentation may be on an indirect (associative) base or a direct (behavioural) base. Also similar to consumer markets, we can use a variety of bases together in order to obtain more precise segmentation in the industrial market.

More recently, the relatively more neglected area of industrial market segmentation has seen a number of potentially powerful industrial segmentation frameworks emerge, specifically based on a step-by-step, hierarchical approach to segmentation. An example of this type of approach is that developed by Wind and Cardozo[11] and illustrated in Figure 6.8. Basically, the approach is that industrial markets be segmented in two stages. The first stage includes formation of macrosegments, based on characteristics of the organization. The second stage involves dividing those macrosegments into microsegments, based on the characteristics of the decision-making units (DMUs).

This hierarchical approach enables an initial screening of organizations and selection of these macrosegments which, on the basis of organizational characteristics, provide potentially attractive market opportunities. Organizations which may have no use for the given product or service can be eliminated. Starting with the grouping of organizations into homogeneous macrosegments also provides a reduction in total research effort and cost. Instead of examining detailed buying patterns and attempting to identify the characteristics of the DMU in each organization individually, such analysis is limited only to those macrosegments which passed the initial screening.

Figure 6.8
An approach to
segmenting indus-
trial markets.
Source: adapted from
Wind, Y. and Cardozo,
R., 'Industrial market
segmentation',
*Industrial Marketing
Management,* **3**, March
1974, p. 156.

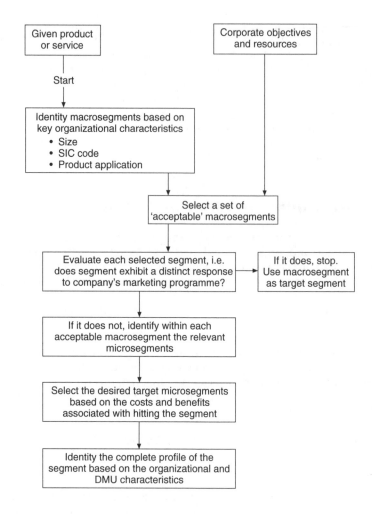

Once a set of acceptable macrosegments has been formed, the marketer may divide each of them into microsegments, or small groups of firms, on the basis of similarities and differences among DMUs within each macrosegment. Information for this second stage will come primarily from the sales force, based on salespeople's analysis of situations in particular firms or from specially designed market segmentation studies.

It is argued that the outcome from this segmentation model should include: a *key dependent variable* on which firms can be assigned to segments, i.e. the bases for segmentation: and a *set of independent variables* which allow a marketer to predict where along the key dependent variable a particular group of customers may lie, as well as providing a greater insight into the key characteristics of the segment.

This concept of successively combining industrial market segmentation bases giving, hopefully, more and more precise and hence meaningful segments is taken even further in the model developed by Shapiro and Bonoma[12]. Their 'nested' approach is shown in Figure 6.9.

This approach identifies five general segmentation bases which are arranged in the nested hierarchy shown. Moving from the outer nests towards the inner, these bases are: demographics, operating variables, purchasing approach, situational factors and personal characteristics of the buyer. We shall examine each of these in turn.

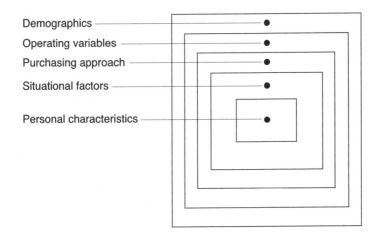

Figure 6.9
A 'nested' approach
to industrial market
segmentation.
Source: adapted from
Shapiro, B.P. and
Bonoma, T.V., 'How to
segment industrial
markets', *Harvard
Business Review,*
May–June 1984, pp.
104–110.

Demographics This category represents the outermost nest, which contains the most general segmentation criteria. These variables give a broad description of the segments in the market and relate to general customer needs and usage patterns. They can be determined without visiting the customer and include industry and company size and customer location.

Operating variables The second segmentation nest contains a variety of segmentation criteria called 'operating variables'. These enable more precise identification of existing and potential customers within demographic categories. Operating variables are generally stable and include technology, user/non-user status (by product and brand), and customer capabilities (operating, technical and financial).

Purchasing approaches One of the most neglected but valuable methods of segmenting an industrial market involves customers' purchasing approaches and company philosophy. The factors in this middle segmentation nest include the formal organization of the purchasing function, the power structure, the nature of the buyer/seller relationship, purchasing policies and purchasing criteria.

Situational factors Up to this point the model has focused on the grouping of customer firms. Now it moves to consider the tactical role of the purchasing situation. Situational factors resemble operating variables, but are temporary and require a more detailed knowledge of the customer. They include the urgency of order fulfilment, product application and the size of order.

Buyers' personal characteristics People, not companies, make purchase decisions, although the organizational framework in which they work and company policies and needs may constrain their choices. Marketers for industrial goods, like those for consumer products, can segment markets according to the individuals involved in a purchase in terms of buyer/seller similarity, buyer motivation, individual perceptions, and risk management strategies.

These then are some of the major approaches to identifying market segments in both consumer and industrial markets. The next step in target marketing is, having identified market segments, an evaluation of the attractiveness of these segments as a prelude to selecting target markets.

Segment evaluation: choice of targeting strategies and market targets

As we have already seen, determining whether, and on what basis, a market segments is only the first step in the process of target marketing. Once we have identified market segments we must also select a targeting strategy and then, if appropriate, select specific market targets. During this process we must also evaluate the relative attractiveness of the different segments. These steps are now discussed.

Evaluating market segments

Whenever a market segments – and we have seen that most markets do – then as part of its overall marketing strategy a company must decide on **targetting**, which of these segments it wishes to serve and on what basis. In order to do this, the strategic marketer must first evaluate the market segments that exist.

This evaluation process broadly involves assessing the attractiveness of the various segments in the market in order to determine which are worth serving. Kotler[13] suggests two major factors for assessing the relative attractiveness of market segments, namely:

- The overall attractiveness of the segment, e.g. size, growth
- Company objectives and resources.

We now consider each of these in more depth starting first with the attractiveness of the market segments.

Segment structural attractiveness

A number of factors influence the relative attractiveness of a particular segment for a company. Each of these factors should be assessed by the marketing manager before making targeting decisions. The main factors are as follows:

1. Segment size and growth   Although the larger segments are by no means always the most attractive (especially to the smaller company), an evaluation of market segments should always include an assessment of current size, together with existing and potential future growth rates. As with market size, the most attractive segments are not always those that have the highest existing or potential future growth rates. Indeed, even a segment which may be in decline may, because of lower levels of competition, offer attractive sales potential to the company able and willing to supply it. A good example of this is the supply of spare parts for old model automobiles. After a certain period of time, the original equipment manufacturers may feel that the declining demand for such spares no longer justifies supplying the market and, subject to meeting any statutory or contractual requirements with regard to supply, then withdraws. This leaves the market open to other smaller specialist suppliers who, for a time at least, can make sufficient profits to justify the investment.

Although the size and growth of a segment is a key factor, the idea of segment structural attractiveness extends beyond the notion of evaluating the attractiveness of a market segment from a purely volume perspective to that of long-term attractiveness in terms of profitability. Here we can usefully use Porter's framework for the competitive structure of an industry (discussed in Chapter 4) to indicate some of the other key areas for assessing segment attractiveness.

2. Extent of segment competitive rivalry   Some market segments are characterized by intense and frequent rivalry, perhaps because they are high growth, high profit, but often because they are in decline with overcapacity. Clearly, a more competitive segment will tend to be less attractive, particularly to the new entrant, unless it has some distinct and sustainable advantage which it can use to compete.

3. Barriers to entry or exit   These were discussed in Chapter 2 when we analysed competition. It was pointed out then that the most competitive segments – and the ones with the lowest profit margins – are those with low barriers to entry and high barriers to exit. What initially appears to be a very attractive new segment can, if entry barriers are low, quickly become overcompetitive, and ultimately, unprofitable.

4. Threat of substitutes   This is another aspect of competition. The existence of many substitute products invariably reduces the attractiveness of a segment. The appraisal of substitutes should take in not only existing substitutes, but also the possibility of future ones. Predicting or forecasting likely substitute products is difficult, but the techniques of technological forecasting (TF), which we discuss later, can be useful here.

5. Bargaining power of buyers   Some otherwise attractive segments are made less attractive by the bargaining power of buyers in the segment. In many of the retailing segments of the UK, the bargaining power of the large multiples is such that profit margins for suppliers can be very slender. As with substitutes, not only current bargaining power of buyers should be assessed, but also likely future developments in this area should be anticipated.

6. Bargaining power of suppliers   This is the reverse argument of the previous factor. Assessing segment attractiveness should also take into account the extent to which present suppliers (of materials, plant, finance, labour and so on) exercise strong bargaining power. Again, an assessment should also be made of the likely future trends and changes.

7. Company objectives and resources   The final key area of segment evaluation concerns the extent to which the segment(s) equates with a company's long-term objectives and strategic plans and its resources or skills.

Targeting strategies

Having evaluated the relative attractiveness of different market segments we are now in a position to select a targeting strategy. A company can select from three broad strategies with respect to targeting. These three strategies are *undifferentiated* target marketing, *differentiated* target marketing, and *concentrated* target marketing, each of which we shall now examine.

Undifferentiated marketing   This strategy is based upon ignoring any segmentation in the market. Instead, a 'blanket' approach is used with a marketing strategy aimed at the entire market rather than any single, or combination of, segments. A firm will usually produce one undifferentiated product, relying upon mass advertising and distribution to reach as many buyers as possible. Undifferentiated marketing is most suitable where demand for a product is relatively homogeneous. It should also have the potential to yield significant economies of scale in both marketing and production. Increasingly, companies are recognizing that the existence of disaggregated/

heterogeneous demand, referred to earlier, is rendering this global approach to market segmentation and targeting increasingly unsuitable.

 Differentiated marketing This strategy is based not only upon the recognition that different segments exist in a market, but also upon a decision to target several or all of these. The company therefore designs a separate marketing programme for each market segment it decides to serve. Because each market segment is specifically targeted, the company expects to increase overall company sales and market share. Any such increase must be compared with the greater costs of having many individual marketing programmes.

 Concentrated marketing This strategy also recognizes the existence of different market segments, but instead of serving several of these, a concentrated marketing strategy focuses marketing effort on just a single market segment. In this way, economies of scale in both production and marketing can be achieved, whilst at the same time more nearly meeting the needs of target group customers. The disadvantage of this strategy is that it renders a company vulnerable should anything threaten sales in the selected market segment.

Many factors can affect the choice of an appropriate targeting strategy. Smaller companies with fewer resources often have to compete by specializing in certain segments of the market and thus pursue a concentrated marketing strategy. Competition will also affect the choice of strategy. Where competitors do not segment and target respective customer groups, a strategy of concentrated or differentiated marketing can produce a significant competitive advantage. The choice of marketing strategy is ultimately a question of comparing the costs and benefits of each approach.

The selection of specific target markets only concerns those companies that decide to pursue a concentrated or differentiated targeting strategy. With those two strategies, a company must decide which of the segments in the market it is best able and willing to serve. This decision must of course be based on the outcome of the previous evaluation process.

Product positioning and market development

The final stages of target marketing involve the development of positioning strategies together with a supporting marketing mix.

In their seminal work in this area, Ries and Trout[14] suggested that positioning is essentially 'a battle for the mind'. In other words, positioning takes place in the mind of the customer. Because of this, Hooley and Saunders[15] believe that positioning is about the psychology of the customer and understanding how people perceive products and brands. Product positioning therefore takes place in the mind of the customer as the buyer. A customer-oriented focus is essential for effective product positioning.

The concept of product/brand positioning is relatively simple (even if researching and applying it is not) and is applicable in both industrial and consumer markets. The key aspects of this approach are based upon the following precepts:

1   Products and brands have both objective and subjective attributes. Examples of objective attributes might include those in Figure 6.10. Examples of subjective attributes include those in Figure 6.11.
2   Purchasers use such attributes when choosing between products and brands in a particular segment.

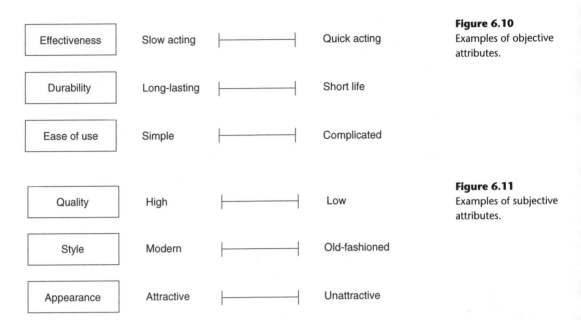

Figure 6.10
Examples of objective attributes.

Figure 6.11
Examples of subjective attributes.

3 The customer has individual ideas about how competitive products or brands rate on each attribute, i.e. 'positioning' takes place in the mind of the customer.

Using these precepts, it is then possible to establish:

1 Which are the important attributes in choosing between competing alternatives.
2 How the customer perceives the position of competitive products in relation to these attributes, and therefore the most advantageous position for the company within the segment of the market.

For example, let us assume that a company seeks to enter the market for 'instant coffee', in which there are already competitors producing brands A, B, C, D, E, F and G. The company must establish what the customers believe to be the appropriate attributes when choosing between brands in this market and the perceived position of existing competitors with respect to these attributes. If we imagine that the important attributes have been found to be 'price' and 'flavour', a possible positioning map (also called a brand map) might be drawn as shown in Figure 6.12. With this information, the company must

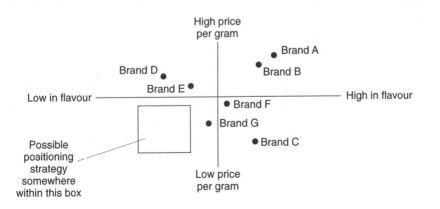

Figure 6.12
Hypothetical positioning map: instant coffee market.

decide where to position its product within this market segment. Possibilities are contained within the box, the parameters of which are low to medium price per gram and low to medium in flavour. Perhaps a 'caffeine free' product could also be considered? Such a product would give the new brand a distinctiveness, as opposed to positioning the brand next to another and fighting 'head on' for market share.

What is the most appropriate position for the new coffee brand depends on a number of factors. For example, as outlined earlier, we must assess the relative attractiveness of a particular position in a market for the new brand. Similarly, and related to this, we must assess the relative strengths of existing competitive brands in the market and whether we want to tackle this competition head on or not. Finally, we must consider what our objectives for the new product are, particularly with regard to brand image.

Once we have assessed brand positioning in the market and determined where we wish to position our products and brands, the final step in the process of segmentation, targeting and positioning involves the design of marketing programmes which will support the positional strategy in selected target markets. In our 'instant coffee' example the company must therefore determine what price, flavour (product) distribution and promotional strategy will be necessary to achieve the selected position in the market.

In the instant coffee market, 'Carte Noir' is positioned as a distinctly up-market and sophisticated product compared to its competition.

All of the elements of the marketing mix for this brand serve to support this positioning strategy. The packaging is designed to convey an image of quality. The brand name itself suggests an air of sophistication. Although not necessarily the most expensive brand, neither is it the cheapest on the market. Finally, the promotion of the brand exemplifies the unique selling proposition extolled by the brand's marketers.

This simplified example illustrates positioning a new producer based on product attributes. However, there are several alternative ways to position new products and brands. For example, a product may be positioned on the basis of uses/applications, e.g. a car engine oil might be positioned as primarily for use in winter. Alternatively, a new product or brand can be positioned by associating it with particular groups of users, e.g. as being predominantly for use by 'executives'.

Finally, positioning can be achieved by deliberately positioning with respect to a competitor. More often than not, this will be done by positioning with respect to the leading brand/competitor in the market using the attributes (good or bad) of the brand leader to make direct comparisons with the new brand and hence develop predetermined perceptions with regard to the new product.

Although positioning is particularly crucial when developing and launching a new product for a market, it is also relevant to the management of existing products and brands. Because markets evolve and change over time, including for example, changes in customer tastes, competition etc,. the marketer must continuously assess the effectiveness of existing positioning strategies for products and brands. Often, existing brands will need to be repositioned to reflect changing market dynamics. Some of the most common repositioning strategies are as follows:

Repositioning with existing segments

This approach to repositioning is often done in order to revitalize a brand which is losing sales/market share and/or has approached the end of its product life cycle. This type of repositioning does not target new customers but seeks rather to update the image and/or features of a brand. A good example of a brand which has been updated consistently over its life is the Oxo cubes brand which has changed its image, particularly through its advertising, to reflect changing social and family attitudes.

Repositioning to attract new customers

Sometimes a company may deliberately reposition a brand in order to attract new customers. This may often involve significant changes to one or more of the marketing mix elements. Again, this may be done to take account of market dynamics and/or to revitalize flagging sales. A good example of repositioning is the Lucozade brand which over time has been repositioned from its original positioning as a product for the sick to a brand which is essentially for the fit and healthy, particularly where they participate in exercise and/or sports activities. A consideration in repositioning brands in this way is the effect it has on existing customers and sales.

Innovative repositioning

Sometimes a marketer can create a new position in a market for a brand by introducing new criteria for brand choice based on attributes in which the marketer is strong. So, for example, Volvo have kept ahead of their competition by deliberately positioning their products on the basis of the 'safety' attribute. Sometimes, the innovative marketer can come up with entirely new attributes to use in such a repositioning exercise. So for example, Daewoo successfully introduced the notion of 'no hassle' showroom staff in order to sell their cars.

Competitor depositioning

In this approach the strategy is essentially based on repositioning competitor brands rather than actually changing the position of one's own brand. Essentially, this means altering the perceived position of competitive brands from the perspective of the customer. Understandably, competitor depositioning normally means repositioning competitor brands in a less favourable light. Competitor depositioning should be approached with caution as it can involve legal implications where, for example, a competitor brand is denigrated through, e.g. media advertising etc. It is normally safer to deposition competitors by more subtle and sometimes veiled comparisons involving competitor brands.

Summary

In this chapter we have examined some of the key concepts in the interrelated areas of defining market boundaries and target marketing. We have seen that the delineation of market boundaries is a prerequisite of strategic market planning and, in particular, the implementation of target marketing. Many companies still define their markets on the basis of product or industry classifications. Simple though this approach is, it can unfortunately lead to a myopic view of markets. At the other extreme we have generic need-based definitions of market boundaries which, although offering several advantages over product/industry-based definitions, are usually too broad to be used for strategic planning purposes. In between these relatively narrow and very broad based definitions of market boundaries is the delineation of markets on the basis of a combination of customer functions, technology and customer groups. This approach affords a much more useful perspective on market boundaries to the planner, enabling, as it does, the basic building blocks of a market to be assembled and analysed.

Recognition of the fact that markets are comprised of individual blocks of demand in turn led us to consider the increasingly important area of segmentation, targeting and positioning in modern marketing strategy. We have seen that the importance of what we collectively call 'target marketing' stems from the fact that demand in most markets is heterogeneous. There are a number of advantages associated with the effective use of target marketing, but, in particular, a company is able to spot marketing opportunities and avoid excessive competition. A market may be segmented using any one or a combination of bases, both associate and direct in nature. However, the base(s) used should lead to clearly distinguishable market segments which may be selected as market targets to be reached with a distinct marketing mix. Used effectively, target marketing can, and does, lead to improved profitability. This is done by tailoring marketing efforts more specifically to customer needs, whilst at the same time selecting market segments which can be best defended against competition.

Key terms

Automatic interaction detection (AID) [p143]
Cluster analysis [p143]
Market segments [p144]
Target marketing [p144]
Life cycle/stage segmentation [p149]
Geodemographic segmentation [p151]

Lifestyle segmentation [p153]
Psychographics [p153]
Targeting [p160]
Undifferentiated marketing [161]
Differentiated marketing [p162]
Concentrated marketing [p162]

Questions

1 What is the importance of defining the business, and what approaches can be used in order to achieve this?
2 Why is target marketing so important to the contemporary marketer, and what are the criteria for effective segmentation?
3 Why have marketers become increasingly concerned about traditional methods of designating social class?
4 What bases can be used to segment industrial markets?
5 What are the criteria for evaluating market segments, and what are the different targeting strategies which a marketer may use?

References

1. Day, G. S. and Shocker, A. D., *Identifying Competitive Product-market Boundaries: Strategic and Analytical Issues*, Marketing Science Institute, Cambridge, Mass., 1976.
2. Levitt, T., 'Marketing myopia', *Harvard Business Review*, **38**, July–August 1960, pp. 45–56.
3. Abell, D. F., *Defining the Business: The Starting Point of Strategic Planning*, Prentice-Hall, New Jersey, 1980.
4. O'Shaughnessy, J., *Competitive Marketing: A Strategic Approach*, 3rd edn, Routledge, London, 1995, p. 105.
5. Day, G. S., Shocker A. D. and Srivastava, R. K., 'Customer-oriented approaches to identifying product markets', *Journal of Marketing*, **43**, 1974, pp. 8–19.
6. Hooley, G. J. and Saunders, J., *Competitive Positioning*, Prentice-Hall, Hertfordshire, 1993, pp. 162–164.
7. Dibb, S., Simkin, L., Pride, W. M. and Ferrell, O. C., *Marketing: Concepts and Strategies*, Houghton Mifflin, Boston, 2000, p. 208.
8. Fifield, P., *Marketing Strategy*, 2nd edn., Butterworth-Heinemann, Oxford, 1998, p. 134.
9. 'A new age of media analysis', *Marketing Week*, March 30, 2000, pp. 40–43
10. O'Shaughnessy, J., *Competitive Marketing: A Strategic Approach*, 3rd edn, Routledge, London, 1995, pp. 205–209.
11. Wind Y. and Cardozo, R., 'Industrial market segmentation', *Industrial Marketing Management*, **3**, March 1974, pp. 142–164.
12. Shapiro, B. P. and Bonoma, T. V., 'How to segment industrial markets', *Harvard Business Review*, May–June 1984, pp. 104–110.
13. Kotler, P., *Marketing Management: Analysis, Planning, Implementation and Control*, 9th edn, Prentice-Hall, New Jersey, 1997, p. 269.
14. Ries, A. and Trout, J. *Positioning*, McGraw-Hill, New York, 1981.
15. Hooley, G. J. and Saunders, J., op. cit, p. 169.

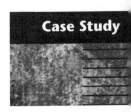

Case Study

The holiday market represents a highly segmented and targeted market. So, for example, we have the Saga type holidays aimed at the over 50s and designed obviously to fill this group's needs. On the other hand we have, for example, Club Med and Club 18–30, the latter in particular suggesting the age group these two operators are targeting.

You have been appointed as the new marketing manager for a large travel group offering a range of holiday packages aimed at several parts of the market. The group includes

package tour operations, a nationwide chain of travel shops and a fleet of aircraft.

One of the fastest growing parts of the travel market in recent years has been the cruise market. Once the domain of the privileged few, cruises are now available to a much wider target market as costs have come down and, in some cases, incomes have risen.

Until now, the company that just been appointed you has not been part of the cruise market. It now realizes it may have made a mistake in this respect and wishes to enter this market as soon as possible. The company has negotiated the provision of two cruise ships for the next season, which will sail round the Mediterranean and the Caribbean respectively. The ships have just been refurbished and offer the most up-to-date facilities. Other companies in this market have been predominantly targeting the middle-income groups. However there remains a part of the market which is aimed only at the luxury end, with high prices and prestigious ships.

The company has asked you to give them some preliminary advice about how to segment this market and which target segments might be most appropriate, and why. It also wants to know how its product offering in this area might be positioned so as to differentiate it from other existing competitors.

QUESTION

1. Prepare the advice and information which your company is seeking.

7

Product and innovation strategies

Chapter objectives

After reading this chapter you will:

▶ Appreciate the strategic significance of product and innovation decisions.

▶ Understand the nature and scope of product and innovation strategies.

▶ Be familiar with the critical factors in the management of innovation.

▶ Understand the key steps in the development and launch of new products.

▶ Be familiar with recent developments in the strategic management of products and innovation.

Introduction

So far we have discussed the analysis which precedes, and is essential to, the development of detailed marketing programmes designed to meet corporate and strategic marketing objectives. In this, and several of the following chapters, we will consider strategic decisions concerned with planning and implementing elements of the marketing mix; namely, product, price, promotion and place decisions. In this chapter, we start with the product element of the mix.

Firstly, we examine the nature and scope of product strategies and through this process clarify the different levels and components of product decisions. We shall see that product policy involves both wide-ranging and fundamental strategic decisions.

Products probably convey to customers more about the company than any other form of marketing activity, and not only are they the source of revenue and profit today, but as Blythe[1] points out, new products will also be one of the most important factors in terms of success in the future. As we shall see, a product can be a piece of heavy machinery with physical characteristics or it can be a service with intrinsic characteristics such as management consultancy. The common denominator between all products whether physical or intangible service is that they need to meet the needs and requirements of the customer and supply the customer with satisfaction. Product decisions effectively determine the upper limit to a company's profit potential, the rest of the marketing mix determines the extent to which this potential is achieved. It is essential therefore, to effectively manage the whole of a company's product mix. In the current highly competitive marketplace however, companies are under increasing pressure to continuously develop new products and services that are both timely and responsive to customer needs. Most successful businesses must have the ability to develop new products and services to meet the changing needs of a dynamic marketplace. To meet the demands of the customer therefore, more emphasis is being placed on the development of new products and hence it is this aspect of product management which is particularly stressed in this chapter.

Elements of product strategy

In their chapter on marketing planning and product policy, Adcock *et al.*[2] suggest that product policy is a key area of corporate and operational decision making. In order to illustrate the range of decisions which this 'key area' encompasses, it is useful to consider product strategy as a hierarchy of related decisions ranging from product item to product mix elements. We shall also briefly consider the nature and importance of service products, though a more detailed discussion of service product characteristics and the marketing of service products is included in Chapter 17.

Product item decisions

The first level of product decisions concerns individual products or services which a company manufactures and markets. Of course, some companies produce only one product, but increasingly most companies are multi-product.

 A **product item** is, by definition, any item that can be considered as a separate product entity and that may be distinguished in some way from other products that the company produces, irrespective of its relationship to those other products. A product item will normally have a separate designation in the seller's list. Provided that any product differs in some way from another, either through modification or market application, it may be regarded as a product item. At the product item level, product decisions include, for example, design quality, features, packaging and branding.

Product line decisions

 Individual product items that are closely related in some way to one another are classed as **product lines**. The relationship could be, for example include, different variations of the same basic product, e.g. the range of different fillings as product items in a range of Marks & Spencer sandwiches – the product line. Also a range of (a) industrial and (b) domestic air conditioning filters as two product lines contain product items for different end use applications.

Product line decisions involve the marketing planner in considering, in particular, the number of product items in a selected product line. For example, Ford Motor Company must determine how many models on 'the Focus line' they should ideally offer, and what the nature of these variations should be, e.g. engine variations, trim variations and accessory variations.

Product line decisions of this type are not as easy as they may seem. A careful, detailed evaluation of demand and cost interrelationships between individual products in the line is vital. A clear sense of balance is needed; if too many variations in a line are offered costs increase substantially, but if a product line contains too few variations customer satisfaction may be unfulfilled through lack of variety. In highly competitive multi-product markets, it is essential to maintain balance within each product line to achieve and maintain market share. Product lines should be focused on target markets to achieve market concentration and to maintain competitive advantage.

Management of the product line means frequent appraisal of the range of product items in each product line, determining whether they are too extensive or too constrained. Policy must be set to add and delete items from product lines to meet financial targets and yet to maintain customer service levels. This is often a dilemma that is difficult to resolve. Frequently, opportunities may arise to extend the product line either by moving up market by adding higher quality products to the line and/or meeting 'budget market' requirements by adding on economy lines. A clear rationale is needed for such decisions. Over time there is a tendency for product lines to extend in size as new products are added but older (and frequently outmoded) ones, for a variety of reasons, are not deleted. Again, this calls for clear policy guidelines on the addition or deletion of product items from established product lines.

Product mix decisions

A **product mix** constitutes the sum total of individual product items and product lines which the company markets. It is common to describe the product mix with the terms 'width' and 'depth'. This enables an analysis of the 'constituency' of the product mix to be made. The following example, shown in Figure 7.1, is from Lancaster and Massingham[3]. This hypothetical company manufactures and markets three separate product lines – fountain pens, cigarette lighters and wrist-watches. Within each product line the company offers a number of separate product items.

This situation is typical of many diversified companies with multiple product lines. In this case, the product mix represents the sum of the firm's products – in this case, 30 products. The number of product lines is three. **Line depth** refers to the number of products in each line – 9, 13 and 8 respectively – with the average depth being 10. **Line width** refers to the number of product lines which a company has to offer.

By using the product mix concept a strategic assessment of the company's product offering can be made. For example, product line three could be extended (and hence

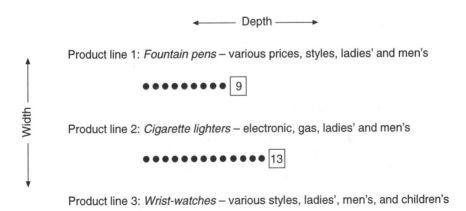

Figure 7.1
A hypothetical product mix for Personal Products Ltd.
Source: Lancaster, G. A. and Massingham, L. C., *Essentials of Marketing*, 2nd edn, McGraw-Hill, London, 1993, p. 201

the product mix) by adding, say, digital watches. The company can also assess the extent to which products in the same line are complementary or which compete with each other and hence which, if any, might be deleted.

Decision about new products must reflect consistency with existing product lines and items in relation to previously determined marketing objects set for product provision in specified markets. Conversely, is any one product so valued in terms of image and reputation that its deletion will damage the product line or indeed the total mix? Ultimately, the addition to the width of the mix and the depth within each product line should be compatible with the planned long-term marketing strategy. Short-termism, opportunism and entrepreneurial decisions taken for early cash recovery may be damaging to the company's financial and market position in the medium to long term.

Product mix analysis is a vital part of the strategy review. In the case of our hypothetical company shown in Figure 7.1, the following are a few possible strategic options:

1 Augment the product line by adding rollerball pens. This would remove some measure of exclusivity and represent a strategy of being 'all things to people' – a bid to serve the whole market for ink-based writing implements.
2 Delete all but the most expensive men's lighters from line two. This would have the effect of making the company a market specialist in men's lighters – aiming at an exclusive market segment.
3 Delete lines one and two and become a specialist in a single product line – wristwatches. In such a situation, options one and two would still be available to the company.
4 Delete all but one product and become expert in its marketing and production.
5 Add another product line. In the case of Personal Products Ltd, it could be a new line of pens aimed at the designer or graphics market.

Given the existing product mix and the options available, the company must begin to take product decisions which are in line with long-term strategy and which are consistent with that mix. The introduction of ball-point pens could influence the perception which the consumer has of the company as a whole. Low-cost disposable pens might not be consistent with the firm's reputation for high quality lighters. Similarly, the firm may be technically capable of producing an industrial line, but lacking in the marketing expertise required to serve this new market efficiently.

Analysis of the product mix thus examines every aspect of the company. Every decision has financial, technical, marketing and market implications. The critical nature of product strategy becomes more apparent when one considers the consequences of failure and the necessity for success.

The strategic choice options that relate to product mix decisions should be carefully considered through a set of evaluation criteria so that decisions taken are rational and not purely emotional or opportunistic.

Implementing product strategies

It is now necessary to consider the ways in which the decision to choose any of the above options is taken, recognizing also the absolute necessity for new products.

If, at any time, the rate of new product development and launch is not equal or superior to the rate of product deletion or obsolescence, the company will lose profits rapidly and ultimately will be unable to survive. A long-term view of product strategy must, therefore, be taken.

As O'Shaughnessy[4] points out, product strategy is central to all company decisions and should emanate from and support the overall objectives of the company. Because organizations have different, and often multiple, objectives there exists a wide variety of possible product strategies which according to the objective(s) might be selected to support them. This notion, together with the range of possible product strategies which O'Shaughnessy suggests, is shown in Figure 7.2.

Summarizing our discussion of product item, product line and product mix decisions, together with the range of possible product strategies shown in Figure 7.2, it can be seen that product decisions are complex and multi-faceted. In addition, as indeed with each of the marketing mix decisions, product decisions need to be consistent with and in support of overall company objectives and strategies. Clearly, product strategies need to be evaluated in relation to both the strengths and weaknesses of the company itself, and to the opportunities and threats which are prevalent and likely in the future. Finally, product strategy involves the management of existing successful products, the elimination of obsolete or non-profit making ones and the development and introduction of new products. Each of these elements of product strategy and management is important to the achievement of company objectives. However, the pace of change, fierce competition and the product life cycle itself all heighten the significance of the new product development and innovation process, and it is to this particular aspect of product strategy and management that we now turn our attention.

Service products

In recent years, in many economies, we have seen the growth of service industries, and indeed in some economies the service sector is now the largest sector. As we have already seen, there is no difference between the more tangible physical products and their service product counterparts with respect to their importance in overall marketing strategy, or in the need for both physical and service products to meet customer requirements. Virtually all of the elements of product strategy and management outlined already in this chapter, and, subsequently apply equally to service products. However, service products do have characteristics which set them aside from their physical product counterparts and which, in turn therefore give rise to additional considerations in their marketing.

The term 'service product' encompasses a myriad of different types of products and markets in which they are sold, but essentially a service is an intangible product involving some deed, performance or effort that cannot be physically possessed by the customer. The most important distinguishing characteristics of services is that they are essentially intangible, they are often consumed at the same time and place they are supplied, and customer and supplier often directly interact during the sale and consumption process. Because of these characteristics we often find additional important elements in their marketing which are often referred to as the 'extended marketing mix'. In addition to the conventional 4Ps which by now we are familiar with for the marketing of physical products, when marketing service products an additional 3Ps, making 7Ps in all, may be added to the marketing mix. These three additional Ps are:

'People': because of direct contact with customers in marketing services, service provider's staff (people) are an important element of the marketing mix for services.

'**Physical evidence**': the intangible nature of service products means that customers often use other evidence such as the physical facilities of the service provider, their promotional and other literature etc., as evidence of the potential quality of the service.

'**Process**': in services marketing, how the service is provided is important. So, for example, systems for serving customers, dealing with their orders etc. take on a particular significance in services marketing.

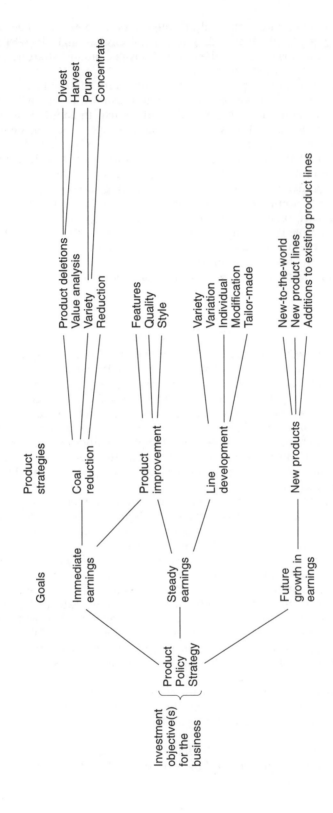

Figure 7.2 Company objectives and the range of product strategies.

Source: O'Shaughnessy, J., *Competitive Marketing: A Strategic Approach*, 3rd edn, Unwin Hyman, Boston, 1995, p. 334.

As mentioned earlier we shall be considering the special characteristics of service products and the additional marketing mix elements associated with them in more detail later in Chapter 17. In reality, most products have a mixture of both tangible and intangible components. In some cases the service element in the marketing of a manufactured product is the most important factor in competitive success because it is the only means of differentiating between different products. In reality there are few products that do not have a personal dimension involved somewhere along the line.

New product development and innovation

Already in this text, including of course this chapter, we have had occasion to raise the importance of new product development or, as we shall often refer to it here, innovation. For the sake of completeness, we reiterate some of the arguments we have developed which serve to illustrate the importance of innovation in corporate and marketing strategy.

Firstly, the pace of technological, market, social and economic change is accelerating. One of the most important implications of this accelerating change for marketing management is the shortening of product life cycles. Simply stated, successful products stay successful for shorter periods of time.

An additional factor contributing to the shortening of product life cycles, and indeed the pace of change itself, is increasingly aggressive competitive behaviour. Successful new products are quickly copied and/or improved upon by competitors in order to retain their competitive edge in markets.

In many markets the new competition is speed of innovation and new product development. Honda, for example, is confronting its competitors by increasing the speed at which it can bring a new product to market. This not only allows Honda to respond to any changes in market demand more rapidly, but also it enables it to undermine both the cash resources and the confidence of its competitors by product proliferation. Amongst the best in the car industry, product development times needed to design and launch a new model have reduced from an average of five to six years in the early 1990s to just over 30 months now.

Taken together, all these factors illustrate the need for continuous innovation. Today, most organizations must either innovate or go out of business. Clearly then, innovation and the new product development which such innovation gives rise to is not just desirable but is essential to long-term market and competitive success.

However, an additional factor which serves to heighten the importance of the process of innovation, or more specifically of effectively managing this process, is the attendant risk associated with new product development. Put simply, a high proportion of new products fail in the marketplace. Needless to say, with so many possible interpretations as to what constitutes a 'new' product and also what constitutes 'failure', estimates of new product failure rates vary enormously. Taking some of the most conservative estimates of new product failure rates we can say that they are at least 20 per cent for industrial product companies and 40 per cent for consumer products. Often these conservative estimates are far exceeded.

Clearly, these potentially high rates of failure, when combined with the often high costs and investments required to develop and launch new products, make this area of marketing a risky business. It is crucially important, then, that the process is managed effectively. Before we look more specifically at the steps in developing and launching new products, we need to set the planning framework for innovation. We also need to establish the range of innovation activities in which a company can potentially participate. Finally, we need to assess and draw upon what is now a considerable body of research and evidence as to the critical factors in managing innovation which have largely been derived from studies into successful versus unsuccessful innovation.

The meaning and scope of innovation

'Innovation' may be defined as 'the bringing in of novelties' or 'making changes in', definitions very much in accord with what, in a business, most managers would see. In practice though, the term encompasses a wide range of activities, differing widely in scope, focus, cost and risk. One way of distinguishing between different types of innovation – and therefore innovative activities – is in term of the degree of 'newness' of the product. Seven types of innovation can be classified in this way:

1 Entirely new products.
2 Improved performance products.
3 New application products.
4 Additional functions products.
5 Lower cost products.
6 Restyled products.
7 Repackaged or renamed products.

Entirely new products

 Often referred to as **'new-to-the-world products'**, these are innovations that perform an entirely new function and therefore, potentially at least, create entirely new markets. A good example would be television, which for the first time allowed the transmission of audiovisual signals.

These types of innovation are, in fact, comparatively rare. They also pose the highest risks and often incur the highest costs.

Improved performance products

These are innovations which improve the performance of an existing function. This type of innovation is much more common than the 'new-to-the-world' type, and is often the prime objective of innovation research and development activity.

It is important to note that 'improved performance' itself encompasses a wide range of different types of innovation. At one extreme, improved performance may involve the development of use of a brand new technology (e.g. digital watches); at the other, it may mean an extension or improvement of the technology currently used, by improved design or better materials.

New application products

A considerable amount of 'innovative' activity in marketing involves funding or developing new applications for existing products. The amount of development activity required can vary enormously. In some cases, the technology or product may be applied with little or no further development (the areas of technology are gradually used in more and more applications), whereas for other products or technologies widening the applications scope of the product requires substantial research and development work.

Additional functions products

This type of innovation may be used to improve performance and/or extend functions of existing products. Typical is the addition of extra product features such as a re-dial facility on the domestic telephone, which adds to what earlier telephones could do.

Lower cost products

This again can be seen as a variation on the 'improved performance' product – a new product which performs exactly the same functions as a previous product, but at a lower cost. A lower cost product may enable the marketer to extend the applications of the product by reaching more buyers for whom the product was previously either too expensive and/or not cost effective. Innovative activity aimed at reducing product cost is common in the computer market.

Restyled products

Often 'new products' are no more than an update or change in styling to old ones. This type of innovative activity is prevalent in the car and clothing markets: a progressive innovation which generally involves lower costs – and lower risks – than the 'new-to-the-world' type of innovation. However, what started as a low cost, low risk modification can turn out to become a major investment carrying high risk. This may not have been the original intention.

Repackaged or renamed products

At the opposite extreme to the entirely new product is the 'new product' which is a result of repackaging, renaming or rebranding. Although requiring careful planning and management, this type of innovation involves fewer management issues than those which are raised by the development of products which are entirely new. One could argue that such products are not new at all, and should not be treated as innovations. The test of what constitutes a 'new product' – and the degree of 'newness' – is the extent to which the market (i.e. customers) *perceive* the product to be new. A repackaged and/or rebranded product, if perceived as new by the market, is in a sense an innovation and should be marketed as such.

Repackaging, renaming and rebranding are tactical aspects of product innovation. They are really part of a 'product regeneration' strategy.

We can now see that 'innovation' encompasses a wide range of different type of activity, ranging from the development of entirely new products and technologies to the repackaging of existing ones. Clearly it is the entirely new products which pose the greatest problems in terms of effective management and attendant risk, as shown in Figure 7.3. It is with managing this high risk type of innovation activity that much of what follows in this chapter is concerned.

Having established the variety of innovation activities we now turn our attention to some of the issues in the management of innovation, in particular the 'ingredients' in the successful management of innovation and some of the current issues influencing the future environment for innovation and new product development.

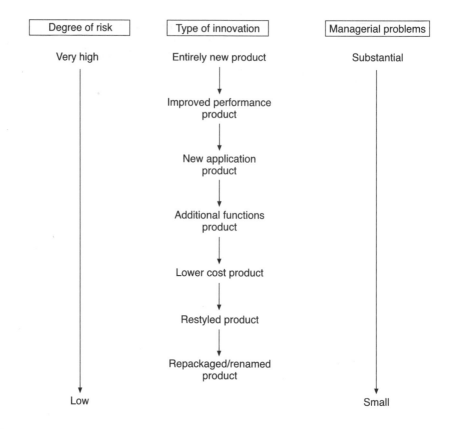

Figure 7.3
The continuum of
product innovation.

The management of innovation: critical factors

Innovation is crucial to long-term success in an organization, yet the risks are high with significant rates of new product failure. The managerial issues and problems to which this dilemma gives rise are considerable.

Success and failure in innovation: some empirical evidence

A combination of the recognized importance of innovation and the high risks of failure has meant that this area of company activity has attracted a substantial amount of attention and research in recent years. Much of this research has focused on attempts to look for empirical evidence that will establish the key ingredients in the successful management of innovation. There are no 'recipes' for certain success in innovation, but research has been instrumental in establishing some of the critical factors in the process. By way of example, we have outlined a selection of the research programmes in this area, together with a brief summary of their findings.

Project SAPPHO

One of the earliest systematic studies of success and failure in new product development was Project SAPPHO. Under Cyril Freeman[5] at the University of Sussex, an extensive and detailed research programme was designed to investigate the key factors for success in innovation. Twenty-nine pairs of similar innovation projects were examined; in each pair one project was successful and the other a comparative failure. Using a carefully designed statistical analysis, Freeman and his team were able to establish a pattern of factors which appeared to distinguish between success and failure in the various pairings. Project SAPPHO found that the successful innovator tended to be distinguished by the following five elements:

1 The successful innovators had a much clearer idea of user needs.
2 Successful innovators put much more effort into marketing their innovations – not just at the original idea stage by looking for gaps in the market, but throughout the process of development and launch.
3 Successful innovators paid much more attention to the development stage of their innovations than those innovators who failed. This often meant that the development work proceeded more slowly, but it was more effective.
4 Successful innovators were much more willing, and indeed able, to use outside help and advice in developing their products. However, most tended to perform more of the practical development work in-house.
5 Successful innovators were distinguished by a high degree of commitment to their innovations. Usually a senior manager with substantial activity in the organization was in charge of the successful innovation in each pair.

Successful product launches

Morley's[6] study of over 2,000 new product launches is one of the most comprehensive to date. This study found that only one in seven of the new product launches researched could be considered successful when considering sales and market share. Those that were successful exhibited the following characteristics compared to their less successful counterparts:

● Sustained heavy promotion during the first three months of launch
● More extensive and rigorous market research
● Less reliance on exaggerated claims for the new product to consumers
● More awareness and receptiveness to distributors' needs and wants
● Use of a well-known company and/or brand name.

Extensive though this study was, the conclusions drawn about successful new products are very much along the lines of what one would expect. For example, it is understandable that new products with a well-known company or brand name and which are heavily promoted would stand more chance of success than their lesser-known weekly promoted counterparts. However, a further finding from Morley's study with regard to successful new products is, at least at first sight, perhaps more surprising, namely that:

● Prices for successful new products tended to be above average for the sector.

Amongst the most difficult of markets in which to succeed with new products is the grocery, particularly the luxury foods market. Despite this, the Ben and Jerry's brand of ice creams, which by any stretch of the imagination is not the cheapest of product ranges in this product category on the market, continue to be extremely successful. One of their latest launches, 'Caramel Chew Chew' ice cream, once again is doing well. The brand's marketers have refused to be drawn into a price war against their competitors and therefore continue to support the brand's positioning in the marketplace to good effect.

The McKinsey report

A slightly different approach to investigating innovative success is exemplified by a report from McKinsey & Co.[7] which sought primarily to establish the essentials of a well managed company. They found certain factors associated with the success of a number of firms acknowledged as being leaders, especially in product innovation. (The ten companies selected in the study were International Business Machines, Emerson Electric, Texas Instruments, McDonald's, Hewlett-Packard, Johnson & Johnson, ZM, Digital Equipment, Procter & Gamble and Dana.)

The eight key factors for success McKinsey found were:

1   A bias towards action.
2   Simple line and team staff organization.
3   Continued contact with customers.
4   Productivity improvement via people.
5   Operational autonomy and the encouragement of entrepreneurship.
6   Simultaneous loose and tight controls.
7   Stress on one key business value.
8   An emphasis on sticking to what it knows best.

A summary of critical factors in successful innovation

These three studies are a sample of empirical research done in this area. What emerges from these and other studies is that there are a set of critical factors in successful innovation which point the way to key areas for managing this activity. One of the best summaries of these ingredients is that offered by Twiss[8], who lists seven critical factors:

1   A market orientation.
2   Relevance to the organization's corporate objectives.
3   A source of creative ideas.
4   An effective project selection and evaluation system.
5   Effective project management and control.
6   An organization receptive to innovation.
7   Commitment by one individual or a few individuals.

As Twiss points out, there will always be cases where innovations succeed in spite of poor management, but absence of one or more of the above factors is more likely to lead to innovative failure. In fact, it appears that companies seem to be learning to manage the process of new product development – and especially the idea generation and screening stages – much more effectively than in the past. A number of pundits nevertheless believe that successful new product development will become more difficult in the future. On the other hand, the rewards for successful innovation remain.

The future environment for new product development

In an excellent résumé of the future for new product development, Merle Crawford[9] has isolated four sets of factors or trends that will influence the future for new product development:

1   Reduced reward factors.
2   Increased cost factors.
3   Increased difficulty factors.
4   Positive market factors.

Reduced reward factors Crawford argues that a number of trends will tend to reduce the rewards (and the incentive) for product innovation in the future. They include:

- The increased use of segmentation, and therefore smaller markets
- The increased speed of competitive response, and therefore reduced period of price advantage
- Shorter product life cycles.

All of these factors serve to make innovation less rewarding (financially) for the innovator.

Increased cost factors The increased pace of technological progress has greatly increased the costs of pioneering new technologies and products. Some of the more advanced technologies are in fact beyond the resources of many individual companies. We are thus likely to see a much greater use of collaborative developments between companies and/or companies and government in the future.

Increased difficulty factors These factors are tending to increase the uncertainty and level of difficulty associated with innovation:

- Increased government regulations pertaining to new technology
- The patent process, which is slow and not too reliable
- To some extent, society itself has become much more critical of constant innovation with its emphasis on 'newness', often at the expense of tradition
- Managers, too, are increasingly being urged to produce short-term results rather than the long-term commitment which much innovative activity requires.

Positive forces On the other hand, Crawford argues that a number of factors will tend to promote the progress of new product development in the future:

- Despite the reaction towards new products and technologies, markets (and many customers) are still very responsive to them
- Linked to this, the profit opportunities from successful new product development are still huge
- In general, managers are now better trained to cope with the uncertainties associated with innovation.

Strategies for innovation

Later we shall look at the stages in new product development, from idea generation to commercialization and launch. The first prerequisite to developing and launching new products is to determine the overall strategic approach to innovation and its use within corporate strategy. Twiss[8] distinguishes the following possible strategies for innovation:

1 Offensive strategy.
2 Defensive strategy.
3 Licensing strategy.
4 Interstitial strategy.
5 Market creation strategy.
6 Maverick strategy.
7 Acquisition of personnel.
8 Acquisition of companies.

We need to look at all of these to see what is involved in the variety of corporate approaches to innovation strategies described by Twiss.

Offensive strategy

This strategy is usually high risk, but with a high potential pay-off, and requires an effective research and developing department with a high degree of innovation, a strong marketing element which can recognize new market opportunities, and an effective production element which can rapidly change these new product ideas into actual commercial products.

Twiss suggests that in most cases a strong research orientation and the application of new technologies will need to be appreciated and brought into effect by the company. This type of strategy is usually undertaken by larger companies, and occurs most often in an industry dominated by a small number of major companies.

Defensive strategy

This is, in effect, the opposite of the offensive strategy: it is a low risk, low pay-off strategy. The company offering it needs an established market share, and has to be able to maintain profit levels, even when involved in heavy price competition, through low manufacturing costs. At the same time, enough technological ability must be available to react to swift technological advances by the competition.

The defensive strategy is best suited to companies whose strengths are in marketing and production rather than research and development.

Licensing strategy

A licensing strategy is also known as 'absorbtive strategy', and allows the company to make profits by buying the technological innovations of another company, so reducing the need for an effective in-house research and development department.

As Twiss suggests:

> There is little gain from discovering what can be obtained from another source more cheaply.

Much advantage can be gained by not relying wholly on in-house research and development.

Licensing out your own technology to competing companies also has its advantages. It may reduce the company's market share in the long run, but large licensing fees can be obtained from the sale of an innovation which the competition would develop and match itself eventually in any case.

Interstitial strategy

 An **interstitial strategy** aims to avoid direct competition confrontations. Instead, the company analyses existing market leaders in order to discover their strengths and weaknesses and related gaps in the market. This technological strategy fits in with a more general 'niche marketing' corporate strategy, and it is usually smaller companies in a large and expanding market which apply it.

Market creation strategy

The company may be in the position to create a completely new market because of technological advances facilitating the development of entirely new products. This strategy has the advantage of there being little initial competition and so can be very profitable. However, as Twiss observes, these opportunities are comparatively rare.

Maverick strategy

A '**maverick strategy**' is one which is applied to a product which, owing to technological advances, will reduce the total market size for the old product. This strategy is best explained by an example, adapted from one quoted in Twiss.

Compton Parkinson developed and introduced the long-life bulb into the market. Compton Parkinson was not a market leader and had no great dependence on the old shorter life bulb and so it suffered no great loss from the subsequent reduction in the light bulb market. Osram, however, was a market leader, but did not attempt to develop a revolutionary new type of light bulb as they were already heavily committed to the old type and would only harm themselves if they introduced such an innovation.

A maverick strategy, therefore, allows a company to apply new technology to someone else's market, so benefiting their own company but harming others in the market with a subsequent reduction in total market size. This type of strategy will succeed in the long run only if the company follows its maverick strategy with an offensive strategy to retain its technological lead over the competition.

Acquisition of personnel

Rather than licensing to gain a competitor's innovations, a company could instead try to 'poach' the opposition's personnel. This strategy is not regarded as being wholly ethical by many companies, even though it is a relatively low cost method of acquiring technology and can prove to be very fruitful. A company cannot, however, base its whole strategy on being able to acquire personnel from the opposition. A further problem, if one reflects upon this approach, is the fact that such personnel will tend to rate low on loyalty and will probably be equally likely to leave your company if they are given a better offer to go elsewhere.

Acquisition of companies

An alternative to acquiring personnel is to acquire the whole company, through either a takeover or a merger. Small companies tend to be highly creative, entrepreneurial and strategically offensive. They do, however, have limitations regarding research and development funds, and may not be very effective in production and marketing. This makes such companies attractive and relatively easy targets for large companies who are less likely to create such innovation and adopt such offensive strategies themselves. The takeover of an already established small company is also much less of a risk to the large company than trying to develop the technology itself.

As we can see from the Twiss typology of innovation strategies, there are a number of alternatives for achieving innovation objectives. Clearly the overall innovation strategies adopted have a major bearing on the focus of new product development and the means of achieving product innovation. Once again, the selection of appropriate innovation and new product development strategies will depend on a host of factors, including company, competitor and customer considerations. However, a key input to innovation strategies and decisions is technology itself, and in particular the way that technology is developing and/or is likely to change in the future. No discussion of innovation, and particularly the formation of innovation strategies, would be complete, therefore, without some consideration of technological forecasting.

Although all of the strategies for innovation suggested by Twiss can be found in today's marketplace there is no doubt that in recent years licensing strategies have been very popular.

The Dutch company, Philips, in particular have pursued this strategy to good effect. Philips have a very strong technology and innovation base and have been responsible, therefore, for many of the most successful 'new-to-world' products. Examples of Philips' inventions range from the cassette tape through to the laser disc. Leading consumer goods companies throughout the world, including Sony and others, have been allowed to license Philips' technologies, and as is the intention with licensing, to the benefit of both parties.

Technological forecasting

Few companies would consider making decisions about investment without considering what the future might hold and how it might affect the profitability of the proposed investment. The allocation of corporate funding to innovation is an investment decision, i.e. committing resources now with a view to a return in the future. In addition, that future is likely to be very different from the circumstances which pertain today, particularly with respect to the nature and performance of future technologies. The pace of technological change, which we have so often referred to, and the high risk and high cost of developing new products means that, however difficult, some effort to forecast the future with respect to technology is essential.

What to forecast?

Perhaps the first issue in considering technological forecasting is the question of what, actually, we need to forecast. As with any forecast – sales, the weather or economic forecasts – the purpose of a forecast is to improve decision making. A technological forecast might be used to make better decisions in one or more of the following areas:

- Levels of research and development spend
- Overall innovation strategy – offensive vs. defensive
- Allocation of resources to specify product innovation programmes – which technologies to invest in.

In order to help in these and other innovation related decisions, the decision maker would ideally like to know the answers to the following four questions:

1 'What will be the nature of future technology as it relates to my business?' – a *qualitative* aspect.
2 'What will be the performance level of future technology?' – a *quantitative* aspect.

3 'What time-scale are we talking about, or when will it happen? – a *temporal* aspect.
4 'What is our assessment of the likelihood of the events described in the first three questions?' – a *probability* aspect.

Armed with the information which the answers to these four questions provides, the decision maker will be in a far stronger position to make informed (and therefore better) decisions about innovation. The techniques of technological forecasting are aimed at generating this sort of information.

Techniques of technological forecasting

The techniques of technological forecasting are many and varied. We confine this section to a brief description of the more frequently used categories, together with an indication of their relative merits and drawbacks, as detailed overview of forecasting and its implications for the process of marketing planning is provided in Chapter 14.

Trend extrapolation This is one of the simpler techniques of technological forecasting. It consists of using past technological trends to predict future levels of performance in a technology. Imagine, for example, that we are concerned to predict likely levels of future performance in computing technology, where 'performance' is measured in terms of 'speed of calculation'.

The first step is to ascertain what the past trend in this performance parameter has been, plotting past trends in this performance over time. As with the time series analysis method of sales forecasting, the performance figures over a time period will fluctuate, but beneath this is a trend which the forecaster wishes to know in order to apply the forecast. If improvements in technological performance do not follow a trend then it is impossible to forecast the future using past performance, but there is considerable evidence to show that technological progress does indeed tend to follow a regular pattern or trend when performance is plotted over time. The essence of the extrapolation technique is illustrated in Figure 7.4.

In using trend extrapolation for technological forecasting, care should be taken with respect to three factors:

1 *Selection of the parameter of performance*
   Care should be taken to ensure that the performance characteristic selected is one which truly does represent the 'correct' measure of 'functional' performance, i.e. one which is not technology specific and is related to the needs of the marketplace.
2 *Sufficient and accurate historical data*
   As with any forecasting technique which relies on past data to predict the future, forecasting accuracy relies on both the quantity and quality of this past data.
3 *Factors which may cause discontinuities in the shorter-term trend*
   While there may be substantial continuity in the long-term progress of technological performance, in the shorter term (say over one to five years) there can be substantial discontinuity. The 'race' to put a man on the moon in the early 1960s (possibly for political reasons) hastened the development of many technologies, as increased resources were devoted to this aim.

Overall, the merit of this technique of technological forecasting is that it is relatively straightforward to understand and apply. The major disadvantage of the technique is that it provides only the quantitative and temporal aspects of information on new technology that the decision maker requires.

Figure 7.4
Trend extrapolation
forecasting.

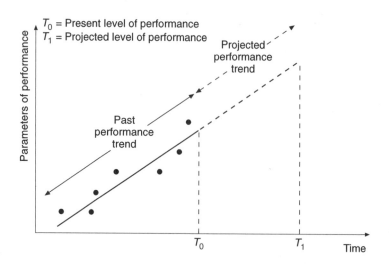

 Delphi forecasting   In **Delphi forecasting** the forecaster recruits a team of experts in the technology and, using a questionnaire, solicits their opinions as to likely future technological developments. The questions may relate to matters of a technological breakthrough (such as new developments in pollution-free engines or the treatment of cancer). In addition, the respondents may also be asked to predict likely time-scales, levels of performance, and estimates of probability.

This method of forecasting can be used to provide answers to all of the four questions which the forecaster would ideally like answered. Another advantage of this method is that the respondents do not meet face to face (as in a committee). Therefore, any 'bandwagon' effect of majority opinion is eliminated.

A Delphi forecast is normally 'played' in a number of rounds. Once the original (first round) questionnaires have been circulated and completed, the results are summarized and then re-circulated to the respondents who are then asked to reconsider their forecasts in the light of the summarized results. The questions themselves may become more pointed as a result of feedback. The rounds of questioning continue until a consensus emerges and/or sufficient useful information is available to make effective innovation decisions.

The advantages of Delphi relate to the fact that it can provide information relating to all of the four areas in which the decision maker is interested. The major disadvantages are associated with difficulties in designing an unambiguous set of questions, and with the selection of the panel of experts.

 Scenario writing   This first became widely known through the work of 'think tanks' such as the Hudson Institute in the United States. Now many companies have such 'think tanks' where a team of experts is responsible for forecasting possible future technological developments based on a wide-ranging technological and environmental analysis.

Normally a number of possible scenarios will be generated, each one then being considered further with respect to probabilities and implications. Scenarios considered highly probable and with a significant projected impact on the organization – e.g. a future technological and/or market threat – may form the basis of research and development programmes.

Relevance trees   These are used systematically to explore all the possible routes to achieving given stated technological objectives. The process starts by defining the desired objectives and then tracing backwards to determine possible viable routes for achieving the objective, and the implications for research and development. A

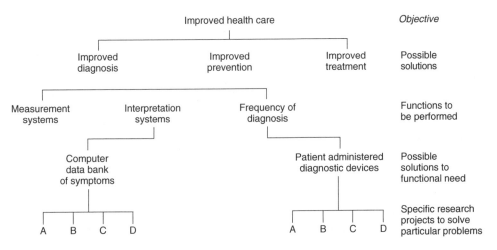

Figure 7.5
A relevance tree for improved health care.

simplified example is shown in Figure 7.5, where the stated objective is 'improved health care' by a computer company which is involved in this market.

Needless to say, a complete relevance tree will be much more complex than this simplified version. The relevance tree approach can be used:

● To explore the feasibility of various technological decisions
● To establish the optimum research and development programme according to feasibility, cost and timing considerations
● To determine and select between detailed research projects.

These are just a few of the variety of techniques of technological forecasting. Our discussion has been necessarily brief regarding this somewhat specialist area though we have described how it might be used in delineating strategies for innovation. Technological forecasting remains somewhat under-utilized in innovation planning, especially in British and European companies. Certainly the techniques have their limitations, but in the future more and more companies are likely to have to use them if they are to cope with a technologically uncertain future.

Developing and launching new products

So far we have set the background to new product development decisions. Not all innovation strategies will involve the in-house development of new products, but where this route is selected our evidence on successful new product development suggests that a systematic approach to this process is essential. The following sequence of steps in new product development is that proposed by Kotler[10] and enables us to outline some of the key marketing issues involved at each stage of developing a new product:

● Idea generation
● Idea screening
● Concept development and testing
● Marketing strategy development
● Business analysis
● Product development
● Market testing
● Commercialization.

Idea generation

Good ideas are the life blood of new product development. Clearly this raises the question 'What constitutes a "good idea"?', but our evidence on the mortality rates involved in developing new products means that we often need a lot of ideas before we are likely to find one which constitutes a market winner. Cannon[11] suggests that the willingness and ability to effectively tap as many sources as possible, both internal and external to the organization, is a major factor in the successful management of new product development. Two key aspects are involved in increasing the number of ideas for new products, namely:

1   An effective scanning process for new ideas which systematically collects ideas for possible new products from the widest range of sources possible.
2   The use of the techniques of 'creativity' to encourage idea generation.

Although both these approaches should be used to generate ideas, the adoption of creativity techniques, such as lateral thinking, synectics and brainstorming, despite their potential, have as yet not achieved widespread acceptance in industry. Hence we shall concentrate on the 'scanning' element of idea generation.

Scanning for new ideas: sources

As mentioned earlier, scanning for new ideas should encompass both internal company sources and external sources. The most obvious, and indeed primary, sources of new product ideas in an organization are those departments primarily, in one way or another, charged with this responsibility. They include:

●   Technical departments – primarily research and development and/or design departments
●   The marketing department
●   In some organizations, the new product development department.

In some ways, however, it is sources of ideas outside of those 'responsible' departments which represent some of the potentially richest and frequently untapped sources of new product ideas. Some of these other sources are now outlined.

Employees

Beyond marketing, research and development, and new products, there are usually many employees with substantial potential for being helpful as sources of new product concepts. Sales personnel are an obvious group, but so are manufacturing, customer service, packaging and, in the case of the general consumer, any person who uses the products. These people need to be told that their ideas are wanted, and special mechanisms must usually be constructed to gather these ideas.

Although employee suggestion systems do turn up ideas, the most useful suggestions come from employees whose work brings them in contact with the customers and their problems. Sales people know when a large order is lost because the firm's product is not quite what the customer wanted. Complaint-handling departments also become familiar with consumers' use of products.

Dun & Bradstreet, with a good new product track record, was recently reported as stating that most of its new product ideas came from field personnel. Eligible Dun & Bradstreet personnel can receive significant financial rewards for suggesting an idea that goes national[12].

Customers

By far the most productive source of external new product concepts is the customer or user of the firm's products or services, though their ideas are usually only for product improvements. Many approaches are used to gather consumer ideas, but the most popular are 'on street' and mail surveys, continuing panels and special focus groups.

Resellers

Depending on the industry, brokers, manufacturers' representatives, industrial distributors, large jobbers and large retail firms may be worthwhile information sources. Many industrial agents are so skilled that they serve as industrial advisers to their clients.

Suppliers/vendors

Large suppliers near to the beginning of the production chain often provide advice to their customers. For example, many manufacturers of plastic housewares are small and look to the large plastic firms for advice. Virtually all producers of steel, aluminium, chemicals, metals, paper and glass have technical customer service departments which give advice to their customers.

Competitors

Competitors' activities are of interest, and competitors' products may be an indirect source of a leap-frog or add-on new product. Leaf[13] suggests a five-step approach to studying competitors' products:

1   Purchase the competitive product.
2   Tear down the product, literally: remove every nut, bolt and weld, and get back to the basic pieces.
3   Reverse engineer the product: while tearing down the product, figure out drawings, parts lists and manufacturing methodology.
4   Build up the costs: using available labour, material and overhead costs, estimate exactly what it cost the competitor to make.
5   Establish economies of scale: given known and estimated production runs combined with selling prices, estimate the competitors' profits.

Miscellaneous

Among the many other sources of new ideas to the firm are the following:

- Consultants
- Advertising agencies
- Market research companies.
- Universities/colleges
- Research laboratories
- Governments
- Printed sources.

As a penultimate point on scanning for ideas, it is worthwhile mentioning that appropriate records for all ideas put forward, but not used, should be kept, since they may be of value in the future.

Finally, we should note that although we have been concerned here to discuss ways of generating more ideas for new products, it is important to note that the quality as well as the quantity of ideas is important. The ideas need to be relevant to overall corporate objectives and strategies. Crawford[14] has suggested the notion of a 'product innovation charter' to ensure that idea generation is conducted within this framework. The product innovation charter specifies, as a prelude to idea generation, the goals of new product development, the product/market areas to which new product development should be aimed, and the corporate objectives towards which the new product development programme should contribute.

Idea screening

The second stage in new product development is the preliminary assessment of ideas with a view to determining which should be dropped and which retained for further development. This crucial step is normally referred to as 'product screening'.

Screening of new product ideas using suitable research techniques is a means of increasing the quality of managerial decisions, since selection based on judgement is more likely to result in two sorts of error as follows:

1 A company may make a *drop-error*, i.e. fail to develop an idea with potential. The losses due to such errors are frequently unquantifiable.
2 A *go-error* occurs when the company lets a poor idea proceed to further development and commercialization.

The risk element in new product decision making can never be eliminated. New product screening methods are used to reduce the risk, but are nevertheless imperfect since there is always an element of judgement. The use of pre-specified screening criteria and product idea rating systems, i.e. a formal screening approach, can help. Below are two of the more frequently used screening techniques.

Criteria checklists

The simplest form of screening technique is the use of a checklist of all the criteria to be taken into account in evaluating the product:

- Corporate objectives, strategies and values
- Marketing criteria
- Financial criteria
- Production criteria.

Each one of these broad areas is then broken down into a number of sub-criteria for evaluation, e.g.:

Marketing criteria

- Extent of clearly defined market need
- Estimated size of market
- Estimated product life
- Competitive position
- Estimated launch costs.

Profiling or merit number systems

A development of the checklist approach is the use of either profiling, or merit number systems. Here the criteria to be used for assessment are given a numerical weighting according to their judged relative importance. Each new product idea is then scored against each of the pre-established criteria, say on a 1 to 10 basis, with 1 being a poor score and 10 the highest possible (i.e. a strong product idea). Scores and weightings are then multiplied to give an overall score for the product idea. A profiling system uses exactly the same approach but the weighted total scores against each criteria are presented in the form of a visual profile for each new product idea.

Comments on formal screening systems

The benefit of such formal systems is that they force assumptions (and prejudices, vested interests, etc.) about new products into the open. They also induce systematic – and, to some extent, more objective – appraisal of new product ideas, where over-enthusiasm and excitement can blind management to potential pitfalls.

Although we have discussed screening as the second stage in new product development, screening effectively takes place throughout the development of a new product, right up to (and after) launch. The idea of preliminary screening is to spot 'no win' products early, before development resources are wasted.

Effective screening, as we have seen, requires the consideration of a wide number of criteria. It is important to have a wide range of viewpoints and skills from different functions in the organization. Analysis of past failures points to the overenthusiasm of either research and development and/or marketing as a prime cause of 'go-errors'.

Concept testing

Crawford[15] suggests that there are a number of purposes associated with **concept testing**. Firstly, it tries to identify the sure loser so that it can be eliminated from further considerations. For some people this is the only use for concept testing. Secondly, presuming that the concept passed the first test, its second purpose is to get some estimate, even a crude one, of the sales or trial the product would enjoy. This has brought some contention amongst researchers to the subject.

Crawford states that the most common format for gathering respondents' reactions in purchase form is a five-point scale:

1   Definitely would buy.
2   Probably would buy.
3   May or may not buy.
4   Probably would not buy.
5   Definitely would not buy.

It is customary to combine the number of people who answered that they probably or definitely would buy and to use that number as an indication of group reaction. This is sometimes called the 'top-two-boxes' figure.

It is not particularly important whether precisely that many people would or would not buy the product. In the first place, the product that will eventually be offered will almost certainly be different from the description offered in the interview, as much development and further testing need to be done. However, if the firm doing the research has an inventory of percentages from past studies, the figure from the current study may provide a good indication.

Research methods in concept testing

However the specific data is phrased or analysed, the methods generally used for concept testing and development are neither new nor difficult. There are the following types:

Personal interviewing This can either be done by the customary personal interview survey or by the increasingly popular focus group. In a focus group, a creative researcher approaches a group of people in a controlled situation with a concept statement which is discussed or refined. According to its supporters, the focus group technique is a powerful tool in the new product development process and in the hands of a skilled researcher can be used to achieve an in-depth understanding of consumer behaviour, attitudes, perceptions and reactions to new product concepts.

Arising from the growing importance of concept testing, many researchers are using a sequenced system of interviewing. In this approach they start with several focus groups, themselves in a sequence from quite exploratory to confirmatory. Then for consumer products the testing is carried over into individual interviews in shopping arcades or homes, and for industrial interviewing the people involved in the buying decision are interviewed on site.

The point is that the research method is constructed differently to fit each situation, frequently varying considerably within a given firm.

Telephone interviews With today's computer-based interviewing technology, the quicker, cheaper telephone is tending to replace the traditional in-home personal interview. However, telephone focus groups have not yet been reported as being effective.

Mail Portfolios of concepts can be mailed to potential users, though sample selection and response are a great problem with this method. Some researchers have reported successful mail tests of new product concepts, especially where combined with a telephone follow-up.

The Internet Increasingly, the Internet is being used in researching new product concepts. The most obvious advantage of researching in this way is speed of response, but in addition the interactive nature of the Net allows new product concepts to be explored with a wider range of potential customers.

Information gathered in concept testing

Exactly what information should be gathered in a concept development study is entirely a function of the situation, but several general issues are suggested by researchers:

- Current practice in the category. Thus, for a new concept in an established product field, one would want to know how the customers responded to the old product.
- Attitudes towards current options. One would want to know not only what the

respondents like about what they are getting now, but their opinions on the options they reject.
- Any specific experience prior to this time that seems relevant to the concept about to be discussed.
- Do the respondents understand the concept?
- Reactions to the concept. This set of information can run quite deep, including positioning, hidden thoughts, probable uses visualized, reactions of others to the idea, further information wanted about it and the degree of use disruption.
- Changes that the respondent would make in the concept, even if in only rather vague verbal form.
- Comparative data to be used in relating this idea to others previously studied. Purchase intentions come in here, but so do many other scorings, e.g. how the concept compares with other current favourite types.

Advantages and limitations of concept testing

Crawford[15] summarizes many of the advantages and limitations of concept testing. Advantages of the concept test prior to proceeding further are:

1 It can be undertaken quickly and easily, well before prototypes are available.
2 It provides invaluable information for later decisions about the product, e.g. applications, user types, preferred attributes etc.
3 Proven market research technology exists.
4 It is reasonably confidential since small samples are taken and most concept particulars can be kept exclusive.
5 The truly bad idea is easily detached, particularly if there is one clear reason for it being so.
6 The research permits further orientation to buyer thinking, misunderstanding and prejudices.
7 Segments and positioning can be developed in tandem with the concept.

Notwithstanding these attributes, concept testing still has weaknesses:

1 Communication is treacherous. There are many opportunities for misunderstanding new items – newness, vague concepts and multiple attributes. Ziegler[16] suggests that one of the problems might be that traditional concept-testing techniques may not be effective for researching many of the new technology based products now coming onto the market.
2 One is never exactly sure of any one statistic when measuring.
3 People find it difficult to react to entirely new concepts without a learning period. The stimulus is very brief and any opinions given might thus not be a true reflection of reality.
4 The testing occurs long before marketing, so many variables in the situation may change by the time the product is marketed.
5 Considerable interview skill is required, especially in focus groups, though it looks deceptively simple. There is thus a danger of misinterpretation.
6 Certain attributes cannot be measured in a concept test, e.g. rug texture or softness produced by using a fabric conditioner.
7 It is very difficult to establish the validity or reliability of a concept test.
8 The testing procedure is somewhat false. It lacks a 'full' environment. People are asked to be judges and endorsers.

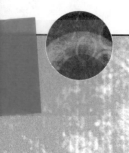

Concept testing for new products can be particularly difficult when the new product is unlike anything else on the market. In this situation it is very difficult for the consumer to have any frame of reference against which to judge the concept. Examples of products which fall into this category include the new wire-less mobile phones and the drink Red Bull, which was completely different to any of its predecessors on the market. Products like these require very careful attention to the context and application of concept testing techniques.

Marketing strategy development

If the results of the concept testing stage are encouraging, the next step in the new product development process is the formulation of preliminary marketing strategy plans for the product launch. Aspects covered by this would include:

- Preliminary marketing objectives
- Delineation of possible market targets
- Product positioning strategies
- Preliminary marketing mix decisions
- Preliminary budget estimates.

By now, the new product will have progressed to the stage where it is possible to assess more firmly its likely sales and profit potential. At this stage, few resources may have been committed to the project. However, the stage is rapidly being approached where further progress may involve substantial investment – including, for example, investment in pilot plant, the development of prototypes, and so on.

Before a decision can be made about the product development stage, a careful and detailed analysis of the business potential of the new product is required. If the results are satisfactory, the stages of product development and market testing, preceding market launch itself, will take place.

Business analysis

The ultimate measure of the success of any business venture is whether or not it generates profits. As far as possible, a company must be sure that the launch of a new product will contribute to the profitability of the firm. For this reason the company invariably conducts some analysis of the likely financial outcome as a central issue in the 'go/no go' situation.

The general approach to this business analysis is to compare alternative new projects, either with each other or some in-company standard, using criteria which give some suggestion of future profitability.

Like screening, business analysis is a process and not an event. Business analysis involves the estimation of likely sales and profit levels. This stage precedes the development of the product itself, so in later stages (and particularly in test marketing) initial estimates of the business potential of the product are likely to become firmer as the information on which to base the estimates becomes clearer. Product development will also enable more accurate cost estimates to be made, including direct and investment costs. Business analysis and test marketing can thus be thought of as a continuation of the screening process carried out earlier in the development of the product.

Business analysis requires that estimates be made for the product in three areas:

- Sales
- Costs
- Margins, profits, return on investment and cash flow.

Sales estimates   This is probably the most difficult of the estimates required in business analysis, but it is nevertheless an essential stage. The estimate of sales should include, in volume and value terms:

- Estimates of likely total market potential
- Estimates of company demand
- Time-scales (i.e. the pattern of sales).

As Kotler[17] points out, the sales pattern for products will vary according to whether the product is a once and for all purchase, an infrequently purchased product, or a frequently purchased product such as a fast-moving consumer food product. Some of the approaches referred to by Kotler for estimating sales of consumer durables and consumer non-durables have proved to be remarkably accurate.

Estimating costs   Cost estimates are usually easier to make than sales estimates – and usually more accurate. Companies nonetheless continue to underestimate the costs of product development (e.g. the Concorde aircraft development, which was estimated at £250 million and eventually cost £2,000 million). All costs need to be estimated, including direct costs, total investment costs, and overhead marketing costs. It is also important to estimate the timing of costs in order to plan cash flow. It is wise to build in a substantial contingency element in the estimation of both fixed and variable costs to reduce the impact and embarrassment of undercosting a new product development.

Margins, profits, return on investment and cash flow   Once sales and cost estimates have been made we can then estimate a number of financial aspects of performance. Not only should absolute profits be estimated, but so should the return on investment of the project. Conventional investment analysis techniques are applicable here including discounted cash flow and calculation of payback periods.

- *Payback period*
  This is defined as the time required to pay the initial investment and is calculated by summing predicted successive yearly net profits until the original outlay is exceeded. Provided the information is at hand, this technique is quick and simple to use. However, it does not take into account the likely life of the product and cannot be an adequate measure of profitability.
- *Return on capital*
  This is defined as the percentage annual net profit to the net assets employed in the product. The analysis is applied to each year of the forecasted life cycle and provides a means of direct comparison with alternative investment options. Account is then taken of the changing value of money over time.
- *Discounted cash flow*
  This technique takes into account the time value of money by, in effect, weighting

the value of cash flows by an amount which depends on when they occur in relation to the initial investment, i.e. money received during the early part of the life cycle is considered more valuable than that received years later. This technique has gained universal acceptance as a means of investment appraisal.

Often the conventional capital investment appraisal techniques give insufficient evidence to allow the decision maker to take the development decision to the next logical stage.

There is a significant and substantial difference between the venture capital required to set up the development and the working capital requirement needed to maintain the necessary levels of marketing activity after the launch stage. Projections for working capital needs are therefore vital.

It is essential also to consider the financial tension new product introductions can have upon the liquidity position of the company. There is a lagged effect during market development that can place companies into severe liquidity crises. This effect is attributable to the rate of growth.

Survival through innovation, growth and competitive advantage as an interactive triangle, bounded by time, cannot be ignored. The financial implications of innovation and new product development in simple terms calls for a clear understanding of (1) start-up capital needs and (2) working capital required to stay in business. It is vital that a cash budget is therefore developed to forecast incomes and expenditures pertaining to the project and which impact upon the company's entire product portfolio.

Pre-tax profits, i.e. the bottom line, and return upon capital invested are goals for achievement. The means of their achievement is through an effective budgetary control system with coincident variance analysis based upon the forecasted cash needs of the project to survive and achieve growth. Cash flow forecasting is therefore essential.

Margins are often eroded through an inability accurately to determine costs and cost behaviour in relation to output. A clear comprehensive understanding of fixed and variable costs in relation to projected levels of performance is equally vital to establish a financial control climate within which the new product development communication process can be nurtured.

Absolute profits are often disappointing in the short term. Therefore, objectives have to be set clearly in relation to the time horizons of the development plan to monitor progress towards targeted profits.

Early attention to these aspects of financial control is advised to provide an effective balance between marketing enthusiasm and the requirements to achieve and maintain a statutory financial position for the enterprise.

Product development

If business analysis points to a favourable decision, the next major step is product development. Investment in the development of the product will now rise substantially. Once a physical product – for example, a prototype – has been developed, further testing, both technical and consumer, should be carried out. Even at this stage an objective and critical view needs to be taken about further investment in the product.

Test marketing

The penultimate stage before full scale commercialization and launch is test marketing. In test marketing the new product is tested in a way which involves the consumer purchasing in a 'normal' shopping situation. This process is therefore conducted towards the end of the development process when the concept, product and marketing strategy are at a relatively refined stage. The principal objective of the test marketing exercise is, as with other forms of new product research, the reduction of risk in any subsequent decisions that are made.

The need for this expensive research must be carefully considered. Jobber[18] suggest that the overall purpose of test marketing is:

To reduce the risk of a costly and embarrassing national launch mistake.

In a somewhat unusual context for new products, one of the most embarrassing launches in recent years was that of British Airways new tail fin designs. British Airways felt that it was time to move away from the traditional red, white and blue British flag design on their aeroplane tail fins, replacing them with a series of ethnic and abstract designs designed to appeal to a more cosmopolitan and global flying public. The result was felt by many to be a public relations disaster. Although the concept had been researched, and it would admittedly have been difficult to conduct true test marketing in this situation, a smaller-scale roll-out of the new designs would probably have quickly established that consumer reaction to them was unfavourable.

The major argument in favour of test marketing is that it measures consumer behaviour in a real situation. The results give an indication of overall consumer response to the marketing mix, whereas product testing measures only individual aspects. Test marketing also removes the major problem in all product research, which is that the consumers know that they are being studied, and this alters the response accordingly.

By definition, the exercise takes place in an area substantially smaller than that covered by the market. Choice of area is dependent on the nature of the product. Since the objective is to create a scaled down version of the national launch, test markets for products developed by major companies in the consumer field generally take place in areas defined by the target market coverage. Test marketing is a theme to which we return in Chapter 13.

Increasingly, companies are looking to cut the costs (and time-scale) of market testing by using laboratory test or simulated market tests. In industrial product markets product user tests and/or dealer tests are common.

Commercialization

The final stage of new product development is 'commercialization', or bringing the product to the market. Kotler et al.[19] point out that if the company goes ahead with commercialization, it is likely to begin to incur its highest costs, involving as it does investment in both plant and production and marketing costs. As a consequence, even more care and planning is required if the product is to succeed: many otherwise excellent products have failed because of an inadequately managed launch phase.

Amongst the key questions to be addressed at the launch stage are the following:

1   *When to launch?*
    Timing of new product launches is critical. Too early and the market or product may not be ready; too late and the opportunity may have passed or a competitor has arrived in the market.

2 *Where to launch?* (coverage)
A major decision at the launch stage is the geographical coverage of the launch. For example should we launch on a local/regional basis first or should we instead go national or even international?

In fact, the 'where' decision involves the selection and timing of areas for launch. In some cases it pays to go first for the more profitable segments of the market only. In others, circumstances will dictate an all-over launch attack to cover the whole market simultaneously. Critical to this decision is the existence – or absence – of competitors (how quickly can they or might they move in?) and company resources.

3 *How to launch?* (launch plans)
By this stage a detailed plan of attack for the launch should be drawn up, including sales forecasts, budgets, allocation of resources and detailed timings. Most important of all, perhaps, at this stage is an understanding of target markets and the processes of *diffusion* and *adoption*.

It is vital to get these key issues at the launch stage right as they provide the platform on which the product's future performance will be built. In addition, as Green *et al.*[20] have shown, changes to the product's competitive position after entry may be very difficult and expensive to achieve. Because of this, Green and her colleagues have developed what they called 'An Entry Strategy Performance Model' (Figure 7.6 below) which attempts to capture what they feel are some of the key determinants of performance for a new product and which must therefore be considered at the entry and commercialization stage.

(a) *Adoption*

The '**adoption** process' relates to the stages:

- Awareness
- Interest
- Evaluation
- Trial
- Purchase.

that every prospect for a new product has to pass through in the buying perceptions of the consumer. These are important processes when we aim our initial marketing and, more importantly, what we say or stress in our marketing communications. If a prospect has already passed through the awareness stage of adoption, then our advertising copy must seek to encourage interest in the product or brand.

Individuals differ in their attitudes towards new product acceptance. Of particular interest and relevance to the new product market are the '**innovator**' and '**early adopter**' categories, because by definition these are the first to adopt new products and services and so represent prime market targets.

Despite considerable research, little evidence has emerged to support the notion of a generalized attitude to innovativeness, i.e. it tends to be product specific. However, if a company can identify likely innovators within a product market, initial marketing programmes should be targeted at this group.

(b) *Diffusion*

Diffusion processes relate to the speed and extent to take-up of a new product. In most circumstances the new product marketer is interested in securing the widest take-up at

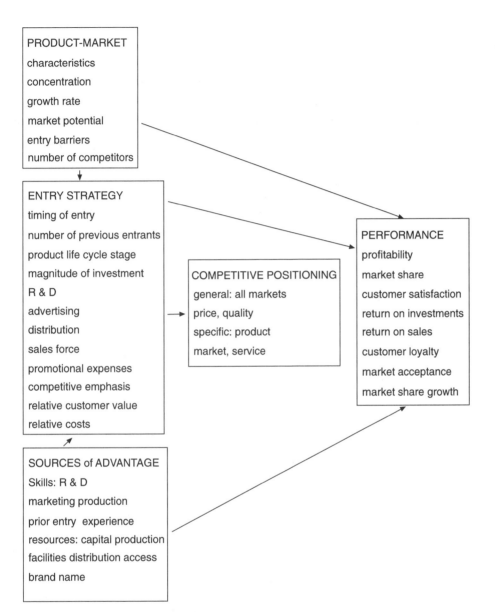

Figure 7.6
An entry strategy
performance model.
Source: Green, D.,
Barclay, D. W. and
Ryans, B., 'Entry strat-
egy and long-term
performance: conceptu-
alization and empirical
examination'. *Journal of
Marketing*, October
1995, Volume **59**, 4, p.
6.

the highest possible rate. Clearly, diffusion is related to the adoption process of individual customers, but five particular product characteristics will tend to favour a more
rapid and extensive adoption (and therefore diffusion process):

- *Relative advantage:* The greater the perceived advantage of the new product to
  customers, the faster it will diffuse.
- *Compatibility:* The greater the extent to which the new product is compatible with
  existing customer lifestyles, values and uses, the faster it will diffuse.
- *Complexity:* the more complex the new product is to understand or use, the slower
  will be its rate of diffusion.
- *Divisibility:* the ability of the new product to be tried or used on a limited scale

before full commitment, the faster it will tend to diffuse.

- *Communicability:* the easier it is for the advantages or features of the new product to be demonstrated or communicated by early purchasers to other potential purchasers, the faster will be the rate of diffusion.

Recent developments and thinking in new product development and innovation

Perhaps as we should expect, in an area of marketing which by its very nature is characterized by change, in recent years a number of key developments have been taking place regarding the management of new product development and innovation. In part, these developments reflect improvements in our knowledge regarding the key factors in managing this process more successfully, and in part, they reflect changes in the competitive and market environment. Some of the more important of these developments are outlined below.

Design and new product development

The design of a product is now a major source of product differentiation in an increasingly competitive market place. The importance of design in new product success has of course long been recognized by some, however, perhaps not since the 1930s has design been more strategically used to gain advantage in the market place. Block[21] has suggested that a distinctive design can render older competitors obsolete and make later competitors appear shallow copies. He also suggests that more durable product designs can have an impact on both users and non-users for many years. To be durable a product design does not have to be complicated, a good product design is one which satisfies the needs of the customer and makes a product eye-catching in the marketplace.

In addition to being one of the principal means of differentiating a company's products from those of its competitors the product design process also determines product attributes such as functional capabilities and product lifespan. Similarly, the life cycle cost of a product is significantly influenced by how it is designed. Product design affects ease of manufacture and product serviceability. Simplifying product designs results in many benefits and not only reduced costs but the marketing benefits of improved quality and potentially shorter product development lead time. Lee and Sasser[22] have suggested that the total cost of producing and delivering a product is largely determined by the design of the product itself. At the time of design completion only 5 per cent of the budget for new product development may have been spent, but 80 per cent of the remaining budget has been committed through the design.

 How products are designed has changed significantly in recent years. Customer focused designs are replacing the expensive, slow, and above all, product oriented engineer dominated design processes of the past. Neff[23] has proposed that **quality function deployment** (QFD) be introduced to ensure customers' ideas are incorporated into the product design process from the outset. Marketing of course, has the responsibility of relating customer requirements to technical departments including design, so in a well run organization, marketing research should be used to evaluate the marketability of new designs at an early stage. Customer requirements in fact should be translated into technical requirements at each stage of product development but it is at the early design stages that they are most important. Competitive benchmarking is also an approach which can be used to ensure that proposed new product designs improve on those of competitors in aspects which have greatest importance and value to customers. The effect of quality function deployment in an organization requires potentially far-reaching changes in how a company operates with respect to design and new product development. In essence it requires different functional groups to interact simultaneously to identify and solve problems and hence much greater teamwork and communication, particularly between marketing and design functions is required. An example of how quality function deployment can be used in the new product design and development process is outlined by Lockomy and Khurana[24]. In particular, they stress the significance of the role of quality function deployment in integrating functions horizontally through the process of design and new product development. This notion is illustrated in Figure 7.7 below.

It is suggested that one of the key advantages of implementing a system of quality function deployment is that 'a pioneer' in a market can charge premium prices in the early years of a product's lifecycle, then use process improvement initiatives to generate savings in later years.

Overall the effective management of the design process is essential if products are to compete successfully in the marketplace. More and more companies have come to realize this and have elevated their design function to a more important role in the overall process of innovation than that afforded it in previous years.

Speed and flexibility in the new product development process

With competitive environments changing so rapidly, and in particular with changes in markets, technologies, and user needs, as we have already seen, causing product life cycles to become even shorter, there is an increased premium on speed and flexibility in managing new product development. Because of this, companies have sought to find ways of improving their performance with respect to both these attributes. The most important way in which companies have sought to increase their performance in the speed and flexibility in new product development has been to move from the traditional sequential approach to product design and development to one which is characterized by shorter overlapping phases between the different stages of new

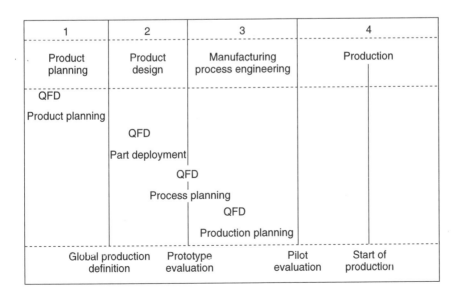

Figure 7.7
Product development cycle and quality function deployment (QFD) key events.
Source: Lockomy, A. and Khurana, A., 'Quality function deployment in new product design' *International Journal of Quality and Reliability Management,* **12,** 6, 1995, p. 75.

product development and with interaction and feedback from cross-functional and multi-functional areas. Takeuchi and Nonaka[25] have suggested an holistic approach to new product development where several phases of development overlap. This idea is shown in Figure 7.8 below.

With the sequential approach to product development the new product goes through each phase in a step-by-step manner, moving from phase to phase only after all the requirements of each phase have been completed. The 'Type B approach' shown in Figure 7.8 has moved from the traditional sequential approach to a process where development overlaps at the borders of each phase. The final truly holistic approach shown in Type C of Figure 7.8 is where the different phases of product development run together. This inevitably means an end to functions being specialized where marketing examines the customer needs, engineers select the design, and production are asked to build the product. Instead of this process which is akin to running a relay race with each function passing the baton from one to another, rather the new product development process is organized around multi-functional teams who take charge of the product development process, developing products, manufacturing processes, and marketing plans simultaneously to collapse time. The increased speed of product development which this can give rise to can represent a major source of competitive advantage. For example, Ray[26] cites the case of Canon. In the early 1980s Canon's top management set an objective of reducing product development cost and time by 50 per cent. Ultimately, Canon reduced its development costs by 30 per cent and achieved its objective of reducing time to market by the 50 per cent figure. This enabled Canon to increase its market share by 10 per cent over a ten-year period. Similarly, when Yamaha threatened Honda's leadership in the motorcycle market, Honda unleashed 30 new motorcycle models within a six month period, effectively thwarting the Yamaha threat.

Similarly, Brassington and Pettitt[27] cite the example of Renault. By bringing all of the new product development activities for a new model into what they refer to as a 'technocentre', Renault reduced both the time and the costs of new product development. Brassington and Pettitt suggest that costs for Renault have been cut by up to 25 per cent and development times for new products reduced from nearly eight years to just three.

Inter-company collaboration in new product development

As many products become more complex and their design and manufacturing demands more and more resources, some companies are increasingly turning towards collaboration for the development of new products. Each of the collaborating companies concentrates on those activities which reflect their competencies, the product develop-

Figure 7.8
Sequential (A) versus overlapping (B and C) phases of new product development.
Source: Adapted from Takeuchi, H. and Nonaka, I., 'The New Product Development Game,' *Harvard Business Review*, **64**, 1, p. 139.

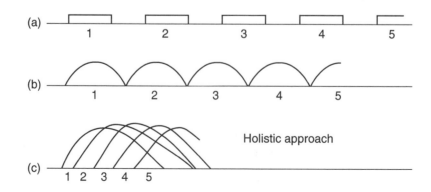

ment process therefore is shared between the different members of the supply chain. Collaboration is increasingly being promoted as an effective strategy in dealing with some of the more problematic aspects of the product development process. Littler and Leverick[28] suggest that collaboration offers the means to secure access to technologies, skills or information, to share the costs and risks of product development and once again reduce the time taken to develop products. Styles[29] contends that the pooling of resources and capabilities can generate synergistic growth between organizations, either in terms of developing a current product or service offering, or through the creation of an entirely new venture. Collaboration between different companies for new product development has, as already suggested, when discussing licensing, been on the increase in recent years in addition to licensing, joint ventures or strategic alliances have been particularly prevalent and popular. This is particularly the case for new technology and therefore high cost/high risk products. Trott[30] suggests that collaboration for new product development is set to increase in importance in the future.

One of the most successful examples in recent years of a strategic alliance between companies to develop new technology and products is that between Kodak, Fujifilm, Minolta, Nikon, and Canon to develop the extremely expensive but ultimately extremely successful Advanced Photographic (APS) System. These companies combined to share the development costs up to the point where the technology was proven. They then went their separate ways in developing specific products and features on cameras incorporating the new technology. The technology would probably never have been developed unilaterally by the companies in the industry.

The Internet and new product development

We have already referred to the use of the Internet in the concept testing stage of new product development. Internet technology allows a much more flexible approach to the process of innovation but its biggest advantage is that the marketer can involve the customer in the process. In a way, this means that the Internet provides a basis for the introduction of the quality function deployment process referred to earlier. This interactive nature of the Internet enables the marketer to solicit customer participation in the product development process and at the same time reduce development times. The following represent some of the ways in which increased flexibility and customer involvement are achieved in new product development using the Internet:

- The database can be used to identify key innovators in the market. The company can then communicate with the selected customers so as to gain information about their particular needs and the implications of these for the product concept.
- Product concepts and the customer's response to these can then be fed into the design process and again the outcomes in the form of design options can be evaluated directly and immediately with customers.
- Ultimately, as product development progresses, customer needs can be integrated with technical solutions using both the Intranet and the Extranet to integrate the process and to encapsulate customer response as the project evolves.

Summary

In this chapter we have examined the product area of the marketing mix, including the crucial area of innovation and new product development.

We have seen that product decisions lie at the very heart of marketing strategy development. Product management starts with the management of existing products and includes decisions about product items, product lines and the overall product mix.

When it comes to innovation and new product development, the logic of the product life cycle provides the imperative for a constant search for new products. In short, companies must innovate or face decline. However, new product development is inherently risky and may in itself court disaster. We need therefore to be aware of the critical factors in successful innovation and follow systematic steps in the new product development process.

The importance of new product development in today's competitive environment has caused companies to look at ways in which the product development and innovation process can be improved. Because of this, in recent years we have seen several significant developments in this area of strategic marketing. In particular, companies have recognized the importance of the design function in new product development and in particular the importance of relating design to all the elements of new product development from manufacturing through to the final marketing of the product. Similarly, considerable attention has focused on how to reduce product development times, in particular through more effective teamwork and better sequencing through the new product development process. Thirdly, the increased cost and problems of new product development has led many companies to enter into collaborative ventures with other members of the supply chain to develop new and improved products. Finally, we have seen how the Internet is becoming increasingly important and useful in new product development. It is both helping to speed up and also qualitatively improve the process by facilitating consumer interaction and responses throughout the new product development process.

Key terms

Product item [p170]
Product line [p170]
Product mix [p171]
Line depth [p171]
Line width [p171]
Physical evidence [p175]
Process [p175]
New-to-world products [p176]
Interstitial strategy [p183]
Maverick strategy [p183]

Delphi forecasting [p187]
Scenario writing [p187]
Relevance trees [p187]
Screening [p191]
Concept testing [p192]
Adoption [p199]
Innovator [p199]
Early adopters [p199]
Diffusion [p199]
Quality function deployment [p201]

Questions

1 Using examples, explain each of the following terms:

   (a) Product item
   (b) Product line
   (c) Product mix.

2 Using examples, explain the different types of innovations which can be found in markets.
3 What are the possible alternative strategies for innovation?
4 What are the key steps in developing an launching new products?
5 What are some of the most important recent developments in the area of new product development and innovation?

References

1. Blythe, J., *Essentials of Marketing*, Financial Times Management/Pitman, London, 1998, Chapter 6.
2. Adcock, D., Bradford, R., Halborg, A. and Ross, C., *Marketing Principles and Practice,* 3rd edn, Financial Times Management/Pitman, London, 1998, p. 336.
3. Lancaster, G. A. and Massingham, L. C., *Essentials of Marketing*, 3rd edn, McGraw-Hill, 1993, p. 201.
4. O'Shaughnessy, J., *Competitive Marketing: A Strategic Approach*, 3rd edn, Unwin Hyman, Boston, 1995.
5. Freeman, C., Rothwell, R., Horsley, A., Jervis, V. T. P., Robertson, A. B. and Townsend, J., *Success and Failure in Industrial Innovation*, Centre for the Study of Industrial Innovation, University of Sussex, Brighton, 1972.
6. Morley, C., 'Set for a Splash', *The Grocer*, 3 April 1999, pp. 28–29
7. McKinsey & Co., 'Putting excellence into practice', *Business Week*, July 1980, pp. 20–32.
8. Twiss, B., *Managing Technological Innovation*, 4th edn. Pitman, London, 1996.
9. Crawford, C. M., *New Products Management*, 2nd edn. Irwin, New York, 1992, pp. 22–25.
10. Kotler, P., *Marketing Management: Analysis, Planning, Implementation and Control*, 9th edn. Prentice-Hall, New Jersey, 1997.
11. Cannon, T., 'New product development', *European Journal of Marketing*, **12**, 3, pp. 48–64.
12. Admec, R. T., 'How to improve your product success rate', *Management Review*, **70**, pp. 21–34.
13. Leaf, R., 'How to pick up tips from your competitors', *Director*, February 1978.
14. Crawford, C. M., *New Products Management*, 5th edn, Irwin, New York, 1997, pp. 64–85.
15. Crawford, C. M., *New Products Management*, 5th edn, Irwin, New York, 1997, Chapter 9.
16. Ziegler, B., 'Old market research tricks no match for new technology' *The Wall Street Journal*, November 1, 1999, p. 131.
17. Kotler, P., *Marketing Management: Analysis, Planning, Implementing and Control*, 9th edn, Prentice-Hall, New Jersey, 1997, pp. 323 324.
18. Jobber, D., *Principles and Practice of Marketing*, McGraw-Hill, Maidenhead, Berkshire, 1995, p. 308.

19. Kotler, P., Armstrong, G., Saunders, J. and Wong, V., *Principles of Marketing*, 2nd European edn, Prentice-Hall Europe, 1999, p. 622.

20. Green, D., Barclay, D. W. and Ryans, A. B., 'Entry strategy and long term performance conceptualisation and empirical examination', *Journal of Marketing*, October 1995, **59**, 4, pp. 1–16.

21. Block, P. H., 'Seeking the ideal form: product design and consumer response', *Journal of Marketing*, July 1995, **59**, 3, pp. 16–29.

22. Lee, H. L. and Sasser, M. M., 'Product universality and design for supply chain management', *Production Planning and Control*, **6**, 3, May/June 1995, pp. 270–277.

23. Neff, R., 'Number one and trying harder', *International Business Week*, December 2nd 1992, pp. 26–29.

24. Lockomy, A. and Khurana, A., 'Quality function deployment in new product design', *International Journal of Quality and Reliability Management*, **12**, 6, 1995, pp. 73–84.

25. Takeuchi, H. and Nonaka, I., 'The new product development game', *Harvard Business Review*, January 1986, **64**, 1, pp. 137–146.

26. Ray, M. B., 'Cost management for product development', *Journal of Cost Management*, Spring 1995, **9**, 1, pp. 52–59.

27. Brassington, F. and Pettitt, S., *Principles of Marketing*, 2nd edn, Pearson Education, Harlow, Essex, 2000, p. 365.

28. Littler, D., and Leverick, F., 'Joint ventures for product development: learning from experience', *International Journal of Strategic Management and Long Term Planning*, **28**, 3, 1995, pp. 58–68.

29. Styles, J., 'Collaboration for competitive advantage: the changing world of alliances and partnerships'. *International Journal of Strategic Management and Long Term Planning*, **28**, 5, 1995, pp. 109–112.

30. Trott, P., *Innovation Management and New Product Development*, Financial Times Management/Pitman, London, 1998, pp. 251–254.

Case Study

John Mackerel is disappointed. His company has just withdrawn its latest new product after three months of trying to market the product unsuccessfully.

The company markets a range of what could be termed 'lifestyle products' using a direct mail brochure. The company markets interesting and different consumer products, many of which have some kind of novelty value. So, for example, the company markets a rainwear range for dogs and cats, an automatic odour protection device for the bathroom, and a make-your-own birthday cards kit. In its outdoor product collection it markets a range of garden lights in the shape of garden gnomes, a self-erecting clothes drier, and a battery-powered flower seed collector. Its range of products now extends to over a hundred individual items including solar-powered nose-hair clippers and painless earwax removal systems.

Needless to say the company is always looking for new product ideas as the essence of keeping sales moving is novelty and interest.

The product just withdrawn after three months in the brochure was an extended toe-nail clipper whereby a person could cut his/her nails without having to bend down. Obviously not all new products succeed, but the disappointment for Mackerel is that this is now the tenth new product in a row which has failed and he is worried that the company is losing its touch.

New product ideas come from an in-house team, which comprises of the three directors of the company including Mackerel. All three directors have technical/engineering backgrounds. Customers are not consulted at the stage of idea generation as it is felt that

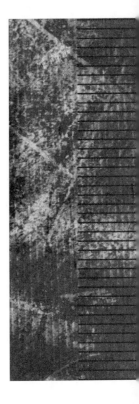

they would be unable to grasp many of the concepts at this early stage.

The idea-generation sessions take place on the last Friday of every month and usually result in ten to twenty ideas for new products. As the owner and founder of the company, Mackerel takes it upon himself to select which, if any, of these ideas should be taken further with a view to including them in the brochure. Mackerel uses his own judgement in this screening process; after all, the growth of the company has been down to his feel for the market.

Once a product idea is selected, Mackerel and his team find someone who can make the product and it is incorporated in a the brochure. Mackerel believes that the best test of a new product idea is whether it sells or not. Because of this, no market research is done between selecting a product idea and its inclusion in the brochure. However, a small sample of customers is contacted at random by mail and asked to complete a questionnaire regarding their views on the products in the brochure.

Mackerel is seriously worried about the recent product failures and is wondering if a different and perhaps more systematic approach to developing new products for the brochure might be appropriate. He is therefore looking for advice about what the company might be doing wrong and how it might improve its new product development procedures.

QUESTION

What are the strengths and weaknesses of this company's approach to developing new products for the brochure, and how might it improve its success rate for future new products?

8

Pricing strategies

Chapter objectives

After reading this chapter you will:

▶ Appreciate the strategic significance of pricing decisions in marketing strategy.

▶ Understand the approaches to pricing of the economist and accountant, together with their contributions and limitations in the context of setting prices.

▶ Apply a framework to pricing decisions based around the key inputs to these decisions.

▶ Understand the main pricing methods and their relative advantages and disadvantages.

Introduction

Price is a crucial element in competitive marketing strategy. The price of a company's products and services represents the vehicle for that company to achieve its financial objectives. It is through price and volume that revenue is generated. Price equates to the financial sacrifice that the customer is willing to pay to purchase the product or service desired.

Mercer[1] has no doubts about the role of pricing in marketing; he suggests that:

Pricing is probably the single most important decision in marketing. Perhaps this view is debatable but most would agree that pricing is certainly one of the most stressful decisions for the marketer.

One of the reasons why pricing should be such a stressful area for the marketer can, in part, be attributed to the considerable amount of uncertainty which is often associated with pricing decisions and strategy. Pricing is an important but complex area of decision making.

It is with a view to examining this complexity and, by way of analysis, reducing the uncertainty and stress associated with pricing decisions, that this chapter is aimed.

The pressures of today's market environment place increasing burdens on management. It is important, therefore, that the decision maker has a framework for making pricing decisions.

We start by examining briefly the traditional economist's view of price and pricing decisions to illustrate both the shortcomings and potential contributions of the economist's theory of pricing decisions as a prelude to discussing more strategic pricing approaches for the decision maker.

The economist's view of price and pricing decisions

Traditionally the economist has looked at price and pricing decisions from the perspective of price being determined by the interplay of demand and supply factors. At a broader level, the economist views prices and pricing decisions as an 'allocatory' mechanism, with prices being used as the signal to solve the basic problem of an economic society: namely, the allocation of scarce resources between competing users and individuals in that society in such a way that those resources are used in the most effective way. From the perspective of the price setter, traditional economic theory suggests that the 'optimum' price is that which equates marginal costs to marginal revenue so as to 'maximize' profits.

This summary of the economist's view of price and pricing decisions is most striking by its relevance, or rather lack of it, to the practising marketing manager. In short, although the economist has some useful concepts to offer the marketing manager when it comes to setting prices (for example the relationship between demand and price) much of what traditional economics has to offer in this area of decision making is not very helpful.

The main problems associated with the bringing together of the theoretical and practical side of pricing can, in the main, be explained by the apparent reluctance of the economist to take full cognizance of the implications associated with the setting of either a particular price, or an overall pricing strategy, when considered in the context of an organization and its overall corporate and marketing objectives.

Brassington and Pettitt[2] suggest that the economists' models of pricing do not take into account the reality of the marketing situation. Essentially, the economist's viewpoint is based on a set of assumptions which, in many cases, are unrealistic and hence would be difficult to apply in the business environment.

An example of such an assumption is when the individual customer is considering the price of a given product. Economic theory suggests that this customer will act in a totally rational economic manner, such that his or her total utility (or satisfaction) is maximized. In deciding whether or not to 'try' this product our 'totally rational' consumer will carefully equate whether or not buying the product at the asking price set will maximize his or her utility. In making this judgement, the economist 'assumes' that the consumer has 'perfect information' about both the prices and utility of all other competitive products in the market and that price is the only consideration in choice. Clearly these are unrealistic assumptions.

Another example of unrealistic, and hence unhelpful, assumptions is that which we mentioned earlier in our introductory summary of the economist's concepts of pricing; namely the assumption of 'profit maximization'. Although profits are of course an essential element of long-run survival in many organizations, and as such are likely to be enshrined in overall corporate and marketing objectives, these are much more likely to be couched in terms of a required level of profits rather than 'profit maximization'. More importantly, it is well known that there are many other objectives which a company might pursue through its pricing strategies. For example, if a company wanted to maximize market share or even wanted just to survive, a very different set of prices would be delivered than if the objective were to maximize profits.

Again, we can see that the assumptions of the traditional economist, in this case as to the objectives of the price setting exercise, are somewhat restrictive and hence potentially unhelpful to the practical price setter.

Set against this seemingly dismissive view of the economist's approach to price and pricing decisions is the fact that in some areas the economist has provided a number of useful concepts and tools for the marketing practitioner when it comes to making pricing decisions. In particular, as we shall see, the economist has made an important, if only partial, contribution to price setting in the area of the relationship between price and demand. Notwithstanding this contribution, it is perhaps hardly surprising that a gulf has opened up between the theoretical/economist viewpoint and the practical/marketing side of pricing. It is important, therefore, that we develop a structure for strategic pricing decisions which is helpful to the marketing manager and which can be implemented in the 'real world' of business.

We shall now turn our attention to what we consider to be the framework of such a structure.

A framework for pricing decisions: key inputs

The starting point for developing a useful pricing structure is the delineation of a framework for pricing decisions. Specifically, we need to establish the key inputs to pricing decisions. Although there are a myriad of possible considerations in arriving at a price for a product or service, the following are considered to be the key inputs for the pricing decision maker:

- Company and marketing objectives
- Demand considerations
- Cost considerations
- Competitor considerations.

We shall discuss each of these in turn.

Company and marketing objectives

As was mentioned earlier, pricing decisions are salient to the achievement of corporate and marketing objectives. Hence it is essential that pricing objectives and strategies are consistent with and supportive of these objectives. Alfred Oxenfeldt[3], in Table 8.1, illustrates both the potential range of pricing objectives and their clear relationship to overall corporate and marketing objectives.

This selection, from an even wider range of possible pricing objectives which Oxenfeldt delineates in this seminal article, illustrates the fact that the pricing decision maker must establish what objectives the pricing strategy is to achieve. We can also see that, according to the precise objectives, we might arrive at very different prices for our product and services. Where a company has multiple objectives, pricing strategies may need to consider trade-offs between different possible price levels such that these different objectives are met.

In addition to these broader corporate objectives, pricing decisions must also reflect and support specific marketing strategies. In particular, pricing strategies need to be in line with market targeting and positioning strategies, which were outlined in Chapter 5. Clearly, if a company produces a high quality product or service aimed at the top end of the market, with a prestige image, it would not make much sense (indeed it would probably be a major mistake) to set a low price on the product even if cost efficiency allowed this. Pricing therefore must be consistent with the other elements of the marketing mix and the selected positioning strategy. Effectively, the selection of company and market objectives, market targets and the formulation of a positioning strategy begin to constrain or delineate the range of pricing strategies and specific price levels.

A good example of how price must reflect and support the overall positioning strategy of the company is the price set for the Aston Martin DB7. The car is positioned at the top end of the market and with just 250 made and sold in the UK each year, needless to say the emphasis is on exclusivity. Most people of course associate Aston Martin with the James Bond character, again emphasising the racy and prestigious image intended.

Prices ... start at £85,000!

Table 8.1 Pricing and corporate/marketing objectives

Pricing to maximize long-run profits
Pricing to maximize short-run profits
Pricing to expand market share
Pricing to maintain a price leadership position
Pricing to discourage potential new entrants
Pricing to avoid the attention of government and legislators
Pricing to establish and maintain dealer loyalty
Pricing to improve corporate image
Pricing to improve the sales of weaker products
Pricing to discourage price wars

Demand considerations

Our second key parameter affecting pricing decisions is essentially customer based. The upper limit to the price to be charged is set by the market – unless, of course, the customer must purchase the product and we are the sole supplier. Effectively, then, at least in competitive markets, demand, i.e. the price which customers are both willing and able to pay, is a major consideration in the selection of pricing strategies and levels. As mentioned earlier it is in the analysis and interpretation of demand and demand schedules that the economist has much to offer the marketer in terms of concepts and techniques.

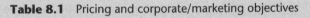
Ideally, the marketing manager needs to know the **demand schedule** for the products and services to be priced. The demand schedule relates prices to quantities demanded and can be illustrated by the use of a simple diagram, as shown in Figure 8.1.

Figure 8.1
Examples of simple demand curves.

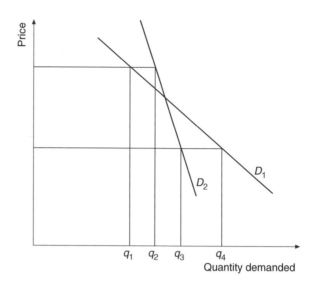

The demand curves in Figure 8.1 indicate the number of units which can be sold at any given price. In addition, the slope of the demand curve is directly related to the price sensitivity of demand. Demand curve D_1 in Figure 8.1 slopes less steeply than D_2 where demand is more price-sensitive. Even simple demand curves, therefore, represent potentially very powerful tools for the pricing decision maker, showing, as they do, both the number of units that can be sold at any given price and, of course, the effect on this quantity of any changes in price. However, price is only one of the determinants of the demand for a product or service. In addition to price, the following represent some additional factors which combine to determine demand:

- Income/budget of the purchaser
- Attributes of the product
- Tastes of the purchaser
- Price of other products
- The time factor.

Income/budget of the purchaser

The ability of the purchaser to buy products and services according to income levels and purchasing power converts the buyer's needs and wants into actual purchasing. The economist refers to this willingness *and* ability to purchase as 'effective demand'.

For an organizational buyer, the ability to purchase is directly related to budget requirements and constraints set on the purchaser.

Attributes of the product

Demand for a product or service, and indeed the price the customer is willing to pay, is related to the attributes of competitive products being offered. Demand for a product is therefore closely related to how the customer perceives the various attributes of competitive products. These attributes include physical/tangible attributes of the product or service in question: for example, quality features, packaging etc., and 'non-tangible' attributes, such as brand/corporate image and status.

Tastes of the buyer

Related to attributes, another factor affecting demand is the tastes of the buyer. Although a somewhat nebulous concept, nevertheless 'tastes' are a powerful influence on demand. Changes in taste can give rise to the growth of entirely new markets and indeed the total demise of mature ones. An illustration of this point is the growth in popularity of four-wheel drive cars over recent years.

'Tastes' can also be of an industrial nature with 'tastes' here being associated with such variables as the emphasis on productivity improvements, quality management and employee care and protection.

Price of other products

The price of competitive products is a key area affecting demand. Inevitably buyers tend to consider prices of substitute products when evaluating the effect of prices on demand. However, if the consumer has to spend more disposable income on 'essential' items due to increases in the prices of these items, e.g. food and mortgage repayments, then the effect on the consumer's disposable income demand for other apparently unrelated products can be affected. Clearly, in the case of substitute products, how the price of one good compares to the price of another is central to the selection process of the buyer.

The time factor

When discussing the demand for a product or service we must take into consideration the time factor, i.e. demand must be specified for a given time period. For example, it is conventional to distinguish between 'short', 'medium' and 'long run' time horizons when discussing demand. Certainly demand can, and does, vary over these different time periods. The time period must be explicit when evaluating demand concepts in the context of marketing.

From the perspective of the pricing decision maker, it is essential also to assess the sensitivity of demand. From our discussion of the slopes of the demand curves shown in Figure 8.1, you will recall that the slope of the demand curve indicates what the effect on quantity demanded will be for any given change in price. This effect is referred to as the *price elasticity* of demand. It is to the concept of 'elasticity' that we now turn our attention.

Elasticity of demand

One of the most important concepts of demand for the price setter is *elasticity*. In general terms, **price elasticity of demand** measures the magnitude of the responsiveness or sensitivity of the quantity demanded of a product to a given change in some demand determinant.

Elasticity can be expressed by:

$$E = \frac{\% \text{ change in quantity demanded}}{\% \text{ change in any demand determinant}}.$$

The demand for a product to be responsive, or not, to changes in price can be summarized as a function of:

- The number and closeness of substitutes
- The necessity of the purchase to the buyer
- The importance of product performance to the buyer
- The cost of switching suppliers.

The number and closeness of substitutes Of all the determinants of price elasticity of demand, this is probably the most important. If the product in question is in competition with a number of others which are similar in quality, perform similar functions and are being offered at a lower price, then it follows that demand for the lower priced product would be greater.

The marketer can modify the price-sensitivity of demand for the company's products and services by differentiating them from those of competitors. For example, the market can be 'desensitized' to differences in price by, say, better quality or improved packaging.

Unless a company is in a position both to compete and win purely on a price basis, every effort should be made to gain a competitive edge by differentiating products and services from close substitutes.

The market for detergents and cleaning products such as washing powders, washing up liquids, bleaches and so on, is one of the most competitive in the world. In an effort to avoid competing purely on a price basis, companies in this market have therefore made substantial efforts to differentiate their brands in some way from those of competitors.

A good example of a brand successfully differentiated from its competitors is Fairy Liquid. For many years Fairy Liquid successfully based its differentiation on its 'kindness' to the hands of the user. When other brands began to blur this differentiation through their marketing efforts, introducing their own claims for gentleness in use, Fairy Liquid switched the differentiation to one of the brand being long-lasting and therefore value for money compared to its competitors.

In this, as in many other markets, the marketer is constantly striving for new and credible ways to differentiate products and brands.

The necessity of the purchase Some product categories are essential purchases for the consumer, whereas others can be classified as luxuries. For example, food, water and electricity are 'essentials'. Total market demand for products and services in this category tend therefore to be less sensitive to changes in price than those products and services which we count as luxuries. We should note though that price-sensitivity for individual products and brands, even within the 'necessities' category, can be extremely price-sensitive where there are available substitutes. In addition, we should note that what is a 'luxury' for one consumer may be a 'necessity' (or utility good) for another, depending on their respective incomes, attitudes and lifestyles.

The importance of product performance In certain industrial markets, where the buyer is primarily concerned with the performance specifications of the product, demand will tend to be inelastic with regard to price. If a situation arises where the product fails and the buyer would suffer severe penalties in the form of cost, production time or convenience, then demand would be inelastic to price.

The cost of switching suppliers Hutt and Speh[4] have pointed to the importance of 'switching costs' in industrial markets. For example, in some situations an industrial user of a component part may align certain part specifications of its products to that of the supplier. The firm may have also made a heavy investment in tooling charges or in installing a supplier's equipment, e.g. a computer system. The cost here of turning to another supplier would clearly be prohibitive and not in the best interests of the purchasing organization.

Cross elasticity of demand

As far as demand is concerned, products can be related in any one of a number of ways. First, they may be competing products or substitutes, in which case, an increase in the purchase of one product may result in a decrease in the demand of another product. Next, when products are of a complementary nature, then an increase in demand for one product may result in an increase in demand for another product. Finally, when two products are of an independent nature then a purchase of one product will have no effect on the demand of another product.

Cross elasticity of demand is a measure for interpreting the relationship between products. Cross elasticity measures the percentage change in the quantity demanded of a product to a percentage change in the price of another product, shown by:

$$\Sigma xy = \frac{\% \text{ change in quantity of } y}{\% \text{ change in price of } x}.$$

Possible shapes of demand curves

In all instances, marketers need to be aware of the way in which customers react to a given price level. There are a number of possible shapes for demand curves. Each curve illustrates how a particular set of customers react to a change in price by plotting the price of the product against the level of sales of the product. In plotting these curves, all other factors are kept constant in line with the assumptions of the microeconomic theory of pricing. A variety of possible shapes for demand curves are shown in Figure 8.2 (a)–(d).

Figure 8.2(a) is our traditional economist's demand curve. Assuming 'rationality' on the part of consumers, the lower the price the higher the quantity demanded. In fact, many markets are characterized by this shape of demand curve.

Figure 8.2(b) also shows a frequently encountered demand curve, though one which is often not appreciated by the pricing decision maker who uses traditional economic principles. Here, lowering the price of a product increases demand up to a point, but below this threshold the desirability of the product and hence demand decreases due to the suspicion of 'poor quality' signalled by the lower prices. Of course, these suspicions may or may not be justified, but it is the customer's perception which counts.

Figure 8.2(c) shows a market where, regardless of the price charged, demand remains unchanged. This seemingly 'unrealistic' market situation is in fact characteristic of markets where the customer must purchase the product and where there is only one supplier of that product, i.e. a monopolistic situation.

Figure 8.2(d) illustrates a market where increased prices result in increases in demand. Markets where this might occur are those where the consumer is eager to signal that the product is affordable, the higher price being an indicator of the prestige and status of the buyer.

Figure 8.2
Possible shapes of
demand curves.

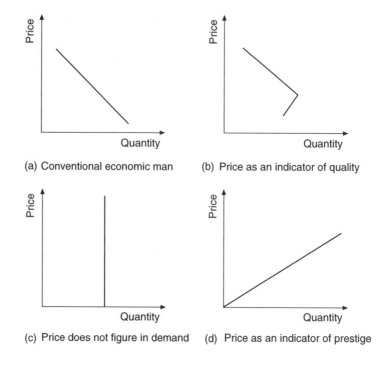

(a) Conventional economic man   (b) Price as an indicator of quality

(c) Price does not figure in demand   (d) Price as an indicator of prestige

In summary, demand and the understanding of price/volume relationships is crucial to pricing decision making. In practice, and particularly for new products, estimating these relationships can be difficult.

It is essential in analysing demand to examine the buyer's 'perception of value' as the key to demand and pricing decisions – a factor we shall return to later in this chapter.

Cost considerations

If demand considerations effectively set the upper limits to price, then cost considerations determine the lower limits. Accurate, relevant, up-to-date cost information is essential to form pricing strategy.

Accurate cost information allow the pricing decision maker to identify costs on a very specific basis directly related to each product, activity or customer. In this way, management is able to make informed decisions about pricing to target market segments.

Relevant cost information is information which is presented and analysed in such a way as to be pertinent and useful to marketing decision making. In particular, the cost analysis should enable the marketer to distinguish between fixed and variable costs and the relationship between these and volume. The importance and use of the distinction between fixed and variable costs can be illustrated by a simple breakeven chart, an example of which is shown in Figure 8.3.

 Fixed costs are those costs that do not vary with the level of output, and are therefore represented by the horizontal fixed cost curve in Figure 8.3. **Variable costs**, on the other hand, are those costs which are more or less directly related to production or sales. Increases in output or sales will lead to a proportional increase in these costs. Taken together, fixed and variable costs combine to give total costs, as shown in Figure

8.3. The remaining information contained in a breakeven chart is the revenue curve. This shows the total revenue which will accrue to the company at a given price-quantity combination.

The **breakeven point** is the point at which total revenue exactly matches the total costs, i.e. there is neither profit nor loss. This information on cost revenue relationships can be very useful to the pricing decision maker.

For example, one use of breakeven analysis is to compare the breakeven points associated with different possible prices for a product. This is shown in Figure 8.4. The

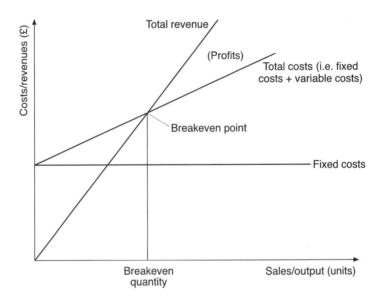

Figure 8.3
A simple breakeven chart.

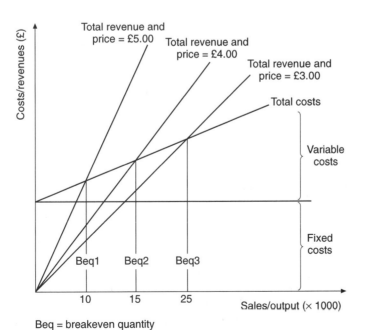

Figure 8.4
Breakeven versus different prices (not to scale).

effect of charging a higher price is to steepen the total revenue curve and as a consequence lower the **breakeven quantity**. The pricing decision maker can then evaluate the effect of charging different prices in terms of what these different prices and breakeven points mean to the company. Specifically, the information given by a breakeven chart includes:

- Profit (or losses) at varying levels of output
- Breakeven point at varying prices
- Effect on breakeven points and profits (or losses) if costs change.

Breakeven points can also be calculated using the following information:

Selling price per unit − variable cost per unit = contribution per unit

$$\text{Breakeven quantity} = \frac{\text{Total fixed costs}}{\text{Unit contribution}},$$

e.g. Selling price = £20
Variable costs   = £10
Fixed costs   = £50,000
Contribution   = £20 − £10 = £10.

Therefore,

$$\text{Breakeven quantity} = \frac{50\,000}{10} = 5000 \text{ units.}$$

The notion of **contribution** is also a valuable addition to the pricing decision. It illustrates that in the short run, at least, it may be advantageous to sell a product at a price which is less than the full cost of producing it. The distinction between fixed costs and variable costs is particularly useful where a company is attempting to penetrate a market with a new product. It is also useful in times of recession where prices have to be cut to maintain demand. The essential issue is to cover variable costs, at least, and to have a clear understanding of the contribution to fixed costs and profits.

Although fixed, variable and total costs are of major importance to pricing decisions, it is also useful to consider how these costs change with different volumes of output, i.e. the so-called economies of scale and experience curve effects which we considered earlier.

Kotler[5] et al. suggest that if a company has a downward-sloping experience curve, i.e. costs fall as a function of production experience, then the company should adopt an aggressive pricing strategy based on increasing volume through low prices. Kotler however does point to the fact that this type of aggressive pricing strategy is not without its risks, including for example aggressive competitor reaction and the creation of a down-market image.

Although costs are just one of our inputs in pricing decisions, in fact in many organizations they are often given more emphasis than any of our other factors in setting prices. As we shall see shortly, cost-based pricing, although severely criticized, is still probably the most widely used approach. Before looking at cost-based versus other approaches to pricing, together with their respective merits, we need to look at our final key input to pricing decisions: competitors.

Competitor considerations

The importance of competitor analysis in strategic marketing planning was examined in Chapter 2. No pricing decision can be taken in isolation from the nature and extent of prevailing or latent competition in any industry. The most important considerations with regard to competitor pricing include:

- Competitors' prices, including discounts, credit terms and terms of trade
- Competitors' resources, especially financial
- Competitors' costs and profit margins
- Likely competitor responses to our pricing strategies and decisions
- Likely potential competitors and barriers to market industry entry
- Substitutes from other industries
- Competitor marketing strategies, especially targeting, positioning and product differentiation.

Three of the most important competitor considerations which directly affect the extent to which an industry will be price competitive are:

- The number of competitors
- The degree of product differentiation between competitors
- Freedom of entry.

For example, where there is only one supplier, i.e. a monopoly, then the pricing decision maker has substantial discretion over price. On the other hand, where products are undifferentiated, price competition is likely to be fierce. Finally, where competitors can enter an industry with relative ease, then the price setter will have less discretion over price and may be forced to set lower prices than might otherwise be the case in order to deter new entrants.

In summary, we have outlined four key inputs to pricing decisions – company, cost, customer and competitor considerations. Clearly, there are many other considerations, ranging from those involving distributor and channel arrangements to possible legal considerations in price setting. We now turn our attention to how prices might actually be set, i.e. pricing methods.

Pricing methods

There are several key methods which a company can use to set prices. Here we distinguish between three broad categories of pricing method according to the emphasis which predominates in the basis for price setting. We shall discuss:

- Internal cost-based methods
- Competitor-based methods
- Customer value-based methods.

Internal cost-based methods of pricing

As mentioned earlier, the most widely used method for determining prices involves setting prices predominantly on the basis of the company's own costs. This method of pricing is often referred to as **'cost-plus' pricing**. In its simplest form, cost-plus pricing involves a company calculating average costs of production and then allocating a specified mark-up, which may be related to rate of return required by the company, to arrive at the selling price.

The major advantage of this method of pricing is its seeming simplicity. However, despite its widespread use by companies, it has long been severely criticized. Before we examine the basis of these criticisms we need to examine further the mechanics of cost-plus pricing, plus some of the reasons why this apparently 'simple' approach to pricing may in fact be more complex than it seems at first glance.

As we have seen, the mechanics of cost-plus pricing involve calculating the variable costs per unit and adding to this an allocation of the total fixed costs. The first problem with cost-plus pricing is in both the calculation and allocation of these fixed costs. Lancaster and Massingham[6] highlight these problems as follows:

> . . . clearly the amount of fixed costs which will be added to each product, and consequently the price, depends on the number of products produced. In turn, the number of products which a firm will produce will, ignoring stockholding, be a function of how many it can sell. How many will be sold, in turn, depends upon the price charged. Pricing in this way then is nonsensical; it means that for a given production capacity, if a company finds that it is selling less and thus cuts its production, its market prices will need to increase. This, in turn, will probably lead to fewer sales, a further cut-back in production and even higher prices. To say the least this is an unsatisfactory state of affairs . . .

In addition, in many multi-product companies the allocation of fixed and semi-variable costs to individual products is often arbitrary.

In practice, total fixed costs are allocated on the basis of either a standard volume or a forecast level of output.

A second problem with cost-plus pricing is the determination of the mark-up. As mentioned earlier, often the percentage mark-up is derived from a predetermined target rate of profit or return. The problem with such predetermined mark-up rates, however, is that they take no account of demand conditions.

If these disadvantages and problems were not enough, where rigid percentage mark-ups are used, and particularly where these are based on internally determined requirements for profit, cost-plus also has the following major disadvantages:

● It ignores demand and market conditions
● It ignores competitors and competitive considerations
● It ignores factors such as target marketing and positioning
● It ignores potential substitutes.

With these disadvantages there must of course be good reason why cost-plus still remains widely used by companies. The advantages are as follows:

● The pricing decision maker does not have to consider the difficult (if essential) area of demand and price sensitivity
● Where other companies are using cost-plus pricing, and provided they have similar costs and mark-ups, it can lead to price stability
● It is often claimed that because prices are directly related to costs it is 'fair' to both competitors and customers.

None of these potential advantages can, in our view, compensate for the fact that cost-plus pricing, certainly in its most rigid form, is not at all market-oriented, and can lead to significant strategic disadvantages in the market.

Variations on cost-plus pricing

It would be strange indeed if at least some companies had not realized the problems of cost-plus pricing. Thus a number of variants on this approach, although still based on costs, may be needed.

 Marginal or direct cost pricing The first of these is where prices are based not on full, but direct or marginal costs. In this way, the problems associated with having to cover costs, and the methods of having to allocate fixed costs, are avoided. This makes use of the notion of 'contribution' discussed earlier in this chapter. Needless to say, in the long run all costs, including fixed costs, must be covered, but marginal cost pricing does at least allow a company to take advantage of market opportunities and to use price as a more strategic tool of marketing. Jobber[7] points out that this approach to cost-based pricing is particularly useful for services marketing where the service cannot be stored, i.e. is highly perishable, such as cinema seats or hotel bedrooms. Prices can then be based on making a contribution to fixed costs by charging prices which cover variable, but not total costs.

Some of the newer airline operators, for example Easy Jet and Ryanair, make good use of marginal-cost pricing in their marketing strategies. These operators will cover their variable costs when selling an airline seat rather than let the plane fly with empty seats. Always provided of course that there are enough 'full price' paying passengers, this is a very effective way of not only making a contribution to profits but at the same time making life very difficult for cost-plus competitors.

 Variable mark-up pricing As an alternative to the fixed mark-up system of traditional cost plus pricing, the percentage added to costs can be varied. This approach has several advantages over the fixed mark-up approach: in particular:

- Mark-up, and hence prices, can be varied to take account of demand, competition and market conditions
- Mark-up can take account of marketing objectives and strategies
- Overall it represents a much more flexible approach.

Despite these variations on rigid cost-plus pricing, it is important to reiterate that all cost-based pricing is an indication of a company that has failed to appreciate the significance of the marketing concept. This is not to deny the importance of costs, and cost information in pricing decisions, but costs are perhaps better used in an evaluative rather than a decision-making role when it comes to considering and setting prices.

Competition-based pricing

This second general method of determining a price uses the price set by competitors in order to orient the pricing decision. This method is based on several assumptions, including that of product image and the position of the company as being the same or very similar to those of the competition.

This method can be improved upon with a slightly more sophisticated method, which involves setting a differential between the company operating this method and the competition.

The marketer may, for example, set a price five per cent below that of the market leader to allow for the market leader's stronger reputation within the industry. This approach to pricing has the disadvantage of being somewhat passive in nature, which tends to restrict the management of the company in terms of individualistic flair and style. Another drawback of this method, which is sometimes known as '**going rate**' **pricing**, is that it tends to ignore the company's own cost and demand situation. Going rate pricing is quite popular, especially in markets where costs are difficult to measure or the response of competitors is uncertain.

However, although it is vital to consider competitors' prices, costs etc. (as we have seen) this information should be used to influence our pricing rather than as a 'formula' for setting it.

Customer value-based pricing

Our third pricing method is one which we feel offers the greatest advantages to the strategic marketing planner. Not surprisingly, it is also the approach which is nearer to what being marketing oriented, in this case with respect to the pricing element of the mix, is all about. Customer or **value-based pricing**, although more complex in nature and application than our first two methods, moves away from the focus on costs or competition and instead concentrates on the customer.

With this approach, prices are determined on the basis of the perceived value of the product to the customer. The basic idea underpinning the value-based approach to pricing is that when customers purchase a product they go through a complex process of balancing benefits against costs.

In consumer product markets, the 'benefits' which the customer derives correspond to the economist's notion of 'utility' or satisfaction and may include both functional and psychological elements. For example, the customer may derive satisfaction, and hence value, from the quality of a product, or a particular product feature such as the remote control facility on say a hi-fi system. An example of a psychological element of value might be the benefit which the customer derives from the status of a prestigious brand name. Clearly, the more benefits the customer perceives a product as offering, the more value the customer will place on this product and the more the customer will be prepared to pay. Again we should note that it is the customer's perception of value that matters and not that of the supplier.

Needless to say, a customer will not purchase a product where the costs are seen as being greater than the benefits. It is important to stress that the costs may include more than just the purchase price, and again it is the customer's perception of these costs that is used in the evaluation process. For example, in assessing the costs of, say, a new car it is not just the initial purchase cost, but also maintenance, insurance, petrol and perhaps depreciation costs that the purchaser may consider. In addition, just as there are psychological benefits so too are there psychological costs. For example, our new car purchaser may well consider the costs of 'loss of status' if an otherwise 'good value for money' purchase might be ridiculed by peer groups. A number of the eastern European car manufacturers face this particular problem in trying to market their models in parts of western Europe. Skoda, in their advertising, actually acknowledges this problem.

It is not too unkind to suggest that perhaps at one time the Skoda was something of a joke. No longer.

Very effective marketing has made the Skoda car one of the success stories of recent years. Product improvements, the backing of Volkswagen and a repositioning of the brand have served to make the Skoda probably one of the best value for money cars in the market. Although the car is still low priced compared to some of its competitors, this low price base has been turned to advantage by the company by building the value for money aspect. Many customers who are attracted to this car and become brand loyal see themselves as being very astute in their choice of this car. After all, they argue, they are securing all the advantages of a Volkswagen product at a Skoda price.

With these points in mind, the marketer must determine the highest price that the customer will pay, which is:

Benefits − Costs other than price = Highest price the customer will pay

For the pricing decision maker, of course, the difficulty in this method of pricing is in measuring how the customer perceives the product the company is offering against the competition.

One method which can be used to measure how the customer perceives the product the company is offering is to weight product attributes against those of the competition. First, the customer would be asked questions concerning different attributes of a product, e.g. quality or delivery. The customer would then be asked how important each criterion was, e.g. the customer might think that after-sales service is more important than delivery. The customer would then give after-sales service a higher rating than delivery. The customer should next be asked how the organization in question fares in comparison to other companies in the market place on these criteria, and the customer's perceived value of different competitive offerings calculated.

As we can see, competitor C has the highest overall value rating. On this basis, therefore, it should be able to charge higher prices than competitors A and B for the product. If, say, the average price for this particular product in the industry is £10.00 and the average value rating is 33.3 then company C should be able to charge £10 × 36.5 ÷ 33.3 = £11.00 approximately, and still be competitive. If all three companies set their prices proportional to their value rating, then they would all be offering the same value to price. However, if company C sets a price of less than £11.00 it should begin to steal market share from its competitors because it will be perceived to be offering better value for money. This illustrates just one method of analysing how the customer perceives the relative benefits of the products on offer.

Taking this approach a stage further, it is useful to establish the Economic Value of a product to a Customer (EVC). **Economic value pricing** is potentially very powerful, though to date has principally been used in pricing industrial products and does require extensive market research.[9]

Essentially this approach to value-based pricing requires the pricing decision maker to analyse the following:

1   How the customer uses the product.
2   The financial benefits which the product offers to the customer in each particular usage situation.

3 The costs involved over the lifetime of usage of the product.
4 The cost/benefit trade-off.

Each of these is discussed below.

How the customer uses the product

Different customers may use the 'same' product in different ways and hence make different cost/benefit evaluations. For example, one contractor may run earth-moving machinery 24 hours a day and will hence place a premium on a machine which offers greater reliability and/or a supplier with good parts back-up in order to minimize 'down time'. Another, perhaps smaller, contractor in the same business might, on the other hand, only operate its machines say 12 hours a day, but may not be able to afford a permanent team of mechanics. This contractor is likely to place much more emphasis (i.e. value) on supplier/dealer servicing facilities. In short, the marketer must study and understand how the product fits into the operation of the customer.

Benefits

When we understand how the customer will use the product we can then proceed to evaluate and 'cost out' the financial benefits of the product to the customer.

Focusing on the benefits a product has to offer will help develop a more detailed picture of the overall desirability of the product being offered. When analysing the benefits the product gives, it is useful to break the benefits into core product benefits and augmented product benefits. The core attributes could be quality, reliability or other functional aspects. The augmented attributes could be delivery, service, guarantees offered by the supplier or maintenance break-up. Focusing on physical and core attributes only is all very well, but it can lead marketers into the trap of marketing the features of the product as opposed to the benefits which the product has to offer.

Costs

Just as benefits can be a group of core and augmented attributes, perceived in differing ways by different customers, so the same can be said for costs, in that costs are not just the price which the customer forgoes.

One aspect of this is when a buyer decides to change from an existing supplier to a cheaper source. The buyer may think of lowering cost, but in actual fact the opposite may be the case, as the alternative products may not be of as good a quality as the previous products or the new supplier may not be able to deliver the goods on time. The lost time from reject products and the subsequent breakdown in the production runs will make any savings achieved on price irrelevant. Total lifetime operating costs, including residual value of the product, should be calculated for each customer.

Trade-off between benefits and costs

If the customer makes a trade-off between costs and benefits it would seem sensible for the selling company to do the same. The simplest method is by analysing only the core attributes and price, e.g. price and reliability. With this analysis the marketer once

again may fall into the trap of marketing product features as opposed to product benefits. Once again, it is important therefore that the selling company looks at the use of
the product and evaluates this in conjunction with costs and benefits offered.

As the customer looks at price as part of the overall product package, so too must
the marketer. If the firm wishes to adopt a value-based approach to pricing it must
follow certain guidelines:

● A commitment to the philosophy that the customer chooses products by measuring product benefits against product costs
● An understanding that the benefits involve a great deal more than the core attributes, and that in many choice situations it is the augmented product benefits
which differentiate products
● A realization that the costs involve more than just the purchase price alone
● Cognizance of the fact that different customers view costs and benefits in different
ways.

Certainly customer/value-based pricing involves much more analysis, time and
effort than either cost-based or competitor-based pricing, but it is essentially marketing
oriented. In addition, and because of this, value-based pricing is also useful in guiding
other elements of marketing strategy. For example:

1 Value-based pricing can help in market segmentation and targeting, with marketing efforts being focused on those parts of the market (customer groups) where the
   perceived value of a company's offering is highest.
2 Value-based pricing can point the way to developing effective promotional and
   selling strategies. It is important to remember that the customer must be made
   aware of, and then convinced about, any extra value that your products or services
   can potentially offer.
3 Value-based pricing can be used in the early stages of designing and developing
   new products and services with a conscious effort being made to 'build in' value to
   the product or service for the envisaged target market.

Other considerations in setting prices

So far in this chapter we have discussed the major inputs to the pricing decision and
the relative merits of different pricing methods. In arriving at a final price, however, a
number of other considerations may influence the decision. These are outlined below.

Price/quality relationships

In the absence of other information, price is often used as an indicator of quality. The
pricing decision maker must be careful to ensure – particularly for a new product – that
a low initial price does not put off customers because they suspect the quality.

'Psychological pricing'

In many product markets prices are set to end in an odd number (e.g. £4.99 instead of
£5.00). There is some evidence that customers then see the product as falling into the
lower priced category (i.e. £4.00) rather than the higher one, to which it is actually
much nearer (i.e. £5.00).

Other products in the line/mix

In the multi-product company, many products have interrelated costs and/or demand. When setting a price on an individual product in the line, consideration should be given to the overall profitability of the product mix. So, for example, we might decide to set a lower price on an individual product than we might otherwise do because it helps to sell other, perhaps more profitable, items in the line.

Other elements of the marketing mix

As with all of the marketing mix elements, it is important that pricing reflects, and is consistent with, other elements of the mix. A high quality, expensively packaged product may be looked at with some 'suspicion' by potential buyers if it also carries a 'bargain' price tag.

Product life cycle

As we have already seen the competitive situation for a product changes throughout the life cycle of a product. Each different phase in the cycle may require a different strategy. Pricing plays a particularly important role in this respect. We now discuss some of the ways in which price may be used at various stages of the product life cycle. Once again, it should be noted that considerable care should be used in interpreting the possible strategic implications of each of the life cycle stages.

Pricing in the introductory stage of the life cycle With an innovatory product its developers can expect to have a competitive edge, at least for a period of time. With innovatory new products, a company can elect to choose between two extreme pricing strategies:

- Price skimming: the setting of a high initial price
- Price penetration: the setting of a low initial price.

1. Price skimming The setting of a high initial price can be interpreted as an assumption by management that eventually competition will enter the market and erode profit margins. The company therefore sets the high price so as to 'milk' the market and achieve the maximum profits available in the shortest period of time. This 'market skimming' strategy involves the company estimating the highest price the customer is willing or able to pay, which will involve assessing the benefits of the product to the potential customer. This strategy has in the past been successfully carried out by firms marketing innovative products with substantial consumer benefits.

After the initial introduction stage of the product the company will tend to lower the price of the products so as to draw in the more price conscious customers. When a company adopts this kind of strategy the following variables are usually present:

- The demand for the product is high
- The high price will not attract early competition
- The high price gives the impression to the buyer of purchasing a high quality product from a superior firm.

2. Price penetration The setting of a low price strategy or 'market penetration strategy' is carried out by companies whose prime objective is to capture a large market share in the quickest time period possible.

The conditions which usually prevail for penetrating pricing to be effective include:

- The demand for the product is price sensitive
- A low price will tend to discourage competitors from entering the market
- Potential economies of scale and/or significant experience curve effects.

Pricing in the growth stage For a period of time after the initial introduction of the new product, the market will continue to grow. The fact that new companies are entering the market means that the market will be divided between the competing companies, but as the market is still growing the new companies may not take any sales away from the innovator for some time. When new companies come in to the market they tend to emphasize non-product attributes of their product, as opposed to the innovator. If this occurs, the innovating company will usually lower the price of its own product so as to discourage competition.

Pricing in the maturity stage As the market for the product continues to expand and develop, the use of the product becomes more widespread, and with the entrance of new competitors the price of the product will tend to become of increasing importance in competitive strategy. A new supplier entering the market, or an existing company can only increase its market share, by taking share away from other companies. The means for achieving this, however, is often on the basis of price competition, since by the time the market reaches the mature stage, product and other forms of differentiation may have been eroded away.

Pricing in the decline stage During the decline stage, the price-cutting initiated in the maturity stage will tend to continue. At this stage, a careful appraisal of profit margins will need to be made. Prices may be eroded to the point where either total or even only marginal costs are no longer being covered. As we considered in Chapter 6, at this stage in the product life cycle, decisions as to whether to harvest or divest the product need to be made. These decisions will in turn need to take account of possible ways of reducing costs so as to try and maintain profit margins.

Other interested parties

Finally, pricing decisions will need to take account of a variety of other parties that might be interested in or be affected by the pricing decision. For example, there may be legal aspects to pricing decisions, with possibly government departments and/or 'watchdog' bodies playing a key role in pricing decisions. For example, some of the recently privatized companies in the UK, such as the gas, electricity and water companies, have to meet quite stringent regulatory requirements with respect to their pricing. A further 'interested party' to take account of in pricing decisions is the distributor. Where products and services are marketed using intermediaries we need to remember that in many markets the final selling price may not be determined by the producer, but by these intermediaries. For example in the UK, there is now no longer a resale price maintenance. This means that a supplier to a retailer can only recommend a retail price. Obviously the final price set by the retailer, who adds a 'standard' mark-up to products, can be influenced by the prices charged to the retailer, so to this extent the supplier of the product can try to influence the final market price. But to the extent that intermediaries are free to set their own prices, effectively in many instances, the marketer often has no control over final price.

Additionally, when considering intermediaries and pricing we must also determine factors such as credit terms and discounts as part of the pricing strategy.

Many branded-product marketers have recently been at least worried and in some cases incensed by their inability to force their distributors to sell their brands at the prices they would like.

Recently, the Tesco supermarket chain were selling Levi jeans at pounds off the manufacturer's 'recommended' prices. Challenged by Levis, Tesco won the right to sell the brand at these reduced prices in their stores subject to certain conditions being met.

Perfume houses, haute couture clothing brands, books, over-the-counter pharmaceuticals, are all examples of where the branded marketer has effectively lost control over the prices charged.

Some clues to effective pricing strategies

It is quite interesting and puzzling why many companies fail to price effectively even when they otherwise employ very effective marketing strategies. The reason is they do not apply to their pricing decision the same fundamental principle of marketing that they apply to other marketing decisions. The fundamental principle is that success in marketing comes from understanding how customers evaluate your marketing decisions, since the customer's response to those decisions will ultimately determine their success or failure.

Many managers correctly reason that by creating exceptional value through careful attention to their customers, they can reduce the importance of price in the buying decision. They also reason that price is of primary importance to their companies. They conclude, therefore, that it is quite appropriate to evaluate product, promotion and distribution strategies from their customer's perspective while evaluating pricing from the company's perspective. They forget about the customer when pricing, focusing instead on the company's need to cover costs, to maintain cash flow, or to achieve a target rate of return. Clearly this is a serious strategic mistake and goes a long way towards explaining why many pricing decisions are ineffective from a strategic marketing point of view.

The customer's goal is to obtain the most value for their money. For commodities, that often means buying the cheapest offering. For differentiated products, that often means paying a little more for the perceived superiority of a particular brand. Whether the product is common or unique, customers will base their decisions on the value of the transaction to themselves rather than to the selling firm. A few pence difference in price may be of great importance to a firm selling millions of units, while being of little consequence to a customer who buys just one, yet that will not stop potential customers from rejecting any price that is a few pence more than they are willing to pay. Customers are not concerned with the seller's need to cover production costs, to improve cash flow or to meet a target rate of return. Their concern is to get their money's worth.

An effective pricing strategy is not possible unless co-ordinated with the other elements of marketing strategy. The crucial relationship between pricing and other aspects of marketing is especially crucial with new products.

Like most marketing decisions, pricing is an art. It depends as much on good judgement as on precise calculation. But the fact that pricing depends on judgement is no justification for pricing decisions based on hunches or intuition. Good judgement requires understanding. One must comprehend the factors that make some pricing strategies succeed and others fail.

The manager must understand how costs, price sensitivity and competition determines a product's pricing environment. In some companies when the time arrives to make a pricing decision, managers simply meet at specified time and make a decision. They do not study the firm's costs to find out how they will change with changes in sales. They do not talk first to potential buyers to learn what role price will play in their purchase decisions, and they do not analyse the past behaviour and likely actions of competitors. Consequently, the pricing process becomes almost exclusively internally oriented and ignores key information necessary to setting effective prices.

Finally, all too often price is considered and implemented as an essentially tactical decision. Clearly there are times when price can be, and indeed has to be, used tactically, particularly when reacting to competitors' price changes. Even then though, as Jobber[10] points out, the marketer must know when to follow competitor price changes and when to ignore them. As Nagle and Holden[11] demonstrate, even tactical pricing decisions need careful consideration before implementing them.

Developments in pricing concepts and practice

It is tempting to think that pricing is one of the less dynamic areas of the marketing mix with regard to concepts and practice. After all, one might think, pricing is either cost-based, demand-based or competitor-based and the considerations in pricing decisions are in many ways just the same as they were ten years ago. In fact, however, pricing is just as dynamic as any of the other elements of the marketing mix. Perhaps the broad category of factors affecting prices and the range of pricing strategies do not change, but the nature of these factors and their specific impact and implications for the marketer do. In addition, pricing offers the opportunity for the marketer to conceive of extremely innovative ways of pricing. Some examples will serve to illustrate this dynamic face of pricing.

In many countries the marketer's power to set prices and control them at the consumer level have been substantially reduced. As we saw in our earlier example regarding Levi jeans, changes in legislation and in the atmosphere concerning competition have meant that distributors now have almost limitless freedom over the prices they charge for the products and brands they are selling. In Europe the European Union has enforced changes in pricing practices on marketers in the Union. In the UK, for example, for many years now there has been consumer concern about the prices charged for cars sold in the UK compared to prices charged for the same models in the rest of Europe. This concern became so great that legislation has been recently introduced to force the car companies to reduce their prices in Britain.

Still on the theme of Europe, one of the most significant developments which will affect marketers' pricing strategies in Europe in the future is the Single Currency and the Euro which is the basis of this. At the moment only three countries including Britain have not already joined the single currency. Obviously there are arguments both for and against joining, but there is no doubt, in or out, that the creation of the single currency must be a major factor in setting prices in the future.

Consumers nowadays are much more motivated and sophisticated in their desire to compare and contrast prices, thereby obtaining the best value for money. Today's consumer is much more willing, therefore, to shop around in order to get the best deal. Bargaining and negotiation, once the almost exclusive domain of the continental and international customer, has become commonplace in Britain, even at the retail level. Moreover, developments in communication and information technology are facilitating the ease with which a customer can conduct a compare and contrast prices exercise. Yet again, the ubiquitous Internet is playing a part in this process. From the comfort of their own home, Internet surfers can easily access information on different manufacturers' prices thereby obviating the need actually to trail round the shops.

In the context of innovative approaches to price, successful marketers are always looking for new ways to make it easier for the customer to buy with respect to payment, and/or ways in which to offer better value for money. Recent years have witnessed all sorts of financing and payment schemes for purchasing expensive consumer durables. Cars, jewellery, holidays, and even houses can all now be purchased using a myriad of different payment methods. We have leasing, leasing and buy-back schemes, tracker mortgages, timeshares, and so on: all examples of pricing strategies designed to make it less 'painful' for the customer when it comes to paying.

These, then, are just some of the ways in which we can justify the contention that pricing is one of the most dynamic elements of the marketing mix.

Summary

Pricing strategy is the first element of the marketing mix we have considered. Although they are often treated as such, we have seen that pricing decisions are more than just a 'mechanical' exercise of adding margins for profit on to costs. Price setting must become an integral part of the marketing strategy of the company and must be consistent with corporate and marketing objectives and other elements of the mix. In addition to these inputs to pricing decisions, the marketer must also consider demand, cost and competitors.

Although both cost-based or competitor-based pricing methods can be, and are, used, they both suffer from major weaknesses. By far the most useful and marketing oriented approach to pricing is one which, whilst not neglecting costs and competitors, is essentially based on customers and their perception of value.

A whole set of complex factors affect pricing decisions, making this in fact one of the most complex and difficult areas of strategic market planning. If anything, this complexity is compounded by the dynamic nature of pricing with so many developments affecting the pricing process.

Key terms

Demand schedule [p211]
Price elasticity of demand [p213]
Switching costs [p215]
Cross elasticity of demand [p215]
Fixed costs [p216]
Variable costs [p216]
Breakeven point [p217]
Breakeven quantity [p218]

Contribution [p218]
Cost-plus pricing [p219]
Marginal or direct-cost pricing [p221]
Variable mark up pricing [p221]
Going-rate pricing [p222]
Value-based pricing [p222]
Economic value pricing (EVC) [p223]

Questions

1 What are the key inputs or considerations to the pricing decision?
2 What are the main internal cost-based methods of pricing and what are their advantages and limitations?
3 Some feel that customer value-based pricing is the only way to set prices. What do you understand by this approach to pricing, and how can it be implemented by the marketer?
4 How might pricing strategies and tactics change over the life cycle of a product?
5 Why is pricing such a dynamic element of marketing, and what are some of the major changes and trends affecting this area of the marketing mix?

References

1. Mercer, D., *Marketing*, 2nd edn., Blackwell, Oxford, England, 1996, p. 240.
2. Brassington, F. and Pettitt, S., *Principles of Marketing*, 2nd edn, Pearson Education, Harlow, Essex, 2000, p. 416.
3. Oxenfeldt, A. R., 'A decision making structure for price decisions', *Journal of Marketing*, 37, January 1973, p. 50.
4. Hutt, M. D. and Speh, T. W., *Business Marketing Management*, 5th edn, The Dryden Press, Orlando, 1995.
5. Kotler, P., Armstrong, G., Saunders, J. and Wong, V., *Principles of Marketing*, 2nd edn, Prentice-Hall, Europe, 1999, p. 689.
6. Lancaster, G. A. and Massingham, L. C., *Essentials of Marketing*, 3rd edn, McGraw-Hill, London, 1999, p. 241.
7. O'Shaughnessy, J., *Competitive marketing: a strategic approach*, 2nd edn, Unwin Hyman, Boston, 1988, p. 354.
8. Kotler, P., *Marketing Management: Analysis, Planning, Implementation and Control*. 6th edn, Prentice-Hall, New Jersey, 1988, p. 508.
9. Anderson, J. C., Jain, D. C. and Chintagunta, P. K., 'Customer value assessment in business markets: a state-of-practice study', *Journal of Business-to-Business Marketing*, 1, 1, 1993, pp. 3–29.
10. Jobber, D., *Principles and Practice of Marketing*, McGraw-Hill International (UK). 1994, pp. 348–353.

11. Nagle, T. T. and Holden, R. K., *The Strategy and Tactics of Pricing*, 2nd edn, Prentice-Hall, Englewood Cliffs, NJ, 1995, pp. 10–35.

Case Study

Bessie Bass has been the accountant in ACME Engineering for over 20 years. During that time one of her responsibilities has been to help set prices for any new products launched by the company. In her view this has never posed any problems either for herself nor for the company over this period of years.

As an experienced cost and management accountant, Bass has taken the approach of estimating the average cost of producing any new product and then simply adding on a predetermined mark up for profit set by the company managing director in line with required rates of return. In her view, and for all these years so far, in the company's view, this pricing method has worked well and has a number of advantages. Bass feels it is the simplest method and it also 'ensures' that costs are covered and a profit is therefore made. Finally, she sees it as a 'fair' method of pricing which can be justified both to customers and the outside world.

Obviously, over this twenty year period not all of the new products launched by the company have been successful. But of the unsuccessful ones no one has ever pointed the finger at price as being a reason for failure. After all, how could the price be wrong if it was based simply on a factual assessment of average cost with a fair margin for profit added?

Bass therefore has never had to think or consider the effect or otherwise of price on product success and failure, and has left these considerations to the design team and the marketers who are after all responsible together for new products.

Things have now changed.

As a result of appointing a new marketing manager who has had a new innovative product developed quickly, Bass has found her position as regards pricing decisions challenged. The new marketing manager has simply asked Bass for some cost estimates. When Bass asked how these were going to be used and proposed a price for the new product based on these estimates, she was told that the new product would be priced using a customer-value based method. Bass had never heard of this.

It was explained that for the new product it was necessary to establish the economic value of the product to the customer (EVC) and that Bass was expected to help in the costing side of this.

Bass was now extremely worried. Not only did she wonder why it was not sufficient to use cost-plus again, but also she had no idea what establishing the economic value of the product to a customer meant and what information and analysis would be required to establish the EVC.

QUESTION

1. What arguments can be used to justify a customer-value based pricing method as opposed to the simpler cost-plus method?
2. What information and analyses will be required to assess the EVC of the new product, and what problems might there be in using this approach to pricing?

9

Promotional strategy

Chapter objectives

By the end of this chapter you will:

▶ Appreciate the scope and role of promotional decisions in marketing strategy.

▶ Understand how the communication process works.

▶ Be familiar with the key steps in marketing communication strategies.

▶ Understand the considerations and issues in planning and managing the individual elements of the promotional mix.

▶ Be aware of some of the developments and trends in promotional strategy.

Introduction

In this chapter we look at the strategic issues associated with planning, implementing and controlling the firm's promotional strategy.

We start by looking at what underpins a sound promotional strategy, and indeed the essence of promotion itself; namely, the *communication process*. We shall see that the tools of promotion used in marketing involve communicating with a predetermined audience in order to elicit the desired response. Understanding the nature and meaning of the communications process and its relevance to marketing objectives and strategy is a prerequisite to planning promotional efforts.

Having established the underpinning concepts of effective marketing communications we then move on to discuss the various tools of promotion available to the modern marketer, or as it is usually referred to, the *marketing communications mix*. Starting first with an outline of the major promotional tools, and factors affecting the choice of these, we shall discuss each of the promotional tools in turn and their respective uses in marketing strategy.

233

Throughout we need to remember that the promotional element of marketing strategy is potentially one of the most potent elements of the marketing mix available to the marketer. Partly because of this, the promotional spend represents one of the largest spend areas of marketing activity, with budgets running into millions for some companies. Unfortunately, it is also one of the more difficult areas of marketing to manage well. As a consequence, a considerable amount of promotional spend is wasted each year by marketers. It is at some of the causes of this wasted spend and possible ways of reducing it that much of this chapter is aimed.

Understanding marketing communications

The communication process

Effective planning of the promotional elements of the marketing mix requires an appreciation of how the communication process works. This process is summarized by Lancaster and Massingham[1] as incorporating the following questions:

'Who says what?'
'In what channel?'
'To whom?'
'And with what effect?'

These deceptively simple questions effectively encapsulate both the elements and the process of communication. The four basic elements, together with the process, are shown in Figure 9.1.

Implications of the communication process

Although this is a simplified representation of the communication process, it illustrates a number of key points.

Figure 9.1
A simple model of the elements and process of communi-cation.
Source: adapted from Lancaster, G.A. and Massingham, L. C., *Essentials of Marketing,* McGraw-Hill, London, 1999, p. 289.

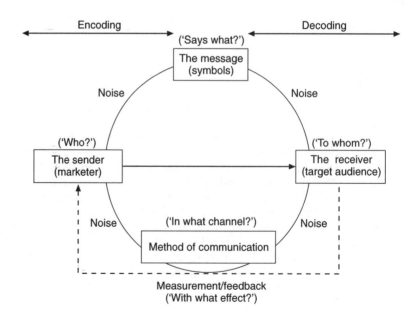

First, communication starts with the sender having a message or meaning to send or share with an intended audience. In order to share this message or meaning the communicator requires **encoding** these into signs and symbols which incorporate the message or meaning. These signs and symbols can be, for example, visual, such as words and pictures, or oral, such as speech and other sounds. In fact, there are many ways in which the message or meaning can be encoded. In order to be effective, however, the encoding process needs to be done in such a way that the target audience can readily interpret (decode) the intended meaning. In other words, the encoding process must take into account, and be consistent with, the target audience. A good example of the importance of this point in marketing communications is where a company is communicating, say through advertising, across international, and hence cultural, boundaries. We all know that what may be readily understood in one culture may be interpreted in very different ways in another. We shall be looking at some of the key aspects of International Marketing later in Chapter 18 but first let us briefly examine some of the possible problems of communicating across national frontiers in marketing.

International marketers in particular have encountered problems in the past because they have not encoded meanings in a way which allows for accurate under-standing of the target audience. For example, the market name 'Nova', a small popular car marketed in the United Kingdom, would probably not have been appro-priate in the Spanish market, where the name literally translates as 'no go'. Even in the domestic markets, communication is most effective where the symbols used are consistent with the target audience. For example, advertisements aimed at the so-called 'Yuppie' market segments so prevalent in the 1980s and early 1990s would now be perceived as being brash and inappropriate to the softer, less up-front and in-your-face lifestyles of the new millennium. The symbols of the financially successful young city trader driving a Porsche and using a gold credit card with laddish abandon are now less appropriate to the same target audience of today. Hence more appropriately encoded messages are being used to appeal to these market segments.

The encoded messages are delivered through a variety of possible *media channels*. Conventionally we think of media channels as including, for example, television, commercial radio, newspapers and magazines, and posters. But in addition to these, messages are also delivered via a company's sales force, and the other elements of the marketing mix. Indeed, as we shall see, one of the key planning areas in marketing communication is *media planning*. Not only are media one of the major costs in promo-tional budgets but the plethora of choice with respect to media, their scheduling and their coverage makes the choice of channels for communicating intended messages a key one.

As we have already seen, communication is aimed at a receiver. In marketing communications, the receiver is the intended target audience. This audience may be customers (or at least potential customers), but organizations may also wish to commu-nicate with other publics, including financial institutions, shareholders, the local community, governments and so on. Irrespective of the target audience, effective communication requires that the encoded message be decoded by the intended recipi-ent. Needless to say, for effective communication, this **decoding** process needs to result in the target audience accurately receiving and interpreting the message which the sender intended. A number of factors can serve to detract from the accuracy of the decoding process.

First of all, receivers often have predetermined attitudes which in turn influence how they perceive messages. For example, a confirmed Labour voter will, because of strong attitudes, tend to have expectations about what he or she will receive in a party political broadcast on behalf of the Conservative party. Because of this, our 'Labour party receiver' will tend only to hear what he or she 'expects' to hear, and will subconsciously add to or remove important meanings when decoding the message. In communication terms, this process is referred to as selective perception and distortion. The important point to stress here is that only by understanding the decoding process, and some of the factors which affect it, can the sender ensure that messages are received and interpreted as intended.

In order to ascertain that messages have been received and interpreted accurately and have had the intended effect, another important element in the communication process is feedback. Feedback in communication may occur in a number of ways. For example, in a conversation between two individuals, the sender can receive feedback through verbal or non-verbal affirmation. The receiver may nod his or her head, or give other non-verbal signals, to indicate that the message has been received and understood. Alternatively, we can ask the receiver to affirm verbally that accurate communication has taken place. Clearly, feedback is easiest when both sender and receiver are in direct contact and preferably can see one another. In these situations we have a two-way communication. However, in much of marketing communications there is often no direct personal contact between sender and receiver. In this type of situation it is much more difficult to gauge the effect of the intended communication and indeed the extent to which it has been received as intended. In terms of managing the marketing communication process, however, accurate feedback is one of the most important elements of the process. Only through feedback can we ascertain the effectiveness of communication. As we shall see, the measurement of effectiveness of marketing communication is essential. For example, by measuring the effectiveness we can determine if often substantial promotional budgets are well spent. In addition, accurate feedback enables marketing management to improve further communication with target audiences.

The final element of our communication process is **noise**. Noise in communication is anything which serves to reduce the quality of communication, and it can occur in any part of the system. Our earlier discussion of selective perception and distortion in the decoding process is an example of noise. A major source of noise in marketing communications is that introduced by other senders of messages. For example, each one of us is, every day of our lives, constantly bombarded with messages from marketers, each vying for our attention and our spending power.

In addition to this source of noise, however, are other attractions for our attention. For example, television advertisers have long been worried about the increasing tendency for viewers to 'zap' to another channel with their remote control when the expensive advertisements appear during the commercial break.

Noise may also appear in the feedback process when, for example, interviewer bias creeps into a market research exercise designed to evaluate the effectiveness of communications.

In summary, therefore, for successful marketing communications, the marketer needs to understand the process of communication. In fact, our model of communication, shown in Figure 9.1, is a simplification of reality and should not be viewed as a marketing communications planning tool. However, the model does illustrate that for effective communication the sender requires to know the target audience and the purpose of the communication. Messages need to be sent in a way which the target audience can interpret as intended. The communicator must send these messages through the appropriate media to reach the intended audience with the use of the feedback channel to monitor audience response. Finally, every effort must be made to reduce or counteract noise in the system.

Marketing communications

Having briefly outlined the process of communication, we can now turn our attention more specifically to marketing communications, and in particular to the elements of planning marketing communication strategies. Perhaps not surprisingly, given the emphasis throughout this text, our contention is that the promotional elements of the marketing mix must be planned and managed in a systematic and strategic manner if they are to be effective. In order for marketing communication to become strategic, it needs to be planned and implemented in a way which is consistent with and supportive of overall corporate and marketing strategies.

Marketing communications therefore must be considered as part of the total marketing strategy and its impact must be considered with the overall marketing objectives. Furthermore, as Doyle[2] points out, the communications mix as a whole must be planned together to integrate each of the major components.

In turn, Mercer[3] suggests that promotion must also be seen in the context of the rest of the marketing mix. Indeed, the other elements of the marketing mix themselves often have a strong communication element. These are considered further below:

Product communication

In terms of communication, a company's products are an important element. For many consumers, products represent symbols denoting characteristics of lifestyles, personality and so on. Packaging, in particular, communicates certain things to the market, including status, quality, atmosphere and image. A product's physical properties or brand name can communicate an image too.

Place communication

Distribution channels, too, can communicate messages to the market. For example, certain distribution channels or outlets, such as Harrods, may communicate quality and status. Others, such as Next, may communicate certain lifestyles.

The state of the company's warehouses may communicate messages to the market. For example, untidy warehouses may create a bad image amongst potential customers, whereas well-stocked and well-managed warehouses may build confidence.

Physical distribution, too, can convey message. For example, the state of a company's fleet of delivery vehicles can convey powerful messages. In fact, many companies now pay considerable attention to the livery of their vehicles, often managing this element as part of a total corporate image package.

Prices and communication

As we saw in Chapter 8, particularly for new products, or for brands with which a customer has no previous experience, pricing conveys powerful signals to the market. In this situation, the price of a product may signal the perceived quality of a product or service. Similarly, regular discounting of brands can lead to the consumer forming an image that the brand is in some ways inferior.

We have taken time to discuss the communication elements of these other parts of the mix because they illustrate an important point about planning marketing communications, namely, that virtually everything a company does, or says, potentially communicates something to the market. Because of this, an effective marketing communications strategy requires more than just the strategic management of the promotional elements of the mix. Marketing communications must be part of an integrated communications strategy with the promotional tools being integrated with overall marketing strategies, and in particular, with other elements of the marketing mix.

Having established this, we can now turn our attention to the overall management of marketing communications before looking in more detail at the management of each of the promotional tools.

Planning marketing communications strategies

As in the other areas of the marketing mix, strategic management of marketing communications requires a systematic and ordered approach. A number of approaches which fit these criteria have been developed. Although these approaches vary in their precise detail, there is sufficient commonality between them to propose a generalized framework that is integrated with other elements of marketing strategy. This framework is shown in Figure 9.2.

Figure 9.2
Steps in planning communication strategies.

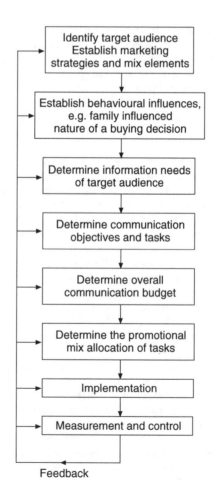

Identify target audience
Establish marketing
strategies and mix elements

Establish behavioural influences,
e.g. family influenced
nature of a buying decision

Determine information needs
of target audience

Determine communication
objectives and tasks

Determine overall
communication budget

Determine the promotional
mix allocation of tasks

Implementation

Measurement and control

Feedback

Target audience, marketing strategies and mix elements

Not surprisingly, effective marketing communications starts with the selection of the target audience and the delineation of broad strategies and marketing mix elements designed to achieve objectives in these target markets. In this chapter we are primarily concerned with communication aimed at customers. But, as we have seen, communications may be aimed at any one or a combination of several target audiences. We have also seen that the specific promotional elements of the marketing mix need to be part of, and consistent with, the communication elements of the remaining marketing mix elements. Unless and until the target audience is delineated, it is impossible to proceed, at least in any effective way, with the remaining elements of the marketing communications planning process.

Behavioural characteristics of target audience

It is not sufficient simply to delineate target audiences: the marketing communicator must also understand the target audience. There are many pertinent factors here, but if we take an example, in planning effective marketing communications the marketer needs to understand the buying decision process, i.e. how customers buy. The importance, in more general terms, of understanding this process was discussed in Chapter 4. In the context of communication decisions, the stage at which the target audience is in the buying decision process begins to provide important information for planning communication. For example, in the case of the new product, communication will have to stimulate the start of the buying process by encouraging problem or need recognition. Alternatively, if the target audience includes mainly already regular purchasers of the product in question, our marketing communications might be aimed at minimizing post-purchase dissonance.

In addition to understanding how the target market buys and the stage of the buying process they have reached, it is also important to understand who is involved in the purchase process. For example, in Chapter 4 we saw that we can usefully distinguish between different roles in the buying process. So if, for example, we are launching a new brand of breakfast cereal, it is important to distinguish between 'influencers', 'deciders', 'purchasers' and 'users'. Of course, all of these roles might be embodied in the one target group but, as we have seen, both in consumer and industrial markets these roles may also be filled by a range of individuals.

Sometimes it is also important to establish existing preferences, attitudes and so on of our target audience. For example, given that very often with marketing communications we are concerned with image, it might be important to establish our target audience's current image of the company and/or its products.

Establishment of information needs

Much of the preceding analysis of the target audience should help the marketing communicator to assess the information needs of customers. For example, analysis of the search, and alternative stages of the buying process, will help to establish where our target market looks for information, the degree of reliance on word of mouth versus marketer-dominated sources of information, and the type of information sought.

Determining communication objectives and tasks

Taken together, each of the previous steps in planning communications strategies will help to contribute to the establishment of specific, and where possible, quantified communication objectives. Given our earlier discussion of the communication process, the marketer must determine what effect the communication is intended to achieve. The problem here is that the range of possible objectives for marketing communication is virtually endless. However, marketing communication objectives are best thought of in the context of what are often referred to as 'audience response repertoires'. These are similar to our stage or step models of buyer behaviour, in that they posit that the buyer passes through a series of stages or steps *en route* to making purchase decisions. A variety of such audience response repertoires have been developed. Two of the earliest and best known in marketing communications are Strong's **AIDA** model[4] and Lavidge and Steiner's **Hierarchy of effects model**[5]. More recently, Jones[6] has suggested that marketing communications in general, but advertising in particular, has a much weaker effect on consumer behaviour than the earlier models such as AIDA have suggested. One model which reflects this view of a weaker effect for advertising is the so-called **ATR model**, with the initials ATR standing for the steps of Awareness, Trial and Reinforcement. This model suggests that advertising works by first creating awareness, which may then lead to the tentative trial of the advertised product by the customer. Having trialed the product the customer can then be reinforced or reassured about the purchase through further advertising. These three models of how advertising might work are shown in Figure 9.3.

These models of the step-by-step process can be used to help determine appropriate communication objectives, although it is important to stress that they need to be interpreted and applied with care. For example, customers need not necessarily always pass through the stages of the various models in the manner prescribed. Factors such as nature of purchase, previous experience, time pressure and so on can all affect the nature and speed of a consumer's progress through the various stages. Bearing this in mind, by using audience response models the marketing communicator is able to set communication objectives in terms of what is required to move the target audience through the various steps in the process. So, for example, in the AIDA model, if the target audience is at the early stage of the buying process the primary objective of communication will be to bring the company and its products to the attention of

Figure 9.3
Examples of audience response repertoires.

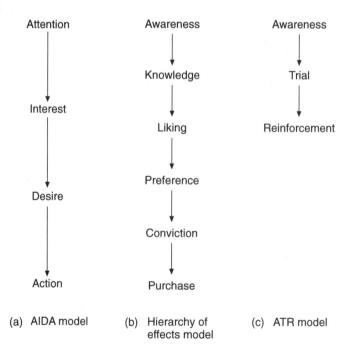

| (a) AIDA model | (b) Hierarchy of effects model | (c) ATR model |

customers. Alternatively, at later stages, the objective of marketing communications may be to produce action. We shall examine further these stages of hierarchy models of audience response when we look more closely at advertising.

As with all objectives, it is important to couch these in quantitative terms whenever possible. Clearly this makes the final stage of measurement and control much easier. It also allows preliminary cost estimates to be made regarding the research required to meet the objectives, thereby facilitating budget decisions for communication.

In setting objectives for marketing communication, it is important to remember that rarely can a consumer be moved through all of the various response stages by a single promotional campaign. Because of this, like corporate objectives, communication objectives may need to include both long-term and short-term objectives.

Determining the communications budget

Having decided the communication objectives we are now in a position to determine the budget required to meet those objectives. There are many ways of setting a communications budget.

A method that is often used is that of taking a percentage of sales, either current or projected. This represents a very simple way of setting budgets for communication. However, the problem with this approach is that communication budgets will be high when sales are high, and low when sales are low. Needless to say, this often-used approach does not make sense.

Another approach is to set the budget at the same level as that of the competition, or at least on a *pro rata* basis using market share. The problem here is that this approach both assumes that competitors have similar objectives, strategies and so on, and that they are budgeting effectively in the first place. Neither of course might be the case.

As mentioned earlier, setting clear and quantified objectives for communication allows us to determine what tasks need to be done to achieve these objectives and further allows these to be costed. Not surprisingly, this method of determining communication budgets is often referred to as the 'objective and task' approach.

Determining the promotional mix: allocation of tasks

This stage of our communication planning model requires decisions to be made regarding the allocation of the communication tasks, and hence the communication budget, to the wide variety of promotional tools available to a company.

As mentioned earlier in the chapter, communication tools are, in fact, embodied in all of the elements of the marketing mix. However, in the promotional area of the mix itself, marketers conventionally distinguished between four major tools of promotion. Collectively these four elements are referred to as the **promotional mix**. These four elements are described and defined by Kotler[7] as follows:

1 *Advertising*:
   any paid form of non personal presentation and promotion of ideas, goods or services by an identified sponsor.
2 *Sales promotion*:
   consists of a diverse collection of incentive tools, mostly short term, designed to stimulate quicker and/or greater purchase of particular products/services by consumers or the trade.
3 *Public Relations/Sponsorship*:
   involves a variety of programmes designed to promote and/or protect a company's image or its individual products.

4 *Personal selling*:
oral presentation in a conversation with one or more prospective purchasers for the purpose of making sales.

Within these conventional four broad categories of promotional tools, Kotler also identifies a myriad of more specific tools, shown in Table 9.1.

Each of the four major promotional tools, with their different characteristics, have their own advantages and disadvantages which, together with the precise nature of the communication tasks, means that the marketing decision maker should be able broadly to determine the most appropriate mix.

For example, advertising, sales promotion and publicity are usually the most cost-effective tools at the buyer awareness stage, more so than 'cold calls' from sales representatives. Advertising is highly cost-effective in producing comprehension, with personal selling coming second. Buyer conviction tends to be influenced most by personal selling, followed by advertising. Placing an order is predominantly a function of the sales call, with an assistance from sales promotion.

However, it has to be admitted that these are very broad generalizations. In fact, determining the most appropriate promotional mix is one of the most complex of the communications planning decisions. Additional factors which will influence this decision include, for example:

- Company objectives and resources
- The stage in the product life cycle
- Competitor considerations
- Type or product market.

Table 9.1 Examples of promotional tools

Advertising	Sales promotion	Public Relations	Personal selling
Print and broadcasting ads	Contests	Press Relations	Sales presentations
Packaging – outer	Games	Speeches	Sales meetings
Packaging – inserts	Sweepstakes	Seminars	Telemarketing
Mailings	Premiums	Annual reports	Incentive programmes
Catalogues	Samples	Charitable donations	Salesmen
Motion pictures	Fairs and trade shows	Public relations	Samples
Magazines	Exhibitions	Corporate Communication	
Brochures and booklets	Demonstrations	Sponsorship	
Posters/leaflets	Couponing		
Directories	Rebates		
Reprints of ads	Low interest financing		
Billboards	Entertainment		
Display signs	Trade-in allowances		
Point of purchase displays	Trading stamps		
Audiovisual material			
Symbols and logos			

As an example, if we take the type of product market, Figure 9.4 illustrates how the usage of each promotional tool might vary for a variety of product markets.[8]

As can be seen, at the two extremes of fast-moving consumer goods versus capital and industrial goods, the promotional mix differs greatly. In particular, the emphasis switches from a primarily non-personal, advertising dominated promotional mix for fast-moving consumer goods to one dominated by personal selling in capital and industrial goods.

Perhaps there is nothing surprising in this. After all, much industrial buying involves the purchase of large volume and/or technical products. Organizations are perhaps less susceptible to 'glitzy' advertising and will want to negotiate on a personal face-to-face basis.

However, we must be careful in forming, or subscribing to, any preconceptions about the relative influencers and hence use of various promotional tools in any given situation. For example, we have already discussed the reasons for the emphasis given to the personal selling elements of the promotional mix in industrial markets. This does not mean that advertising should be discounted in such markets – even though in practice it often is. We know, for example, that in industrial markets advertising helps substantially to increase the effectiveness of personal selling by increasing the awareness of a company and its products and thereby reducing the difficulty and costs of selling 'cold' to customers.

In addition, it is important to stress that is it not only a choice between advertising and personal selling, or some combination of these. As Table 9.1 illustrates, there is a wide range of very effective promotional tools to choose from and the more proactive marketers and their agencies are constantly searching for new and improved ways to promote their products and services.

In this constant search for new and effective promotional tools we have seen the development of more direct ways of marketers communicating with their target

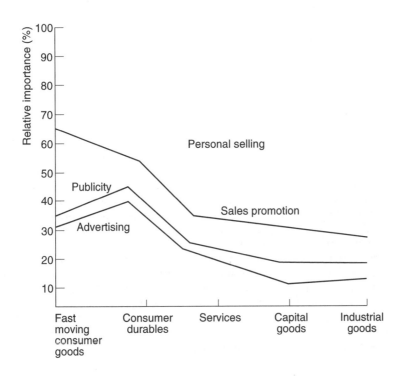

Figure 9.4
Relative importance attached to promotional tools across different production markets.
Source: Abrath, R. and Westhuizen, B., 'A promotional mix appropriation model', *Journal of Industrial Marketing*, 1985, p. 215.

audience. So rapid and far-reaching have been these more direct forms of promotion that Kotler *et al.*[9] suggests that they can now be considered as the fifth element of the promotional mix. Perhaps not surprisingly, this fifth element of the promotional mix is referred to as direct marketing.

Direct marketing includes some of the most dynamic and innovative tools of marketing communication and is set to continue to grow in importance as an element of the promotional mix in the future. We shall therefore be considering this relative newcomer to the promotional mix tools in more detail later in the chapter. In common with the other broad categories of promotion, direct marketing includes several types of promotional tools, some of the more important of which are direct mail, telemarketing and, increasingly, the Internet.

Implementing the promotional mix

Having determined how the communication tasks are to be allocated between the different elements of the promotional mix, the next step is to develop detailed action programmes for each of the promotional tools being used. This will entail the development, for example, of advertising, sales promotion, personal selling, direct marketing and publicity programmes. As we have seen, these separate programmes will also need to be coordinated one with another and with the other elements of the marketing mix. More often than not, advertising, sales promotion, direct marketing and publicity programmes will be developed and implemented with an outside agency. Needless to say, therefore, careful selection and briefing of an appropriate agency is essential, as is a close and effective working relationship.

Planning and implementing each area of the promotional mix is in itself a complex process requiring a detailed understanding of the issues and steps involved, together with a knowledge of the variety of promotional tools within each area. In this chapter, we shall look in more detail therefore at the strategic issues in designing and implementing advertising, sales promotion, direct marketing and publicity campaigns. The management of the personal selling element of the promotional mix is discussed in Chapter 12.

Measurement, control and feedback

The last stages of effective communication management are concerned with the measurement of the effectiveness of marketing communications against predetermined objectives and standards. As we shall see when we consider some of the individual elements of the promotional mix, evaluating the effectiveness of communication can be problematical, but with such substantial spends involved it is important to control this area of marketing. According to how effective, or otherwise, the communication programme has been, some readjustment may be necessary. Measurement and control should not simply assess the extent to which communication objectives have been met, but should also provide information or reasons for any variances. This can then be used to adjust the communications programme.

In summary, marketing communications is a vital and costly element of marketing strategy. In order for this part of the marketing mix to be cost-effective it needs to be planned and organized in a systematic way. It also needs to be coordinated with the strategies and tactics for other elements of the marketing mix. In the remainder of this chapter and in Chapter 12 we shall examine in more detail the strategic management of each of the five major promotional tools – advertising, sales promotion, direct marketing, publicity and personal selling.

Advertising

Perhaps one of the first promotional tools we tend to think of, and certainly one of the most visible in our daily lives, is that of advertising. Partly because of this high visibility, advertising is also one of the most controversial elements of the promotional mix. There are those, both in management and amongst the general public, who believe that much advertising is either a waste of money or immoral or both. We shall start by examining what advertising is (and is not) before looking at how advertising works. Our main concern, however, is to point to how advertising can be managed so that it is cost-effective and helps support both overall and marketing communication strategies.

What is advertising?

Earlier we gave a definition of advertising which contained a number of key elements which both distinguish it from the tools of promotion and, at the same time, indicate its key characteristics. These key elements are outlined below.

Non-personal   Unlike personal selling, advertising affords no direct personal contact with the customer. Although this is a limitation, especially in industrial markets, it does mean that the advertiser has much more control over what is said and to whom.

Paid for by an identified sponsor   Unlike publicity, advertising is directly sponsored and paid for by the advertiser. Although the consumer may not be aware of the company behind the advertisement for a particular brand, the consumer is aware that advertising is intended to create a favourable response on the part of the consumer and as such is clearly identified as being for commercial or organizational gain on the part of the sponsor.

Promotion of ideas, good or services   This element of the definition is to a great extent shared by the other tools of promotion. It does illustrate, however, that advertising is not only relevant to fast-moving consumer goods: indeed in recent years we have witnessed an increased use of advertising by organizations as diverse as the major charities and political parties. What is most notable about this part of our definition though is that the word 'promotion' rather than 'selling' is used. Although some advertising is intended to create a sale in its own right, such as in classified advertising or some forms of direct marketing, most advertising is but a part of the process of moving consumers nearer to making a purchase.

A final distinguishing characteristic of advertising compared to, say, personal selling and to some extent direct marketing, which is not highlighted by Kotler's definition, is that it is normally aimed at a mass audience, i.e. it is *mass communication*.

In the case of the commercial advertiser, it is true to say that the ultimate objective of spending advertising monies is to increase sales and profit. As we shall see, however, we must be careful not to exaggerate the power of advertising in this respect. As we have constantly stressed, advertising is but a part of the communications mix; and the communications mix, in turn, is a part of overall marketing strategy. Perhaps this point is best evidenced, albeit in a somewhat negative way, by illustrating what advertising cannot do; for example:

● Advertising cannot secure repeat business for a product or service which does not represent value for money

- Advertising cannot remove the problem of insufficiently trained or motivated sales staff
- Advertising cannot work if the brand is not in the stores when the consumer wants it.

We could go on, of course, but the point is that advertising is only powerful, if indeed it is, when it and the rest of the communication and marketing strategy, are well planned, implemented and integrated. Furthermore, viewing sales as the objective for advertising is, again with some exceptions, a narrow and hence, from a planning perspective, dangerously limiting view. We shall return to this point later, but in discussing what advertising is (and is not) it is important to recognize that the term 'advertising' covers many different types of activity. For example, advertising may be classified on the basis of sponsor/audience. On this basis we can distinguish between, for example, retail advertising, manufacturers' trade advertising, and manufacturers' consumer advertising. Similarly, we might categorize the different types of advertising according to objectives, as described below.

The objectives of manufacturers' consumer advertising might be to create preference for a specific brand; that of retail advertising to create traffic through a store.

The objective of manufacturers' trade advertising might be to encourage dealers to stock a product, announce important forthcoming price deals or new product launches, or simply to increase trade confidence and loyalty.

With government advertising, the objectives can vary from presenting public information through to exhortations to behave or vote in a certain way.

Local newspapers give a good idea of the range of classified advertising, from 'announcements' such as births, deaths and marriages, through to the sale of products and services.

With such a range of different types of advertising it is difficult to pin down the precise nature of advertising and hence how advertising might work. Perhaps one of the most useful ways of distinguishing between broad categories of advertising, not surprisingly, is on the basis of the *intended communication effect*. In this way we can distinguish between three main categories of advertising; namely, *'informative'*, *persuasive'* and *'reminder'* advertising.

1 *Informative advertising* can be used in a variety of ways. It is particularly relevant when, for example, a company wants to tell the market about a new product, suggest new ways of using an existing product, or informing the market of changes to the product, e.g. price changes.
2 *Persuasive advertising* is used to build up a brand following. So, for example, it might be used to encourage customers to switch brands. Persuasive advertising is also used when potential customers have unfavourable attitudes towards a product or company, in an attempt to change these attitudes.
3 *Reminder advertising* is advertising which is aimed at, for example, maintaining brand loyalty. It can also be used to encourage previous customers who have ceased to buy the product or service to return to purchasing.

A good example of the widening scope and application of advertising is the recent advertising campaign to attract new recruits to the police force in the UK. For the first time ever, the Home Office used nationwide television advertising to attract these new recruits. This national campaign was backed up with a series of newspaper advertisement and other 'sales' promotion techniques.

How advertising works: behavioural models of advertising

Given the plethora of types of advertising, and the underlying complexity of the behavioural issues involved, it is perhaps not surprising that there exist a number of views, often conflicting, as to how advertising works. From our perspective, the importance of attempting to understand how advertising works is that by doing so we can improve our planning, implementation and control of this element of promotion. In this respect, the audience response repertoire models which we looked at earlier in this chapter have proved to be the most fruitful, even if, as is the case, they are somewhat controversial.

The three examples of possible audience response repertoires shown in Figure 9.4, i.e. the AIDA model, the Hierarchy of Effects model, and the ATR model, are typical of a range of such behavioural models designed to explain how advertising, or more generally communication, works. Although, as we can see from these three examples, the precise nature and number of steps in the various models may vary, the essence of these models of how advertising works is essentially the same. Specifically, they share the common characteristics of suggesting that advertising, as an element of marketing communications, works by nudging the audience through a series of steps or stages in the buying process, *en route* to making a purchase decision. As already outlined, the first two of these, the AIDA and the Hierarchy of Effects models, suggest that effective advertising can potentially at least exert a powerful effect on the customer creating, in the case of the AIDA model, 'desire' and 'action', and in the Hierarchy of Effects model, 'conviction' and 'purchase'. The ATR model, however, although based on a step-by-step process, again suggests that the effect of advertising, even where it is effective, is much weaker than in the first two models, serving only to encourage 'trial' and/or create 'reinforcement'. Two further, and each in their own way, very influential models of this type are Colley's[10] 'DAGMAR' model, and Rodgers'[11] 'Product adoption model'. These are shown in Figure 9.5. As with our three previous models of this process, the suggestion is that by understanding these steps, and by knowing where our target audience currently is in the sequence, we can better plan, implement and control our advertising decisions.

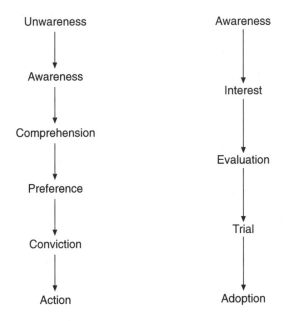

(a) The DAGMAR model   (b) The product adoption model

Figure 9.5
Two further models for the consumer decision process.

For example, in Colley's model DAGMAR stands for *D*efining *A*dvertising *G*oals for *M*easured *A*dvertising *R*esults. In other words, based on a concept of the relationship of advertising to a sequential process of buying behaviour. Colley suggested that it was possible to define precise and quantified objectives for advertising. In turn, these objectives would help delineate and determine the types of advertising required, including what was to be said and through what channel. Finally, performance could be measured against these objectives to ascertain the extent to which they had been attained. We shall return to the suggested uses of these models shortly when we examine the management of advertising under 'Campaign planning'. Before we do this, however, it is important to outline some of the disadvantages, limitations, and hence criticisms, of these sequential models.

The first criticism of this type of model is that they are not based on empirical evidence. In other words, they represent hypothetical constructs which may or may not reflect reality. It is certainly true that, at least at the time of their initial development many of these models lacked any empirical support. However, by now many of them have been extensively tested and, on the basis of this, subsequently developed and refined. The evidence, however, is mixed. Certainly some consumers do pass through the stages shown in the models. However, they need not necessarily always and inevitably do so. Kristian Palda,[12] in particular, has criticized the hierarchy model, suggesting that consumers may actually first purchase a product and then become convinced about its value.

A second criticism of the models is that they are difficult to operationalize. For example, although they may point to a level in the hierarchy at which advertising should be aimed, it is still necessary to develop a specific campaign. Many of the models lack the detail as to how best to achieve an objective. Refinements to some of these basic models, such as the DAGMAR MOD II, and the Leon Burnett Continuous Advertising Planning Programme (CAPP)[13] are two examples of attempts to operationalize hierarchy models further. There still remains, however, the difficulties associated with measurement. Severe conceptual problems are still associated with constructs such as awareness, conviction, preference and so on.

In addition, some still believe that these models focus on the wrong dimensions. Specifically, it is sometimes argued, sales and not communication effects are the underlying objective of advertising. So, for example, in the absence of a direct and measurable relationship between awareness, or attitudes and sales, the models will tend to focus attention and spend on objectives which may not be related to sales.

A final and interesting criticism is that these models tend to restrict creativity in advertising by overspecifying what has to be achieved. Certainly many very successful and respected practitioners and writers on advertising subscribe to the view that the creative element, which effectively establishes and sells the brand image and/or appeals to the emotions, is the most important element of successful advertising.

At this stage of the debate regarding how advertising works and the usefulness, or otherwise, of the models described, it is perhaps safest to say that the arguments remain unresolved. Certainly we have gone some way to understanding the complex process of how advertising might work and how, therefore, to manage it more effectively. The stance taken here on this debate is that the models are useful provided they are applied and interpreted with care and a great deal of common sense, but much more research is needed before we can reach definitive conclusions.

Managing advertising: campaign planning

The following represent the six basic elements of managing the advertising effort:

- Identification of the target audience
- Determination of clear, realistic and measurable objectives for advertising
- Determination of the advertising budget
- Message selection/creative platform
- Media selection and media scheduling
- Control and evaluation of advertising effectiveness.

Before discussing each of these, once again it is important to stress that the planning and implementation of advertising, as with all the promotional elements, needs to be set against the rest of the marketing mix and be consistent with overall marketing objectives and strategy. In addition, external factors will also need to be taken into account, including, for example, social and legal constraints, the attitudes and ideas of the advertising agency, competitors and, of course, customers, and particularly their needs and motives. Finally, the overall role and emphasis given to advertising, together with some indication of the preliminary budget for advertising, should be set in the overall context of the promotional mix. This wider framework for advertising decisions is shown in Figure 9.6.

Figure 9.6
Managing advertising: a systematic approach.
Source: adapted from Aaker, D.A. and Myers, J.G., *Advertising Management,* 2nd edn, Prentice-Hall, New Jersey, 1982, p. 30.

Identification of target audience   Identifying the target audience is the first step in planning advertising campaigns. Much of what follows in campaign planning stems from this essential step. Together with overall marketing and promotional objectives, the target audience determines, for example, creative context, media planning and scheduling.

As we have seen, frequently used methods of defining target markets include demographic factors, age, sex, income and social class. However, particularly useful for advertising decisions are the more behavioural/psychological bases; for example, the previously discussed ACORN type systems and particularly the newer 'lifestyle' approaches to classifying target markets. This is because these bases give us a fuller, richer description of target markets, encompassing not just consumer characteristics such as their age and sex, but also their personalities, spending habits, attitudes, interests and opinions. Where information on these aspects is not available, market research will be required to establish a full profile of target customers.

Setting advertising objectives   Once we have determined the target audience for our advertising, we need to determine what our advertising is intended to achieve with that audience. In broad terms, and using our earlier classification of types of advertising, our advertising might be intended to inform, persuade or remind. Whilst this might be useful in beginning to delineate the reasons and role of advertising in the overall marketing and communications mix, these broad classifications are not a sufficient guide to the next steps in the advertising management and campaign planning process. Ideally, we need to specify precise communication goals for advertising. Needless to say, this is where our earlier models of the sequences in buyer behaviour related to communication are useful. For example, Colley's earlier described DAGMAR model translates into some 52 possible communication goals for advertising. Notwithstanding the controversy over these models, they are helpful in setting specific objectives for advertising couched in terms of objectives for communication designed to move customers through the buying stages. These objectives should, whenever possible, be defined in quantitative terms and specify a time-scale.

Determining advertising budgets   Earlier in this chapter we briefly discussed some of the approaches to determining the overall budget for marketing communications, together with some of the factors that would determine the allocation of this overall budget to the individual elements of the promotional mix. Having gone through the process of broadly determining the thrust or emphasis of promotional strategy between the different promotional tools, we should have at least a preliminary idea as to how much of the total budget will be allocated to advertising. However, at this stage, and taking into account our first two steps of advertising management, we now need to refine this process to arrive at a precise budget for advertising. In fact, the advertising budget can be arrived at on the same variety of bases as the overall budget for communications, i.e. based on percentages of sales and or profits, based on competitors' spend or based on the objective and task method. Once again, the only justifiable method is the objective and task approach. Indeed, this is a distinct advantage if setting clear and quantified communication objectives for advertising in the preceding stage.

Once we have a thorough understanding of what our advertising objectives are, these can then be translated into specific tasks for advertising, and in turn those tasks costed in conjunction with the advertising agency.

Deciding on the message/creative platform   The creative element of advertising is an area which potentially has the greatest impact on the success or failure of an advertising campaign. Unfortunately, it is also an area which, despite considerable research, generates considerable controversy as to what makes a successful creative advertisement.

The basic direction for the creative programme is provided by the product strategy, which defines the market position towards which (for consistency) the product is to be directed. Advertising objectives are the second vital input to the creative programme. They influence both what the advertising says and the manner in which it is presented. The third input to the creative programme is information developed in the consumer, product and market analysis. In particular, the creative programme should be based upon a clear description of the characteristics of the target consumer and the problem that the consumer is trying to solve. It also depends on detailed information about the product to be advertised and detailed information about competitive products.

It is here that the manufacturer and the advertising agency have to decide what the advantages of the product are when compared with those of its competitors. Is it less expensive? Is it of improved quality? Is it smaller or larger? Does it have new features? Does it offer a new experience? Does the product have several outstanding advantages to offer the consumer? If it has one truly outstanding feature that can be exploited in the advertising, this is sometimes referred to as the **unique selling point** or proposition (the USP).

There are three essential steps in developing a creative programme:

1 Determine the content of the message. The advertising content serves the advertiser by carrying out the strategy and objectives set for the product. The content serves the consumer by providing useful information about solving problems.
2 In addition to deciding what is to be said, the programmes must consider how it is to be said.
3 The creative programme must determine how the advertising will be produced.

The advertiser also faces numerous difficult choices in weighing up the promise or appeal. It has been suggested that the advertiser should use rational appeals when their prospects face utilitarian problems and emotional appeals when problems are social or psychological! Research evidence indicates that fear appeals raise consumer defences if the problem is a vital or unavoidable one, but fear appeals may be effective with less important problems.

Increasingly advertising agencies are using less of an intuitive subjective approach to developing the creative content of ads, and instead of turning to a range of market research tools designed to improve the design of creative content based on careful and systematic research. Perhaps what is surprising is that it has taken so long for advertising agencies to start to use more systematic research based approaches to creative content. For example, it is over 30 years ago now since one of the most successful advertisers Leo Burnett[15], advocating using in depth interviewing techniques to provide information on suitable copy platforms. Similarly, as long ago as the 1960s Maloney[16] developed a framework for designing copy content based on encouraging representative target customers to associate with the type of reward or benefit they expected or hoped to get from either having used/consumed the product or service in question, or whilst using the product or service in question, or from an aspect of the product or brand in question which was 'incidental' to the use experience.

Although there is considerable controversy over their use, fear appeals have been used particularly in trying to change certain types of behaviour in society. Examples of government-sponsored advertising with this aim in mind have included campaigns to stop people smoking, change their sexual habits and behaviour in order to prevent the spread of Aids, and to encourage drivers not to drink.

Determining media selection and scheduling This element of advertising management should be prepared concurrently with the budget decision. A wide variety of
media vehicles are available to the advertiser these days, especially in the developed
economies. For a detailed and practical appraisal of the variety of media and their characteristics you are advised to read one of the specialist advertising texts such as Smith[17]
or Aaker *et al.*[18] Media planning, however, is made easier by adherence to the preceding
steps in our advertising management programme. Overall marketing strategy, advertising objectives, budgets and creative strategy all serve to delineate and point to the
required media strategy. Above all, media strategy is determined by the target audience.

A four step media planning approach begins with:

1 A definition of media requirements, specifying the target audience, the required
   exposure, creative requirements of the media, and the budget available.
2 The next step is to select the medium to be used against the media requirements.
3 The third step is to select specific media vehicles, again utilizing the media requirements in order to gauge their effectiveness.
4 This final step is to specify the size or time length of the advertisements and the
   timing of their appearance.

The selection of media is a specialized task. As Davies[19] suggests, with such a variety
it is difficult for a non-specialist to decide which of the various media are best suited for
a particular campaign. There is considerable competition between the various media
and, to provide a service to advertisers, most of the media owners publish information
about their media and its coverage/audience. We shall examine sources of such information shortly, but generally, media selection requires asking and answering a number
of questions:

● To whom is the appeal to be directed and what kind of appeal should be made? On
   the basis of the decisions made, the media department (usually in the advertising
   agency) will begin to examine the characteristics of the available media.
● To what extent are the various media categories and vehicles appropriate to reaching the target audience and the particular appeal selected?
● What is the credibility of the various media vehicles?

Having decided upon a shortlist of the various media which appear to be suitable
for the campaign, the media buyer must then consider which ones or which one is the
'best buy'. It is rare for only one medium to be selected. Usually the best results are
obtained by using a combination of various media.

When the media buyer prepares the shortlist, he or she will also prepare a cost
comparison. This will be based on the rates issued by the media owners. A summary,
which may show the cost per thousand readers or viewers in the 'target' market for
each of the media, will be submitted to the advertiser with the agency's advice. At this
stage, the decision will be taken.

In recent years there has been a trend towards 'media shops'. Before the arrival of
these independents, the agencies had to run their own media departments, which has
probably accounted for a disproportionate amount of total overheads compared with
their overall billings. These media independents, however, are able to book space or
time and thus specialize in this kind of work. Starting an agency with a proper media
team can be costly, but it becomes increasingly more economic to employ a team the
larger the agency grows.

An agency has to consider whether it gives a better service through continuing to
use an independent media shop or by integrating the function 'in-house'. Some would

argue that media handling should operate within an advertising agency and be part of the total process, with creative and media staff working directly with each other in the same environment.

We mentioned earlier that a number of sources are available to help in the task of media planning and buying. Some of them are provided by the media owners themselves. The more important of these are now outlined.

British Rate and Data (BRAD) This gives information on issue date and price, copy date, circulation, mechanical data and the advertising rates of:

1 National daily newspapers.
2 National Sunday newspapers.
3 Provincial daily newspapers.
4 London and provincial newspaper groups.
5 Weekly newspapers.
6 Consumer publications.
7 Trade, technical and professional publications.

Advertising rates and other relevant information are also included on:

1 Television.
2 Radio.
3 Posters.
4 Transportation.
5 Cinema.
6 Telephone directly advertising.
7 Local free distribution papers.
8 House-to-house distribution.

Media Expenditure Analysis Limited (MEAL) MEAL produces a monthly report which covers product groups within product categories; analysis of advertising expenditure by category, product group and brand; and product group, product description and expenditure via press, television and agency.

British Audience Research Bureau (BARB) TV audiences in the UK are measured through a system of audience research known as BARB (the British Audience Research Bureau). BARB monitor a sample of 4500 homes using a special meter installed in each household. The meter records which stations are turned on and using a hand-held remote control unit, a record is made of who is watching the programmes at any one point in time. This data is then downloaded from the monitors direct to BARB for analysis.

BARB provides a monthly chart involving the top programmes as well as publishing a weekly top ten of the most popular programmes. In addition, it publishes weekly regional lists of the top programmes and the monthly ratings share of each channel.

Radio Joint Audience Research (RAJAR) Established in 1992 RAJAR measures and analyses radio audiences in the UK.

Cinema and Video Industry Research (CAVIAR) With an exotic sounding name, CAVIAR produces statistics on cinema and video audiences.

National Business Readership Survey This is commissioned by the *Financial Times* and the results arc published at six-monthly intervals. The purpose of the survey is to help in the planning of advertising aimed at business people in Britain.

Audit Bureau of Circulation (ABC) Most large publishers belong to the ABC, to which their auditors return the sales figures. The Bureau has the right to investigate them, and random checks are, in fact, made. The Bureau issues an ABC Certificate at the end of each half year. This gives the ABC figure for the publication and is published in about April and October each year by the ABC in the *Circulation Review* issued as a supplement to the British Rate and Data (BRAD). More recently ABC also measure and verify web site traffic.

We have now discussed the first five of the six steps in advertising planning. We have deliberately avoided discussing the mechanics of producing an advertisement. Once all these planning stages have been completed then the advertising must be produced, the media booked, and so on. Normally, both the planning and production of the advertising will be done in conjunction with an advertising agency. Agency selection, briefing and organization are outside the scope of this text and once again interested readers are advised to consult a specialist text in this area. This leaves us with the final stage of managing advertising: namely, evaluation and control.

Evaluating and controlling advertising Given the importance and expense of advertising, it is vital to assess how effective it is. Again, this is where the importance of the previous stage of setting clear and quantified objectives comes in. You will recall that when we discussed objectives for advertising, it was suggested that, although sales and profits may be the ultimate reason for advertising (at least in the profit making organization) there are distinct difficulties in relating these to advertising. Furthermore, because of this, it was suggested that advertising objectives be set in communication terms, e.g. increasing recognition and brand awareness. It is also important to recognize that advertising, and particularly the creative/copy content of advertising, be evaluated prior to actually implementing the campaign as well as post-campaign. Lancaster and Massingham[1] (pp. 317–319) give an overview of the range of research techniques available for both pre-testing and post-testing advertisements. Briefly, though, the overall approach to evaluating and controlling advertising is set out below.

The evaluation programme begins by defining the elements and decisions to be evaluated, including elements from the budget programme, the media programme and the creative programme. Next, an *effectiveness evaluation procedure* is designed for each element. This must include specification of a standard as a base for comparison – when actual performance is measured it will be compared to the standard to determine whether or not performance is satisfactory.

For each programme element to be evaluated the evaluation programme should specify the *measurement technique* to be used. For example, the *media audience measurement* evaluates the effectiveness of media programmes, the *recognition and recall tests* measure the effectiveness of individual advertisements, and techniques such as *consumer and retail audits* measure the effectiveness of overall campaigns.

Some developments in advertising research and practice

Perhaps inevitably advertising concepts and methods represent one of the most dynamic areas of marketing. The importance of advertising in marketing coupled with the amount of marketing budgets and resources devoted to this area, have meant that it is an aspect of marketing which attracts considerable research attention in an effort to extend our knowledge and ultimately management expertise in this area. In short, we are constantly increasing our knowledge about how advertising works (or perhaps as importantly – it sometimes does not work) in order to manage advertising more effectively. In addition to developing our knowledge about advertising in general and television advertising in particular, this is greatly affected by trends and changes in some of the macro-environmenal factors identified earlier in this text, and particularly technological trends and changes. Some of the more important developments and trends in advertising research and practice are outlined below.

The proliferation of advertising/advertising clutter

Increases in the availability and types of media, more advertisers, and greater advertising spends have all contributed to a proliferation of advertising activity and messages in most societies. Consumers are now inundated with advertising and the result is that it is much more difficult to gain the attention or interest of consumers and often the commercial message intended by the advertiser is lost. This phenomenon is known as 'clutter' and is an increasingly difficult problem. Clutter occurs when the number of advertisements to which an audience is exposed, reduces the audiences' interest in, and/or capability to receive, any particular advertisement. Several studies have shown that clutter is a problem and is increasing. For example, Kent[20] investigated clutter with respect to television advertising on UK network channels. His results showed that television is highly cluttered with advertisements for directly competing brands, and that this damaged the ability of the target audience to recall particular advertisements. The suggestion is that advertisers attempting to seek target audiences may be inadvertently compromising the effectiveness of their advertising. The conclusions of this and other similar experiments are essentially that highly cluttered times should be avoided and advertisers should negotiate for greater protection against clutter. Other experiments suggest that consumer recall of brands is adversely affected to a greater degree by clutter than is consumer recognition.

Direct response television/interactive digital television

Direct response television (DRTV) represents one of the fastest growing but still comparatively underdeveloped aspects of advertising. It is still a little understood type of advertising and research is only now beginning to indicate how such advertising works best and hence how to manage it most effectively. In an early study in this area, Carter[21] found that longer direct response advertising (60–90 seconds) was much more efficient than shorter ones. She also found that advertisements which displayed a telephone number for more than ten seconds were six times as efficient than those which displayed a telephone number for less than ten seconds. A voice-over of the telephone number gave a much better response.

Carter's research represents an example of how we are gradually improving our knowledge in this new area of advertising. Many advertisers now use DRTV but are unsure about the basic rules. Despite this, DRTV advertising is set to grow particularly in fast moving consumer goods.

Developments in technology are facilitating the growth of two-way communication of television advertising with target audiences. Admittedly, this interactive television advertising for products is still in its infancy but is destined to grow in the future with the growth of digital technologies.

Zipping, zapping and muting

Related to the proliferation of advertising, and particularly television advertising, coupled with the advances made in technology there are new problems confronting the television advertiser. Virtually every modern home now is likely to have a television set with a remote control and a video recorder. These items have led to the phenomena known as '**zipping, zapping and muting**'. Zipping is the term given to the fast-forwarding of advertisements either on pre-recorded or taped video cassette. Zapping is the term for channel-hopping, and Muting is turning the sound on the set down. All of these activities are much easier of course with the use of a remote control. Advertisers have become increasingly worried about these phenomena because obviously they potentially reduce the effectiveness of any given advertising spend. However, the effects on advertising of these phenomena are much more complex than we might imagine. For example, Gilmore and Secunder[22] found as a repetition of a zipped advertisement increased, so did its recall. However, product recognition and product recall depended on having seen the product advert before seeing the zipped advertisement. Therefore, they concluded, a zipped television advertisement can lead to product retrieval and reinforcement of previously learned information. This recognition and retrieval can have a positive effect on attitudes towards a product. This simply illustrates that the implications of zipped, zapped, and muted advertising still needs extensive research with regard to their potential implications for the marketer.

Fragmentation of media

Technology in particular has led to an explosion in the range and types of media available to the advertiser. Again, this is particularly true in television advertising. The growth of satellite and cable television in many countries means that audience figures for many programmes are much smaller and often more specialized than they have been in previous years. Whilst on the one hand this means that the advertiser can reach fewer potential customers through television advertising, on the other hand they are able to target selected audiences much more accurately. There are many implications of this fragmentation of target audiences but for example many marketers are now moving away from widescale 'blockbuster' promotions on national TV networks towards more selective promotional campaigns involving much more of an emphasis on 'push' rather than 'pull' promotion. Another key development in the proliferation of advertising media has been the phenomenal growth in the worldwide global internet system. More and more advertisers are now using the global web sites to promote their products and companies.

In summary, we have seen how advertising strategy fits into the overall marketing and promotional strategy, together with the steps in its effective planning and management. We shall now consider three more of the promotional tools – sales promotion, direct marketing and publicity – before looking at the personal selling element in the following chapter. Much of the framework for planning sales promotion, direct marketing and publicity, i.e. the need to relate these to an overall promotional and marketing strategy considering target customers, competitors, social/legal factors and so on, apply in the same way as for advertising. Similarly, these elements of promotion too must be planned systematically with clear, measurable objectives, effective control and evaluation etc. For these three further elements of the promotional mix, therefore, we shall confine ourselves to looking at the strategic use of these tools in marketing.

Sales promotion

Recent years have witnessed a continuing growth in the use of **sales promotion** both in consumer and industrial markets. In fact, in consumer markets the total UK spend on sales promotion outstrips the spend on media advertising.

Paul Smith[23] suggests that a key distinguishing feature of sales promotion compared to, say, advertising, is that it is action-oriented, whereas Fill[24] describes sales promotion in the following way:

> Sales promotion seeks to offer buyers additional value as an inducement to generate an immediate sale.

Davidson perhaps best captures the key distinguishing features of sales promotion as a marketing tool when he suggests that essentially sales promotion is an immediate, orderly incentive to purchase, having only a short-term or temporary duration.

Scope and objectives of sales promotion

As advertising has become increasingly competitive and the population has developed a resistance to it, the use of sales promotion has increased. There is scope for a greater variety of different activities with promotions and it is possible to create a promotion which singles out one's own company from its competitors. Advertising is partly circumscribed by the media which can be used. This should not be taken to mean that sales promotion is likely to be more effective than advertising, but merely that a wider scope offers a greater number of promotional options.

As we have seen, the role of sales promotion is to encourage purchase by temporarily improving the value of a brand. However, it is part of the overall marketing mix and should tie in with advertising, product performance, pricing etc. In general, the purpose of advertising is to improve dispositions towards a brand, while the objective of sales promotion is to translate favourable attitudes into actual purchase. Advertising cannot normally close a sale because its impact is too far from the point of purchase; but sales promotion can and does.

Sales promotion is often managed in isolation from the other elements in the marketing plan and is sometimes used inappropriately. It has become important because of self-service, competition, consumer behaviour, e.g. impulse buying, brand loyalty and switching, and the need to gain scarce shelf space through retailer support. Consumer promotions at the point of sale can now be termed 'the silent salesman'.

When it comes to considering the range of sales promotion tools, we are faced with an almost bewildering variety. Even if space permitted, it is not our intention to discuss every type of possible sales promotion technique. Collectively, these tools of sales promotion are often referred to as 'below-the-line', with advertising being known as 'above-the-line' expenditure. Two excellent reviews of the full range of sales promotion tools are those given by Smith[25] and Fill.[26] The intention here is to point to the uses of sales promotion in marketing planning, together with some of the issues which arise in attempting to manage this element more effectively. In doing so, of course, we shall be describing and discussing some of the more frequently used tools of sales promotion. With such variety of sales promotion techniques, however, we need to be sure that the planning of sales promotion is systematic. Below, we outline the key steps in planning sales promotion, indicating, where appropriate, some of the possible sales promotion techniques which are available to the marketer.

Planning sales promotion

As you would expect, the starting point in planning sales promotion is the identification of the target audience and the specific objectives we intend our sales promotion to achieve.

Sales promotion can be aimed at one or more of the following:

- Consumers
- The 'trade' (retailers, wholesalers, distributors etc.)
- The sales force.

In consumer sales promotion, typical objectives for sales promotion include, for example, encouraging customers to switch brands, encouraging customers to try a new product and encouraging heavier purchase/consumption. It is interesting that much of the literature on sales promotion relates to the use of this tool in markets for fast-moving consumer goods. However, sales promotion is also prevalent and effective in industrial product markets, through the use of, for example, trade fairs, executive gifts, sponsorship and so on.

Unfortunately, many industrial marketers tend to look upon some of the techniques of sales promotion used in consumer products marketing as being somewhat 'cheap' and dubious and hence inappropriate to their business. This is a pity. Sales promotion can play an important part in any market where competition is fierce and where, because of this, relatively minor 'incentives' to purchase might swing the balance in favour of a particular supplier.

In trade sales promotion, objectives might include, for example, encouraging the trade to stock a new line, encouraging them to stock more of an existing line, or encouraging them to put more effort into selling a company's brands to the final customer. Of course, the trade will only be interested in doing any of these if it is profitable to them. Clearly it is of no value to a trader to have large stocks of products which do not move off the shelves. Because of this, effective trade sales promotion needs to be supported by effective marketing, including sales promotion efforts to the trade's customer. More importantly, the trade will need to be convinced that there is a market for the product.

Promotion aimed at the company's own sales force might include the following objectives: stimulating greater effort to support a new product launch, encouraging the opening of new accounts and encouraging more visits per day. In other words, sales promotion is used here to motivate the sales force.

We can see from the above that, often, achieving a given objective may require the targeting of sales promotion at all three parties. Clearly, where this is the case it needs to be effectively coordinated and controlled along with other elements of the marketing and promotional mix.

Having established what the sales promotion is intended to achieve and with whom, the next step is to select the most appropriate and cost-effective sales promotion tools. Again, with such a variety of possible tools available, this is not easy. Each of the tools tends to have its relative advantages and disadvantages and there is little consistent empirical evidence to suggest which tools work best in which situation and why. In most circumstances, it is advisable to make use of a specialist sales promotion agency, when devising sales promotion programmes.

As an indication of the types of sales promotion tools available for each target audience, we now briefly outline some of the major tools used for each of consumers, trade and sales force.

Examples of consumer sales promotion

Coupons The consumer must be in possession of a coupon or voucher of a particular value which can then be 'redeemed' at a local store to obtain the product or products named on the voucher at the usual price, less the value of the voucher. There is usually a deadline, and the offer often applies to a particular size in the range of products, which usually means that the consumer, in order to take advantage of the offer, must purchase the product within a shorter space of time than normal. The effect of this is to increase the rate of stock-turn for both the retailer and the manufacturer.

One problem is, of course, that the majority of redemptions are made by people who would have bought the product anyway and so, to that extent, the value of the scheme is doubtful. But where the voucher constitutes an introductory offer on a relatively new product, the 'bargain' element often persuades consumers to switch brand loyalties, in the hope that this is not just a temporary switch.

 Self-liquidating offer   An example of this would be where a manufacturer of tinned food purchases a quantity of kitchen knives from a supplier at a price of £1 per knife. The food manufacturer then 'offers' to sell the knives to the consuming public at the cost price of £1 or thereabouts, plus five labels from a particular size of the tinned food.

Again, the advantage to the retailer and the manufacturer is that the rate of stock-turn is increased, and the consumer also benefits by being able to purchase the knives at trade price. This type of operation is termed 'self-liquidating' because all the capital used by the manufacturer in purchasing the knives is returned by the consumer.

Sampling   Many manufacturers, again particularly in the areas of fast-moving consumer goods, give away free samples of their products. The sample is very often of a smaller size than the normal pack size and it is hoped that customers will try the product, like it, and purchase the product in future. Once again, this operation is usually reserved for new entrants to a market and it also has the advantage that if consumers are given a tablet of soap, for example, they are most unlikely to buy their usual brand that week, or until they have used the free gift.

Bargain packages   There are two main forms of this promotional technique. One is where the product is advertised at a particular price but the pack is marked '5p off', which means that the purchase price will be reduced by that amount, but only on the products so marked, which is another way of saying 'whilst stocks last'. Again, many people take advantage of this type of offer, but they include all the regular purchasers of the product, many of whom just stock up with the product at the bargain price but then do not purchase the product again until their own stocks have been run down, by which time there is probably another 'offer' on the same product. Where a pack is marked, e.g. '5p off', these are often known as 'flash' packs. Legislation has, however, been recently enacted which makes it more difficult for manufacturers to use this tactic. Many are now switching to the tactics of, for example, '10% extra free'.

The second form of this technique is where the offer is advertised as 'two for the price of one' and very often, attached to the large size pack (of toothpaste, for example) is a smaller sized pack. This method does not help the retailer so much as the manufacturer, who is able to increase the turnover of the large packs, sales of which may have been sluggish, and at the same time maintain the turnover of the smaller pack. Again, this also means that very little of the toothpaste of competitors will be purchased by the same customer during the next few weeks.

Where one pack is attached to another (often smaller) pack, this is known as the 'limpet' method. The title is self-explanatory.

Give-aways   This is often aimed at the younger end of the various market segments, and has been used extensively by breakfast cereal companies. Into every packet of cereal is put a small toy or gift in an attempt to use the influencing power of children in this market.

Trade promotions

Some of the more frequently used trade promotions include the following.

Discounts/cash allowances   A percentage discount or cash allowance given for each case purchased.

Additional products with order   Extra products given with each unit ordered, e.g. if a case of 12 is purchased, two extra products are given free.

Merchandising allowances   A merchandise allowance which compensates the retailer for featuring the manufacturer's products.

Advertising allowances/cooperative advertising   An advertising allowance compensates the retailer for featuring the manufacturer's products in the retailer's newspaper advertisements; alternatively, the supplier may organize collaborative advertising with the trade.

Exhibitions   Exhibitions are, in some trades, almost obligatory. A well known example in the UK is the Ideal Home Exhibition, which is held annually. It features all possible goods which can be used in a home, and exhibits 'model homes' which are fully furnished and which can be visited and inspected.

The bulk of exhibitions are industrial and they include such examples as the Motor Show, the Office Equipment Exhibition, the Hardware Trades Fair and a variety appropriate to other industries. Many of the exhibitions are mounted solely for the trade and the public are not allowed admittance.

Sales force promotion

This is a growing area for the application of sales promotional techniques and some of the more frequently used techniques are:

- Sales contests
- Bonus prizes
- Sales incentives and gifts.

Many marketers are now 'bundling' their promotional offers, i.e. they are using several promotional tools together in a campaign. For example, a two-for-one offer on a brand may also be combined with a promotional offer of another free complementary product with the purchase, such as a free bolognese sauce with a pasta purchase.

One can understand of course why such bundled promotional campaigns are successful, at least in getting customers to purchase or switch brands, in as much as they offer the consumer excellent value for money. On the other hand, though, they are very expensive for the marketer.

With such a wide variety of sales promotion tools to choose from, it is important that the most cost-effective ones are selected. The most appropriate tools in this respect will vary according to a number of factors including, for example, type of product market, specific sales promotion objectives, target audience, and the emphasis of the marketing strategy, e.g. 'push' versus 'pull' strategies. It is also important to recall we have stressed that very often all three areas, i.e. consumers, trade and sales force, will be targeted. You will recall therefore that these multi-faceted campaigns must be coordinated.

Before the full-scale sales promotion is launched, as with advertising, it is advisable to pre-test the promotional vehicles selected. This can be done relatively quickly by using, for example, focus groups, selected in-store tests or full-scale test marketing. If the testing is successful – indicating that the sales promotion will achieve the required objectives – the full-scale campaign can be implemented.

The final stage, of course, is evaluation and control. Often the formal evaluation of sales promotion campaigns is overlooked by marketers. The chief factor in assessing the success of a sales promotion campaign is usually the effect on sales. However, this should also be compared with both the costs of the campaign and alternative ways of spending these monies, e.g. on other elements of the promotional mix.

In measuring the sales effectiveness of sales promotion, it is important to monitor sales over a longer period than the duration of the campaign itself. The reason for this is because there is often a 'lagged' effect. If the promotional campaign has been aimed at generating a short-term increase in sales and market share, any such increases will often be followed by a down-turn in sales and market share compared to those that pertained immediately before the commencement of the campaign. This drop is due to customers having stocked up as a result of an effective sales promotion campaign. After a time, sales will return to normal, albeit at a new and hopefully higher level than before the campaign. In addition, Doyle and Saunders[27] have also pointed to a possible 'lead' effect. This is where, in anticipation of the sales promotion, customers delay the purchases they would otherwise have made. Similarly, salespersons may hold back on selling effort if they expect a sales contest with prizes to be introduced in the future. These complications do not detract from the need to evaluate and control sales promotion: indeed they add to it.

Some developments in sales promotion, research and practice

As with the advertising area of the promotional mix, so too, sales promotion is constantly being researched and new tools and techniques being developed. Some of the more interesting of these are outlined below.

In-store sales promotion: promotional kiosks

In-store sales promotion is of course a widely used type of sales promotion activity. Traditionally, in-store sales promotion has used techniques such as in-store leaflets, demonstrations, merchandising and so on. Allied to developments in Information Technology, a number of companies have experimented with promotional kiosks. As the term implies these are in-store kiosks which potential customers enter and are presented with visual and verbal information regarding the products in store, their features, uses, unique selling points, stock availability etc. Increasingly interactive video is used in these kiosks. Some of the advantages claimed for in-store kiosk systems include:

● They provide a means of showing an extended range of products.
● Customers can be encouraged to consider alternatives if the desired item is not in stock.

- The customer can browse through the range of products and in some cases can actually pay for specific products in stock.
- They can be used to offer a 24 hour 'through-the-wall' shopping service like automatic teller machines now used extensively for banking services.

A variation on the promotional booth are the touch screens now increasingly being used in some of the large grocery supermarket stores.

Sainsbury's have experimented with a touch screen promotional technique in several of their stores in the UK. The touch screens are usually located in the entrance foyer of the stores and are activated by the customer swiping their loyalty card through the sensor. Having done this, the customer is then able to trace through the promotional offers in the store on that day. The use of the customer's loyalty card, backed up through the database system, enables the promotional offers displayed to be to a degree tailored to the personal shopping profile in terms of product and brand choice of the individual customer. If the customer is interested in any of the promotional offers on the screen then he/she presses the screen to indicate this and the appropriate promotional coupons are issued.

Packaging design

Although packaging is not only a sales promotional tool, as we have seen, it is a potentially very powerful area of promotion for a product. Time and time again exceptional and innovative packaging design is able to demonstrate market share and profitability improvements for the marketer. Even more companies are now turning their attention to the potential for this **below-the-line promotion** element of marketing. Blair and Rosenburg[28] have shown the potential impact of effective packaging design. For example, they cite the effect of a re-designed package for McVities Jaffa Cake product. When this long established product was languishing in the market the company rejuvenated the product packaging and market share rocketed. In the UK a reform to the Trademarks Act has allowed 3-D shapes, sounds, and smell to be registered as trademarks. The rush of applications is testament to brand owners' perception for the need to re-design packaging design and the need to protect this as quickly as possible.

More extensive and sophisticated use of point of sale material and in-store merchandising

A trend, rather than a shift, in the use of sales promotion in the marketing communications mix is the increasing recognition of the importance of **point of sale** (POS) and in-store merchandising activities. Several factors account for this including:

- The increasing power of retailers in many sectors and the ensuing fight for limited shelf space.
- Research evidence[29] which shows that up to 70 per cent of customers make their brand choices in store.
- A recognition of the need to reinforce brand differentiation at the point of sale.

As a result, in-store merchandising and POS, once to some extent the cinderellas of marketing communication, are now becoming increasingly sophisticated and fully integrated into the promotional mix being planned as a key part of a brand's long-term positioning.

Hewlett Packard used POS techniques very effectively in their launch of a new CD writer. The POS strategy was planned well in advance as part of the overall promotional campaign for the product. POS material was specifically designed to be appropriate to different types of retailer who in turn had different target customer groups. The POS techniques were seen as being essential to the overall communications campaign and proved to be very successful.

Increased use of information technology

Once again, developments in information technology are having a major effect on the marketer, in this case in the area of sales promotion. For example, more sophisticated and powerful databases are enabling much better targeting of sales promotion campaigns. Earlier we described the use of touch screens in Sainsbury's stores which enables promotional offers to be linked to individual customers' purchasing patterns. Many retailers' loyalty schemes, and the ensuing databases which stem from them enable the marketer to identify targets for promotional campaigns much more effectively. Similarly, the effects of a given promotional campaign can now be rapidly and accurately measured and evaluated using developments in information technology. This enables the marketer to evaluate a campaign while it is ongoing and make any modifications to increase the effectiveness of the campaign.

More emphasis on building loyalty

Perhaps surprisingly for a promotional tool, which is often used to encourage short-term brand switching on the part of customers, increasingly sales promotion is now being used to encourage/develop company, brand or store loyalty. We have already mentioned the use of the most obvious promotional tool in this respect, namely the use of loyalty cards, particularly in the area of retailing but this is just one approach to using promotional techniques to engender customer loyalty. The growth in the recognition of the importance of customer loyalty is linked to the growth of relationship marketing which is discussed in Chapter 17. At this stage, it is sufficient to note that marketers have become aware of the value of customer loyalty as a marketing asset and have put more effort into building and maintaining this loyalty therefore. Sales promotion campaigns which can lock in customers have therefore increased in recent years. There is a danger, however, that customers can become loyal to the loyalty scheme rather than to the marketer or the brand.

There is no doubt that the introduction of their loyalty card scheme was one of the factors in Tesco becoming the largest grocery supermarket retailer in the UK. Launched in the 1990s, Tesco's loyalty card was amongst the first such schemes in the UK. Many of its competitors felt that the scheme would be a short-term gimmick and that customers would quickly tire of it. Not long after, however, these competitors realised that the scheme was very successful and quickly moved to introduce their own schemes.

Somewhat controversially a considerable amount of sales promotion aimed at building customer loyalty is aimed at children. Research[30] has shown that children are particularly susceptible to some sales promotional campaigns, especially for example the use of free gifts, T shirts, models etc. This susceptibility is heightened where the campaign can be linked to, say, a film character or theme. For example, some of the most successful sales promotion campaigns of the late 1990s made use of the interest in anything to do with dinosaurs.

Direct marketing

Our third major elements of the promotional mix is our relative newcomer, namely direct marketing. In fact, in some ways of course, direct marketing is not new. After all, the direct mail catalogue as a basis for marketing products has been around for hundreds of years. However, there is no doubt that the use of direct marketing techniques has grown considerably in recent years. As in the other major categories of the promotional mix, direct marketing encompasses a plethora of different tools and techniques. We should also remember that as well as being a promotional tool, direct marketing can also be considered under the place element of the mix as a channel of distribution in its own right.

Some of the major tools of direct marketing together with recent developments in this area are outlined below.

Direct mail

As with direct marketing itself, direct mail is not a new tool of promotion, but again it has been a major growth area. Many factors have fuelled this growth of direct mail, but of particular importance in this respect have been access to more accurate, detailed and up-to-date mailing lists allied to extensive database systems on consumers. Obviously most direct mail involves the marketer sending out promotional material through the mail system direct to the home or offices etc. of target customers. Increasingly however, direct mail is using the newer forms of mail delivery including, for example, fax mail, e-mail, and voice mail. These newer forms are destined to be the growth areas in the future for direct mail. Greater accuracy in mailing lists and more sophisticated databases on customers already referred to have made such mailings much more cost effective in recent years. Obviously a major issue in direct mail marketing is response rates. Response rates can be very low indeed and are typically round about the 0.5 per cent level. Direct mail campaign planners know that one of the most critical factors in success is getting the addressee to open the envelope as opposed to simply junking it into the wastepaper basket. Not surprisingly, this has led to the somewhat unfortunate description of direct mail by some as 'junk mail'. This somewhat derogatory term has been reinforced by the fact that the sheer growth in direct mail in recent years has meant that most consumers in many developed economies are now inundated with direct mail on a daily basis. Careful targeting, and skill in the design of the direct mail package can significantly increase the percentage of consumers who will open the direct mail envelope, but remember this is still only the first step. Walker[31] has suggested that some 83 per cent on average of consumers in the UK did not read the direct mail they had actually opened. Again, skilful design of the direct mail package can increase the percentage of consumers who proceed to at least read the promotional material. There is no doubting, however, that direct mail remains one of the most unpopular techniques of promotion amongst many consumers. More research, improved techniques and an increased social and customer conscience on the part of direct mail marketers – preferably backed up with an effective regulatory system – are essential if direct mail is to achieve its potential as an effective promotional tool.

Catalogue (mail order) marketing

Essentially a form of direct mail marketing as the term implies, catalogue, or as it is often referred to, mail order, marketing involves the customer using a brochure or catalogue to place direct orders. Often the catalogue will be part of a mailshot, or alternatively the catalogue may have been provided by the retail outlets of the company concerned. A large number of catalogue marketing companies still use agents who generate orders from amongst their friends and acquaintances. Forms of direct marketing have been around for a long term, and after a brief lull in popularity during the 1970s and 1980s, the 1990s and the first part of the new millennium have witnessed a return to popularity of this way of purchasing some products and services. In part, this is due to increasingly busy lifestyles of many customers, making it impossible or difficult for them to visit retail outlets. In addition, the mail order marketers themselves have improved their marketing techniques. The catalogues are now usually very well produced and are used by up-market brands and retailers whereas at one time mail order had very much a down-market image. Finally, new and easier methods of payment such as telephone credit card payments have helped facilitate a resurgence in popularity of this direct marketing method.

A good example of effective catalogue marketing in the UK is the NEXT company's catalogue. Although essentially a retailer, NEXT appreciate that many of their customers are busy working women for whom shopping through a catalogue at home represents a significant advantage. NEXT were one of the first companies to move up-market with catalogue marketing. Their catalogues are expensively produced and designed to show their fashion products in the best possible light. Back-up systems for the catalogue marketing activities of the company include easy delivery, payment and return systems.

Telemarketing

This form of direct marketing has come a long way in recent years. The following British Telecom description of telemarketing from a study by Rines[32] captures the essence of this type of direct marketing:

> The systematic use of telephones to achieve business objectives in sales, customer care, market growth and cash flow management.

Telemarketing's importance as a marketing tool is underlined by a growth rate, in the UK at least of approximately 20 per cent per year over the past five years. The advantages of Telemarketing include easy and widespread access to customers in their own homes or offices; low cost per contact compared to personal selling; and the ability to contact customers outside normal shopping hours.

However, like direct mail, telemarketing has developed something of a poor image. Many householders and for that matter businesses, resent unsolicited telephone calls to sell something. There are codes of practice in the industry regarding the use of this tool, but the more unscrupulous telemarketers can often be accused of 'pestering' customers in their own homes. The advantages of telemarketing mean that it is likely to continue to grow but it does need careful management and self-regulation.

When setting up a telemarketing system staff must be recruited and suitably trained. In addition suitable equipment, in particular software packages, must be acquired. In the first instance many newcomers to telemarketing use agencies at least, as the first step.

Direct-response television (DRTV)

Mentioned earlier under the advertising element of the promotional mix, television adverts which are intended to produce a direct sale through an order by the customer can also be included as part of direct marketing. Although **direct-response television** marketing can be used for example to build brand awareness or develop a customer database, most frequently it is used to generate an immediate sale. For example, the viewer may be given a telephone number to ring in order to place a direct order. Direct-response television marketing is growing. It is particularly suited to fundraising marketing, for example for charities, causes etc. It is also increasingly widely used for products such as CDs, chatlines, and novelty products.

Online marketing: The Internet

Perhaps the most significant recent development in direct marketing, online marketing using a computer, a modem and the Internet has been the fastest growing form of direct marketing in recent years and is set to grow phenomenally over the next decade. There are so many developments and uses of these electronic forms of online marketing now that the reader is advised to consult a more specialized text on this form of marketing. Originally, a US phenomenon and still the more widely used there, other parts of the world and particularly the UK are rapidly catching up. Virtually every product or service that one can think of can now be bought directly through the Internet. As mentioned earlier, products and services such as books, travel, entertainment, have proved particularly suitable for this type of marketing, but now one can purchase houses, cars, education, and even cosmetic surgery over the Net. Admittedly, there have been some major disasters as regards some of the newer Internet companies and there are still problems for the consumer in purchasing using this medium: security, non-delivery, for example. However, again every marketer nowadays must consider the implications and applications of the Internet to their businesses and their marketing.

These then are the first three major elements of our promotional mix. In the final part of the chapter we now turn our attention to the fourth element, namely publicity and public relations, and sponsorship.

Public relations and sponsorship

Perhaps at one time amongst the most neglected promotional tools, recent years have witnessed an increasingly professional approach to managing this area of marketing communications. The term public relations has now virtually replaced the old term that used to be used for this area and type of promotion, namely publicity, although publicity, somewhat confusingly, is sometimes still used to denote these activities.

Public relations is in fact a broader concept than publicity and in many ways encompass most of the activities of what used to be termed publicity.

Sponsorship is often included either as a promotional category in its own right or sometimes as a sales promotion technique. However, we feel that because sponsorship is normally associated with promoting the company's image and name amongst its publics, it is most appropriately considered alongside the other public relations activities.

We shall now outline the main issues in managing these elements of the promotional mix in turn.

Public relations

Public relations is essentially about promoting the image of a company or its products and services. Unlike most promotional activities sometimes public relations does not involve the company in any direct costs. So, for example, the company may issue press releases with a view to having these published for free if the publisher feels that the release is sufficiently newsworthy and/or interesting to their readers. The fact that it is sometimes not paid for, however, does not mean that it is unimportant and should not be integrated with all the other elements of a company's promotional mix. In addition, we must not be misled by the old adage that there is 'no such thing as bad publicity' (to use the old term). This is simply not true. Bad publicity can have, and has had, most serious effects on many companies' image and sales.

The launch of the now highly successful Mercedes 'A' Class model was marred by bad publicity. The so-called 'moose test' conducted by some Scandanavian countries and designed to test the ease with which a new model can be steered around an object such as a moose appearing on the highway showed that in its original design form the 'A' Class was susceptible to rolling over in some circumstances.

The tests and the failure of the 'A' Class to pass them made worldwide news. In short, the publicity for the safety conscious and highly respected engineering image of Mercedes was a disaster. The product had to be recalled and redesigned.

Having said this, Mercedes handled this publicity problem in an exemplary manner and in some ways, it could be argued, actually made the best of any bad publicity which they had engendered.

Public relations tools include the following:

1 *Press release*
   This is basically news which the company issues in objective, journalistic form. It may well be printed in the form in which it is received by the editor.
2 *Press conference*
   This takes the form of a meeting where a major announcement is made and at which guests are invited to ask questions. A press conference may be given in preference to a press release if the matter under review merits some explanation which may not be covered adequately in the press itself.

3 *Press receptions*

These are different from the above. They are not a substitute for a press release. It is at press receptions, which are major events in themselves, that important announcements are made, e.g. a new model of a car. Such receptions are normally well planned and guests receive 'programme invitations'.

4 *Facility visits*

Representatives, usually belonging to the media, are given the opportunity to inspect some special aspects of a firm's operations. Such a visit can involve a tour around a new factory.

Clearly, effective public relations management requires building up good and trusting relationships with opinion leaders, especially in the press and magazines.

As already mentioned, publicity is misunderstood because it is often confused with public relations. In fact, publicity is a tactical tool within the broader framework of public relations. Public relations can be defined as the deliberate, planned and sustained effort to establish and maintain mutual understanding between an organization and its public. In this context, public relations has a wider role to play than simply publicity. In particular, it is often aimed at publics other than the consuming public. For example, public relations may extend to the financial community with financial public relations, the local or wider community with community relations, the workforce itself with industrial relations, and finally relationships with policy makers, such as local and national governments and politicians.

In addition to the tools we have mentioned, public relations also makes use of special events, lobbying and audiovisual and written materials. As Kotler[7] points out, in the past public relations and marketing practitioners have not always worked well together, with the PR people seeing their job as essentially non-commercial, a public service if you like. However, public relations, especially where companies are increasingly under attack for their 'antisocial behaviour' in areas such as 'green' issues, can be a very potent marketing tool. Increasingly, in the future, what will be required is a recognition of the marketing communication role of public relations. This will mean that public relations will have to be brought more into the fold of overall marketing communications planning with clearly specified marketing communications objectives for public relations, well managed campaigns, and effective evaluation and control.

Sponsorship

As already mentioned, sponsorship is sometimes viewed as being a sales promotion activity, but we consider it to be best described alongside public relations activities.

Sponsorship involves a company in supporting in some way something or someone that it feels will help in the overall marketing and sales of its products or services, albeit indirectly. The 'something or someone' that is sponsored can be a person, for example a sportsperson, an event, for example the Olympics, a cause, for example Aids prevention, and so on.

Over the past ten years commercial sponsorship has been one of the most rapidly growing areas of promotion. There are many reasons for this. For example, sponsorship of a particular event or person enables the sponsor to achieve much more cost-effective awareness with the target audience generated by the event or by the publicity associated with the individual than might otherwise be possible through conventional promotional tools such as advertising. So, for example, approximately 250 million people eventually see the Oxford/Cambridge University boat race, a massive audience for any sponsor at what in advertising circles is a relatively small outlay.

Thousands of millions of pounds are now spent annually by marketers on event and celebrity endorsement contracts. Tripp and Jensen[33] have suggested that the use of such promotion is based on the premise that source effects play an important role in persuasive communication. They give examples of the potential impact of such endorsement upon High Street sales. When Michael Jordan, the US basketball star, signed a multi-million pounds sponsorship contract with Nike, the training shoes manufacturer, the company's market share increased by 20 per cent over the previous quarter. However, their research also points to the possible detrimental effects of celebrities becoming involved in promotion, especially where a celebrity is involved in multiple product advertising. In particular they indicate two key points:

1   The number of products a celebrity endorses negatively influences consumers' perceptions of the endorser's credibility.
2   The number of exposures the celebrity endorser has to be public must be carefully monitored if it is not to have a negative impact upon attitude towards purchase intention.

Clearly then, Sponsorship based on celebrity endorsement in particular is not a panacea for marketers. Another risk associated with using celebrities to endorse products is if, for some reason, the reputation or image of the celebrity becomes 'tarnished', this may be a potentially detrimental effect on the sponsor's image.

Summary

In this chapter, four of the major tools of promotional strategy have been examined. The fifth element, personal selling, forms the focus of our next chapter.

In order to understand, and therefore plan, the promotional element of the marketing mix, it is important to appreciate how communications, for this is what promotion is, works. We have seen that marketing effectiveness is highly correlated with the effectiveness with which the marketer communicates with the target audience, and that this in turn requires coordinating all the variety of ways in which this communication is achieved. All of the elements of the marketing mix, and not just the promotional elements themselves, potentially contribute to this process. In particular though, advertising, sales promotion, direct marketing, public relations, sponsorship and personal selling must be seen as a total marketing communications package and managed from this perspective. When it comes to managing the individual elements of the promotional mix, although there are differences in application, purpose and implementation, the overall process is the same. Clear objectives must be set, couched preferably in communication terms and, wherever possible quantified. On this basis, budgets can be set and promotional campaigns developed. Each of the promotional tools and the overall marketing communications strategy must be carefully evaluated and controlled. Only by following a systematic, planned and coordinated approach to marketing communications can what is an enormous spend area of strategic marketing be justified and improved.

Questions

1 What are the main elements of the communications process, and how does an understanding of these elements help the marketer develop more effective marketing communications?
2 Outline the key steps in the planning of communication strategies.
3 Compare and contrast the so-called 'strong' versus 'weak' theories of advertising.
4 Using examples, indicate the sorts of situations, products etc. where each of the following promotional tools might be best used:

   (a) Advertising
   (b) Sales promotion
   (c) Public relations
   (d) Sponsorship.

5 Using examples, discuss why direct marketing has become such an important tool of marketing promotion.

References

1. Lancaster, G. A. and Massingham, L. C., *Essentials of Marketing*, 3rd edn., McGraw-Hill, London, 1999, p. 289.
2. Doyle, P., *Marketing Management and Strategy*, 2nd edn, Prentice-Hall International, Hemel Hempstead, England, 1998.
3. Mercer, D., *Marketing*, 2nd edn, Blackwell, Oxford, 1996, p. 310.
4. Strong, E. K., *The Psychology of Selling*, McGraw-Hill, New York, 1925.
5. Lavidge, R. J. and Steiner, G. A., 'A model for predictive measurements of advertising effectiveness', *Journal of Marketing*, October 1961.
6. Jones, J. P., 'Over-promise and Under-delivery' *Marketing and Research Today*, November 1991, pp. 195–203.
7. Kotler, P., *Marketing Management: Analysis, Planning, Implementation and Control*, 9th edn, Prentice-Hall, New Jersey, 1997, p. 642.
8. Abrath, R. and Westhuizen, B., 'A promotional mix appropriation model', *Journal of Industrial Marketing*, 1985, pp. 212–221.
9. Kotler, P., Armstrong, G., Saunders, J. and Wong, V., *Principles of Marketing*, 2nd

European edn, Prentice-Hall, London, 1999, p. 757.

10. Colley, R. H., *Definitive Advertising Goals for Measured Advertising Results*. Association of National Advertisers. New York, 1961 and 1983.
11. Rodgers, E. M., *Diffusion of Innovations*, Free Press, New York, 1962.
12. Palda, K. S. 'The hypothesis of a hierarchy of effects – a partial evaluation'. *Journal of Marketing Research*, **3** (1) February 1966.
13. Burnett, J., *Promotion Management*, Houghton Mifflin, New York, 1993.
14. Maloney, J. C., 'Attitude measurement and formation'. Paper presented at the Test Market Design and Measurement Workshop, American Marketing Association, Chicago, Illinois, 21 April 1966.
15. Burnett, L. Co., *Communication of An Advertising Man*, Leo Burnett Co., Chicago, 1961, p. 61.
16. Maloney, J. C., *Marketing Decisions and Attitude Research in Effective Marketing Coordination*, ed. G. L. Baker Jr., American Marketing Association, 1961, pp. 595.
17. Smith, P. R., *Marketing Communications: An Integrated Approach*, 2nd edn, Kogan Page, London, 1998.
18. Aaker, D. A., Batra, A., and Myers, J. G., *Advertising Management*, 4th edn, Prentice Hall, New York, 1999.
19. Davies, M., *The Effective Use of Advertising Media*, 4th edn, Business Books, London, 1992.
20. Kent, R. J., 'Competitive versus non-competitive clutter in Television Advertising', *Journal of Advertising Research*, March/April, 1993, pp. 40–46.
21. Carter, M., "Direct Response Ads', 'Gain Respect'", *Marketing Week*, July 1, 1994, pp. 24–25.
22. Gilmore, R. F. and Secunda, E., 'Zipped TV commercials boost prior learning', *Journal of Advertising Research*, Nov/Dec 1993, pp. 29–38.
23. Smith, P. R., op. cit., p. 296
24. Fill, C., *Marketing Communications*, 2nd edn, Prentice-Hall, Europe, 1999, p. 360.
25. Smith, P. R., op. cit., Chapter. 12.
26. Fill, C., op. cit. Chapter. 19
27. Doyle, P. and Saunders, J., 'The lead effect of marketing decisions', *Journal of Marketing*, February 1985, pp. 54–65.
28. Blair, M. H. and Rosenburg, K. E., 'Convergent findings increase our understanding of how advertising works', *Journal of Advertising Research*, **34**, 1994, May/June, p. 35.
29. 'Power Points' *Marketing Week*, February 3, 2000, pp. 43–47.
30. Miles, L., 'Childish Things', *Marketing Business*, December/January 1999, pp. 36-38.
31. Walker, J., 'Mailing against the wind', *Marketing Weekly*, September 9th, 1994, p. 41.
32. Rines, S., 'Telemarketing calling the shots', *Marketing Weekly*, September 19th, 1994, p. 33.
33. Tripp, C. and Jensen, T. D., 'Effects of multiple product endorsement', *Journal of Consumer Research*, **20**, 4, 1993, March, p. 548.

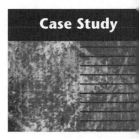

Case Study

Tony Trout is the recently appointed Marketing Director of Global International PLC. Global are a multinational marketer of sports equipment, selling a range of well-known brands in virtually every part of the world.

As a company, somewhat unusually compared to their competitors, Global have never considered commercial sponsorship for the company or any of its brands. In fact, several of the company's branded products are used by the leading sports persons in a number of sports. So, for example, Jerry Sprat (currently the world's number 1 tennis player from the US) uses the company's 'Spinner' brand of racket. Similarly, most of the Australian cricket

team use the company's 'Crackem' brand of bat. Finally, their basketball brand, 'Big'N'Bouncy' is the official ball of the American Basketball Association. None of these brands or usages are connected in any way with any form of sponsorship.

The company has considered sponsorship several times during its history, particularly as it has seen its major competitors use this form of promotion to good effect. The main reason why the company has not considered sponsorship before is that the chairperson, the original co-founder of the company, feels that any form of sponsorship is demeaning to the company and its products. The view held by the chairperson is that a good product will sell itself, in some ways a viewpoint substantiated by the selection of many of the company's brands by leading sports persons and sports organizations without any sponsorship. In addition, there was a feeling at least in some parts of the company that sponsorship through product endorsement by a leading sports person was not particularly effective in as much as everyone knew that this person would be in receipt of large sums of money for endorsing the product. In other words, there was a source credibility problem. Finally, there was always a concern about what would happen to the company and/or brand image if, as so often seemed to be the case, there was some sort of scandal with the sponsored party.

Tony Trout is a firm believer in sponsorship. His previous company used it to excellent effect despite one or two problems. Global spend large amounts of money on advertising and sales promotion. He has decided to make his case to the rest of the Board for introducing sponsorship as a major part of the promotional mix. He needs to prepare his case for this at the next Board Meeting.

QUESTION

Prepare Tony's case for sponsorship.

10

Channels of distribution

Chapter objectives

By the end of this chapter you will:

▶ Appreciate the importance and role of channels of distribution in marketing strategies.

▶ Understand the functions of intermediaries.

▶ Comprehend key elements and decisions in distribution channel design.

▶ Be able to evaluate the different configurations of channel structure.

▶ Be familiar with some of the more recent trends and developments in channels of distribution.

Introduction

The next two chapters review what is often referred to as the 'place' element of marketing strategy. Consumers are often unaware of the methods through which they receive goods. Indeed, the channel structure is often very complex and performs many functions.

Before we discuss in depth the structure of marketing channels, it is perhaps useful that we look at their emergence and the functions they perform. Four distinct functions can be identified, and these are described below.

The consumer wants cycle

The word 'channel' has its origins in the French word for canal, which in marketing terms can be interpreted as a route taken by products as they flow from their point of production to points of intermediate and final use. Marketing is a key factor in a continuous cycle that begins and ends with consumer wants. It is the role of the marketer to interpret consumer wants and combine them with empirical market data, such as the location of consumers, their numbers and their preferences, to form the basis for manufacture. The simple notion is that on completion of the manufacturing process, the finished product is moved into the hands of consumers, and the cycle is complete when the consumer obtains the satisfaction resulting from product ownership.

The producer-user gap

Despite the growth of direct marketing discussed in Chapter 9, in today's complex economy, the majority of producers do not sell directly to the final users. Between them and consumers stands a host of marketing intermediaries. The distribution channel serves to bridge the gap, geographically speaking, between producers and users. Marketing channels thus play an integral role in the operation of the marketing concept.

Relationship between marketing channels

The relationships among channel members are greatly influenced by the basic structure of the channel itself. Such marketing channels can be described as sets of interdependent organizations involved in the process of making a product or service available for use or consumption.

Demand stimulus

Inevitably, in addition to marketing channels satisfying demand by supplying goods and services in the right location, at the correct quantity and price, they should stimulate demand through promotional activities of the units (retailers, manufacturers and wholesalers). In this way, a marketing channel should be viewed not only as a demand satisfier, but also as an orchestrated network that creates value for the user or consumer through the generation of form, possession, time and place utilities.

In this chapter, therefore, we shall start by examining the ways in which distribution systems are designed and how channel policy is determined, depending on the degree of market exposure sought by a company.

Distribution system design

More and more, the starting point for marketing channel design is the ultimate consumer, indicating a shift away from manufacturer-driven designs. Inevitably, although an understanding of consumer purchasing patterns is essential, there are other factors that influence channel organization. Several factors can be identified:

- There may be a restriction in the choice of outlets available to manufacturers and suppliers; for example, retail outlets may already have been secured by existing, well established manufacturers.
- Channel design will be influenced by the number, size and geographic concentration of consumers. If customers are few in number but large and geographically concentrated, it may be that direct channels will be suitable. If, however, the opposite is true and customers are well dispersed, the mechanics of direct channels

become increasingly difficult and inevitably there will be a need for a large number of intermediaries.

- Product characteristics will affect the channel design. Industrial goods manufacturers tend to use direct channels, but there are other factors that can influence the decision. Perishable goods, for example, need to be turned over quickly; therefore direct methods are often applied. In contrast, non-perishable, non-bulky goods can be more readily handled via indirect channels.
- Some products are more suited to indirect channels because of the environmental characteristics. Thus in certain lines of trade – for example, furniture – manufacturers' representatives are particularly well adapted to serve producers and customers because of their ability to carry full lines of complementary products assembled from a variety of manufacturers.
- Some organizations have limited discretion on marketing channels owing to economic conditions and legal restrictions.

It is important here that we consider the strategic impact of the distribution channels on a company. Needless to say, any decision made regarding the channel will have a long-term effect on the company. The whole of the marketing mix will at some stage be affected by the choice of the marketing channel. For example, the price of goods will be affected depending on the number of levels between the manufacturer and the end user. Any decisions to alter the marketing channels for products will more than likely be long-term decisions. Therefore it is important that existing channel structures are constantly reviewed in order to exploit opportunities.

Strategic channel choices

We mentioned earlier that an important consideration towards the formulation of channel policy was the degree of market exposure sought by the company. There are several choices available to a company that can be identified:

- *Intensive distribution*
  Products are placed in as many outlets as possible. Such an **intensive distribution** strategy is most commonly used when customers wish to purchase goods frequently; for example, household goods such as soap, newspapers or toothpaste. Such wide exposure of products gives the customers an opportunity to buy and very often the image of the outlet is not vitally important. The aim of such a strategy is to achieve maximum exposure for the products.
- *Selective distribution*
  Products are placed in a more limited number of outlets in defined geographic areas. Instead of widespread exposure for the products, **selective distribution** seeks to show products in the most promising or most profitable outlets only.
- *Exclusive distribution*
  Products are placed in the hands of one outlet only in a specified area. **Exclusive distribution** often brings about a greater partnership between seller and re-seller and results in a great deal of loyalty. Part of the agreement usually requires the dealer not to carry competing lines, and as such the result is a more aggressive selling effort of the company's products.

We can see, therefore, that there are several key decisions to make when determining the company's distribution system. Its importance is perhaps underlined by the fact that the choice of a distribution channel does have an effect on all elements of the marketing mix and as such any decisions could have long-term effects.

Types and classifications of channel

It is often argued that the marketing channels can be characterized according to the number of channel levels. Each institution which performs some work to bring the product to the point of consumption is included in every channel; the number of intermediaries involved in the channel operation determines on how many levels it operates.

There are four main types of channel level existing in consumer markets (see Figure 10.1). The first three levels (zero, one and two) do not require explanation. The three-level channel usually constitutes three intermediaries, usually comprising a 'jobber' (merchant wholesaler) who intervenes between the wholesaler and retailer. It is the jobber's role to buy from wholesalers and sell to smaller retailers, who are not usually serviced by the larger wholesalers.

Within each marketing channel, the intermediaries are connected by several types of flows. These can be classified as follows:

1 *Physical flow*
  This flow describes the movement of physical products from raw materials to the final consumer. For example, in the case of a towel manufacturer, the raw material is the cotton yarn which flows from the grower via transporters to the manufacturers' warehouses and plants.
2 *Title flow*
  This flow is the actual passage of ownership from one channel institution to another; using the same example as above, i.e. the manufacturing of towels, the title to the raw materials passes from the supplier to the manufacturer. Title to the finished towels passes from the manufacturer to the wholesaler or retailer, and then on to the final consumer.
3 *Information flow*
  This flow involves the directed flow of influence from such activities as advertising, personal selling, sales promotion and publicity from one member to other members in the system. Manufacturers of towels direct a promotion and information flow to retailer or wholesalers, which is more commonly known as a trade promotion. Additionally, this type of activity may be directed to the end consumer and is often referred to as an 'end user' promotion.

We can now consider the classification of marketing channels.

Conventional marketing channels

Stern and El-Ansary[1] describe conventional marketing channels as:

> networks comprising isolated and autonomous units, each of which performs a traditionally defined set of marketing functions.

Figure 10.1
Channel
relationships

Zero level channel
Manufacturer –► Consumer

One level channel
Manufacturer – – – – – – – – – – – – – – – – – – ► Retailer – – – –► Consumer

Two level channel
Manufacturer – – – ► Wholesaler – – – – – – – – – ► Retailer – – – –► Consumer

Three level channel
Manufacturer – – – ► Wholesaler – –► Jobber – – – –► Retailer – – – –► Consumer

Coordination among channel members is through the bargaining process, and consequently membership to the channel is relatively easy and loyalty is low. As such, this type of network does tend to be very unstable. As Erdem[2] has pointed out, members of conventional channels rarely co-operate; rather, each channel member tends to work independently of the others.

Decision makers within conventional channels are more concerned with cost and investment relationships at a single stage of the marketing process, and as such are usually committed to established working practices.

Vertical marketing systems

Vertical marketing systems (VMS) are in complete contrast to conventional channels. In vertical marketing channels, channel members co-ordinate their activities between the different levels of the channel in order to reach a desired target market[3].

The essential feature of a vertical marketing system is that the primary participants both acknowledge and desire interdependence, and view it as in their best long-term interests. For the channel to function as a vertical marketing system, one of the member firms must be acknowledged as the leader. This leader is typically the dominant firm and can be expected to take a significant risk position. It usually has the greatest relative power within the channel.

Corporate vertical marketing

Corporate vertical marketing is defined as one that owns and generates two or more traditional levels of the marketing channel.

In fact in many economies corporate vertical channels have arisen primarily as a result of a desire for growth on the part of many companies through vertical integration. Two types of vertical integration are possible with respect to the direction which the vertical integration moves a company with respect to the supply chain. So, for example, when a manufacturer buys, say, a retail chain, this is referred to as forward integration with respect to the chain. Backward integration then, is moving upstream in the supply chain. For example, when, say, a retailer invests in manufacturing, or a manufacturer invests in a raw material source. Although the end result of such movements is a corporate vertical marketing channel, often the stimulus to such movement is less to do with channel economies and efficiencies as such, and more with for example, control over access to supply or demand, entry into a profitable business or overall scale and operating economies. It is now felt that much of the vertical integration activity which took place during the 1990s in many economies, in fact resulted in lower overall profitability levels, and in some cases, the demise of the companies involved in the vertical integration as companies overextended themselves and/or moved into areas where they had little expertise or strengths. Because of this, many companies have turned their attention towards contractual systems for achieving growth and more control through the vertical channel marketing system.

Many companies wish to formalize their role obligations within their channel networks by employing legitimate power as a means of achieving control. This is often achieved by the use of contractual agreements. Dibb[4] *et al.* suggest that the contractual vertical marketing system is now the most popular arrangement partly because channel member roles and responsibilities are covered by legal (contractual) agreements.

We must remember that nearly all transactions between business are covered by one form of contract or another, and as such the contractual agreement determines the marketing roles of each party within the contract. Indeed the locus of authority usually lies with the individual members, but not exclusively.

The most common form of contractual agreement are *franchises* and *cooperative* and *voluntary groups*.

Franchise systems are increasingly popular and have fastest growing forms of marketing, and the basis for such agreements is common. A parent company will grant an individual or a relatively small company the right or privilege to do business in a prescribed manner over a certain period of time in a specified place. The parent company is often referred to as the franchiser and may occupy any position in the channel network. We can identify four basic types of franchise system:

- Manufacturer-retailer franchise (the best example is probably franchised service stations).
- Manufacturer-wholesaler franchise: for example, Coca-Cola, who sell the drinks they manufacture to franchised wholesalers, who in turn bottle and distribute soft drinks to retailers.
- The wholesaler-retailer franchise, typically exemplified by drug stores.
- The service-sponsor retailer franchise, exemplified by National Car Rental companies, McDonald's and Kentucky Fried Chicken.

There are thus many different types of franchise arrangement; for example, McDonald's insists that all of its units purchase from approved suppliers, provides building and design specifications, provides or helps locate finance for its franchisees, and issues quality standards that each unit must adhere to in order to hold its franchise. Other companies, however, are not as stringent in their demands of franchisees.

Irrespective of the patterns of different franchising systems, they all share a set of common features and operating procedures as follows:

1 A franchise essentially sells a nationally, or often internationally recognized trade name, process, or business format to the franchisee.
2 The franchisor normally offers expert advice on, e.g. location selection, capitalization, operation, and marketing.
3 Most franchise systems operate a central purchasing system at the national or international level to enable cost savings to be made at the individual franchise level.
4 The franchise is subject to a contract binding both parties.
5 This contract normally requires the franchisee to pay a franchise fee and royalty fees, but the franchisee owns the business as opposed to being employed.
6 The franchisor normally provides initial and continuous training to the franchisee.

As already mentioned, contractual vertical marketing systems, and particularly franchising, have been one of the fastest growing areas of marketing activity and distribution arrangements. Clearly this would not have occurred if there were not substantial advantages which derive from the franchising system. As we would expect, from a system which essentially involves two independent parties voluntarily agreeing to contract with each other, these advantages accrue to both the franchisee and franchisor. The main advantages are as follows beginning with the franchisees.

Some key advantages for the franchisees

- The franchisee gains the benefit of being able to sell a well-known product or service which has been market tested and known to work.
- The franchisee enjoys access to the knowledge, experience, reputation and image of the franchisor. Because of this the franchisee is able to enter a business much more easily than setting up from scratch. The learning curve is shortened, expensive mistakes can be avoided, and overall there is less chance of business failure.
- Although the franchisee has the backing of what is often the large organization of the franchisor, the franchisee is still essentially an independent business with all this implies for enjoyment and motivation.
- The franchisee is helped by often national or international advertising and promotion by the franchisor which would be beyond the means of a small independent business.
- The franchisee enjoys the use of the franchisor's trademark, continuous research and development, and market information.
- The franchisor will normally provide a system of management controls such as accountancy, sales and stock control procedures, etc.

Some of the main advantages accruing to the franchisor are as follows.

Some key advantages for the franchisor

Recruiting a network of franchisees enables rapid growth as wider distribution can be achieved with less capital.

- The individual franchisee is, as already mentioned, more interested and motivated than the hired manager might be.
- The franchisor secures captive outlets for this products or services, especially in the case of trade name franchising and private labels.
- Franchise fees and royalty fees provide a regular stream of income for the franchisor.
- The terms of the franchise contract normally give the franchisor substantial control over how the franchise is operated. Normally, the franchisor can terminate a franchisee's contract should he find the relationship unsatisfactory. The costs of such terminations are likely to be much less than if the franchisor were operating corporate owned facilities and where the staff involved were on the payroll. Normally the terms and restrictions on location and sale of the business by the franchisee ensure that the franchisor is able to maintain territorial exclusivity for its franchisees.

These advantages then explain why Kotler *et al.* comment on the rapid growth of franchising as a system of distribution. Of course there are also potential disadvantages and pitfalls to franchising both for franchisee and franchisor, however, the franchise relationship is such that it combines the strengths of both small and large scale businesses. The franchisee is the small businessperson who is able to respond to local market conditions and offer personal services to customers. The franchisor passes on economies of scale in national advertising and bulk purchasing. Not surprisingly, Falbe and Dandridge[6] suggest that for a franchise to be successful both parties need to work towards a common goal and avoid conflicts. This in turn, they suggest, requires frequent and open communication between franchise partners if the franchise system is to meet rapidly changing market conditions while maintaining the integrity of the system.

We often think of franchising as being confined to consumer products, in particular fast food, mainly of course due to the success of franchisers such as McDonalds, Kentucky Fried Chicken and others.

However, franchising is used for a wide range of products, and in both consumer and industrial markets. Other examples of hugely successful franchising operations include Prontoprint, Interflora, Dynorod and Benetton.

Voluntary and cooperative groups emerged in the 1930s as a response to chain stores. However, the scope of the cooperative effort has expanded from concentrated buying power to the development of a vast number of programmes involving centralized consumer advertising and promotion, store location and layout, financing, accounting and, in some cases, a total package of support services.

Generally, wholesaler sponsored voluntary groups have been more effective competitors than retail sponsored cooperatives, primarily because of the difference in channel organization between the two. In the former, a wholesaler can provide strong leadership, because it represents the locus of power within the voluntary system. In the latter, power is diffused throughout the retail membership, and therefore role specification and allocation of resources are more difficult to accomplish. In voluntary groups, the retail members have relinquished some of their autonomy by making themselves highly dependent on specific wholesalers for expertise. In retailer cooperatives, individuals retain more autonomy and thus tend to depend much less strongly on the supply unit for assistance and direction.

Administered vertical marketing

The **administered vertical marketing** system typically does not have the formalized arrangements of the contractual system or the clarity of power dependence of the corporate system. The member organizations acknowledge the existence of dependence and adhere to the leadership of the dominant firm, which may operate at any level of the channel. Large retail organizations (a prime example is Marks & Spencer) typify this system.

In administered systems, units can exist with disparate goals, but a mechanism exists for informal collaboration on inclusive goals. Decision making occurs by virtue of the interaction of channel members in the absence of a formal inclusive structure. However, the locus of authority still remains with individual channel members.

As in conventional channels, commitment is self-orientated, but there is at least a minimum amount of system-wide orientation among the members.

McCammon[7] observes:

> Manufacturing organizations . . . have historically relied on administrative expertise to co-ordinate reseller marketing efforts. Suppliers with dominant brands have predictably experienced the least difficulty in securing strong trade support, but many manufacturers with 'fringe' items have been able to elicit reseller co-operation through the use of liberal distribution policies that take the form of attractive discounts, financial assistance, and various types of concessions that protect resellers from one or more of the risks of doing business.

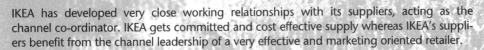

One of the best examples of a successful administered vertical marketing system in recent years is that of the furniture and lifestyle retailer, IKEA.

IKEA has developed very close working relationships with its suppliers, acting as the channel co-ordinator. IKEA gets committed and cost effective supply whereas IKEA's suppliers benefit from the channel leadership of a very effective and marketing oriented retailer.

We must observe that administered vertical marketing systems are one step removed, in an analytical sense, from conventional marketing channels. In an administered system, coordination of marketing activities is achieved by the use of programmes developed by one or a limited number of firms.

Successful administered systems are conventional channels in which the principles of effective interorganization management have been correctly applied.

Before we go on to discuss how such marketing channels are effectively coordinated, it is perhaps important that we discuss the structure of channels.

Structure of marketing channels

The marketing channel is an immensely complex structure. This has two basic aspects:

1   The placement of intermediary types in relation to each other.
2   The number of different intermediary levels or stages included in the channel.

'Placement' of intermediaries concerns the order in which they occur. The levels, or stages, in a channel refer to how many different separate types of intermediary are involved. In general, each intermediary type, such as retailers as a group, constitutes a level. The types of intermediary and the number of levels thus determine the structure of a marketing channel.

There are several types of channel structure available and they are often very dependent on the type of goods. A typical example of structures for consumer goods such as food and clothing is shown in Figure 10.2. We need to consider this figure very carefully, because it is based on three assumptions:

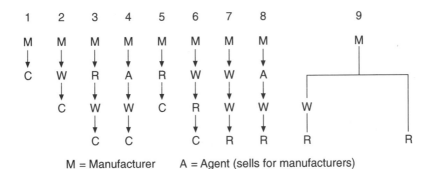

Figure 10.2
A typical example of structure for consumer goods.

1   The channel consists of complete organizations.
2   Manufacturers' agents and selling agents are included with the merchants even though they do not take title.
3   Physical movement follows exactly the movement of ownership.

Before we can fully understand the marketing channel, it is important that we understand the underlying reasons for the emergence of channel structures. Four logical steps can be identified for the emergence of intermediaries, as follows:

1   The efficiency of the process can be increased via an intermediary.
2   Channel intermediaries arise to adjust the discrepancy of assortments through the performance of the sorting processes.
3   Marketing agencies hang together in channel arrangements to provide for the routinization of transactions.
4   Channels exist to facilitate the searching process as well as the sorting process.

Each one of the above factors needs to be considered carefully.

Rationale for intermediaries

As the number of transactions increases, the need for intermediaries becomes greater. We referred earlier to the marketing channel as a 'canal', in which is contained the physical flow of products. Because of the complex array of organizations' intermediaries operating within a channel, which may be involved in one or all aspects of channel functions, the channel may also be visualized as a chain-link arrangement, in which each intermediary unit is in effect one link. Manufacturers are dependent on the effectiveness of their intermediaries if their channels of distribution are to meet their marketing goals.

Certain intermediaries of a marketing channel specialize in more than one function. Their inclusion primarily depends on their superior efficiency in the performance of basic marketing tasks. Such intermediaries, through their experience, specialization, contacts and scale, offer other channel members more than they can achieve on their own.

However, this type of specialization does lead to some important behavioural concepts, described below.

Position and role   Each channel member chooses a position or location in the channel. In a channel context 'role' refers to the functions and degree of functional performance expected of the firm filling a position.

Channel intermediaries have many roles. One is to perform the distribution function at a lower cost per unit than could the manufacturer, who is the intermediary unit most distanced from the consumer, and to balance the production efficiencies of the supplier with the purchasing needs of the customer.

A second is to break down the large volumes produced into the small quantities bought. For example, a retail furniture company might place an order for 100 suites of furniture, but the individual buys only one.

It is also important to remember when we consider the selling process, that the number of intermediaries can reduce the number of transactions contained within the selling process.

Figure 10.3 shows that given four manufacturers and ten retailers who buy goods from each manufacturer, the number of contact lines amounts to 40. If the manufacturers sell to these retailers through one intermediary, the number of necessary contacts is reduced to 14.

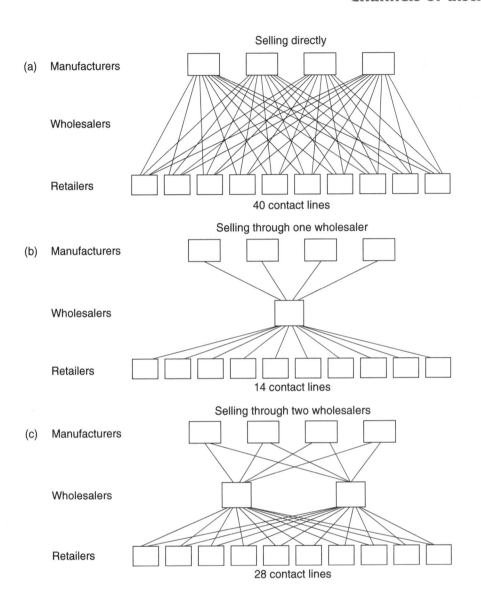

Figure 10.3
The economics of intermediary systems.

However, the number of contacts will increase as the number of intermediaries increases. For example, if the number of wholesalers was increased to two, necessary contacts will increase from 14 to 28. Similarly, four wholesalers will require 64 contacts. Thus, the greater number of intermediaries will result in diminishing returns on a contact basis.

Assortment and sorting   In addition to increasing the efficiency of transactions, intermediaries smooth the flow of goods and services by creating possession, place and time utilities. This smoothing requires that intermediaries perform a sorting function to overcome the discrepancy that arises between goods produced by manufacturers and goods demanded by the consumer.

In addition, intermediaries bring together a range of similar or related items into a large stock, thus facilitating the buying process. A supermarket will buy in 6000 to

10000 lines to provide shoppers with choice, and a builders' merchant will provide everything (from sand to light fittings) that the builder can use, on occasion even assembling some parts.

In this way, intermediaries play a very important role in facilitating the flow of products from the manufacturer to the consumer.

Routine transactions   The cost of distribution can be minimized if transactions are routinized. In effect, through routinization, a sequence of marketing agencies is able to hang together in a channel arrangement or structure. A good example is automatic ordering, whereby the cost of placing orders is reduced when retail inventory levels reach the necessary re-order point.

Searching   Buyers and sellers are often engaged in similar activities within the marketplace. There is a degree of uncertainty if manufacturers are unsure of customer wants and needs, and consumers are not always sure what they will find. In this respect, marketing channels facilitate the searching process in two ways:

1   Wholesale and retail institutions are organized by different product groups; for example, fashion, hardware, grocery.
2   Many products are widely available from wide ranging locations.

Flows in marketing channels

When we discuss marketing flows, there will be times when the word 'function' could be used, but in terms of this chapter, we shall refer to marketing 'flows' in channels as a more descriptive method of describing movement. In this way, we can show that the various intermediaries that make up a marketing channel are connected by several distinguishable types of flow, summarized in Figure 10.4, which depicts eight universal flows. This figure shows that physical possession, ownership and promotion are typically forward flows from producer to consumer. Each of these moves is 'down' the channel; a manufacturer promotes the product to a wholesaler, who in turn promotes it to a retailer, and so on.

Figure 10.4
Marketing flows in channels.

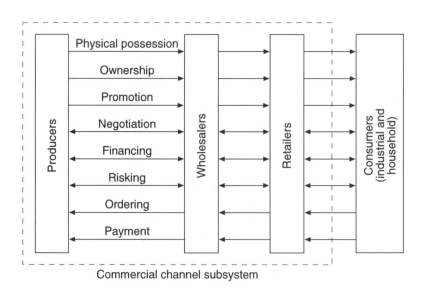

Commercial channel subsystem

Negotiation, financing and risking flows move in both directions, whereas ordering and prepayment are backward flows. Financing is perhaps the most important of all these flows: at any one time, when stocks are being held by one member of the channel, financing is in operation. When a wholesaler takes ownership and takes physical possession of a portion of the output of a manufacturer, the wholesaler is essentially financing the manufacturer.

This notion can be highlighted if the costs of stock are considered. Stock held in stores as dormant stock is 'dead money', but if this stock is freed via a wholesaler, the 'dead money' is freed for reinvestment.

The furniture industry exemplifies the flow. Traditional furniture retailers operating on a sold-order basis choose not to participate in the backward financing flow. However, 'warehouse' furniture retailers do participate in this flow directly, and thereby receive benefits from manufacturers in the form of lower prices and preferential treatment. This backward flow of financing is not solely associated with stockholding – another example is prepayment for merchandise.

The forward flow of financing is more common. All terms of sale, with the exception of cash on delivery and prepayment, may be viewed as elements of the forward flow of financing.

In addition to these flows there is the information flow. Typically, information regarding product attributes is passed 'down' the channel, often with the dominant channel member having great influence on this function. Marketing information is passed 'back' up the channel. In addition, information flows horizontally, i.e. with intermediaries operating at the same level, such as fibre manufacturers, communicating for mutual benefits.

Channel co-ordination

However well designed a marketing channel is, it is vitally important that it is organized and coordinated in a proper manner. Without such coordination, the activities and flows within it will not operate in an efficient and effective manner, and as a result the full potential of the system will not be realized.

In this part of the chapter, we will discuss effective coordination and the objectives of channel management. Emphasis is placed on understanding the relevant behavioural dimensions of interorganizational relations, because it is through this understanding that the manager can learn how to organize, manipulate and exploit the resources available.

The long-term objective of channel management is to achieve, at a reasonable cost, the greatest possible impact at the end user level so that the individual members of the channel can obtain satisfactory returns (e.g. profits, market share) as compensation for their specific contributions. The behaviour of intermediaries within any given structural arrangement should thus be directed towards achieving high yield performance.

Once the marketing management of an organization isolates the market targets to attack, and the products and services which it must supply in order to satisfy needs and wants in those various segments, the question of how best to make the products and services available for consumption arises.

Figure 10.5 clearly identifies four major steps which represent the co-ordination process. The first step is to determine the level of service outputs demanded by end users of the commercial channel system. The service outputs that are among the most significant in distribution are lot size, delivery or waiting time, market decentralization or spatial convenience, and breadth and depth of product or service assortment.

The second step involves identifying the marketing tasks that need to be carried

Figure 10.5
Stages in the
channel coordination
process.

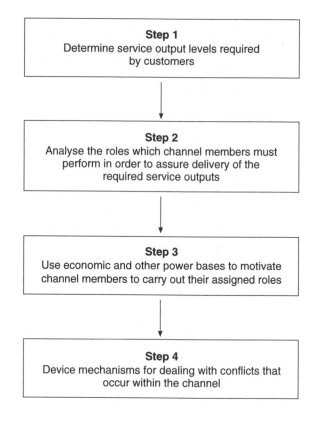

Step 1
Determine service output levels required
by customers

Step 2
Analyse the roles which channel members must
perform in order to assure delivery of the
required service outputs

Step 3
Use economic and other power bases to motivate
channel members to carry out their assigned roles

Step 4
Device mechanisms for dealing with conflicts that
occur within the channel

out in order to achieve the service outputs, and which channel members have the capability to perform the tasks. Management must then determine whether, through the use of channel control strategies, it will be able to control the behaviour of existing channel members or whether it will be compelled to integrate channel flow vertically so that the required service outputs are provided to end users. The latter notion will not, however, guarantee that the desired outcome is achieved. Therefore, a major issue in channel management relates to where and what extent marketing flow participation should be assumed in order to generate the desired service outputs. For example, if car buyers need financing, the manufacturer, the retailer or some outside intermediary can provide it. But the output – in this example, lending services – must be readily available if the consumer is going to feel comfortable in considering a specific purchase requiring financing. In a situation where no channel intermediary is willing to accept the risk of financing, the initial supplier may have to assume the flow. That is, it would prefer to specialize in those flows which it can perform best and rely on others to invest their capital in flows which they can perform at a comparative advantage. This example shows how it is possible to consider marketing channels as a means of dividing labour.

The third step in the coordinative process is to determine which strategies should be used to achieve the desired results, irrespective of whether management decides to invest in integrating functions or whether it deals with independent companies.

In essence, power is the ability to get somebody or something to do a task. It can be defined in terms of how one channel member can exert influence on another channel member. Such use of power is the mechanism by which congruent and effective roles become specified, roles become realigned, when necessary, and appropriate role performance is enforced. There are several bases of power, which include rewards, coercion and expertness.

The fourth step involves setting up mechanisms to deal with conflict issues which will arise in channels so that the channel will continue to provide the desired service outputs even if channel members disagree. Very often channel members perform unique roles. Thus, manufacturers specialize in production and national promotions, while retailers specialize in merchandising, distribution and promotion at a local level. This specialization means that channel members become reliant on each other in order to achieve objectives. Inevitably, this means there has to be a great deal of cooperation between channel members, and without it, the task will not be completed. Brassington and Pettitt[8] not only highlight this need for co-operation but also the fact that such co-operation doesn't always come easy:

> A climate of cooperation is perhaps the most desirable within a channel system. It does not just happen, but needs to be worked on and cultivated with positive cooperation, signs and signals.

There is, however, a danger that there will be conflicts of interest, and it is very possible that distribution channels will exhibit levels of conflict.

Ideally, channel members should attempt to coordinate their objectives, plans and activities with other intermediaries in such a way that the performance of the total distribution system to which they belong is enhanced. However, there is much empirical evidence to support the view that such integrated activity throughout the length of the marketing channel is rare:

1 Channel participants are not concerned with all the transactions that occur between each of the various links in the channel.
2 Channel intermediaries, in particular, are most concerned about the dealings that take place with those channel members immediately adjacent to themselves from whom they buy, and to whom they sell.

Channel intermediaries are thus not, in fact, functioning as enlisted member components of a distribution system, but are operating independently, making decisions concerning methods of operation, functions performed, clients served, and objectives, policies and programmes adopted.

Channel conflict

We have stated already that a marketing channel should be a set of interlocking and mutually dependent elements. We have also stated that it is in the interests of all the members of a channel for there to be a substantial degree of co-operation. In fact, an almost inevitable feature of marketing channels is potential conflict between channel members. This should always be taken into account by marketing firms in the strategic design of their channel arrangements.

It is, however, possible that healthy competition can lead to conflict. A major task in channel management is to seek ways to manage this conflict. Channel structures and relationships can be designed in such a way that the potential for conflict is reduced, and if conflict is inevitable, then management must manipulate conflict in the interests of the company.

Channel conflict can be described as a situation in which one member of a distribution channel perceives another member as an adversary, engaging in behaviour designed to injure, thwart or gain scarce resources at its expense. Conflict in distribution channels can occur in many different forms. We can identify at least three types of distributive conflict – horizontal, intertype and vertical.

1 *Horizontal conflict*
   Horizontal conflict is related to competition among similar types of intermediaries at the same level in the channel – two household textile stores in competition with one another, is one example of such conflict.
2 *Intertype conflict*
   Intertype conflict refers to competition among different types of intermediaries at the same level in the channel. This sort of competition has intensified since the advent of 'scrambled merchandising' by retailers (where retailers add new product lines which are unrelated to their normal lines of business; supermarkets have added homewares and clothing to their product lines, offering the consumer a wider product range and achieving higher margins). Intertype is a significant variety of conflict because it reflects one manner in which industries remain efficient and respond to changing market conditions.
3 *Vertical conflict*
   Vertical conflict refers to competition among the different levels of a channel. Such problems among channel members can be devastating to existing co-operative relationships.

Whilst there are several reasons for channel conflict, what is more important to channel management are the underlying causes for conflict. There is rarely a single reason for conflict when stress arises in the management of channel institutions. Stress and conflict can be present in a dormant state for an indefinite time; times of change cause existing stress to peak, leading to open hostility among channel members. Doyle[9] points out that some conflict is inevitable in most channels and may even be positive in that it can prompt needed changes to the channel. He also points out, however, that conflict can quickly get out of control, usually leading to severe problems in the channel.

Our earlier example regarding some retailers selling manufacturers' brands at lower prices than these manufacturers would wish is a good example of vertical conflict in the channel. There is no doubt that the selling of brands such as Levis, Calvin Klein, Sony and so on at prices much lower than those recommended by their manufacturers and marketers has given rise to considerable vertical conflict in the channel.

Goal incompatibility

All channel members would appear to share a common goal – maximizing the efficiency and effectiveness of the total system. However, each firm exists as a separate legal entity, each with its own employees, owners and other interested parties who help shape its goals and strategies. Some firms' goals may be incompatible with the aims and objectives of other channel members. This incompatibility will be a primary cause of stress which will ultimately result in conflict.

The distribution of channel profits is a typical example here. Each institution will desire the highest possible profit for the whole channel and the natural tendency will be towards co-operation to achieve maximum profit levels. However, each individual firm can be expected also to desire the largest obtainable share of the total channel profits. The predictable result is conflict over the allocation process.

Even if goals are compatible there may be disagreements about certain methods employed: all channel members may agree that increases in volume of a product are desirable, for instance, but may disagree on the means employed to accomplish it. Wholesalers may desire more shelf space for better positioning of products in retail stores; retailers may feel that more advertising and promotional effort by the manufacturer would accomplish the objective of an increase in sales. The result is conflict over which method to use.

Position, role and domain incongruence

The concepts of position, role and domain need to be recognized by channel members. In a channel consisting of a manufacturer using wholesalers to sell to retailers, there is a consensus of opinion about the roles and domains of each party. If, however, the manufacturer decides to serve larger retailers directly, positions will be respecified. Changes in position specification, or poorly defined positions, can precipitate conflict among channel members.

Where roles vary, all channel members must understand and agree upon the expected behaviour of the respective firms. In situations where consensus does not exist, conflict can be expected. Because each role represents a code of conduct defining the channel member's expected contribution, adequate performance is critical to maintaining harmony within the channel system. Inadequate performance, or failure to behave in the prescribed manner, frustrates attempts by one firm to predict what the other will do. This frustration is a major cause of channel conflict.

Conflict may also arise when there is a lack of agreement concerning the organizational domain. If channel members do not know, or do not agree on, the domain of other firms in the system, the result is frustration and an inability to achieve goals.

If domains overlap, and two or more firms lay claim to the same functions, products or customers, extreme disagreement will probably result in open hostility.

Communication breakdown

Communication breakdowns may cause conflict in two distinct ways:

1 The failure of one firm to pass on vital information to other channel members. A manufacturer wishing to maintain a competitive advantage may decide not to announce a new product until a national distribution programme has been developed; retailers on the other hand, need information about new products as soon as possible, in order to prepare their own strategy for the introductory period.
2 Noise and distortion within the message process. In channels, 'noise' often arises from confused language connotations: when channel members attach different meanings to language and terminology, stress results and the potential for conflict increases.

Communication breakdowns are particularly common in specialist business areas. This sort of noise arises because functional specialists develop a terminology of their own, which means little to others outside that business environment. Unclear communication with a non-specialist may play a major part in developing conflict: the specialist should always ensure that communications have been understood.

Differing perceptions of reality

Different solutions to mutual problems can lead to confliction behaviour. Even when channel members have a strong desire to co-operate and goal agreement exists, conflict can occur when perceptions of the real facts differ.

Each channel member brings to the relationship different backgrounds and prejudices; facts are likely to be interpreted according to prior experience. All members may agree that the channel is not functioning as effectively as desired; each channel member may perceive a different reason for this lack of effectiveness. Manufacturers may feel that a retailer's lack of stock is due to failure to maintain adequate safety stock levels and realistic reorder points. The retailer may feel that inventory policies are realistic and that the problem is caused by the manufacturer's inability to meet scheduled delivery times. Each party is interpreting the situation based upon experience and natural prejudices associated with its own position and role.

Ideological differences

Sometimes there may be a fundamental ideological conflict in channels which stems from big business and small business perceptions of management, particularly concerning the appropriate level of sales effort. So, for example, a manufacturer may be so satisfied with the performance of a wholesaler in a given territory that pressure is exerted on the wholesaler to expand the line of business. The wholesaler may be satisfied with allowing the business to continue to run in its present form.

In this way, the pressures exerted by the manufacturer will lead to stress in the relationship, and perhaps to conflict. If this is an established channel, it is in the interests of everybody to settle the dispute or misunderstanding in whichever way is possible.

There are several methods of resolving conflict, and it is an essential task of management to seek ways to manage conflict. Ways need to be found to avoid conflict becoming dysfunctional and to harness the energies in conflict situations to produce solutions. Doyle[10] also suggests that ideally channel members should agree strategies for resolving any conflict in advance.

The specific strategy employed will depend largely on the cause of the conflict. We have already discussed the major causes of channel conflict, and depending on which underlying cause is identified, different strategies in isolation will be employed. Another important factor towards the resolving of the conflict will be the weight of power of the channel member seeking to resolve the conflict. There are, however, several conflict solving strategies, and these will now be described.

Problem solving

Two important problem solving techniques exist – the adoption of superordinate goals and the improvement of the communications process.

1   *Adopting superordinate goals*
    This refers to a goal or goals that are greatly desired by all members caught in the conflict. Very often, **superordinate goals** cannot be achieved by an individual member of the channel, but the concerted efforts of all parties are required. Such disputes become more pronounced when the channel is confronted by an external threat, and conflicts among members of channels also seem to dissipate when alternative channel systems arise.

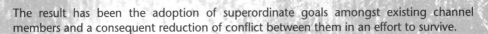

The threat to existing channel members of new channel arrangements for car retailing in the UK has brought about a reduction in some of the conflict between the conventional channel members which used to exist. The car manufacturers and their dealers are being challenged by the fact that consumers are increasingly purchasing their new cars through a variety of new channels. These include, for example, sourcing their new cars from other countries where the prices may be much lower; the growth of so-called car hypermarkets where the cars are often sourced on the grey market; and finally, of course, the ubiquitous Internet which is increasingly being used as a channel for new car purchase in the UK.

The result has been the adoption of superordinate goals amongst existing channel members and a consequent reduction of conflict between them in an effort to survive.

Conflict resolution of a permanent nature requires an integration of the needs of both sides to the dispute so that they find a common goal without sacrificing their basic economic and ethical principles. What is difficult is to develop a goal or common interest on which all parties can agree.

2   *Communications process*

A number of methods exist to alleviate *communications noise* in distribution channels. A more efficient flow of information and/or communications in channels permits members to find solutions to their conflict based on common objectives. All channel communications are efforts to decrease conflict (or avoid it altogether). The use of sales representatives by a manufacturer to convey information from wholesalers or retailers implies that the manufacturer is trying to encourage the attainment of both individual and common goals: the function of the sales representative has often been described as that of the 'problem solver'.

Persuasion

This implies that the institutions involved draw upon their power resources or leadership potential. If effective channel management is to be achieved, it is very often the case that there will be a need to locate an institution or an agency within the system that is willing to assume a leadership role. In this instance, channel leadership is viewed as the intentional use of power to affect the behaviour of other channel members in order to cause them to act in a manner that contributes to the maintenance or achievement of a desired level of performance. Very often, channel control results from channel leadership. Furthermore, like channel power, the level of channel control achieved by one firm over others in a channel may be issue-specific. For example, while the manufacturer may have control over pricing, retailers may have control over stock levels in the channel. Whether or not control can be exerted depends very much on the power base of each channel member.

By its very nature, persuasion involves communication between conflicting parties. Emphasis is on influencing behaviour to resolve conflict; the primary intention is to avoid or reduce conflict concerned with domain.

Usually, persuasion allows channel members to reach a consensus concerning relevant domains, and results in agreement without formal bargaining.

Bargaining/negotiations

The major difference between bargaining and persuasion is that in the bargaining process, very often stress continues to exist in the system long after agreement is reached.

In negotiation, no attempt is made to satisfy fully a channel member. Instead the objective is an 'accommodation', stopping conflict among members. Such as compromise may resolve the episode, but not necessarily the fundamental stress over which the conflict erupted. If stress continues, it is likely that some issue will cause conflict again at some later date.

Compromise is one means by which bargains can be reached in the channel. Each party gives up something it desires in order to prevent and end conflict. Often compromise is necessary to reach domain consensus, where persuasion and negotiation draw upon the abilities of the involved parties to communicate.

Politics

Here, politics refers to the resolution of conflict involving new organizations in the agreement reaching process.

Mediation involves a third party, usually to secure settlement of a dispute by persuading the parties either to continue their negotiation or to consider recommendations made by the mediator. Mediation involves operating in the field of the conflicting parties in such a way that opportunities are perceived that otherwise may have been missed. The very fact that solutions are being offered by a mediator – that is, somebody external to the dispute – can often lead to a settlement if both parties deem the solutions acceptable. Effective mediation keeps the parties together and clarifies facts so that the communication process does not break down. We need to remember that whilst mediators offer solutions to disputes, channel members are not obliged to accept the solutions.

In arbitration, however, the solution suggested by the third party is binding upon the conflicting parties. Arbitration can be compulsory or voluntary, and when it is the former, parties are required by law to submit their dispute to the third party and be bound by the decision. Voluntary arbitration is a similar process whereby parties are bound by the decision, but the dispute is submitted voluntarily.

We should note here that the whole question of relying on law enforcement to settle disputes in distribution is suspect, because it is doubtful whether solutions enforced by law can be applicable to future channel disputes in very different circumstances. Indeed, in channel management, these mechanisms are not greatly used because of the inability to find a neutral third party whose decision would be accepted by everybody involved in the dispute.

Diplomacy

Channel diplomacy is often referred to as the method by which inter-organizational relations are conducted, adjusted and managed by 'ambassadors', envoys or other persons operating at the boundaries of member organizations. Normally, channel members rely upon diplomatic procedures, especially in non-integrated systems. Channel diplomats should be the eyes and ears of the firms they work for, and should report anything which may be of interest to their firms.

Such 'diplomats' are commonplace in distribution channels, often at executive level. In this way, the diplomat's power base is such that it is obvious to the parties with whom the diplomat will interact.

In general, we must remember that the objective of effective channel management and the generation of conflict management strategies is to provide more rational and functional collective decision making within the channel. Channel leadership is often a prerequisite for effective management, and in some instances control will need to be exercised within the system.

The dynamic nature of channels

Just as we have seen that all marketing is characterized by constant change and therefore a need for the marketer in turn to adapt to these changes, so too marketing channels are subject to constant change and innovations. In fact, channels represent probably one of the most dynamic areas of marketing, and are constantly evolving to meet changing customer and market needs, which in turn reflect underpinning wider changes and trends in, for example, demography, lifestyles, etc. The marketer who fails to be aware of the changing nature of marketing channels and therefore fails to respond to them is in danger of becoming uncompetitive. It is not possible to outline all the important changes which are taking place with respect to channels of distribution but as examples of some of the recent developments in channels which are indicative of the innovation and changing nature of this area of marketing we can briefly explore the growth of so-called *multi-channel systems*. The growth of direct marketing, as previously discussed in Chapter 9, and finally the growth of Internet purchasing.

The growth of multi-channels

Many companies are now using a variety of channel arrangements to reach their target customers. Whilst at one time companies tended to use only one type of channel configuration in their marketing, now they may use several. The use of what Kotler[11] calls **multichannel systems** can be for a number of reasons, e.g.

- To increase market coverage by reaching new customers.
- To reduce the costs of selling to certain customers where, for example, these customers require, say, less service than that provided through the company's normal channels.
- To achieve a more customized service to particular customers than would normally be available through the company's normal channels.

Therefore in multichannel marketing a company might sell to one group of customers using telephone selling and no intermediaries, whilst another target group of customers may well be marketed to through a network of dealers because these customers require after-sales service and technical advice.

Although there are distinct advantages to be gained through using several different channel configurations to different target customers, multichannels can give rise to increased costs where they are not effectively controlled. They also can give rise to problems of conflict between different channel members where several channels are used.

The growth of direct channels

In Chapter 9 we discussed the growth of direct marketing. We pointed out that besides being an element of the promotional mix, direct forms of marketing can also be considered as sales channels. Obviously then, the growth of direct marketing methods such as catalogue selling and direct mail are examples of developments in channels as well as promotion. In addition to the direct marketing channels discussed in Chapter 9 however, another key area of growth in direct distribution is the development of home shopping.

Internet channels

Although strictly speaking not channels of distributions as such, in as much as goods of course cannot be delivered through the modem, there is no doubt that the Internet is bringing about significant changes to existing channels. We have already mentioned some of the products/markets where the Internet has already been significant in changing purchasing and hence distribution arrangements. Traditional booksellers, travel agents and record stores such as Virgin are all having to cope with major changes in how customers purchase these products and services, and the fact that more and more of this 'shopping' and purchasing behaviour is taking place via the Net.

The success of Amazon, the Internet bookseller, has shocked some of the more traditional book retailers. From virtually nothing, Amazon has built substantial sales in a very short space of time. Needless to say, without having to support expensive retail outlets, Amazon have also been able to undercut the prices of many of the conventional book retailers.

Although still in its infancy in many countries, home shopping is set to be one of the most important developments in channels over the next few years. Of course shopping at home is not new, after all, mail order has been around for a long time. The newer forms of home shopping, however, take this concept of selecting goods at home and then ordering them one step further. Needless to say, the developments in home shopping are based around developments in Information Technology and communication, and in particular the ubiquitous personal computer. Access to, and use of, cheap computing power at home has enabled the marketer to begin to develop systems of real time shopping where the customer calls up descriptions and even pictures of products on their home computer screen using a modem. The customer can search through such computer based 'catalogues' and then place an order over the Internet or telephone, including direct payment through, e.g. a credit card and have the selected item delivered direct to their homes. More recent developments in this area are based around virtual reality shopping. Again, using the computer, the home shopper calls up the virtual reality shopping mall onto their screen and then can move into different selected outlets in 'the mall', taking virtual reality trips down the different aisles in the selected retail outlet, and even selecting products as required from the 'shelves' for closer inspection. As with conventional mail order the customer may then place an order through the Internet and have the selected products delivered and their account debited. At the moment such virtual reality shopping is in its infancy but it is not likely to be long before at least a proportion of everyone's shopping is done in this way, and certainly some of the major retailers ranging from the multiple grocers to the major clearing banks are investing heavily in this area.

A more conventional, but just as fast growing an area of home shopping has been the growth of the shopping channels on the television. Cable television in particular has fostered the growth of this particular type of home shopping. For example, in the United Kingdom most of the Cable television companies have a shopping channel where customers can view products and services and buy direct using only the television, their credit cards, and the telephone. Clearly home shopping using the television is very advantageous, particularly for the elderly and infirm, and again it is likely that this particular type of home shopping will continue to grow in the future.

Summary

The need for effective distribution channel management is never more clear than when economic conditions are not good. We need to remember that distribution arrangements are often relatively long term in nature; therefore, any channel decisions are strategic decisions and not necessarily tactical or operational.

The inevitable consequences is that manufacturers need continually to monitor the distributive environment and reassess their existing channel structure with a view to exploiting and capitalizing on any changes.

Clearly, channel strategy must be derived from channel objectives, which vary amongst companies. Commonly, such objectives are derived from profit growth, return on investment, sales growth and many others. Because of the strategic nature of channel decision, the decision to change channels is infrequent, mainly because such a move would be considered high risk, and it often requires the approval of very senior executives within the company. We also need to consider the way in which a company is perceived in the marketplace; any change in channel selection can radically affect the perception of the company.

We discussed three major strategies – intensive, exclusive and selective. Each strategy has merits depending on the type of product made by the company. We need to remember that despite the relative advantages and disadvantages of each strategy, there is often a trade-off in selecting the strategy for a company.

For example, if a company decides on a strategy of intensive distribution, in many ways the company loses some control over the marketing of its products. In order to maintain control of its own destiny, the company needs to assume greater participation in each of the marketing flows.

On the other hand, as channel members move towards exclusive distribution, role expectations become more sharply delineated. There is greater effort required in careful bargaining over rights and obligations in order to achieve participation in each of the marketing flows. It is important to note here that exclusive strategies are not one-way agreements, and implicit in such agreements is a core of mutual support – that is, each of the parties gains something from the agreement. Thus, benefits and costs are normally divided.

We also discussed how channels could be classified based on participant acknowledgement of dependence. Primarily, we discussed the differences between the conventional marketing systems based on isolated and autonomous units and the vertical marketing system whereby the primary participants both acknowledge and desire interdependence and view it as in their best long-term interests.

Summary – continued

During the discussion on the role of intermediaries in the management of channels, we concluded that each channel member had both a position and a role. For the purposes of this chapter, 'position' is defined as where each channel member chooses to locate in the overall scheme of things and 'role' refers to the functions and degree of functional performance expected of the firm filling the position.

As in all forms of organization, the interaction of people, companies, organizations etc. will inevitably lead to some form of conflict. We discussed the most common types of conflict that emerges in distribution channel management; for example, there is a strong chance that role performance will deviate, at least occasionally, from that which is expected, because of situational factors and differing personal expectations of channel members.

Conflict is caused by goal incompatibility, domain dissensions and differences in perceptions of reality as well as by the level of interdependence in the system. We discussed these at length in the chapter, and whilst conflict can be a positive social force which often results in innovation, it needs to be effectively managed so as not to prevent a system from achieving its stated objectives.

We discussed several methods of managing conflict, which, if handled properly, would result in more rational and functional collective decision making within the channel. We need to understand that there will always be some element of conflict when organizations interact and 'pure' competition will never be achieved. Thus, in order to achieve long-term viability, inter-organization management is critical for marketing channels.

Wilson, Gilligan and Pearson[12] perhaps sum up distribution best when they state that distribution can be seen to present opportunities for gaining distinctive competencies relative to competitors. While an enterprise can offer good products at competitive prices, communicated effectively to the right people, all these factors are let down if the products are not available in the right place and at the right time.

Finally, we need to remember that changes in the structure and operation of channels have emerged and will continue to change in response to external and internal issues. Without doubt, the role of intermediaries and the whole subject of channel management are likely to change also.

Having established the nature, purpose and management of the marketing channel, we now need to set this in the wider arena of managing business logistics, of which the channel is but one important part.

Key terms

Intensive distribution [p297]
Selective distribution [p297]
Exclusive distribution [p297]
Vertical marketing systems [p297]
Corporate vertical marketing [p297]

Administered vertical marketing [p297]
Franchises [p280]
Multichannel systems [p293]
Superordinate goals [p2990]

Questions

1   What are the major strategic channel choices available to the marketer with regard to distribution system design?
2   What is the difference between vertical marketing systems and conventional marketing channels, and why have vertical marketing systems become more popular?
3   Using examples, identify the different basic types of franchise system.
4   What is meant by 'flows' in marketing channels and what is the significance of these for channel design and management?
5   Using examples, discuss the different types of conflict which can occur in channels of distribution and how these might be minimized.

References

1. Stern, L. W. and El-Ansary, A. I., *Marketing Channels*, 2nd edn, Prentice-Hall, Englewood Cliffs, N.J., p. 307.
2. Erdem, S. A. and Harrison-Walker, L. J., "Managing Channel Relationships": Towards an identification of effective promotional strategies in vertical marketing systems', *Journal of Marketing Theory and Practice*, 5, 2, Spring 1997, pp. 80–87.
3. Erdem, S. A. and Harrison-Walker, L. J., op. cit. pp. 80–87.
4. Dibb, S., Simkin, L., Pride, W. M. and Ferrell, O.C., *Marketing Concepts and Strategies*, 4th European edn, Houghton Mifflin, Boston, 2001, p. 363.
5. Kotler, P., Armstrong, G. Saunders, J. and Wong, V., *Principles of Marketing*, 2nd European edn, Prentice-Hall, Europe, 1999, p. 903.
6. Falbe, C. M. and Dandridge, T. C., 'Franchising as a strategic partnership: issues of co-operation and conflict in a global market'. *International Small Business Journal*, 10, 3, 1992, pp. 41–43.
7. McCammon, B. C., Jr., 'Perspective for distribution programming', in L. W. Stern and A. I. El-Ansary (eds), *Marketing Channels*, Prentice-Hall: Englewood Cliffs, N.J., p. 45.
8. Brassington, F. and Pettitt, S., *Principles of Marketing*, 2nd edn, Pearson Education, Harlow, Essex, 2000, p. 484.
9. Doyle, P., *Marketing Management and Strategy*, 2nd edn, Prentice-Hall, Hemel Hempstead, Herts, 1998, p. 328.
10. Doyle, P., op. cit. p. 328.
11. Kotler, P., *Marketing Management: Analyses, Planning and Control*, 9th edn, Prentice-Hall, New Jersey, 1997, pp. 551–552.

12. Wilson, R. M. S. and Gilligan, C. with Pearson, D., *Strategic Marketing Management, Planning, Implementation and Control*, Butterworth Heinemann: Oxford, 1992, p. 401.

Case Study

Starfish Products produce a range of fashion jewellery products. The founder of Starfish Products, Julie Flounder, started by making jewellery has a hobby at home. Eventually Julie began to sell some of her jewellery at small craft fairs in the district in which she lives. Right from the start, the jewellery proved to be very popular, especially amongst the age group 14–18. The jewellery was low priced but well made and very fashionable. Quite simply, Julie discovered that not only was she good at making jewellery but that she had a feel for the market and the jewellery fashions that would sell to the younger target market.

From this humble beginning, in just three years Julie has expanded her business and sales to the point where she now works full-time herself and employs three people helping her make the jewellery in a small workshop.

At the moment Julie is still selling mainly through craft fairs and the like, but now at much larger ones and nationwide.

Julie now wants to expand the business, demand is still strong and she has retained her flair for judging the market. She has the option to move to larger premises where she could take on more production staff, she also has a small budget set aside for promoting her products. Her main problem, she feels, at the moment with regard to expanding the business is distribution.

She feels that to expand the business quickly she needs to secure retail outlets on a national basis through which she can sell her products. Or, alternatively, she has wondered if a franchising operation might be the answer, possibly with sales direct to customers in their own homes rather like Tupperware or Ann Summers parties.

QUESTION

What distribution alternatives might be available to Julie to expand her business, and what are their relative advantages and disadvantages?

11

Logistics

Chapter objectives

By the end of this chapter you will:

▶ Appreciate the importance of managing the physical flows of products, services and information into, through, and out of the organization to its customers.

▶ Understand the meaning and scope of physical distribution and logistics management.

▶ Be aware of some of the more recent developments and trends in production and manufacturing, and in particular the growth of 'lean manufacturing' and 'just in time' systems and their implications for marketing.

▶ Be familiar with the steps in designing and operating a business logistics system.

▶ Appreciate the role of Information Technology and the marketing aspects of logistics management.

Introduction

This chapter considers what, in many ways, was until recently an unexplored and undeveloped aspect of marketing and corporate strategy; namely, the physical flows of products, services and information into, through and out of the organization to its customers. Clearly, physical distribution and logistics are part of the place element of the marketing mix and therefore should be considered and planned alongside the subject of Chapter 10, i.e. marketing channels. Indeed, as we shall see, a major impact, and hence consideration, of channel strategy and design is on the flows referred to above. It is now recognized, however, that the effective management of physical distribution and logistics can and does have a substantial impact on a company and its customers' levels of costs, efficiency and effectiveness. As important, from our perspective, is the fact that these elements of distribution, if well planned and implemented, are powerful competitive tools and can be used therefore to build a sustainable competitive advantage in the difficult markets of today.

Throughout, we shall emphasize a total systems approach to physical distribution management which, together with channel design decisions, is now most often referred to as marketing logistics.

Background to the growth in importance of physical distribution and logistics

We have already suggested that it is only relatively recently that physical distribution and logistics have begun to attract management attention. Some of the major reasons for this increased attention are as follows.

A continued search for cost savings/high costs of distribution

Rightly, all companies are concerned to search for ways to reduce costs. Since the industrial revolution, much of this search for cost savings has centred on the production area. Labour-saving technology, replacement raw materials, effective production planning and so on have all accounted for considerable managerial time, effort and expertise in order to reduce costs and improve output. All of this attention, however, has meant that increasingly the potential for further cost savings in these areas has become somewhat limited. If management is going to continue to look for cost savings, therefore, it will have to look elsewhere.

Doyle[1] has suggested that typically distribution costs can account for up to 20 per cent of sales. Not surprisingly then, in the search for further cost efficiencies in companies, physical distribution and logistics have figured highly.

More recently, however, a number of factors have prompted companies to explore this 'continent' more closely. As a result, it has become increasingly clear that not only is there substantial potential for improving efficiency and reaping cost savings but – perhaps more importantly for the marketer, this area also offers substantial potential for developing sustainable competitive advantage.

Perhaps what is surprising is that if physical distribution potentially accounts for such a large proportion of costs, why has it, as suggested, been such a neglected area for so long? Part of the answer to this lies in the fact that, as we shall see, conventionally the individual elements of physical distribution and logistics have been dealt with in a fragmented and piecemeal way, with separate parts of the business incurring what appeared to be relatively small costs of distribution. As a consequence, information on the total costs has not been available and/or has disappeared in the accounting system.

In addition to this, as a generalization it is fair to say that some of the major costs of physical distribution have accelerated recently. For example, one of the major elements of cost, transport, is increasingly expensive as the road, sea and air networks become increasingly congested. Similarly increases in fuel prices throughout the world have become a major cause for concern.

The emergence of a total systems (logistics) view of distribution

We have just seen that one of the reasons why distribution, despite its high overall cost, remained comparatively unexplored was the fact that conventionally it was organized and managed in a piecemeal fashion. Based partly on experience during military conflicts, it began to be recognized that effective and efficient distribution depended on **logistics**, an integrated approach to all of the elements which helped to move products and services to the right place, in the right quantity and at the right time. It was increasingly recognized that 'optimizing' one part of the system, for example inventories of stocks and work-in-progress, might have a detrimental knock-on effect on other parts of the distribution system, thereby reducing, not increasing, the efficiency and effectiveness of the system as a whole. Such systems thinking is, as we shall see, an essential component of modern logistical management. But at this stage it is sufficient to note that systems thinking, as applied to distribution, has proved a powerful impetus to the developing importance of this area.

Improved concepts and tools of logistics management

Hand in hand with the development of the total systems approach to distribution has gone the development of more sophisticated and powerful tools of analysis. The notion of interrelationships in the total system of distribution, again as we shall see, makes the problems of managing this total system difficult and complex. Developments in modelling, allied to more powerful and accessible computer power, enable this complexity to be managed. In short, we now have the tools to handle the logistical system in its entirety. Later on we shall see how the information technology (IT) revolution has impacted on the management of physical distribution and logistics.

The potential for competitive advantage: the notion of customer service

As already indicated, perhaps the most important reason for the growth in importance and interest in physical distribution and logistics, and certainly the major reason for including it here, is the fact that the logistics system offers substantial potential for achieving a competitive edge and hence winning and keeping customers. Particularly in industrial markets, where products may be relatively undifferentiated and prices and margins cut to the bone, companies might find that they can gain a competitive edge by using their logistical system to improve customer service levels. Jobber[2] suggests that customer service standards should be given 'considerable attention' as they may be crucial in customer choice. This in turn may allow a company to increase the volume of sales and/or to increase prices. Because of this, identifying appropriate levels of and types of customer service to be achieved by the logistics management system is a key aspect of planning in this area.

Trends and developments in manufacturing and purchasing: lean manufacturing and just in time purchasing and production

In the same vein, a number of developments and trends in industrial manufacturing and hence purchasing have heightened the importance attached by many customers to the service elements of the logistics systems of their suppliers and potential suppliers. Some of these were touched on in Chapter 4 when we looked at organizational buyer behaviour. But, for example, with modern continuous flow and large batch manufacturing systems a stock-out situation of even a relatively minor and inexpensive component may incur substantial costs in down time. This potential problem is heightened where, as they increasingly are, a firm's customers have moved towards the implementation of 'lean manufacturing' and/or the related 'just in time' purchasing and production. These two developments in contemporary manufacturing and purchasing are so important to the marketer, and in particular to the design of the logistics (and as we shall see in Chapter 12 the selling) elements of the marketing mix that we need to consider them in a little more detail.

In recent years perspectives on what constitutes an efficient and effective production process in a company have undergone considerable changes. Many factors have given rise to these changes in perspective but in simple terms they have been as a result of increased competition and more demanding customers. One of the major implications of these factors has been the recognition that production needs to be built around flexibility, whilst at the same time achieving cost efficient production and consistent quality of output. Lancaster[3] has suggested that this flexibility of the production process is essential because

> 'it transforms production operations enabling one machine to produce a wide variety of models and products – it provides the corporate capability to produce more varieties and choices even down to offering each individual customer the chance to design and implement the 'programme' that will yield the precise produce, service or variety that is right.'

Womack[4] *et al*. have termed these new production processes *'lean production'*. Often referred to also as '**lean manufacturing**' these new production processes are fundamentally different from the previous traditional mass production processes developed by companies such as Ford. Bolwijn and Kumpe[5] suggest that this new production is part of an overall change in world manufacturing. They describe a number of developments over the past 40 years. The first stage of development was based on the notion of the *'efficient firm'* where cost and price was all important. The emphasis on production was on producing competitively priced products on a mass-production scale. As a result of increasing competition, however, the end of the 1960s saw the need for the *'quality firm'* which was the next development in the evolution of production. The third and most recent development, he argues is the transition to our *'flexible firm'*. Much of manufacturing industry is now passing through this third phase which involves a distinct change in the production process with flow production and small batch runs of a wide assortment of products operated by teams of multi-skilled employees. Increasingly companies are now turning to this new form of flexible lean production based on flexible cells and working arrangements. Accompanying this growth of lean manufacturing has been the introduction of '**just in time**' (JIT) systems of manufacturing and purchasing. First used most extensively in Japan, JIT has not made major inroads into the West. As the terms implies, in the context of manufacturing and purchasing, JIT is based on a company securing supplies of raw materials and components needed for the manufacturing process at the precise point in time when they are required to enter this process. Dion *et al*.[6] have defined JIT as:

> 'an inventory control system which delivers input to its production or distribution site only at the rate and time it is needed. Thus it reduces inventories whether it is used within the firm or as a mechanism regulating the flow of products between adjacent firms in the distribution system channel.'

The JIT approach contrasts with the more conventional approach to stockholding delivery and manufacturing which was based essentially on a *'Just in Case'* principle. Oliver[7] provides a useful comparison between the Just in Case and Just in Time approach which is shown in Table 11.1.

The implications of the introduction of JIT systems for the marketer have been

Table 11.1 Just in Case versus Just in Time

Issue	Just in Case	Just in Time
Official goal	Maximum efficiency	Maximum efficiency
Stocks	Integral part of system – a necessary 'evil'	Wasteful – to be eliminated
Lead times	Taken as given and built into production planning routines	Reduced to render small batches economical
Batch sizes	Taken as given and economic order quantity is calculated	Lot size of *one* is the target – because of *flexible* system
Production planning and control	Variety of means – MRP models existing system and optimizes within it. Information 'pull' for hot orders	Centralized forecasts in conjunction with local pull control
Trigger to production	Algorithmically derived schedules. Hot lists. Maintenance of sub-unit efficiencies	Imminent needs of downstream unit via Kanban cards
Quality	Acceptable quality level. Emphasis on error detection	Zero defects. Error prevention
Performance focus	Sub-unit efficiency	System/organization efficiency
Organizational design	Input-based. Functional	Output based. Product
Suppliers	Multiple, distant; independent	Single or dual sourcing Supplier as extension

Source: Adapted from Oliver, N. (1994), 'JIT: issues and items for the research agenda', *International Journal of Physical Distribution and Materials Management*, 13, pp. 3–11.

many and wide-reaching. But in the context of the logistics element of the marketing mix, successfully supplying a customer using a JIT system fundamentally alters the design and operation of the whole logistical process of the supplier. For example, to supply successfully to a JIT system needs precise synchronization from supplier right through to production units to retailers to consumers. In turn, this synchronization requires a full exchange of information, so the supplier is fully aware of raw material deliveries and the need for component deliveries to manufacturers. Manufacturers also need to know that they will receive deliveries at the right time. Lynch[8] has shown how JIT systems require close contact between suppliers and customers. Increasingly, this contact and the exchanges of information involved utilize computer linkages.

Womack *et al.*[9] have shown that at a consumer level this system can work through retailers who provide information to manufacturers in two forms: firm orders and tentative orders. Working through retailers in this way means that the company can respond very closely to customer needs and changes in the market. Thus, in the volume car market in Japan, nearly all cars are made to orders taken in the distributor's showroom and lead times are as low as 10 days.

Clearly, where a manufacturer is using a JIT system, delivery, and hence logistics performance of the supplier, is crucial and its importance heightened. A company which can perform well on its delivery, therefore, has a strong competitive edge over those suppliers who cannot. In fact, for many companies these days, an inability to supply JIT deliveries means that a supplier would simply not be considered.

These trends towards lean manufacturing and JIT are themselves of course indicative of the recognition on the part of the customers of the substantial costs, and hence potential cost savings, associated with elements of their own logistical systems including, for example, stocks of raw materials, work-in-progress, the consequences of stock-outs, and defective raw materials and components from suppliers.

The result of these factors is that logistics service is now a key factor in supplier choice in industrial markets. Evidence for this is presented in a variety of studies in the UK, the rest of Europe and the US. Table 11.2 is taken from a study by Perreault and Russ[10] and discussed in Hutt and Speh.[11] This study indicated that logistical service was high on the list of supplier evaluation criteria, in fact ranking second only to quality. As we shall also see, another implication of these factors is also the need for much closer working partnerships between suppliers and customer and hence the growth of Relationship Marketing, to which we shall return to in Chapter 12.

A company at the forefront of developing Just-In-Time techniques in its relationship with suppliers is the Toyota Motor Company. Toyota has over the years built up very close relationships with its component suppliers, many of whom are, as a result of these close relationships, actually sited next to the Toyota production units which they supply. Toyota was one of the first companies to recognise that effective supply chain management could be a key factor underpinning competitive success.

The nature of physical distribution and logistics

So far, we have established the importance of physical distribution and logistics without actually specifying what these terms mean. We shall now examine the scope of this area of business activity, at the same time distinguishing between the somewhat confusing terms used to describe it.

At its simplest, the subject of **physical distribution** and logistics can be defined as having the right quantity of an item, in the right place, at the right time. Perhaps in marketing terms we could also add 'at the right price', but we shall return to the price, or rather to be more accurate, the right cost, later.

This deceptively simple description of physical distribution and logistics in fact belies the complexity of the decisions and planning required to achieve this objective. In addition, defining this area of business activity in this way does not actually provide any insights or guidance as to how to manage it. Finally, as we have seen from the importance attached to logistics service, physical distribution and logistics are not, as this definition implies, passive tools. Physical distribution and logistics can be important demand creators (as well as customer losers). Product availability, prompt delivery, and efficient and accurate order processing are just a few of the services which can help capture and keep customers. Hence determination of the nature and level of physical distribution service elements is crucial to the effective planning of this area of marketing if it is to be used as a demand generating marketing tool. In this way, physical distribution and logistics can be considered in just the same way as the product, price and promotional elements of the mix. This concept is shown in Fig. 11.1. Some of the

Table 11.2 The importance of logistics service in how purchasing managers evaluate suppliers

I The importance of logistics service:

Supplier characteristics	Ranking
Product quality	1
Distribution service	2
Price	3
Supplier manager	4
Distance to supplier	5
Required order size	6
Minority/small business	7
Reciprocity	8

II What happens when a stock-out notice for a product is received? Purchasing managers switch to another supplier 32 per cent of the time. Over a two-year period, 50 per cent of the purchasing managers stopped using a supplier because of slow or inconsistent service.

III What happens if a rush order is not acted upon by the supplier? After only one such inaction on a rush order, 42 per cent of the purchasing managers would change suppliers. If this problem happened several times, 54 per cent would change suppliers.

elements which comprise physical distribution can be used, through service levels, to influence demand as shown.

However, there are others. Before examining and exploring these and other elements which contribute to customer service, however, we now need to clarify the distinction and relationships between the terms we have to date used interchangeably; namely, physical distribution and logistics. In addition, to explain the business meaning of the latter term, we also need to introduce the concept of materials management.

'Physical distribution', 'logistics' and 'materials management' are often used as alternative terms when discussing flows of materials into, through and out of an organization. In fact, although they are interrelated, the scope of each of these terms, together with their interrelationships, is shown in Figure 11.2.

As we can see, *physical distribution* relates primarily to those elements which facilitate the flow from the company to its distributors, retailers, final customers or all three. **Materials management**, on the other hand, is primarily concerned with those elements which facilitate the flow of goods, raw materials etc. into and through the organization. *Business logistics management* encompasses all of these elements in a total systems view of the 'place' element of marketing.

The term system is used to denote the fact that *all* of the elements need to be integrated and planned as a whole in order to achieve specified objectives. We shall return

Figure 11.1
The demand
creating role of
physical distribution
efforts.
Source: Adapted from
Ballou, E.H., *Basic
Business Logistics,* 2nd
edn, Prentice-Hall, New
Jersey, 1987.

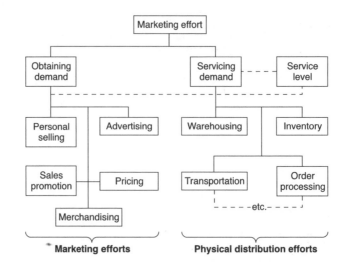

Figure 11.2
The relationship
between materials
management,
physical distribution
and logistics.
Source: Firth, D.,
*Profitable Logistics
Management,* McGraw-
Hill, Ryerson, Canada,
1988.

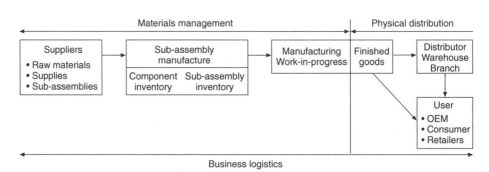

to the implications of this sentence shortly, but we can see that the most comprehensive and useful term to use in order to plan and coordinate the place elements of marketing is business logistics and we shall now use this term throughout the rest of our discussion of this part of strategic marketing. It is also important to stress that in addition to the physical flows of materials into, through and out of the organization shown in Figure 11.2, a business logistics system also includes flows of information and planning and decision-making systems. For example, sales forecasting is an important information and planning input to the logistics system as are, for example, order processing procedures, production scheduling and planning, quality control, and so on. We can now define business logistics as follows:

> A total system approach to the management of all those activities required to acquire, move and store raw materials, in process inventory and manufacturing inventory from the point of origins to the point of user or consumption.

Implications of the total systems approach

Before considering the design and planning of the business logistics system and its relationship to marketing strategy, we need briefly to consider some of the major implications of the total systems approach to business logistics.

Complexity

The first and perhaps most obvious implication of the total systems approach to business logistics is that the web of interrelationships it introduces poses considerable problems in its planning and management, particularly when trying to optimize the performance of the system. This is one reason why the growth of business logistics, as mentioned earlier, has been partly dependent on the development of suitable planning tools and particularly the use of computers and information technology.

Trade-offs between elements

A second and extremely important implication is that in trying to optimize the performance of the total system we are invariably confronted with trade-offs between the different elements. For example, attempts to optimize the performance of one part of the system, without regard to the other elements, will usually result in lower performance for the system as a whole. We may, therefore, have to trade off optimum performance in one or more elements of the business logistics system (optimum in the sense of when considered from the perspective of that element in isolation) in order to optimize overall performance. An example of this would be where we try to minimize the costs of, say, holding raw materials inventory by cutting down the stocks of these. If we cut these too far, we might find that the effect is to increase costs elsewhere in the system. For example, we might lose production through stock-outs, customers through not being able to fill their orders, and so on. The systems approach to business logistics invariably involves trade-offs throughout the system. Recognition of this is an essential step forwards towards more effective planning and control of business logistics.

Effective coordination and organization

Related to both complexity and trade-offs is the need in a systems approach for the individual elements to be effectively coordinated and planned as a whole. The problem here is that very rarely are organizations structured in a way so as to achieve this. The far-reaching nature of the elements of the business logistics system invariably means that it cuts across functional boundaries. Marketing, production, purchasing and accounts are just some of the functions that will affect, and be affected by, the elements of the system. Some companies, of course, have distribution managers, but very often their responsibility is limited to factors such as route scheduling, fleet purchasing and maintenance and so on. Other, if fewer, companies have a manager in charge of all of the physical distribution activities and another responsible for materials management. Fewer still have a manager or department responsible for business logistics. However, for the reasons stated earlier, this number is likely to grow in the future.

Potential for conflict

Both the trade-off element and the need for effective coordination and organization mean that implementing and managing of business logistics system can give rise to potential conflict between different functions in the system. In turn, this means that there must be adequate systems and mechanisms for reducing and resolving this conflict. One approach is to install a manager with line authority over functions affecting the overall efficiency and effectiveness of the system. Unfortunately, this approach is likely to increase conflict in the system and the business logistics manager is more likely to have to use persuasive argument and effective planning in dealing with the various functions. In addition, the system will require the establishment of operating rules and policies which guide decisions in the different parts of the system. These should cover aspects such as, for example, purchasing procedures, re-order levels, customer service levels, and so on.

Finally, an effective business logistics system will require involvement, support and direction from the corporate planning level if conflict is to be minimized. Decisions at this level can then be implemented further down at each level of management. Ballou[12] has suggested that effective management of the business logistics system needs to be carried out on three levels – strategic, tactical and operational – as shown in Figure 11.3.

Need to incorporate relationships outside the organization which affect the system

The final important implication of the systems view of business logistics is that the system must be planned and coordinated, taking into account relationships outside the organizational system which affect its planning and effectiveness. In systems terminology the business logistics system is an 'open system'. Of particular importance to the design and management of the system are suppliers into the system, intermediaries (channel members), and at the other end, customers.

The growth in the importance of logistics planning, together with the increasing complexity and hence specialist skills required to develop these plans, has led to the development of specialist logistics companies. For example, Tibbet and Britten, one of the market leaders in logistics planning, will plan and execute a complete logistics system for a client company. More and more companies use an outside specialist for their logistics. A company like Tibbet and Britten will take responsibility for every facet of the distribution chain management, right through from planning to actually delivering the products from a fleet of lorries to the customer's warehouse.

Figure 11.3
Levels of management in the business logistics system.
Source: Ballou, E.H., *Basic Business Logistics,* 2nd edn, Prentice-Hall, New Jersey, 1987.

Level of management

Top management (Director, distribution manager) — Strategic planning

Middle management (Traffic and inventory control managers) — Tactical planning

Supervisory management (Warehouse foreman, truck fleet supervisor) — Operational activities

Designing and operating the business logistics system: marketing strategy implications

Introduction

Having established the need for a business logistics view of distribution, together with what this means, we can now turn our attention in more detail to the design and operation of the business logistics system. As you would expect, the perspective of our discussion here is taken from that of the implication for strategic marketing. In other words, we are going to be looking at business logistics in the context of how it should be managed to gain maximum competitive advantage. The first thing to note in this respect is that the planning, operation and control of business logistics in a company is not, and should not be, the responsibility of marketing management. The detailed design and operation of business logistics, as we have said, should be the responsibility of the business logistics or distribution director. Some marketing texts go into great detail regarding the concepts and techniques of managing business logistics, including, for example, details on how to calculate economic order quantities (EOQ), models for warehouse siting, identifying cost points, and so on. These, in our view, are not the task of the marketing manager or department. Nevertheless, as we shall see, the overall design, implementation and control of the business logistics system needs to *start* with the output of the system and what we want to achieve in this respect. The output of the business logistics system is customer service, and it is around customer needs for service that we need to start to design the 'optimal' system.

Starting with customer needs: the service output

As you would expect in a marketing oriented company, companies that have adopted the marketing concept should start the design of their business logistics system by identifying the types and level of service from the system that customers desire and are willing to pay for. Kotler[13] refers to this approach as 'marketing logistics thinking'.

Starting with customer needs, not only is it consistent with a marketing oriented approach (which, remember, should pervade all business decisions) but it also recognizes what we referred to earlier in this chapter as logistics being a 'demand generating' tool.

When we think of service outputs from a business logistics function, we immediately tend to think of factors such as speed of delivery, reliability of delivery, and goods being delivered undamaged. Certainly these are important elements of potential customer service, particularly, as we have seen, with the growth of just-in-time management.

However, there are potentially a large number of elements of customer service which the design and running of the business logistics system can affect. Firth *et al.*[14] list those shown in Table 11.3.

Ballou[15] on the other hand, identifies possible service elements at the 'pre-transaction', 'transaction' and 'post-transaction' stages, as shown in Table 11.4. Pre-transaction elements are associated with establishing good relationships with the customer, for example, written policy statements regarding delivery and the associated conditions can be provided for every customer inquiry and/or when the order is initially received. This will cover aspects such as ordering and delivery procedures, procedures for sending goods back and so on. In this way, customers know precisely what they are getting in terms of logistical service.

Transaction elements are those elements that are directly concerned with delivering

Table 11.3 Common measures of customer service

- Order cycle time
- Consistency of order cycle time
- Availability of product
- Order status information
- Flexibility to handle unusual variations
- Returns – damaged and surplus goods
- Response to emergencies
- Freedom from errors

Source: Firth, D., *Profitable Logistics Management*, McGraw-Hill, Ryerson, 1988.

Table 11.4 Elements of customer service

Pre-transaction elements	Transaction elements	Post-transaction elements
1. Written statement policy	1. Stock-out level	1. Installation, warranty, alterations, repairs, parts
2. Statement in hands of customer	2. Ability to back order	2. Product tracking
3. Organizational structure	3. Elements of order cycle	3. Customer claims, complaints
4. System flexibility	4. Time	4. Product packaging
5. Technical services	5. Trans-ship	5. Temporary replacement of product during repairs
	6. System accuracy	
	7. Order convenience	
	8. Product substitution	

Source: Ballou, E.H., *Basic Business Logistics*, 2nd edn, Prentice-Hall, New Jersey, 1987.

the product to the customer, and affect things like lead times, order accuracy, and so on.

Finally, post-transaction elements affect the logistics support a customer receives after purchasing the product, and includes elements of service such as return of faulty products, complaints and warranty provisions.

In addition to the service elements shown above, individual industries, and even individual customers, may have their own special service requirements. The strategic marketer must also constantly search for innovative logistics service features which, provided the customer values them, can provide a new competitive edge. Federal Express, Avon and, in the UK, the retailers B&Q and Argos, are all examples of companies that have carved a profitable position in the market through innovative logistics programmes designed to give additional customer service. In order to illustrate how the business logistics system potentially impacts on customer service, we shall consider an example of just one aspect of logistics service level – order cycle time – and illustrate how this might relate to some of the elements of the business logistics system and their design and management.

Order cycle and time (lead times)

We are all familiar with the frustration we feel when, having selected a product and a supplier, placed the order (and possibly paid our deposit) we have to wait four weeks for delivery of, say our gleaming new car. In industrial markets, frustration is compounded by the fact that time, literally, is money. Because of this, the length of time which elapses between an order being placed and the customer receiving the product or service, the order lead time, can be a crucial element of customer service. As a result, decreasing order lead times can be a potential source of competitive advantage.

If, for example, we found that the average lead time in our industry was five days, and if we determined that by decreasing this to say three days we would have a significant competitive edge (i.e. customers would value this) what elements of our business logistics system might we potentially look to for us to decrease the order lead time? In fact, there are many areas we might consider in order to achieve this objective, for example:

- *Inventory levels*
  The first area we might look to in order to decrease order lead time is on levels of inventory. If, for example, we only keep limited or possibly no stock, i.e. we only produce to order, then clearly the order time is increased by at least the length of time of the manufacturing cycle. Quite simply, we can decrease order lead times by increasing inventory at the appropriate points in the business logistics system. This might be done at factory, wholesaler or retailer levels, or all three as appropriate.
- *Order transmission*
  A second area of our business logistics system which affects order lead times is the length of time it takes for us, the supplier, to receive the order. In fact, developments in modern business communications potentially make this less of a problem, but at the very least, we need to make sure that there are no unnecessary delays in our receiving the order.
- *Transport*
  A third possible element affecting order lead times is the mode and organization of transport used to deliver products to customers. We might, for example, look to faster modes of transport, e.g. air freight instead of road, or we might increase the size of the fleet, or re-plan delivery routes.

Many companies have developed systems for reduced lead times. Benetton for example have a computer system which enables them to gather data from their franchised outlets on a continuous basis with regard to what is selling in the shops. This data is analysed overnight and translated into a production schedule based on which products, colours etc. of garments are selling. Benetton holds stocks of 'grey' finished material which can then be quickly dyed in the factories according to fashion demands. In this way, Benetton are able to substantially reduce the lead times required to respond to fashion and customer demand.

These are just some of the possible areas we might look to in our business logistics system in order to reduce order lead times. In fact, there are many other areas we might potentially look to in the system, both singly and in combination. So, too, with the other elements of logistical service levels to customers; having determined what the service level should be we can then proceed, though with some complexity, to design an appropriate system. According to Lambert and Stock[16], the output of a logistics system is the level of service received by the customer, but having accepted this notion specifically what steps should we take in implementing this notion and what are the considerations in designing the optimal business logistics system? Figure 11.4 outlines the steps in this process. We now examine each of these steps in turn.

Step 1 – Establishing the importance of logistical service elements to customers We have already stated that the design of the business logistics system should start with customer needs with respect to the service elements provided by the system. Because of this, therefore, it is important to establish what these are. For example, do customers require speedy delivery or is reliability of delivery more important? Do customers require flexibility in dealing with, say, special orders or do customers require only standard products, and so on? Not only is it essential to establish the customer's service needs, but also

Figure 11.4
Designing the business logistics system.

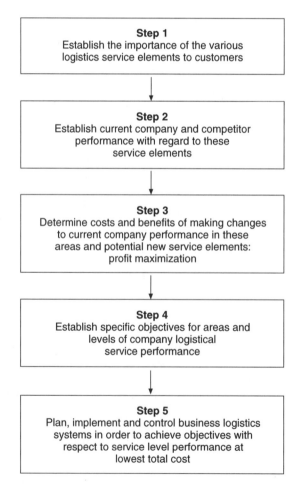

Step 1
Establish the importance of the various logistics service elements to customers

Step 2
Establish current company and competitor performance with regard to these service elements

Step 3
Determine costs and benefits of making changes to current company performance in these areas and potential new service elements: profit maximization

Step 4
Establish specific objectives for areas and levels of company logistical service performance

Step 5
Plan, implement and control business logistics systems in order to achieve objectives with respect to service level performance at lowest total cost

the relative importance attached to each need. Both needs and relative importance of course may vary between different industries, different customers, and even for different products supplied to the same customer. For example, on this last point we may find that certain components are more critical to a customer's production process than others, with a consequent increased importance attached by the customer to the reliability of delivery of these particular components. Similarly, if we take order cycle or lead times discussed earlier, in some industries, such as the automobile industry for example, order lead times must be kept to a minimum. In fact, this is an industry where most suppliers must increasingly supply on a JIT basis. These differences in the degree of importance attached to logistical service elements by different customers or industries can potentially be used by a supplier to segment and target markets where the basis of segmentation is differences in sensitivity to different service levels. What is important throughout this process is the need to establish the importance of the various elements from the customer's perspective. But this is a perspective, the importance of which we have stressed throughout this text.

Step 2 – Establishing current company and competitor performance with regard to service elements The second step of designing the business logistics system is to establish how well (or badly) the company and its competitors are performing in areas of logistics services seen as important by customers. In general terms, we need to be performing as well in these areas as our competitors. Any significant underperformance is likely to result in lost sales and market share. However, even if we are performing as well as our competitors, this is not to say that customers will be happy with current levels. Indeed they may be distinctly unhappy about the service they are receiving from current suppliers. In other words, there may be significant marketing opportunities available to the company which is able and willing to improve service performance. On the other hand, in assessing competitor performance we also need to look carefully at areas where we are significantly outperforming our competitors in order to assess whether or not our extra performance is justifying the additional cost of providing it. This brings us to the third and most difficult step in designing the business logistics system.

Step 3 – Determining cost and benefits of making changes to current company performance in levels of logistical service: profit maximization Before we can make decisions about specific objectives for service elements and the design of the logistical system to achieve them, we need to assess carefully the likely costs and benefits and hence profit potential, associated with different service levels. This brings us to a very important point about the overall design of the logistics system. You will recall that earlier we stressed the fact that logistical services can be important demand generators. However, improvements in these services are also likely to be costly to the firm providing them. In determining the appropriateness, or otherwise, therefore, of current company logistical services and any proposed changes in these, we need to assess the likely impact on company profits. In other words, the optimal logistics system is not likely to be one which operates at lowest cost, as we may be losing too many sales. On the other hand, nor is the optimal system likely to be one which generates the greatest demand, as these sales will probably be generated at too great a cost. Put simply, the optimal business logistics system is one which generates the maximum profit or, more specifically, as it has been put, 'where the logistics contribution is maximized'. In turn, this requires that the company understands the relationships between service levels and demand, and service levels and costs. We can then determine whether to increase or decrease service levels to generate maximum contribution. This notion of optimizing the profit contribution of the logistics system is shown in Figure 11.5. We can see from

Figure 11.5
Cost, revenues and
contribution vs.
service levels.

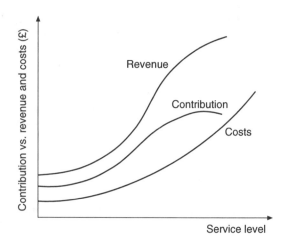

the figure that maximum contribution is obtained neither at the lowest nor the highest service levels. Too low a level of service and we are losing revenue; to high and we incur too high costs for the extra revenue generated. In theory, maximum contribution is obtained where the marginal cost of additional service levels is equal to the marginal revenue generated by these additional service levels. Needless to say, in practice, actually deriving the demand response function (revenue) curve with respect to different levels of service can be difficult. Nevertheless, our earlier steps of identifying customer service requirements and current company and competitor performance in this area should at least give some indication of the likely response to increases or decreases in service levels.

In practice, therefore, as we have stressed throughout, the system should be designed from a demand perspective. Essentially, based on our earlier analysis of customer needs, we should define our service level objectives based on the role we have determined for logistical services in our overall competitive strategy. The design of the total logistics systems should then be aimed at delivering this predetermined level of logistical services at minimum cost.

Step 4 – Establishing specific objectives for areas and levels of logistical services
Overall objectives for logistical service levels will need to be translated into specific objectives for the various areas of logistical service. The variety of possible customer service elements were outlined earlier in Tables 11.2 and 11.3, but, for example, we will need to set quantified objectives for order cycle times, response to emergencies, consistency of order cycle time and so on.

Step 5 – Planning, implementing and controlling the logistics systems From a marketer's perspective, at this stage we can now pass the responsibility for the detailed planning, implementation and control of the logistics system over to the logistics experts. Their task is to design the system to give the desired level of service support in each of the elements of our prescribed customer service strategy. This will involve the planning, implementation and control of factors such as purchasing, inbound transport, production planning, inventory control, warehousing, order processing, outbound transport, and so on. We should be careful not to seem to be suggesting that it is only at this stage that the logistics experts should be involved. Even though customer and market needs must be paramount throughout the design of the logistics system, this can only be achieved through the co-operation and expertise of functions such as materials management, production planning and control, and so on. In addition, we will need the help and co-operation of the channel members and suppliers, who must therefore be consulted. We should also note that the continued operation of an effective logistics system requires ongoing information from sales and marketing including, for example, sales forecasting, customer feedback and competitor information. Of all the elements of the marketing mix, perhaps the 'place' element requires more inter- and intra-firm communication and co-ordination than any other.

As mentioned earlier, having established what types and levels of customer service the logistics system is to provide in order to support our competitive market strategy, the task of the logistics manager is to provide this at minimum cost. It is not our intention, nor indeed from a marketing strategy perspective is it necessary, to discuss the details of operating the logistics system, but it is important for the marketer to understand and recognize the existence of what we referred to as 'trade-offs' between the elements of the logistics system.

In a sense we have already come across the notion of a trade-off, but in this case for the system as a whole, where the costs of the total system are traded off against revenue. In planning and operating the system, however, the logistics manager must also make trade-offs between the individual elements of the system in order to achieve the desired levels of customer service at minimum cost. This, in turn, will require what logistics planners refer to as a total cost approach to distribution and recognizes the interdependence between the demands of logistics activities. So, for example, minimizing costs in one area, say inventory, may lead to more than proportional increases in another, say transport. Once again, we see the importance and value of a total systems approach to logistics.

Effective planning, implementation and control of the business logistics system is greatly enhanced by the introduction of a service policy and quantified service standards. Again, these need to be determined on the basis of customer and market needs.

The service policy should include written statements concerning the level of customer service in the form of promises to customers which the company will fulfil. These can represent both a powerful promotional tool in helping to secure and keep customers, and also inform staff as to the role and value of a logistics service in overall company and marketing strategy. Policy statements may be relatively simple, such as 'all orders received by noon will be shipped the same day' or more elaborate, covering in detail factors such as time, condition of goods, order communication, service contingencies and so on. The policy statement may then be translated into detailed operating standards for the logistics system. In turn, these standards form the basis of the logistics control system, against which logistics inefficiencies and out of line service situations can be quickly addressed.

Developments and trends in logistics

A number of developments and trends in the area of logistics have important implications for the marketer with regard to the design and operation of their marketing logistics systems. Some of the more important of these developments and trends are outlined below.

Information Technology and logistics

We have already seen, several times, in this text the impact of developments in Information Technology (IT) on marketing management. This impact is particularly pronounced in the area of logistics with IT acting as an enabling factor in more effective logistics management. There are a number of major trends which are having an impact on the use of IT in logistics. Integration and flexibility are vitally important. Advance transaction processing systems which enable management to monitor inventory at all locations throughout the organization are commonplace. The levels of flexibility and sophistication in software is continually being enhanced, enabling organizations to now manage the whole supply chain system to give them a competitive advantage. We have seen developments such as Electronic Data Interchange where customer and supplier can interact through an on-line system in order to conduct transactions. Electronic data interchange of course is not an especially new concept, but increasingly the emphasis on the way it is being used is moving from one-off tactical benefits to realizing the strategic benefits, that is its use for developing closer supply chain relationships. Suppliers and customers are now able to work more closely together for mutual benefit by co-ordinating integration. A series of developments in IT now enable a totally paperless supply chain.

Much of the IT hardware now available is smaller, faster, and cheaper enabling it to be implemented in parts of the logistic process that were previously never considered because of space and cost considerations, for example, the use of hand held bar code scanners. Various developments such as point of sale terminals, satellite tracking, electronic funds transfer, and once again, EDI systems have resulted in substantial gains in logistical efficiency.

Another area of IT developments which has affected logistics management is the developments in mobile communications, for example, growth of cellular technology based mobile voice communications, developments in digital service provision in this area offer the possibility of both voice and data services.

Finally, developments in computing power and software systems have enabled the marketer to cope with some of the complexities of managing the interactions and trade-offs which we have seen are part of the logistics problem.

Channel partnerships/supply chain management

Our earlier example of the Toyota company illustrates that the notion of developing channel partnerships with a view to managing the overall supply chain is not new. However, more and more companies, like Toyota, are now beginning to develop effective channel partnerships and supply chain management.

In part, this is linked to the application of information technology in as much as this technology facilitates the complex management and exchanges of information required for effective channel partnerships and supply chain management. Channel partnerships can and do take many forms, ranging from simple information sharing and joint facilities such as warehousing through to joint management of the whole supply chain by its members. Buzzell and Ortmeyer[17] point out that **supply chain management** includes every facet of the supply chain from raw material suppliers through to and including customers.

Effective supply chain management requires different approaches with regard to effective management. As one would expect, much greater trust between the different members of the supply chain is required together with exchanges of information. This is one reason for the growth of the relationship marketing approach which we have mentioned several times already and which will be explored in more detail in Chapter 17. As a result of supply chain management, some companies now use a very small number of suppliers, so these have to be 100 per cent reliable. As mentioned earlier, the output of the logistics system is the level of service received by the customer, so effective supply chain management must reflect this. An interesting further development in this area which reflects this output based view is the growth of what is referred to as the concept of **enhanced consumer response** or ECR.

Efficient consumer response (ECR)

As so often, initially developed in the US, efficient consumer response (ECR) represents the application of total supply chain management, initially and still predominantly used in the manufacturing supply chain, to the retailing sector.

Varley[18] reports that many of the leading marketers in the retail supply chain are now adopting the ECR concept with some of the UK's leading supermarket retailers in particular being at the forefront. By working in close partnerships with other members of the supply chain – not only as regards logistics, but also in areas such as promotion, product development, packaging and so on – the retailers have found that non-essential costs can be cut out of the system. Many retailers, therefore, are managing the total supply chain in partnerships with their suppliers. In applying the ECR concept, again one must remember that the output of the system is customer service. After all, the concept centres on efficient consumer response and indeed is called this. One must be careful therefore, not to overemphasize cost minimization in the design and operation of the system. Laarhoven and Sharman[19] suggest that all too often the application of ECR focuses on short-term cost savings which can detract from longer-term benefits and in particular improved customer service.

> The so-called 'fuel crisis' in the UK during the month of September 2000, together with some of the panic buying which this crisis caused, led to many supermarkets having, at least for a short time, empty shelves with regard to some basic commodities such as bread, milk and sugar. In part this problem was exacerbated by the fact that the supermarkets had introduced logistics systems based on their suppliers delivering as many as four times a day in order to keep the costs of stock holding and product deterioration down as low as possible. This cost-based Just-In-Time system of supply and delivery works fine under normal conditions, but once there was any problem with regard to securing deliveries the system tended to collapse.

The Internet

Although essentially part of the trends and developments in information technology discussed earlier, the Internet is sufficiently important in terms of its impact on logistics planning and management to be considered separately.

In some ways the Internet is proving to be a 'double-edged sword' with regard to conventional and accepted wisdom about planning logistics systems. As already mentioned, over the last twenty years the trend in logistics planning has been to try to minimize the level of stock held throughout the system. One of the problems for many of the Internet marketers, however, and indeed a major criticism at this still early stage of the development of Internet companies is that although it is easy to place an order with these companies, many of them have simply literally failed to deliver. In the run up to Christmas 2000 for example, some disgruntled customers who had ordered their Christmas presents via the Internet found that they were not going to be delivered until the middle of January. Internet supply therefore, if anything, requires the holding of larger stocks than would be considered 'normal' in conventional channel systems. But the Internet is also having many beneficial effects on managing logistics. Remember effective supply chain management requires above all good communication between channel members; to the extent that the Internet facilitates this, then one can see the advantages which accrue from the application of this technology to logistics.

International/global sourcing

International aspects of marketing are covered in more detail in Chapter 18. A trend with regard to logistics and supply chain management has been the growth of a much more international and even global outlook with regard to sourcing. In part this is a reflection of a more global outlook in every facet of many companies' operations, but it has also been facilitated by developments in communication, transport and infrastructure which now make it much easier for the marketer to consider sourcing components and supplies from any part of the world according to which offers the best competitive advantage.

These, then, are just some of the developments and trends in the logistics and supply chain management area of marketing. Once again this is a very dynamic area and we can expect to see many developments which will affect this area in the future.

Summary

In this and the previous chapter we have examined the issues and opportunities which arise out of the management of the 'place' element of the marketing mix. Specifically, in this chapter we have examined the management of the physical flow of products, services and information into, through, and out of the organization to its customers. Although, for a long time, a neglected element of competitor strategy, it is now increasingly recognized that 'physical distribution' represents not only a substantial cost element in most companies, but also, managed as a total logistical system, can be a powerful competitive tool. A number of factors have served to increase this importance: for example, the changes in purchasing practices, and in particular the growth of just-in-time systems. The result is that logistics service is now a major issue in supplier choice. Effective management of the logistics service in marketing requires a total systems approach to be used. Inevitably, this makes the management of this area much more complex and requires effective coordination and organization of a large range of elements, often cutting across different functional areas of the company. The start of logistical decision making is, needless to say, customer needs. Specifically, the logistics system should be designed around a predetermined level of customer service. In turn, both levels and elements of customer service need to be based on a careful appraisal of customer requirements, and in particular what levels of service they value and will pay for, and what competitors are currently offering in this respect. Levels of customer service can then be translated into likely costs (to the marketer) and benefits (to the customer). The service level should be designed so as to maximize the logistics contribution.

Logistics management is changing. Developments in technology have enabled much more sophisticated systems of logistics management. We have also seen the growth of total supply chain management and consequent increases in the number of channel partnerships. Total supply chain management is extending from the manufacturing sector into retailing, particularly with the introduction of the ECR concept. Finally, the Internet is beginning to affect supply chain management and decisions, as is the growth of international and global sourcing.

Key terms

Logistics [p301]
Lean manufacturing [p302]
Just in time (JIT) [p302]
Physical distribution [p304]

Materials management [p305]
Supply chain management [p316]
Enhanced customer response (ECR) [p316]

Questions

1 Why has the effective management of physical distribution and logistics become so important to today's marketer?
2 What is the relationship between materials management, physical distribution and logistics, and how do these different elements affect customer satisfaction?
3 What are the key steps and considerations in designing and operating the business logistics system?
4 What do you understand by the term 'trade-offs' in the design and operation of the business logistics system?
5 What are some of the major trends and developments in the area of physical distribution and logistics?

References

1. Doyle, P., *Marketing Management and Strategy*, 2nd edn, Prentice Hall, London, 1998.
2. Jobber, D., *Principles and Practice of Marketing*, McGraw-Hill, Berkshire, 1995, p.487.
3. Lancaster, G. 'Marketing and engineering', 'Can there every be synergy'? *Journal of Marketing Management*, 9, 1993, pp. 143–144.
4. Womack, D. 'Developments in production', *Business Quarterly*, 1992, pp. 19–22.
5. Bolwijn, P. T. and Kumpe, T., 'Manufacturing in the 1990s – productivity, flexibility and innovation'. *Long Range Planning*, 23, 1990, pp. 44–57.
6. Dion, P. A., Banting P. and Halsey, L. M., 'The impact of JIT on industrial marketers' *Industrial Marketing Management*, 19, 1990, p. 42.
7. Oliver, N., 'JIT: issues and items for the research agenda' *International Journal of Physical Distribution and Materials Management*, 13, 1991, pp. 3–11.
8. Lynch, R., *Corporate Strategy*, 2nd edn, Pearson Education, Harlow, Essex, 2000, p. 399.
9. Womack, D., op. cit., p. 25.
10. Perreault, W. D. and Russ, F. A., 'Physical distribution' in 'Industrial purchase decisions', *Journal of Marketing*, 40, April 1976.
11. Hutt, M. D. and Speh, T. W., *Business Marketing Management*, 5th edn, The Dryden Press, Chicago, 1998.
12. Ballou, E. H., *Basic Business Logistics*, 2nd edn, Prentice-Hall, New Jersey, 1987.
13. Kotler, P., *Marketing Management Analysis Planning Implementation and Control*, 9th edn, Prentice Hall, New Jersey, 1997, p. 591.
14. Firth, D., *Profitable Logistics Management*, McGraw-Hill, Ryerson, Canada, 1988.
15. Ballou, E. H., op. cit., p. 85.

16. Lambert, D. and Stock, J., *Strategic Logistics Management*, Irwin, 1997.
17. Buzzel, R. D. and Ortmeyer, G., 'Channel partnerships streamline distribution', *Sloane Management Review*, 22 March, 1995, p. 85.
18. Varley, P., 'Trend Spotter', *Supply Management*, 4 March, pp. 14–16.
19. Laarhoven, P. and Sharman, G., 'Logistics alliances: The European experience', *McKinsey Quarterly*, **1**, 1994.

Case Study

David Crabbe is feeling the pinch. He is the marketing manager in a company supplying components to companies that in turn supply some of the major car manufacturing plants in the UK. His customers' customers include therefore companies such as Rover, Ford, and Toyota. He has had several complaints recently from his customers concerning the level of service his company is providing with regard to some key areas.

These key areas include the following:

* *The order cycle time:* this is now felt to be too long compared to what the industry requires. Companies like Toyota and Ford are constantly looking for reductions in this time from Crabbe's own customers.
* *Order status information:* customers are complaining that it is difficult to get information regarding the status of a particular order when they enquire. Currently a customer can only enquire about order status via the telephone or a fax.
* *Responding to emergencies:* Crabbe's company is simply not felt to be flexible enough when it comes to dealing with unplanned events, such as emergency orders.
* *Damaged goods:* Crabbe's customers are beginning to insist on a zero defects policy. Currently, the defect rate is approximately 0.5 % of all products delivered.

QUESTION

What steps can Crabbe take to improve the design and operation of the business logistics system in his company?

12

Sales management

Chapter objectives

By the end of this chapter you will:

▶ Understand the role and importance of the selling function in the marketing programme.

▶ Know the different steps in the selection, training, and organization of the sales force.

▶ Appreciate the considerations in planning the salesforce structure and territory and journey planning.

▶ Be aware of the elements of the personal selling process.

▶ Appreciate the different ways of controlling and evaluating the sales force including remuneration systems.

▶ Be aware of the changing nature of personal selling and the developments taking place in this area of marketing.

Introduction

Selling is a universal activity. Everybody sells something as people have done throughout history. One may sell a product, a service or even an idea. In a modern market economy, selling is even more important and has become a sophisticated activity.

Selling can simply be described as an activity to make a sale. Personal selling is more than this. General selling can be done remotely through mail-shots or advertisements. Personal selling is done face-to-face. This demands good interpersonal skills and training. Personal selling is a highly professional activity, but it varies. Everyday purchases in shops generally require a low degree of personal selling, unless it is the type of large, infrequent purchase that makes dialogue between the buyer and seller inevitable. High involvement goods thus require a high degree of personal selling. Capital equipment being sold by one business to another is a perfect example of this.

Much deliberation is required. Here the salesperson must possess a number of qualities: sound product knowledge, together with a knowledge of customer requirements (requirements in terms of performance, delivery, credit arrangements, price ceilings and so forth). Modern market economies are based on constant selling, whereas in less advanced societies, selling is low level, and often amounts to subsistence-based bartering.

Modern selling thus creates many benefits, such as the division of labour and economies of scale. There are also certain factors that distinguish selling in modern civilizations from that in more primitive ones.

In this chapter we shall examine the important role of the saleforce in overall marketing activities and the relationship between the marketing and selling functions.

We shall be looking at some of the key steps in managing the salesforce through from recruitment and training to territory design, sales call planning, and control and remuneration. Also introduced are the steps in personal selling and the considerations in managing these effectively. Finally, we examine some of the emerging trends in selling and sales management.

Role of the sales force

The sales force and selling within the marketing function differ according to the type of organization. Some companies do not have a sales force in the normally accepted sense. For instance, a firm selling its products by mail order may or may not have locally resident agents.

It may seem superfluous to specify that the role of the sales force is selling and obtaining orders but, in fact, there are situations where the salespeople are unaware of the details of the placement of orders, as in the following examples.

Companies which sell pharmaceutical products It is the task of the company's medical representative(s) to call on doctors and persuade them to prescribe the products that the representative is selling. Doctors are not actually involved in the purchase of drugs, but they prescribe them and chemists dispense them. The sales are made, as a rule, to chemists' wholesalers who, in turn supply retailers or chemists, who dispense them on receipt of doctors' prescriptions. More and more drugs once available only on prescription are now available without prescription from chemists and even off the supermarket shelf.

Companies which sell building construction material Architects, like doctors, do not buy materials but specify what should be used. It is the task of the sales force to encourage architects and other specifying authorities to include the company's products in the final specification. Contractors then submit tenders in the hope of being awarded the contracts for construction of the building.

Although selling is the main task of the sales force, there are other tasks involved. These include:

- Obtaining information
- Maintaining and creating goodwill
- Building business for the future.

Depending upon the type of organization, a sales force may consist of a few salespeople with infrequent contact, or many salespeople operating in a highly organized system with regular and frequent contact. The latter would apply to companies selling consumer expendable goods, such as food, where it is necessary to have a regular, day-to-day feedback of information. On the other hand, a company which sells and installs expensive machinery, such as agricultural vehicles, needs comparatively fewer sales-people. Therefore, it is more appropriate to have a team of engineers who can sort out any problems which the customers may face, especially during installation and proving trials.

The sales force provides a flow of information back to the company's head office, which can also be a major influence in operating a sales force successfully. Some companies need to know what is happening 'in the field' if they are to keep up with sudden changes in demand. This is especially true in the 'novelty' trade, where 'fads' come and go very quickly.

Personal selling is a form of marketing communication and, as such, is part of the firm's communication or promotional mix. As we have seen, the communication mix is also made up of non-personal communication: for example, advertising and sales promotions. Advertising and personal selling are complementary activities, personal selling providing communication inputs not offered by advertising and other non-personal selling. The communications mix decided upon will depend on the type of organization and/or product concerned.

Generally, personal selling is more important in industrial marketing. As much as 80 per cent of the total marketing budget is spent on personal selling in many industrial marketing situations because of the necessity of a one-to-one relationship. This is because of:

1. The technical complexity of the product
2. The commercial complexity of the sales negotiations
3. The degree of commercial interdependence and interaction between the buying and the selling firm.

These factors are not present in many consumer marketing situations and consequently personal selling, although important, is less so. More of the marketing budget in consumer markets is spent on non-personal communications. For instance, we all must be aware of the vast amount of expensive advertising for products such as lager, coffee and detergents – good examples of non-personal selling. Such direct consumer advertising attempts to 'pull' these goods through the distribution channel. Personal, face-to-face selling, attempts more to 'push' goods through the channel.

Types of sales force

There can be a great variety in the types of sales force required to carry out the sales function. The managing director of a small company may be personally involved in selling, since he or she knows best what the company can handle. This is especially so with companies engaged in subcontracting.

The main types of selling situations are for consumer goods to channel members, industrial goods and retail selling.

Consumer goods to members of the channel

The sales force which sells consumer goods to members of the channel are usually well organized. Consumer goods require regular contact between sellers and buyers because they are repeatedly sold and, unless regular contact is maintained, there will be a tendency for the buyer to deal only with sellers who call regularly.

Consumer goods may be divided into 'FMCGs' (fast-moving consumer goods), which include products such as food, cigarettes, confectionery and consumer durables, such as refrigerators, washing machines and television sets.

The main characteristics of consumer sales forces is that they must be organized to provide regular coverage and undertake to service their customers both regularly and reliably.

Even so, there are wide variations between the *kinds* of sales force which are used, depending on whether selling is to retailers or wholesalers. The former requires a comparatively large sales force which will call upon customers at predetermined intervals. The latter requires fewer salespeople calling at frequent intervals.

In some cases, the salespeople may sell to the wholesaler and then call on the retailers, obtaining 'transfer orders' which the salespeople then pass on to the wholesaler to deliver.

Large sales forces may consist of anything from hundreds to even thousands of salespeople. For example a firm which sells cosmetics direct to homes and offices may have hundreds of salespeople. They are, of course, likely to be part time, but it is a formidable total. Because of the size it is customary to organize a large sales force into regions with a regional sales manager, and regions are split into areas with an area manager in charge of individual sales representatives.

It is important to note that although selling consumer products, the buyer, a channel member such as a retailer or wholesaler, is of course a business customer. As such, the processes and considerations which pertain to organizational buyers apply. For example, the sales person is dealing with professional purchasers, using systematic buying processes, purchasing in large quantities and so on. Because of this there can be considerable overlap between selling consumer goods to these types of buyers and selling industrial goods which is discussed below.

Industrial goods selling

Unlike consumer goods, industrial goods tend to be made to individual specification and customers' needs have to be satisfied on an individual basis. Much of the work of industrial sales forces is taken up with finding prospective customers. Often the goods are not repeatedly sold or they sell at such infrequent intervals that, by the time a customer is ready to re-order, the machine has been modified and improved to such an extent that it is an entirely new model.

Industrial salespeople are often qualified technicians or engineers and have worked in a factory which produces the type of goods that they sell. With such a background, they are normally well able to discuss their customers' problems. Consequently, they usually keep in touch with past customers to help sort out any service problems which may arise. If they do this efficiently, they may obtain recommendations for new customers.

Products other than machinery may be sold by industrial sales forces, e.g. raw materials such as iron and steel and coal, semi-processed or finished products such as copper ingots, or billets and coke products. They may include chemicals, yarn for spinning or components made on a subcontract basis for other manufacturers.

As mentioned earlier, sales forces for industrial goods are usually technically oriented and are organized to satisfy the customers' requirements. This can pose problems. For instance, salespeople who sell construction material may be summoned at short notice to a 'site' conference. This is a conference on the construction site which might have been called by the consulting engineer to deal with a specific problem.

Retail selling

It is easy to forget that despite the ubiquitous nature of self-service in many retail outlets a considerable amount of selling activity takes place in this setting. Furthermore, these selling activities are not confined to expensive durable goods such as cars, CD players, holidays and so on, but also relate to many much lower value items such as, for example, shoes, clothing, and even non-durables such as say, foodstuffs and meals. Selling activities, then, can be just as important in overall marketing strategy in the retail context and in selling to the public as they are in selling, say, expensive industrial products and services to the business customer. In fact, selling in a retail setting requires as much skill, albeit perhaps applied in different ways, as any other type of selling.

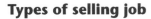

Think back to the last time you purchased a pair of shoes in a retail outlet.

How helpful was the person who served you? Did they have any influence over whether you bought or not? Did they suggest a particular pair of shoes? Did they get you to spend more than you intended? Did they also get you to purchase another item, for example, polish with the shoes? Will you ever return and buy another pair from the same retailer?

Shoe retailing companies are fully aware of the importance of selling activities to customers in their retail outlets. Staff are often trained in how to sell to customers including encouraging customers, to trade up and extend their purchasing.

Types of selling job

There are many types of selling job. One of the classic descriptions of selling positions was formulated by Robert N. McMurry.[1]:

1. The 'salesperson's' job is mainly concerned with delivering the product, e.g. milk, beer, bread, lemonade etc. He or she possesses little in the way of selling responsibilities. Increases in sales are more likely to stem from a good service and a pleasant manner.
2. The salesperson is predominantly an inside order taker, e.g. the sales assistant in a retail outlet. Opportunities to sell are rather limited, as customers have in many cases already made up their minds.
3. The salesperson is predominantly an order taker but works in the field, e.g. the wholesale or retail grocery salesperson. Selling the account, e.g. a large retail chain, is usually done by senior executives at head office. The field sales person simply records and processes the customer's order and makes sure the customer is carrying sufficient stock. Again, good service and a pleasant personality may lead to more orders, but the salesperson has little opportunity for creative selling.
4. In missionary selling, the salesperson does not actually take orders but rather builds up goodwill, educates the actual or potential user and undertakes various promotional activities, e.g. salesperson for a pharmaceutical company.
5. In technical selling, many companies in the industrial market use sales engineers

or sales people with technical knowledge where product and application knowledge is a central part of the selling function.

6. Creative selling involves both tangible and intangible products and services, e.g. vacuum cleaners, washing machines, encyclopaedias, insurance, banking and investment advice. The last three are more difficult because the product cannot easily be demonstrated.

There will be other selling positions which do not fall distinctly into one of the above categories. The main point is that there is a range of selling jobs, from the relatively simple routine sales function to highly complex sales situations. However, the classifications can serve a useful purpose in such areas as the recruitment, selection, training and remuneration of salespeople.

Such classifications of the nature and range of selling positions are useful in as much as they provide clues to the effective management of sales and selling activities. For example, they can help point to the right recruitment and selection procedures; the different selling positions also may require different training and remuneration schemes for sales persons. Perhaps not surprisingly, then, since McMurry's early classification scheme several other schemes have been developed. For example, Donaldson[2] has developed what he refers to as a 'modern' classification of types of selling job encompassing some twelve categories of selling, ranging from 'industrial direct' through to franchise selling. In another scheme, Anderson[3] identifies three categories of selling encompassing 'order taking', 'order supporting', and 'order getting' categories.

Perhaps one of the most interesting and useful views of different selling jobs is that proposed by Pickton and Broderick[4], illustrated in Figure 12.1 below together with examples of selling categories derived from this classification scheme.

As can be seen, Pickton and Broderick's classification system is based on two key dimensions, namely on the one hand the degree of communication and relationship building skills required and on the other, the degree of complexity and the value of the sales involved. For example, one type of selling job in this system is 'key account

Figure 12.1
Types of selling categories
Source: Adapted from Pickton, D. and Broderick, A. *Integrated Marketing Communications,* Pearson Education, Harlow, Essex, 2001, p. 558.

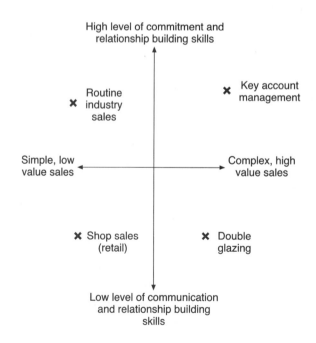

management', where high levels of communication and relationship building skills are required and where the transactions are relatively complex and involve high values. At the other extreme is the example of the category of selling called 'shop sales' (retail), which involves simple low-value sales where the level of communication and relationship building skills needed are low. An interesting aspect of this classification system is how it uses relationship building skills as a key dimension. We shall return to the notion of relationship marketing and the skills required on the part of the sales person in Chapter 17.

Role of selling within marketing

Selling is of course only one of a number of tactical activities within the marketing function. Co-ordination of these various activities is essential to carry out the marketing policy effectively. Thus, no one activity is more important than the other. Any relative difference in importance which might exist would depend on the companies and/or industries involved.

A successful sale depends on whether or not the product concerned fulfils the requirements of quality and availability. Packaging is also important. The product also needs to be competitively priced. Such information needs to be presented by a salesperson during face-to-face contact or by means of a catalogue or brochure.

Relationship with marketing research

Marketing research provides information about the market for goods and services. As we have already seen marketing research finds out what people want and why they want it. This information may result in policy changes or even changes in the product itself. Much of the information obtained from marketing research is fed to the sales department and can be used by the sales force to counter competition. On other occasions, the sales force, because of the close contact with the public, can be used to provide information for the marketing research department (or marketing intelligence). In such a case the kind of information which is obtained is usually of a limited nature. Salespeople do not tend to make good researchers.

It is common practice in most companies which use marketing research for the findings to be passed to the sales department for comment and sometimes for verification.

The marketing research department should never be regarded as a watchdog of the sales force but rather as a source of information which can be put to good use.

Relationship with other elements of the promotional programme

The relationship of the sales force to the other aspects of promotion should be one of mutual co-operation. There are various ways in which co-operation can be achieved. For example, the sales force could obtain agreement from the customer for the company to use the customer's window space for displaying promotional materials. The promotional department can make the task of the sales force easier by 'softening up' the customer through the pressure of advertising. This also applies to organizational buyers, who are also susceptible to advertising approaches.

As mentioned earlier, both personal selling and various kinds of publicity activity, such as advertising, are forms of marketing communication. All forms of marketing communication are interrelated and all elements in the firm's marketing communications mix have a specific part to play in the overall scheme of things. Non-personal communication, in the form of advertising, public relations and sales promotions will hopefully push the customer, previously unaware of the firm's products, into buying them. It is then the role of personal selling to capitalize on the preceding communications and finally close the sale. Hence, personal selling and other forms of publicity should all contribute to an overall marketing communications strategy.

In order to achieve this, it is essential that the selling function be managed effectively. Sales management, which covers recruitment, selection, training, and planning and control of the sales effort, is a critical area in most companies and it is to this area and the elements within it that we now turn our attention.

Recruitment strategy

There is no such thing as a typical salesperson. Likewise as we have already seen sales work varies enormously. The suitable salesperson will vary in accordance with the product/service to be sold and the nature of the selling situation.

We can, in general terms, set out four key elements in the hypothetical job description.

1. *Responsibility*
   The representative will be responsible directly to the sales manager.
2. *Objective*
   To achieve the annual sales target across the product range in the area for which the salesperson is responsible, as economically as possible and within the limits of company policy.
3. *Planning*
   To know company policy alongside having an ability to plan and achieve the defined objectives within the limits of that policy. To submit this plan to higher management.
4. *Implementation*
   - To act as an effective link between customer and head office
   - To organize own travel itinerary effectively
   - To develop skill in comprehensive selling
   - To maintain and submit accurate records
   - To gather market intelligence and report this to head office
   - To assess the potential of his or her area in terms of time available for visits, outlets for company products and the activity of the opposition
   - To protect and promote the company image
   - To protect the company's business by avoiding unnecessary expense
   - To be a good team member, so setting a good example and maintaining loyalty towards superiors.

Role of the salesperson

Companies are often judged by the quality of the salespeople they employ. Most customers do not see any representative of the companies with whom they deal other than the salesperson who calls on them. It should be remembered that frequent changes of representative can have an unsettling effect upon customers and their ordering habits. In a sense, the salesperson can be described as a 'company ambassador'. It is more reassuring for the customer if the same salesperson calls regularly in order to build up a good working relationship. It can thus be seen that the salesperson has an important role to play. The salesperson is responsible for upholding the company's image and occupies a position of considerable trust. He or she is relied upon to provide goods which are suitable for the purpose for which they have been purchased, supply them when required, and charge a fair price for them.

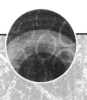

As a service marketer, companies like McDonalds in particular recognize that their sales and service staff perform an 'ambassadorial role' for the company in their direct contact with customers. This role is acknowledged and reflected, therefore, in the company's selection, training and motivation systems.

Because of the differential performance between 'good' and 'average' sales staff, which may be as high as 30 per cent (Lancaster and Jobber)[5], it is important that the right type of person is selected for the job. This is not as easy as may at first appear – nearly 50 per cent of sales managers find recruiting good sales staff difficult. The best way to tackle recruitment of sales staff, as in other work areas, is by adopting an ordered and logical approach. The key steps in such an approach are as follows:

1. Preparing the job description.
2. Preparing the personnel specification.
3. Identifying recruitment methods/means of contacting likely candidates.
4. Designing and applying suitable selection procedures.

We can now turn our attention to each of these steps with specific reference to sales personnel.

Preparing the job description

The job description is an essential tool of any sales manager for five basic reasons:

1. It is a means of checking that all the duties in the sales organization are covered.
2. It enables selection decisions to be made.
3. It provides the criteria against which to appraise staff performance and identify training needs.
4. It can provide motivation because the salesperson knows the precise limits and opportunities of the job, thus making him or her feel more secure.
5. It provides a basis for the advertisement.

The job description should include the following:

- Job title
- Job location
- Prime job objective
- Person to whom the successful applicant will be responsible
- Subordinates (if any)
- Duties of the position

- Evaluation of performance.
- Remuneration (sometimes).

The job description needs to be drawn up on the basis of a careful analysis of the job itself. What follows is the much more difficult task of preparing a personnel specification for this job.

Preparing the personnel specification

The personnel profile will reflect the type of person required to fulfil the job description. This sets out the qualities, skills, experience etc. which the ideal salesperson is required to possess. Some of these can be objectively appraised (experience, qualifications etc.), but some are more subjective and consequently difficult to appraise.

Quantitative factors These are age, education, experience, special qualifications (e.g. languages), intelligence and health. Such factors are relatively easy to identify. Because of this, and because other relevant factors are more difficult to identify and measure, an applicant may be selected on the basis of having the right qualifications and experience and being the right age. However, it must be stressed that there is no natural relationship between possession of the right quantitative factors and sales ability.

Character traits Some of the traits here might be:

- *Industry*
  This basically means the willingness to work hard and long to achieve results.
- *Perseverance*
  This can be related to industry in that it means an ability and willingness to see a job through to its conclusion, particularly under circumstances where it may take two years or more to secure and order, e.g. selling capital goods.
- *Ability to get along with others*
  Any job involving interpersonal relationships requires this ability, but it is especially important when the job entails dealing with different levels of the company's hierarchy and different types of people.
- *Loyalty (to the company)*
  If a buyer thinks that a salesperson exhibits a lack of confidence in the product and company, he or she may not buy.
- *Self-reliance*
  This means the ability to take decisions on one's own and to be decisive. It is important to recognize the degree of self-reliance in an applicant because it would be counter-productive to employ a person with little self-reliance in a job which requires a great deal of it. Not all jobs require self-reliance (e.g. shop assistant), whereas some jobs require a great deal (e.g. export sales person).
- *Empathy*
  This means the ability to feel as the customer does. We know that this is one of the most fundamental quality traits required of a salesperson and the basis of continued sales success. This quality enables the salesperson to produce the behaviour most appropriate to the situation – the best sales approach, for instance, or the best way to interrelate with a particular customer.
- *Persuasiveness*
  By this we mean the ability to get people, through discussion, to agree to do something or to change their opinions, attitudes or behaviour. A salesperson should be

able to moderate the level of persuasiveness to suit the situation, using it when it is necessary to arouse interest, but letting it 'idle' at other times to avoid being offensive or too 'pushy'. Empathy is helpful here.

- *Flexibility*
  The salesperson must be flexible in the selling approach and adjust to temperamental differences among customers. By flexibility, we mean the capacity to change, to modify one's behaviour when the situation so requires it; to change pace; to change emphasis in a sales talk; or to change sales tactics. Rigid minded people would probably be both unhappy and unsuccessful in sales work.
- *Resilience*
  The ability to 'bounce back' and be cheerful, especially when one has been demoralized by, say, an offensive and aggressive buyer, or if disappointed by a failure to secure a sale, or loss of a sale.

Job motivation

Money and security   Selling jobs vary in the ratio of money and security. Some salespeople expect to be directly rewarded by results. This type of person is best suited to a sales position paid on a commission-only basis, or perhaps part salary, part commission, with the level of reward related to the level of risk. Routine, straight salary sales jobs suit a person who feels security is more important than risk taking.

During the 1990s in the UK, many financial products sales persons were remunerated on a commission only basis. In selling products such as pensions and life insurance schemes, the inducement to sell in return for high commissions resulted in many inappropriate schemes being sold to unsuspecting customers. Now referred to as the pensions mis-selling era, the effects of this are still impacting the financial services industry. As a result of what is acknowledged as mis-selling in many situations new legislation was introduced and many of the financial services companies have removed or substantially modified their remuneration schemes that were based on commission only.

Selling jobs vary tremendously in the degree to which they confer social status, e.g. door-to-door selling is perceived as ranking low in social terms.

Power   Generally speaking, selling positions do not offer much scope for the exercise of power.

Perfection   Jobs which involve detailed specifications, such as selling drugs to doctors or dealing with architects, would be suitable for a salesperson with this type of motivation.

Competitiveness   The importance of this quality depends on how the company views the selling task. The salesperson is seen as an individual with a built-in capacity to succeed or fail. If this is not the case, a spirit of competitiveness may be an advantage if the company runs contests for salespeople.

Desire to serve This trait must be present in all salespeople. Every salesperson must serve customers, although it must be recognized that this must be done in accordance with stated company objectives, e.g. profitable sales.

Emotional maturity

1. *Dependence*: If the selling job is highly structured, it will not matter to any great extent if the salesperson is dependent.
2. *Disregard of consequences*: This can be particularly dangerous if a salesperson is liable to promise delivery dates to customers which he or she knows cannot be achieved.
3. *Self-discipline*: This will need to be high in selling jobs where there is little direct supervision.
4. *Degree of selfishness*: This may be a useful trait where the sales force is remunerated by individual commission.
5. *Exhibitionism*: This could be valuable where the salesperson has, for example to demonstrate the product to audiences.
6. *Willingness to accept responsibility*: This will be a requirement where a salesperson makes major commitments on behalf of the company.

Signs of emotional maturity would be:

- The ability to accept criticism when justified
- To be successful without being obnoxious
- To learn from failure
- To be moderate in expressing opinions
- To avoid wide fluctuations in mood.

We can see from this list that a personnel specification for a sales job may include a number of factors which are difficult to appraise and assess in a candidate.

Lancaster and Simintiras[6] have conducted research from the point of view of salespeople. This indicated that the best efforts by salespeople do not always lead to performance maximization and such factors as role clarity and social interaction with management can lead to greater job satisfaction, rather than simply financial reward. Moreover, many of the qualities which might be looked for in a candidate may derive from the specific job itself than from the manager's preconceived notions of what constitutes a 'successful' salesperson. Research by Jobber and Millar[7] suggests that sales managers did indeed have such preconceived notions, which translated into the qualities they were looking for in job applicants. It is not suggested that this is wrong on the part of sales managers; after all, we would expect an experienced sales manager to have some idea of the essential qualities required to sell in that person's industry. However, it should be carefully noted that stereotyping of the 'ideal' sales person is dangerous where it is not based on hard facts and evidence.

Recruitment

The elements of a sound recruitment policy are:

1. *Continuity*
   Sometimes recruitment is not so much a search for the most suitable candidate but a last minute effort to fill an existing vacancy.

Ideally firms should operate a continuous policy of looking for recruits, and encouraging their staff to be on the look-out for promising material.

Some companies, especially those involved in the marketing of FMCGs, employ mobile salespeople to 'fill in' when another salesperson is sick or on holiday. After an initial trial period of proving their ability, they are often moved to a permanent territory, as and when a vacancy occurs.

2. *Economy*

The national media are not necessarily the most economical route to new recruits, although they constitute the most popular method. The aim is to generate sufficient candidates to ensure an appropriate selection, and this may be achieved by other means. For example, specialist journals will draw forth particular marketing groups, which should be of reasonable calibre and at a reasonable cost. It is wise to keep each method and medium under constant surveillance so that the most appropriate can be used for best results, thus avoiding unnecessary expenditure and time wasting through using the wrong method.

3. *Practicability*

Short-, medium- and long-term personnel requirements should be built into the overall marketing plan – that is, what you need now and in five to ten years' time. In this way, recruitment can be made in a practical and realistic way.

In order to satisfy future requirements, different types of salespeople should be recruited. Not all salespeople, for instance, wish to become supervisors, or indeed would make supervisors, however good they are as salespeople. A top salesperson, in fact, is not the ideal material for supervising, being rather singular in his or her methods of achieving high sales targets; this often means disliking responsibility and control systems.

Both types are necessary for the company's success – the potential supervisors as well as the top salespeople – so a recruitment programme should cater for these needs.

4. *Experimenting*

Many companies use an established routine when recruiting, but it is not necessary to be so restrictive. A little imagination and experimentation in trying different mixes of methods and media may reap dividends.

Contacting potential recruits is the real problem. How to do this depends on:

1. Type of job being offered.
2. Type of person who will fill the job.
3. Salary or wage to be paid.
4. Future prospects.

Other things being equal, you should be able to attract sufficient applicants at a reasonable cost to fill the vacancy.

Approaches to recruitment

In-company sources   One of the obvious sources is the company's sales office. Many of the clerks in the sales office have a thorough grounding in the company's methods, products and policies, and if they have the right temperament to be salespeople they are likely to be successful.

But there are other departments in the company, and these should not be neglected. Many a good salesperson has emerged from the shop floor. This is a particularly good source when the product is one where a thorough knowledge of the manufacturing process is of value when selling.

There are obvious advantages in recruiting from within:

- You will already know the person, and so have some idea of the individual's habits, attitudes and temperament
- You will need to spend less on training and introduction
- You will be helping to promote better relations within the company.

Not enough companies encourage applicants from within. The following may be the reason why this is so:

- Departmental heads are reluctant to release what are usually their best people
- It is difficult to cope with any failures
- Many marketing managers have inflexible ideas about 'sales potential'.

Even employees themselves often seem reluctant to apply for a sales job within the same firm because:

- They feel their present departmental head might feel slighted, and it would prejudice their present standing should an application fail
- Too many have misconceptions about the dubious glamour and lack of security of the sales job
- They feel that they would not like to leave their colleagues.

In fact, these problems are less formidable than those encountered when recruiting externally in the normal way. It seems that internal managers dislike associating their name and reputation with someone carrying their personal recommendation.

There are ways in which home-grown talent can be produced:

- Ask your personnel department to check records of personnel against the new profile for the job
- Ask your colleagues if they know of any likely candidates
- Promote interest through the house journal
- Hold regular informal discussions and talks on selling and marketing subjects.

Outside sources The most frequently used outside source is advertisements. Most companies at some time or other advertise for personnel. When advertisements are used, care should be taken in devising them. They should always give clearly the qualifications that are required, the locality of employment and the approximate benefits.

Advertisements may be used in:

- The national press
- The local press
- The trade and technical press
- Recruitment agencies
- Professional and Executive Recruitment (PER).

Advertisements for marketing personnel may, for example, be seen in the *Marketing Week* published by Haymarket Publishing. Recruitment agencies and PER do advertise, but it is possible to apply directly as they may have a position in their files that is suitable for the applicant.

Another source is that of personal recommendation. This may come from friends, customers, employees, trade associations or educational establishments.

Many educational institutions have a session commonly known, for reasons of its regularity, as the 'milk round'. A period is put by for firms to visit the college campus and talk to final-year students who are interested in working in their particular area or industry.

Selection procedures and techniques

The importance of the salesperson has already been emphasized and it is during the selection procedure that the calibre of the people engaged is decided upon.

The two processes of recruiting and selecting salespeople are closely interrelated. However, they are different enough to merit separate consideration.

1. The aims of *recruitment* are to determine the ideal kind of individual wanted for a particular job and to make available an array of candidates.
2. The aim of *selection* is to screen the candidates, matching each with the profile for the job and selecting the individual who matches best.

Although there are many techniques of selection, by far the most important selection tools are the application form and the interview. These are now discussed in more detail.

Application forms

It is helpful to have standard application forms for candidates. The advantages of having such a form are that all the required information can be listed and any omissions are immediately apparent. A standard form also makes for easier comparisons between candidates. The kind of information which is required will vary between companies, but most forms follow a general pattern. A further advantage is that they can be completed and sent in prior to interviews so that the interviewing panel has time to study and compare them. The task of going through many application forms and selecting candidates for an interview is formidable, and any means which can make the work simpler without lowering the quality of the selection is beneficial.

It helps if unsatisfactory candidates can be eliminated as early as possible to reduce the workload involved in processing unnecessary applications. The application form aims to do this. Quantitative factors should be assessed first, resulting in rejections of applicants who do not meet the essential requirements. An examination of an applicant's educational record and subsequent career might highlight clues as to character traits, job motivation and emotional maturity.

Some application forms also invite applicants to write a letter in support of the application, which will indicate how well the applicant expresses reasons for wanting the position.

Interviewing

Structured interviewing 'Short-listing' is the most important stage of the selection process. It is up to the interviewer to decide what information is to be collected and how this is to be done. The interview should be structured by using an *interview record* *form*, on which details of the interview are recorded. It consists of, in the first instance, questions which explore work history, and secondly, more personal areas.

Planning the interview   The interview should be planned to enable coverage of the following areas: work history, education, family background, domestic, social and financial situations, and health.

The interview   This should begin by informing the candidate of the purpose of the interview and the length of time it should take. A detailed explanation of the job should be given and the candidate allowed the opportunity to ask questions. Next, questions should be asked about the candidate's present or last job, widening out into a detailed questioning of the candidate's work history.

Questions which can be answered by a 'yes' or 'no' should be avoided, as this should have been elicited in the pre-interview stage. It is far more fruitful to ask open-ended questions using such words as 'why', 'how', 'where', 'when' and 'what', e.g. 'Why do you think that you can do the job?', 'What makes you think that we should employ you as opposed to anyone else?, or 'What do you know of our company?'.

When all the necessary information has been gathered, the interview should be brought to an end and the candidate told the date by which the outcome will be known.

Group interviews   Some companies now favour the group interview technique. In this case, the candidates on the short-list are requested to attend at the same time. The candidates are told of a subject or topic – usually a controversial one – to discuss. Senior personnel staff and/or sales staff are brought in to listen. Each senior staff member is usually assigned a particular candidate and the staff member assesses the candidate by means of a rating chart (Figure 12.2). The group interview is usually followed by a conventional interview.

Rating charts   Some companies use a rating chart when carrying out interviews. These are completed by the senior sales personnel at a group interview. Most companies are reluctant to engage a candidate on the basis of a single interview and the possibly fallible judgement of the interviewer. This method provides second opinions and facilitates comparisons between interviewers.

The rating chart has standard headings, the candidate being awarded scores under each heading. The complexity of the chart varies according to the type of job on offer and the calibre of candidates required. A simple chart is shown in Figure 12.2.

Figure 12.2
Rating chart.

	0–3 Unsuitable	4–7 Marginal	8–10 Possible	Total
Appearance				
Knowledge				
Self-expression				
Loyalty				
Intelligence				
Experience				
			Grand total	

The interviewers compare their scores after the interview and then decide upon which candidates to short-list. Candidates are thus more relaxed at a second meeting and interaction between the personalities should be less hindered by nervous tensions, enabling a clearer judgement to be made by both parties. This may help in explaining why some experienced interviewers claim that candidates appear to change between first and second interview.

Interview checks Many of the interview questions elaborate on the information already given on the application form and usually concern candidates' background and work experience. However, there are also often check questions intended to test some particular quality or claim made by the candidate.

An example of a check question would be one that tests the candidate's sense of loyalty. Typically, this would elicit comments about relations with previous employers. If in the answers the candidate discloses that all his previous employers were incompetent, unreasonable and unfair, the interviewer is likely to conclude that the candidate is not only disloyal to previous employers but that he or she is perhaps the one at fault.

Training

The belief that salespeople are born and not made sometimes leads to a neglect of training – anyone newly recruited as a salesperson needs to undergo a period of training.

It is untrue that a new recruit can learn merely by 'sitting with Nellie'; that is, by observing the skilled performance of an experienced salesperson. There is much more to it than that. Just consider whether one could learn to drive a car by the same technique. It is much wiser to provide a training programme which sets out to achieve the objectives of giving knowledge and developing selling skills.

Hewlett Packard have experimented with schemes to train their sales persons by sending them out to actually work in their customers' organizations, so as to develop real insights and empathy on the part of the sales person as to the customer's needs and problems.

Development objectives

Setting objectives in terms of development can be done by identifying the gap between the expected level of performance of salespeople and their current standards. First find out what their current standards are, then determine the expected level of performance from the job description.

Knowledge goals The knowledge goal would be in terms of learning the general company history and background. At the end of a salesperson's training, he or she should have achieved defined knowledge goals (e.g. must be able to name six major benefits of a particular product and explain how these benefits are derived from the relevant product features). This knowledge goal would reflect a statement in the job description which states: 'The salespeople must be fully knowledgeable about the products and their applications'. Another example might be where a job description states: 'The salesperson must ensure that the company's products are well displayed'. The knowledge goal here would be in terms of learning merchandising techniques and in-store promotion schemes. A final example might be where the salesperson is required to represent the company at trade shows and exhibitions and make presentations when required.

Skill goals Skill goals are spelt out in terms of what the salesperson needs to do. If we recognize the three examples of the section on knowledge goals, we can identify the required skill goals. In the first example the skill goals would be an ability to relate product features to consumer needs and to find and interest new customers. In the second example, the skill goals would be concerned with display building and selling merchandising ideas. In the final example, the skill goals would be related to public speaking ability and use of audiovisual aids.

Major areas of knowledge and skill

The company and its procedures These involve areas such as company history, organization structure, product mix and company policy towards customers. This is all relatively straightforward. However, there could be problems, e.g. the commission system employed by the company – the salesperson needs to know and understand the system from the viewpoint of how it can affect an individual's earnings and why it is constructed in this particular fashion. Failure to clarify this will mean that the commission will not act as an incentive.

Product knowledge The important areas here are product application(s) and related consumer benefits. It is of little use that the sales person possesses a sound knowledge of the mechanical aspects of a machine without appreciating how the features of the machine can be translated into benefits to the customers, e.g. cost reduction, time saving, increased efficiency, less maintenance and ease of servicing.

Market knowledge Such knowledge must involve continuous updating in relation to competitors' products in order that the salesperson can talk with 'conviction' to buyers.

Sales techniques This must not be restricted to a study of the sales interview only, but widened to include the salesperson's role, pre-sales preparation and after-sales servicing.

Work organization Spending more time with customers can mean obtaining more business. The salesperson should therefore be trained in the use of work organization techniques so that more time is spent with the customer and less time on travelling or waiting.

Reporting Reports from the field are an essential aspect of selling. Good reports can help a company to determine and take appropriate action in such areas as customer relations, competitive activity and market changes.

Place of training

The company factory and offices should be used for training in basic company procedures and product knowledge. The company training premises (or a hotel) can be used for training in initial sales techniques, work organization and some product applications. The main sales skills development, in the form of continuous training, is best done out in the field. Outside trainers can also be used.

Method of teaching

Observation alone is insufficient as a training method. Although lectures, film shows, books demonstrations, case studies, videos and seminars are useful, these are just a beginning. The salesperson will derive the greatest benefit from actual participation in sales situations or simulations. Although this is trial and error learning, it can be very effective if feedback is provided quickly. Ideally, this should be by closed circuit television. Tape recorders, although useful, lose the visual impact.

Initial training programme

There are several clearly identified areas of the sales job which should be included.

- *Marketing concept and role of the sales force*
  The main aim here is to inform the salesperson of his or her role in the overall company effort.
- *Nature of selling*
  The salesperson must be clear about what selling actually is, its role in the company and the basic requirements of the job.
- *Communications*
  Selling undoubtedly involves grasping the skills and techniques of communication if the salesperson is to establish a rapport with the prospective customer, e.g. by asking questions, treating prospects as 'real' people by speaking the same language and listening. The salesperson must also be taught skills in reporting and talking on the telephone. The importance of skills in asking questions to identify customer needs is now increasingly recognized especially when dealing with major sales. In this respect, the very successful and now widely used **SPIN model** of selling developed by the Huthwaite Research Group and described by Rackham[8] emphasizes the importance of questioning skills in identifying customer requirements in the selling process, and hence the overall need for strong communication skills on the part of the salesperson.
- *Preparation for selling*
  This must be done well in advance of meeting the customer.
- *Prospecting*
  The importance of finding new business, known as **prospecting**, should be emphasized and the salesperson should be given guidance on how to obtain it.
- *Opening the sale*
  Research has shown that first impressions are important. On meeting the customer, it is important that the salesperson conveys the right initial impression; otherwise, the sale might be quickly lost.
- *Making sales presentations*
  The persuasive powers of a salesperson are critical to success. This does not just mean verbal skills, but skill in handling visual aids and demonstrations.
- *Dealing with objections*
  The salesperson should be trained in what to say and how to reply to a whole variety of issues and complaints raised by customers upon such matters as price or delivery.

- *Closing the sale*
  Knowing how and when to close a sale is an art. A really good salesperson is a skilled performer and is a diplomat, negotiator and psychologist. Although experience plays a large part, **closing** techniques can be taught. Training enables the salesperson to recognize verbal and non-verbal cues which indicate a close is appropriate and how to proceed. For instance, left too late, information might be divulged which could cause the 'customer' to change his or her mind. On the other hand, too early a move may leave one unprepared for an objection from the customer that had not been covered.
- *Work organization*
  The salesperson must be trained in the effective use of time through the use of journey planning and day planning routines.

Field training

Field performance assessment There should be a set of standards against which a salesperson's performance in the field can be evaluated. The job description and related knowledge and skill requirements should provide the necessary criteria.

Role of the manager The manager or supervisor should sometimes accompany the salesperson on a normal day's work and should observe, but not interfere.

Appraising the salesperson's performance After the period of observation, the manager and salesperson should get together to discuss the latter's performance. The appraisal can be formalized through the use of an appraisal form, which will include product knowledge, selling method, work habits and organization, mental attitude, development needs and general commitments. Figure 12.3 shows a typical appraisal form.

The salesperson, when being appraised, can be given marks or a letter rating. There is also a section for the last grade awarded, to see if there has been an improvement, no change, or a decline in standard since the last appraisal. The salesperson should be allowed to see the comments and then both the salesperson and the manager should sign the form. The appraisal form system is popular within the salesperson context.

The advantage of the appraisal form is that it acts as a record of abilities. It can also be compared with the previous year's results to see if progress has been made, and act as a basis for quantifying qualitative attributes.

The manager must now communicate to the salesperson the action required to correct the deficiencies. This can be done by role playing with the salesperson, reference to the initial training programme or manual, or simple instruction.

This action may take many forms. It may require the salesperson to study the company product literature more deeply. This may be one situation where observation of a skilled performance may be educational for the salesperson. Perhaps the manager could take the next call to demonstrate the correct method. However, care must be taken to carry out any follow-up action in the spirit of helpful constructive co-operation rather than allowing it to become a process of negative criticism.

The sales manual

The sales manual, issued to salespeople for reference, can be used to improve performance. This contains full information on method of operation and helps guide the

APPRAISAL FORM

Grade

	A	B	C	D	E	Last grade
Product knowledge						
Selling method						
Work habits						
Organization						
Mental attitudes						

A = Excellent   D = Below average
B = Very good   E = Poor
C = Average

Date: ....

Signature of manager: ....

Signature of salesperson: ....

Department: ....

Figure 12.3
Salesperson appraisal form.

salespeople in their duties. It is a confidential document which includes such matters as:

- A statement on company sales policy and methods
- Background information about products (but not formulae)
- Prices, terms and conditions of sale
- Distribution method
- Publicity and display policies
- Regulations regarding use of company vehicles
- Rules governing expenses
- Sickness and accident rules
- Journey planning procedures
- Rules for granting credit and obtaining trade references
- Account collection procedures
- Order procedures
- Rules governing the issue of samples
- Methods of requisitioning stationery and supplies
- Reporting and correspondence procedures.

The sales manual can be a useful reference source both for initial training and for established salespersons.

Personal development and continuous training

One-off training is not a sufficient requirement to produce a salesperson. Continuous development by means of updating courses, seminars and conferences ensures that the salesperson is well equipped to deal with changing marketing conditions.

Current market conditions, competitors' activities, company publicity policies and specific sales objectives can be imparted to the salespeople at a special training session. This could take place at a training centre or a hotel – somewhere where there will be no interruptions. Such sessions should be held at regular intervals and have a specific agenda or theme. Such sessions should not be seen to give the impression of questioning the efficiency of the sales force.

Sales force structure

There are two aspects to this element of sales force management, namely:

1. Determining the overall structure of the sales force.
2. Territory design and journey planning.

A sales force can be organized in several ways. The most common methods of organization are outlined below.

Geographically-based sales force

Each salesperson has a geographical area in which the company's products are sold. The main advantage of this structure is that as the salesperson's responsibility is clearly defined, the territory is intimately known and, in co-operation with management, its sales potential can be fully developed. The salesperson can also develop business and personal ties with the locality. Finally, if the territory is of a manageable size, expenses can be economized.

This type of structure may not be effective where a company's product and customer types are many and varied, or, where salespersons are required to collect marketing intelligence.

Product-based sales force

This is the most suitable organization if a company's products are technically complex (e.g. electronics industries, capital equipment); for businesses where the company sells numerous products (e.g. the grocery business); or where the company produces completely unrelated lines (e.g. highly diversified companies).

This structure requires the salesperson to be knowledgeable about product applications. However, if products are brought by many of the same customers, duplication of effort occurs by having different specialist representatives travelling repeatedly over the same route. The extra costs incurred as a result must be borne in mind before such a division is made.

Customer-based sales force

Customers vary according to type of industry, size, distribution channels, company etc., so a sales force may be organized according to the type of customer. A thorough understanding of the customer is necessary for this approach. However, there may be a resulting overlap of territory if customers are spread evenly throughout the country.

This approach is becoming increasingly popular, especially in 'key account' structured selling efforts which are discussed later.

Territory management – the two levels

Territory management itself can be thought of at two levels:

- At one level, it is the planning, allocating and delineating of territories within the total area with which the company is concerned. This is the task of the sales manager.
- At the second level, it relates to how each salesperson manages his or her own territory. The aim is to realize the full business and sales potential of that territory by careful planning and organization.

We shall look at overall territory and design and management first.

Overall territory design

Importance of a basic principle The 'territories' are generally thought of as being geographical units although, as mentioned previously, they may be organized on the basis of both products and customers.

The most important principle about territory design is to ensure that it provides the most effective form of contact. Even if this may result in several salespersons from the same company calling on many customers in the same locality, this may still be the most effective (i.e. profitable) policy to follow.

The 'sales engineer' It is no longer valid to design territories simply on a numerical allocation system. Because of the complexity of the various factors required, some companies employ executives whose main task is to 'build' territories, and readjust them as situations demand. These executives are known as 'sales engineers', even though they are not strictly engineers in the accepted sense.

The 'building' analogy is taken further by the development of specialist organizations which will design territories by using sales 'bricks' (a geographical area in which all known buyers are listed). The bricks are generally about equal in sales potential. For example, one brick may contain 10 buyers of furniture and another brick may have 15. In such an example, the brick would have been calculated on the basis that the 10 buyers are, on average, slightly more sizeable than the 15, but the total purchasing capacities are about the same.

Sales bricks can be constructed for almost every kind of industry. As the bricks are built up, they can be transferred in units from one territory to another. However, to design territories using the brick principle is a long and painstaking task, and not many companies can afford the time or expense to use this method.

'Sales engineers' may also help in the mounting of special promotional schemes. These promotions can be mounted at very short notice and may be targeted down to individual customer level.

As preparation for the promotion, information regarding the customer's buying potential is collected. In a complicated scheme, this may involve many different levels of incentives linked with different grades of buying potential. Once this is done, schedules listing all the customers with the appropriate incentive which is related to the customer's known buying potential are prepared.

Factors which determine territory design

Not all factors involved in territory design are clear-cut. Many pragmatic or personal factors contribute to the final design. For example, if a customer has a distinct preference for a particular salesperson, or conversely, a known dislike for a particular salesperson, then it would be politic to ensure that the preferred salesperson makes the visit. These problems are best dealt with as they arise.

Some practical factors are as follows:

Potential business   An estimate needs to be made of the amount of business which is available in the territory. The estimate should include the total business and the share which the company may expect to obtain.

Number of active customers   Assuming the company is already doing business in the area, it should be possible to count the customers or to make an estimate of them. If the company only deals direct, then counting will be simple. If the goods are sold through wholesalers, an estimate or some research may be necessary. As well as the numbers of customers it is also necessary to assess or calculate the amount of business which each does.

Number of potential customers   These are prospects with whom the company is not yet dealing. The estimate should be realistic and it may be necessary to grade them in terms of potential. If they deal with competitors, it may not be possible to convert them.

Location of customers   Knowing where existing and potential customers are located is important.

Method of distribution   Sometimes territories have to be designed around goods distribution facilities.

Sales situation   Territory design may depend on the existing sales situation. For example, if the workload of an existing salesperson is too heavy in a well-developed area, it may be if necessary to divide up the area into two smaller areas. A run-down area, on the other hand, might need a salesperson to concentrate on building it up.

Frequency of call   Several factors need to be considered before deciding how often a salesperson should make a visit. These factors include the size of the territory, ordering frequency, the level of stock the customer is prepared to carry and the individual buyer.

Mixture of trade   When companies sell to several different trades, the decision may be made for each salesperson to deal with a single trade or, alternatively, to have a balanced mixture of trades.

Identifiable boundaries   To avoid any disputes about territory boundaries, these should be clearly defined so that salespersons and nearby colleagues recognize and know which territory belongs to whom.

Limitations   This is a broad restriction. Some companies offer regional rights, and the salespersons' territories need to coincide with the regions because they work in collaboration with franchise holders. An example could be the salespeople of companies which sell flooring or roofing material but do not install it. Usually they have arrangements with flooring and roofing contractors who do the installation. It is not essential for territories to coincide with such franchise holders or contractors, but it does make the co-operation and co-ordination easier if a regular working partnership can be established.

Economics of representation   Economic viability is a crucial factor in the delineation of territories. Usually there is a rough calculation of boundaries and an estimation of likely business. This is related to the total cost and expenses incurred in working the territory, and the profitability calculated. Only at this point can a realistic assessment and subsequent decision be made regarding the viability of the new territory.

However, a long-term view should be taken, taking into consideration any possible future growth of the territory. Low profitability, or even a loss, may be tolerated in the interests of higher potential at a later stage. Some companies prefer to use 'brokers' to do the selling for them because of the relatively high total costs of employing a sales representative. This is particularly so in the food trade.

Territory development

The development of territories applies not only to newly formed ones but to all existing ones as well. Salespeople should search for ways in which an existing territory can be developed. They need a constant awareness of what is going on in their own territory, as well as frequent perusal of appropriate trade directories.

The salesperson's activities should extend to visiting trade and technical exhibitions, making contacts with trade and professional associations, and examining the activities of competitors and the possibility of working with associated industries.

Factors to consider in revision of territories   No sales territory should be assumed to be permanent. Several factors may point to the necessity of revising an existing territory. These are:

- Change in consumer preference
- Intrusion of competition
- Diminution in the usefulness of chosen distribution channels
- The complete closure of an outlet or group of stores
- Increases in cost of covering territories.

Changes should not be instigated until a thorough investigation of the sales effort has been carried out. Falling sales is one indicator that something is wrong, but the fault may lie with an ineffective selling and promotion effort rather than a faulty territorial structure.

Other reasons may include lack of systematic planning by salespeople; for example, too much time may be spent in non-selling activities, e.g. travelling. Representatives may also only be calling on customers who offer the greater buying potential. A lack of enthusiasm may also be a factor, which might be due to inadequate or poor supervision. Perhaps existing distributors of the product have begun to be disenchanted with the company, its products or its policies. A reappraisal of market potential and consumer acceptance, perhaps by means of a market survey, would be the best action to take before any revision of territories is carried out.

Just how much revision is necessary, once a decision has been made, will depend on the need to increase coverage and sales, or to reduce costs. Needless to say, the sales force should be fully informed about any changes and the reasons for them.

The role of the salesperson in territory management

Once the overall design of territory (size and number of customers) is agreed with the sales manager, the salesperson can play an important role in helping the sales manager to achieve maximum sales effectiveness. Indeed, this achievement will depend on self-management by the salesperson. Some of the more important aspects for the salesperson and manager to consider are now listed.

Know the decision maker

It is important not to waste time by contacting the 'wrong' person in a company. The 'right' persons for the sales person to see are the key members of the decision making unit (DMU). It is not always clear just who these people are, especially in industrial and commercial fields, so it is advisable to find out first from the company itself; for instance, a secretary may be able to suggest the most suitable contact.

As we saw in Chapter 5, often the decision is not taken by one person but several. This is especially the case where large capital expenditure is concerned. Different sales tactics will, of course, have to be applied to different members of the DMU.

Carry out research

It is up to sales personnel to carry out relevant research regarding the buyer and the buyer's company. This creates a good impression and is easily done from market intelligence sources.

Make appointments when possible

Appointments save time, especially when they are part of an organized travel plan. Ideally, the next appointment should be arranged while the salesperson is actually with the prospect.

Make record cards work

Assuming they are kept properly and regularly updated, record cards can be an invaluable source of information. Essential data on a record card would be:

- Name and address of company
- Telephone number
- Name of contacts and their position within the company.

In addition, a salesperson should record information on:

- Type of business
- Size
- Number of employees
- Best days and time to call
- A record of what has taken place
- Date for the next call.

Many companies send copy invoices to each salesperson for recording on customer record cards.

Keep a diary

A diary is a valuable part of a salesperson's planning strategy, especially regarding future appointments.

Organize the territory

A map is an invaluable aid when journey planning. The territory can be divided into sectors, with the salesperson making regular calls in one sector at a time, thus cutting down on travelling.

Plan each interview

Once an appointment has been made, it is important not to waste the effort by lack of planning. The interview needs just as careful planning as other areas of work. Before the interview, a decision should be made as to the overall aim, although the salesperson should have realistic expectations of just how to close a sale within the allotted time. All necessary documents and samples should of course be taken to the interview.

Careful planning will enable the salesperson to know just what will be needed at the interview, according to the aims. Some possible aims are:

- To get a final decision
- To arrange for a demonstration to take place
- To obtain consent to carry out a survey
- To provide sales benefits
- To find out about competition
- To find out the decision maker.

Journey planning

Companies rarely attach the same importance to the improvement of salespeople's productivity as they do to raising factory output or streamlining office procedures. We have seen, however, that planning, activity controls, and better organization of the salespeople can all help the sales force become more productive. In this connection, the systematic planning of journeys is particularly important to avoid waste of effort and to get the maximum return from a salesperson's time.

Journey planning is a management responsibility, although the assistance and advice of each salesperson must be obtained for best results. Journey planning involves the following:

- Developing a call frequency
- Establishing priorities in terms of both customer value and customer potential value
- Minimizing travelling time

- Evolving a call pattern
- Assessing the workload
- Combining a programme with flexibility.

We shall look at each of these in turn.

Developing a call frequency

Each salesperson will have a mixture of accounts of varying size. An account worth more money deserves more attention than an account worth a little. Not only will the big customer need more help with the purchasing schedule, but that customer will also require advice on processing, distributing, merchandizing and the like. It should be remembered, moreover, that most buyers allocate only a certain amount of time to seeing salespeople. The more time you spend with a customer, the less time will that customer be willing to give to a competitor! You should ensure that each customer and each live prospect on each territory is allocated a **call frequency**. Some should receive a visit as frequently as once a week, and others say once every three months, or according to the sales journey cycle.

Establishing priorities

Customer value   It is important that your sales force recognizes the cost per minute of their selling time. Customers should be given priority according to the value of the business done with them. Accounts that order in small quantities hardly justify a call. It might even be worthwhile abandoning such accounts altogether, or linking them with the wholesaler, as the cost of invoicing and administration may exceed the profit.

Customer potential   Because of the prestige which goes with 'landing' a big account, it is all too easy to concentrate on customers with this potential. This means giving these 'big' customers a great deal of attention and perhaps offering inducements like a price concession. This concession should be thoroughly thought through unless the aim is to, say, use hitherto unfilled production capacity. Access to decision makers is often difficult and any actual interview time will probably be very limited.

Minimizing travelling time

Eliminating waste in travelling time is a responsibility of sales management as well as the salesperson. Management should ensure that:

- The salesperson is not sent out for unduly long periods dealing with complaints, debt collecting and deliveries
- The salespeople's cars are properly maintained
- Overnight accommodation allows for private telephone calls and a reasonable entertainment allowance
- Field visits by management actively involve the salesperson
- Territories are not too large for one salesperson. (It is sometimes better to appoint an agent in remote districts.)

Evolving a call pattern

Having graded customers according to their value or potential value, the salesperson should now be able to develop a call pattern. The basic call pattern will centre around the most significant accounts. For instance, if these involve a call frequency of alternate weekly visits, then this is the basis for the call pattern. Over a two month period the salesperson will be able to allocate (say) the second, fourth, sixth and eighth weeks to less significant accounts, the remainder being devoted to key customers. With proper organizations, it will be possible for the supervisor to know where the salesperson can be located on any day of any week. Such a routine is called the 'sales journey cycle'.

Obviously there are certain idiosyncrasies which have to be taken into account. These range from practical considerations such as early closing days, market days, whether the salesperson is dealing with say refrigerated goods, or fitting in with the buyer's own preferences. Provision will also have to be made for 'time out' when the salesperson may be required by management to attend training courses, conferences, exhibitions and so on.

Assessing the workload

An assessment of the workload is necessary to ensure that a salesperson's effort is not wasted by too many calls for too short a duration. A decision should be made as to the optimum number of visits which can be made each day, allowing for achievement of the salesperson's full quota. If it is discovered that the salesperson is making more visits than this, then it may be necessary to take on extra staff or to revise the boundaries.

Combining a programme with flexibility

Any programme, once decided upon, should allow for some element of flexibility. Occasional changes of activity will benefit the salesperson and help the company reach certain sales targets. Activities may take the form of test marketing and task force selling (a number of sales people on one territory aiming at saturation in selling so as to build up sales quickly) or any of the following special promotions:

- Developing a certain market segment
- Forestalling a competitive activity in a given area
- Forestalling competitive promotional activities
- Introducing a new product
- Training a new recruit
- Balancing the product mix
- Moving obsolete products from stock
- Announcing a revised price structure
- Entering a new market
- Opening new accounts.

Participation in these periods of activity will mean that the salesperson is not available for some routine visits. A well planned, flexible programme should enable the salesperson to vary the intensity of calls on less significant accounts, rather than neglecting the more important ones.

The general sales sequence

Planning is essential if personal selling time is to be maximized and other less important considerations minimized (but not at the cost of neglect). At a simple level one must:

1. Adopt a general plan for sales interviews, i.e. a sales sequence
2. Adopt a specific plan for each individual interview.

The general sales process or sequence is really only a basic framework – it must be flexible and adaptable, as each individual sales situation will be different and present its own problems. The following sales sequence is only a guide to the types of procedures a salesperson should follow.

Preparation

The salesperson should have a good general knowledge in all the following areas:

1. *The company* – its systems, procedures, prices and terms
2. *The product* – especially new products and/or uses for existing products
3. *Market knowledge*
4. *Customer knowledge* – general knowledge of customers and the maintenance of a good customer record card file
5. *Equipment, samples and sales aids* – the salesperson should make sure that he or she has all the right equipment, including order books and trade directories
6. *Journey planning* – an organized journey plan giving details of appointments and other calls. This should cover existing customers and time for generating new business or prospecting
7. *Personal preparation* is also important in terms of appropriate appearance.

First impressions

First impressions are usually very important. A good salesperson will usually open a sales meeting in a pleasant yet businesslike way. Time is important, but so is being polite. Likewise, good personal selling also involves listening as well as asking questions. It is also about being accommodating. If a buyer sets a time limit, this should be respected – though an offer to stay longer is often necessary and can be useful.

Mention should also be made at this early stage of other business to be discussed, such as expediting of invoices due for payment. These matters should be dealt with in a clear way. Indeed, it is often best if these matters can be discussed and settled at the beginning of the sales meeting in the knowledge that it will then be simpler to discuss the real business on hand.

Preparation and demonstration

Sales personnel should examine their products carefully and make a list of the major selling points. The most important of these will be those that give some advantage over competitors' products. In the presentation and/or demonstration the salesperson should concentrate on the unique sales propositions (USPs) that are appropriate to that particular customer's needs and interests.

In a sales situation involving the need for a sales presentation or a demonstration, the salesperson should be prepared for this and secure the potential customer's active involvement. What should be avoided is running both the demonstration and presentation together, as this can lead to confusion. The salesperson should use terms that the customer can understand. During the presentation the salesperson should ask questions and listen to the answers in order to probe the customer's interests further.

Some products are impossible to demonstrate. In such cases the salesperson should use models or audiovisual aids.

A salesperson should never be too 'long-winded', or sales can easily be lost. What should be done is to watch for buying signals, and then to try, as far as is decently possible, to close the sale.

Negotiation

The principal rule of **sales negotiation** for the salesperson is that of knowing the limits of acceptance and non-acceptance. The salesperson may negotiate with the customer on such things as price, discounts, credit and selling rights. Often the final margin of negotiation is retained by the sales manager.

The salesperson should get as much information as possible about the buyer's needs and the level of potential business, i.e. what is the potential volume of business going to be worth?

As in all forms of trade, concessions should be held back as long as possible. If not, they cease to be concessions.

Negotiation is a key element of many sales persons' activities. However, not all selling involves, or rather allows for negotiation. Pickton and Broderick[9] point out that if the terms of agreement between seller and buyer cannot be varied by the parties, then the process is simply one of selling or 'persuasion' rather than negotiation.

Overcoming objections

Objections in sales interviews fall into two categories:

1. Objections which arise from faults of the salesperson; proper preparation should overcome such objections.
2. *Commercial objections*
   These objections relate to such matters as price, credit and delivery etc. This type of objection is the most usual, but a good salesperson should be able to learn techniques with which to handle them. An objection on commercial grounds can also be a disguise for a real objection. It can also be a buying ploy. When it is a disguise, or excuse, it is up to the salesperon to discover, by shrewd questioning, what the real objection is. A good salesperson can use customer objections to close a sale. One must be careful in using customer objections to close a sale, however, particularly where the customer is a professional and/or skilled buyer. Organizational buyers for example will through experience, learn to recognize when salespeople are using objections as a closing technique and can feel insulted and therefore antagonized if this is not done tactfully and carefully.

Closing a sale

The objective of most sales interviews is to obtain a sale. There are a variety of sales closing techniques, which the salesperson needs to know, as well as how to use them. Experience here is the best teacher. Of the many techniques, there are four that are generally used.

1. Basic close: when the salesperson thinks that he or she has a sale, start filling in the order form.
2. Alternative choice: offer a choice as a trial close, e.g. 'Do you want grey or black?'.
3. Summary questions: from a prepared list, ask the buyer: 'Is this a problem?'. Here an answer of 'no' represents a step towards closing the sale.
4. Closing on a final objection: if a final objection still exists, identify it then offer to do something about it. The customer cannot then object to anything else.

Following up the sale

There are two elements to this:

1. To avoid the loss of the contract.
2. To bring about repeat business.

After closing a sale it is important that the salesperson 'ties up' loose ends, e.g. delivery times. To this end a follow-up call should be made, and if any unforeseen problems occur the salesperson can then rectify them, and so not lose the sale.

After-sales service

Many products require after-sales service. Some manufacturers rely on their dealers to offer this (e.g. the motor trade). In this case the manufacturer should be satisfied that dealers are capable of providing the required level of service, although for many products after-sales service is an important element in the marketing mix and needs to be costed into the final selling price of the product.

Effective communication

We saw earlier the importance of communication skills on the part of the salesperson. Good communications require good listening skills as well as speaking skills. Charts, models, brochures and the like may also help in the sales process.

Sales personnel can be trained to be good speakers, knowing what to say, how to say it and when to say it. However, an aptitude for speaking does not necessarily make for a professional salesperson. Listening to what the customer has to say is the best guide to knowing how to speak yourself. Listening and speaking are dual parts of the same process – effective communication.

Salespeople, as well as developing selling skills, develop technical expertise which is applied during the presentation process. It is possible that there will be occasions when a customer might ask questions that appear to be particularly simplistic. Salespeople deal with a limited number of products but a large number of customers, so what might be an unusual problem to one customer may seem routine to the salesperson. Every sales situation is different and the professional treats it as such. Much patience might then be required in explaining to the buyer what, to the salesperson, is a simple matter.

Non-verbal communication

As has been spelt out, listening during a sales interview is of great importance. Beyond this, showing the customer that you are listening is also of great importance. This can be done by non-verbal communication: eye contact, facial expressions and other forms of 'body language'. Using such non-verbal clues, the salesperson is able to signal understanding of what the customer is saying without actually speaking. The salesperson who is really adept at using non-verbal communication can, to some extent, regulate the speed of the conversation and the depth and detail of the customer's discussion, without verbal interruption.

When we feel that we have something important to say, we tend to say it. In turn we expect others to respect us, and so listen to us. What we do not expect is that people will talk while we are speaking, or show other outward signs of lack of interest. Indeed, this can be highly embarrassing. Customers thus need to be listened to. This point is of paramount importance to the professional salesperson. It is emphasized because salespeople, by their very nature, tend to be talkers rather than listeners.

The psychology of talking

Often in talking there is a feeling of control. One is asserting one's beliefs and with this there is a feeling that by doing so one will succeed. This is satisfying one's own needs. Often it has the problem of ignoring the needs of others. Salespeople aim to satisfy others. They offer goods and services that fit precise requirements. Such requirements can be practical or can relate to less tangible buyer behavioural needs.

Managing and controlling the sales force

We have thus far examined those elements of sales management which encompass recruitment, selection and training of sales personnel. Additionally, we have looked at the important area of organizing and structuring the sales force, specifically looking at such factors as territory design, journey planning and bases for structuring a sales force. We have also looked at the sales sequence.

In this section, we shall examine further some of the additional elements of sales management, including setting sales quotas, evaluating and controlling the sales effort, and the design of remuneration systems.

Setting sales quotas

'Sales targets' and quotas' are terms often used to mean the same thing. The *target* which is given to a salesperson is, strictly speaking, something which should be aimed for. A **sales quota** is something which should be achieved, but the difference is really minimal. Whichever term is used, the salesperson should be given clear indication of the level of performance that is expected to be achieved.

Need for joint consultation   If a salesperson's quota is fixed with his or her co-opera-tion, there is more likelihood of its being acceptable. It also raises the salesperson's level of confidence in the management, unlike a quota which is imposed. This latter situa-tion may result in resentment and an unwillingness to co-operate with management that fails to consult its salespeople on such an important matter. The salespeople, after all, are expected to meet any quotas set.

The individual salesperson is the best person to help in setting realistic estimates of what can be achieved. It is helpful, therefore, for both parties if the area, branch or regional manager sits down with the salesperson and, by consulting the list of customers, they estimate sales for each customer.

This not only applies to fixing new quotas, but also to any changes in quotas which may be necessary. The salesperson needs to appreciate why changes are neces-sary; the arbitrary raising of quotas which may be unjustified in the eyes of the salesperson does nothing to foster mutual trust between management and staff. The salespeople are not unreasonable and do realize that quotas may become out of date because of inflation and a developing market. However, a cut in earnings resulting from arbitrary alterations is understandably not appreciated.

Setting the sales quota   Sales volume achieved in the previous period is a good start-ing point when setting a sales quota. However, one must be aware of factors which may influence future sales – changes in demand, business conditions, marketing and sales policies, territory potential and competitive actions. Because of these, adjustments may have to be made to the figures for the previous period.

The sales quota should be an accurate measure of the market potential tempered by workload and experience factors. Territories are differentiated by the density of the market. A rural area will involve a salesperson in more travelling time between calls than a salesperson working in an urban area. The amount of physical effort and time involved, that is, the workload factor, should therefore be taken into consideration when setting quotas.

The experience of the individual salesperson, as well as the experience the company has in a particular market area, make up the 'experience' factor. Higher sales targets will be expected from the experienced salesperson, while even an inexperienced salesperson will find sales easier if the company is well established in the market area.

Sales quotas stem from the sales forecast and are used for the following reasons:

- To set targets of performance
- To monitor this performance
- To serve as incentives
- To serve as a basis for payment to the sales force.

Analysing sales performance

Unlike performance measurement in the production department, which usually deals with material which can be seen and relatively easily measured, the salesperson's activi-ties can neither be seen by head office nor, in some cases, can they easily be measured. Some sales operations are simple, e.g. in mobile shop (or van) selling the number of calls made, number of orders obtained, and value of the orders can be calculated reasonably accurately. Some sales contacts of a more long-term nature are more compli-cated than this, and are thus far more difficult to calculate.

Although performance standards are necessary in order to ensure that the sales force is operating efficiently, they need to be applied with considerable forethought and in consultation with the salesperson from the outset. They should also be relevant to the kind of operation being conducted. Examples of the kind of performance standards which can be applied are detailed below.

Sales analysis and performance analysis Sales analysis begins with a detailed breakdown of the company's sales records, whilst performance analysis seeks exceptions or variations from planned performance.

Sales analysis is merely the listing of facts and figures, but performance analysis is the comparison of predetermined standards with actual results. It can be useful in:

1. Pinpointing operating problems
2. Identifying areas in which the company may be performing very well.

The continuous use of sales and performance analysis enables operating problems to be detected *before* they become serious. What they cannot do is uncover the root cause of the problem, nor can they provide the solution.

Before going on to an example, we shall define what is meant by a 'sales performance index'. This is computed by dividing actual sales for an area (or salesperson, product etc.) by the sales quota and then multiplying this figure by 100, i.e.

$$\frac{\text{sales (for area, sales person, etc.)}}{\text{sales quota}} \times 100.$$

Performance indices enable marketing management to compare what 'ought to have happened' with what did happen.

Analysis by product line Analysis of sales (for evaluating purposes) is based on a geographical breakdown. Another way in which total volume can be analysed is by product line.

Analysis by customer category Sales may also be analysed by customer categories. The sales manager can request sales data broken down by:

- Industrial customers
- Key customers
- Customer types
- Channels of distribution.

Market share analysis Analysis of sales, no matter how detailed, may not be enough. The analysis may present a favourable picture as far as sales volume versus quota is concerned. Actual sales can be equal to, or over, the quota and yet the firm may be losing position to a dangerous extent because the market in which the firm is operating is expanding at a greater rate than the firm's expansion of sales. This situation is illustrated in Figure 12.4.

Evaluating performance – quantitative standards

The effectiveness of the salesperson is evaluated against some predetermined set of performance standards. To help the sales manager determine whether or not corrective action is required, the control technique deals with three elements:

Figure 12.4
Market share
analysis.

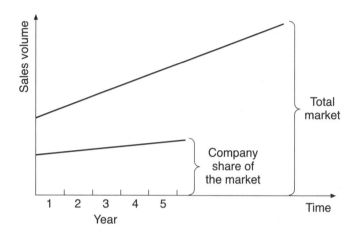

1. Information on performance.
2. Standards.
3. Evaluation of performance (against standards).

While the types of standard used in a given company will vary, most are linked to the following:

- Sales volume
- Profit contribution on sales/product mix
- Number of calls made
- Number of calls for an order
- Percentage of quota achieved
- Number of service calls made
- Amount of market intelligence gathered.

All these performance standards (targets against which results are measured) are quantitative measures of performance. Such standards, when communicated to the sales force, become a basis for sales planning.

Where, then, does sales management obtain information about the salesperson's performance?

- *Reports*
  1. Call reports, showing which customers were visited, competitive brands used, best time for calling, degree and type of resistance, results achieved and future account promise
  2. Expense reports, showing a breakdown of expenses incurred
  3. New business reports, showing new accounts opened and potential new business – this evaluates the extent and effectiveness of the salesperson's prospecting work
  4. Lost business reports, showing what business was lost and why
  5. Work plan reports, showing what calls the salesperson will make and the routing he or she will use for a future specified period. This provides a basis for comparing plans with achievements
  6. Reports on a local market condition and competitive activity. Care must be taken when interpreting and evaluating this report because the salesperson sometimes distorts the local picture.

- *Observation*
  Here the district sales manager actually goes out with the salesperson and observes him or her in the real situation. This can be a meaningful input into the evaluation–control system.

Checklist of quantitative standards for performance evaluation

1. *Sales*
   - Sales volume in money terms
   - Sales volume in previous year's sales
   - Sales volume in units
   - Sales volume to quota
   - Sales volume in relation to market potential
   - Sales volume by customers
   - Sales by outlet type
   - Sales by product or product line
   - Sales volume per order
   - Average sales volume per call
   - Amount of new account sales
   - Amount of repeat sales.
2. *Accounts*
   - Percentage sold to existing accounts
   - Number of new accounts
   - Number of accounts lost.
3. *Profit*
   - Net profit by salesperson.
4. *Orders*
   - Number of orders delivered
   - Number of orders booked
   - Number of cancelled orders.
5. *Selling expense*
   - Compensation in relation to sales volume
   - Salesperson's expenses in relation to sales volume or quota
   - Total direct selling expenses per sales value.

Evaluating performance – qualitative standards

How can a salesperson be assessed qualitatively? Consider the following measures:

1. How does the salesperson demonstrate knowledge of markets, competition, the company's lines and each customer's business? How does he or she apply this knowledge?
2. How does the salesperson break down the quota given into separate goals, customer by customer?
3. How does the salesperson create effective plans of action?
4. How capable is the salesperson in the 'art' of preparing and making selling presentations?
5. How well does the salesperson deal with awkward customers?
6. How well does the salesperson evaluate results and take corrective action?

These questions are at the base of qualitative evaluation.

Other qualitative measures of performance might be in the areas of:

- Motivation
- Personality characteristics – general manner, speech, appearance, tenacity, patience, temperament
- Contribution to the flow of market intelligence
- Managerial ability
- Personal development
- Self-organization (time management).

As Lancaster and Jobber[10] point out, qualitative measures are necessarily more subjective. Nevertheless, they are important and useful.

Remuneration

Since profitability is so important, sales managers need to seek ways to stimulate salespeople to sell more profitably, especially by means of equitable remuneration methods. Thinking in terms of profitability is a move away from the more traditional commission schemes geared to turnover. The three main methods of remuneration are commission, salary plus commission, and salary only, although there are many variations.

Commission

Payment by commission only is a simple method. If the salesperson works, and gets results, he or she gets paid. The advantages of a commission-only scheme are that the employer knows exactly how much sales expenses will be, and the salespeople know that they will only get paid if they work. This is simple, but there is a strong element of insecurity in a commission-only system. It is not wholly satisfactory, in that sometimes the salesperson may not wish to work, and the employer is then left without any sales coverage. Much, of course, depends on the nature of the product and the way it is sold. As mentioned earlier, another disadvantage of commission-only remuneration is the potential danger of 'over' or 'mis-selling'.

Salary and commission

This is the most common method of payment. Commission is taken to include any form of bonus or profit sharing. If offers more security to the salesperson. The proportion of salary to commission will vary depending upon the company and its product.

Salary

Another common form of remuneration is salary only. Although it may appear to be lacking as a means of creating incentive, it is popular with salespeople who prefer a more straightforward lifestyle. It must be considered that some situations are more suited to this type of payment. Sometimes it is not possible to establish just what has been sold by some salespeople, or perhaps the total sales effort is not down to the salesperson but to estimators or background technical personnel. Often (in the case of capital goods) the time delay between inquiry and receipt of the order is too long for commission payment to be an incentive. This method of payment is particularly suited to complex buying and selling situations.

Variations

There are many variations to the methods cited, which include:

1. A basic salary plus commission above a certain figure. Here the salesperson, once the target has been reached, can start to earn commission on amounts above this.
2. A basic salary plus an escalating scale commission. Here the salesperson receives a salary plus a commission; for example, $1/_2$ per cent on the first £5000 sales, 1 per cent on the next £5000 and $1^1/_2$ per cent on amounts over this. The figure could be related to monthly sales targets.
3. A basic salary plus a commission on the type of outlet sold to. Here again the salesperson receives a salary plus a commission as follows (as an example):

   - $1/_2$ per cent on all wholesale orders
   - 1 per cent on all multiple orders
   - 1 per cent on all co-operative orders
   - $1^1/_2$ per cent on all independent orders
   - $1^1/_4$ per cent on all department store orders.

Incentives

Incentives (other than commission schemes) include methods such as group incentives, where a team of salespeople form a group and, if the group fulfils its performance, all members benefit.

Some companies prefer incentives which benefit the salesperson's family. These may be in the form of holidays or gifts, such as domestic appliances, children's presents, clothes etc.

The main point to be borne in mind is ensuring that the pay and benefits structure corresponds with:

1. The company's market segments.
2. The company's stage of development.
3. The company's goals and objectives for the future.

A company can implement a marketing strategy via remuneration. It can remunerate differently for different kinds of work. Remuneration can be weighted towards missionary work (seeking out new customers) as this work will undoubtedly involve more time and effort than servicing existing clients.

If a company's marketing objective is not specifically that of growth, expanding the customer base through missionary selling is less important. The company may wish to put maximum effort into account servicing in order to consolidate its existing customers. The remuneration policy would reflect this objective.

The remuneration programme may need to be adapted in various ways in the case of companies selling multiple products. Salespeople working on a commission plan, understandably, tend to concentrate on the products which offer the most commission. Setting sales targets by volume is only partially the answer, since the tendency for salespeople will be to concentrate on higher value products. One solution is to offer higher commission on sales of a particular product or perhaps extra commissions or bonuses for sales of excess or obsolete stocks the company may wish to off-load.

Creatively designed incentive plans are useful for achieving corporate and marketing objectives other than sales volume, which is the usual key objective for commission or bonus payment. Straight salary may be a poor motivator for increased sales, but it may be instrumental in helping to achieve other company objectives, since the salesperson, being free of the pressure to sell, can concentrate on these other objectives. A competitive straight salary is also a key way of obtaining good sales staff.

By using various forms of financial incentive in imaginative ways, the sales manager can motivate the sales force to ensure that the company's objectives will be carried out. This is a powerful marketing tool which is often not used to its full potential.

The company should have a clearly defined remuneration policy which will help achieve at least the following objectives:

- To attract sales personnel of the right calibre
- To encourage sales personnel to achieve their job objectives
- To reward sales personnel in accordance with the value of their contribution
- To prevent losses made through dissatisfaction with levels of pay
- To encourage good sales personnel to stay with the company
- To enable sales personnel to move up or across departmental, divisional or company boundaries (where a company is part of a group).

Motivation of employees by their supervisors is extremely important. It is easy for busy managers to overlook the fact that financial needs are rather less important to the salesperson than the need for security, status, job satisfaction and a sense of group belonging, especially since the salesperson may not readily admit this. It must be remembered that salespeople tend to work alone, unsupervised for long periods of time and visits to supervisors tend to be brief and infrequent.

It is very important to provide clear objectives and standards. Management by objectives (MBO) enables managers to lay down a clearly and precisely defined sales job. Setting realistic sales targets in co-operation with the salesperson makes their achievement more likely, and the salesperson has a clear idea of what is expected. Clearly defined objectives and strategies enable management to evaluate the sales force on their ability to get results.

Sales force size

Calculating the optimum sales force size is one of the basic tasks of sales management. A number of factors need to be taken into account:

1. The firm's financial resources.
2. The number of customers to be reached.
3. The average number of calls required per customer, per week, per month.
4. The average number of calls that can be made by a salesperson in a given period.
5. The distribution policy of the firm – does the company operate a policy of exclusive, selective or mass (intensive) distribution?

Sales office administration

Function

The main function of sales office administration is to support the sales force. This is done by the regular supply of information, following up of queries and prompt attention to matters arising in sales representatives' reports.

Responsibilities

These will vary according to the nature of the company and the products it sells, but most sales offices have the following responsibilities:

- Preparation of a budget of activity in financial terms for the forthcoming budget period
- Planning of administration of the sales office and the sales force
- Organization of the day-to-day work – consisting of handling orders, correspondence, complaints; administering to the needs of the sales force; control and administration of the sales force in matters such as the scrutiny of expenses and reports
- In some companies there may be an estimating department to which all inquiries are submitted. This is sometimes the responsibility of the sales office
- Distribution arrangements and arranging for the handling and storage of goods
- Keeping records of progress and sometimes the ledger accounts of customers.

The above matters are mostly directly concerned with sales. In smaller companies, the sales office also has responsibility for market research and publicity. These two responsibilities are quite specialized, and even if they are the responsibility of the sales office it is usual for specialized personnel to be employed to deal with them.

Organization

The organization of a sales office must fit the needs of the situation. The organization is usually under the control of a sales office manager, who is responsible for the overall supervision of the office. The sections for which he or she is responsible can include:

- A general correspondence section. This deals with quotations, general correspondence, complaints, requests for information and queries about orders
- A section responsible for maintaining records of customers' accounts and correspondence
- A sales statistics section
- A planning section (which is responsible for co-ordinating and communicating the sales plan)
- Particularly in industrial companies, there will sometimes be sections for marketing research and publicity.

Developments in selling and sales management

Amongst the more important trends and developments in selling and sales management we would identify the following:

The growth of key account management

Recent years have witnessed a growth in the use of key account management (KAM) approaches to organizing the selling process. Many factors underpin this growth, but some of the more important ones are the trend towards more centralized buying, a shift in the balance of power, particularly in retail markets, towards the buyer; but above all, perhaps, the recognition that it simply makes good marketing sense to identify and manage your key accounts.

Millman and Wilson[11] suggest that a **key account** is

any customer of strategic importance to the supplier.

It is important to note that this definition does not necessarily mean large customers or even the most important in terms of share of sales, but rather those customers that can affect the future of the company in some important way.

In a way, of course, all customers are important, but it is useful to assess the differences and the bases regarding the extent of this importance between different customers.

Key account selling requires the development of special selling and sales management skills, so key account selling heightens the consultative and ambassadorial roles of the sales person. In addition, the salesperson must have regular meetings and communication with key account customers – key account customers require much more support than their non-key counterparts.

Telesales

We have earlier discussed the growth in telephone marketing (telemarketing). We know that this form of direct marketing has increased dramatically in terms of usage in recent years. As Starkey[12] reminds us, although only one facet of the overall process of telemarketing, selling (telesales) is a key part of this process. **Telesales** can involve dealing with calls in (to the company) or calls out (to the customer). Primarily, the increase in use of telesales is because of the potentially lower costs. However, these lower costs can only be justified to the extent that teleselling actually creates sales. Like key account management, teleselling requires special skills and training. In addition, there is a danger of alienating some customers when using telesales staff to contact customers at home. In this respect there are ethical and legal issues involved with this type of selling.

The Internet

In a sense the Internet removes the need for selling, certainly in the sense of personal selling. One might wonder, therefore, why we have included it as a development in selling in this chapter. It is primarily the fact that the Internet does potentially remove the need for a sales force that we have felt it important to include this section. Admittedly the major impact of the growth in Internet marketing will be the reduction in the size of many companies' sales forces, but on the more positive side the Internet is proving to be a powerful aid to generating sales leads in companies. In addition, the Internet can provide a powerful communication tool when managing the key account customers mentioned earlier.

Relationship marketing

Again, several times we have mentioned the importance and the growth of relationship marketing. Remember, a detailed discussion of the reasons for this development, together with the implications for the marketer, are the subject of Chapter 17. In the context of this chapter however, it is important to point out that one of the most important areas of marketing that relationship concepts have affected is that of personal selling and sales management.

At several points in this text we have highlighted the changing nature of markets and marketing and in particular the increased competition in most markets. We have also pointed to the emergence of much more co-operation and inter-dependence between suppliers and their customers as evidenced by the growth in strategic alliances mentioned in Chapter 7 and developments such as lean manufacturing JIT production which we have examined in Chapter 11. With greater consumer choice it is increasingly realized that customer loyalty can no longer be relied upon unless positive steps are taken by the marketer to develop and hold such loyalty. According to Sasaki[13] marketing must seek to try to develop customer loyalty by integrating customers into the company and trying to develop a new relationship between the company and its customers. According to McKenna[14] there has been a fundamental shift in the role and purpose of marketing from manipulation of the customer to genuine customer involvement, from 'telling and selling' to communication and sharing knowledge. Lancaster[15] argues that the emphasis in marketing has shifted from a perspective which is concerned primarily with generating sales on a one-off basis to one which looks for longer term and interactive exchanges between the company and its customers based on true partnership and sharing.

As a result of these changes in markets, marketers have realized that they must now develop new approaches to their customers. In particular today's marketing environment requires that the marketer develop a new more co-operative approach to dealing with customers and in particular the development of close long term relationships with them. The wider consequences of this so-called relationship marketing is discussed in more detail in Chapter 17, but at this stage we should note some of the key implications of relationship marketing with regard to the process of selling.

Relationship marketing requires a fundamentally different approach to the process of selling than that found in the transaction marketing approach. The following represent some of the shifts in emphasis and perspectives in the selling process when a company moves towards a relationship marketing approach.

- The sales person must take a longer term perspective than that of simply making a one-off sale when dealing with customers.
- Effective relationship selling requires much more of a team effort, not only between individual members of the salesforce but between the salesperson and other functions in the supplying company.
- The sales person must be proactive with customers, for example, calling or visiting customers at times other than when they think the customer is ready to place an order.
- The salesforce must act as a problem solver rather than an order taker or even an order winner.
- The sales person must act as an exchanger of information between his or her own company and the customer, and the customer and his or her own company.
- The emphasis must be much more on levels of customer service than simply low prices when attempting to generate sales.

All of this means that the skills and attitudes required for successful selling, or put another way ideas of what constitutes an effective salesperson and selling process is changing. The relationship salesperson for example must be skilled at listening to

customers and interpreting their problems. Job satisfaction (and incidentally remuneration) for the salesperson must be geared much more to developing customer
loyalty and trust rather than immediate one-off sales. The importance and impact of
the growth of relationship marketing on selling is such that Kotler[16] has defined the
relationship approach as the latest step in the evolution of the sales force. There is no
doubt that relationship marketing is set to continue to change the nature of selling to
an even greater extent in the future.

Summary

This is one of the longer chapters in the book, which perhaps reflects the importance of selling within the communications mix and indeed within the wider
context of the marketing mix. It is felt that selling is too often relegated to a
minor component within the wider remit of marketing. In most companies,
particularly non-end product manufacturers, it is the singular more important
element of the mix (and the most expensive). Face-to-face communication will
always be essential in commercial transactions. More to the point, such contact
involves human beings, with their idiosyncratic ways, which makes the subject
of selling complicated, dynamic and extremely interesting.

Some of the more significant developments in recent years have been the
growth of key account management, telesales, relationship marketing and of
course the ubiquitous Internet.

Key terms

Prospecting [p339]
SPIN model [p339]
Closing [p340]
Journey planning [p347]
Call frequency [p348]

Sales negotiation [p351]
Sales quota [p353]
Key account [p362]
Telesales [p362]

Questions

1 What are the major types of sales force, and what are the differences between these types as regards the nature of the selling process and the sorts of skills and activities involved?

2 Why are effective recruitment and selection procedures and techniques so important when considering sales staff, and what are the key steps in these processes?

3 What types of training might be required for sales staff in a company, and what key areas should be covered in an initial training programme for new sales staff?

4 What are the key steps in the general sales sequence, and what activities and skills are involved at each of these stages?

5 What are some of the key developments in selling and sales management, and what are some of the major implications of these for the selling process?

References

1. McMurry, R. N., 'The mystique of super-salesmanship', *Harvard Business Review*, March–April 1961, **26**, pp. 114–132.

2. Donaldson, B., *Sales Management: Theory and Practice*, 2nd edn, MacMillan, London 1997.

3. Anderson, R., *Essentials of Personal Selling*, Prentice-Hall, London, 1995.

4. Pickton, D. and Broderick, A., *Integrated Marketing Communications*, Pearson Education, Harlow, 2001, pp. 557–558.

5. Lancaster, G. A. and Jobber, D., *Selling and Sales Management*, 5th edn, Pitman, London, 2000.

6. Lancaster, G. A. and Simintiras, A., 'Job related expectations of sales people: a review of behavioural determinants', *Management Decision*, **29** 2, 1991, pp. 32–48.

7. Jobber, D. and Millar, S., 'The use of psychological tests in the selection of salesmen: a UK survey', *Journal of Sales Management*, 1984, pp. 66–89.

8. Rackham, N., *SPIN Selling*, Gower, 1995.

9. Pickton, D. and Broderick, A., op. cit., p. 561.

10. Lancaster, G. A. and Jobber, D., *Selling and Sales Management*, 5th edn. Pitman, London, 2000.

11. Millman, T. and Wilson, K. J., 'From key account selling to key account management', *Journal of Marketing Practice, Applied Marketing Science*, **1**, 1995, pp. 9–21.

12. Starkey, M. W., 'Telemarketing' in D. Jobber (ed.) *CIM Handbook of Selling and Sales Strategy*, Butterworth-Heinemann, Oxford, 1997.

13. Sasaki, T. 'How the Japanese accelerated new car development'. *Long Range Planning*, **24**, 1991, p. 17.

14. McKenna, R., 'Marketing is everything', *Harvard Business Review*, January–February, 1991, p. 70.

15. Lancaster, G. A., 'Marketing and engineering: can there ever be synergy?', *Journal of Marketing Management*, **9**, 1993, pp. 141–153.

16. Kotler, P., *Marketing Management: Analysis Planning Implementation and Control*, 9th edn, Prentice Hall, New Jersey, 1997.

Case Study

Peter Guppie is at a crossroads in the development of his business. Eighteen months ago, Peter left his job as a successful salesperson for a large software producer to set up his own company. Over this period his new company has gone from strength to strength. So much so that he knows that he now has to take on more staff. In particular, Peter will need to employ several new sales people.

Although Peter has always been successful in selling and indeed much of his new company's growth is down to his personal selling skills, he has never before had to manage a sales force, and certainly not for his own company. Within the next three months, however, Peter will have to decide what sort of persons he needs, recruit and select them, and finally train and manage them. Quite simply, despite his extensive experience as a sales person, he is worried about where to start. He recognizes the importance of getting this right as the whole future of his company will depend on the qualities and management of his sales force.

QUESTION

Advise Peter regarding what you feel are the key elements in recruiting and managing his new sales force.

13

Marketing information systems

Chapter objectives

After reading this chapter you will:

▶ Understand the importance of information in effective marketing planning.

▶ Appreciate the nature and meaning of the marketing information system and its role in providing information for decision making.

▶ Be aware of the principal problems and pitfalls in designing the marketing information system.

▶ Appreciate the contribution of contemporary marketing information system technology to information provision and processing.

▶ Be familiar with the key sources of information and inputs to the marketing information system including the marketing research process.

▶ Appreciate some of the key recent developments in this area.

Introduction

Remember marketing orientation places customers at the forefront of planning activities. As such, it is a philosophy of total business thinking and is not merely confined to the realms of the marketing department.

Organizations face changes and challenges from outside as well as inside their boundaries. The role of marketing is to anticipate and identify such changes and advise the organization on how to respond to challenges in the context of a competitive marketplace.

 Marketing needs information to carry out this task. Marketing research collects information and a **marketing information system** (MkIS) analyses and acts on such information. According to Kotler[1] a marketing information system consists of:

People, equipment, and procedures to gather, sort, analyse, evaluate and distribute needed, timely and accurate information to marketing decision-makers.

This, and other definitions, of a marketing information system highlights two important points. First, the marketing information system is more than just marketing research. In fact, as we shall see, information provided by marketing research is but one input to the marketing information system, albeit a crucial one. The second key point which Kotler's definition highlights is that the whole purpose of the marketing information system is to enhance the marketing manager's decision making. Both of these important points about the marketing information system we shall return to later.

In practice, an MkIS provides a store of historical customer data. This produces better efficiency internally due to better organized data, thus ultimately leading to more effective strategic improvements; better identification of opportunities that might lead to the development of new products and services; and the development of better long-term relationships with customers arising from increased customer loyalty.

To achieve this requires a study of an organization's current information base and its ability to monitor existing marketing activities. It also needs the ability to use information to match the dynamics of a changing market and to report such changes to marketing management in order that appropriate planning action can be taken.

Information requirements

An organization's strategy, planning and operational control will only be as good as the information that is available to the decision maker. A situation analysis is one method of considering these activities and changes and relating them to the operations of the organization. Means must be found for environmental scanning, studying the marketing system and giving the results of such intelligence gathering to key decision makers. This forms the basis for strategic decisions on marketing which are then monitored to ensure that objectives are achieved. The MkIS thus provides the medium through which information is collected, channelled, focused and communicated.

Information requirements depend upon a number of factors:

- The type of industry or environment
- The size of the organization
- The marketing decisions to be taken
- The dynamics of the industry or environment.

It is therefore difficult to generalize about the individual needs of an organization. However, such information is collected from internal and external sources, and thus will include customer, market and competitor information. Quite often this information exists but is not in a form suitable for use by marketing. Much is collected for invoicing purposes only, where its value is not recognized. Customer inquiries and customer complaints need to be channelled into the MkIS to ensure that they are valued and used for planning and controlling marketing operations.

Information on existing customers will form the core of the database. For example, a typical invoice records information which can be used by marketing (see Table 13.1).

Table 13.1 MkIS utilization of accounting invoice information.

Information	Marketing use
Customer name	Identification
Customer address	Geodemographic profiling and census data
Date of sale	Tracking of purchase rates, repurchase identification
Items ordered	Benefit/need analysis, product clusters
Representative's name	Representative performance monitoring
Quantities ordered	Heavy/light user, crude segmentation
Price	Value calculation of profitability
Discount (if any)	Price sensitivity
Terms and conditions	Customer service needs, special requirements

As the volume and sophistication of information collected increases, so an organization will build up its database of existing and potential customers, which will allow the application of more sophisticated targeting and segmentation strategies through a more thorough understanding of buying behaviour in the marketplace.

The nature of the marketing information function has changed over recent years, and so too has the technology available to marketing managers. Microchip and computer technology have made information readily accessible and communicable – for instance, through the laser scanning of bar coded grocery products at supermarket checkouts.

The current developments in new technology have created revolutionary changes to achieve a business climate to check accuracy and validity of information.

Decisions support systems (DSS) were introduced in the late 1970s and these are designed from the viewpoint of an individual decision marker. McDaniel and Gates[2] have stated that the characteristics of a true DSS are that it is:

- Interactive – simple instructions are given and results are generated on the spot
- Flexible – it can sort, regroup, total, average and manipulate data in many ways
- Discovery orientated – it helps managers probe for trends, isolate problems and ask questions
- Easy to learn and use.

The MkIS is thus seen as an invaluable aid to decision making, and as such it plays its part as a specialized subset of the corporate management information system (MIS).

The MkIS and the MIS

The term **Management Information System** (MIS), along with that of MkIS, is synonymous with data processing. Dibb et al.[3] have has defined an MIS as being:

> The framework for the day-to-day management and structuring of information gathered from sources both inside and outside an organization.

Figure 13.1
Marketing information system.

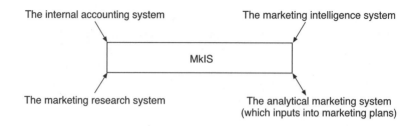

Lucey[4] stresses the decision making of the MIS:

> A system to convert data from internal and external sources into information and to communicate that information, in an appropriate form, to managers at all levels in all functions to enable them to make timely and effective decisions for planning, directing and controlling the activities for which they are responsible.

The MkIS is in fact a sub-system of an organization's MIS. Lancaster and Massingham[5] suggest that an MkIS is a system used to generate and disseminate an orderly flow of pertinent information to marketing managers. Marketing research is concerned with the task of generating information, whereas the MkIS is focused on managing the flow of information to marketing decision makers. This we have already seen, is highlighted in Kotler's and Lucey's definitions. This distinction is important because information is worthless unless it is relevant and effectively communicated.

The operation for MkIS is illustrated in Figure 13.1. It can be seen that an MkIS consists of four subsystems:

1. The internal accounting system. This is a system that reports orders, sales, dispatches, inventory levels, and cheques receivable and payable.
2. The marketing intelligence system. This is a set of procedures and sources used by executives to obtain their everyday information about pertinent developments in the marketing environment.
3. The marketing research system. This is the systematic design, collection, analysis and reporting of data findings relevant to a specific marketing situation facing the company.
4. The analytical marketing system. This is a system for analysing marketing data using statistical procedures and mathematical models. This analysis subsequently feeds into marketing plans.

Subsystems 1, 2 and 3 are all data collection methods, whereas subsystem 4 is an analytical method. Together they provide a framework for marketing managers to frame their thoughts into tactics, and to assist top management in seeing the important elements of a particular situation and examining the relationships between these elements. A successful MkIS will also provide a structure for analysis, planning and control of a given set of activities. It is important to note that creating an MIS and MkIS for any business is a complex process with no standardized solutions.

Need for MkIS

We have seen that today marketers must emphasize the building of long-term relationships. We have also seen that this has been part-brought about by the widespread adoption of a 'just-in-time' (JIT) management philosophy. Lead times are becoming increasingly shorter across a range of goods and services, and greater emphasis is being placed upon supplier reliability and less upon such factors as price.

Lancaster[6] points out that these trends have affected all aspects of marketing. Normally dominated by the idea of the unique selling proposition, corporate marketing is now being forced to practise the small business philosophy of staying close to customers, understanding and meeting their needs and treating them well after the sale. Through having an MkIS it is becoming possible to apply these principles in practice in that without an effective MkIS in many organizations, the contemporary marketer could not manage.

Proctor and Gamble is a company that is using an effective marketing information system to get close to customers and their needs. An example is their use of their marketing information system to target Pampers users with sales promotion campaigns.

Problems of MkIS design

Research undertaken into the uses of information in decision making by organizations suggests that integration of computer processes with decision making is difficult. Feldman and March[7] summarize their findings as follows:

1. Much of the information that is gathered and communicated by individuals and organizations has little decision relevance.
2. Much of the information that is used to justify a decision is collected and interpreted after the decision has been made, or substantially made.
3. Much of the information gathered in response to requests for information is not considered in the making of decisions for which it was requested.
4. Regardless of the information available at the time a decision is first considered, more information is requested.
5. Complaints that an organization does not have enough information to make a decision occur while available information is ignored.
6. The relevance of the information provided in the decision-making process to the decision being made is less conspicuous than is the insistence on information.

In short, most organizations and individuals collect more information than they use, or can reasonably expect to use, in the making of decisions. At the same time, they seem to be constantly needing or requesting more information, or complaining about inadequacies of information.

The authors go on to conclude that either organizations are systematically inept, or have severe limitations in understanding the nature of information and decision making. A situation therefore exists where turbulent environments are increasing the need for information on the changes taking place, yet information technology does not always make the contribution it could to providing this information in a form suitable for decision makers.

The technical problems of designing and implementing an MkIS are many, but it is the problems faced by the user of the system which are of most importance to the marketing manager. These problems can be summarized under the headings of misinformation, lack of user orientation, the nature of management decision making, the user-system interface and organizational problems.

A final set of problems relates to the difficulties of integrating the system into the organization. Often systems are designed which fail in their implementation, not due to any failures of the system, but because of the designer's ignorance of organizational theory. This is likely to be a particular problem with marketing systems where the interest and influence of marketing is often felt across formal departmental boundaries. This 'boundary spanning' role is an essential aspect of an integrated marketing approach, but is often resisted by departments who jealously guard their own power in the form of the information they control. Clearly, in this instance management support at board level is necessary in order to overcome these problems. Overcoming these problems therefore, and particularly the problem of 'too much' information from the system needs careful system design.

A well designed information and decision support system should have the following characteristics:

- The system should be based on a careful appraisal and analysis of the decision-making requirements of marketing management. This involves establishing, for example what types of marketing decisions are made, what sorts of information are required for these decisions, and how this information is to be supplied. Clearly this involves consulting the end users of the system before it is designed and implemented.
- The system should be designed to be 'user-friendly'. Information is wasted if it cannot be, or is not, used. A major problem in the provision of information to marketing management is that often the system is designed to suit the information specialist rather than the actual decision maker.
- The system should be designed so as to be 'interactive'. In other words the system should allow analysis rather than merely retrieval of information. This means that the system should be model rather than data oriented.
- The system should be cost effective. As mentioned earlier, information costs money. An effective system of marketing information supply should be based on a careful evaluation of how the system will contribute to more cost effective marketing decisions.

It is by paying attention to these key areas of the design of the marketing information system that the potential problems of having too much information and/or the system being too costly can be minimized. If the marketing information system is not designed with these elements in mind the marketing manager may suffer from information overload.

Application of an MkIS

Tactical applications The most obvious applications are in such areas as customer loyalty measures, the generation of sales leads, testing price levels and promotional effectiveness. A more detailed application is in customer segmentation. When analysing the most suitable or profitable consumer profile for a product or service, the analyst can locate a list of actual and prospective customers with those characteristics. Promotional material can then be targeted to the specific needs of the identified market segments.

Sales force activities can be better co-ordinated by selecting the contact tactics most suitable for different groups of customers. Customer loyalty can be built up through

Table 13.2 Strategic application of an MkIS

Competitive opportunity	Marketing strategy	Role of information
1. Changing the basis of competition	Market development or penetration Increased effectiveness/better margins, alternative sales channels Reducing cost structure	Prospect/customer information Targeted marketing Better control
2. Strengthen customer relationships	Tailored customer service Providing value to customer Product differentiation Create switching costs	Know customer needs 'Individual' promotions Response handling, identify potential needs Customers as 'users' of your system
3. Strengthen buyer/supplier relationships	Superior market information Decreased cost of sales Providing value to supplier Pass stockholding onto supplier	Internal/external data Optimization of sales channels Measure supplier performance Identify areas of inefficiency
4. Build barriers to new entrants	Unique distribution channels Unique valued services Create entry costs	Knowledge of market allows improved service/value 'Lock in' customers, suppliers and intermediaries Immediate response to threats
5. Generate new or substitute products	Market-led product development Alliance opportunities New products/services	Market gap analysis Customer dialogue, user innovation Information as a product

logging all customer contacts. This will provide an opportunity for repeat sales and maximizing sales of other company product lines.

Strategic applications Increasingly, information is now being used to develop strategic plans. O'Connor and Galvin[8] describe a variety of strategic applications of information for marketing purposes, including segmentation targeting, new product development and direct marketing strategies

An effective MkIS generates huge amounts of customer and market data. It thus has the potential to input into marketing policy. Porter's[9] framework provides us with a guide when identifying competitive opportunity areas and an MkIS can be seen to operate strategically when its information is used in the ways illustrated in Table 13.2.

Developments in marketing information systems technology: databases

Perhaps as one would expect, technological developments, and particularly those associated with information technology, are having a major impact on marketing information systems. In the main, these developments are underpinned by increasingly cheap but sophisticated computing power which is facilitating improvements in data collection, storage, manipulation, and retrieval. Examples of how new technologies are helping in this respect are computer-assisted telephone interviewing, improved access to secondary data sources through on-line CD-rom services and once again, of course, the Internet. Related to all of these areas, one of the most significant developments has been in the area of database technology.

Databases

As Withey[10] *et al.* point out, developments in information collection, storage and analysis are now making information one of the most important competitive assets a company can have. The key to this information revolution is the use of databases in marketing. Essentially a **database** represents a pool of information on markets and customers which can be interrogated and analysed in order to facilitate improved marketing decision making.

Of course, databases are not new; after all, a system of manual sales records kept on customers in a filing cabinet is a database. Modern databases, however, are now extremely powerful and sophisticated.

A database can be built from a variety of sources. Examples include customer orders, loyalty cards, customer enquiries, subscription lists, ad hoc market research studies, and a host of secondary sources. There is now a wealth of information available to marketers. However, this wealth of information has in the past been a problem rather than an asset in that all too often marketers have simply been overwhelmed by data. Not only do modern database techniques and technologies help to overcome this problem, but also we now know much more about the key factors in developing and using successful databases. Withey *et al.*[11] suggest that in developing a database attention needs to be paid to the following:

- Clear and specific objectives for the database, including types of information required and why
- Effective systems and strategies for data capture
- Effective systems for data storage, including database maintenance
- Effective systems of analysis and interpretation of data to provide information for decision making.

Data capture involves systems for providing and collecting data for the database and includes many of the sources mentioned above. Marketers have become much more sophisticated in data collection in recent years, again facilitated by more extensive use of computing and information technology. It is important to remember that in many countries there is often legislation relating to the collection and use of data on customers which is designed to cover customers' rights in several respects with regard to data on them.

Data warehousing is a term used to describe collecting data on customers and markets from several possible sources in a company and storing it in one central database. This idea has developed because many companies have different departments in the organization, each of which have their own databases that are not made available to the rest of the organization.

Remember that a database should provide information for improved decision making. Again, developments in information technology and computing have helped facilitate the analysis and interpretation of data for this purpose. Marketing managers can now use statistical analysis and modelling techniques to look for important patterns of cause and effect in the database. This is referred to as 'data mining'.

Data mining enables the marketer to use database information in very powerful ways, improving the effectiveness of aspects such as segmentation and targeting, promotional and particularly direct marketing strategies and, as will be discussed further in Chapter 17, the development of relationship marketing strategies including customer retention and loyalty strategies.

Some companies, because of the nature of their business, often have considerable information on their customers which can effectively be used through data mining. Banks and credit card companies are particularly good examples. A company like Federal Express has a wealth of information encompassing not only their card holders' personal details but also what purchases they are making, at what price, how often, and from where. Imagine how information like this can be used by the marketer.

It is vitally important to ensure that databases are regularly maintained and updated. Customers and information on them is changing all the time and if the database contains inaccurate information we run the risk of making wrong decisions or even embarrassing ones.

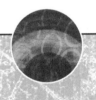

One of the most embarrassing (for the company but not for the customer) distressing effect of obsolete database information is where direct mail, for example, is sent to a deceased person's address. Obviously offering the chance of a 'holiday of a lifetime' is not much use to someone who has passed away twelve months earlier.

It is not possible to describe in detail here all the techniques for ensuring database maintenance, but for example, many companies reference their data against third-party lists to ensure its accuracy. Other companies use external consultants to ensure that the database is maintained.

Inputs to the MkIS

Up to now, the discussion has centred upon the MkIS in the context of a tool of marketing management. The three inputs to the MkIS (see Figure 13.1) are now examined individually, commencing first with the internal accounting system.

The internal accounting system

Internal company data can be a most fruitful source of information. However, it is often not utilized as fully as it should be. The administrative and documentary procedures of a firm will vary from company to company, but most systems will start with the customer's enquiry and end with the customer's invoice. With careful analysis, it is possible to build a picture of the overall system from individual employees to the total departmental system and ultimately to the firm as a whole.

Many records are kept by individual members of staff 'unofficially' in case a question is asked about something or for some other contingency. These unofficial sources may be very useful and only identified through careful probing. It is often surprising exactly what information is kept and maintained for personal use of this kind.

Data from marketing/sales departments

The marketing and sales departments are the main points of commercial interaction between an organization and its customers. Consequently, a great deal of information should be available, including:

1. *Total sales*
   Every company keeps a record of its total sales over a defined time period; for example, daily records, weekly records, monthly records and so on.
2. *Sales by products*
   Very few companies sell only one product. Most companies sell a range of products and they keep records of each kind of product or, if the range is large, each product group.
3. *Territorial sales*
   Sales statistics are invariably kept by individual sales territory. This is partly to measure the progress and competence of the salesperson (sometimes to influence earnings because commission may be paid on sales) and also to measure the degree of market penetration.
4. *Sales by trade classification*
   Many organizations classify customers by trade, such as textiles, engineering or chemicals. This will give some indication of market penetration for each class when compared to the official census of distribution which analyses sales by trade classifications.
5. *Sales volume by market segment*
   Such segmentation may be geographical or by type of industry. This will give an indication of segment trends in terms of whether they are static, declining or expanding.
6. *Sales volume by type of channel of distribution*
   Where a company has a multi-channel distribution policy, it is possible to calculate the effectiveness and profitability of each type of channel. This also allows for trends to be identified in the pattern of distribution and to be taken into account in planning future channel requirements. Such information allows marketing management to identify and develop promising channel opportunities and results in more effective channel marketing.
7. *Sales volume over time*
   This covers actual sales and units sold. Such information will enable seasonal variations to be identified, and inflation cost adjustments can be taken into consideration.
8. *Pricing information*
   Historical information relating to price adjustments by product allows the organization to establish the effect on demand of price increases or decreases and to judge the likely effects of any future price changes.

9. *Communication mix information*
   This includes past data on the effects of advertising campaigns, sponsorship, direct mail programmes or exhibitions, levels of expenditure on marketing communications, and the effect on sales of increases or decreases in such expenditure. Such information can act as a guide as to the likely effectiveness of future communication expenditure plans.
10. *Sales representative's records and reports*
    Sales representatives should keep a visit card or file on every 'live' customer. In addition, sales representatives often send reports to the sales office on such matters as orders lost to competitors and possible reasons why, as well as on firms that are holding future purchasing decisions in abeyance. Such information could help in determining future levels of demand or point to possible necessary improvements in marketing strategy.
11. *Inquiries received and quotations sent*
    Buyers send inquiries to potential suppliers. Each potential supplier sends a quotation. Such information may be useful in terms of establishing a pattern of inquiries that mature into purchase orders. Such a pattern will also expose the level of economic activity in the marketplace.

Other records

Sales records from the internal accounting system are clearly of most direct use for the MkIS. Other departments also have records that may be of direct value, and these include:

1. *Materials purchased*
   This information relates to purchase records and reflects the raw material and components side of what the company manufactures. Profitability measures can be established from such analyses.
2. *Wages records*
   Knowing the proportion of direct labour that goes into prime cost (prime cost being made up of direct labour, direct materials and direct expenses) can give a guide to manufacturing productivity.
3. *Dispatch records*
   This department will have logged details of goods dispatched and methods of transport. Such information will allow the company to build up a picture of logistical effectiveness.
4. *Accounts department*
   The management accountant will be able to provide cost data on areas of interest, as well as other documents such as past management reports which will be kept either on file or stored on a 'dead file' for a considerable period of time. In addition, past budgets, complete with variance analyses, will show budgeted figures against actual figures.
5. *Departmental plans*
   Not only is past and current internal information available to marketing, but so are short-, medium- and long-term plans of individual departments. Future planned activity and changes in company policy or methods of operation can be evaluated and taken into account.

The sources of information available from the internal accounting system are not all-embracing. They do, however, represent, the most obvious data that can be of use within an MkIS. Other departments, too, can input valuable data and such information can be collected from Research and Development, Personnel and, of course, Production, where measures of output and productivity can be used. The list is virtually endless, but the problem might be one of an 'information explosion', with much information being so irrelevant that users will find it of little value. However, a fully co-ordinated corporate MIS, of which the MkIS is a component part, will be an invaluable aid to strategic corporate planners as well as to marketing planners.

The marketing intelligence system

As described earlier, the marketing intelligence system is concerned with the collection and analysis of ongoing developments in the marketing environment. A variety of sources of information can be used in this part of the information system, but the main sources are usually secondary sources available to the marketer. For a fuller description of some of these key sources of **secondary data**, data collected by others for other purposes, the reader should consult, for example, Brassington and Pettitt[12], who provide an excellent summary of some of the key sources of Europe-wide data available to the marketer.

Government sources

We shall first examine what, for most researchers, is probably the most important and valuable of external sources of secondary data. Among the more important and potentially useful sources of UK government data, we include the following.

Census of population   This is taken every 10 years during the year that ends with the digit '1' (e.g. the 2001 census), with a 10 per cent sample being taken during every year that ends with a '6'. It collects information on numbers in the population, including age, sex, marital status, socio-economic class, country of birth and economic activity.

The Economic Activity Tables contain statistics about the occupied population based on their personal occupations and the employed population classified into branches of industry. Key statistics, covering age, distribution, socio-economic status, housing conditions, housing tenure, car ownership and many others, are available for each of the 106 000 enumeration districts (i.e. precisely mapped areas containing approximately 150 households each and based on wards and parishes).

These statistics have been extensively used in the past by marketing organizations in order to evaluate potential markets and form the basis of geodemographic segmentation bases such as ACORN groupings, which were discussed in Chapter 6.

Monthly digest of statistics   This contains information on national income and expenditure; population statistics; labour; social services; production; agriculture and food; energy; chemicals; textiles; construction; retailing and catering; transport; external trade; wages and prices; entertainment; and overseas and home finance.

Annual abstract of statistics   This contains information on area and climate; population statistics; social conditions and services; education; labour; energy; industrial materials; building and construction; manufactured goods; agriculture and fisheries; transport and communication; retail distribution; balance of payments; personal income; expenditure and wealth; finance; and prices.

Business monitors The object of individual business monitors is to bring together the most up-to-date official statistical information covering production, imports and exports relating to a particular industry:

1. The *Production Series* covers such items as food, drink and tobacco; coal and petroleum products; chemicals and allied industries; metal manufacture; engineering; textiles; clothing and footwear; printing and publishing; timber; furniture; pottery; glass and cement.
2. The *Service and Distribution Series* covers food shops; clothing and footwear shops; durable goods shops; catering trades; and finance houses.
3. The *Miscellaneous Series* covers motor vehicle registrations; cinema; insurance companies; overseas travel and tourism; acquisitions and mergers; and company finance.

Census of distribution Although it is called a census, this series samples various retail outlets, e.g. grocers, confectioners, tobacconists, newsagents, clothing and footwear shops, and furniture and electrical goods shops. It provides information on numbers, sizes, type and turnover of shops.

Census of production This series samples establishments engaged in manufacturing, mining and quarrying, electricity, and gas and water supply. It provides information on employment, wages and salaries, stocks, capital expenditure, purchases of materials and fuel, sales, and work done.

Economic trends This is published monthly and contains information on the value of imports and exports; volume of retail sales; index of production; new car registrations; retail prices; gross domestic product; personal disposal income; saving and borrowing; consumer expenditure; investment; relationship of stocks and output; and changes in stocks.

Family expenditure survey This is prepared annually with the co-operation of a sample of about 7000 households. The survey collects information on weekly expenditure on about 100 grouped items, and analyses it according to household income, household composition, occupation and age of the head of the household.

Overseas trade statistics of the UK This involves a summary of imports and exports by commodities and countries.

Social trends The Central Statistical Office produces an annual report which covers population; employment; leisure activities; personal income and expenditure; social security; welfare, health; education; housing; environment; justice and law; and public expenditure.

Yearbooks These are published by certain government departments. They contain a variety of information in no specific format.

It must be remembered that government statistics are collected for the purposes of government, and not specifically for marketing firms. Consequently, such statistics may not always fit a particular marketing purpose and may have to be extensively modified or retabulated to be of use. A further point is that fact that many of these statistics have been collected by the government for general macroeconomic policy making. For such decision making, broad aggregates of data are usually sufficient and the various government agencies will often use a number of assumptions and conventions when compiling statistics which can affect their valid-ity, especially when they are used out of context in situations other than those for which they were originally compiled. Whilst government statistics are a very valu-able source of information, they must be used with due caution when making marketing plans.

International sources

These sources are very well established and the most prominent ones are now discussed.

The United Nations Apart from its political role, the United Nations operates through many other agencies. Those which concern the industrial and trade researcher are the United Nations Development Programme (UNDP) and the United Nations Industrial Development Organization (UNIDO), both of which are mainly concerned with helping the progress of developing countries. Each has an international staff and each is engaged in a wide variety of international operations.

To support these operations, regular researches are undertaken and reports are published on industrial and commercial problems throughout the world.

International bodies Apart from the organizations sponsored by the United Nations, there are some which are associated with the UN and others which are independent but co-operate. Some of the main ones are:

World Health Organization (WHO) This is mainly concerned with world health prob-lems, such as combating disease and giving advice and guidance on hygiene. Its activities are of particular interest to marketing people who are engaged in the pharma-ceutical trade.

International Labour Office (ILO) The main occupation of this organization is trying to find work and create employment in under-developed areas. To a certain extent, its activities run parallel with those of UNDP and UNIDO, but it concentrates mostly upon employment and training labour.

The World Trade Organization This is mainly concerned with international negotia-tions on trade and tariff reforms, but also issues many useful publications on trade and industry.

European Through Eurostat Union (EU) This is mainly concerned with the development of trade and industry in Europe. It issues a wide range of publications on trade and industrial issues. These are mainly, but not exclusively, concerned with Europe. Since non-European countries have ties with the European Union, some publications also have studies and reports on other countries' activities.

Food and Agricultural Organization (FAO) This is mainly concerned with food and agri-culture, as its title indicates. Associated with this is the use of fertilizers and insecticides.

Organization for Economic Co-operation and Development (OECD) This organization's objective is to achieve in Europe the highest sustainable growth, employment and standard of living, to contribute to economic development and to expand world trade on a multi-lateral and non-discriminatory basis. As a result, the OECD produces many publications, e.g. *Food Marketing and Economic Growth* and *Organizing and Operating a Voluntary Food Agency.*

Statistics of trade associations and other bodies   There is a wide variety of statistics on particular trades or industries, issued by trade associations, chambers of commerce and other bodies. Generally, these statistics are issued only to the members of such associations, depending on what they make or sell.

The data available from these sources are more detailed than government statistics, and relate to a narrower field. Thus, the statistics issued by a trade association for tool manufacturers will include figures – for volume or value, or both – of the production of various tools in the UK, and of imports and exports (with countries of origin and destination). They will probably also show which rival countries that manufacture tools export them to which other countries, and this will give valuable leads as to the areas where there is a market for such products.

Other published information   Statistics are only part of desk research. A great deal of other information can also be obtained from published reports, year books and reference books on relevant subjects. This is a very wide field, but the trained researcher will soon learn where to look for such information and will often find the information services of technical and reference libraries to be of great help.

Official handbooks   There are a number of official books giving a mass of general background information on a country. An example is *Britain – an Official Handbook*, issued by the Stationery Office. Similar publications are available for most countries and are very often obtainable free from information departments of embassies. If one is carrying out research relating to a particular country, such a handbook will supply general background data.

Directories   There is a wide range of trade and regional directories, listing, often with some basic details, businesses in a particular trade or a particular town or area. Even a classified telephone directory can yield a lot of information.

Economic surveys   Most governments and many banks and chambers of commerce publish economic reports on specific markets. Some of these are of a general nature, but quite a number of them refer to an industry or particular group of industries. Firms of stockbrokers often issue reports on a particular industry, mainly in relation to those firms whose shares are quoted on the Stock Exchange.

Sometimes the findings of research sponsored by a firm or trade association are published and available. Many reports are brought out by national or local newspapers.

The availability of such reports varies; they may be for private circulation to clients or members only, for sale to anyone interested, or freely available.

Companies House   Information about all UK limited companies can be accessed here in person or through agencies which conduct searches for a fee.

Miscellaneous   This includes company annual reports, promotion and publicity literature, and competitors' price lists. Visits to trade exhibitions are a good way of gathering this sort of material as well as giving the opportunity to study competitors' products and promotional material at first hand.

A further source of information that we can include under this section is published market research reports. These can be purchased when required, examples being

Economic Intelligence Unit reports, *Euromonitor*, Henley Centre for Forecasting reports and MINTEL publications surveys.

If we take MINTEL as an example, these are reports that cover a number of different markets, usually four or five in each publication, although periodically a whole issue is devoted to one market. They give many useful comments, statistics and predictions, and all the work is carried out by market researchers, either employed by MINTEL or commissioned from other professional market research firms.

'Off-the-peg' research data

In addition to the variety of published secondary research data which has been discussed, a company may decide to make use of syndicated research data usually purchased from a marketing research company which itself has carried out certain surveys. This type of data is a 'hybrid', falling somewhere between true secondary data and primary data.

The difference between this type of data and **primary data** collected by the company itself through primary research is that the data are normally not collected for an individual client, but rather are sold to whoever will buy. For this reason, such data is often referred to as **'off-the-peg' research data**. Some examples are now detailed.

Consumer panels   serve the purpose of providing manufacturers and advertisers with a continuous check on the market and a record of the behaviour of consumers and their reactions to changes in products, methods of marketing or advertising. They comprise a reasonably permanent set of consumers, usually consisting of a sample of women, selected on a statistical basis to represent accurately a cross-section of non-working women in the country.

In the UK, the Attwood Consumer Panel consists of 5000 women in Great Britain and 500 women in Northern Ireland. Members of the panel are defined by age, ACORN class, social class and district. Each member of the panel is given a diary in which she records information.

The women report the following facts concerning the product in the diary:

- Brand name and description
- Number of items brought
- Size and weight of each item and price
- Day of purchase
- Type of outlet
- Full description of any 'special offer'
- Information on flavour of product, type and colour of container, if applicable.

The women return the diary to the market research organization weekly. The market research organization sells reports of this activity to individual manufacturers. The diaries are intended to reveal:

- The performance of brands
- The total number of people buying specific products
- Sales volume by type of shop and geographic area
- The effect of promotions, price changes or competition
- Consumer purchasing patterns concerning brand switching.

Brand barometers are a service offered by market research firms to subscribers on a quarterly basis. Brand barometers each cover a particular market, examples include the private motorists market and the household products market.

In each market barometer a range of products is covered. For example in the household products market, product areas such as pet foods, bread, cereals, cleaning materials and so on are encompassed. In brand barometers respondents are questioned regarding their purchases or otherwise of each product category. Where respondents indicate that they have purchased within a commodity class they will be questioned as to when, what brand, and from which retail outlet etc. Data in brand barometers is analysed in a variety of ways including geographic area, age, social class, and Acorn categories.

Inventory audits of retail sales This well tried method of research (retail audits) was first started by the A.C. Nielsen Company. The basic principle is that an inventory is made at regular intervals of the stock and purchases of certain products at selected retail outlets, in such fields as food, confectionery and cigarettes. This detailed inventory is carried out by field researchers with the co-operation of the retailers concerned, who are remunerated for their help. The audits are therefore accurate, and provide a picture of what the trade buys and sells and the quantities it carries in stock.

Once the manufacturer's products leave the factory, there is a time lag before they are bought and consumed. The longer this gap becomes, the more difficult it is for the producer to exercise control over supply to meet the changes in demand and modify production.

By the process of adding purchase invoices to opening stocks and then deducting closing stocks, the sales of each item can then be determined.

The reports issued to subscribers are generally along these lines:

1. Retail purchases by brand and by product.
2. Retail stocks by brand and by product.
3. Consumer sales by brand and by product.
4. Percentage of shops handling the product.
5. Percentage of shops out of stock of various brands.
6. Retail and wholesale prices of various products.
7. Average size of retail order from average retailer.
8. Proportion of retailers buying direct from manufacturers and from wholesalers.
9. Display material, promotions and advertising carried out for various brands.

This is now a very competitive market and several companies provide retail audit type services and data.

On-line information sources

Increasingly information is available on-line. Websites and commercial CD-rom sites enable the marketer to access a wide range of information sources quickly.

The marketing research system

This is the final input to the MkIS and the method used can be one, or a combination, of observation, experimentation and survey research. We shall now examine each of these in turn.

Observation

This approach to the generation of primary data is based on watching and sometimes recording market-related behaviour.

Observational techniques are more suited to investigating what people do rather than why they do it. An example of this approach might be the posting of a researcher in a retail outlet to observe patterns of shopping behaviour. Another example is the use of meter-recording devices in television audience research.

Observational research may vary from the simple, non-permanently recorded personal approach to the use of complex, non-personal and permanently recorded ones, including the use of eye cameras and video cameras.

A major advantage of observational techniques in market research is that they may be used without the observed respondent's knowledge. This is particularly useful when such knowledge would influence or bias the results, or where perhaps respondents would not be willing to participate at all. Understandably, use of observation without the knowledge of the respondents raises a number of ethical and legal issues.

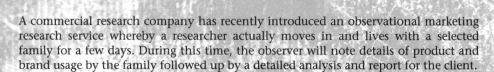

A commercial research company has recently introduced an observational marketing research service whereby a researcher actually moves in and lives with a selected family for a few days. During this time, the observer will note details of product and brand usage by the family followed up by a detailed analysis and report for the client.

An interesting if somewhat extreme example of observational research techniques in action.

Experimentation

This is a more formal approach to primary data collection. As in any experimental design, the essence of this approach is to determine causal relationships between factors and to support or refute hypotheses about these relationships. The most usual marketing research application is that of test marketing. This is a research technique in which the product under study is placed on sale in one or more selected localities or areas, and its reception by consumers and the trade is observed, recorded and analysed.

Performance in these test markets gives some indication of the performance to be expected when the product goes into general distribution. Performance includes two aspects:

1. The likely sales and profitability of the product when marketed on a national scale.
2. Feasibility of the marketing operation, by which we mean the soundness and integration of all the elements that enter into the marketing operation.

It is often an economic necessity to reduce new product risk by using one or more small and relatively self-contained marketing areas, wherein the marketer can apply a full-plan marketing strategy in order to gain at least a reasonably reliable indication that the product can be sold profitably in the eventual total marketplace.

For a more detailed consideration of test marketing, any good marketing research textbook will give details as to the practical implications.

The problem with the experimental approach to marketing is the difficulty of designing and administering the experiment in a scientific way. It is particularly difficult to control extraneous factors which might affect the test results.

Survey research

This approach to collecting primary data is what is generally regarded as constituting marketing research. Survey research, based on sampling and questioning respondents, represents, both in volume and value terms, perhaps the most important method of collecting data.

Survey research is used for a variety of marketing problems and decisions, including such aspects as

- Customer attitudes
- Customer buying habits
- Market trends
- Potential market size.

Unlike experimental research, survey research is more often aimed at generating descriptive rather than causal data; unlike observational research, survey research usually involves the respondent.

Because of the importance and diversity of survey research in marketing, it is on this particular aspect that we now concentrate.

Sampling   Contact with consumers and dealers is fundamental to marketing research. Except in very restricted markets, it would be both impracticable and too expensive to interview more than a proportion of the total number. This total number is known statistically as the 'universe' or the 'population'. In marketing terms, it comprises the total number of actual and potential users of a particular product or service. The total number of consumers who could be interviewed is known as the 'sample frame', whilst the number of people who are actually interviewed is known as the 'sample'.

Scientific sampling techniques aim to achieve samples which are reflections, in miniature, of the universes from which they are drawn. In other words, the sample should be a microcosm of the 'universe'.

If we can define clearly the universe or population to which the study will relate, we have then to see if there is a suitable frame. If random or systematic sampling is to be used in a market survey, the availability of a suitable sampling frame is of prime importance. In practice, there are few really satisfactory sampling frames. National lists, such as the Register of Electors, quickly fall out of date, while commercial directories and professional registers are only reflections of subscribers or members, who may not represent the entire population.

Five criteria are important when evaluating sampling frames:

1. Adequacy.
2. Completeness – which should indicate *all* the units of a population under survey.
3. Accuracy – totally up-to-date sampling frames are rarely available. The frame may contain units which no longer exist, e.g. the Electoral Register will contain people who have moved home.
4. Duplication – bias will result where names of sampling units occur more than once, e.g. some firms may have multiple listings in telephone directories.
5. Convenience – sampling lists should be accessible and suitable for sampling purposes.

It is not the purpose of this text to explain the various methods of sampling or the calculation of standard error as this knowledge is subsumed. Basic statistics texts will explain such options as random sampling, systematic sampling, multi-stage sampling, cluster sampling, stratified sampling and quota sampling, along with an understanding of how deviation or bias can enter into a sample and its potential effects upon the results of a survey.

Contact methods The method of contact chosen is usually a balance between time, the degree of accuracy required and costs. These include personal interviews, postal surveys and telephone interviews.

1. *Personal interviews*
   These can be divided into more formal 'on-street' surveys using structured questionnaires and a less structured 'depth' or 'focus' interview format.
2. *Postal surveys*
   These demand a very straightforward formalized questionnaire, since personal intervention is not possible to explain any questioning areas which might not be clear.
3. *Telephone interviews*
   An increasingly popular medium owing to the relatively low costs, especially for industrial marketing research, where respondents might be widely scattered geographically.

The contact medium – the questionnaire A good questionnaire cannot be designed until the precise information requirements are known. It is the vehicle whereby the research objectives are translated into specific questions.

The type of information sought, and the type of respondents to be researched, will have a bearing upon the contact method to be used, and this, in turn, will influence whether the questionnaire is a relatively unstructured schedule of discussion points for depth interviewing or a structured closed-ended type questionnaire for 'on-street' interviews.

Qualitative research

Marketers are obviously concerned with the collection and analysis of quantitative data on their markets and customers. Data such as market size, numbers of competitors, average purchasing prices, and so on all provide quantitative data on market facts. However, marketers are also interested in qualitative data on markets and customers.

Qualitative data encompasses areas such as underpinning customer attitudes, customer perceptions and beliefs, psychological and sociological influences on consumer behaviour. **Qualitative research** techniques are aimed at providing these sorts of information.

Over the years, marketers have tried several tools and techniques for researching these often complex and more difficult to get at qualitative aspects. Many were begged, borrowed, or adapted from the psychologist and sociologist. In the 1960s for example, marketers began to use what became collectively referred to as motivation research techniques. Examples of specific techniques used included thematic apperception, Rorschach ink-blot tests and word association tests. During the 1980s and 1990s many of these techniques fell by the wayside and motivation research in general was used less and less by marketers who felt it to be unscientific and discredited. Two techniques of qualitative research which did remain viable and have been even more widely used, are the focus groups and depth interviews, discussed in Chapter 5.

Recently however, marketers have once again begun to look at innovative research techniques to gather and analyse qualitative data. Futures research described earlier in the text is a good example here. In the main, marketers are becoming more amenable to innovative techniques of qualitative market research if they afford them insights into the underpinning behavioural processes and attitudes of their customers.

Guinness is a good example of a company which has been willing to try out new techniques of qualitative research to try and find out their customers' innermost thoughts. Guinness's research company have used techniques such as role playing, psychodramas and psychodrawing in this process. Some of the findings from this research have found their way into multi-million pound advertising campaigns for the Guinness brand.

Industrial marketing research

Marketing research is traditionally associated with consumer goods. However, industrial goods marketers face similar problems to consumer goods producers, for example assessing market size and share; identifying customer needs; ascertaining the most appropriate price structure; and determining the level of competitive activity.

As we saw in Chapter 5 the principal differences between consumer and industrial (or organizational) buyer behaviour are motives for purchase and the context within which buying takes place. With this background in mind, it is useful to consider some differences in emphasis in relation to marketing problems:

1. Marketing mix emphasis, where purchasers of consumer products are more affected by appearance, packaging and advertising and often buy on impulse. Industrial goods purchasers are more concerned with quality, performance, specifications, price and delivery.
2. Different end uses of industrial products, which include finished articles like machine tools or fuel injection systems for cars, and components which need further work performing in order for them to fit into an end product (e.g. castings which will then require machining and polishing).
3. Customer requirements which can vary according to how closely they specify (e.g. some specify dimensions, materials and tolerances whereas some may simply purchase standard parts of materials).

Having sketched the background, it follows that industrial marketing research is more concerned with researching individual buyers and more use is made of depth interviews. These are costly, as more skilled interviewers must be used and respondents tend to be more widely scattered. Such disadvantages are offset against the 'richer' data that can be generated.

In industrial marketing research it is less possible to generalize, as too much depends on such factors as numbers of potential customers. For example, a total market may only contain say six large buyers who make 70 per cent of all purchases, and 50 small buyers who make up the other 30 per cent. In such a situation it would probably be sensible to census survey the six large buyers and sample the 50 smaller buyers.

This is, of course, a very general overview of industrial marketing research. For a more detailed treatment of the subject the reader is advised to consult a specialized marketing research text.

Export marketing research

As we shall see in Chapter 18 there are added complexities when marketing across international frontiers. This includes the process of marketing research. Differences in the availability and quality of secondary data are important considerations, so care should be taken to verify the accuracy of such data.

Social and marketing practices can differ widely between countries, as can political and commercial institutions and, of course, language.

In researching export markets, it is important to note that conditions may vary from country to country so that each has to be looked at individually. It is important not to assume that because a product or service is a commercial success in one country that it will automatically be so in another. This is true even of countries which, for political or historical reasons, share similar customs, lifestyles and languages.

There are many examples where, because some basic – albeit apparently small – difference has been overlooked, a great deal of money and effort on the part of the exporter has been wasted. Even within a country, regional variations may be sufficient to require a different marketing strategy. These variations add to the complexity of research in international markets, and should be considered at a very early stage in research design. As a simple example we can define potential export markets:

- Geographically
- Administratively (by divisions imposed by the company)
- By economic zones or trading blocs
- Politically.

These extra dimensions add complexity and more uncertainty to the marketing research situation.

The research brief and the research proposal

It is important to ensure before research is commissioned and undertaken that the objectives, scope, time-scale and costs of the proposed research are fully understood and agreed. This is of particular importance when the marketing research is to be undertaken by an outside market research agency. The document which accompanies this stage of the research procedure is known as the **research brief**.

The research brief should specify the nature of the problem to be investigated, the objectives of the research, research methods, analysis of results, time and budget. Most importantly, these aspects of the research must be understood and agreed between the party commissioning the research and those who will undertake it.

A good brief, must:

- Mean the same to both parties
- Not ask for irrelevant information
- Define the population to be sampled

- State the accuracy required
- State the variables to be measured and how these relate to the problem
- Specify analyses
- Clearly state the objectives of the research.

Once the research brief has been discussed and agreed, the marketing research team can then draft the *research proposal*. The main considerations here are to:

- Restate the problem to confirm understanding.
- Specify the research methods and reasons for choice.
- Specify the sample method/size/construction/frame.
- Specify the interviewing method/location/supervision.
- Specify the data processing methods.
- Specify the anticipated analyses.
- Specify the length of the survey and costs.

The various stages through which marketing survey operations pass are as follows:

1. Deciding upon the objectives of the research.
2. Choosing the methods which will be used to conduct the research.
3. Selecting and training the interviewers.
4. Deciding upon and selecting the sample.
5. Preparing the questionnaire.

We have already discussed these five stages, but there are also further responsibilities:

6. Checking, analysis and tabulation of the results
7. Interpretation and presentation of the findings of the marketing investigation.

These responsibilities are important because the conduct of marketing research and the decisions arising from them are the cornerstones upon which subsequent marketing policies are based. It is, therefore, important for an activity which can have a major influence on the future prosperity of a company to be organized and controlled effectively.

Summary

In this chapter we have explored the reasons why it is becoming increasingly important for marketing management to have up-to-date information to carry out its tasks. Marketing is becoming increasingly proactive, and *must* seek to identify changes and trends in the macro-environment and then translate these into action plans. In order to carry out this task, the concept of the marketing information system (MkIS) has been developed and this forms an integral part of the corporate management information system (MIS).

Tactical and strategic applications of an MkIS have been investigated and discussed. The practical technological tools of a modern MkIS have also been examined.

Summary – continued

Inputs to the MkIS were seen to be:

- The internal accounting system
- The marketing intelligence system
- The marketing research system.

These have been discussed in detail with particular emphasis upon the marketing research system.

The output from the MkIS is the analytical marketing system. This forms the information that inputs into marketing plans.

Key terms

Marketing Information System (MkIS): [p367]
Decision Support System (DSS): [p369]
Management Information System (MIS): [p369]
Database [p374]
Datacapture [p374]
Data warehousing [p374]

Datamining [p375]
Secondary data [p378]
Primary data [p382]
Off-the-peg research data [p382]
Consumer panels [p382]
Brand barometers [p383]
Qualitative research [p386]
Research brief [p388]

Questions

1   What is a marketing information system? What are the main sub-systems in such a system? And why do marketers increasingly need such information systems?
2   What are the main problems in designing a marketing information system, and how can these problems be minimized?
3   What is a database, and how can such databases be used by the marketer to improve the effectiveness of marketing strategies?
4   Explain each of the following in the context of marketing research:

   (a) Observation
   (b) Experimentation
   (c) Survey research
   (d) Sampling
   (e) Contact methods.

5   What is the research brief, why is it important, and what should the research brief encompass?

References

1. Kotler, P., *Marketing Management: Analyses, Planning, Implementation, and Control*, 9th edn, Prentice Hall, New Jersey, 1997, p. 110.
2. McDaniel, C. and Gates, R., *Contemporary Marketing Research*, West Publishing Co: New York 1991, pp. 132–133.
3. Dibb, S., Simkin, L., Pride, W. M. and Ferrell, O. C., *Marketing Concepts and Strategies*, 4th European edn, Houghton Mifflin, Boston/New York, 2001, p. 169.
4. Lucey, T., *Management Information Systems*, 5th edn, DP Publications: Lincolnwood, Illinois, p. 23.
5. Lancaster, G. and Massingham, L., *Essentials of Marketing*, 3rd edn, McGraw-Hill, London, 1999.
6. Lancaster, G. A., 'Marketing and engineering: can there ever be synergy?' *Journal of Marketing Management*, **9**, 1993, pp. 141–153.
7. Feldman, M. and J. March, 'Information in organisations as signal and symbol', in R. Galliers (ed.), *Information Analysis: Selected Readings*, Addison-Wesley, Wokingham, 1988.
8. O'Connor, J. and Galvin, E., *Marketing and Information Technology*, 2nd edn, Financial Times, Pitman, 1999.
9. Porter, M., *Competitive Advantage*, Free Press, New York, 1985.
10. Withey, F., Lancaster, G. A. and Ashford, R., *Marketing Fundamentals,* Butterworth-Heinemann, 2000, pp. 211–113.
11. Withey, F., *et al.* op. cit.
12. Brassington, F. and Pettitt, S., *Principles of Marketing*, 2nd edn, Pearson Education, 2000, p. 227.

Case Study

Jim Lamprey is feeling under pressure. His desk is covered with market research reports, data from the accounts department regarding sales and profits figures, sales representatives' records and reports for the last three months, and any number of secondary reports, including government publications, Chamber of Commerce reports and bank reports pertaining to his company's product markets. His problem is he simply cannot make sense of what it all means. His boss, the marketing director, has asked Jim to sort through all this information, which was previously on the marketing director's own desk, and to come up with a report that makes sense of it all. The marketing director's view is that there is plenty of information to go on and that some of it must mean something for the company. Jim is not even sure what information his marketing director wants, and why, let alone what the format and precise content should be.

Having studied at the local university for a Chartered Institute of Marketing qualification, which in fact helped get Jim this job as a marketing assistant, he is convinced that the company needs a properly designed marketing information system. He is aware, however, that the marketing director feels it is simply a question of getting lots of information and then sifting through it. Jim feels his first priority will be to explain to his director the nature and purpose of a modern marketing information system in a company and the key facets in the design and operation of such a system. He has decided to write a brief report setting out his thoughts on these matters for his marketing director.

QUESTION

Write the report.

14

Sales Forecasting

Chapter objectives

By the end of this chapter you will:

▶ Understand the role of sales forecasting in the marketing planning process.

▶ Appreciate the distinction between short-, medium- and long-term forecasting.

▶ Be aware of the use of the sales forecasts by the different functional areas in the business.

▶ Know the relationship between sales forecasts and sales budgets.

▶ Be aware of the major types of forecasting techniques available to the marketer.

Introduction

The task of business management would be simpler if industry was not in a continual state of change. This change is reflected in increasing competition, precipitated to a large extent by the growth of global competition which has increased over the last decade. Business tasks are becoming more complicated. There are trends towards to more innovation within businesses and circumstances in general are tending to change more rapidly. This makes it increasingly important and necessary for organizations to predict their future prospects in terms of sales, costs and profits.

Aid to marketing planning

Forecasting is said to be the act of giving advance warning in time for beneficial action to be taken. The value and importance of this advance information is a cornerstone of planning activity. Modern businesses are aware of sales forecasting and its overall purpose, but many managers still do not pay due regard to its importance. Only in recent years has the value of forecasting become clear. This has resulted in the development of sophisticated techniques that can be applied directly to businesses.

Davidson[1] suggests that anticipating the future with a view to dealing with it now is a fundamental task of marketing.

In order to predict the future we must examine the past to observe trends over periods of time and establish the degree of probability to which these trends are likely to repeat themselves in the future. Thus all forecasts are wrong; management must be aware of this fact and decide upon the degree of inexactitude that can be tolerated when planning for the future.

Incorrect forecasting (or no forecasting) is at the base of many of today's business failures. In pre-marketing orientated times, goods could be sold on company reputation alone and forecasting was not too important. In this more competitive era sentiment does not apply, and firms that do not attempt to make an accurate forecast on which to base their future production will find it increasingly difficult to survive.

Richard Branson's People's Lottery, which bid unsuccessfully to replace the incumbent Camelot in running the National Lottery in the UK, included detailed forecasts of estimated players for the new format proposed. These forecasts were essential in the bid process but also in planning the implementation systems required to operate the lottery such as, for example, the number of lottery machines in retail outlets.

When attempting a forecast we must essentially forecast for a specific market segment, the segment at which the marketing effort is aimed. One can forecast demand for, say, the world market for a particular commodity, in the knowledge that the company's marketing effort only covers certain segments of the domestic market. The skill lies in determining what percentage of that total potential market is likely to accrue to the company, given its known marketing effort and market segments. It is here that management planning must determine the resources that must be apportioned to individual parts of the business in order to achieve the forecasted sales.

Forecasting occurs at different levels – internationally, nationally, by industry etc. – until we ultimately reach a specific product forecast. Normally a company does not have to produce general international or national forecasts on such matters as economic growth or inflation. These are usually provided by governments and other agencies. Company forecasters simply take these forecasts and adjust their individual forecasts in the light of these macro level predictions. In some industries, forecasts for the industry are sometimes supplied in general terms by an agency such as a manufacturers' association. Such forecasts for the industry are sometimes termed market forecasts, as opposed to a sales forecast, which pertains to an individual company.

Management planners are thus only interested in a forecast when it relates to the individual firm and specific products or services, because it is from there that they can prepare their plans and budgets. It is this pragmatic level of forecasting in which we are interested; what makes the situation better is that management can now place more confidence in forecasts, because more sophisticated techniques are now available with the aid of computers. Miles[2] has shown that increasingly information for forecasting is available on a global basis from global market research companies. These can provide more timely and accurate data to assist in management planning.

Short-, medium- and long-term forecasting

We are interested in these three types of forecast because they are directly concerned with forecasting for sales and marketing management.

Short-term forecasts These are usually made for tactical reasons, and they include production planning and control, short-term cash requirements and seasonal sales fluctuations. This latter factor can be very important for production, whereas the general trend may be of less consequence. Such forecasts are for periods of less than one year, with a normal range between one and three months.

Medium-term forecasts These are made for minor strategic decisions in connection with the operation of the business. They are important in the area of business budgeting, and it is from this forecast that company budgets are built up. Incorrect forecasting can, consequently, have serious implications for the rest of the organization, for if it turns out to be over-optimistic, the organization will be left with unsold stock and will have overspent on production. Money will be owed to the bank and other creditors, and stock may have to be sold at a loss to raise money to satisfy these creditors. Many bankruptcies among smaller firms can be ascribed to insufficient attention being paid to medium-term sales forecasting. This forecast is used for such matters as the staffing levels required to achieve the expected sales, the amount of money to be spent on selling effort, and short-term capital requirements (for such items as more machines to be purchased to meet increased production). The time period for medium-term forecasts is normally one year.

Long-term forecasts These are for major strategic decisions to be taken within an organization, and they relate very much to resource implications. They deal with general rather than specific items, and rely more heavily in their computation upon such factors as government policy, social change and technological change. They are, therefore, concerned more with general trends, and, in the light of these trends, attempt to predict sales over periods greater than two years. In some strategic, heavily capitalized industries, predictions need to be for a decade or more. The danger here is that for these lengths of time the forecast cannot be more than vague, but planners in retrospect blame the forecast when things go wrong (often for reasons completely outside the possible knowledge of the original forecaster), and forecasting thus receives a bad name.

Corporate objectives

A major reason for forecasting is to provide a basis for long-range plans. Businesses must plan in order to achieve goals established on the basis of long-term forecasts, and these plans will affect various functional aspects of the business. At the base of such plans is long-term profitability, for without this the company may not be able to meet its future commitments in achieving the planned-for sales. Company planners will have to assess whether or not such potential sales can be achieved within the confines of the business as it stands and, if not, what resources will be needed in order to achieve these sales.

Medium-term forecasts are also used for business planning, but less so for strategic reasons. They are of particular importance for costing and, through the sales budget, for marketing management in controlling the marketing function while it goes about achieving the forecasted sales. With a reasonably accurate sales forecast such plans will be more realistic, and when they are put into action they should work.

Management decisions within a manufacturing concern, together with such external changes as new technology, fashion and the cost of raw materials, affect the accurate prediction of future sales. It is the accuracy of this prediction that can single out the successful firm from the unsuccessful. In the current competitive climate there is little margin for error, and efficiency of operation is a major factor for success. Consequently, prediction of a change in demand is essential for continued prosperity. If a company is able to forecast a change in demand, and also the extent of that change, then it can plan ahead to operate in the most efficient and profitable manner.

Managers are surrounded by a multitude of factors that can affect the future operation of the business. By using the best available forecasting method, they can assess their present position and provide more accurate predictions for the future. Whatever the circumstances surrounding the situation in which the manager makes a forecast, there is one clearly defined objective, which is to profit eventually from this prediction in terms of cash or knowledge.

Companies prepare for change by planning. This requires forecasts to be made, and then an assessment of how these planning goals are to be reached. In practice, the sales forecast acts as the planning base upon which all internal forecasting and budgeting takes place. The effect of considering expected levels of sales in making such decisions is to reduce uncertainty and lower costs. Forecasting is thus central to the planning process and should not be used as a substitute for effective decision making, or management will tend to react to short-term fluctuations as they affect sales instead of developing long-term strategies. The company should first work out its selling plan, because this is really what is going to determine the level of sales. For example, a price reduction can be expected to influence a company's share of the total market, and such considerations should be noted by the sales forecaster. Consequently, the forecaster predicts what will happen for a set of decisions in a given set of circumstances, whereas planning states that by taking certain actions, the decision maker can alter the subsequent events relating to a particular situation. Thus, if a forecast is made which predicts a fall in demand, management can prepare a plan to prevent sales from falling. The future is not unchangeable; if it was, there would be no real point in either forecasting or planning.

The objective of the sales forecast is to predict a company's sales for some period in advance, and this can be done in one of two ways.

1. It can predict the company's sales directly (called a sales forecast).
2. It can forecast the total market and then determine the company's market share (called a market forecast).

For most companies, the latter course is the most logical, because a company's future strategy will affect its market share. Consideration must also be given to what competitors are doing, and in many cases sales action by one manufacturer will merely cancel out similar action by another.

It has been said that forecasting is often a fruitless adventure, but the difficulty of forecasting should not be used as an excuse for inactivity. Davidson[3] feels that it is realistic to anticipate the future. Forecasting is not a 'crystal ball' that enables the manager to foresee the future more clearly. It is an aid to more informed and better decision making.

Functional objectives

Forecasts are needed for a variety of purposes, including production planning; ordering raw materials; ensuring a steady supply of trained operatives; controlling stocks or inventories; estimating short-term cash requirements; and a variety of other reasons. All of these applications have different 'time horizons'. That is, the forecast is needed at different times before the event if it is to be of any practical value. The sales forecast is thus not merely used for planning marketing; it has company-wide applications.

Marketing personnel prepare, or *should* prepare, the sales forecast. The emphasis is deliberate, because in many companies sales forecasting is left to the finance department, as they have an immediate need for the forecast for business budgeting purposes. When forecasts are left to finance departments in this manner it is an abrogation by marketing of its responsibilities. Marketing, above all other business functions, should be in the best position to ascertain potential sales – including downturns and upturns – of which accountants will be less aware, since they are further removed from customers than the marketing department. Forecasting is a risky business, which is all the more reason why Marketing should not abrogate its responsibilities.

We now consider the business functions that are most directly concerned with sales forecasts.

Production needs forecasts for each product line in order that manufacturing can be planned and scheduled on an orderly basis. Thus machines and manpower can be more effectively utilized. When 'Transport' is organized by 'Production', it is helpful to have advance warning of bulky or awkward items that have to be packed and moved, particularly when overseas considerations are involved. In the longer term, Production needs to make decisions on levels of plant operation in order to be able to meet production levels to achieve the planned-for sales. Production's main need will thus be for accurate short-term forecasts for production planning and control.

Personnel needs forecasts in order to be able to ascertain staffing levels in the future. It will then be able to recruit personnel to achieve the forecasted sales. There will be training implications for employees taken on to achieve an increase in sales, so the concern of personnel will be mainly in respect of the medium-term forecast, but the long-term forecast will be needed for formulating management succession plans.

With accurate forecasting, *Purchasing* requirements can be met on a more timely basis, and since the forecast will give the purchasing officer more time in which to purchase (rather than having to wait until the requisition is received from production) he or she may be in a position to purchase on a more favourable basis because of the increased lead time. The purchasing department can also operate more effective stock control for raw materials and part manufactured goods and work out optimum stock levels. The danger of overstocking, with the risk of deterioration and obsolescence, will be less, and because less stock will need to be carried, this will result in a saving on working capital. Better forecasting will also avoid the possibility of stock-outs resulting in disruption to the production programme. In general, the purchasing function will be more interested in short-term forecasts, although the medium-term forecast will be of value. Clearly the techniques of JIT management discussed in Chapter 11, have altered the nature of the forecasting process here.

Finance needs forecasts in the medium term to establish budgets based on the planned-for sales. Here accuracy is important, because if the forecast is incorrect, then all the company budgets will be incorrect, with consequent overspending in the case of an optimistic forecast. Cash requirements to fund working capital need to be budgeted, and an incorrect forecast could mean that the company has to make a request to the bank for increased borrowing. Many bankruptcies are a result of a shortage of working capital, and better forecasting could, in many instances, have avoided such an event. In the long term, Finance needs to engage in long-range profit planning and must predict income flow. It must make provision for long-term capital needs in terms of plant, machinery etc., and here the long-term forecast is of importance if the organization is to be ready to produce appropriate products in the correct quantities.

It has been demonstrated that *Marketing* should make the forecasts, and it needs these forecasts in order to plan promotional campaigns and plan sales strategies to complement these campaigns. It needs the forecast in order that the correct types of sales and marketing personnel can be recruited and trained to achieve the planned-for sales. Remuneration plans will also need to be formulated, particularly when these are linked to sales targets or sales quotas, and these targets or quotas will be a reflection of the sales forecast broken down among individual sales personnel. When 'off-the-shelf' delivery is offered to customers, the sales forecast will help to determine maximum/minimum stock levels, and here an incorrect forecast will result in either stock-outs (and possible loss of custom) or overstocking (with a resultant drain on working capital). In the longer term, goals can be set in the marketing channels. Channel arrangements tend to be of a more stable, long-term nature, and if potential sales are predicted to be much higher in the long-term, then a new channel arrangement may be called for. Thus, Marketing is in need of short-, medium- and long-term forecasts.

Technological forecasts as discussed in Chapter 7, are required by *Research and Development*. The design, features and technology of products will affect their sales, and from time to time such products will need to be updated or changed. It might be that a particular product line is becoming obsolete, and in such a case Research and Development will need to plan and develop a new product or make modifications to the existing product in conjunction with marketing research. Only by doing this will an organization be able to keep ahead of, or apace with, its competitors and continue to produce a product that is satisfactory for the marketplace. Marketing, through the medium of marketing research, will liaise with Research and Development and from medium- and long-term forecasts will coordinate new product developments and ultimately product launches.

With an accurate forecast, departments can plan more effectively with the reassurance that these plans can be carried through and actioned, and they will not have to be modified in the light of an inaccurate forecast.

There is thus an interrelationship and interdependency between the plans and operations of each of the above functions, because they are all based on the sales forecast. If the original sales forecast proves to be incorrect, then it will affect each and every function within the business, because each department uses the sales forecast as its starting point. The importance of an accurate and timely sales forecast cannot be overemphasized. What we must do is reduce the extent of their wrongness, or at least provide guidelines as to the extent to which they are likely to be incorrect.

Sales budgets and their uses

Budgets, which are also discussed in Chapter 15, stem from the sales forecast, and the sales budget is the vehicle through which sales are generated. Thus the sales budget comes after the sales forecast, and this is a representation of each salesperson's sales broken down by product type, by customer type and by individual territory. The sales department budget then follows, together with other departmental budgets; although we use the term 'sales department budget', its true description reflects more than purely selling. It includes forthcoming investment in promotion, such as different forms of advertising, displays, exhibitions, consumer and trade promotions etc.; investment in distribution, which includes intermediaries and facilities such as warehousing and physical distribution of finished goods to customers; marketing research expenditure; and selling expenditure and all the various costs that go into winning orders. For definition purposes, cost accountants subdivide the sales department budget into the selling expense budget, the advertising budget and the sales department administrative budget. The reader will, of course, realize that the above terms reflect production orientation, and better descriptions should be found for each of the subdivisions which reflect a more modern marketing orientation. However, accountants use the above terms, and it would be a difficult task to alter these universally accepted descriptions now that they are so firmly established.

A budget differs from a forecast in that it is a representation of what is planned to happen, whereas a forecast is concerned with what is expected to happen. The forecast is far more uncertain, because it is affected by extraneous factors, whereas the budget is to do with internal matters, and these can be controlled directly by the organization. The relationship is explained diagrammatically in Figure 14.1.

It has been explained that the budget is derived from the sales forecast, and business budgeting cannot commence until the forecast has been agreed. Budgeting requires detailed planning of all duties to be undertaken during the budget period (normally one year ahead). The total sales budget is divided among the individual product lines to be sold in terms of apportionment of expenditure on advertising, packaging, personal selling etc. The way the total sales budget is apportioned is, of course, a decision for marketing management.

It is important to ensure that the sales budget co-ordinates with other budgets in the organization. For instance, the sales budget should not plan to achieve more sales than production is budgeted to manufacture. Budgets must also be flexible to allow for changing conditions or unforeseen circumstances, and some companies prepare more than one budget as a contingency measure. Thus flexibility is important, and if, during the budget period, it seems as though another set of circumstances is likely to prevail, then the budget should be altered to cover such a contingency.

When actual expenditure differs from the budgeted expenditure, the departmental manager must explain the deviation. Cost accountants refer to each item of cost as a budget or cost centre, and they describe these differences as 'variances'. The term used to describe this process of control is 'management by exception', and the philosophy implies that only when events do not go as planned does an investigation need to be made. Budgeting is not merely a matter of planning; it is also used as a method of control. Furthermore, realistic evaluation cannot take place unless detailed plans have been agreed before the budget period.

In short, budgets provide a financial statement of the company's plans and policies, and reflect the co-ordinated efforts of all departments (or cost centres) within the organization. The sales department budget is thus the marketing function's share of the company budget and this, in turn, is broken down into constituent parts covering promotion, selling, administration etc. and allocated between each product within the range of products.

Figure 14.1
The sales budgetary procedure.

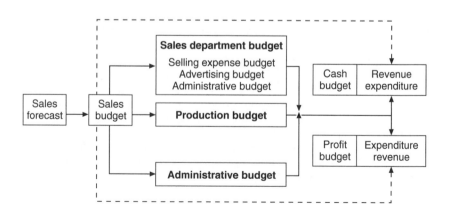

Need for profit planning and its derivation

Profits need to be planned on the premise that in a well run organization they should grow. Actions within the company that can bring about such profit growth include better working practices (or the provision of incentive schemes to bring about increased productivity); computerization, with resultant efficiency in the performance of clerical tasks; automation in the workplace; better stock control of raw materials, components and finished goods with resultant savings in working capital; standardization and variety reduction exercises to bring about a reduction in inventories, less obsolescence and better quality control; and many further cost saving exercises.

Sales forecasting must precede such exercises, and it is again emphasized that such forecasts should be as accurate as possible, for such efforts as those just described are time-consuming and costly in their implementation. To be meaningful, they should take place in the light of probable production, which is based on the forecast.

Companies need to plan in order to make provision for fixed and working capital expenditure. Such fixed capital expenditure plans are necessary because old assets deteriorate, new additional plant and buildings may be needed to accommodate increased production, and new production methods may become available, rendering the old plant and machinery obsolete. Similarly, working capital needs to be planned, and this means forecasting stock investment because sales can fluctuate on a cyclical basis or for economic or other reasons. As a result, raw materials, components and finished stock levels will fluctuate in accordance with demand. Working capital, in terms of liquid cash assets, must be planned to accommodate the value of stocks to be held plus the costs of holding such stock.

The sales forecast precedes all planning, and the need for fixed and working capital expenditure forecasts has just been outlined. Once this has been done, it is necessary to translate all of these statements showing how they will affect the finances of the business. This is called the **cash forecast**, which encapsulates the sales forecast and resulting business plans in terms of money. Preparation of the cash forecast is a specialized cost accounting activity, but it starts with the basic premise that profits should increase the amount of cash in the business. Therefore, a net profit figure is forecast, and from this is taken away corporation tax, increases in stock and work in progress, loans and overdrafts repaid, dividends and interest, increases in debtors, decreases in creditors, and expenditure on capital equipment. To the end figure must be added sales of assets, receipts from share or loan issues, decreases in stock and work-in-progress, depreciation, increases in creditors and decreases in debtors. The amount left at the end is profit, and how it is distributed is a decision for the board of directors. The fact is that a plan is needed in order that business management can organize its activities in a responsible manner, and such planning, of necessity, stems from the sales forecast.

Forecasting techniques available

There are two basic techniques available:

- *Objective*
  These methods are of a mathematical or statistical nature.
- *Subjective*
  These methods are based on experience and judgement and are based more upon intuition than analysis.

The wide acceptance of objective techniques in recent years is primarily because objective methods have developed a record for accuracy and thus have inspired confidence in the managers who use them as an aid to decision making. As already discussed in Chapter 13, the development and adoption of computer systems by many companies has created a facility that can compute forecasts and also store historical data that can be retrieved rapidly and efficiently as required. Subjective methods are still highly intuitive and there can be no question that the 'art' of objective forecasting is more advanced. Marketers, though, are increasingly recognizing that the pace of change in the marketing environment and the increased uncertainty which this gives rise to is making the use of more intuitive techniques more appropriate.

Forecasting has already been introduced in Chapter 7 in the context of new product development and technological forecasting when the techniques of scenario writing, relevance trees and Delphi were discussed. For a more detailed discussion of forecasting, Lancaster and Massingham[4] provide a practical overview and Lancaster and Lomas[5] provide a detailed guide to individual forecasting techniques. Kotler[6] provides an excellent overview of the major concepts in demand measurement and forecasting including a taxonomy of the different types of market demand.

The following discussion relates to specific practical and managerial problems that can be encountered when using such techniques.

Objective methods

 Moving averages   This method of time series analysis involves the compilation of the arithmetic average of a number of previous consecutive points in a time series. It is best employed in a situation where an extrapolation of a trend that is gradually increasing or decreasing is present. It has a low cost with ease of manual computation. Problems occur in the choice of the number of points to average, and the effects of a non-typical item in the time series. Seasonality and cyclical trends can be catered for by the application of relevant indices – provided they are known.

The major disadvantage of this technique is that it is purely quantitative in its approach and thus extremely introspective. It does not take into consideration any salient factors in the environment that may affect future sales.

 Exponential smoothing   Using a moving average has the problem that it gives equal weight, or significance, to all the items in a time series. More recent points in a time series will represent the present situation more accurately than older items, and it is therefore only logical to attach more significance to more recent items by using a weighting method. The different weight attached to an item in a time series can be calculated either simply by using an arithmetic progression or, more sophisticatedly, by using a geometric progression. When a geometric progression is used and a graph drawn, the raw sales data are smoothed into an exponential curve; hence the name 'exponential smoothing'. In the case where an arithmetic progression is used, this is simply known as a weighted moving average.

Exponential smoothing provides a forecast which is equal to the old one, plus or minus some proportion of the past forecasting error(s). There are many variations of exponential smoothing, ranging from the very simplistic to the more complex methods involving a greater number of data points and proportions of forecast errors. Once again, these techniques, because of their highly statistical nature, lend themselves particularly to purely quantitative data, thus neglecting many other important market factors.

A more realistic prediction is gained through the use of this technique because it allows for new factors and influences that have emerged in the most recent sales period.

Trend projections   By fitting a trend line to a mathematical equation it is possible to make forecasts about future sales using the equation. Figure 14.2 shows four typical growth curves a firm may experience.

The danger of using the trend approach alone is that, when the analyst extrapolates, the assumption is that what affected sales in the past will continue to affect sales (and in the same way) over future periods. An adequate number of past measurements or observations are also required for adequate statistical significance, but care must be taken not to include too many past observations or history will be too heavily weighted. Trend projections, like moving averages and exponential smoothing, are not ideal for short- or medium-term forecasts. They are more fitting for predicting a 'broad sweep' trend over the long term.

The Box–Jenkins forecasting method is a special case of exponential smoothing in which the time series is fitted with an optimizing mathematical model that attributes minimal error to historical data. Once the model has been identified and constructed, the parameters must then be estimated.

Of the available statistical routines, this is one of the most accurate and flexible in that it can cope with almost any type of data pattern. However, accuracy involves complexity, which, along with flexibility, results in a relatively high cost and the need for a skilful operator with plenty of time to reap the full benefits of this technique. As

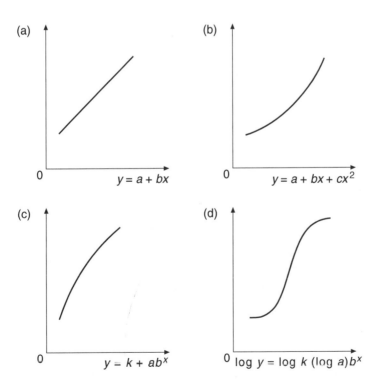

Figure 14.2
Company growth curves.

(a) $y = a + bx$

(b) $y = a + bx + cx^2$

(c) $y = k + ab^x$

(d) $\log y = \log k \, (\log a)b^x$

this method's accuracy is limited to the short term, it is not very often used in practice, as there are many other cheaper and easier techniques which can be employed that, although they do not give as much accuracy, are often adequate for short-term decisions.

 Spectral analysis   Incorporated in the classification of spectral analysis is the technique of Fourier analysis, where a time series is mathematically decomposed into its constituent sine wave forms. Thus, from the one time series a spectrum of time series is produced having the name 'power spectrum'. The mathematical complexities of this method put it beyond the use of all but the most competent analyst, whose skill and understanding of the technique are imperative for its successful implementation.

 X-11 technique   X-11 is similar to spectral analysis in that it decomposes the original time series into a spectrum of time series. However, it only separates out the seasonal and cyclical trends, and then fits a time series to the remainder. It takes the best of spectral analysis and Box–Jenkins and combines them in one technique. Used by a skilled analyst, it rates as one of the most effective short- to medium-term forecasting methods, with its ability to identify turning points being a major asset.

Causal methods   Though still objective techniques these methods all involve some degree of subjectivity.

 One of the best known causal methods is that of **regression analysis**, which attempts to assess the relationship between at least two variables – one (or more) independent and one dependent – the purpose being to predict the value of the dependent variable from the specific value of the independent variable. The basis of this prediction generally is historical data.

This method starts from the assumption that a basic relationship exists between two variables, and the least squares method of estimation is used to formulate the mathematical relationship which exists.

Various forms of regression analysis are in existence, one being multiple regression analysis, where any number of variables are considered at one time. Another form is stepwise regression analysis, where only one independent variable is considered at one time.

The value of this technique is difficult to assess other than in individual cases, as the accuracy is dependent upon the degree to which the independent variables explain characteristics of the dependent variable. This relationship may vary considerably, but as computing becomes easier and cheaper the value of regression analysis is increased dramatically on a cost/benefit basis.

Through techniques such as regression analysis, The Newspaper Society have established clear links between their different life stage categories outlined earlier in Chapter 6 with levels of demand for a range of products. Mothercare shoppers, for example, are almost four times more likely to have pre-school aged children than the national average.

 Econometric models are an extension of the regression technique whereby a system of independent regression equations is evolved. These equations describe a particular sector of economic activity whose parameters are usually estimated simultaneously. Generally, these models are relatively expensive to develop, the precise cost being dependent on the amount of detail incorporated in the model. However, the inherent systems of equations in such models express far better the causalities involved than an ordinary regression equation, and thus will predict turning points more accurately.

Input–output models are particularly applicable in the field of industrial marketing, since they are concerned with the inter-industry or interdepartmental flow of goods or services in the economy of a company and its markets. The technique is based on the theory that the output of one industry comprises the basic inputs of products and materials of another, thereby providing an inter-industry/interdepartmental flow of goods and services within the economy/industry. The major efforts required by this type of model are not in the operation of the model, but in the collection and presentation of data. This is because tables and government statistics showing the extent to which one industry obtains its basic inputs from another are very broadly defined in standard industrial classifications.

The cost of these models in producing a sales forecast, especially when they are combined with econometric models to produce economic input–output models, is often prohibitive for the smaller company. Large organizations can often justify the expense of such a model for medium-term (and particularly long-term) sales forecasts.

Diffusion indexes use the many economic indicators available that represent general economic activity, or the activity within a particular industry or product class. By formulating an index, based on a certain combination of these indices, an indication of future trends can be compiled. The accuracy and applicability of the index can be tailored to fit specific requirements – such as predicting turning points in the short term – by the choice of appropriate economic indicators. A forecasting technique of this nature can be accurate and cheap to apply in certain industries and product classes.

Tied indicators are used where the sales of one product are closely related to sales of another product and the sales trend of one product precedes that of the other. The preceding product is the indicator, and in the case of leading indicator models, the sales of more than one product may be utilized along with indicators of general economic activity. The leading indicators generally increase or decrease prior to the pending increase or decrease in the dependent variable and they usually take the form of a time series of economic activity. As a forecasting method the only real value of this type of model is in its ability to predict turning points rather than as a predictor of future trends in general.

Life cycle analysis is particularly applicable where there is no historical data. Sales of similar products are analysed over time and usually a particular 'S' curve (see Figure 14.2d) is found to apply for a certain product class. The phases of product acceptance by the various groups – such as innovators, early adopters, early majority, late majority and laggards – are essential to the analysis. Consideration of the concepts of life cycle analysis by individuals is often more valuable than a thorough detailed expert analysis, as the database for this type of model is conceptually weak. A manager can readily appreciate that the product has to pass through the various stages in its life cycle and subjective opinion is thus likely to be as accurate as any expert analysis.

Subjective methods

Market research   This is usually done by studying a representative sample of a market which involves the systematic formal procedure for evolving and testing hypotheses about a market. For any valid information to be obtained, two reports must be made over a period of time so that one can be compared with the other and conclusions drawn. This necessitates the collection of a relatively large amount of market data from questionnaires, surveys, published statistics, marketing intelligence reports and time series analyses of market variables. Due to the relatively high cost of this technique, it is only used in cases where there is a considerable financial risk, which generally means in large companies. The major application of this technique for sales forecasting is in the area of predicting new product sales by investigating consumer reaction to a new product.

The Delphi method   This technique involves the marshalling of expert opinion to cope with the problems of eradicating the 'bandwagon effect' of majority opinion. Its workings and implications were discussed in Chapter 7.

Panel consensus   This technique is not unlike the Delphi method, except that the panel of experts are encouraged to communicate and discuss matters in relation to the future prospects of what is to be predicted. Developed primarily for long-term forecasting, this method is rarely used due to the problems of personal and social bias influencing the members of the panel. Methods of this nature often do not arrive at a true consensus of opinion because of the effects of such bias.

Experts are not infallible. Recent predictions regarding the growth in access to the Internet in the UK have proved to be much too conservative. Growth rates in the diffusion of this technology into UK households have been much higher than the experts predicted, even as little as twelve months ago.

Visionary forecast   'Visionary' forecasters or 'futurologists' attempt to prophesy through personal opinion and judgements. The method is characterized by subjective guesswork and imagination, and in general the methods used can be described as non-scientific. A set of possible scenarios about the future is prepared by a few experts in the light of past events. At one time, visionary forecasts were felt to be too subjective to be used in marketing decision making. However, as mentioned earlier, the pace of chance and the dynamic nature of the marketing environment has begun to make companies appreciate some of the advantages of visionary forecasts even though they may sometimes be wrong.

Many believe that at least in part the success of Microsoft to date in being ahead of its competitors in many areas is down to visionary forecasts. The company has a system whereby senior managers are encouraged to think about the future in the widest possible sense, including, for example, social trends and developments, and how these developments, might potentially open up new opportunities for Microsoft for future product development.

Historical analogy This is a comparative analysis of the introduction and growth of similar new products that bases the forecast on similarity patterns. By comparing a new product with a similar previous new product, forecasts of future sales performance can be made. This technique, however, is conceptually weak, as a true new product will not be similar to any previous product, and even a new version of a product will probably not be similar enough to make any comparison really valid.

Sales force opinion Members of a sales force are in constant contact with customers, and are in a position to predict their buying plans, attitudes and needs. An obstacle to gaining true estimates is that salespeople often tend to be pessimistic, owing to their compensation system. It is common practice for salespeople to be remunerated according to the degree to which they attain sales quotas which, in turn, are based on sales forecasts. Thus it is in their own interest to underestimate future sales, resulting in low quotas and possibilities of high compensation. In fact though, Jobber and Lancaster[7] has provided some evidence that being involved in the sales forecasting and hence quota setting process can actually increase salesforce motivation therefore making the achievement of agreed sales quotas more likely.

However, this method does have the advantage of being relatively cheap and easy to introduce and administer through the existing sales organization.

Appropriateness of technique chosen

There can be no general conclusion drawn as to which is the best forecasting technique to employ, but it is certainly true that a forecast should consider both objective and subjective aspects. The analyst can only consider what is required, and the resources available, and try to match them against a method that will provide the best result.

The techniques just considered cover a range of objective and subjective, quantitative and qualitative techniques that require various resources and data for their employment. It is the situation, within various constraints, that should determine the method to be used for forecasting, not external constraints of cost, simplicity and personal preferences.

Measures of value or volume?

In theory, a manager should use sales forecasting where the benefit is greater than the effort needed to generate a forecast. Most managers are aware of this and it is the problem of measuring the effectiveness of a forecast that is the major obstacle: a manager can accurately cost the use of a forecasting technique in terms of current time and money, but not the benefits that could possibly be enjoyed in the future.

One of the first problems the analyst has to face when preparing a sales forecast for a product or product group is: What units should measurement of future sales be in? Even if a total market prediction is undertaken, the forecaster still has to determine what units to use for the forecast. In most commercial situations this results in a choice between value and volume, dependent upon whichever is the most consistent over time and likely to provide the most accurate measure of future sales, assuming data are available in both forms.

Volume measures are likely to be confusing where the product mix is not homogeneous, e.g. two products may have similar physical characteristics that classify each of them as one single unit, but they may have widely differing sales values. A volume measure may state a market of so many units, but the value of this market could vary to a large extent as the value of the constituent units is not precisely known. However, volume forecasts have the advantage of not being affected by inflation or deflation, because once a physical unit is defined it is not affected by external factors.

On the other hand, value predictions can be adjusted for variations in the buying power of a currency, but the application of many of the available inflation/deflation indices is not representative of the same fluctuation experienced by the product. Indices are invariably computed on the basis of price changes and therefore reflect only one aspect of inflation/deflation, and neglect to compare the product with other products. The consumer can be regarded as having a disposable income for which many companies compete by means of their products, and a consumer's choice of product is a function of that consumer's perception of the worth of that product in relation to other products. A price increase index does not reflect the inflation/deflation experienced by a product in relation to other products.

Importance of accurate forecasts

Should actual sales fall short of, or exceed, forecasted sales, management must investigate the reasons for the difference, and from their inquiries determine whether or not it is necessary to adjust the sales forecasting technique. Thus sales forecasting is a continuous process. The changing nature of the economic and physical environment means that forecasts should be under continuous scrutiny and revision. Every projection can be improved, and in competitive situations even fractional increases in accuracy can be translated into higher profits.

It has already been said that all sales forecasts are wrong: they only differ in the extent of their wrongness. Perfection is unattainable, and the organization must decide what level of accuracy is required within predetermined time and cost constraints. Management must fix the level of inaccuracy that can be tolerated, and this will allow it to compare cost with value when selecting the appropriate technique.

An illustration of how this notion of comparing the costs of different techniques of forecasting can be traded off against their degree of accuracy in order to arrive at the best-value techniques is illustrated in Figure 14.3.

Figure 14.3
The cost-sophistication trade-off.

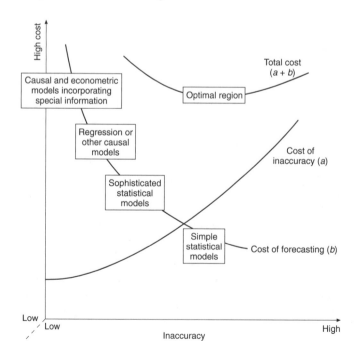

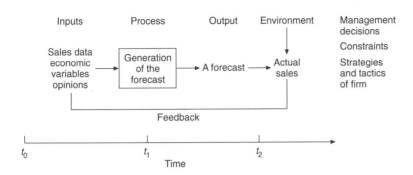

Figure 14.4
The sales forecasting system.

The sales forecasting system

Sales forecasting involves the determination of the expected levels of sales in the future, based on past and present sales data, the intentions of management and environmental influences upon the enterprise. The forecasting of sales can be regarded as a system having inputs, a process and an output. This may be a simplistic viewpoint, but it serves as a useful tool for the analysis of the true worth of sales forecasting as an aid to management, and is illustrated in Figure 14.4.

The time factor

It could be said that the main concern of forecasting is the elimination of the phenomenon of time, in that it attempts to negate the effects of time by the logical and probabilistic determination of future events. To appreciate this, you only have to consider the effect time has on the validity of inputs to a forecasting technique. In Figure 14.4, at time t_0 all the inputs may be correct, but by time t_1, when they are collated, some may well have varied to reflect changing situations, yet this is not shown in the inputs to the forecasting process. Certainly by time t_2 (the lead time) the inputs could be totally inaccurate due to changes in the market and this is without considering the changes that may occur in the projection time of a forecast.

Although the analyst may strive to reduce the lead time for a forecast to a minimum in order to ensure that the output is based on the most recently available data, any forthcoming changes in the inputs will ultimately occur in the projection time. As forecasting should be a continuous process, analysts should constantly be updating the inputs to reflect any changes and produce revised forecasts. It is thus the job of the analyst to reduce lead time to an optimum point where a forecast is based on the latest data without sacrificing accuracy, or involving disproportionate costs for the value of the prediction obtained. On the whole, quantitative methods lend themselves to economical revision far more readily than qualitative techniques, owing to the nature of the data involved and the cost of generating and processing them.

A common fallacy is that forecasting is an activity that takes place at periodic intervals, such as once a year, and ceases entirely between these intervals. In fact, in order to reflect changes in the environment and internal structure of the firm, forecasts should be continually evaluated and revised to maintain their credibility. Such factors as price alterations by competitors, government legislation, technological breakthroughs, changes in the firm's own advertising strategy and alterations of any one of the factors in the marketing mix which had not been previously foreseen can substantially alter sales.

Sometimes, a forecast can be rendered totally wrong by completely unforeseen events which would have been impossible to forecast using any method.

In an earlier example we referred to the fuel crisis in the UK during the early weeks of September 2000. Panic buying caused sales of some products to increase by up to 75 per cent over a three-day period. None of the companies affected by this could have forecast such a dramatic interest in short-term sales.

The importance of the feedback loop cannot be overemphasized. For the ongoing forecasting process, the feedback loop constitutes a major input to the forecasting process, as can be seen by considering the value attached to error analysis in many quantitative methods. In the case of qualitative techniques, significant weight is attached to any variance between what was forecast and what actually occurred, and the related reasons. Future forecasts often then attach considerable significance to the reasons for past performance and try to incorporate these in any new forecast. The feedback loop is thus the control on the process.

Summary

Forecasting is of utmost importance to business, as it is the precursor to all planning activities and lies at the base of strategic planning. This strategic plan determines how the company will go about achieving its share of the total forecasted sales. Thus sales forecasting and strategic planning go together.

Sales forecasting does, however, have three principal dimensions: short-term (about three months), medium-term (normally one year) and long-term (usually two years minimum and a lot longer in some industries). Each of these dimensions is for specific tactical or strategic purposes.

Once the sales forecast and the strategic plan have been agreed, business budgeting can take place and the sales budget is the medium through which sales are generated.

Forecasting thus lies at the base of all company planning. It is of paramount importance that this forecast is the best than can be produced within the resource constraints of the company, for if the sales forecast is incorrect in the first place, then the whole planning exercise will have been in vain.

Key terms

Moving averages [p400]
Exponential smoothing [p400]
Trend projection [p401]
Spectral analysis [p402]
X-11 technique [p402]
Regression analysis [p402]
Econometric models [p403]

Input–output models [p403]
Diffusion index [p403]
Tide indicators [p403]
Panel consensus [p404]
Visionary forecasts [p404]
Historical analogy [p405]

Questions

1 Why is it important to attempt to forecast the future with regard to sales, and how are these forecasts related to corporate and functional objectives?
2 Outline the major objective techniques of forecasting.
3 Outline the major subjective techniques of forecasting.
4 What is meant by the notion of a trade-off between accuracy and costs in the selection of forecasting techniques, and how can this trade-off be made so as to ensure the best value for money?
5 What are the major elements and requirements of the sales forecasting system?

References

1. Davidson, H., *Even More Offensive Marketing*, Penguin, London, 1997, p. 223.
2. Miles, L., 'Single market research', *Marketing Business,* July/August, 1994, pp. 40–44.
3. Davidson, H., op. cit. p. 228.
4. Lancaster, G. A. and Massingham, L. C., *Essentials of Marketing*, 3rd edn, McGraw-Hill, London, 1999, pp. 154–170.
5. Lancaster, G. A. and Lomas, R. A., *Forecasting for Sales and Materials Management*, Macmillan, Basingstoke, 1985.
6. Kotler, P., *Marketing Management: Analysis, Planning, Implementation and Control*, 9th edn, Prentice Hall, New Jersey, 1997, pp. 130–145.
7. Jobber, D. and Lancaster, G., *Selling and Sales Management*, 3rd edn, Prentice Hall, Harlow, 2000, p. 383.

Case Study

Rita Wray cannot believe what she has just heard. Having joined Scalar Products as a market analyst and planner she has just been informed that the company has no sales forecasting system. She cannot understand how the company has managed to operate effectively without one. Her boss, however, a very competent technical engineer who has over the years moved through sales and into marketing in the company, believes that all forecasts are simply a waste of time. His view is that what is going to happen will happen and no amount of forecasting will affect this. Moreover, he has pointed out that in his experience forecasts are usually wrong and so it is better to do without them. Although Rita has already pleaded her case regarding the need for and uses of sales forecasts, her boss is adamant that she should spend her time on other 'more useful activities'. Rita, however, feels that she cannot effectively do her job with regard to helping prepare marketing plans without an effective system of sales forecasting.

QUESTION

How can Rita persuade her boss that sales forecasts are not only useful but essential in the marketing planning process, and what types of forecasts and forecasting techniques might be useful in any newly established system of forecasting?

15

Implementing strategic marketing: organization and resources

Chapter objectives

By the end of this chapter you will:

▶ Understand the importance of, and the steps in, implementing strategic marketing plans.

▶ Be aware of the relevance of managing human and financial resources in the implementation process.

▶ Appreciate the need for skills on the part of marketing manager in communicating, motivating, and leading marketing and other staff.

▶ Understand the meaning and importance of internal marketing in the implementation process.

▶ Understand the approaches to determining overall marketing budgets and the allocation of the budget to individual elements of the marketing mix.

▶ Be familiar with the alternative ways of organizing the marketing function and appreciate the increasing importance of newer forms of marketing organization structures, and in particular the growth of Strategic Alliances.

Introduction

Up to now in this text we have looked at some of the key steps in, and components of, strategic marketing planning, together with some of the major tools of analysis. However, even the most detailed and carefully evaluated analysis is wasted unless and until it results in the development of action plans which are then **implemented**. Johnson and Scholes[1] highlight this importance of implementation:

> Strategic analysis and choice are of little value to an organization unless the strategies are capable of being implemented.

This implementation stage requires that the following be planned and managed effectively.

First of all, the *human resources* required to implement strategic marketing plans need to be planned and managed. All plans are dependent upon human resources for their implementation, and marketing plans are no exception. Not only must there be sufficient human resources, a quantitative aspect if you like, but also these human resources need to be sufficiently skilled and trained to complete their organizational tasks. Moreover, even if the human resources are potentially adequate in both numbers and requisite skills, these skills need to be pointed in the right direction. This in turn means that both effective communication and leadership skills are important in implementing strategic marketing. Similarly, even if marketing and sales personnel possess the requisite skills and training necessary to devise and implement strategic marketing plans, they must be willing to exercise these skills. In other words, motivation of human resources is crucial. Thirdly, in the area of human resource management implementation of strategic marketing in order to achieve customer satisfaction requires that the efforts of individuals, both within the marketing function and between marketing and other company personnel, be co-ordinated, particularly when it comes to the second of these (i.e. co-ordination between marketing and other functional areas of the business), for there can often be problems of conflict. Effective conflict resolution is, therefore, a crucial aspect of effective implementation.

In recent years an increasing recognition of this need to involve everyone, and not just marketing personnel, in the achievement of customer satisfaction, has given rise to the notion of 'internal marketing within organizations'.

A second key area of implementation also relates to resources, but this time *financial resources*. Plans cannot be implemented (nor, as we shall see in the next chapter, controlled) without ensuring that there are adequate financial resources. If strategic marketing plans cannot be financed, then the plans themselves are unrealistic and will need to be changed. For this reason the preparation and role of *marketing budgets* is a crucial part of implementing strategic marketing.

Finally, the effective implementation of strategic marketing requires appropriate organizational structures. In fact, the organizational structure for marketing directly affects some of the human resource management issues already mentioned. Such as co-ordination and communication, both within marketing and between marketing and other functions. However, it also affects such strategic issues as ability to respond to market change and the extent to which an organization is customer oriented.

Certainly there are other issues in implementing strategic marketing, but the three outlined here, namely, managing human resources, planning and allocating financial resources in the form of marketing budgets, and structuring the marketing organization, are amongst the key issues and hence form the subject of this chapter.

Implementation and human resources

Even with the advent of sophisticated computing power, improved concepts and tools of analysis, and elaborate systems of decision making and control, the effective implementation of strategic marketing plans is still reliant on that most important, if difficult to manage, of a company's resources, namely its human resources. Because of this it is important that those individuals charged with the responsibility of achieving effective strategic marketing ensure that their human resources are effectively managed. Some of the more important elements of managing human resources in the implementation of strategic marketing plans are outlined below.

Analysis and comparison of existing human resources compared to those required to implement strategic marketing plans

One of the most important steps in managing the human resource aspect of strategic marketing planning is to analyse and assess the current human resources of the organization against those required to implement proposed marketing strategies. This analysis and comparison has both quantitative – for example, do we have sufficient numbers of salespeople to implement the plan? – and qualitative – for example, are they adequately trained and skilled? – aspects. Perhaps, needless to say, the quantitative aspect is somewhat easier to assess than the qualitative aspect, though in practice neither assessment is easy. In making both assessments the marketing planner needs to think through the human resource implications of the marketing strategies. Specifically, the assessment will need to be based on a careful analysis of marketing strategies in terms of 'what needs to be done', 'by whom', 'where' and 'when'. This analysis can then be translated into specific human resource requirements, both quantitative and qualitative, and a comparison made of existing versus required resources. Where an imbalance exists, then either the plan must be modified and/or the human resource element 'altered'. Where the imbalance errs on the side of insufficient human resources (either qualitative or quantitative) and the decision is to alter the human resource rather than the plans themselves, then effective human resource management is likely to involve one or more of the following elements:

- Recruitment and selection
- Training and development
- Redeployment and redundancies.

Clearly, in the broadest sense, management of these elements is conventionally the responsibility of the personnel department rather than of the strategic marketing planner. In addition, and in line with this wider perspective, we should also note that we are not only concerned with the adequacy or otherwise of human resources in the marketing function. The implementation of strategic marketing plans is also likely to have human resource implications in other functional areas, including, for example, production, quality control and distribution. As with any other management function, however, it is important that the strategic marketing planner be involved in the evaluation, selection and development and training of personnel, which are crucial to the achievement of plans.

Having ensured that the necessary human resources for the achievement of strategic marketing plans are available and/or being made available, a second crucial aspect of implementation which pertains to human resources is their allocation.

Allocation of human resources

In the implementation of strategic marketing plans, key decisions will need to be made regarding the allocation of human resources. This requires a detailed assessment of what tasks are required to be achieved in the implementation of strategic plans, followed by the allocation of individuals with the necessary skills and authority to achieve these tasks. In simple terms, we are discussing the allocation of responsibilities. Objectives will need to be translated into a series of tasks to be achieved. Initially these tasks may be allocated on a functional level for (for example, to the marketing research function), but eventually they will have to be translated into specific responsibilities and tasks, and individuals allocated to the achievement of these tasks. Especially in the multi-product, multi-divisional company there will always be a problem of scarce resources. Decisions, therefore, will have to be made as to which products/divisions will be allocated resources. Having made this difficult decision, invariably in consultation with other senior management in the company, it is then important that individuals in the human resource structure of the company are involved in the process not only of implementing marketing plans but where appropriate, formulating them. This, in turn, requires effective communication.

Communication in implementing strategic marketing plans

A major obstacle to the effective implementation of marketing plans is lack of communication between those responsible for formulating marketing plans and those responsible for implementing them. So it is important that there be effective, and preferably two-way, communication between individuals in the organization. The need for effective communication pertains to both vertical communication, i.e. between successive layers in the management/organizational hierarchy, and horizontally, i.e. between different functions in the organization. For example, in horizontal communication it is vital for marketing management to secure the co-operation of other functional areas in the achievement of marketing plans. Very often, as we shall see, the achievement of marketing and corporate objectives, based on placing the customer at the centre of organizational decision making, can often cause resentment and hostility from other functional managers, who often perceive marketing to be usurping their authority and power in the organization. A key element in reducing this hostility and resentment is two-way communication. Other functional managers preferably need to be consulted about, and at least apprised of, marketing strategies and plans and their full co-operation sought.

Similarly, it is important that there be adequate, and preferably two-way, communication between the various management levels within the marketing and sales functions. For example, it is pointless spending substantial time and resources on sophisticated marketing planning systems if marketing objectives and plans are not communicated throughout the marketing management hierarchy. Even better than communicating plans through the hierarchy after they have been determined at the higher levels is a system of planning which involves all levels of the hierarchy in the planning system itself. In this way there is bound to be much more communication between the vertical levels in the hierarchy, accompanied by a greater commitment to the achievement of the plans which result from the communication. It is to this aspect of 'commitment' to the achievement of marketing plans, which is a further key element of implementation, that we now turn our attention.

Motivation and leadership in implementing strategic marketing plans

Underpinning much of what we have already discussed concerning the importance of human resource aspects in implementing marketing plans are the related issues of *motivation* and *leadership*.

As was mentioned in the introduction, even if staff have the necessary skills needed to implement marketing strategies, they must be willing to exercise these skills. The extent to which individuals will be willing to exercise their skills is significantly influenced by the leading and motivating skills of senior management. Both leadership and motivation involve complex issues, many of which are beyond the scope of what is, after all, a text on strategic marketing. However, as we have already seen, two-way communication is an important element in securing motivation. In turn, the willingness to exercise such two-way communication implies a more supportive leadership style on the part of management. In addition, it is important that the reward system of the organization supports and encourages a more strategic approach. All too often, in many companies, the reward (or rather 'punishment') system encourages short-term, tactical thinking and efforts rather than longer-term, strategic thinking.

We should not forget that the tasks of motivating and leading for the marketing manager also extend to individuals outside the organization itself. For example, distribution channel members will need to be motivated to achieve organizational plans, as will, say, marketing research agencies and advertising agencies. A problem here, of course, is that such outside agencies will have their own objectives and management styles, which may conflict with those of the marketing manager's organization. In the same way, even within the organization, the marketing manager will need to understand and be able to deal with conflict between marketing and other functions. Conflict resolution, therefore, is our final key human resources consideration in the implementation of strategic marketing.

Managing conflict in implementing strategic thinking

We have already seen that there exists potential for conflict, both within and outside the organization, in the implementation of strategic marketing. The skills required to avoid and/or resolve this conflict are central to the effective implementation of marketing strategies. But to understand this centrality we need to be aware of some of the bases for such potential conflict.

As noted, the primary basis for potential conflict between the internal marketing function of an organization and outside agencies and organizations stems from the fact that outside agencies and organizations have their own objectives and management styles. In short, of course, they are essentially separate organizations. The problem of such conflict in the context of strategic marketing planning stems from the fact that it can make it difficult, and sometimes impossible, to implement otherwise carefully prepared marketing plans. For example, the achievement of an objective of, say, increased market share on the part of the organization may be very much reliant on the sales and promotion efforts of distributors. On the other hand, distributors will have their own objectives, and in fact may view the final customers as their responsibility rather than of their suppliers' responsibility. Unless marketing management appreciate the potential for and sources of such conflict, marketing strategies are likely to be somewhat less effective. Marketing plans should be designed from the outset to minimize such potential conflict. However, where and when conflict does arise the marketing manager will need to be skilled in resolving it. These skills involve interaction and essentially comprise the ability to resolve conflicts amicably and to the mutual benefit of both parties through effective dialogue and influencing skills.

These interacting skills are equally, if not more, important within the organization where, if anything, the potential for conflict between marketing and other functions in the implementation of strategies is even greater.

There are two major and interrelated reasons for internal conflict between marketing and other functions in the company. The first is the need, under the marketing concept, for all departments and personnel to 'think customers'. In some cases this may require a department to consider the effect of its actions on customers and not just on its own internal functioning and efficiency. So, for example, the production function may be most efficient, in terms of production, with long, uninterrupted runs of standardized products. However, customers (and in the long run at least, the supplying organization itself) may be best served by more custom-made products produced in smaller batches and with a more flexible approach. Moreover, this dichotomy is heightened by the simple fact that longer production runs of more standardized products make the life of production staff, including the production director, that much easier. Needless to say, the view taken here is that the issue should be resolved in favour of meeting customer needs rather than in the interests of the production department. Understandably, however, this view, although sound in marketing terms, can give rise to real conflict. In fairness, it is also important to understand the problems of functional managers in such a situation. Viewed from their perspective, meeting customer needs may, in their terms, lead them to do a worse job than if they were left to their own devices. The potential for this sort of conflict exists between marketing and virtually every other function in the business which does not view customer satisfaction as one of its prime responsibilities and objectives.

The second reason for inter-functional conflict between marketing and other functions is in reality the other side of the coin to that just described. Nothing is more frustrating for marketers than the fact that whilst they may not see customer satisfaction as part of their remit, there is no doubt that virtually every other function in the business has the 'ability' (knowingly or not) to affect customer satisfaction – for better or worse. So, for example, an otherwise sound marketing strategy may be less than successful in its implementation, or at the worst, a total failure, because of the actions (or lack of them) of another function. A good example would be where marketing plans require the co-operation of, say, the research and development department in only developing new products for which there is a clearly specified market need and which moreover must be developed on time to match strategic windows. Unless the R&D function is totally committed to this strategy then the achievement of marketing plans is likely to be thwarted. Unfortunately, all too often R&D is likely to resent such customer-driven programmes for research, preferring instead to pursue research which is scientifically 'more interesting'.

The question remains that, if there is such scope for wide-ranging and potentially damaging inter-functional conflict in the implementation of marketing plans, how should it be resolved? One approach would be to give Marketing the final and formal authority over all activities which actually and potentially impinge upon the achievement of customer satisfaction through marketing plans. Simple though this may sound, however, in practice it would mean that virtually every decision in the organization would be made by Marketing. Attractive though this may at first glance seem to marketing management, in fact in most organizations it would be a recipe for disaster. Not only would most marketing managers be incapable (or unwilling) to accept this range of responsibilities for decision making in functions where they have little or no expertise, but it would also tend to lead to a heightening of mistrust, antagonism and, ultimately, even greater conflict.

We are back, therefore, to what were referred to earlier as 'interacting skills'. The effective resolution of such conflicts depends upon the ability of marketing planners to *persuade* the management of other functions of the sense and soundness of their marketing plans and their requirements in implementing them. Ultimately their success in this persuasion process is down to a combination of interpersonal and planning skills, the latter meaning that marketing planners must convince other functions on the basis of sound and clearly communicable analysis. In addition, however, as we shall see later in this chapter, certain types of organizational structure can lend themselves to increasing inter-functional planning and co-operation.

In the best run companies, however, the centrality of customer needs to all organizational planning and decision making is an accepted part of the company culture. This degree of customer orientation is rarely achieved overnight and requires top management support and an effective action programme in order to implement it.

Kotler[2] lists the following steps in building a company-wide 'marketing orientation'.

1. Convincing the management team of the need to become customer focused.
2. Appointing a top marketing officer and a marketing task force.
3. Securing outside help and guidance from, e.g. consultancy firms.
4. Changing the reward structures in the company towards performance in building more loyal and satisfied customers.
5. Hiring suitably trained and experienced marketing talent.
6. Developing strong in-house marketing training programmes.
7. Installing a modern marketing planning system.
8. Establishing rewards for the best annual marketing plans.
9. Re-organizing away from product-centred company structures to market-centred company structures.
10. Shifting from an emphasis on departmental activities to an emphasis on process/outcomes.

Building an organization-wide marketing culture, in itself not a simple task, is not guaranteed to remove all the possible sources of conflict. Probably nothing can ensure this, and in any event some degree of conflict, or at least competition, is healthy in an organization – if kept within bounds. In addition, as we have seen, the effective management of conflict is only one of a number of complex human resource issues to which the implementation of marketing strategies gives rise.

Internal marketing

Earlier, we mentioned the notion of **internal marketing** in implementing marketing plans. Many facets of building a company-wide marketing orientation mentioned above in the implementation of strategic marketing plans, but in particular the co-ordination of other functional areas and the need to minimize conflict in the achievement of customer satisfaction, have come together in the notion of internal marketing.

According to Dibb[3] internal marketing refers to:

> The managerial actions necessary to make all members of the marketing organization understand and accept their respective roles in implementing the marketing strategy.

Some of the steps suggested by Kotler to achieve a company-wide marketing orientation are essentially steps in implementing internal marketing. However, contemporary views regarding internal marketing also stress the importance of looking at and treating internal company employees as 'customers'. In other words, a key distinguishing feature of internal marketing is the idea that the concepts and techniques initially designed to be applied to external customers are used internally with respect to company employees. So employees become 'customers', jobs become 'products', internal communication becomes 'promotion', identifying the needs of different functional groups within the organization becomes 'segmentation', and so on.

This internal application of marketing concepts and techniques, Lings and Brooks[4] point out, serves to improve communication throughout an organization, at the same time increasing motivation. But above all, internal marketing can bring about an increased awareness of, and commitment to, the importance of satisfying external customers and the plans that the company has for achieving this.

One leading building society in the UK uses internal company videos, produced on a monthly basis and available to all staff, to inform them of developments in marketing plans and any notable marketing successes during the month. Individual staff and/or departments are signalled out for praise where they have made a particularly valuable contribution to marketing plans and customer satisfaction.

The idea is to improve communication throughout the organisation, raise levels of awareness and motivation, and above all, secure a commitment to external customers.

Although internal marketing is relevant to all organizations it is felt to be particularly important in service organizations where the people element is so important and potentially has such a key effect on the achievement of marketing plans. We shall therefore return to this aspect later in Chapter 17 when we discuss the special characteristics and issues in services marketing.

We shall now turn our attention to our second major issue in implementing marketing strategies, and again it is a resource issue. But this time the issue is more technical than human in nature, namely the issue of financial resources or, more specifically, marketing budgets.

Implementation and financial resources: marketing budgets

If the management of human resources is the first key strand in successful implementation of marketing strategies, the second key strand is the management of financial resources. A key step in assessing the necessary financial resources to support marketing strategies is the preparation of marketing budgets. In fact, the preparation of marketing budgets is itself a key element of marketing planning and forms the basis of much of an organization's control procedures.

Ultimately, in most organizations the effectiveness of strategic marketing planning is measured in financial performance. At some stage, therefore, the marketing plan must contain financial projections, certainly in terms of both costs and revenues, and in many cases, conventionally, profits. The word 'conventionally' in the context of profits is used because, increasingly, marketing is not solely responsible for profits – it is being suggested that a better measure of marketing performance would be gross margin or some measure based on contribution. At the very least, however, most marketing budgets contain both revenue forecasts and the estimated costs of the marketing programmes.

Approaches to determining marketing budgets

As mentioned above, conventionally, the marketing budget sets out sales revenue, less costs, to give profits. An example of a simple marketing budget for a single product company is shown below:

	£
Sales revenue	————
Less non-marketing variable costs	————
Contribution	————
Less marketing costs:	

- Advertising
- Sales promotion
- Selling
- Distribution
- Marketing research

Total marketing costs	————
Adjusted contribution	————
Less fixed costs	————
Net profit	————

In our example, the various elements of the marketing costs are derived from detailed budgets for each element of the marketing programme, i.e. there will be separate budgets for advertising, sales promotion and selling. Note also that fixed costs are deducted after calculating the adjusted contribution for marketing. The reason for this are discussed in more detail later, but essentially derive from the problems of allocating fixed costs to elements of marketing expenditure. The question here, though, is how the overall marketing budget is arrived at and then how to allocate this overall budget to each element of the marketing mix. Amongst the most frequently discussed methods for setting the overall budget are:

Affordable or given-sum method This involves allocating an amount for marketing expenditures based on what the company can afford. The interesting point here is that often this amount may be determined by personnel outside marketing. The problem with this approach is that the amount allocated may not bear any relevance to that required to meet marketing objectives.

Percentage of sales This may be based either on past sales or, more frequently, on future (forecast) sales. In fact, determining marketing (and many other company) budgets on a sales forecast is probably the most frequently used basis. The problem here, of course, is that sales (and hence sales forecasts) are themselves influenced by the marketing budget. In other words, sales forecasts should be based on marketing budgets and not the other way round.

Following competitors In some organizations, both total and individual elements of the marketing budget, for example advertising, are based on what competitors are spending (competitive parity). Certainly, competitor considerations are important in all marketing decisions. However, blindly following the competition for decisions such as marketing budgets is nonsensical and dangerous. Different organizations have different objectives, strategies and resources profiles.

Sales response function Here marketing expenditures are based on expected or envisaged sales to various levels of marketing expenditure. The theoretical notion is that marketing expenditure should be increased to the point where the marginal sales return is equal to the marginal marketing expenditure. Whilst this is theoretically sound, in practice it is virtually impossible to determine the optimum spend. It is simply too difficult to estimate the various marginal sales response functions.

Objective and task Essentially, budgets are determined on the basis of the tasks required to be achieved in the marketing plan. This approach has a number of distinct advantages and is therefore often suggested as being the most appropriate. The major advantages are as follows:

- It ensures that budgets follow from and are consistent with the marketing plan
- It forces the planner to consider the cost implications of suggested strategies
- It is not based on arbitrary or historical bases as are many other approaches to budgeting
- Unlike the sales response approach it is practical

Brassington and Pettitt[5] point out that in setting budgets there is:

A need to balance precision against flexibility.

Having set the overall budget, the next step is to determine the allocation of this to the individual elements of the marketing mix.

Allocating the budget to individual elements of the marketing mix

Having set the overall budget for marketing, this budget must then be divided between the various elements of the marketing mix. This is a problematical area for the marketing manager. Why this is, and some of the ways of resolving these problems can be high-lighted by looking at the setting of the promotional budget as an example of the issues in this allocational problem. Many of the problems which are outlined for the promotional budget also apply to allocating the budget to the other areas of the marketing mix.

 In principle the allocation of the overall budget to the individual elements of the marketing mix should be determined by the **law of diminishing returns**. In the case of the promotional budget therefore (and indeed the other elements of the marketing mix) budget resources should be allocated up to the point where additional marginal expenditure on promotion gives rise to an equal marginal return in terms of revenue. The law of diminishing returns suggests that increased expenditure on promotion will give rise to ever decreasing returns in terms of revenue, i.e. marginal revenue will diminish until it ceased effectively to exist.

This seemingly obvious concept is in reality almost impossible to apply in practice for the simple reason that the marginal return from promotional (and other marketing budgets) is extremely difficult to measure. So, for example, in the case of promotional activity, increased sales revenue after increasing the budget allocation to promotion may in fact be due to a number of possible reasons other than this increase in promotional spend. Other reasons for an observed increase in sales revenue may be, e.g. an increase in competitor prices, an increase in consumers' disposable income, special offers by the retailer rather than the manufacturer etc. Similarly, increased spending on promotional activity may take some time to come through in terms of increased sales revenue.

These problems of measuring the effects or attributing causality to promotional spends also apply to the other elements of the marketing mix although it is true to say that there are differences between the elements of the mix with regard to the relative ease of measurement of some of the effects of budget changes.

The recognition of these problems, however, coupled with a similar recognition of the importance of effective budget allocation between the different elements of the marketing mix has led to considerable interest in how to improve this process of resource allocation. Once again, developments in marketing models allied to the use of more powerful computing facilities has led to the growth of ever more sophisticated methods for determining budget allocation. In particular, the use of mathematical models in the budget allocation process has increased substantially in recent years. If we take our example of the promotional budget therefore, this might involve, for example, combining data on consumers with media characteristics, objectives for market share, and records of past results. Regression models based on this data and information can be used to develop models of the likely cost effectiveness of a variety of advertising budgets in an attempt to optimize the promotional spend. Kotler[6] lists several examples of statistical tools and mathematical models which can be used to improve the budget allocation process.

In concluding this section, we have seen that an important aspect of implementing strategic marketing is the marketing budget. Although most marketing budgeting is done either on an affordable basis or on the basis of past/forecast sales, budget setting is more logical if undertaken on a task-related basis. Once the overall budget for marketing is set, it must then be allocated between the different elements of the marketing mix.

We now turn our attention to the final aspect of implementing marketing strategies, namely, the organization of the marketing function.

Organizing the marketing function

Earlier in this chapter we discussed some of the important elements of managing human resources in the implementation of marketing plans. Many issues raised in this discussion, for example the importance of effective communication and minimization of conflict, are in turn influenced by the structure of the marketing department and its role within the overall corporate structure of the organization.

The importance of the marketing organization structure

In discussing Sony's investment in China in the late 1990s, Lynch[7], illustrates the important and close links between strategies and organizational structures. The marketing organization structure provides the framework for the implementation of marketing strategies and is fundamental to their success or failure. Any number of studies of the relationship between organizational structure and the effectiveness of marketing and other strategies confirm the importance of organizational structure. Amongst some of the more influential of these studies are those by Chandler[8] and Channon[9], whose respective studies in the US and in the UK demonstrated the fact that a company's organizational structure will change according to the strategies adopted over time. More importantly, companies whose structure did not adapt to strategy were less successful than their adaptive counterparts.

Procter and Gamble have recently undertaken a major restructuring of their marketing organization on a global basis. We need not concern ourselves with the details of this reorganization here, but it is interesting that Procter and Gamble have obviously felt that the existing structure is a major reason for poor performance in some areas in recent years. As a result, the company have been prepared to spend millions of dollars and undergo traumatic changes that have been difficult, painful, and costly in an attempt to achieve a better marketing structure.

Clearly, then, organizational structure is central to the implementation of marketing plans. For the remainder of this chapter, therefore, we shall consider the alternative marketing organization structures available to an organization. We shall confine ourselves to the marketing function itself, although it is important to recognize that the organization of marketing has wider ramifications and needs to be set against the important task of determining the structure of the organization as a whole.

Although there are any number of possible variations for organizing the marketing function within a company, the following represent the basic alternatives, together with the major advantages and disadvantages of each.

Functional structure Perhaps the simplest form of organizational structure for marketing, as the name implies, is a structure based upon the different functions of marketing. Each function, e.g. market research, advertising and sales promotion, and selling, will have a separate manager, each reporting to the marketing manager or director as the case may be. Co-ordination and control is achieved through the functional authority of the marketing manager. Although simple, this type of structure can lead to tactical rather than strategic approaches. It is also more suited to stable, simple environments and smaller, often one-product companies.

Product-based structure Again, as the name implies, these are marketing organization structures based on the products of a company. A variety of product-based structures are possible. One of the most vaunted and hence widely used of product-based structures is that of the **brand manager** organization. Essentially, the development of this type of structure was a response to the problems of managing individual products or brands in the multi-product company. The brand manager system introduces additional layers of management into the marketing organization structure. Brand managers are responsible for developing marketing plans for their own particular brands and are responsible for sales and sometimes profits. The advantages of this system of organization include the following:

- It allows close control of individual brands with someone assuming responsibility for their marketing
- It provides a good basis for training future marketing managers
- It enables fast response to market conditions and changes.

On the other hand, there are disadvantages:

- It can lead to excessive competition for resources
- It can encourage tactical rather than strategic planning
- It is costly to support in terms of staff
- The brand manager typically has responsibility without authority.

Other forms of product-based structure include product divisions and product teams, the latter being a response to some of the disadvantages associated with traditional brand management structures. Perhaps one of the most significant forms of marketing organization in recent years, in part as a response to the limitations of the brand manager system, has been the emergence of 'category management/category teams'.

Category management/category teams

Dewar and Schultz[10] believe that the time of the product/brand manager system of marketing organization has gone. Once such a successful and therefore widely used form of marketing organisation, the product or brand management system is now felt to be no longer appropriate to today's marketing environment. There are many factors in the marketing environment that have caused this shift away from brand management including more deal-prone customers, a resulting lowering of brand loyalty, and the growth of own brands in large and powerful retailers. A response to this in some companies has been the adoption of so-called **category management** systems.

Category management groups products together under a category manager. There are various bases on which this grouping may take place. Some companies, reflecting the power and importance of the supermarkets, group their products and brands according to their section or even aisles in the supermarket. A manager is then responsible for this category of products. Another way of grouping products for category management is to group brands by product area and application; for example, all detergent and cleaning products may come under a category manager. Category management is felt to help avoid the sometimes narrow concentration on individual brands that a brand manager system can lead to. It also mirrors better the systems of purchasing and merchandising in many retail operations. A development of this type of organization is the use of **category teams** where each category manager has a team of marketing people, including brand managers, sales managers, marketing research specialists, and even specialists from other functional areas of the business as appropriate. The team performs all the necessary functions to market a particular category of products.

Market-based structures   In this type of structure, the marketing organization is structured around markets or customers rather than products or functions. Many believe that this represents the most marketing oriented way to organize the marketing function. Some of the major companies that have adopted this approach include IBM, Xerox, General Foods and General Electric. Different companies have used a variety of approaches to organizing around customers, some establishing customer divisions and others establishing strategic business units. The basis of market-centred structures is that different customer groups or markets have different needs and requirements for competitive success. A market-based structure enables these different needs to be catered for more than do other marketing organization structures.

On the down side, market-based structures can be costly to introduce. For example, where previously a simple sales force has sold to a variety of customer groups, a market-based structure requires a separate sales force for each customer group. Similarly, a market-based structure places additional demands on the marketing information system to disaggregate data on individual customer groups.

Matrix structures   In this type of structure a combination of other marketing organization structures is used. For example, marketing may be organized on a combination of products and markets. The company would have both product managers responsible for the effective marketing of their particular product range, and market managers responsible for individual customer groups or markets. This type of structure is particularly well suited to the company with considerable diversity in both products and markets, but it can be costly and may give rise to potential conflict between product and market managers.

How to select the marketing organization structure

With such a variety of possible organizational structures to choose from, the problem for the marketing planner is how to decide which is the most appropriate, i.e. 'which works best?' The simple, if somewhat frustrating answer to this question is: '... it all depends'. The so-called contingency school of organizational theorists has demonstrated that there is no 'one best way' to structure all organizations.

Factors which will affect the choice of the most appropriate structure will include:

- Company size
- Rates of environmental change
- Product/market diversity
- Complexity/predictability of the environment
- Marketing and corporate strategies.

Unfortunately, given its importance to the achievement of strategies, to date there has been little consistent empirical research done on the characteristics of 'successful' marketing organization. However, contributions such as that by Peters and Waterman[11] and Aaker[12] are beginning to shed more light on this complex issue.

Extending the marketing structure: the emergence of strategic alliances

One of the key developments in contemporary business in recent years has been the growth of so-called 'Strategic Alliances' between companies. These were mentioned earlier in Chapter 7 in our discussion of innovation strategies. It is not possible or appropriate to detail all the reasons for the emergence of such alliances, the different formats they may take, their operation, and their advantages and disadvantages here, but it is the case that strategic alliances have many implications for the contemporary marketing manager including, in the context of this chapter, the implementation of marketing plans and strategies. In addition, as already indicated, the number of strategic alliances is set to grow. It is important therefore to consider some of the issues which such strategic alliances give rise to with respect to these organizational aspects of marketing. We shall start by outlining what a strategic alliance is.

Essentially, a strategic alliance is where two or more independent companies voluntarily enter into an agreement in order to collaborate together to achieve common objectives. There are many possible reasons behind forming such alliances. For example, these days often the largest companies cannot afford to develop new technology and products on their own. Similarly, a company which may wish to enter a new overseas market may find that it has neither the skills nor the resources to do so unilaterally. These are examples of where companies may seek to enter into partnerships with other companies in order to overcome these resource and other problems. The overriding aim behind alliances is to achieve competitive advantages in the increasingly competitive environment. Badaracco[13] lists several specific motives which may give rise to strategic alliances including, e.g. filling out product lines, cutting costs, reducing risks, accelerating product speed to market, building flexibility, guiding the migration of knowledge, and monitoring or neutralizing competition. These advantages which can accrue from businesses joining together are summarized neatly by Doyle[14], who states that ultimately strategic alliances should provide the advantage of adding additional value to customers.

An interesting area of strategic alliances in recent years have been those alliances which have involved the coming together of public and private sector companies. In the UK in particular this type of strategic alliance has been particularly prevalent in some industries. Somewhat controversially, these industries have involved the health service sector, the education sector and many civil engineering projects. The Public Finance Initiative was specifically introduced in order to develop public assets such as hospitals using private money. This has been a major area of marketing activity for some companies.

Needless to say, any number of reasons may underpin the forming of a strategic alliance between two or more companies, and there are many implications for the marketing function and the process of marketing management which result from such strategic alliances. From the point of view of marketing organization however, essentially a strategic alliance with another company effectively extends the marketing organization of each company which is party to the strategic alliance and therefore gives rise to additional and new issues in marketing organization and implementation. Some of the more important of these are outlined below.

Webster[15] has argued that in strategic alliances, more emphasis will be placed on the relationship of management skills. To ensure successful strategic alliances, he suggests, marketing can no longer be the sole responsibility of a few specialists in the company, rather, everyone involved in the strategic alliance must be charged with understanding customers and contributing to delivering value to them. This notion is not new, nor is it confined to strategic alliances, but it is believed by Webster and others such as Kanter[16] that the need for this customer oriented culture is particularly critical when two or more companies come together to serve a market.

Another organizational issue which arises out of strategic alliances is that the partners in the strategic alliance must decide which companies will perform the different marketing functions such as market research, research and development; and amongst other activities, new product development, promotion etc. to prevent a duplication of marketing activities and to get the best out of marketing resources and skills. Resolving such allocation of responsibility issues is, needless to say, not easy. Understandably marketing personnel in each company will have vested interests to protect. In addition to this organizing of responsibilities and activities, strategic alliances also require careful attention to be given to factors such as communication between the partners in the alliance and facets such as the sharing of marketing research, technical information etc.

It is fair to say that in many respects concepts and ideas regarding marketing management in general and marketing organization and implementation in particular, have not kept pace with the practice of strategic alliances and the issues and problems which such alliances give rise to. Nevertheless, as already indicated, strategic alliances are set to become increasingly important in the future. Therefore, marketing management will increasingly not only have to consider partnerships with customers, but also integrating partnerships with suppliers and other parties to create new sources of competitive advantage. Hughes[17] has identified several questions when considering whether or not to enter into a strategic alliance, as follows:

1. Will the alliance increase efficiency in production and marketing of products and services?
2. What qualities and skills amongst staff and structures will be required?
3. Will the alliance allow prices to fall and the availability, choice and quality to increase?

Hughes suggests that the overriding test of the worth of a strategic alliance are in its potential benefits to the consumer.

Byrne[18] has suggested that today's strategic alliances may be just an indication of the business organization of the future. This future organization may well be 'the Virtual Corporation'. Under this sort of organizational structure Byrne suggests that temporary networks of companies will join together to exploit fast changing environments and opportunities. Companies will share costs, skills, and access to markets, with each partner contributing what it is best at. He further suggests that the Virtual Corporation will represent the ultimate marketing organizational structure for adding value to the customer and will comprise of neither a central office nor organizational chart, and will have no hierarchy and no vertical integration. The organizational structure will bring together only those core competencies required to serve customer needs and take advantage of marketing opportunities by linking companies' skills together. Whether this organizational structure suggested by Byrne will ever materialize is beyond the scope of this chapter but it does appear that this is the direction in which many companies are headed. What is clear is that the marketing organization structures of the future may be very different to those which prevail today and will require new inter-personal and implementational skills on the part of the marketer of the future.

Summary

In this chapter we have looked at the vital, though often neglected, aspects of implementing strategic marketing plans.

First of all, we examined some of the issues which surround the human resource aspects of implementation. Ultimately, all plans are implemented through people, so it behoves the strategic marketing planner to consider the profile of human resources and the extent to which this is adequate to carry out the plans envisaged. Where the human resources are insufficient, then either the resource must be improved or the plans changed. Improving the human resource base involves recruitment, selection, training and developing, and unfortunately, on occasions, redeployment and redundancies. Similarly, attention needs to be given to allocating human resources. Because of the importance of managing human resources to the achievement of strategic plans, the marketing manager needs to develop skills in communicating, leading and motivating, and handling conflict.

Secondly, we examined the control role of marketing budgets in the marketing planning process. It was suggested that, in many organizations, the process of developing marketing budgets is relatively unsophisticated, often being based on past or forecast sales or on the basis of what is affordable. As a result it was suggested that, although more complex, budgets ought instead to be based on a task-related basis.

Finally, we looked at the organization of the marketing department itself. Simpler types of structure include functional and product based structures but more and more companies are moving towards marketing centred and, in some cases, matrix type structures. However, we should remember that there is no one best way to organize for marketing. Each company needs to assess carefully for itself which type of structure will best enable it to implement successful marketing strategies.

Key terms

Internal marketing [p417]
Sales response function [p420]
Objective and task [p420]
Law of diminishing returns [p420]
Functional structure [p422]

Product-based structure [p422]
Brand manager [p422]
Category management [p423]
Category team [p423]
Matrix structures [p424]

Questions

1   What aspects does the implementation element of marketing planning encompass, and why is it so important?
2   What factors can give rise to conflict in the implementation of strategic marketing plans and how can such conflict be minimized?
3   What is meant by internal marketing, and why is this increasingly felt to be essential in marketing management?
4   Outline and discuss the different approaches to setting the marketing budget, indicating their relative advantages and disadvantages.
5   Outline and discuss the different approaches to structuring the marketing organization, indicating their relative advantages and disadvantages.

References

1. Johnson, G. and Scholes, K., *Exploring Corporate Strategy*, 5th edn, Prentice-Hall, Hertfordshire, 1999, p. 399.
2. Kotler, P., *Marketing Management: Analysis, Planning, Implementation and Control*. 9th edn, Prentice-Hall, New Jersey, 1997, pp. 761–762.
3. Dibb, S., Simkin, L., Pride, W. M. and Ferrell, O. C., *Marketing Concepts and Strategies,* 4th European edn, Houghton Mifflin, Boston, 2001, p. 733.
4. Lings, I. and Brooks, F., 'Implementing and measuring the effectiveness of internal marketing', *Journal of Marketing Management*, **14**, **4**, 1998, pp. 325–351.
5. Brassington, F. and Pettitt, S., *Principles of Marketing*, 2nd edn, Financial Times/Prentice/Hall, Essex, England, 1997, p. 904.
6. Kotler, P., op. cit. pp. 128–129.
7. Lynch, R., *Corporate Strategy*, 2nd edn, Financial Times/Prentice-Hall, Essex, England, 2000, p . 713–715.
8. Chandler, A. D., *Strategy and Structure*, MIT Press, Cambridge, Mass., 1962.
9. Channon, D. F., *The Strategy and Structure of British Enterprise*, Macmillan, London, 1973.
10. Dewar, R. and Schultz, D., 'The product manager: an idea whose time has gone' *Marketing Communications*, May, 1989, pp. 283–285.
11. Peters, P. J. and Waterman, R. H., *In Search of Excellence: Lessons from America's Best-run Companies*, Harper and Row, New York, 1982.
12. Aakcr, D. Λ., *Strategic Marketing Management,* 5th edn, Wiley, New York, 1999, Chapter 2.

13. Badaracco, J. J., *The Knowledge Link: How Firms Compete Through Strategic Alliances*, Harvard Business Press 1991.
14. Doyle, P., *Marketing Management and Strategy*, Prentice-Hall, London, 1994.
15. Webster, F. E. Jnr., 'The changing role of marketing in the corporation', *Journal of Marketing*, **56**, October 1992, pp. 1–17.
16. Kanter, R. M., 'Collaborative advantage: the art of alliances', *Harvard Business Review*, July/August 1994, **72**, 4, p. 96.
17. Hughes, D., *Breaking with Tradition: Building Partnerships and Alliances in the European Food Industry*, Wye College Press, 1994.
18. Byrne, J. A., 'The virtual corporation', *Business Week*, Feb. 8, 1993.

Case Study

Sally Pike, director of marketing at Oyster Products, has called an urgent meeting with her fellow directors of the other functional areas of the business. The overriding reason for calling this meeting is that Pike feels her efforts to improve the marketing standing of the company through improved customer orientation is being thwarted by other functional managers. In addition, and as part of the overall problem, over the past twelve months since Pike was appointed there has been considerable conflict between members of her marketing team and other members of the company.

One of the first things that Pike organised when she was appointed marketing director was an update of the product range, including the introduction of several new products. In Pike's view the product range was badly out of date and was affecting sales and market share. However, the battle that Pike had had to fight in order to get the design team and the engineering and production staff in the company to go along with her ideas had been very bruising indeed. In short, they had initially resisted the new innovations tooth and nail. Pike though felt vindicated now because the new product range had been welcomed by the existing customer base.

This was not the only battle though that Pike had to fight. Over the past twelve months she had battles with finance – over pricing; delivery and distribution – over complaints about customer service; personnel – over some proposed customer awareness training for all company employees which they had turned down; and even sales – over suggestions for increasing call rates on key accounts.

In short, Pike was not happy with the way things were in the company.

The company is currently organised on a functional basis, including her own marketing department. Most of the sales team come from engineering backgrounds and the company is strongly engineering and product oriented. At the moment, she feels that she does not even have the support of the senior management team regarding her views that the company needs to become more customer focused.

QUESTION

What problems and issues might Pike highlight to her follow directors at the forthcoming meeting as regards the marketing organisation and culture in the company, and what proposals might she make in order to try and resolve some of these problems and issues?

16

Evaluating and controlling strategic marketing

Chapter objectives

By the end of this chapter you will:

▶ Understand the importance of evaluating and controlling strategic marketing activities.

▶ Be aware of the elements of the control process and how these apply to the key areas for control in marketing.

▶ Understand the distinctions and relationships between profit control, efficiency control and strategic control in marketing.

Introduction

In this chapter we turn our attention to assessing the efficiency and effectiveness of the strategic marketing effort. The evaluation and control of marketing probably represents one of the weakest areas of marketing practice in many companies. Even organizations which are otherwise strong in their strategic marketing planning have poor control and evaluation procedures for their marketing. There are, possibly, a number of reasons for this. First of all, there is no such thing as a 'standard' system of control for marketing. Other functional areas of management have well-established techniques and systems of control in, for example, production planning and control, financial planning and control, and quality control. With the exception of annual sales and profit control, marketing theory and practice has tended to lag behind in the development of comprehensive evaluation and control procedures. Second, and perhaps related to the above, there is no doubt that the evaluation and control of marketing does present complex problems for the designer of control systems. For example, in large companies several marketing areas, each with different specialists, will need to be controlled. The efforts of sales managers, marketing researchers, advertising personnel, brand managers and so on, will need to be closely co-ordinated if the control and evaluation process is to be successful.

Finally, perhaps more controversially, marketing management has long resisted some notions of control that are widely accepted and indeed welcomed in other functional areas. This resistance has been, and still is, justified on the basis that much marketing activity does not lend itself to traditional control concerns, and indeed can detract from more 'creative' marketing. This argument is rejected here. Certainly, control of marketing, with its myriad of complex interrelationships, is difficult. Control of marketing presents distinct measurement problems, as we saw with, for example, the evaluation of the effectiveness of advertising. We should also be careful not to overconstrain marketing management with control. But control and evaluation of marketing effort are essential, even if it is only part of 'good housekeeping'.

Sponsorship spend is a good example of how some areas of marketing have been notoriously difficult to evaluate and control. Very few marketers have in the past known exactly what they were getting from often substantial spends in this area. To some extent, marketers have colluded in this failure to measure the effectiveness of sponsorship spending as it has enabled them to have more discretion over how much and where a major part of the promotional budget was spent. This is now changing.

Sponsors are now demanding to know what they are getting for their money. Recent large sponsorship deals have involved clauses in the contract which allow the sponsor to withdraw if pre-specified promotional objectives and results are not achieved.

For this reason, a good understanding of the nature of control is needed, not only by the designers of the control system, but also by those being controlled. The issue also of who controls the controllers cannot be overlooked.

The essentials of the control process

The essentials of the control process for any management function are shown in Figure 16.1. We can see that it contains four essential elements, namely:

- Setting specific performance standards
- Locating responsibility for achieving these standards
- Evaluating performance against standards
- Taking corrective action.

In addition, we can see that the performance standards should stem from and reflect the objective, strategies and tactics of the planning process. The corrective action then feeds back to, and potentially affects, the planning process itself, the performance standards, and those responsible for achieving these standards.

Building on our overview of the control process, designing an effective system of control requires consideration of the following aspects.

Information

In Chapter 13 we considered the importance and design of the marketing information system. Clearly, the control process is reliant upon timely, accurate and up-to-date information. In designing the control systems for marketing strategy, the information element should be based on establishing minimum rather than maximum information needs. This will mean improved, not reduced, performance. If we are not careful in the design and implementation of control systems, marketing personnel can spend more time accounting for their activities than performing them.

In addition, information costs money. The control system, of which information is a part, should not cost more than the costs that would be incurred if there were no controls.

Finally, information needs to be analysed and presented in a way which is understandable to managers and subordinates alike. If required, adequate training should be given.

Communication and 'noise' in the system

As shown in Figure 16.1, communication is essential for effective control. Managers need to be made aware of, and accept, the standards of performance against which their activities and those of their own subordinates are to be judged. In addition, rapid feedback of results is important so that differences between required and actual standards of performance can be corrected. Direct communication between manager and subordinates, rather than passing information down a potentially long chain of command, is to be preferred as this minimizes the **'noise'** in the control system which can occur when information is distorted by having it passed down an extended scalar chain of command.

The human aspects of control

Unfortunately 'control' is often viewed by the people of an organization as being negative. If individuals fear that the control process will be used not only to judge their performance, but as a basis for punishing them, then it will be feared and reviled. Another reason for this negative view of control is the fact that the essential process of collecting information for control is often seen by some as detracting from their 'real' work. Salespeople, in particular, often see control in this way. For example, they often resent having to fill in visit report forms which contain essential control information because, as they see it, it leaves less time for selling and/or impinges on their home life.

In order to be successful, the people involved and affected by the control process should be consulted in both the design and implementation stages of marketing control. Above all, they will need to be convinced that the purpose of control is to

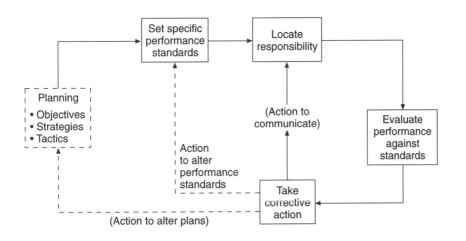

Figure 16.1
An overview of the control process.

improve their own levels of success and that of the company. Subordinates need to be involved in setting and agreeing their own standards of performance, preferably through a system of *management by objectives*.

The control process in action

The strategic control process should enable management to accomplish the following:

1. To allow problems, i.e. deviations from plans and budgets, to be identified at an early stage and on a continuous basis as the plan is being implemented
2. To assess the causes of deviations from standards of performance so that corrective action can be taken
3. To provide an input to the process of identifying and analysing opportunities and threats
4. To provide a positive incentive to staff to improve their performance.

Figure 16.2 shows how the concept of a control process can be translated into action. In the context of a marketing control system, each of the steps involves the following.

 Determining control parameters Determining what to control (the parameters) is the start point of the control process. Overall, sales, costs and profits are the major parameters. But marketing control involves more than just these key parameters. For example, the company may have other key objectives which relate to, for example, social responsibility or innovation/technological reputation. In addition, each of the marketing functions will

Figure 16.2
Steps in the control process.

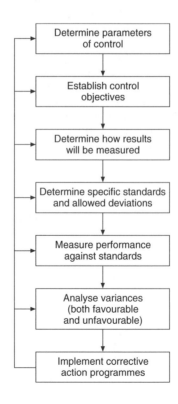

also involve objectives, and hence parameters, which will need to be controlled. The parameters of marketing control must also include those for controlling the marketing objectives and strategies themselves in order to assess if they are still relevant to the marketing environment.

The objectives of control   When we have decided what to control, control objectives can be set. As we have stated, these will encompass functional and financial performance in addition to more qualitative objectives. If planning objectives have been clearly set, the control process can build on these. Each objective must be achieved within a given budget, so budgetary control is essential. Broad control objectives need to be broken down into sub-objectives for each area of marketing activity. Having done this we can then establish specific standards of performance, together with the degree of deviation, if any, which will be tolerated in the system.

Establishing specific standards of performance and allowed deviations   The next step in the control process is to establish specific performance standards which will need to be achieved for each area of activity if overall and sub-objectives are to be achieved. For example, in order to achieve a specified sales objective, a specific target of performance for each sales area may be required. In turn, this may require a specific standard of performance from each of the salespeople in the region with respect to, for example, number of calls, conversion rates and, of course, order value.

Like each standard of performance, we must also try to determine what are allowable deviations for both under- and overperformance. When these allowable deviations are exceeded, then this would initiate some sort of corrective action. Such limits are useful for initiating ongoing control.

Measuring performance   Clearly, standards mean that we must measure performance against them. In addition to determining the appropriate techniques of measurement we also have to determine such things as the frequency of measurement, i.e. daily, weekly, monthly or annually, and the responsibility for measurement, i.e. who should do it. More frequent and more detailed measurement usually means more cost. We need to be careful to ensure that the costs of measurement and the control process itself do not exceed the value of such measurements and do not overly interfere with the activities of those being measured.

Analysing results   The analysis and interpretation of results, prior to taking any action, is one of the most important and yet most difficult steps in the control process. Because marketing is a complex process there is the potential for misinterpreting the causes of variances from standards and hence compounding the problem by taking the wrong corrective action.

The system of marketing control, therefore, requires an information system which is based on disaggregative data so that variances can be broken down into their constituent causes. The system should also allow responsibilities for these variances to be pinpointed so that corrective action can be communicated. The analysis system should also allow sufficient time for detailed analysis to be made so as to avoid taking precipitous actions.

Taking corrective action   The final step in the control process is the implementation of action programmes designed to correct any deviations from standards. There is a temptation to assume that corrective action only needs to be taken when results are less than those required or when budgets and costs are being exceeded. In fact, both 'negative' (underachievement) and 'positive' (overachievement) deviations may require corrective action. For example, failure to spend the amount budgeted for, say, sales force expenses may indicate either that the initial sum allocated was excessive and needs to be reassessed, and/or that the sales force are not as 'active' as they might be. Similarly, overachievement on, say, market share or profitability may mean that overall marketing objectives in these areas need to be looked at again. Clearly, this relates back to the analysis stage of the control sequence, but it shows that *all* significant deviations from standards should be looked at with a view to taking corrective action.

Another question which arises *vis-á-vis* corrective action (and indeed the whole process of control) is timing, i.e. how quickly should corrective action be implemented? This will vary enormously according to the area of control and the nature and extent of deviations from standards. For example, a sudden fall in sales and profits will probably require immediate action. In broader terms, some elements of control will effectively be continuous; for example, the control of sales calls and expenses, which may be carried out on a monthly, weekly or even daily basis. Other areas of control will relate more to the annual planning sequence and will include sales and market share analysis. Finally, we may have control processes which relate to the totality of marketing activities and systems, i.e. a comprehensive examination of the marketing function itself within the organization. In effect, this is a marketing audit, and, as we shall see, it is an essential part of the strategic control process. A full marketing audit will probably be required on a two- or three- yearly basis.

Key areas for control in marketing

Kotler[1] distinguishes four types of marketing control, involving different approaches, different purposes, and a different allocation of responsibilities. (Table 16.1).

Table 16.1 Types of marketing control

Type of control	Prime responsibility	Purpose of control	Examples of techniques/approaches
1. Annual plan control	Top management Middle management	To examine if planned results are being achieved	• Sales analysis • Market share analysis • Marketing expenses to sales ratios • Customer tracking
2. Profit control	Marketing controller	To examine where the company is making and losing money	• Profitability by, e.g. product • Customer group • Trade channel
3. Efficiency control	Line and staff management Marketing controller	To examine ways of improving the efficiency of marketing	• Sales force efficiency • Advertising efficiency • Distribution efficiency
4. Strategic control	Top management Marketing auditor	To evaluate overall marketing planning and implementation systems	• Marketing effectiveness ratings • Marketing audit

Annual plan control

The purpose of annual plan control is to determine the extent to which marketing efforts over the year have been successful. Annual plan control activities are the responsibility of both senior and middle management. Analysis and control will centre on measuring and evaluating sales in relation to sales goals, market share analysis, expense analysis and financial analysis.

Sales analysis

As we have seen in previous chapters, sales performance is understandably a key indicator of marketing effectiveness, and hence an essential element of annual plan control. The marketing budget will specify objectives for sales and according to the company these will be broken down into sales targets for individual parts of the business, customer groups, individual products and/or brands, and ultimately individual salespeople. In other words, sales analysis and control is likely to comprise a hierarchy of standards and control levels, each of which are interlinked, as shown in Figure 16.3.

We can see from this that analysis and control of sales may involve considerable time and effort. Any variance in achieving sales targets at the corporate level are ultimately a result of variances in the performance of individual salespeople. At every level of sales analysis and control, variances must be investigated with a view to determining their causes. For example, at the broadest level variances may be due to one or a combination of volume or price. Put simply, sales revenue may be down on target either because the company has not sold enough and/or because volume has been achieved only on the basis of price cutting. A more detailed analysis of the reasons for volume variances might, in turn, be refined down to volume variances by individual members of the sales force due to, say, poor motivation or bad journey planning.

We can see from this example that throughout the control process we may need to provide disaggregated control information so that broad measures of evaluation and control can be investigated in sufficient detail to pinpoint the causes of possible variances, both favourable and unfavourable, so as to take the necessary corrective action.

Market share analysis

The importance of market share to modern marketing is well known. Indeed, many portfolio techniques of planning are underpinned by the relationship between market

Figure 16.3
The hierarchy of sales analysis and control.

share and cash flow and profits. In addition, and perhaps more importantly in the context of marketing control, marketing objectives, both short- and long-term, are set for market share.

The principal reason for measuring and evaluating market share performance is because it allows a company to assess how well it is doing compared with the overall market and competition. A company might find that while sales volume has declined over the year its market share has increased. Clearly, declining sales volume would still represent a cause for concern. Nevertheless, an increase in market share would indicate that a company is faring better than competitors in a market which has declined overall. This observation would suggest a very different course of action on the part of marketing management than that suggested by a simple analysis of sales.

As the last millennium came to a close, Marks & Spencer were struggling to maintain the sales and profits they had enjoyed in previous years. Perhaps most worrying for Marks & Spencer was their fall in market share. Like most companies, the company realized that even small drops in market share can have a tremendous impact, not only on profitability but also on the market standing and image of a company. Marks & Spencer started the new millennium therefore with a determined effort to recapture lost market share. This has involved substantial restructuring of the company and the introduction of major new lines and store developments, which the company hopes will restore their standing in the market.

As with sales analysis, measurement of market share alone is not sufficient to determine the action(s) to be taken. The evaluation process requires that marketing management determine the reasons for observed levels of company market share and any significant differences and trends. On the basis of this, the marketing manager must then determine the actions required and by whom. Results and conclusions of the evaluation of the annual marketing plan must be discussed with those responsible and a future plan of action agreed.

It is important to recognize that in interpreting market share results, several bases of measuring market share might be needed to provide useful control information for further decision making. For example, Figures 16.4(a)–(d) show how various measures of market share for the same product might produce different pictures of the position of the product in the marketplace. The example shows four possible market share percentages for a hypothetical marketer of car tyres. Figures 16.4(a) and (b) represent this manufacturer's percentage market share by volume and value respectively of the total UK car tyre market. We can see straight away that very different pictures of market share are obtained using these different measures and they may in themselves provide insights into this company's market position compared to competitors.

Figure 16.4(c) represents this company's market share of the replacement (rather than original equipment) UK tyre market. Again we can see that a very different picture of market share is obtained than when using the total UK tyre market as a basis. This simply illustrates that we need to be quite clear about which 'market' we are talking about when we set objectives for market share and how we interpret our performance in this respect.

Figure 16.4(d) uses a measure of market share based on this company's share relative to its largest competitor. As we saw in Chapter 4, relative market share is a key input to many of the so-called 'portfolio techniques' of strategic market planning.

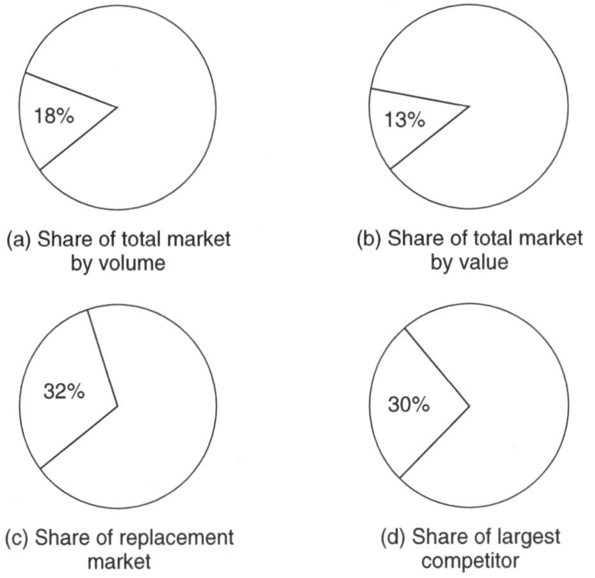

Figure 16.4
Measuring market share: the UK tyre market.

(a) Share of total market by volume — 18%

(b) Share of total market by value — 13%

(c) Share of replacement market — 32%

(d) Share of largest competitor — 30%

Marketing expenses to sales ratios

An important element of the marketing budget is the planned expenditures on the elements of marketing activity designed to achieve budgeted levels of sales. Precisely what these elements comprise, and how they are to be grouped together for the purpose of control and evaluation, will vary from company to company, but common expense areas for marketing would include:

- Sales force expenses
- Promotional expenses
- Distribution expenses
- Market research expenses.

As indicated, each of these groups of expense will comprise a series of activities, each of which may have their own budgeted expense level for the year. For example, promotional expenses may comprise:

- Advertising expenses
- Sales promotion expenses
- Public relations expenses.

Finally, budgeted expenses for each activity may comprise expenses for each product, sales area, customer group and so on. For example, sales force expenses might be broken down into budgeted expenses as shown in Figure 16.5.

As we have seen throughout our discussion of control, the evaluation process in the case of marketing expenses to sales ratios usually starts with broad measures. For example, we should first of all measure and control *total* marketing expenses to sales. We start by determining the standards for marketing expenses to sales together with the upper and lower limits between which we are prepared to allow these expenses to deviate. Ideally, total marketing expenses to sales should be evaluated on a continuous

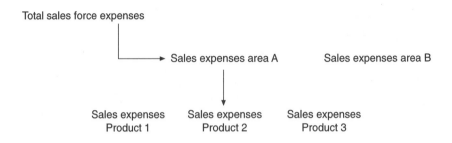

Figure 16.5
Breaking down sales
force expenses.

basis throughout the planning year, normally each month. Where total expenses deviate outside the control limits the reasons should be investigated and corrective action taken. At this stage the broad measure of total marketing expenses to sales will need to be broken down into the previously defined expense areas of sales, promotion, distribution, market research etc. In turn, each of the expense areas can then be further disaggregated in order to pinpoint the precise reasons for deviations from standards. If all this appears to imply a detailed and comprehensive system of marketing expenses control – it does! Provided that the costs of control do not exceed the benefits derived from it, and provided that these benefits are perceived and accepted by those being controlled, then the control system should be as detailed as possible.

Customer tracking

The control elements which we have discussed in the context of the annual marketing plan involve quantitative elements of marketing control. Equally important to the control process are the more qualitative elements of marketing control, and in particular **customer tracking**, the assessment and evaluation of customer feedback and attitudes. Effective marketing control should include the systematic and regular tracking of factors which indicate how customers feel about the company's marketing activities and in particular should highlight any potential problems before they become serious. Examples of information and procedures which would form this part of the control system might include:

- Consumer panel information
- Returns and complaints
- Customer surveys
- Sales force reports.

This last element, sales force reports, is potentially a very valuable source of information on customer attitudes and can highlight early signs of problems. Unfortunately, this element of reporting is often resented by many salespersons, who see it as a chore and a distraction from what they see as their main task of selling. In addition, it might be viewed with some suspicion by salespeople as to how such information might be used for control purposes. Owing to this, care should be taken to ensure that salespeople understand the purpose and accept the value of providing such information.

Customer tracking can be carried out on, say, a monthly basis for such matters as customer complaints, panel data and sales force reports, backed up by customer surveys on a biannual or annual basis. Although most qualitative control will relate to customers, other important publics, such as the local community, watchdog bodies and shareholders, might also usefully be included as part of the qualitative control system.

Profit control: the marketing budget

In addition to the previously discussed control elements of the annual marketing plan, most organizations will, or at least should, be concerned with **profit control**. Already in this chapter we have seen that key areas of marketing control, such as sales analysis and marketing expense analysis, are evaluated against preset standards for both sales and costs. These standards for sales and costs derive from the marketing budget. When we combine the notion of profit control with sales and costs we have the basis of a complete system of budgetary control for marketing.

However, when it comes to the analysis of profits in the budgetary control process, a number of complex and controversial issues arise, not only with respect to the control of profits, but also with respect to the compilation of budgets. We can illustrate these contentions by examining the essence of profitability control.

The focus of profitability control begins with the company evaluating the profitability of different marketing entities. Precisely what these entities will be will vary according to the particular company, and how its profit and cost centres are organized. In addition, the entities may also vary according to the precise purpose of the profitability analysis; but examples of marketing entities would include products, channels of distribution, customer groups and so on. In short, according to Hutt and Speh[2]:

> The essence of profitability control is to describe where the firm is making or losing money in terms of the important segments of its business.

So, let us take a simple example of a one-product company selling to three distinct customer groups as follows:

- Customer Group 1: industrial buyers
- Customer Group 2: institutional buyers
- Customer Group 3: domestic buyers.

A profitability analysis of these marketing entities (in this case, customer groups) would allow marketing management to assess the differences, if any, in profitability between these customer groups and hence the extent to which future strategies and tactics might be designed to reflect this. In order to assess the profitability of these three customer groups we need to be able to associate both costs and revenues with each of them. A simple example will serve to illustrate the problems which can arise when we try to do this for a hypothetical company with its three customer groups.

First of all, let us assume that the overall profit and loss statement for the company is as shown in Table 16.2. As mentioned earlier, if we now want to know the profitability by customer group we have to be able to associate the revenues and costs associated with each. For some elements of the overall profit and loss account this is relatively straightforward. For example, revenues, variable costs, and some elements of marketing expenses, such as sales force costs, marketing research and possibly some elements of the promotional expenses, may be directly attributed to each customer group. This still leaves us, however, with the *fixed costs* and some of the marketing expenses, such as administration and elements of the promotional expenses, which must be in some way *allocated* to each customer group. As Wilson[3] points out, in practice it can sometimes be difficult to identify some aspects of marketing costs.

Certainly, it is possible to devise a way of allocating these remaining costs to our three customer groups, but often, and particularly with fixed costs, the allocation is arbitrary. We may end up with a 'profitability' analysis which is possibly misleading for evaluation and decision making with respect to marketing entities. Related to this,

Table 16.2 The conventional profit and loss statement

	£	£
Sales		100,000
Cost of goods:		
Fixed costs	30,000	
Variable costs	20,000	
Total costs		50,000
Gross margin		50,000
Marketing expenses:		
Advertising	10,000	
Sales force cost	15,000	
Administration	5,000	
Distribution	5,000	
Market research	5,000	
Total marketing expense		40,000
Net profit		10,000

through perhaps more fundamental to the issue of profitability control, is the question of what constitutes an appropriate measure of profitability for marketing entities and marketing effort. Specifically, what we are talking about is the issue of which costs to deduct from revenues for the purpose of marketing profitability control.

In our example, the net profit figure for the company requires the deduction of all costs. Similarly, if we require a net profit figure for each of our customer groups, as we have seen, then the total costs associated with each customer group must be deducted from the revenues derived from that group. For the purposes of control, evaluation and decision making, perhaps a more useful and relevant measure of marketing profitability is *contribution to profit* rather than net profit.

Although there are some differences between the suggested approaches to using these contribution based control mechanisms for marketing profitability, the idea is illustrated in Table 16.3 for one of our hypothetical customer groups. The controllable margin represents the contribution to profits of customer group one, taking into account only those revenues and costs which can be directly attributed to this customer group.

Clearly this is not to deny the importance of net profit to the organization, nor the fact that, in the long run at least, all costs need to be covered. But the contribution approach to marketing budgeting and profitability control recognizes the fact that non-traceable fixed costs lie outside the control of the marketing manager and that to allocate them to marketing entities potentially distorts the picture of the true profitability of these entities, which is after all what we are seeking to establish. Needless to say, a distorted picture also leads to ineffective decision making.

A further broader, but inevitable, issue which the marketing contribution approach raises is whether or not net profits should be included in marketing objectives and budgets, and hence form part of the responsibilities of the marketing department.

Table 16.3 The contribution approach to measuring marketing profitability

		£
Minus	Variable production costs: customer group 1	———
	Manufacturing contribution: customer group 1	
Minus:	Attributable marketing costs for customer group 1	———
	Contribution margin: customer group 1	
	Less the non-variable costs incurred specifically for customer group 1	———
	Controllable margin: customer group 1	≡≡≡

Many believe they should not, in that so many other factors affect net profits which are clearly outside the direct control of marketing. The view taken here is that the contribution method in fact offers a sounder approach to planning and controlling the profitability element of marketing.

Finally, it is important to stress that profitability control requires a carefully designed, predetermined information and control system. In particular, the accountancy system needs to be designed to provide information on costs that can be easily translated into profit performance by the marketing entities of most relevance to the particular organization. Kotler *et al.*[4] acknowledged that budgeting can be extremely difficult but point to the fact that increasingly computer models are being used to facilitate the process.

Efficiency control

As the term suggests, **efficiency control** is concerned with ensuring that each element of the marketing mix, together with their sub-elements, is being utilized as efficiently as possible. Examination of the efficiency of marketing activities may derive from other parts of the control system. For example, we may instigate an examination of efficiency as a result of, say, adverse profitability results for a marketing entity. However, efficiency controls should be built into our marketing planning and control systems so as to make them part of a dynamic system. As an example of how efficiency control might be applied, we can take the example of personal selling.

Personal selling can be evaluated at two levels – first, at the level of the individual salesperson, and second, as we have seen, looking at the total selling effort. The individual salesperson will tend to be evaluated on how well he or she has met performance targets such as:

- Number of sales calls per day
- Strike rate = $\dfrac{\text{Number of orders}}{\text{Number of quotations}}$
- Average order value
- Prospecting success ratio
- Expense targets.

In addition to these quantitative aspects of efficiency, we should also include some qualitative aspects such as, for example:

- Sales skills
- Customer relationships
- Cooperation and attitudes.

The evaluation of the total selling effort is basically derived from the sum of the contributions of all sales personnel. The evaluation of individual sales personnel and the total selling function is often viewed as a negative device for the control of sales-people, this is too narrow a view. A more comprehensive view is that the evaluation process, in addition to providing information about performance, can also be used to motivate and encourage sales personnel to plan their sales campaigns more efficiently and effectively. Hence evaluation brings considerable benefits both to the organization as a whole and to the individual salesperson.

This sort of detailed evaluation and control of marketing efficiency should be applied to each element of marketing mix activity, including advertising, sales promotion and distribution.

Strategic control

 The **strategic control** of marketing planning process pertains to the control of the strategic planning process itself. According to Kotler,[1] two main tools are available to marketing management for strategic control:

1. The marketing effectiveness rating review.
2. The marketing audit.

Control of marketing effectiveness

Control of marketing effectiveness is essentially aimed at evaluating these areas:

- The extent to which the company is customer-oriented
- The extent to which the different functions are integrated with the marketing function, and the extent to which the marketing functions themselves are co-ordinated one with another
- The effectiveness of marketing information systems
- The extent to which there is a strategic perspective to marketing planning, the quality of current strategies and the efficacy of contingency planning
- The extent to which marketing plans are communicated to lower levels, the speed of response to marketing developments and the use of marketing resources.

As we can see, control of marketing effectiveness is wide-ranging, complex and requires considerable management judgement and skill. A questionnaire approach can be used, with marketing effectiveness being scored against a prepared checklist of questions. Total scores are obtained and the organization scored on a scale of marketing effective-ness ranging from poor to superior.

The marketing audit

 Even more wide-ranging than even a marketing effectiveness rating is a full **marketing audit**. The major purpose of a marketing audit is to examine and evaluate periodically, in the light of current circumstances, the marketing objectives and policies which have been guiding the company. A marketing audit is essentially a systematic, critical and impartial review and appraisal of the total marketing operation – of the basic objectives and policies of the operation and the assumptions which underlie them, as well as of the procedures, personnel and organization employed to implement these policies and achieve the objectives.

The audit should also include a careful analysis of the company's marketing environment. Recommendations for improving marketing performance should be a major outcome from the audit process.

Any company carrying out an audit will be faced with two kinds of variable. First, there are variables over which the company has no direct control. These usually take the form which can be described as *environmental and marketable variables*. Secondly, there are variables over which the company has complete control. These can be called *operational variables*.

The process of auditing is usually associated with the financial side of the business and is conducted according to a defined set of accounting standards, which are well documented and easily understood. The total business, moreover, can also be audited, though this process is more complicated and demands considerable powers of judgement. A marketing audit is part of this larger audit and is concerned with the collection and analysis of information and data essential to effective problem solving. As Lancaster and Massingham[5] point out, the marketing audit should be concerned not only with marketing performance but with the overall marketing philosophy in the company. For it to be beneficial, an audit should be carried out on a regular basis and the company should not wait until things start to go wrong.

Carrying out the audit

You will recognize that we have come full circle in the marketing planning process. We began this text by discussing the importance of analysing the environment, followed by an internal appraisal of the company itself. In addition, we stressed the importance of both customers and competitors. We can now remind ourselves of some of these factors by looking at how they form part of the marketing audit.

Auditing the environment   Three distinct elements of the environment are relevant to the marketing audit:

1.   Business/economic and market factors
2.   Competitors
3.   Customer needs and wants.

In the context of the marketing audit, we will now briefly describe some of the factors that will need to be assessed under each category of environmental factors.

Business/economic and market factors   The following elements should be examined during a marketing audit:

- Demographic trends are important to the audit, since it is people who make up markets. A change in the size of the population, its age distribution or its regional distribution may have implications for the type of industry the company is in.
- Markets require purchasing power as well as people. The company should audit the main economic trends. For example, high inflationary pressure may lead to a change in customer expenditure patterns, or an impending shortage of raw materials vital to the firm's business may result in the firm having to increase its costs.

- As we have seen, one of the most dramatic forces shaping people's destiny is technology. Each new technology creates major long-run consequences. The marketer should audit any major changes occurring in product or process technology that can affect the company.

- Any changes in the political/legal environment should also be audited. This environment is made up of laws, government agencies and pressure groups that may influence and constrain organizations and/or individuals. There is a substantial amount of legislation regulating businesses, which protects companies from each other, protects the larger interest of society against unbridled business behaviour and protects customers from unfair business practices.

- As we have seen, the society that people grow up in shapes their basic beliefs, values and norms. The major cultural values of the population are expressed in people's relationships to themselves, others, institutions and society. Companies need to anticipate cultural shifts in order to identify threats. For example, people vary in their attitudes towards corporations, government agencies and other institutions. Most people accept these institutions, but there may be a point in time when they become critical of them and less trusting. A company finding itself in such a position would need to find new ways to win back confidence, perhaps by reviewing advertising communications.

During the 1997 election campaign the Labour party realized that many voters had for various reasons become critical of political parties and less trusting regarding politicians. In part, therefore, their advertising campaign was aimed at trying to find new ways to win back confidence by stressing an increased emphasis on integrity in the new Labour party.

- In addition to these major forces, an examination of trends in the markets the company serves is necessary to reveal what is happening to the market size. It may be increasing or declining, with major segments behaving differently.

Competitors   We looked at competitor analysis in some depth in Chapter 2. As a first step in auditing its competitive environment a company must find out who its direct and indirect competitors are, their objectives, strengths and weaknesses. The industry structure, its growth and the number of competitors in the industry help determine the degree of rivalry between the different firms. The determination of a threat of entry of new firms and the threat of substitute products provides a basis for analysing indirect and possible future competition. However, barriers such as economies of scale tend to deter new entrants. The bargaining power of suppliers refers to the ability of the industry's raw material suppliers to demand higher prices or better terms, and the bargaining power of buyers refers to the ability of the industry's customers to effect price reductions using their combined strength. These are also important factors that can cause competition. The interaction of these forces determines the intensity of competition within the industry, and should be audited on a regular basis.

Customer needs and wants   In Chapter 5, we stressed the fact that any company wishing to achieve a profitable and durable penetration of a market must base its marketing strategy upon a thorough understanding of customer needs and wants. It must also make itself thoroughly familiar with the buying processes utilized by the customer and the factors that influence customers in their choice. This requirement holds for all companies, no matter what their products or the markets to which their efforts are directed. We should remember that industrial or organizational customers will not be buying on their own behalf, but on behalf of an organization, and will respond to a different set of circumstances from an individual. It is always the needs of the ultimate user that must be recognized and satisfied with the product/service. A monitoring of needs in an attempt to identify opportunities and any unsatisfied needs is also required.

The internal audit   The internal part of the marketing audit should be a comprehensive and detailed look at how effectively the marketing part of the organization is currently responding to the environment, and its potential to do so in the future. The audit should encompass:

* Marketing objectives and strategies
* The organizational structure for marketing, including interfaces with other functions
* Marketing systems and procedures, including those for marketing information and control
* Marketing mix elements, i.e. how effective are product, price, place and promotion?
* Sales, market share and profitability analysis.

There is no such thing as a definitive checklist for a marketing audit. Each company must determine for itself what constitutes the detail of an appropriate audit. However, in order to illustrate in more detail the scope of an audit, we give below an illustrative checklist for a marketing audit.

1. *Business and economic environment*

Economic	Inflation
	Unemployment
	Energy prices
	Price volatility
Political/fiscal/legal	Availability of materials, etc.
	Nationalization
	Privatization
	Trade unions
	Taxation
	Duties/levies
	Regulatory constraints, e.g. labelling, quality, safety etc.
Social/cultural	Demographic issues, e.g. age distribution etc.
	Changes in consumer lifestyle
	Environmental issues, e.g. pollution
	Education
	Immigration/emigration
	Religion etc.
Technical	New technology/processes
	Energy saving techniques
	New materials/substitutes
	New equipment
	New products, etc.

The market

Total market	Size (value/volume)
	Growth (value/volumc)
	Trends (value/volume)

Characteristics	Developments etc.
Products	Principal products bought How they are used Where they are used Packaging Accessories etc.
Prices	Price levels/range Terms and conditions of sale Trade practices Special discounts Official regulations etc.
Physical distribution	Principal methods Batch sizes Mechanical handling Protection etc.
Distribution channels	Principal channels Purchasing patterns Geographical disposition Stocks Turnover Incentives Purchasing ability Needs Tastes Profits Prices paid etc.
Communications	Principal methods Sales force Advertising Exhibitions Public relations Promotions New developments etc.
Industry practices	Inter-firm comparisons Trade associations Trade regulations/practices Links with government Historical attitudes Image etc.

Competition

Industry structure	The companies in the industry Their make-up Their market standing/reputation Their capacity to produce, market, distribute Their diversification Their origins and ownership New entrants Mergers and acquisitions Bankruptcies

| | International links |
| | Strengths/weaknesses etc. |

Industry profitability   Historical data
Current performance
Relative performance of competitors
Structure of operating costs
Level of investment
Return on investment
Pricing/volume
Sources of funding etc.

2. *Internal audit*

Sales   Total (value/volume)
By geographical location
By industry/market segment
By customer
By product etc.

Markets   Market share
Profit margins
Marketing procedures
Organization structure
Sales/marketing control data

Marketing mix variables   Market research
Product development
Product range
Product quality
Unit of sale
Stock levels
Distribution
Dealer support
Pricing/discounts/credit
Packaging
Samples
Exhibitions
Selling
Sales aids
Point of sale
Advertising
Sales promotion
Public relations
After-sales service
Training and development

Systems and procedures   Marketing planning system, e.g. is it effective?
Marketing objectives, e.g. clear, consistent with corporate objectives?
Marketing strategy, e.g. appropriate for objectives?
Structure, e.g. are duties and responsibilities clear?
Information, e.g. adequacy of marketing intelligence, its presentation?
Control, e.g. suitable mechanisms?
Communications, e.g. effective? in all areas?

Interfunction efficiency, e.g. between functions/departments?
Profitability, e.g. regular monitoring and analysis?
Cost effectiveness, e.g. are functions/products continually
reviewed in attempts to reduce excess costs?

We can see from this list that the marketing audit is far reaching and potentially complex. It encompasses not only marketing performance but also the underpinning objectives and strategies of the company. Enis and Garfein[6] illustrate once again how computing power is coming to the rescue with regard to dealing with the complexity of the full marketing audit. In terms of conducting the audit, Ferrell *et al.*[7] highlight the importance of ensuring that the elements of the audit match the elements of the marketing strategies which underpin it. The implication of this is that the precise nature of the marketing audit and the elements contained therein should be company-specific, reflecting the individual strategy of that company. We must be careful though in the application of audit 'checklists', including, it must be stated, that of our own included in Chapter 19. Checklists are useful but should be used with care and discretion in selecting those elements which are appropriate to a particular company and its situation.

Summary

The final, but often neglected stage of strategic market planning is the control process. Not only is control important to evaluate how we have performed but it completes the circle of planning in that it provides the feedback necessary for the start of the next planning cycle.

Control is often viewed with suspicion by those whose activities are being controlled and so needs to be implemented with some sensitivity by senior management. In particular, it is important to involve people in the setting of standards and in the process of determining and agreeing corrective action.

Every element of marketing should be controlled using both quantitative and qualitative standards for performance. The most obvious areas of control relate to the control of the annual marketing plan and include sales control, control of market share, control of expenses and customer tracking. In addition, profitability control is an essential element of marketing control, preferably using a contribution rather than net profit basis.

Control of marketing efficiency involves potentially detailed analysis of each and every element of the marketing mix. Again, although some of these are difficult to evaluate, for example the efficiency of advertising spend, it is possible provided clear objectives and standards of performance, which are essential stages in the control process, are established.

Finally, the control process should stretch to the evaluation of the effectiveness of the marketing process itself in the organization. The marketing audit represents the most comprehensive process of marketing control and seeks to assess the entirety of a company's marketing system with a view to establishing what future strategies and actions will be required to match an ever changing and turbulent marketing environment.

Key terms

Noise [p431]
Control parameters [p433]
Customer tracking [p438]
Profit control [p439]

Efficiency control [p441]
Strategic control [p442]
Marketing audit [p443]

Questions

1 Why is the evaluation and control of marketing probably one of the weakest areas of marketing practice in many companies, and what can be done about overcoming this weakness?
2 What are the essentials of the control process, and what should the strategic control process enable the management of a company to accomplish?
3 Using examples, outline the main types and areas of marketing control.
4 Why is market share analysis often used as one of the main control and evaluation areas of marketing, and what are the problems of using it?
5 Outline the nature and purpose of the marketing audit and discuss the steps in carrying out such an audit.

References

1. Kotler, P., *Marketing Management: Analysis, Planning, Implementation and Control*, 9th edn, Prentice-Hall, New Jersey, 1997, p. 765.
2. Hutt, M. D. and Speh, T. W., *Business Marketing Management*, 5th edn, Dryden Press, Chicago, 1995, p. 546.
3. Wilson, R. M. S. *Strategic Marketing Management*, Butterworth-Heinemann, 1998.
4. Kotler, P., Armstrong, G., Saunders, J. and Wong, V., *Principles of Marketing*, 2nd European edn, Prentice Hall, Europe, 1999, p. 115.
5. Lancaster, G. A. and Massingham, L., *Essentials of Marketing*, 3rd edn, McGraw-Hill, London, 1999, p. 357.
6. Enis, B. and Garfein, S. J., 'The computer-driven marketing audit', *Journal of Management Enquiry*, December 1992, pp. 306–318.
7. Ferrell, O. C., Hartline, M. D., Lucas, G. H. and Luck, D., *Marketing Strategy*, Harcourt Brace, Orlando, 1999, p. 160.

Case Study

Richard Sole is worried about the latest sales figures for his company. As marketing manager, he is concerned that over a twelve month period sales have dropped by some 10 %. But more than this, he knows that he will have to present and explain these figures to the main board at the company's annual review of results.

He knows that, understandably, the directors will want answers as to why sales have dropped. After all, in the previous five years that the company has been trading, sales have increased every year. The problem is that Richard simply does not know why sales have dropped, nor what this means in the context of the market as a whole.

For the past two years, he has been arguing that the control and evaluation systems in the company, particularly with respect to marketing activities, have been neglected. In arguing for more resources and effort in this area, however, the directors have always been

able to point to the fact that there was no need to put more effort into this area of evaluation and control because sales were constantly rising. Richard now feels caught in a trap in the sense that he is going to have to explain the reasons for a drop in sales, but without having had the support of the necessary control and evaluation techniques required to provide this information.

He is, however, determined to use the situation to reinforce his case for improved control and evaluation techniques, including the resources necessary to implement these. At the moment, the company has in operation only a system of profit control which can be used to examine profitability by product and customer group. In addition, there is a relatively crude system of sales analysis. There is no market share analysis, no systems of customer tracking, no efficiency controls, and no systems of strategic control in the company. Richard is determined to make his case for implementing some of these key areas of marketing control in the company at the forthcoming meeting.

QUESTION

Prepare Richard's case for the types of controls he feels are necessary.

17

Services marketing: relationship marketing

Chapter objectives

By the end of this chapter you will:

▶ Understand the nature and scope of services marketing.

▶ Be aware of the special issues which the marketing of service products gives rise to.

▶ Understand the reasons for the emergence of relationship marketing.

▶ Be familiar with the key concepts and techniques of relationship marketing.

Introduction

Several times already we have touched on what are probably two of the most significant developments to affect the marketing manager in recent years. The first is the continued growth in importance of the so-called service industries with an attendant rise of course in services marketing, while the second is the shift towards what is termed a relationship approach to marketing. Each of these developments have had major implications for marketing theory and practice. So much so that it would be remiss for any contemporary marketing manager not to understand the nature, significance and implications of these two developments. In this chapter therefore, we expand on the nature and meaning of both services marketing and relationship marketing, together with the implications of these two aspects of marketing for the practising marketing manager.

Services marketing

In Chapter 7 we mentioned the growth of service industries, pointing out that in some economies, including the UK and US, the service sectors now predominate. The reasons

451

for this growth need not concern us here except to note that in the future more and more of the developed economies will move towards a preponderance of service industries and products. In short, then, many of the marketing managers of the future will be involved in services marketing. This shift towards services would perhaps not matter if marketing of services was exactly the same as marketing physical products. However, as noted in Chapter 7, although many of the basic principles involved in marketing service products are much the same as for their physical-product counterparts, service products do have a number of characteristics which set them aside from physical products and give rise to additional issues with regard to their marketing and in particular to the elements of the marketing mix. We can now discuss some of these differences and their implications in more detail, first of all what is meant by a service product.

What is a service product: intangibility and non-ownership

Remember the term '**service product**' encompasses a myriad of different types of services. However the definition proposed by Berry[1] is still one of the most effective definitions in capturing some of the key distinguishing characteristics of many different types of service products:

> A service is an intangible product involving a deed, a performance, or an effort that cannot be physically possessed.

There is little doubt that both intangibility and non-ownership are key characteristics of service products, though, as we shall see later there are other characteristics which are also important. Sticking for a moment however with Berry's definition, if we consider for example air travel, which few would doubt is a service product, we can see that the product is essentially intangible and the customer certainly does not take physical possession as such. Admittedly, there are tangible elements to the product. The aeroplane itself, the seat we occupy, the meals and drinks we are served, are all very much tangible aspects of the air travel product. In addition, we do take 'physical possession' of certain elements of the product – for example, the seat, the meals and drinks. But the core benefit that the customer is purchasing is essentially intangible.

This example shows that most products have a mixture of both tangible and intangible components. If we think of tangibility as a continuum, service products are those where the intangible element is predominant. This idea of a continuum of intangibility is frequently encountered in texts on services marketing and is a useful way of evaluating whether the customer is buying what is essentially a tangible product or a service. An example for business products/services from Shostack[2] is shown in Figure 17.1.

A brief list of examples of where the intangible element is dominant, and hence examples of what we would define as service products, includes:

- Fast food
- Hotels
- Holidays
- Travel
- Insurance and banking
- Health care
- Legal/financial advice
- Consultancy
- Personal health and beauty.

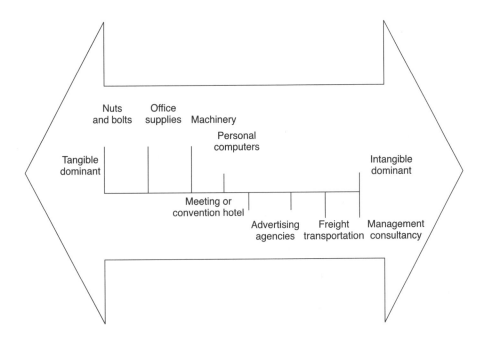

Figure 17.1
A continuum of tangibility and intangibility: business product-service classifications. Source adapted from Schostack, G.L., 'Breaking free from product marketing', *Journal of Marketing*, **41**, April 1977, p. 177.

Clearly, there are literally thousands of different service products. An important fact to note, however, is that although they are usually relatively easy for the marketer to classify as being service or non-service products, ultimately it is the customer who decides whether or not a product or service is being purchased – and hence marketed – according to the relative importance he or she attaches to the tangible versus the intangible elements.

Intangibility then is certainly one of the key characteristics that distinguishes service products. But what about the notion of 'non-possession' referred to in Berry's definition, and what are the other distinguishing or special characteristics of service products that we have referred to? These other suggested special characteristics of service products, including the aspect of non-possession or if you prefer non-ownership, are outlined below. As with the characteristic of tangibility remember that these so-called 'special characteristics' are also a matter of degree and therefore best thought of as a continuum. For each of these characteristics we have also outlined the marketing implications and issues which these characteristics give rise to.

Non-ownership

As explained in our air travel example a characteristic of many services is that they are used rather than owned. Another example is a holiday where we simply use the services of the holiday provider as opposed to taking physical possession of a product.

Non-ownership can sometimes make it difficult for a customer to assess and appreciate all the advantages of purchasing the service. The marketer therefore needs in some cases to pay particular attention to stressing the benefits of non-ownership, such as no long-term commitment and no expensive maintenance, in promotional programmes.

At one time few private car buyers in the UK would have considered leasing a car on a long-term basis as opposed to purchasing one either outright or on credit. However, partly as a way to help customers finance the use of a car, over the last ten years the majority of the major car manufacturers have introduced what effectively are leasing schemes albeit often under other names. An increasing number of customers not only find this a more convenient way of covering the costs of having access to a new car, but are also finding that there are many benefits to not actually taking ownership as such of a vehicle.

Inseparability

Unlike the majority of physical products, services are often consumed at the same point and at the same time as they are produced. For example, when we pay a visit to the hairdressers, with perhaps one or two obvious exceptions, normally the hairdresser 'produces' his/her services while we are there in the hairdresser's premises. Production and consumption are simultaneous and therefore producer and consumer are inseparable. Needless to say, in such a situation the person(s) providing the service become very, very important and in many ways actually are the service product. An interesting aspect of this inseparability of consumer and service provider is that both provider and customer affect the 'quality' of the relationship.

Inseparability places an increased emphasis on the selection and training of the service provider's personnel. The service provider must also be careful to examine the circumstances and processes that can affect the quality of the relationship between provider and consumer.

Perishability

Generally, service products cannot be stored. For example, if a restaurant is not filled for the night, if a hotel room is not booked, or if an aeroplane flies with empty seats, then these services or rather the rooms or seats that the provider was hoping to fill cannot be 'stored' and sold later. The revenue that would otherwise have accrued had the room been let or the aeroplane seat booked has been lost for ever.

The fact that service products have this perhaps surprisingly high degree of perishability makes effective matching of demand and supply of service products particularly important. This is especially so with service products where there are periods of excess demand and/or periods of excess supply. The marketer therefore needs to manage the balance between demand and supply and may use devices such as differential pricing, the development of complementary services, effective pre-booking systems, and the use of part-time staff to ensure effective matching of demand and supply.

Variability

Because service products have a high 'people' content, i.e. there is a significant human element in the provision of many services, the quality of the service product is potentially much more variable than with a physical product. As consumers, we have all probably experienced this variability of services. What the service provider must seek to minimize is the customer experiencing poor service as a result of people variability.

Variability therefore means that the marketer must pay particular attention to quality control. Staff selection and training become very important to the service marketer, as do quality control systems such as customer care.

These then, together with the intangibility and non-ownership characteristics discussed earlier, are some of the distinguishing features of services. We have also indicated some of the implications for the marketer associated with these characteristics. Perhaps the major implication of these characteristics, however, is the notion of an extended marketing mix for service products, which was briefly introduced in Chapter 7 and to which we now return.

The marketing mix for services

The characteristics of service products mean they must be marketed in a somewhat different way from other products. Kotler[3] argues that traditional '4 Ps' marketing approaches often work well for physical products, but additional elements are required in service businesses. Similarly, specialist service marketing experts such as Baron[4] or Lovelock[5] agree that the traditional marketing mix of the '4 Ps' needs to be extended to '7 Ps' for services. These three additional 'Ps' again, you will recall were introduced in Chapter 7 and are 'People', 'Physical Evidence' and 'Process'. We shall now expand on these additional elements in turn.

People

The characteristics of inseparability and variability associated with service products in particular mean that the service provider's staff (People) are an extremely important element of the marketing mix for services. As already indicated, this means that the selection and training of service staff is an important part of the overall marketing effort of the service provider, but in addition it is important that service staff also are adequately motivated and therefore often rewarded, to provide effective and, to the customer pleasing interactions. In particular front-line employees, those who have direct contact with the customer, should exhibit enthusiastic, positive and caring attitudes. Staff should also be, wherever possible, empowered to deal with minor customer complaints as they occur rather than having to refer them to a senior manager or head office before any action is taken. Many companies encourage this by allowing their front-line personnel to refund customers where necessary or provide additional services.

Many of the fast-food retailers such as Pizza Express and McDonalds empower their restaurant staff to deal immediately with any customer complaints. For example, if a customer is unhappy about the quality or even quantity of a meal the front-line staff have the discretion to offer either a full refund, a replacement meal or additional portions.

Physical evidence

Because of the intangibility of services, it can often be difficult for consumers to evaluate service offerings, particularly aspects such as quality and value for money, prior to purchase. In the same way this intangibility can also make it difficult for the marketer to position new service product offerings. Because of this the marketer often needs to 'tangibilize' the service offering by managing the **'physical evidence'** that accompanies the service. Physical evidence includes aspects such as the service provider's buildings/facilities and staff appearance, including personal hygiene and uniforms. Even promotional material and branding strategies can be included as elements of physical evidence that serve to tangibilize a service offering to a customer.

Needless to say, many service marketers are aware of the importance of physical evidence and the use by the potential customer of such evidence to gauge, accurately or inaccurately, things like service quality. Many service marketers therefore place great emphasis on the appearance of their employees, often spending large amounts of their marketing budgets on aspects such as staff grooming and uniforms. In addition, the service marketer must pay particular attention to achieving consistency throughout the promotional mix with regard to things like the use of company colours, logos, etc.

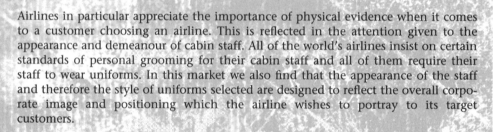

Airlines in particular appreciate the importance of physical evidence when it comes to a customer choosing an airline. This is reflected in the attention given to the appearance and demeanour of cabin staff. All of the world's airlines insist on certain standards of personal grooming for their cabin staff and all of them require their staff to wear uniforms. In this market we also find that the appearance of the staff and therefore the style of uniforms selected are designed to reflect the overall corporate image and positioning which the airline wishes to portray to its target customers.

Process

In Chapter 7 we indicated that 'Process' relates to how the service is provided. Again, inseparability and intangibility are important characteristics underpinning this seventh 'P' of the marketing mix. But the characteristic of variability also underpins the importance of process. The **process** element of the services marketing mix relates to procedures for dealing with customers at the point of contact or before, such as when taking orders and procedures for supplying the service itself including the production processes and organizational systems required to provide the service. The process element of the mix should above all be planned and run to ensure consistency in service delivery in line with pre-determined levels of customer service. Elements such as staff training and motivation are important in the process element of the marketing mix, but so too are the 'technical' systems such as production, ordering facilities, delivery services, and so on. The process element of the marketing mix for services can be a major way of differentiating a service provider from the competition. This, coupled with the fact that successful process systems and services markets are often readily and easily copied, means that the services marketer needs to be constantly looking for new service innovations with regard to the process element.

These then are some of the major distinguishing or special characteristics of service products together with some of the major additional marketing issues and complexities which they give rise to. Again, we should stress that many of the other elements of effective marketing management and strategy, for example the need for effective segmentation and targeting, adequate market research and information systems, are no different for services as opposed to physical products. In addition, both types of marketing are being impacted by the second major development in marketing thought and practice discussed in this chapter, namely the growth of relationship marketing, to which we now turn our attention.

Relationship marketing

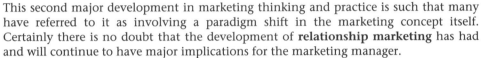

This second major development in marketing thinking and practice is such that many have referred to it as involving a paradigm shift in the marketing concept itself. Certainly there is no doubt that the development of **relationship marketing** has had and will continue to have major implications for the marketing manager.

As so often, there are many different views as to the precise nature and hence definition of relationship marketing. So, for example, Gronroos[6] stresses the element of mutual exchange and trust in relationship marketing as follows.

> Relationship marketing is a process including several parties or actors, the objectives of which have to be met. This is done by mutual exchange and fulfillment of promises, a fact that makes trust an important aspect of marketing.

Stone and Woodcock[7] on the other hand put more emphasis on the more traditional tools of sales, communications and customer care techniques.

> Relationship marketing involves the use of a wide range of marketing, sales, communications and customer care techniques and processes to: identify named individual customers, create a relationship between the company and these customers, and manage that relationship to the benefit of both customers and company.

Perhaps one of the simplest and yet most powerful summaries of what relationship marketing is however, is that provided by Buttle[8].

> At its best, RM (relationship management) is characterized by a genuine concern to meet or exceed the expectations of customers and to provide excellent service in an environment of trust and commitment to the relationship.

Moreover, Buttle goes on to indicate what is involved in successful relationship marketing and the commitment of the company required to generate this success:

> To be successful relationship marketers, companies must develop a supportive organizational culture, market the RM idea internally, intimately understand customers' expectations, create and maintain a detailed customer database, and organize and reward employees in such a way that the objective of RM, customer retention, is achieved.

This illustrates that relationship marketing has major implications for the practice of marketing, including the provision of marketing information, organizational systems and procedures and the elements of marketing strategy. But what are the characteristics of a relationship marketing approach, and in particular, how does relationship marketing compare and contrast with the more conventional so-called 'transaction' marketing approach? In addition, it is useful to consider why relationship marketing has emerged as a suggested new paradigm for marketing, and some of the key implications of this new paradigm for marketing management practice.

The nature of relationship of marketing: a comparison with transaction marketing

The notion of relationship marketing first began to appear in business-to-business marketing, but for reasons we shall see shortly, the relationship marketing approach is now evident in the services sector and is becoming increasingly important in consumer marketing. To understand the nature of relationship marketing, it is useful to compare and contrast relationship marketing with the more conventional and traditional transaction marketing approach.

 Conventional **transaction marketing**, although based on the notion of mutual exchange, is essentially based on the seller offering immediate and hopefully attractive combinations of product, price, technical support, etc. in order to generate a sale. The emphasis, although perhaps implicitly, is on completing this individual transaction and this completion is the measure of success of the exchange. The marketer then moves on to finding the next customer and/or with the same customer generating another individual transaction next time round. The buyer is interested in the best possible value from the exchange and there is little emphasis on customer service or long-term relationships by either party.

Lancaster and Massingham[9] argue that this emphasis in traditional transaction marketing on the one-off exchange is what distinguishes transaction from relationship marketing. In relationship marketing the emphasis switches to developing a longer term and interactive set of relationships between the marketer and customers based on partnership and sharing. Although transactions and of course immediate satisfaction are still important to both parties, in relationship marketing the success of the exchange is the extent to which both parties benefit through co-operation and agreement. In the most successful examples of relationship marketing the two parties grow more trusting, more knowledgeable about each others' interests and needs, and more interested in helping each other. Transactions cease to be negotiated each time and become part of a longer-term routine. The outcome of successful relationship marketing is the development of solid, dependable supplier–customer relationships which form the basis of a marketing network and represent a true marketing asset.

In fact, relationship marketing, as opposed to traditional transaction marketing, can be seen as opposite ends of a continuum in much the same way as we considered the characteristics of services marketing earlier. The distinctions between transaction marketing and relationship marketing already highlighted, together with additional key areas of difference, are well summarised by Kotler[10] and are shown in Table 17.1.

Table 17.1 Transaction marketing versus relationship marketing

Transaction marketing	Relationship marketing
Focus on single sale	Focus on customer retention
Orientation on product features	Orientation on product benefits
Short time scale	Long time scale
Little emphasis on customer service	Significant emphasis on customer service
Limited commitment to customer	High commitment to customer
Moderate customer contact	Extensive customer contact
Quality is primarily concern of production	Quality is concern of all functions

Source: Adapted from Kotler, P., *Marketing Management: Analysis, Planning, Implementation and Control,* 7th edn, Prentice-Hall, Englewood Cliffs, NJ, 1991.

We can see from this table that relationship and transaction marketing are indeed very different in several respects. But why has relationship marketing emerged? What has given rise to this paradigm shift in the concept of marketing?

Reasons for the growth of relationship marketing

The long-established notions of exchange and interaction in marketing provide theoretical antecedents for the emergence of relationship marketing. However, as Lancaster and Massingham[11] point out, the growth of relationship marketing is in fact down to more hard-nosed pragmatic reasons. Put simply, they assert, both marketer and customer have increasingly recognized that relationship marketing, and in particular the requirements needed to develop effective relationship marketing such as the building of strong trust and confidence between the two parties, the exchange of information and effective communication, and mutual support simply makes good sense.

In part, this explains why relationship marketing first began to emerge in business-to-business markets where relationship marketing was seen to make good commercial sense. For the marketer, building long-term relationships with customers can lead to substantially lower marketing and other costs. For example, lower costs are incurred in advertising and promotion in order to attract and keep customers. Selling costs too can be lower, particularly in business to business markets, where salespeople do not have to call on as many prospective new customers. Both implicitly and explicitly relationship marketing focuses on customer retention. Companies have at long last realized the financial value of keeping customers. Cram[12] illustrates that the lifetime value of loyal customers is potentially huge. Similarly, Kotler[13] suggests that today's companies must pay closer attention to their customer defection rates and take strategic steps to keep these rates to a minimum. Relationship marketing is one of the key tools in improving customer retention rates in a company. Estimates vary, but on average it can be up to six to eight times more expensive to create a new customer than to keep an existing one. Not only are business-to-business marketers now aware of the financial pay-off of building long-term lasting relationships with their customers. Increasingly, fast-moving consumer goods (FMCG) too have recognized this importance. As we shall see, because of this one of the key implications of relationship marketing is the emphasis it puts on managing and improving customer retention rates.

Needless to say, however, relationship marketing would not have increased in importance were there no benefits for the customer. In fact, relationship marketing can only be of value where it also bestows important and valued benefits to customers. Again, in the case of business-to-business customers these benefits are often easy to identify, and indeed therefore to communicate, and are largely but not exclusively financial in nature. For example, for the manufacturing customer developing effective relationships with suppliers enables effective implementation of more effective systems of production and purchasing such as Just-In-Time (JIT) systems which were discussed earlier. Similarly, as we saw in Chapter 7, more and more companies are involved in collaborative ventures with regard to developing new products with their suppliers. Clearly this requires effective long-term relationships. Perhaps less obviously though a relationship marketing approach also potentially bestows benefits on the customer in consumer goods markets. Obviously, if a customer feels they can purchase the same brand every time this can substantially help reduce the time and effort required to purchase. Similarly, having a trusted brand reduces the risks to the customer of making a wrong or perhaps ill-advised purchase decision. Finally, many of the relationship marketing campaigns used in consumer markets actually involve some sort of financial inducement for the customer to become involved in a long-term relationship with the marketer. The use of loyalty cards, for example, allied to bonus points in grocery retailing, or similar financial inducements through 'frequent fliers clubs' in the airline industry, illustrate this approach.

Overall, then, as one would expect from any successful relationship, both parties can and indeed need to benefit if relationship marketing is to be appropriate and successful. In this respect, Barbara Bund-Jackson[14] has suggested that the development of a relationship marketing approach is not always appropriate for all customers. Indeed, she suggests that some customers are in fact better managed through the traditional transaction marketing approach. These customers she refers to as **'always-a-share' customers**. These are customers who have low switching costs in terms of changing suppliers/brands and therefore can change relatively easily. Because of this, they do not value long-term relationships with suppliers and indeed prefer to negotiate individual transactions each time a purchase is made. Other types of customers in this category include customers who are making 'one-off' purchases and hence are obviously not interested in supplier relationships. Any would-be supplier, therefore, is always in a position to gain a share of this type of customer's business. Bund-Jackson points out that relationship marketing with such customers is ineffective and indeed inappropriate.

In contrast, she has termed the customers who are best suited to a relationship marketing approach as **'lost-for-good' customers**. The characteristics of such customers are that they have high switching costs in terms of changing suppliers, they tend to have longer time horizons, make a series of purchases over time, and view commitments to particular suppliers as important and preferably relatively permanent. Once a supplier has won this type of account, the customer is likely to remain loyal to the supplier for a long time. If lost, however, the customer often never returns to the supplier, hence the term 'lost-for-good'. An increasing number of customers, particularly in business-to-business markets are such lost-for-good customers. There are many reasons for this; for example, as we have already seen, the growth in JIT in manufacturing industry requires very close co-operation and high levels of loyalty and trust between supplying and purchasing companies. This can only be achieved by both supplier and buyer taking a long-term relationship marketing approach. Obviously one of the first steps in developing relationship marketing, and indeed in determining whether a relationship marketing approach should be used at all, is to identify which customers merit a relationship marketing strategy.

The implications of relationship marketing

There are several far-reaching implications for the marketer associated with the emergence and growth of relationship marketing. Some of the more important of these implications are discussed below. First of all, relationship marketing heightens the need for more effective two-way communication between the marketer and customers. For example, some companies have introduced direct, on-line communication between themselves and their customers. Clearly such communication is facilitated by the use of new information technology including e-mails and the Internet.

A second implication of relationship marketing is that everyone in the supplying company, and not just the marketing function, needs to be concerned with generating customer satisfaction. This heightens the importance of internal marketing in companies. Recently some companies have introduced the notion of '**Total Relationship Marketing**' (TRM). Zineldin[15] suggests that the main philosophy behind the TRM approach is to facilitate, create, develop, enhance, and continuously improve all internal and external relationships with customers, employees and collaborators.

Systems must be in place with relationship marketing to enable constant tracking and assessment of customer satisfaction and needs. Customer databases and the introduction of total quality management are important in implementing an effective relationship marketing approach.

Relationship marketing, as we have seen is based on developing long-term relationships with customers and hence heightens the need for building and maintaining customer loyalty. Although there are many reasons for their introduction, customer loyalty schemes as introduced by many retailers and discussed earlier in this chapter are examples of how companies are concentrating on customer retention. In discussing the importance of managing and improving customer retention rates Kotler[16] discusses three ways in which a company can attempt to build and maintain stronger relationships with existing customers:

1. *Adding financial benefits.* Essentially, as you would perhaps expect, this involves rewarding customers financially for being loyal. For example, frequent customers may be offered additional discounts. Similarly, customers may be given some sort of reward points which they can use, say, to exchange for gifts or lower prices at a later stage. Obviously, the more loyal they are, the more points they accrue.

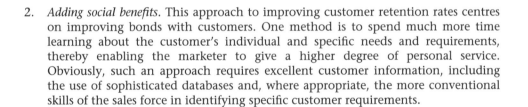

The supermarket group Tesco was amongst one of the first retailers in the UK to introduce a loyalty card system. At first, many of its competitors thought that this was a throwback to the 1960s when consumers were offered stamps with their purchases which they could later trade in exchange for products from a catalogue. Many of these competitors felt that customers would not be bothered to collect their reward points let alone be induced to shop at Tesco because they were available. They very quickly changed their minds when they found that they were losing market share to Tesco partly as a result of Tesco's loyalty scheme. Needless to say many of these competitors were quick to follow Tesco's example when they saw how successful the scheme was proving to be.

2. *Adding social benefits.* This approach to improving customer retention rates centres on improving bonds with customers. One method is to spend much more time learning about the customer's individual and specific needs and requirements, thereby enabling the marketer to give a higher degree of personal service. Obviously, such an approach requires excellent customer information, including the use of sophisticated databases and, where appropriate, the more conventional skills of the sales force in identifying specific customer requirements.

The banking industry has increasingly been using the notion of social bonds to improve customer retention rates. At one time, up to the 1970s and early 1980s, many banks had personal relationships with their customers, with customers often knowing and dealing with a bank manager on a close personal basis. During the late 1980s and early 1990s the banks moved away from this personal approach in an effort to reduce costs and become more like retailers than bankers. Recently, however, some of the banks have been making determined efforts to rebuild bonds with individual customers by learning about their customers' individual and specific needs and by giving personal care. The Natwest Bank for example has introduced a product for its current account holders who may for a fee be given access to a range of banking services which are specifically designed to meet their individual banking needs. In short, personal service is returning to at least part of the UK banking system.

3.   *Adding structural ties.* Although there are several ways in which this approach to building and maintaining stronger relationships with customers can be implemented, essentially it involves providing customer support in the form of expertise and/or equipment which helps customers run their business. At the same time, the expertise or equipment provided helps to lock the customer in to the supplier. In other words, this approach increases the switching costs, mentioned earlier, for a customer. Examples would include companies providing computer software to a customer which helps the customer run a production schedule which is specific to the supplier. Another example would be the supply of electronic data interchange (EDI) systems for purchasing.

These then are just some of the ways in which a company can attempt to build and maintain stronger relationships with their customers. In turn the application of some of the marketing mix elements is affected by the adoption of a relationship marketing approach. As we saw in Chapter 12, personal selling in particular requires a fundamentally different approach under the relationship marketing concept compared to transaction marketing.

Summary

In this chapter we have looked at the special issues associated with the marketing of service products and the reasons for, together with the implications of, the development of relationship marketing. In the case of services marketing we have seen that the special characteristics of services compared to their physical product counterparts does indeed give rise to additional considerations in their marketing. In particular, services marketing requires us to consider an additional '3 Ps' in an extended marketing mix to encompass People, Physical evidence, and Process considerations. One of the most far-reaching developments in marketing recently is the emergence of the so-called relationship marketing concept. Relationship marketing effectively adds another layer to the notion of consumer orientation, and in particular emphasizes the benefits of building long-term lasting relationships with customers based on trust and communication. Initially applied to business-to-business markets, the concept and techniques of relationship marketing have now spread into both services and consumer goods marketing. Marketers now recognize that building long-term customer loyalty and paying careful attention to retaining customers can provide major long-term benefits to both parties.

Key terms

Service product [p452]
Physical evidence [p456]
Process [p456]
Relationship marketing [p457]
Transaction marketing [p458]

Always-a-share customers [p460]
Lost-for-good customers [p460]
Total relationship marketing (TRM) [p461]

Questions

1. Using examples, discuss what you feel to be the key distinguishing characteristics of service products.
2. Discuss the following characteristics of service products in each case indicating the implications of the characteristic for the marketing of service products:
   (a) Inseparability
   (b) Perishability
   (c) Variability.
3. Using examples discuss what is meant by each of the following additional marketing mix elements in services marketing:
   (a) People
   (b) Physical evidence
   (c) Process.
4. Compare and contrast relationship versus transaction marketing.
5. Discuss what you feel to be some of the major implications of adopting a relationship marketing approach for the development of marketing strategies.

References

1. Berry, L. L., 'Services marketing is different', *Business Horizons*, May–June 1980, pp. 24–29.
2. Schostack, G. L., 'Breaking free from product marketing', *Journal of Marketing*, **41**, April 1977.
3. Kotler, P., *Marketing Management: Analysis, Planning, Implementation and Control,* 9th edn, Prentice-Hall, Englewood Cliffs, NJ, 1997, p. 472.
4. Baron, S., *Services Marketing: Text and Cases*, The MacMillan Press Ltd, Basingstoke, Hampshire, 1995.
5. Lovelock, H., *Services Marketing*, 3rd edn, Prentice-Hall, Englewood Cliffs, NJ, 1996.
6. Gronroos, C., 'From marketing mix to relationship marketing: towards a paradigm shift in marketing', *Management Decision*, **32**, 2, pp. 4–20.
7. Stone, M. and Woodcock, N., *Relationship Marketing*, Kogan Page Ltd, London, 1995.
8. Buttle, F., *Relationship Marketing: Theory and Practice*, Paul Chapman Publishing Ltd, London, 1996, p. 13.
9. Lancaster, G. and Massingham, L., *Essentials of Marketing*, 3rd edn, McGraw-Hill Publishing Co, Maidenhead, Berkshire, 1999, p. 340.
10. Kotler, P., *Marketing Management: Analysis, Planning, Implementation and Control*, 7th edn, Prentice-Hall, Englewood Cliffs, NJ, 1991.
11. Lancaster, G. and Massingham, op. cit. p. 343.
12. Cram, T., *The Power of Relationship Marketing – How to Keep Customers for Life*, Pitman Publishing, London, 1994.
13. Kotler, P., *Marketing Management: Analysis, Planning, Implementation and Control*, 9th edn, Prentice-Hall, Englewood Cliffs, NJ, 1997, p. 720.
14. Bund-Jackson, B., 'Build customer relationships that last', *Harvard Business Revenue*, November–December, **63**, 1985, pp. 120–128.
15. Zineldin, M., 'Exploring the common ground of total relationship management (TRM) and total quality management (TQM), *Management Decision*, **37**, 9, pp. 709–718.
16. Kotler, P., *Marketing Management: Analysis, Planning, Implementation and Control*, 8th edn, Prentice-Hall, Englewood Cliffs, NJ, 1994, pp. 48–52.

Stephen Collop has recently joined Marine Services Ltd, a specialist consultancy company providing technical advice and services to marine exploration companies. Stephen's background, somewhat unusually in this industry, is entirely in consumer services marketing. The company has employed him for this expertise and experience, believing that it is lacking in its knowledge and application of up-to-date marketing ideas and techniques being used so successfully in other industries. Marketing in the past in this company has been dominated by people with technical backgrounds and an in-depth knowledge of marine biology, marine engineering and marine exploration.

The idea to introduce a marketing specialist to the company came from the managing director of the company who has recently attended a couple of courses at the CIM College in Cookham, Berkshire. The first of these courses was on services marketing and although not exclusively concerned with technical and consultancy services, the course had provided what the managing director felt were useful insights into some of the additional considerations in marketing service products, including the notion of an extended marketing mix to include People, Physical Evidence and Processes. The managing director realised that these were just as potentially important in the hard-nosed world of marine exploration as they appeared to be in the fast food and other consumer service industries. Certainly he felt there was food for thought as to how some of the ideas from these service industries could be applied to the company and its markets.

The second course attended by the managing director focused on the concept of relationship marketing. The course leaders had stressed the move towards relationship marketing in many industries and the way that relationship marketing tools and techniques could be used to help build customer loyalty and retain customers. This was of particular interest to the managing director as current relationships with customers in the industry seemed to be characterised by antagonism and lack of co-operation between the companies in the industry and their customers including Marine Services Ltd. Again, the managing director felt there was potential to apply some of the ideas about relationship marketing to the company and its markets.

Having appointed Stephen Collop with the specific job remit to develop and apply service and relationship marketing concepts and techniques to the company and its marketing, the managing director has asked Stephen as his first task in the company to produce a brief (maximum two page) outline report outlining how these concepts and techniques could be of value in the company's future marketing. He has informed Stephen that he will be presenting this report to a meeting of the company directors and senior managers at the next monthly meeting. He has also warned Stephen that he can expect some reservations and even antagonism regarding the use of some of the more recent marketing ideas in what is after all a very traditional and conservative company.

QUESTION

Prepare the outline report.

18

International marketing

Chapter objectives

By the end of this chapter you will:

▶ Understand the importance of international and global aspects of marketing to the modern marketer.

▶ Appreciate some of the key factors which have given rise to the growth of international marketing.

▶ Be familiar with the different possible levels of involvement in international marketing.

▶ Understand some of the key differences and additional complexities encountered when developing marketing strategies for international markets.

▶ Comprehend the key decision areas in planning international marketing strategies.

▶ Appreciate the importance of, and difficulties associated with, researching and appraising international markets.

Introduction

It would be virtually inexcusable to consider any marketing management text to be complete without a chapter on the international aspects of marketing – why is this? Put simply, international, and in fact increasingly global marketing activities continue to grow, to the extent that virtually every marketing manager in today's competitive environment is involved in, or at least affected by, these international and global aspects. For this reason, the contemporary marketing manager who does not understand the nature and significance of international marketing, and at least to some extent, how to plan strategically for these markets, is quite simply deficient in the skills required of a modern professional marketing manager.

This chapter therefore seeks to address some of these key issues and skills required when managing marketing programmes in international markets. It is important to stress that, necessarily when only devoting a single chapter to this topic, we are only able to give an overview of the issues and skills associated with international marketing management. As such therefore, we are focused on what we believe to be some of the key contemporary issues in international marketing and some of the key decision areas and considerations when developing marketing strategies in these markets. Students and/or managers who, for a variety of possible reasons, are interested in and/or need more detailed knowledge in this area, are advised to consult one of the many excellent specialist texts in what is an increasingly complex area of marketing. We shall start by examining some of the background to the growth in international trade and marketing and some of the reasons put forward as to why companies and nations become involved in such trade and marketing.

The growth of international/global marketing

One of the most striking business trends of the past 30 years has been the increase in internationalization; that is, the growing number of firms that participate in international trade. Of course such international trade is not new, after all, nations have traded ever since the start of commerce. However, the 1990s was really the first decade when companies around the world started to think globally. It was during the 1990s that time and distance – dimensions which have been shrinking for centuries between countries – began to become really compressed. The advent of ever faster transport and communication systems which in turn have led to vastly increased travel and therefore more cosmopolitan consumers, have served to 'shrink' the world even further. So much so that some writers now refer to the so-called 'global village'. Needless to say, in the new millennium this shrinking will continue aided and abetted by technologies such as the Internet.

Although many companies such as Nestle, IBM, Shell, Toshiba and others have been conducting international marketing for decades, global competition has now intensified to the extent that even purely 'domestic companies' that have hitherto never thought about international marketing are, if nothing else, potentially and actually affected in their marketing by global competitors.

In addition, the importance of international trade to governments and their economies, has meant that more and more firms are being urged to internationalize thereby selling more of their products abroad and as a consequence adding to a positive balance of payments. This 'urging' has resulted in many governments offering material encouragement to companies to become involved in international marketing through, for example, grants and loans, offers of expert advice etc. Finally, global markets themselves have changed, and are changing with developments such as the enlarged and potentially at least in the future even more co-ordinated European Union, now with the majority of the member states having adopted a single currency. The development and temporary decline of the so-called 'tiger economies' of the Pacific rim, and the collapse of Communism and ensuing growth of more liberal economies in eastern Europe have given rise to significant new opportunities for companies willing and able to take advantage of them and threats for those who are not. These and other developments largely explain the increased activity and therefore importance of international marketing but do not, of themselves, explain basic reasons and motives for companies becoming involved in international markets. It is useful in our understanding of international marketing management to identify some of these key underpinning reasons and motives.

The prime motive for a company becoming involved in international trade and marketing is essentially profitability. This though is a very simplistic view of the reasons and motives for becoming involved in international marketing and we shall therefore return to some of the added complexities and considerations in making this decision later in this chapter. However, related to the profitability issue, the economists have long known some of the prime reasons for international trade.

Adam Smith of course, was the first major writer on international trade. He produced the theory of **'absolute advantage'** in which he argued that the nation exported those products in which it had an absolute cost advantage over foreign competition and imported the products in which it had an absolute cost disadvantage. This, he argued was not only common sense but actually, through the specialization in production and trade which it gave rise to, would actually increase the wealth and well-being of each participating nation. Other economists developed Adam Smith's basic thesis to include considerations of comparative costs rather than absolute, or the notion that trade was largely explained by relative factor endowments such as land, labour, capital and entrepreneurial skills possessed by a nation. These legacies concerning the notions of absolute, comparative, and factor endowment considerations to explain international trade are still to be found in more recent explanations of international marketing and trade. So for example, Porter[1] has explored competitive advantage between nations on the basis of their relative skills and resources.

The major conclusions of these theories are that an examination of price, cost structures, and factor endowments between countries will indicate which products and services they are likely to export and import.

Other contributors have amended these basically economic theories. Some for example have highlighted the fact that many of the more traditional economists' theories of trade are essentially 'supply side' theories only. They point out that demand patterns may reverse or at least affect trading flows which we might otherwise predict on the basis of classical economics alone. So, for example, we may find that the demand for a product in a country may be so high that, despite the country possessing a comparative advantage, demand exceeds supply. Instead of being a net exporter the country becomes a net importer, often from higher cost foreign suppliers. Similarly, we know of course as marketers, that markets are not homogeneous as the classical economists assumed. They are often segmented, which means a nation can be both an exporter and importer within the same product group. Brand image reinforces this phenomenon. For example, the UK exports cars but imports substantially more than it exports. Much of this trading flow results from the plant location strategies of US, Far Eastern, and European multi-national vehicle manufacturers, complicating the more simplistic notions to explain production and trade suggested by the classical economists. Another example would be that Sweden, which has a comparative advantage in luxury cars such as the Volvos and Saabs has a comparative disadvantage in small, medium and budget cars.

Perhaps one of the most interesting alternative trade theories to explain international trade and marketing is that developed by Wells[2]. He suggested that international trading in products and services follows a pattern that was broadly similar in nature to that of the product life cycle with which we are already so familiar. Essentially he suggested that many products and services follow a pattern that can be divided into four stages as follows:

1. Innovation and Exporting:
   New products and innovations are developed in the most 'advanced' economies essentially for domestic consumption. However, these countries will quickly begin to export the new products and services to other 'less developed' economies.

2. Start of Foreign Production:
   As the market for the new product or service begins to grow in the importing countries, companies in these countries begin to start their own production to take account of local demand.
3. Foreign Production Becomes More Competitive in Domestic Markets:
   As production and demand in the previously importing country grows, factors such as economies of scale and experience curve effects begin to make domestic production much more cost competitive compared to imports.
4. Foreign Production Becomes Competitive in Export Markets:
   In this final stage the previously importing countries become competitive in export markets to the extent that their products begin to substitute for the original innovators'/exporters' products in their own markets. In effect we have come full circle with the early producers and exporters becoming net importers.

Wells further suggests that this pattern of trade is repeated over time with successively less developed, and therefore lower cost economies becoming in turn the foreign producers and eventually net exporters to the countries which previously imported to them.

Many empirical studies have in fact confirmed this 'pecking order' over time. Lancaster and Wesenlund[3] have modified and extended Wells' basic theory to suggest that as the cycle of trade from one group of countries to another progresses, sales of the product or service in question gradually increase. However, Lancaster and Wesenlund's evidence still supports the basic notion of a product life cycle at work for international trade.

Notwithstanding the insights which these various theories of international trade have provided us with, with regard to the reasons and motives for international marketing, as mentioned earlier, the prime motive, as far as the individual company is concerned, to become involved in this area of marketing is the potential for increased profits. It is this potential which largely explains the reasons why a company might move from purely domestic marketing to some involvement in international markets. However the term, 'international marketing' can involve very different levels of involvement in international markets and therefore very different issues for the participating company with regard to, for example, strategic marketing planning. Before we consider some of these issues in more detail, therefore, and to continue the development of our understanding as to the reasons and motives for international marketing we need to explore further this notion of different levels of involvement in international marketing.

International marketing definitions: levels of involvement in international marketing

Clearly international marketing essentially involves marketing across national boundaries. This simple notion, however, belies the potential complexities of defining precisely what international marketing is and involves. On the one hand marketing across national boundaries may simply involve a company passively responding to an unsolicited foreign order received from, say, an independent broker. The company involved in this transaction simply sells its product or service to the broker with little effort, additional considerations, or long-term commitment. On the other hand, at the other extreme, marketing across national boundaries may involve a company devoting all, or most of its resources, to foreign market activities with substantial commitment to markets across the globe and with production or marketing in many countries. Clearly the term 'international marketing' can, and does, encompass a wide range of different activities and commitments even though products and services are still essentially being sold across national boundaries. Lynch[4] for example distinguished between European companies which at one extreme were concerned primarily with their domestic sales and markets, and, at the other extreme, European companies operating on a world stage such as Philips, GlaxoSmithKline and SKF. These different types of international marketing essentially stem from the different levels of involvement and commitment which a company makes to its international marketing activities. These different levels of involvement may usefully allow us to explore and categorize the different types of activities and commitments encompassed when marketing across national boundaries.

1. **Casual or accidental exporting** This type of international marketing entails the lowest levels of commitment and involvement by a company. In fact, as in our earlier example, it essentially comprises of a company responding to largely unsolicited foreign orders and there is no real commitment to international marketing.
2. **Active exporting** Here, a company makes a positive commitment to its international marketing with an ensuing higher degree of involvement. Not only is there an active recognition that foreign markets exist and represent possible marketing opportunities, but because of this attempts are made to cultivate sales across national boundaries in a proactive manner. However, even this type of export marketing tends still simply to apply the marketing principles to exporting a product which the firm is already selling in its domestic market. Because of this, overall corporate strategy does not really reflect foreign market importance and activities although minor adjustments may be made to the company's strategy to accommodate these.
3. **Committed international marketing** This level of commitment to international marketing involves the greatest degree of involvement on the part of the company. Markets across national boundaries are a key consideration in the marketing strategy of the company. International marketing activities are an integral part of the overall marketing programme. Organizational systems, structures and procedures may be developed specifically for the purpose of enhancing international marketing operations and profitability.

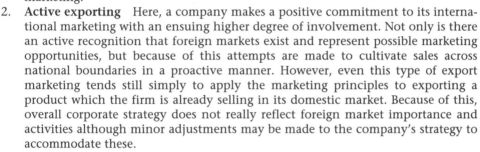

Of all the examples of committed international marketers, the Coca Cola company has to be one of the best. For many years now international marketing activities form the centre of the company's overall marketing programme. All of the company's organizational systems, structures and procedures are purposely designed to enhance international marketing operations and profitability.

Clearly then the level of involvement and commitment by a company to its 'marketing across national boundaries' can vary considerably which means that no single simple definition of what constitutes international marketing can adequately encompass the possible range and scope of activities involved in this area of marketing.

Related to this notion of different levels of involvement, and therefore types of international marketing, is the notion of different types of company perspectives and approaches to organizational structure and systems with regard to its non-domestic marketing.

The *export marketing company*, as suggested in our earlier discussion of levels of involvement, is a company which simply sells its products overseas. This company may or may not have a separate export marketing division but essentially uses the same marketing strategies in both its domestic and export markets.

The *international company* is one whose headquarters are located in one country and where share ownership is dominated by the nationals of that one country. However, this sort of company views international marketing in a much more positive manner and has been more central to their overall strategy and profits. Marketing strategy tends to emanate from the company headquarters, although they may own marketing operations in other countries which in turn may reflect the particular requirements of each of the foreign markets and customers.

The *multinational company* is a relatively recent phenomenon in world markets but Schlender[5] and many others provide testimony to the growth of this type of global organization. The **multinational company** (MNCs) may be defined in a number of ways but it is generally agreed that they have the following characteristics.

- They treat the various national markets in which they operate as if they were one. In other words they do not see a distinction between domestic and global marketing opportunities.
- They have a single management strategy that guides all their various operating companies throughout the world.
- They think and operate in what Wind *et al.*[6] termed a '*geocentric*' manner, that is to say that they are essentially world oriented in their approach to their marketing and planning. We shall return to Wind *et al's*. notion of geocentric versus other types of perspectives on international marketing activities when we consider alternative organizational systems and structures for international marketing later in this chapter, but essentially the multinational company which will predominantly have a geocentric perspective will be concerned to achieve complete integration of its marketing strategies throughout the world. Lascu[7] refers to this as the most extreme type of international involvement. Increasingly the multinational corporations are practising global marketing. The global marketing company views the world as a whole as its market and the firm develops a global marketing strategy.

Clearly, both the level of involvement and the commitment by a company to its international markets and the associated different perspectives regarding these markets which have just been outlined constitute one of the key and indeed perhaps the first decisions by a company regarding its international marketing strategy. Simply stated a company must decide whether it is going to be either a passive exporter or a fully fledged global marketing operation, or of course any number of levels of involvement and commitment in between. However whilst this is obviously a crucial determinant of virtually every other aspect of a company's international marketing operations and strategies, in fact we know that the decision to 'go international' is often not a rational '**searching after business**' opportunity but rather the result of a series of chance decisions and many companies go through a process of gradually evolving their international marketing operations. So, for example, in the first stage a company begins by filling unsolicited orders but does not seek to export actively. In the next stage the company may actively seek out export markets but exporting still remains a small part of its business. If the exporting is successful, however, the company becomes established in one or more export markets and exporting becomes a major activity. The company may then begin to invest in production and other facilities in overseas markets and eventually the company move towards becoming a fully fledged global marketer.

Progression through the stages of involvement in international marketing is by no means an automatic one. Marks & Spencer, for example, despite early forays into overseas expansion including the opening of stores in France, North America and the Far East, have never really developed into a full-blown international retailer. IKEA, on the other hand, have progressed through successful expansion of their international operations.

In fact, although this gradual evolution of international marketing is how many companies develop their global marketing activities in fact, as always, it is far better if the organization plans a systematic development of its activities into the international arena. A firm may enter into marketing across national boundaries passively due to problems in their domestic market or actively by seeking attractive opportunities abroad. We shall consider some of the reasons for deciding to 'go international' shortly, together with some of the factors that should affect this choice if it is to be planned, as suggested, systematically as part of the overall strategic planning process for international marketing. Before we do this however it would be useful to consider what, if anything, is different or 'special' about the management of international marketing compared to its purely domestic counterpart. In other words, aside from its importance to today's markets because of global opportunities and competition, we consider it necessary to have a separate chapter on the management of international marketing activities. We shall now briefly consider these differences.

International marketing management: differences and special issues

Thankfully, most writers agree that the main concepts and techniques of marketing management apply both in domestic and also in foreign markets. So for example, many of the steps in strategic marketing planning already outlined in this text such as analysing opportunities and threats, assessing strengths and weaknesses, research and appraising markets and customers, segmentation and targeting, the management of the marketing mix, and the implementation and control of marketing plans apply equally whether one is operating in purely domestic market situations or exclusively in foreign market situations or any combination thereof. However, even though the principles of marketing management are the same for international and domestic marketing there are at least some additional important issues or complexities which arise once a company begins to extend its marketing operations beyond its national boundaries and which are therefore not encountered at least to the same extent, in purely domestic marketing. In addition, there are one or two areas of marketing management and planning where there are inherent differences between domestic and international marketing management. Below we have summarized what we feel are some of the most important differences and special issues involved in international marketing compared to purely domestic.

A comparison of domestic and international marketing management and planning

Domestic	International
1. Single language and nationality	Multi-lingual/multi-national/multi-cultural

2. Relatively homogeneous market	Fragmented and diverse markets
3. Data usually accurate and easily available	Data collection a formidable task requiring significantly higher budget and personnel allocation
4. Political factors relatively unimportant	Political factors frequently vital
5. Relative freedom from government interference	Involvement in national economic plans; government influences company plans
6. Individual company has little effect on environment	'Gravitational' distortion by large companies in small countries
7. Chauvinism helps	Chauvinism hinders
9. Relatively stable business environment	Multiple environments, many of which are highly unstable but may be highly profitable
9. Uniform financial climate	Variety of financial climates ranging from over-conservative to wildly inflationary
10. Single currency	Currencies differing in real value and stability
11. Business 'rules of the game' understood	Rules diverse, changeable and unclear
12. Management generally accustomed to sharing responsibilities and using financial controls	Management frequently autonomous and unfamiliar with budgets and controls

We can see from this that there are indeed differences between domestic and international marketing management. Many of these differences and/or additional complexities stem from simply operating in markets with a different environment to that encountered in the domestic market. Of particular significance in this respect are the differences which arise from the cultural and social elements of the environment. Because of this importance we have considered these forces and factors in more detail below.

Cultural and Social Forces in International Marketing

There is no doubt that many of the additional complexities and problems faced by the international marketer compared to the purely domestic marketer stem from differences in the cultural and social environment which the marketer must face when marketing in foreign countries. Because of the potentially extremely significant, for marketing, influences of cultural differences when marketing across national boundaries, cultural and social forces, which in any event are always important considerations in developing marketing plans in fact take on a heightened importance.

We know of course that how people consume, their needs and wants, and the ways in which these wants are satisfied are significantly determined by culture. Cateora[8] defines culture as the 'human-made part of human environment – the sum total of knowledge, beliefs, art, morals, laws, customs, and any other capabilities and habits acquired by humans as members of society.' In a similar definition Ferraro[9] defines culture as 'everything that people have, think, and do, as members of their society. Because cultures are potentially so different between countries, cultural forces and factors take on a particular significance for the international marketer. Below are just some of the possible areas or aspects of culture where there may be important differences when marketing in foreign markets:

Social organization
Norms and values
Religion
Language
Education
Arts and aesthetics.

Sometimes seemingly relatively small and subtle differences in cultural habits and practices can be important in marketing products in different cultures. For example, attitudes towards body hair differ between even relatively geographically proximate European countries. In the UK for example, most women shave their under-arm hair, whereas most German women do not. Obviously a company like Gillette needs to take this difference into account in preparing its marketing plans for the different European countries.

The marketer must understand the implications of these possibly different elements of culture for developing marketing strategies. So, for example, there may be very different norms and values pertaining to say gender roles, or the use of sex in advertising when marketing in a foreign country. Similarly, religious morals and taboos may have a significant impact on what is acceptable marketing practice in a country.

It is important to recognize of course that within any national culture there are often a number of sub-sets of culture, so for example in the UK there is quite a distinct cultural difference between the north and south regions of the country which affect purchasing behaviour often in direct and observable ways but sometimes in quite subtle ways. In addition to geographical sub-cultures, of course, cultural sub-sets will often also be created by, say different racial groups within a country, for example, the Chinese in Malaysia, Italians in the US etc.

Sub-cultures have now become prime targets for many marketers within countries. In the UK for example, the Asian sub-culture, once a neglected and underserved part of the market now represents a major market segment. Such sub-cultures have their own particular marketing needs and as such represent substantial opportunities for the marketer willing and able to cater for these.

There are several key concepts relating to culture which become especially important when marketing across national boundaries. These are as follows:

1. **Self reference criterion** (SRC). This notion emphasizes the fact that it is all too easy to use all one's own cultural experience and values when developing and implementing marketing plans in another country. When confronted with a situation or a set of facts we assess this situation or facts on the basis of our own knowledge and experiences usually based, understandably on our experiences within the culture in which we were raised and with which we are most familiar. This can give rise to largely unconscious but potentially disastrous mistakes in international marketing strategies.

A simple example is the word 'Pet'. In many societies this word is used in an affectionate manner to describe domestic animals or even, in some societies, loved ones. In France however, the word *pet* means, in certain circumstances, flatulence, simple cultural differences like this can be potentially very significant in developing marketing programmes and in this case naming or branding of products. It is important to isolate the differences in cultural values between your own culture and the new culture. Inevitably we use our own criterion and culture frameworks to assess markets but these may not be appropriate when marketing in a foreign market.

Unfortunately, at least for their marketers, there are plenty of examples of 'misnamed' products or unfortunate advertising slogans including for example:

'Nova' – Vauxhall's small car which in Spanish means literally 'no go'.

'Pschitt' – A French soft drink brand which probably needs no explanation.

The 'Come alive with Pepsi' campaign slogan translated in some countries into 'Pepsi will bring your relatives back from the grave.'

2. **High and low context culture**. Clearly, different cultures and societies differ in terms of certain aspects of their development. Some have referred to the differences between high and low context cultures which in turn has implications for various facets of their cultural elements. A good example would be in the use of language. Chee and Harris[10] suggest that language is a major factor distinguishing one culture from another. Moreover, it is not only the formal written and oral structure of the language but also symbolic communication which they refer to as 'silent languages'. These are ways of communicating in a culture other than through verbal communication. Silent languages include aspects such as **Time**, e.g. the use of deadlines, scheduling appointments etc. and **Space**, e.g. conversation difference in communication. Some estimates suggest up to 90 per cent of the communication in high context cultures may take place through silent rather than spoken language. For example, in some cultures arriving late for a meeting is a sign of respect, in others it is a sign of power. Self-reference criteria usually create more difficulty with silent languages than with spoken ones. Spoken languages are often obvious in their differences whereas silent languages are much less obvious and yet have potential significant impact on marketing.

3. **Cultural sensitivity of products and services**. Whilst culture is potentially important to all products and services and hence to all marketing plans, some products are more *'culturally sensitive'* than others. For example, most food products are likely to be very sensitive to cultural differences. Food usage, preparation and consumption and indeed overall attitudes towards food in general often differ significantly between cultures and sub-cultures. For example attitudes to drinking coffee in Italy and France are still very different to those in the UK. Clearly, some products are taboo for social and/or religious reasons in some cultures. Generally speaking, consumer products are more culturally sensitive than business to business products but even in business to business markets Harte[11] suggests there are distinct rules of social and business etiquette that marketers need to appreciate and adhere to when conducting business in other countries.

Cultural differences then probably represent one of the most important areas of increased complexity compared to purely domestic marketing. Clearly, as we have seen, there are other differences and complexities but as already suggested, the overall concepts and principles of marketing remain the same. However, obviously some of the decision areas involved in planning international marketing also differ from purely domestic ones. We can now turn our attention to the key steps and decision areas in developing international marketing plans.

International marketing strategies and decisions

As in purely domestic marketing international marketing strategies must be systematically planned and implemented. The following represents the key steps and decisions in planning and implementing international marketing programmes.

1. **The extent of involvement and commitment to international markets** i.e. does the company wish to become involved in international markets, and if so, to what extent, e.g. does it intend to be simply at the one extreme a passive exporter, or at the other extreme, a global marketing company.
2. **Foreign market selection** here the company must decide which markets it wishes to enter. The company must determine not only which specific markets offer the best opportunities but for example how many markets it wishes and is able to enter.
3. **The method of market entry** this involves determining how the foreign market(s) is to be developed.
4. **The marketing mix strategies to be used** as in domestic markets this involves decisions regarding as a minimum the 4Ps and, in the case of service products, the 7Ps of the marketing mix. Here we will consider only those issues involved in managing the marketing mix which stem from the marketing of products and services across national boundaries.
5. **Marketing organization and implementation for developing international markets** here the company must decide factors such as organizational systems and procedures including its orientation towards international markets.

These then are the key decision areas which we can now consider in more detail. In addition however, to these five key areas, again as in purely domestic markets these decisions need to be based on a careful appraisal of markets including, e.g. market size, customer needs, competitors etc. In short, they need to be based on accurate and up to date marketing research and information. We shall therefore briefly consider a sixth key area, namely the process of *planning and collecting marketing information for international marketing decisions.*

The extent of involvement and commitment to international markets

We have already discussed the notion of different levels of involvement and commitment to international markets. It was suggested that although this is often the result of a process of evolution in many companies it is best ordered as a systematic and considered decision area and indeed the first one in planning international marketing strategies.

Many factors will influence and determine the extent to which a company wishes and/or should become involved and committed to international markets. It is therefore impossible to be specific about what constitutes an appropriate degree of involvement as it obviously varies from company to company and even within a company over time. However, a company should decide in a rational manner the extent of its current and planned future involvement and commitment to international markets, and where for example this commitment and involvement is to increase over time, that this should be done in a systematic and ordered manner. Amongst the factors which will affect these decisions in a particular company are the following:

- Situation in domestic market regarding sales, profits etc.
- Opportunities afforded through international expansion
- Corporate objectives and plans
- Company resources and skills etc.
- Attitudes towards risk
- Outside influences such as, e.g. government incentives, changes in trading blocks etc.

What is most important is that international marketing plans be developed from, and consistent with overall corporate objectives and plans.

Foreign market selection

Having determined how committed and involved a company is to be to international markets, the company must then select specific foreign markets which it intends to concentrate on or target. In many ways of course this is an issue of market segmentation and targeting which we considered earlier in the text. Overall, therefore, it is a question of matching company strengths and resources against potential market opportunities after considering aspects such as competition, market size and growth etc. Of particular importance here, especially for the relatively new or inexperienced international marketing company, is the need to resist the temptation to attack too many markets thereby spreading effort and resources too thinly to be successful. Often, the initial effort should be directed at a single market and this then can be extended to other markets.

Market selection can be based on a number of criteria, three possible ones are as follows:

1. Market potential: e.g. market size and trends, location of competition and their marketing mixes, customer profiles, needs and wants, channels of distribution etc.
2. Market similarity: often a company will select markets which are similar to their own domestic markets. 'Psychological' proximity is often more important than geographical proximity in international markets. Whilst it is understandable that companies would prefer markets similar to their own domestic markets in which they have experience there is a danger that a company may be tempted to take too much for granted and ignore subtle but critical environmental differences. This false sense of security has often produced the most spectacular international marketing disasters.
3. Accessibility: this encompasses both geographical distance and logistics but also includes, e.g. political distance which involves legal and technical import controls, political constraints on business, exchange controls and so on.

Clearly the selection of which markets to enter, and how many, i.e. coverage, is a crucial strategic decision. Overall we are looking for those markets which offer the greatest potential for the company to achieve its overall objectives for its international markets.

A. *Home based production*
Indirect export
  – (1) Trading company
  – (2) Export management company
  – (3) Piggy-back operation

Direct export
  – Overseas agents
  – Overseas distributor
  – Overseas marketing subsidiary

Figure 18.1
Alternative methods of entry.

B. *Foreign production sources*
  – Assembly
  – Contract manufacturer
  – Licensing
  – Joint venture
  – 100% ownership

The method of market entry

As we have already seen, there are a number of ways in which a company can become involved in foreign markets depending on its level of commitment and involvement. Related to this therefore, having decided this degree of involvement and commitment and having determined which foreign markets are to be targeted, the company must determine how it will most appropriately enter these markets. Essentially, there are two broad alternative methods of entry as shown in figure 18.1.

Clearly, each of these methods of entry has its own advantages and disadvantages and must be assessed against a number of criteria. Examples of criteria which may be used to assess the alternative methods of entry are as follows.

Company specific factors
● Corporate goals
● Size of company, resources

General factors
● Number of markets
● Penetration within markets
● Competition

Political factors
● Government restrictions/incentives
● Political risk, stability etc.

Control
● More direct involvement affords greater control

Incremental costs/investment requirements
● Marketing outlay varies directly with method of entry as does investment requirements

Profit and sales potential
● Long-term sales and profit potential associated with each method of entry need to be considered

Administrative requirements
● Documentation, red tape, management and legal time

Personnel requirements
- The more direct the method of entry, the greater the skills required

Risk
- Political as well as commercial

Flexibility
- An optimal choice at one point in time may change over time, long term involvement may require initial flexibility.

The marketing mix strategies to be used

Although there are obviously differences in detail, essentially management of the marketing mix elements in international marketing involves the same 'ingredients', i.e. the basic 4Ps or 7Ps in the case of services, and the same general principles for their management as in domestic markets. Clearly there are some differences, so for example the 'place' element of the marketing mix for international markets is more likely to possibly include more specialized intermediaries in the channels of distribution such as say agents or overseas distributors. Similarly, logistics, because of sheer distance, is likely to be more complex to plan. In the area of the pricing element of the mix, the marketing manager has to consider for example exchange rates when quoting prices and things such as currency regulations and provision for export credit guarantees. Nonetheless, despite these and other added considerations and complexities when marketing in foreign markets, as already mentioned the basic concepts and techniques for managing the marketing mix remain the same. However, there is one major aspect of managing marketing mix elements in international marketing which broadly is not an issue when marketing on a solely domestic basis. This aspect, which is therefore central to managing the marketing mix in international marketing, concerns the extent to which the elements of the marketing mix, and indeed the marketing mix as an overall package, need on the one hand to be modified or adapted to each of the foreign markets in which a company is involved. On the other hand, it can be applied in a standardized manner across all the markets in which the company operates. This aspect has come to be termed the issue of *'standardization'* and it is perhaps the major issue when considering managing the marketing mix in international markets. We will therefore concentrate in our discussion on the management of the international marketing mix on this particular area.

Essentially, when a company operates in one or more international markets a decision must be made as to the extent to which it is appropriate and/or possible to use a standardized versus a non-standardized approach to its marketing mix in these markets. It is appropriate to use Buzzell's[12] interpretation to define the meaning of standardization and non-standardization in international markets.

> In a literal sense, multinational standardization would mean the offering of identical product lines, at identical prices, through identical distribution systems, supported by identical promotional programmes, in several different countries. At the other extreme, completely and 'localized' marketing strategies would contain no common elements whatsoever.

Clearly, it is not always an either/or decision to standardize or not. Very often it is a question of deciding the degree of standardization for the mix as a whole and for each of the individual elements of the mix in particular.

On the one hand supporters of standardization argue that for any given product consumers' interests everywhere are basically the same and therefore standardization is possible. Cateora and Ghawri[13], amongst others, acknowledge that increasingly the world is becoming a global marketplace where, due in particular to improvements in communication and transportation, there has been a trend towards a more homogeneous world market. On the other hand, supporters of more localized non-standard marketing programmes suggest that the differences between consumers and market in different parts of the world are still too great to support a standardized approach. Needless to say there are both advantages and disadvantages to standardization of the marketing mix and the marketing manager must determine what is the appropriate level of standardization given the particular circumstances and the nature of the markets in particular for his/her company. The potential benefits of standardization are as follows.

1. Cost savings
   With standardization a company can achieve larger production runs, spread the cost of marketing and research and development and thus reduce total unit costs.
2. A uniform global image
   Standardization enables the development of a uniform image throughout the world, a consistency in product design, brand name and packaging, in sales and customer service and generally in the image projected to customers is a very powerful competitive weapon.
3. Improved planning and control
   The strategy of global standardization helps facilitate improved planning and control within a company. If all major decisions are made at company headquarters and implemented throughout all worldwide divisions and subsidiaries there is less chance for example of conflicting policies being pursued.

Despite the significant potential advantages to be gained from a standardized marketing mix, there are several factors which render this strategy less suitable and indeed, on occasions may make it impossible to standardize certain elements of the mix. So, for example, there may be legal restrictions which prevent standardizing elements of the marketing mix. Similarly, geographical and/or climatic conditions may prevent standardization. Economic factors too, such as standards of living and disposable income, may make it less effective to standardize the marketing mix elements. Finally, and perhaps most importantly of all, the all important cultural factors may make standardization impossible or ineffective.

As already mentioned, standardization, or rather the extent of it, can only be determined for each particular company at a particular point in time in its overall strategic planning, but it is perhaps one of the key decisions regarding the management of the marketing mix elements in international marketing.

Even a company like McDonalds, who have strived to standardize as much of their international marketing as possible, have to vary the marketing mix in order to meet local needs. For example, there is a non-beef product for the Hindu segment of the Indian market. Their New York outlets cater for the lunch time worker market whereas in Holland they are geared up to family groups. In parts of the Far East they cater especially for the needs of the teenage and 'Yuppie' market, and in the UK they are strongly positioned in the children's birthday party segment.

Marketing organization and implementation for developing international markets

The final element in the strategic management of international marketing is the organization and implementation of international marketing programmes. Organizational structure and culture is of vital importance in international marketing. A highly centralized structure is likely to develop a more standardized approach. A more decentralized structure is likely to lead to less standardization. Majaro[14] has identified three alternative types of organizational structure for international marketing as follows.

1. The 'Macropyramid' structure
   This type of structure is characterized by a strong central 'nerve centre'. All strategic planning is centralized and subsidiaries operate primarily at the management and operational levels. The marketing effort is directed towards a maximum standardization of its mix with strong control procedures from the centre and centralized determination of policy.

   This approach obviously encourages standardization but may be characterized by a degree of inflexibility and a lack of empathy and sensitivity for dealing effectively with local/national business. Local managers may be upset by having to operate within rigid standards of performance.

2. The 'Umbrella' structure
   In this structure, the nerve centre lays down a broad set of objectives in terms of profits, growth and return on investment but local management has the freedom to interpret these objectives and adapt them to local needs and conditions. This organizational structure is based on the recognition that markets and countries differ and that a degree of local independence and freedom of action is more effective than totally centralized control and standardization.

   Although the Umbrella organization is usually very responsive to local needs, it may give rise to increased costs through the need for more adaptations to the elements of the marketing mix and can, under certain circumstances, lead to overfragmentation.

3. The 'Interconglomerate' structure
   In this type of organization central control and planning is exercised almost exclusively with regard to financial matters. Funds are manipulated on a transnational basis with a view to maximizing returns from factors such as exchange disparities. There is strong communication between the centre and the subsidiaries but only as regards financial planning and control and hence marketing tends to be non-standardized but also to some extent, neglected.

Clearly, many factors will affect the choice of appropriate structure for implementing international marketing programmes such as, e.g. company size, number of markets and their geographical spread, management attitudes and culture etc. However, one of the most important determinants of organization, and indeed the overall approach to developing and implementing strategic international marketing plans is the previously discussed level of involvement and commitment to international markets. You will recall that Wind *et al.*[15] have suggested that the company which is totally committed to and involved in international marketing, i.e. the global marketer, will tend to have what they have termed a 'geocentric' approach to its marketing. This is in fact part of these authors' often quoted EPRG schema.

The authors of this schema contend that firms can be classified as having an ethnocentric, polycentric, regiocentric, or geocentric orientation (EPRG) according to the level of involvement and commitment to international markets by the organization. The **ethnocentric orientation** is one which is essentially characterized by a company concentrating primarily on its home markets, i.e. with little or no commitment to international markets. The **polycentric orientation** organizes its international marketing around each host country and therefore has little central control and standardization. The **regiocentric orientation**, as the term implies, organizes its marketing strategies and systems around specific regions either geographical but often political or economic, such as the European Union. As we have seen, the geocentric company looks at the world and its markets therefore in a global context. Such a **geocentric orientation** a global marketing strategy and will tend to have more standardized global marketing programmes. Even the global marketer though needs to be sensitive to different environments. Quester and Conduit[16] suggest that success in international markets very much depends on the marketer's ability to assess and adjust to different and often strange environments.

International marketing research and information systems

As with all marketing plans, international marketing decisions must be based on accurate and up to date information and intelligence. Fortunately the basic approaches to marketing research and marketing information systems are the same internationally as domestically. However, at an international level market research and information gathering are more complex, have wider dimensions and are generally more difficult to plan and control. Some of the operational problems of conducting international marketing research are caused by differences in language and literacy, different cultural values, unreliable or unobtainable secondary data and so on. Careful planning of the research process can, to a large degree, overcome many of these problems.

The information requirements for international marketing obviously depend upon the decisions which are to be taken on the basis of that information, but clearly each of the elements of international marketing strategy outlined here will require marketing research and intelligence. Examples of the information required for some of the key decision areas in developing international marketing plans are briefly outlined below.

	Marketing decision	*Information/Intelligence needed*
1.	Degree of involvement/commitment in international marketing	Assessment of global market demand and firm's potential share in it, in view of local and international competition and compared to domestic opportunities.
2.	Market selection	A ranking of potential markets based on, e.g. market size and growth, political, cultural and economic factors, and extent of local competition.
3.	Market entry method	Size of market, trade barriers, transport costs, intermediary availability, local competition, government requirements and political stability.
4.	Marketing mix strategies	For each market: buyer behaviour, competitive practice, distributors and channels, promotional media and practice, economic factors.

As with all marketing research and information gathering activities, care should be taken in planning these activities. In fact, a systematic approach is even more important when conducting an international marketing research programme. Problem definition and the design of the research brief need to be done as clearly and as tightly as possible so that there is little room for misinterpretation. In developing the research plan, the timing and scheduling of events needs thorough planning to enable the data to be collected, analysed, interpreted and reported upon in a common language and in the most efficient manner. Specification of the analysis and method of interpretation must be standardized to enable international comparison and a meaningful report to be produced. Fortunately, in some ways, obtaining information on international markets can be easier than in domestic markets simply because of the availability of secondary information supplied for example by governments, chambers of commerce, banks, and international organizations. Clearly the availability of such secondary information does differ by country, but most of the developed economies have substantial amounts of secondary information available for marketing research.

Summary

In this chapter we have looked at the increasingly important area of international marketing management. We have seen that many of the principles and practices of marketing management which are used in purely domestic marketing in fact apply when marketing across international boundaries. However, there are some additional considerations and decision areas, of course, when marketing internationally. We have outlined and discussed what these are so that at least you are familiar with the key decision areas in planning international marketing operations.

Key terms

Absolute advantage [p467]
Casual exporting [p469]
Active exporting [p469]
Multi-national company [p470]
Self reference criterion [p473]
Silent languages [p00]
Macropyramid structure [p480]

Umbrella structure [p480]
Interconglomerate structure [p480]
Ethnocentric orientation [p481]
Polycentric orientation [p481]
Regiocentric orientation [p481]
Geocentric orientation [p481]

Questions

1 International/global marketing has been one of the fastest growing areas of commerce over the past thirty years. What factors underpin this rapid growth and why might we expect this growth to continue over the next thirty years?

2 Using examples, explain Wells' international product life cycle for international trade.

3 What are some of the major differences and special issues which arise when considering international as opposed to purely domestic marketing activities.

4 Using examples, explain the following concepts relating to cultural and social forces in international marketing:
    (a) Self reference criterion (SRC)
    (b) High and low context culture
    (c) Cultural sensitivity.

5 Outline and explain the key decisions in planning and implementing international marketing programmes.

References

1. Porter, M. E., *The Competitive Advantage of Nations*, Macmillan, London, 1990.
2. Wells, L. T., 'A product lifecycle for international trade', *Journal of Marketing*, **32**, 1968, pp. 1–6.
3. Lancaster, G. A. and Wesenlund, I., 'A product life cycle theory for international trade: an empirical investigation, *European Journal of Marketing*, **18** (6/7); 1984, pp. 72–89.
4. Lynch, R., *European Business Strategies: The European and Global Strategies of Europe's Top Companies*, Kogan Page, London, 1994.
5. Schlender, B. R. 'Matsushita shows how to go global', *Fortune*, July 11th, 1994, pp. 159–166.
6. Wind, Y., Douglas, S. P. and Perlmutter, H. V., 'Guidelines for developing international marketing strategy' *Journal of Marketing*, April 1973, pp. 14–23.
7. Lascu, D., 'International marketing planning and practice', *Journal of Global Marketing*, **9**, 3, 1996.
8. Cateora, P. R., *International Marketing*, 9th edn, Irwin, Chicago, 1996, p. 89.
9. Ferraro, G. P., *The Culture Dimension of International Business*, 2nd edn, Prentice-Hall, Englewood Cliffs, New Jersey, 1994, p. 17.
10. Chee, H. and Harris, R., 'Global marketing strategies', *Financial Times*, London, 1998, pp. 144–145.
11. Harte, S., 'When in Rome, you should learn to do what the Romans do.' *The Atlanta Journal-Constitution*, January 22nd, 1990, pp. DI, -D6.
12. Buzzell, R. D., *International Marketing*, 6th edn, Prentice Hall, Englewood Cliffs, New Jersey, 2000.
13. Cateora, P. R. and Ghauri, P. N., *International Marketing*, McGraw-Hill, London, 1999, pp. 19–22.
14. Majaro, *International marketing*, Butterworth Heinemann, Oxford, 1996.
15. Wind, Y. *et al.* op. cit. (1973).
16. Quester, P. and Conduit, J., 'Standardization, Centralization and Marketing in Multinational Companies', *International Business Review*, **5**, 4, 1996.

Mary Mullett is pondering a major decision for her UK based company. Twelve months ago, Mary received an unsolicited enquiry from a customer in France. From what was essentially a tentative enquiry regarding simply the possibility of supplying some of the company's products to this customer, this export customer now accounts for some 12% of the company's total sales. Quite simply, this largely passive exporting activity has become very important to Mary's company.

On the basis of this success Mary has to decide whether or not to become more actively involved in other export markets. However, apart from the French market the company has little or no experience of international marketing and markets. Partly due to feedback from the French customer, however, Mary is sure that there is much more potential for the firm to develop its international operations. She is therefore actively researching other markets in Europe both within and outside of the European Union countries.

At this stage, she wants to assess which markets to target for future international expansion. She also has to decide the degree of commitment that she is prepared to make on behalf of the company to international marketing. She is also aware that once she commits beyond the passive exporting stage she will have to consider the appropriate methods of market entry for the countries she selects as the next target markets. Finally, she will have to consider the marketing mix strategies to be used, and in particular the degree of standardisation with regard to the marketing mix.

With little experience in these areas, Mary has sought the advice of an external consultant in international marketing. She is awaiting an initial outline report from the consultant summarising the main considerations in making the decisions that she is currently pondering.

QUESTION

Prepare the summary report for Mary.

19

Analysing case studies

▶ Case study 1: Apex Leisure Limited

▶ Case study 2: Hamid Foods

Introduction

In the preceding chapters we have been concerned to introduce you to the frameworks, concepts, techniques and issues of strategic marketing planning. As was discussed earlier, however, planning is nothing unless, and until, it is put into action.

Most users of this text will, in one way or another, be concerned to apply the principles and techniques to practical marketing problems. No doubt for some users, at this stage the envisaged application will be to case studies on courses on which they are studying and/or for examinations for which they are preparing. Other users will be practising marketing professionals charged with the responsibility of actually preparing strategic marketing plans or, at the very least, inputting to them.

For these reasons, and because the application in many ways is the most exciting and interesting (if most challenging) aspect of strategic marketing planning, this and the following two chapters consist of a framework for analysing and preparing marketing cases followed by two selected case studies which will enable you to practice and develop your skills in tackling such cases and en route seeing how many of the concepts and techniques outlined in earlier chapters apply to 'real life' organizations.

This chapter presents a generalized framework for analysing and preparing cases. It should prove particularly useful to the reader with little experience of how to tackle marketing cases and for those who are preparing for case study examinations.

Then follow two case studies for you to tackle. We hope that for those readers preparing for case study examinations these cases will provide useful practice in applying the tools and techniques for tackling case studies covered in this chapter. However, even if you are not intending to take case study examinations we also hope that you will find the cases helpful in helping you to develop and understand the ideas and skills of marketing management developed throughout this text, ultimately improving your skills as a practising marketing manager. Needless to say, whether you attempt the case studies is entirely up to you but we can assure you that in our view the time and effort involved would be worthwhile.

What is a case study?

A case study is normally a description of a situation, which may be factually based or fictional, which the student has to analyse in order to make recommendations and or answer a number of specific questions. Cases can vary from the very short and simple case to the lengthy and complex ones. They can also be general, encompassing many different areas, or specific, where only a few issues (or possibly one issue) are raised. Finally, cases can be for the experienced or inexperienced manager and for group or individual settings. In short, case studies can vary enormously in nature.

The cases selected here are ones which we believe raise key strategic marketing issues.

Analysing case studies: the key steps

As has just been stated, case studies and what they require in the way of analysis and tasks vary enormously. As was stated, the cases selected here have been chosen to allow readers to explore a variety of strategic marketing issues. It is also important to note that the case studies included in the text pose specific questions for readers to tackle. Needless to say, the specimen answers also address these questions. The fact that our case studies include questions is designed to enable readers to focus more precisely in their analysis on the information and issues in the cases which pertain to these questions. However, many readers in the future, both in examinations and in 'real life' marketing situations, will not, initially at least, know the questions. Rather they will have to sort out for themselves what the key issues in the situation are, as well as their recommendations.

For this reason, therefore, and although our selected cases include questions, what follows is an outline framework for analysing a case study from a strategic marketing perspective. Before looking at it, refamiliarize yourself with the strategic marketing planning framework illustrated in Figure 2.1, on p. 33 above.

Step 1: Reading the case/familiarization

It might sound obvious, but the first step in analysing a case study starts with reading the case and beginning to familiarize oneself with the company, markets, characters and so on. Obvious it might sound, but any experienced case examiner will confirm that all too often it is patently obvious that a candidate has not read the case, at least not thoroughly. Here are some tips on familiarizing yourself with a case study.

1. First of all, read through the case *quickly* several times to familiarize yourself with the situation.
2. At this early stage, do not make any notes. Even if you have been given specific questions on the case, try to keep an open mind as to the key issues. You should simply be considering the facts in the case. Examples of what you are looking for at this stage include the following:

   - Activities of the company: products/markets, etc.
   - Major competitors
   - Company organization, structure, functions, etc.
   - Marketing mix policies: products, price, place, promotion.

Step 2: Situation analysis

This starts the analysis of the case proper using the following procedure:

Assess information in the case   In fact, this is not a discrete step. Throughout a case analysis there is a continual need to assess and reassess the information in a case. However, at this initial stage what one is after is the establishment of a 'data bank' of information which is contained in the case. This data bank can be organized in a variety of ways according to the circumstances of a particular case. For example, where the case study includes questions, the data from various parts of the case can be begun to be assembled under each question topic.

A useful way to begin to build this data bank, and hence to explore key issues for more detailed analysis later in the preparation is, having read through the case several times, to assemble a page by page synopsis of the salient facts of the case as seen by the reader, together with any *initial* thoughts that these facts prompt with respect to possible marketing issues and or case questions if included.

At this stage the strong temptation to prepare 'answers' to the case or questions should be resisted. It is more an issue of organizing the information in a case in a way which makes it easier to use and interpret at a later stage. However, it is important to appraise critically the status of information in a case. Information in a case should be assessed on the extent to which it is:

- Reliable
- Complete
- Precise
- Valid.

The information should also be examined for any 'gaps'. This can prove useful at a later stage in suggesting areas for further market research.

Marketing audit   As we now already know, the marketing audit is an essential step in preparing marketing plans. In the context of a case study, the audit consists of a detailed appraisal of the company in the case and its marketing environment. The aim is to build a complete marketing picture of the company so that a SWOT analysis can be prepared. In carrying out a marketing audit it is useful to use a checklist approach. The problem here is that no checklist can ever be totally complete – nor will every item on a checklist always be relevant to every case. With these caveats in mind, however, in order to help the reader, Table 18.1 includes what is considered to be a useful starter checklist for analysing most cases.

The next stage in a case study analysis is to prioritize the major findings from the audit. We now turn to this next stage, i.e. the so-called 'SWOT analysis'.

Analysing strengths, weaknesses, opportunities and threats (SWOT analysis)
Having completed the marketing audit, the next stage is to analyse and present the information in a format which is useful and relevant to marketing decisions and strategies. This is best done by preparing an analysis of the strengths, weaknesses, opportunities and threats facing the company in the case.

In compiling a SWOT analysis it is important and useful to recognize that strengths and weaknesses essentially stem from the audit of internal company environment, whereas opportunities and threats will stem primarily from trends and changes in the factors covered in your audit of external environmental factors. This is shown in Figure 19.1. This reminds us that a SWOT analysis requires that both 'strengths and weaknesses' and 'opportunities and threats' be appraised together *for the specific company in*

Figure 19.1
SWOT analysis.

External environmental audit

• Macro environment
• Market environment

(analyse for trends/changes

Assess and prioritize
opportunities and threats

⟶ Comparison

Company
Case
Specific
SWOT
Profile

Assess and prioritize
strengths and weaknesses

• Detailed marketing activity
• Marketing systems, procedures
  organization etc.

Internal company environmental audit

the case. For example, rapidly changing technology in an industry can represent *either* an opportunity *or* a threat to individual companies in that industry according to their own particular blend of strengths and weaknesses. Clearly, a company which is flexible, has good planning and forecasting systems, and effective new product planning would probably view rapid technological change as an opportunity rather than a threat.

Similarly, what seem at face value to be, say, apparent strengths in a company, e.g. established products, dominant market share and so on, may well turn out to be weaknesses when set against external environmental trends and changes. For example, dominant market share may be a weakness if new monopoly and fair trading legislation is planned by the government.

Identifying and prioritizing major problems and opportunities: selection of key issues Having made a list of the strengths, weaknesses, opportunities and threats relating to the company in the case, we then need to move on to the next step in the analysis, which is to condense the SWOT even further to product a concise and prioritized list of major problems and major opportunities facing the company in the case, enabling the selection of key issues for the next stage. The relationship between the marketing audit, the SWOT analysis, the identification of major problems and opportunities and the selection of key issues is shown in Figure 19.2.

Techniques for identifying key issues

●   One way in which key issues can be detected is to distinguish between what commonly exists and the desired state for the future.
●   The gap which exists between the SW area and the OT area in SWOT analysis is a rich source for key issues detection.
●   It is important not to consider issues in isolation, for in effect there is usually a causal relationship, which can be quite complex and hence multivariate in origin.
●   Distinction must be drawn between *symptoms* and *fundamental issues* to ensure that the outcomes expected and planned for actually occur.
●   It is useful to distinguish between *existing* issues and *anticipated* issues. For the latter, using the SWOT analysis, this classification can be further divided into areas for opportunity exploitation and areas to avert the risk of implementing threats.

Table 18.1 Marketing audit: checklist of factors

A External/environmental factors

Analyse for current position and trends/changes

A.1 *Macro-environment*
A.1.1 Political/legal/fiscal, e.g.
- Taxation
- Regulatory constraints
- Duty/excise
- Trading blocks
- Patent law
- Labour laws
A.1.2 Economic, e.g.
- Disposable income
- Inflation
- Unemployment
- Exchange rates
- Interest rates
- Taxation
- Currency stability
A.1.3 Social/cultural, e.g.
- Demographic needs
- Education levels
- Attitudes/beliefs/values
- Lifestyle
- Religion
- Consumerism
A.1.4 Technological, e.g.
- Manufacturing processes
- Raw materials
- Innovation and technological change

As they affect the company in the case study

A.2 *Market environment*
A.2.1 Total market, e.g.
- Size ⎫
- Growth ⎬ Volume and value
- Trends ⎭
A.2.2 Competitors, e.g.
- Number
- Strengths/weaknesses
- Barriers to entry/exit
- Strategies
- Profitability
- Shares
- Mergers/takeovers
A.2.3 Customers, e.g.
- Needs/wants
- Buying patterns
- Brand loyalty
- Segments
A.2.4 Distributors, e.g.
- Principal channels
- Trends in channels
- Purchasing strength/power

Table 18.1 Continued

- Location
- Terms and conditions of sale, e.g. margins
- Physical distribution/logistics

A.2.5 Suppliers, e.g.
- Number/types
- Bargaining strengths
- Location

B Internal environment

The internal environment of the company in the case study

B.1 *Detailed marketing activity*
B.1.1 Sales/market share, e.g.
- Total sales (volume/value)
- Market share (volume/value)
- Trends in above
- Sales by products, customer, geographical areas

B.1.2 Marketing mix elements, e.g.
- Prices: pricing strategies, discounts etc.
- Products: range, features, quality, product life cycles, customer service, branding
- Promotion: types, spend, media, sales force activities, organization etc.
- Place: channels used, stock levels, warehousing, delivery systems etc.

B.1.3 Financial aspects, e.g. (see also later notes)
- Profits and margins
- Cost structures
- Liquidity and cash flow
- Asset structure
- Debt/equity structure
- Capital investment levels

B.2 *Audit of marketing systems, procedures, organization etc.*
This part of the internal company audit should encompass the following areas:
B.2.1 Planning systems, e.g.
- Information gathering/marketing research
- Current company and marketing objectives
- Current strategies and tactics
- Control and budgeting systems
- Planning systems – effectiveness and efficiency

B.2.2 Organization and staffing, e.g.
- Overall company and marketing organization structures
- Co-ordination and conflict between marketing and other functional areas, e.g. production, finance, R&D etc.
- Marketing and sales staff: responsibilities, authority, skills and experience

The next stage in a case study analysis is to prioritize the major findings from the audit. We shall now turn our attention to this next stage, i.e. the so-called 'SWOT analysis'.

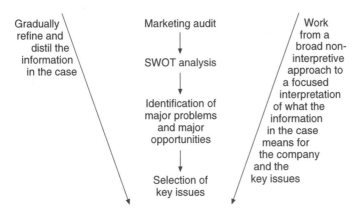

Figure 19.2
From marketing audit to selection of key issues.

- Key issues defined should be **capable of action** and hence they **need to be prioritized** with reference to the scale of the issues specified and the time-scale for overcoming them; hence the use of a time-scale running from the immediate term to the long term over specified years and months is useful.
- In many case studies, key issues may be difficult to define. It is useful, therefore, to distinguish between the following problem areas:

  - Actual explicit issues: provided by clues in the text of the case itself, or in the questions set in the case
  - Concealed issues: identified by your analysis of the case
  - Potential issues, which may arise in the future for the company, and/or on the examination day itself.

- The key issues in case study scenarios must ultimately be assessed in terms of who and what is affected and to what extent the issue is controllable and by whom.
- Key issues can often be highlighted by the imposition of criteria for organizational assessment. It is against such standards that issues which previously had not been identified become revealed.

Further detailed analysis of major issues identified Having identified key issues in the previous step we are then in a position to analyse these areas in more depth, using both the quantitative and, where appropriate, qualitative techniques and tools of market and financial analysis. Applying these tools and techniques will not only provide a deeper insight into the problems and issues facing the company in the case, but may also require redefinition of the problem areas. For example, what from an initial analysis of the case may appear to be a problem of, say, loss of market share may, upon further analysis, turn out instead to be a problem of falling industry sales. Only an in-depth analysis of the information and facts contained in the case enables us to determine what the 'real' problems and opportunities are.

Specifying assumptions and identifying resource constraints Constraints may impose problems upon an organization. They may also provide the limits within which problems can be both identified and researched. By now a detailed analysis of the information in the case should enable us to highlight the constraints, both internal and external, which provide limits to organizational performance and will therefore serve to begin to shape the framework for the subsequent stages, where we begin to develop marketing strategies. For example, the analysis may show that the market as a whole is declining, or that the company in the case has limited financial and/or staff resources, etc. Clearly those types of constraint must be taken account of in shaping future strategies for the company.

Similarly, as in 'real life', often we will have to make assumptions before we can proceed to develop strategies. These assumptions can encompass many and varied areas relating to the case. For example, we may have to make assumptions regarding trends and developments in the macro-environment: say, rates of inflation, or political developments. Or, again, by way of example, we may have to make assumptions regarding, say, future rates of market growth, or resources available to the organization for development. These assumptions are likely to be particularly important in assessing the SWOT analysis. Clearly, we should make as few assumptions as possible, but where it is felt necessary to make assumptions we should be quite clear in our own mind what these are. Indeed, in this initial stage of analysing the case we should explicitly write down our assumptions so that we are reminded of them later on when it comes to proposing actions.

A note on the financial analysis of case studies So far in this chapter we have concentrated on the stages involved in the first step of preparing for an analysis of a case study, namely, familiarization with the case itself and the detailed analyses required to identify key issues in terms of problems and opportunities as a prelude to analysing possible objectives, strategies and action plans in the next step. Clearly, throughout this first step of the analysis we will need to draw upon many of the relevant techniques and concepts of modern marketing which have been discussed in earlier chapters of the text. Most case studies will also require some familiarity with financial analysis. If you feel in need of further basic knowledge of financial aspects of marketing, you are advised to read one of the many excellent texts in this area. However, whilst this text was not designed to provide a comprehensive review of financial techniques, in an analysis of case studies you will probably find that the most useful and used set of financial assessment techniques is **financial ratio analysis**. Hence, in order to facilitate your initial analysis of cases (and if you feel you need it), below we have detailed some of the more useful ratios which you might analyse from case study profit and loss accounts, balance sheets etc.

Some basic financial ratios in analysing case studies

1. *Liquidity ratios*
    These are used to assess the company's ability to meet current financial obligations.
    (a) **The current ratio**
       Formula Current assets divided by current liabilities.

       Interpretation The number of times current liabilities are covered by current assets. This is a fairly crude measure expressing the company's ability to meet current obligations with a margin of safety, which may arise from the varying quality of the current assets, particularly with reference to stocks and the status of debtors. A more critical measure of the company's solvency is the 'quick ratio', known also as the 'acid test'.
    (b) **The acid test**
       Formula Quick assets divided by current liabilities.

       Interpretation The number of times current liabilities are covered by quick assets. Quick assets are cash and 'near cash' items, but *not* stock because it may not be quickly converted to cash. Quick assets are often considered as current assets minus stocks. In most cases this is cash plus debtors, a critical measure which should be in the ratio 1:1.

2. *Profitability ratios*

These are used to assess the company's profit performance with reference to the direct costs and indirect costs of the business and the associated control of both in relation to sales performance.

(a) **Gross profit percentage**

Formula   Gross profit divided by sales, multiplied by 100.

Interpretation   As a percentage of sales revenue, gross profit is the margin created from absolute sales for the period minus the direct costs represented by the cost of sales.

(b) **Net profit percentage**

Formula   Net profit before tax and depreciation divided by sales, multiplied by 100.

Interpretation   Net profit or loss is the result of charging the indirect costs as revenue expenses of the business against the gross profit margin. To present an objective picture the net profit figure is taken before depreciation has been charged and corporation tax deducted.

(c) **Return on total assets**

Formula   Net profit divided by total assets, multiplied by 100.

Interpretation   The ratio measures the rate of profitability achieved on the total assets of the business. Much will depend upon the accuracy of the assets valuation in the company's balance sheet. There is frequent debate over which profit figure to use. The key is to be consistent throughout the analysis. Options include:

- The figure used in the net profit per cent ratio
- Net profit after tax.

In either case, it is considered appropriate to add back the interest charged on long-term debt to demonstrate objectively the company's capacity to produce profits from total asset utilization.

(d) **Return on capital employed**

Formula   Net profit before tax and long-term interest divided by total capital employed, multiplied by 100.

Interpretation   This is considered to be the primary ratio from which family trees of ratios can be extended to form a pyramid. It expresses the efficiency of management and measures its performance to generate a *rate* of return on the total capital and reserve of the business.

(e) **Return on owner's equity**

Formula   Pre-tax profits divided by equity capital, multiplied by 100.

Interpretation   This ratio measures the rate of return on the owner's investment in the business. As a percentage, absolute return can also be measured for every £100 invested.

3. *Funds management*

These ratios are used to assess how efficiently the company uses the available working capital, particularly with reference to inventory holding, debt collection and payment.

(a) **Debtors collection period**
Formula   Debtors divided by sales, multiplied by 365 days.

Interpretation   This ratio determines the time taken by the company to collect debts. It provides a clear indication of the efficiency of credit control.

(b) **Average payment period**
Formula   Creditors divided by purchase, multiplied by 365 days.

Interpretation   This ratio determines the average time taken for the company to pay its bills. The relationship between 3(a) and 3(b) gives an indication of how the company manages cash flow.

(c) **Stock turnover**
Formula   Sales divided by closing stock.

Interpretation   This ratio measures the rate at which stock moves through the business. A more critical measure can be made by taking the cost of sales figure. The ratio is expressed as the 'number of times' stock is turned. If this is then divided into 365 days one can assess the number of days' or months' stock which are tied up on the company shelves. Often less dynamic companies tie up a considerable amount of working capital through poor inventory control.

4. *Ability to borrow*
These ratios demonstrate the position of the company in relation to the level of indebtedness and the management of the capital structures.

(a) **Debt ratio**
Formula   Current liabilities divided by total assets, multiplied by 100.

Interpretation   This ratio measures the percentage value of the current liabilities in relation to the total asset value of the business. This demonstrates the amount of current short-term indebtedness which is covered by the company's assets and hence the company's ability to pay off current liabilities from the sale of total assets.

(b) **Capital gearing ratio**
Formula   Fixed interest capital divided by shareholders' funds, multiplied by 100.

Interpretation   This ratio reflects the percentage of fixed interest capital and business commitments in relation to the shareholders' funds. It shows the relative position of creditors to the business owner's stake in the company. The fixed interest capital figure is also called net debt and is calculated by adding long-term debt to debentures to overdraft and short-term loans less the cash the company has as a current asset.

Step 3: Generation and selection of alternative action plans

The first two steps in the analysis of a case study are essentially focused on assessing where the company in the case is now. This third, and more difficult step, takes us from analysis to action. At this stage we are now required to make a substantial conceptual leap from analysis and problem definition to suggesting alternative solutions and action plans. In preparing action plans, the following aspects from our strategic marketing planning framework in Chapter 1 may need to be assessed, according to the circumstances of the particular case and any specific questions attached. For the purpose of completeness, the key steps are reiterated below.

Defining the business mission   As we have seen, the business mission of a company should precede the setting of marketing objectives and strategies and essentially provides the link between overall corporate objectives and marketing plans.

Defining the business mission requires that two simple but demanding questions be asked and answered as follows:

- What business is the company in now?
- What business should the company be in, now and in the longer term?

We can see from these questions that the business mission is best thought of as a definition of the business. As we now know, many companies define their business either much too narrowly and/or in product terms rather than on the basis of customer needs.

Setting objectives   Objectives provide the basis for the action plans in a case and as such are essential to the process. Broadly, setting objectives involves a company in determining the following:

- What do we wish to achieve?
- In what time-scale?

Remember:

- Objectives should, wherever possible, be *specific* and *quantified*
- Objectives should be *acceptable to* and *agreed by* those charged with the responsibility of achieving them
- Objectives should be *realistic* and *achievable*, pitched neither too high nor too low
- Objectives should be *consistent* and *hierarchical*.

This last point about the need for objectives to be consistent and hierarchical relates to the fact that objectives need to be set at a number of different levels in the organization, and relatedly, encompassing a number of different time-scales, or as they are often referred to, '**planning horizons**'.

For instance, at the corporate level we would expect to find broader objectives encompassing short-, medium- and long-term objectives for the company. Examples of objectives at this level would include objectives for, say:

Corporate objectives	*Short-term*	*Medium-term*	*Long-term*
Profit/Return on Capital Employed			
Productivity			
Market standing			
Social responsibility			
Staff relations			
Innovation			
Sales/market share			

These corporate objectives are, at one and the same time, determined by and in turn feed into and determine objectives for each functional level, including marketing:

Marketing objectives	*Short-term*	*Medium-term*	*Long-term*
Sales/market share			
New product development			
Company/brand image			
Market development			

In turn, at the next level, each functional area needs to break down these broad functional objectives into specific sub-objectives for each area of activity, as follows:

Marketing activity objectives	*Short-term*	*Medium-term*	*Long-term*
Sales objectives			

- By product
- By market

Pricing objectives
Distribution objectives
Communication objectives

Clearly then, objectives at each of these levels need to be consistent.

Initially, at least, it is useful to think in terms of setting the broader higher level objectives relating to corporate and marketing performance, which in turn will later provide a clear focus for action at the more detailed marketing and sales plan levels.

Finally, remember that, as in any company, your objectives should be *flexible*. If circumstances change, then so too must objectives. This includes, of course, any additional information or instructions given to you on the day of the examination.

Identifying and selecting marketing strategies   This stage comprises looking at the alternative broad marketing strategies for achieving objectives. The difficulty and, at the same time, opportunity here is that there are usually several different broad strategies which can be used to meet objectives. Indeed, we may find that we need a number of strategies to achieve our objectives for the company in the case. For example, objectives to increase sales and profits might be achieved through any one, or a combination, of the following broad stages:

1. *Market penetration*
   This strategy is based on increasing sales and profits with **existing products** in existing markets. Sometimes, where the total market is still growing, this strategy may be achieved, for example, through natural market growth. Where markets are static or declining market penetration implies capturing market share.

2. *Market development*
   This strategy is based on a company **entering new markets** with **existing products**. An obvious example is where a company enters, say, new export markets.

3. *Product developments*
   Rather obviously, this strategy is based on developing and launching **new products** for sale in existing markets.

4. *Diversification*
   This strategy is based on **new products** for **new markets**. Diversification can take a number of forms; for example, a company might develop new products which are essentially based on a similar technology to that already used by the company but marketed into totally unrelated markets. Alternatively, and again by way of example, both products and markets may be totally unrelated to the firm's existing operations, e.g. a printing company moving into the package holiday market.

Notes on strategy options

- Again you will appreciate that there are usually any number of strategic options. This gives us the chance to be creative in thinking about a variety of routes that might be chosen to achieve company and marketing objectives.
- The range of strategy options needs to be generated in the context of the case. For example, it is obviously a waste of time looking at strategies which are not suited to the company in the case and/or the environment in which it operates.

Choosing between strategy options   This leads us on to consideration in the selection of strategies. Again, the selection of what you feel to be the best strategies must stem from the details of the specific case and your earlier marketing audit, SWOT analysis, and identification of key issues. Some of the more important factors in selecting between strategies are as follows:

- Company resources/organizational constraints
- Risks associated with each strategy
- Costs of each strategy
- Chances of success.

Certainly some of these, for example risks and the chances of success, are difficult to assess. Overall, however, it is important to try to rank the alternative strategies and select those that offer the most cost-effective way of achieving the organizational and marketing objectives selected for the company in the case.

Marketing action programmes: marketing mix plans   By this stage of the case analysis we should be in a position to begin to develop detailed marketing programmes in order to support broad objectives and strategies. This is best done by detailing plans for each element of the marketing mix in turn. Remember again, though, that each of the elements of the marketing mix must be consistent and co-ordinated one with another. Similarly, of course, the detailed plans for the mix elements must be consistent with and supportive of both objectives and strategies.

As we would expect, therefore, the marketing mix programmes must be developed in relation to the circumstances and facts of the particular case study, again reflecting the whole of the previous analysis.

Notes

- **This step in the case preparation will take a considerable amount of time**. In addition, of course, we will need to be familiar with the relevant concepts and techniques in, for example, promotional planning, product management, including new product development, pricing strategies, and distribution and logistics management.
- **The overall action plans for the marketing mix and, where appropriate, for each individual element of the marketing mix, should specify time-scales and schedules for achievement**. Normally, the planning period for **detailed** marketing programmes will encompass **one year of marketing activities**, i.e. it will be an annual marketing plan. However, again, the circumstances of the particular case and the objectives and strategies which have been selected may dictate the need for both shorter term planning horizons, including the need for immediate action, and/or longer term marketing programmes such as, for example, those needed for new product development.

- Although the detailed plans will cover each of the four Ps of the marketing mix – product, price, place and promotion – we may need to develop these around, say, separate products or possibly different geographical markets, according to how the company in the case is organized. For example, we might need separate plans for the industrial products and consumer products divisions in the company, or for home markets and export markets.

As a guide, here are some factors the detailed marketing mix plans might consider:

Products

- Quality
- Features
- Options
- Style
- Services, installation, warranty
- Packaging
- Range, width and depth
- New product development.

Price
- Pricing strategies, e.g. 'skimming vs. penetration'
- Price changes
- List prices
- Discounts
- Allowances
- Payment and credit terms.

Promotion
- Overall emphasis in promotional mix
- Objectives, strategies and plans for:
  - Personal selling
  - Advertising
  - Sales promotion
  - Public relations and publicity.

Place
- Channel configuration/coverage/levels
- Specific types of intermediaries
- Terms and responsibilities of channel members
- Order processing systems
- Warehousing, storage, stocking and delivery policies.

Note: wherever appropriate and possible we need to develop detailed plans for each of the sub-elements of the mix.

For example, under the promotional element of the mix you will need to develop detailed plans for the advertising element, which may include:

- Objectives
- Copy content/message
- Media decisions
- Timings/frequency
- Measurement of effectiveness/control.

Costing detailed marketing plans   Remember our observation earlier in this chapter about the need to consider the financial aspects of the case and our suggested strategies. As much as is possible on the basis of both the information in the case combined with up-to-date information on marketing costs, we need to determine costs for the proposals.

For example, for the advertising element of the plan we may need to ascertain likely costs and hence the required spend/budgets. Clearly, if these subsequently turn out to be unrealistic in the context of the case, due, say, to the size of the company and a lack of resources, we may need to rethink our objectives and strategies.

Implementation, organization and staffing   This step of our preparation of a case requires us to consider how, and by who, the plans will be implemented. The degree of detail both possible and necessary here will of course depend on the nature of the case, but below are some of the factors that we may need to consider:

- Required organizational structures
- Responsibilities and authority, including chains of command
- Staffing considerations, including numbers, skills/training, redundancies etc.
- Motivation and attitudes of staff.

In many case studies we will probably have to recommend changes in one or more of the above areas. In addition, of course, the recommendations we make for marketing strategies may involve significant change in the company.

Hence, how to manage this change process may be part of the recommendations. In a wider context, these staffing and organizational aspects of the case study are part of effective human resource management.

Remember, too, that staffing and organizational issues also extend to the appointment, liaison with, and appraisal of external agencies and consultants. As we know, particularly in marketing, extensive use is made of such external agencies and we must fully cover these areas in the case.

Expected results, forecasts and control mechanisms   In the past many marketing case studies often required the production of strategic plans in a vacuum where the input was simply the case study material and the output was a well presented strategic marketing plan. However, increasingly organizations are now asking for answers to the following questions:

- When implemented, what will be the tangible results of the proposed action?
- Can these results be quantified?

Therefore, the projected outcomes of marketing plans should be considered not only in terms of qualitative contribution, but also in financial terms. Indeed, in some case studies the questions will often explicitly specify that we must consider the financial implications. However, even where financial implications are not explicitly mentioned, any good marketing plan should encompass them and we should therefore include the financial aspects in our analysis.

Again, the amount of detail we will be able to include in this section will vary according to the information given in the case study, but wherever possible the analysis should encompass forecasts for the following:

- Sales volume
- Costs/margins
- Profit
- Return on capital employed

- Liquidity of cash flow, current ratios etc.
- Debt/asset structure.

Provided we have costed our marketing programmes in the earlier stage of our analysis, we should attempt to prepare a budget for the company as follows.

Example of budget format and forecasts

	Year 1	Year 2	Year 3*
Gross sales revenue (quantities × prices)			
Variable cost of production	_____	_____	_____
Gross contribution	_____	_____	_____
Less marketing costs			
Advertising and promotion			
Sales force			
Distribution and margins			
Packaging			
Customer service			
Marketing research	_____	_____	_____
Net contribution	_____	_____	_____
Less overheads			
Net operating profit	_____	_____	_____

*The number of years you will be required to forecast depends on the circumstances of and information in each individual case.

Finally, in this section of our case study we consider **control mechanisms** plus any **necessary marketing information systems**. The control aspects of the plan should be designed to enable the company to monitor and assess performance against objectives and targets in order that any deviations can be measured and appropriate action taken.

To design a control system for the marketing plan, ideally all the main elements in the plan should have a set of specified controls tailored to fit the plan and the organization. The control systems should enable analysis and problem diagnosis, and specify priorities for feedback, responsibilities and action programmes.

To assist both in the control of the marketing plan and in order to 'fill in' any information gaps identified in your initial analysis of the case study, we may also **need to consider the marketing information systems required**. Again, the precise requirements and the complexity of the system will vary considerably depending on the size of the company in the case and the particular circumstances. We should consider what the marketing planning system needs, in what form, and what is economically feasible within the financial resource constraints of the organization.

Contingency planning The purpose of contingency planning is to force us to think ahead to answer the question of **'what if?'** e.g.

- What if the environment or circumstances change which forces a rethink of our original plans?
- What if our original plans do not produce the expected results?

As in real life, we should consider alternative contingency plans for the company in the case. In preparing these contingency plans we should consider in particular the assumptions which we made in our earlier analysis. For example, if we assumed, say, that the market would grow and this turns out not to be the case, then we need to consider in advance how this would affect our plans. Similarly, perhaps we have assumed that sufficient resources would be available to implement our plans. Again, if this assumption is critical to the plan's success then we ought to consider contingency plans.

We should also consider how flexible our plan is should conditions change and what options are open to the company in the light of anticipated change.

A final note on writing up case studies

Given that most marketing case studies are testing and developing management skills, it is conventional to write up an analysis of a case study in a report-type format. The conventions for structuring a report vary considerably but should you be unfamiliar with report writing/structure we have included a simple outline of how to prepare and structure a report.

1. *Planning a report on a case study*
   The planning stage starts with the purpose of the report, what is to be included, how it is to be presented, and to whom it is to be presented. Sectionalizing the report and the use of clear headings – especially where a case includes a number of separate questions – will help to produce a good report, but so too will starting the report itself with a statement of 'terms of reference'.

2. *Terms of reference*
   At the start of a report it is a good idea to write out the terms of reference so that we can demonstrate that we understand precisely what we have been asked to do. Terms of reference should include the following:

   ● Who the report is for and or by whom it has been requested, e.g. 'At the request of the marketing manager of Smith plc . . .'
   ● The areas to be covered (i.e. the questions), e.g.
     – Methods of entry into overseas markets
     – The promotional mix
     – Pricing strategies
   ● The intended outcome of the report, e.g.
     – To establish strategies for developing export markets . . .
     – To make proposals for a co-ordinated promotional campaign . . .
   ● The constraints/assumptions (if any) which affect the report, e.g.
     – Within a proposed budget for promotion of £50,000 . . .
     – In compiling the report it has been assumed that the rate of inflation will continue to be 5 per cent per annum . . .

3. *Proposals and recommendations*
   Remember that reports are not extended essays but concise statements which set out our thoughts simply and clearly. In most reports it is the proposals and recommendations which are of prime interest (although clearly these must be based on sound analysis).

   All proposals and recommendations should be justified to support them, but do not bore the reader with overcomplicated or in-depth analysis. For the most part, any detailed calculations and analysis, if required in the report, should form part of the appendices.

4. *Structuring the report*
    The conventions for structuring a report vary considerably. Here is one example of a report structure which you could use.

    (a) *Title page* Title of report, to whom addressed, the date, author's name, company etc.
    (b) *Terms of reference* Resume of terms of reference (as above)
    (c) *Contents list* Report structure together with the numbering system which is used throughout the report. Major headings and sub-headings would be shown
    (d) *The main report* This should include the detailed facts and recommendations contained in the report
    (e) *Appendices* So that the main flow of argument is not interrupted by a mass of detail, financial and other data can be summarized or referred to in the report, but attached at the end. As an alternative, we could insert a *summary* of the main findings and recommendations between the title page and terms of reference. This is quite common and useful in report writing.

Above all, it is important that we structure a report to achieve the following:

*   The report should, as far as is possible, be interesting
*   The report should be easy to understand
*   The report should follow a logical sequence, leading the reader along a particular path.

5. *Presentation*
    Presentation is crucial for a report to be well received. Each page must be well laid out to appeal to the reader's eye.
    The use of white space, headings and sub-headings, indentations and report numbering systems should be applied to create maximum impact.

Case 1: Apex Leisure Ltd

'A new company, with a new concept in total fitness', claimed Alan Brooks back in July 1996. Alan Brooks was then the new managing director of Apex Leisure Ltd, based in Bracknell, Berkshire. At that time his statement was made with a vision focussed on a five-year future time horizon. Initially the new private limited company were the sole importers and distributors of multigym equipment for use in sports clubs and gymnasiums around the UK. Their overnight success led to a much bolder move just two years later when a 20-year lease was signed for a new property with vacant possession in the heart of the City of London.

The lease was granted by Wates Estates, who owned the new freehold site – an ambitious complex of residential, office and commercial units which, in architectural terms, could only be described as tastefully futuristic.

The trustees of Wates Estates were reluctant to grant the lease to Apex Leisure Ltd, because their short-term history was insufficient grounds for a solid covenant. Nonetheless, Apex plans for the site were heartening, and with solid trade and bank references, plus a good personal projection on the part of Alan Brooks, his ambition set earlier in 1996 was realized.

On the signing of the fully repairing and insurance lease with agreed five-yearly rent reviews, the 'concept' of the Brooks Health and Fitness Centre was off the ground. A full 12 months of renovation led in July 1999 to the opening of 'The Brooks Club', one of the largest and best equipped fitness centre in the capital city.

Pride, ambition and achievement, however, had to be balanced with the realities of financing the business. Alan Brooks had little training in this area and until 1996 this 42-year-old entrepreneur, father of two, had seven years' relevant experience in retail selling and sales management in the health foods products industry.

The 'easy fortunes' of the multigym business were soon eroded in financing a much larger project. The financial difficulties facing Alan Brooks were typical of the small business whose ambition far exceeds an ability to plan and control business operations:

1. The business was under capitalized.
2. Insufficient working capital needs had been projected.
3. Cash flow forecasting was far too ambitious in the overestimation of revenue and the under estimation of expenditure.
4. Unrealistic planning for breakeven and profit volume considerations.
5. Insufficient professional advice before embarking upon the project.

The supporting bank were very concerned with the trading progress and threatened to foreclose on the business.

So began the history of the Brooks Club, with the near bankruptcy of the business owner. However, the freeholders of the site, Wates Estates, were still committed to the concept of the club and furthermore had successfully completed leases on other units in the complex based upon the fact that these facilities would be available. In December 1999 Wates Estates acquired an 80% shareholding in Apex Leisure Ltd and injected substantial venture capital to rescue the situation. Alan Brooks was retained as managing director but Clare Hepburn was appointed as director of the club, which then was renamed 'Crispins' to reflect, she claimed, the fitness image which should accord with the club.

Clare was a natural choice for the position as she had operated a similar club in Miami, USA, for four years and had just recently returned to the UK.

So with a somewhat chequered history, Crispins opened officially for business on 1st February 2000 and today is managed soundly under Clare's direction, with membership building in numbers and the club growing in stature and local recognition.

At a recent presentation to prospective corporate club members, Clare gave her well rehearsed introduction:

> Why do we focus attention upon corporate *financial* accounts to assess performance? Why are we preoccupied with the bottom line? The answer may be simply, survival!!
>
> If we take a more creative view, then the minefield of human asset accounting leads us to realize that corporate financial health depends upon the well-being of company staff.
>
> In short, it is long since time that companies took a keen look at investment in employees as well as return on investment in future and current capital projects!
>
> Yes, it is time for *British* companies to consider *American* style corporate fitness programmes, because the evidence is building that business enterprises are gaining profitable growth from giving health a high priority.
>
> Recent surveys have revealed that over 35 million working days are lost every year in *Britain* owing to employee heart conditions. The coincident loss of revenue is estimated at £1.5 billion!!
>
> How can we continue to ignore these facts of commercial life? Take, for example, the threat of Japanese competition and the increasingly global challenges. The British are nine times more likely to die from heart disease . . . . Why should we assess the market place as the only field to do battle, when diet and exercise should be the training ground upon which effective and sustained business strategy depends. Do you realize that over 20 people die every hour from coronary failure here in Britain?
>
> So what is to be done?
>
> Well, the evidence relating to successful fitness initiatives are not Japanese in origin, but American!!
>
> Corporate health programmes have been in operation for some years and their effectiveness is beyond doubt. Health care programmes have achieved remarkable results: absenteeism arising from sickness – down 15 per cent in one major multinational after 18 months and 40 per cent down over five years in one major American oil company. Even insurance companies who had a better than average position in the stress ratings of executives claim marked improvements in the number of working days lost after the introduction of health care programmes for male and female staff.
>
> The 'heart' of any corporation is *its people*, corporations must look after their *people's hearts*.
>
> A good example has been set by the British government's Department of Employment with initiatives on to smoking, drinking, exercise, health screening and so on, but it's time now for your companies to look after their employees' hearts. Yes, it's time now to wake up to the problem!! There are simply *too many excuses* that cause corporate health and fitness to be a low priority on the corporate agenda – usually, lack of executive time and the fallacious assumption that staff have to be superfit and hyperhealthy before starting a fitness programme. Maybe the weakest but most frequently cited excuse is 'Well we like the way we are!'
>
> A survey recently completed shows a marked difference in attitude between American and UK companies, the former considering the issue as one of corporate and social responsibility, the latter dispensing with the issue lightly.
>
> Surely, to change attitudes, to change behaviour to overcome complacence, corporate fitness must be packaged to make it attractive – that is where we can help!! Welcome to Crispins.

Following Clare's introduction, the group are then shown the comprehensive facilities – the short tour is also a well rehearsed routine to show the club 'in use', working, rather than empty and in a pristine untouched condition. Visits are timed tactically to achieve the best possible impression to the first time visitor.

The impression created is usually most favourable.

After the visit, the group is normally handed over to the membership secretary who, in a well rehearsed professional manner, concludes the visit with a brief statement of the benefits derived from joining Crispins. The script has been carefully prepared by Clare Hepburn and reads:

> At Crispins a free full health screening is offered to all members, with a confidential interview and the completion of a computerized questionnaire with one of our medical staff.
>
> The survey inquires about eating habits, exercise taken, levels of perceived stress and the areas to which it relates, and lifestyle. A comprehensive medical examination is then given so that an individual assessment is made of each club member. Exercise programmes are now prescribed, after consultation with the club member's local general practitioner (doctor) should there be a specified problem.
>
> A variety of activities will be combined to build up stamina and improve members' fitness. These include aerobics activities, swimming, weight training and use of exercise equipment in our gymnasium. Following this initiation into the world of enhanced fitness many members make fuller use of the comprehensive range of facilities that are offered.
>
> Members soon become addicted to the benefits that are directly derived from getting into good physical and hence good mental shape.
>
> The social atmosphere at Crispins spurs people to adopt a healthier approach to life.

At the end of this typical routine, Clare normally reappears to make a concluding statement:

> It is common practice for our staff to give presentations to companies or to invite them to visit the club and inspect our facilities, but sooner or later companies may take the initiative and come to us and not wait for an invitation. Then we will know we have a successful concept – it is only a matter of time!
>
> Thank you for visiting Crispins today. Our brochure contains comprehensive details of the terms and conditions of club membership.
>
> We look forward to receiving your applications in due course but in the meantime please do not hesitate to contact me or Fiona, our membership secretary, should you have any further questions.

It is company policy *NOT* to sign up new members on the day of the visit. The selling activity is conceived as 'deliberately low profile' to avoid the impression that the 'club needs new members'. Seven days are allowed to elapse before Fiona will make a follow up telephone call to those who have visited the club as potential corporate or individual members.

Wates Estates are delighted with the progress that has been achieved with Crispins and have now realized the potential of diversification beyond the business of estate management, in which they have a 90 year history.

As a trust body, Wates Estates have substantial funds, backed with an equally substantial fixed assets portfolio of freehold property around London and the surrounding counties. One such property is Acotts Manor, a stately home in Berkshire, purchased for an undisclosed sum from the previous owners in 1995. Until recently the property had been leased to and occupied by an American film producer, but is now empty and destined for a new beginning. The appointment of Adrian Scott as business development manager led Sir Douglas Reed, chairman of Wates Estates, to explain their intention:

> At Acotts Manor we need to meet the challenge of the next decade and beyond; we need to build also in new directions. Stately homes, unless open to the public, are a drain on any owner's financial resources and hence the Board of Trustees have decided to take a new challenge, one of substance, we think.

We have commissioned Leonard Grey & Partners for the development, which has already started, and will take place over three to four years in two stages. Firstly, to open Acotts Manor as a model lifestyle centre for getting into good physical and mental shape and secondly, to extend the planned facilities and capacity by building more residential facilities within the surrounding parkland.

Appendix 1: Crispins – an outline of club facilities

1. *Club opening hours*
   6.30 a.m. until 10.30 p.m. Monday to Friday
   10.00 a.m. until 5.30 p.m. Saturdays

2. *Days closed*
   Sundays and public holidays

3. *Sports facilities*
   Swimming pool
   Squash courts
   Fully equipped gymnasium with state of the art machines, including multistation gyms, vertical chest benches, exercise bikes, treadmills, rowing machines, weights and all standard equipment.

4. *Health facilities*
   Sauna baths, male and female (separate)
   Steam baths, male and female (separate)
   Hydro pool and jacuzzi

5. *Group exercise sessions*
   Low intensity aerobics
   Water exercise classes*

6. *Treatments*
   (a) Solarium
   (b) Therapeutic massage

7. *Low calorie restaurant – serving lunch and dinner*
   (closed Saturday)

8. *Bar – serving soft drinks and alcoholic beverages*

9. *Other activities/facilities*
   (a) Periodic lectures on health, heart care and stress management
   (b) Quarterly club magazine outlining past and future events
   (c) Organizing of sports activity holidays
   (d) Doctor in attendance for consultation each weekday evening.

   Note
   At Crispins, individualized exercise programmes are given to all members by qualified and trained instructors.

*To be introduced.

Appendix 2: Crispins – organization chart, March 2001

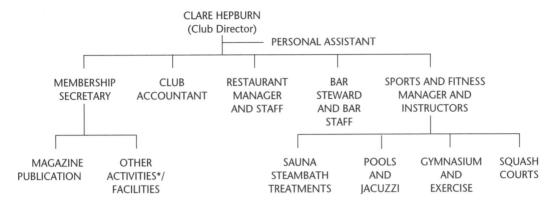

Note

Crispins have geared up staff in anticipation of reaching the membership target of 850 members, so currently there is ample capacity to manage and operate the club.

*See Crispins – an outline of club facilities.

Appendix 3: Crispins – club membership status, March 2001

	Current	Target for December 2001
Total number of members	540	850
Female members	30%	50%
Male members	70%	50%
Individual members	80%	60%
Corporate members*	20%	40%
Membership joining fee	£700	£850
Annual fees per member	£1500	£1800
% payable by credit card	15%	25%
% payable by monthly direct debit	80%	25%
% cash or cheque in advance	5%	50%
Active membership (at least three attendances weekly)	45%	80%
Passive membership (at least three attendances monthly)	35%	20%
Inactive membership (less than one attendance in three months)	5%	–
Subscriptions cancelled	15%	–

*Corporate members pay one membership joining fee of £700 but are required to pay a £6,000 annual fee in return for ten corporate membership cards. All members must be designated by the company. Memberships are not transferable to other employees unless at the express written request of the company. Memberships cannot be bought or sold on the open market.

Appendix 4: Crispins – current membership profile, March 2001

1.

Age/sex	Male	Female
18*–24	19	20
25–34	81	97
35–44	212	40
45–54	60	5
55–64	6	–
	378	162

*Persons under 18 years of age are not eligible to attend the club.

2. *Socio economic groupings*

	AB	C1	C2	DE
Male	313	53	12	–
Female	85	69	8	–

3. *Exercise activity at time of joining*

	No regular exercise	Some exercise	Using a planned exercise routine
Male	213	90	75
Female	45	80	37

4. *Age: weight:height ratio at time of joining*

	% overweight for height within age band	
	Male	Female
18–24	10%	15%
25–34	40%	45%
35–44	70%	40%
45–54	50%	50%
55–64	33%	–

5. *Family status*

	Single	Married	Married with children
Male	65	40	273
Female	70	36	56

6. *Salary levels per annum*

£ sterling	Male	Female
Less than 15,000	–	–
15,000–18,999	–	8
19,000–22,999	26	29
23,000–26,999	38	26
27,000–30,999	42	43
31,000 and above	272	56

7. *Main mode of getting to work*

	Rail	London underground (tube)	Car	Walk	Taxi	Bicycle
Male	212	65	53	3	37	8
Female	70	48	19	12	11	2

6. *Time taken to arrive at the club from home*

Minutes	Male	Female
Less than 10	–	–
10 but less than 20	–	2
20 but less than 30	10	4
30 but less than 40	20	19
40 but less than 50	36	26
50 but less than 60	77	30
60 and over	235	81

9. *Time taken to arrive at the club from the place of employment*

Minutes	Male	Female
Less than 10	59	20
10 but less than 20	90	36
20 but less than 30	173	80
30 but less than 40	37	26
40 but less than 50	19	–
50 but less than 60	–	–
60 and over	–	–

10. *Membership of other clubs/associations* (number)*

Purpose	Male	Female
For general health and fitness	19	26
Business	57	5
Social and entertainment	6	5
For dedicated sports activities	52	11
Others	7	12

*Certain members have more than one other membership

11. *Attendance at any health farm*

	Never	Once only	Once per year	More than once per year
Male	345	27	6	–
Female	90	47	20	5

12. *Main motivations stated for joining Crispins*

	Male	Female
To lose weight	113	83
To learn to swim	17	26
To keep fit	270	162
To take regular exercise	143	102
As a preventive health care activity	216	90
To balance executive stress with bodily exercise	247	71

To regain personal vitality	42	15
To remedy a health weakness	36	12
To recover from a long-term illness	6	2
To help to regain total fitness	137	72

13. *Averaged personal priority rankings of members at time of joining*

		18–24 M	18–24 F	25–34 M	25–34 F	35–44 M	35–44 F	45–54 M	45–54 F	55–64 M	55–64 F
1.	Work	1	1	1	1	1	1	1	2	2	4
2.	An active social life with friends	2	3	3	4	10	8	3	4	6	3
3.	In home entertaining	11	11	2	5	5	4	4	5	3	7
4.	Watching television as a form of relaxation	6	6	9	7	6	5	5	6	5	5
5.	Eating out	7	5	8	8	4	6	7	7	11	12
6.	Family life in general	8	7	4	3	2	2	2	1	1	1
7.	Keeping fit	4	4	7	6	11	7	12	10	8	6
8.	Visiting relatives	9	9	10	9	9	10	6	8	7	8
9.	Holidays taken overseas	5	8	6	10	7	9	10	9	12	10
10.	Attention to personal grooming and attire	3	2	5	2	3	3	9	3	9	2
11.	Maintenance of home and garden	12	12	11	12	8	12	8	12	4	9
12.	Hobbies not involving physical exercise	10	10	12	11	12	11	11	11	10	11

M = Male   F = Female

Appendix 5 transcript of interview conducted by Adrian Scott with Clare Hepburn, March 2001

1. How would you describe the nature of your business at Crispins?
   Reply
   If you are asking for a mission statement, I have this already prepared for our new brochure. It reads:

   The Crispins Club is in the business of providing a wide range of facilities and treatments to assist in the enhancement of people's personal health and fitness and thereby to improve their duration and quality of life.
      Through our collective experience we aim to give the highest levels of caring individual attention to our members in the areas of health and fitness training and planned exercise programmes.
      At Crispins our members' health is a first priority.

2. Within the current resources, what are your expectations for the club?
   Reply
   Firstly, to build membership to the levels targeted; secondly achieve a balanced use of the facilities we provide for our members; and finally, achieve the financial performance budgeted and agreed with our parent company, Wates Estates.

3. What are the main constraints which restrict the achievement of these expectations?
   Reply
   (a). Limited personal time: I am able to devote to personalized promotion to individuals and companies as potential members.
   (b). Members' disposable time and availability of club time are difficult to harmonize.

4. With what degree of efficiency or effectiveness is the club operating?
   Reply
   Well above expectations at this point in time, but well below maximum capacity.

5. Where do you see the club, say, in five years' time?
   Reply
   By that time, operating effectively at maximum capacity, with a sound financial and market standing, productive and continuing to innovate in the fields of personal health and fitness.

6. What do you consider to be the main strengths of Crispins?
   Reply
   Well, there are many, so I'll give them to you off the top of my head. Location, catchment area, accessibility to the London Underground network, Crispins is 'new' with up-to-date facilities, there is total care for members from fitness assessment to individual coaching, easy payment terms, highly qualified staff recruited from the top physical education colleges in the UK, support from major companies, high profile in the locality, Olympic standard swimming pool, excellent security, good quality clientèle.
      I suppose also we have become a lunch time and evening oasis for the gathering of office weary executives.

7. How about weaknesses? What do you consider these to be?
   Reply
   Well, we are only just finding these out as a result of experience. There is a substantial variation in the patterns of club attendance and usage. There are no car parking facilities nearby. Our inactive accounts suggest something is wrong but I don't know what .... yet!
      We have a company policy of taking no outside bookings of club facilities. I am

not happy with this because it frustrates financial performance. This may become acute because our business is seasonal. July, August, December, January and Easter are all low periods. We need to attract more members of the right calibre without appearing too exclusive, yet I do not want to open the floodgates to all comers.

8. How would you assess the future of the club in terms of unexploited opportunities?
Reply
Well, this is difficult because my main concern is reaching our membership targets. Then it is time to plan ahead, and I may need your help.

9. I will be only too happy to help provided you don't view me as someone from head office spying on what you are up to! To return to business, what do you see as the main threats facing Crispins in the future?
Reply
Crispins, as you know, had a shaky start. I have not met Alan Brooks so it is unfair to comment further. However, we are saddled with a five-year rent review and estimates from friends in the property business have considered an increase of 150% to be realistic. This will put considerable pressure on club financing, membership fees and who knows what else. Even though Wates Estates own the freehold, we are expected to bear market level rents. We are an independent profit centre even within Apex Leisure Ltd. I have heard rumours that another club is to be opened in a nearby four-star hotel within the next nine months. This places even more pressure on us to get new members signed up now!

10. Where do you see the key areas of future business potential?
Reply
In the area of corporate health and fitness, and we have the ability to exploit it.

11. I would like to ask you an open question about Acotts Manor. What are your feelings?
Reply
Well, this *is* a catch-all question. Where were you trained? OK, here goes. My initial reaction to your question is that Acotts is simply fabulous. I would love to have the reins and really make it big in the residential health, beauty and fitness market.

The history, location and ambience have been retained; many of the rooms have been retained in the traditions of the period. The business concept is difficult to position. It is a hotel on the one hand, a gourmet restaurant on the other, a health farm for the rich and famous, a sports and fitness centre for the locals. Furthermore, the picture will become even more complex if the time-sharing venture is launched.

I can see that our parent company seeks maximum flexibility in the usage of the facilities and at the same time, to use your jargon, needs maximum capacity utilization – I just hope it works. On the other hand – and now I have run out of hands – from Wates Estates' viewpoint, the site was a burden. Now, after investing, I guess, a very substantial sum indeed, they will get capital appreciation from the site and in time cash flow from the business to cover the fixed and variable costs. Clearly profit is a much longer term goal. I have not been involved in planning. I made one suggestion to build repeat business that was the 'Acotts Gold Card', giving credit facilities to holders and preferential discounts on beauty treatments. This has been adopted, and with 365 days trading on site it may be a substantial benefit.

I would imagine that there has been adverse reaction from local people and as time goes on it will increase the traffic to an otherwise quite rural area.

If the pressure becomes too great the entire site could be disposed of as a going concern. This is typical of acquisitions strategy that is hitting the hotel and leisure market generally.

I hope this is helpful. These are random thoughts only and not what I would call a professional, considered opinion.

Appendix 6: Crispins – club usage analysis, March 2001

Sports facilities

		Hours											
	6.30–8.30		**8.30–10.30**		**10.30–12.30**		**12.30–2.30**		**2.30–4.30**		**4.30–6.30**		**6.30–10.30**	
	Day	Use	Day	Use	Day	Use	Day	Use	Day	Use	Day	Use	Day	Use
Swimming pool**	M	L	M	L	M	L	M	M	M	L	M	M	M	M
	T	L	T	L	T	L	T	M	T	L	T	M	T	M
	W	M	W	L	W	L	W	M	W	L	W	M	W	H
	TH	M	TH	L	TH	L	TH	M	TH	L	TH	M	TH	M
	F	M	F	M	F	L	F	L	F	L	F	L	F	M
	S	–	S	–	S	L	S	L	S	L	S	–	S	–
Squash courts+	Moderate use M to F		Light use M to F		Light use M to F		Moderate use M to F		Moderate use M to F		Heavy use M to F		Heavy use M to F	
					Light use S		Light use S		Light use S		Light use S			

Gymnasium**

Weekdays: 6.30 to 8.30 a.m. light usage; 8.30 a.m. to 4.30 p.m. very light usage; 4.30 to 6.30 p.m. light usage; 6.30 p.m. to 10.30 p.m. moderate usage;

Saturdays: The use is negligible

Group exercise sessions

Low intensity aerobics+ Two one-hour sessions held Tuesdays, Wednesdays and Thursdays, 6.30–8.30. Well attended by ladies

Health facilities

Sauna baths** — No daytime usage. Moderate usage 6.30 to 10.30 p.m.

Steam baths** — No daytime usage. Moderate usage 6.30 to 10.30 p.m.

Hydropool**
Jacuzzi** — The pattern of usage is very similar to that of the swimming pool

Treatments

Solarium+
(30 minute sessions)
Hours 10.30 a.m. to
10.30 p.m.
Close Saturdays — Heavily booked Monday to Friday 10.30 to 4.30 p.m.
Light use only   6.30 to 10.30 p.m.

Therapeutic massage+
Hours 4.30 p.m. to
10.30 p.m.
Closed Saturdays — Light usage until 6.30 p.m. Then moderate usage until 10.30 p.m.

Facilities

Hours

	6.30–8.30		8.30–10.30		10.30–12.30		12.30–2.30		2.30–4.30		4.30–6.30		6.30–10.30	
	Day	Use	Day	Use	Day	Use	Day	Use	Day	Use	Day	Use	Day	Use
Restaurant++	–		–		M	L	M	M	M	M	–		M	L
	–		–		T	L	T	M	T	M	–		T	L
	–		–		W	L	W	H	W	M	–		W	M
	–		–		TH	L	TH	H	TH	M	–		TH	M
	–		–		F	L	F	H	F	H	–		F	L
Bar++	–		–		M	L	M	L	M	L	M	L	M	M
	–		–		T	L	T	M	T	L	T	L	T	M
	–		–		W	M	W	H	W	M	W	L	W	M
	–		–		TH	M	TH	H	TH	M	TH	L	TH	M
	–		–		F	M	F	H	F	H	F	M	F	H

**Free use to members
+Additional charge to members
++Prices at competitive market rates

codes: M = Monday; T = Tuesday; W = Wednesday; TH = Thursday; F = Friday; S = Saturday.
L = light occasional usage; M = moderate regular usage; H = heavy usage.

Appendix 7: Acotts manor – history and location

Acotts Manor, set in 315 acres of peaceful private parkland, has been described as a stately home. It dates back to the 17th century and, like many such manorial residences, has been extended over succeeding years to provide substantial accommodation.

This lakeside Berkshire manor house has 42 bedrooms, a range of reception rooms and an historic library, all steeped in English history. The outbuildings are of especial interest, in particular two huge barns which are claimed to be even older than the original house. In former times owners used the barns for banqueting and more recently, have been open to the general public on public holidays as a revenue earning activity for the owner.

With the comprehensive motorway network which now dissects the country, the manor is within relatively easy reach by car. The manor is within 1½ hours driving time of Central London and somewhat less from the major airports of Gatwick and London Heathrow. Major population centres are hence within easy reach. The nearest Rail station is 33 minutes taxi drive.

Few places in Britain offer the potential for tasteful development, to enable more people to experience part of our English heritage and to enjoy the environment of the English countryside.

Appendix 8: Acotts manor
Stage one development
Target date to open June 2002

Interview conducted by Adrian Scott with Leonard Grey, senior partner and architect of Leonard Grey & Partners, March 2001.

'Acotts is to be transformed, with local planning permission already granted, from a country setting of slow but certain decay, into one of the top six residential fitness and leisure centres in Britain, with conference facilities to seat 80 persons theatre style.

The lakeside location provides for a host of leisure and enthusiastic water activities ranging from sailing, windsurfing, canoeing and fishing to beautiful parkland walks and horse riding. Areas have been designated for clay pigeon shooting, archery and even falconry. To complete the outdoor provision are six grass tennis courts and a nine-hole golf course which is to be extended to 18 holes in the future.

The vagaries of English weather have been anticipated; hence a balanced range of indoor facilities comprise swimming pool, heated spa pools, separate male and female saunas, solarium and eight squash courts. A small gymnasium will be equipped with exercise machines similar to those at the Crispins club for use under the expert guidance of highly trained instructors. Aerobics will be featured as a regular daily activity.

The range of beauty treatments, beauty therapy and beauty culture is planned to be extensive, including personal skin care, body and facial massage, skin analysis and consultation, deep cleansing facials, manicure, nail sculpture, pedicure, aromatherapy, herbal baths, eyebrow trimming and eyelash tinting and perming and associated cosmetology. The hairdressing salon will not only provide traditional cut, style and trim, but also hair examination to determine the strength of hair roots so that appropriate hair treatments can be recommended.

To assist guests attending Acotts, a small shop will be opened within the manor to retail products for skin, body and hair care, biocosmetics and shampoos, natural food supplements for sports people, a limited range of natural dietary foods, vitamins and mineral supplements and homeopathic medicines. For the more studious even a range of health books will be on offer.

Acotts as a centre of excellence will be committed to total health care and in particular is emphasizing the gains from alternative medicine. Acupuncture treatment and reflexology will be arranged by special appointment.

All this means that Acotts Manor is to be a health farm of distinction. Plans are even made to run professional beauty training courses leading to international diplomas with the aim to produce top beauticians and to use the manor as a means of getting export exposure under the guidance of the Acotts professional team.

Two restaurants will be opened to cater for distinct but different needs. 'Bites', with a low calorie menu for weight watchers, which also provides hot and cold non alcoholic beverages 9 a.m. to 7 p.m., and 'Acotts', a refined licensed dining room serving classic English cuisine – open both to residents and non residents.

You may be amazed at the detail I have given you, but I have worked with Sir Douglas for many years, we are close family friends and his wife, Doreen, is a qualified beautician who frequents the top health farms. Her help has been simply tremendous'.

Acotts manor
Stage two development
Tentative date for completion, July 2005

'As you will understand, stage two is even more ambitious.

Planning permission has been applied for and granted for 30 fully equipped timber framed lodges, purpose built, individually sited in the grounds, each to sleep four to six persons. This will develop the current concept of Acotts Manor into a luxury time share complex. By buying into the time share scheme, lodge time owners can become members of Acotts and thereby use the facilities, not just for the period of the time share but each day for the 40-year period of the time share agreement.

With an awareness of the negative publicity that has been given to the characteristic high pressure salesmanship associated with time share ventures, Acotts plan to complete these new leisure facilities first so that the prospective purchaser can view that which is being purchased. Furthermore, a full 30 days period for cancellation has been determined to avoid bad publicity.

The time share lodges are to be fully equipped to a high specification for self catering, including microwave ovens, dishwashers, waste disposal units, etc.

As a touch of Acotts class, Sir Douglas has suggested that the cutlery is to be silver and the dinner place settings in high quality china.

Again the corporate market will be a prime target. A time share week is then not only a holiday but a venue for meetings, client entertainment or even as an incentive for a company's high achievers.

Clearly an additional benefit is the opportunity to exchange for an equivalent site and time availability worldwide under the time share exchange scheme, to which Acotts Manor will be affiliated.

This project is, however, in its infancy. Our priorities are with stage one'.

Questions

In you capacity as Adrian Scott you have been in post four months and are required to report to the office of Sir Douglas Reed, chairman of Wates Estates, on the following:

1. The advice you would give to Clare Hepburn to:
   (a) build membership levels to those targeted for December 2001;
   (b) achieve a more balanced use of the club facilities.
   Then state how this advice, when implemented, would further improve the financial and market position of Crispins.
2. The steps that need to be taken to achieve an effective launch plan to promote the opening of Acotts Manor in July 2002.
3. The form and content of a feasibility study to assess the stage two development plans for Acotts Manor.

Case 2: Hamid Foods

Hamid Foods are manufactured by Hamid Food Industries Sdn Bhd (private limited company) in Malaysia. The company was formed in 1995 to produce a range of ready prepared meals for a local market that was becoming more aware of, and favourably disposed towards, convenience foods. All Hamid Foods then and today are of authentic Asian culture – but with some major differences:

1. They are prepacked ready prepared meals which require no refrigeration.
2. They contain no preservative or artificial colouring.
3. They are conveniently packed in 180 g sizes to serve one to two persons.
4. They require just three minutes 'boil in the bag' to be ready for serving.
5. They are presented, not in tins, but in a convenient packet with an airtight seal – offering a long shelf life to storekeepers and customers.

For many companies, new products involve the full effort and co-operation of a total management structure as well as a wide cross-section of the total work force. New products can involve large-scale investment and a higher than normal risk than many other marketing decisions. Hamid have been fortunate to provide a range of innovative food preparations that are truly 'new' to the consumer, providing a real alternative to foods which are more traditionally consumed in Asian markets.

To date consumer perception of, and rate of adoption for, Hamid Asian Foods has been most encouraging. Distribution within West and East Malaysia has achieved national coverage with retail sales made direct to supermarkets in major population centres.

Export markets have been pioneered with promising results and are targeted to outstrip the domestic market in volume terms within 12 months. Next on the agenda for international market expansion is Western Europe, with the UK from 2002 as a number one priority. The criteria for this development have yet to be fully appraised – but an experimental pilot launch programme will require answers to three basic questions:

1. Is there 'real' consumer need?
2. Do Hamid have the resources and capacity to sustain the development?
3. Is the designated market(s) large enough to generate profit?

These questions answered, the best method of market entry must be decided.

It is pertinent to observe that even today the range of Hamid Foods in existing markets has achieved just the early growth stage in the product life cycle, with competition only from close substitute convenience foods. Yet full product development costs have been recovered and Hamid enjoy a 25 per cent net profit to sales ratio with forecasts of 29 per cent for the next year end.

Sales promotion in domestic and export markets has been directed at creating point of sale product awareness, and to support the domestic-based and missionary sales force activity. To date there has been no above-the-line advertising, but considerable benefit has been gained from well-planned publicity.

It is expected that Hamid-appointed distributors must independently fund local promotion for the Hamid foods they carry in current domestic and overseas markets.

Pricing strategy has been based upon a simple cost-plus full absorption costing model and until real competition emerges net profit objectives will be achieved through this method of pricing. Within this cost-plus approach Hamid have aimed to skim the market on the rationale of product innovation, convenience and the unique selling points mentioned previously. Until the market becomes more elastic this policy will be retained. As new overseas markets are penetrated it is believed that this simple but effective means of pricing will be successful.

Hamid's ultimate goal, through marketing a wide range of foods, is to ensure long-term profitability, but for their existing product offering, the subsequent stages of the product life cycle must now be considered across the mix of markets both at home and overseas. Hamid believe the notion of market share acquisition is mostly irrelevant because it is difficult to define 'the market' – and yet the issue of product positioning must be addressed to fulfil the requirements of an international product strategy.

A real issue to be tackled is that of product presentation. To date all packaging carries the Hamid brand name, the name of the authentic Asian cuisine dish and instructions in Malay and English. The European market may present different conditions. Policy on standardization must be debated before market entry strategy is confirmed.

On the Malaysian domestic market front the sales team are driving hard to acquire stronger distribution. The main trade promotional platform is 90 days' credit for existing accounts and 'sale or return' for an experimental 30-day period for new accounts.

The perennial battle at the retail end is the pressure for profitable shelf space – shelf space among established competitors for other foods and foodstuffs. Supermarkets internationally will usually allocate the linear selling space to a 'hierarchy of brands'. Hamid have to fight hard to get prime selling space in stores.

Hamid are fully aware that the domestic Malaysian market may mature before overseas markets, but are aware also of the need to plan ahead for a time when:

1. Sales will increase but at reduced rates.
2. More product lines will be needed to support the brand base.
3. Prices may soften owing to direct competitive demand.
4. More tactical promotion will be needed.
5. Retail store buyers become more discriminating about the rationalization of the brand and the inventory kept.

Being proactive for these eventualities is of particular concern.

An underlying anxiety during this exciting but turbulent time for the company is that of maintaining the working capital balances of the company. The need for growth means that growth has to be effectively financed. Tensions already exist within the company to maintain an effective cash cycle to avoid the risk of Hamid running into a liquidity crisis as a result of their programme of rapid overseas expansion.

Appendix 1 Transcript of business mission. Discussion with Hamid Managing Director, Ali Harun

1. What business is the company in now?
   Reply
   'The processed food business. We manufacture ready meals in prepacked sealed containers for people who enjoy eating an authentic Asian dish but do not want the bother of preparing it.'
2. What business, then, is the company really in?

Reply

'I suppose we sell convenience foods to the time conscious.'

3. How well is the company doing?

   Reply

   'Very well – but I know we can do much better with the right guidance.'

4. What assumptions have you made about the future?

   Reply

   'Making assumptions is very dangerous – we may make false assumptions and run a high risk. Our main assumptions are to help us forecast sales and hence our budgets for the forthcoming period – but to date these have been exceeded. Either our assumptions have been good or our forecasts too modest.'

5. Where should the company be, say, in five years' time and why?

   Reply

   'Hamid should be known not only in the Far East but also in Western Europe. I can forsee growth into Hong Kong and Singapore, and growth within the European Union especially with the single currency. We simply have to export. The volume market in Malaysia is not large enough to sustain our projected levels of staffing and future capital investment in plant.'

6. What routes will you take to exploit these new countries further?

   Reply

   'This is where I need your help.'

7. What do you think will be the market reaction to your products?

   Reply

   'In Hong Kong it is difficult to say – unless we diversify into some Chinese dishes. In Singapore there is already an indigenous Malay community which is part of the cultural structure of the country – and Chinese people and Indian people living in Malaysia buy our product – so why not in Singapore? In the UK and Europe – well, I don't really know. This is something you can help to resolve. But I do believe that Europe with the proposed UK provision of the EU over the next few years represents probably the greatest potential.'

8. What level of corporate risk is Hamid prepared to take to exploit these markets over the next five years?

   Reply

   'I am not in a position right now to answer this question.'

9 What future direction should the company take?

   Reply

   'I believe it is important to look carefully at our corporate level objectives; then select the best product and market combinations to achieve them both at home and overseas.'

10. What resources will be needed to achieve the intended direction over the next five years?

    Reply

    'Well, labour is not a problem; there is no real shortage. We will need better to formalize our marketing and sales structure to make our company more efficient. Our factory is freehold with room to expand to increase output considerably. I would estimate currently that we are operating at 35 per cent of our production capacity. We have considerably geared up for growth.'

11. What measures will you take to check progress towards company goals for the next five years?

    Reply

    'Again, our planning system is based now on budgetary control. I am sure that this must change, but we again need guidance on how to prepare for such changes.

There will be a number of actions that need to be taken well before five years and I shall be looking forward to receiving your proposals.'

Appendix 2   Hamid export product mix. Statement by Ali Harun, Managing Director

We define our product lines technically as 'retort pouch' food. Using this technology our production system can produce almost any type of food that can traditionally be marketed through cans, paper packs, vacuum packs, plastic film packs and so on. Our product range features authentic Asian food, mainly Malay and Indian cuisine.

Retort pouch food manufacturing is a process of sterilization whereby heat is applied under pressure at a certain temperature and time depending upon the food being processed. Through the food processing system bacteria are destroyed, making the food safe for the consumer up to a period of two years. The opportunities for using this food processing method appear limitless – we are now experimenting with vegetables at the more expensive end of the range, like asparagus.

On the home market sales emphasis is upon traditional Malay cuisine – but the narrow product mix sold overseas has been limited until 2000 to chicken curry, beef curry, mutton korma, prawn curry, beef korma and squid curry, the emphasis being upon Indian dishes.

We have had demand from our export markets for sweet and sour prawns, sweet and sour chicken and for our traditional satay sauce.

The pool of potential product ideas is vast, but as yet we can sell all we are producing. Things will change, so we need an effective means by which we can select the best new product line additions for our expanding overseas markets.

In terms of feasibility, our experimental technical research department have only to perfect the 'cooking process' before we can add to the product range. Development time and costs to add a new product line are very modest compared to those in a traditional manufacturing industry.

We have conducted no market research in the history of the organization – we cannot tell you about market characteristics, size or trends. We watch our competitors in the food canning industry like hawks, though. Our overseas sales have occurred by luck and sound judgement, but lack what others may call sophisticated planning.

Our sales team merely visit potential distributors, agree the terms of the sales contract, set up the system of payment by letter of credit, and we ship. Initially, we tried air freight, but volumes are such that we depend upon containerized transport by road and sea.

I believe it may not be so straightforward for UK market entry. I am convinced that our product lines will sell – but the real question we need to answer is to whom, to get rapid market penetration. Certainly package modifications and other marketing areas need to be explored as part of your brief.

Appendix 3

FAX
From: KNIGHT, LANDERS & MEADOWS
To: ALI HARUN, HAMID MANAGING DIRECTOR

INITIAL THOUGHTS ON UK MARKET ENTRY

1. We need a clear understanding of the level of corporate priority that will be given to the UK and the wider European Union market, so that the scale of the operation can be best determined.
2. We appreciate that staffing resources do not impose a constraint, but will need a clear understanding about the level of finance required for the venture and to be certain that financial constraints will not restrict market penetration and subsequent take off.
3. We are confident to be able to provide market profits, forecasts, identification of target markets and to obtain a measure for the nature of competition. We must answer three questions in depth:

   (a) Who are the buyers?
   (b) Where are they located?
   (c) What motives will induce purchase?

4. This achieved, we will again need to assess the company position with reference to time and ability to exploit the market and consider the level of associated risk involved.
5. It will then be appropriate to revise the company's objectives in the light of more facts about the market and a better knowledge base from which to work.
6. The above pointers will lead to the identification of a number of different market entry options.
7. These options must be assessed across a number of criteria which we must jointly discuss, agree and evaluate.
8. Then we can select and justify the best market entry option for the country and set up the marketing mix and sales plans within a framework of your existing budgetary control system.
9. From experience we have found that market entry plans become frustrated all too often from inadequate communication and a poor flow of information. We must ensure that an information system is in place to our specifications before attacking the UK market.

FAX
From: KNIGHT, LANDERS & MEADOWS
To: ALI HARUN, HAMID MANAGING DIRECTOR

Having consulted our files and spoken to many partners, an interesting scenario has emerged.

During the period 1996–2000 we were retained by a company whose main brand was and is today a household name in the market for Asian pickles, curries and relishes. While the main selling product remains mango chutney, the range is quite extensive and includes lime pickle, hot chilli chutney, Madras curry sauce, chilli and garlic sauce, curry relishes, and so on – all sold through traditional wholesale grocery channels and larger supermarket groups. The company bought a canning plant in London's Docklands area and we were responsible for test marketing a new range of canned curries over six months, through to a National roll out for five product lines.

A year later this was followed successfully with the launch of a range of canned curry powders in three strengths – mild, hot and extra mild. In 1999–2000 they diversified into accelerated freeze dried foods, sold in packets from refrigerated display units; the range includes Chinese foods.

One option for us to consider, clearly among others, to achieve rapid market penetration is to open discussions with our former clients!

FAX
From: KNIGHT, LANDERS & MEADOWS
To: ALI HARUN, HAMID MANAGING DIRECTOR

THE PRICING ISSUE

With growing concern over the company's liquidity position, it is not only the price level which is important but effective credit control and the need also to guard against the vagaries of fluctuating exchange rates, which can convert a profitable consignment into a loss. The current uncertainty with regards to whether or not the UK will eventually join the single Euro currency is also a problem, expecially as the Danes have now voted not to join the single currency in their recent referendum.

With a market leadership position in Malaysia and an assumed positive response from the UK market, which follows other international experience, then it may be appropriate to take a close look at the cost components of meeting a UK order – time to reflect before the price level is set for the first time.

The following checklist will help to avoid the more serious errors and omissions in calculating the profitability of exports:

1. The ex-works price, i.e. the direct cost of manufacture, plus:
   - an allocation of company overheads that pertain to export markets
   - an allocation of total export overheads, e.g. part of export administraiton
   - an allocation of overheads specific to the UK e.g. selling and production costs
   - any relevant agency commission
   - export packing costs
   - an appropriate profit margin.

2. If an fob price is quoted, then the ex-works price is to be supplemented by:

   (a) Transport and insurance to docks/airport
   (b) Handling and other fob charges.

3. If a cif price is quoted, then to the fob price must be added:

   (a) Transport to country of destination
   (b) Insurance in transit.

4. To determine the local market price, additional costs will be incurred:

   (a) Landing charges
   (b) Import duty
   (c) Internal transportation, storage and handling charges
   (d) Distributor mark-ups
   (e) Local turnover taxes.

   Now this will depend upon how far down the channel the company wishes to proceed to achieve market penetration, but additional costs also need to be viewed in perspective.

5. Increased financing costs resulting from delays in transit and payment that are inseparable from even the normal export transaction, increased costs that will arise from the need to finance distributors with inventory, insurances of credit risks, forward exchange cover and a myriad of additional, often unseen, expenses.

These costs will vary from market to market. The common practice of marking up a fixed percentage on cost usually ends up with a disappointing return, especially where logistics have a significant contribution to maintain customer service levels.

It is important to forecast market response, but as yet this is at best a 'guesstimate'. The speed with which orders are filled, the ability to meet emergency orders, the options offered on minimum order sizes, all have cost implications – as does the company's policy on returned goods.

Appendix 4

Home and export markets: product range average selling prices (in M$ equivalents); January 2001

	Malaysia	Australia	Japan	USA	Middle East
Beef meals	2.50	8.35	12.00	6.75	8.00
Lamb/mutton meals	2.80	8.50	14.00	7.75	12.00
Chicken meals	2.35	8.35	11.50	7.25	10.00
Prawn meals	3.50	14.50	20.00	10.00	12.00

No pork dishes – Hamid is a Muslim company
M$ = Malaysian ringitt (dollars)
£1 = M$4.8

Appendix 5

Key financial data (calendar year end): sales revenue M$ (millions)

	1995	1996	1997	1998	1999	2000	2001
Malaysia	0.3	1.1	1.9	2.7	3.8	5.3	5.6
Australia	–	–	–	–	0.2	1.0	1.9
Japan	–	–	–	0.4	1.2	2.5	3.6
USA	–	–	–	–	–	1.3	2.9
Middle East	–	–	–	–	–	0.2	0.5
Total M$ (m)	0.3	1.1	1.9	3.1	5.2	10.3	14.5

M$ Malaysian ringitt (dollars)
£1 = M$4.8

Home and export net profit contribution before tax (calendar year end; per cent)

	1995	1996	1997	1998	1999	2000	2001
Malaysia	(4)	9	19	22	20	12	12
Australia	–	–	–	–	(4)	4	5
Japan	–	–	–	3	5	6	7
USA	–	–	–	–	–	3	4
Middle East	–	–	–	–	–	0	1
Total net profit to sales (%)	(4)	9	19	25	21	25	29

Combined domestic and export business performance (calendar year end)

	1995	1996	1997	1998	1999	2000	2001
Stockturn (number of times)	N/A	6	5	6	6	8	8
Debtors collection period (days)	90	95	97	109	120	128	120
Current ratio	1.7 : 1	3.1 : 1	3.1 : 1	2.3 : 1	1.9 : 1	1.6 : 1	2 : 1
Number of months in overdraft (negative cash flow balance)	12	8	6	5	6	7	5

Appendix 6

Mr Colin Knight
Knight, Landers & Meadows
City Road
London, EC1

17 January 2002

Dear Mr Knight,
Following our recent discussion in Kuala Lumpur, we wish to confirm your appointment on the terms agreed in your initial proposal: that your company would be retained on a one-year contract to assist in the corporate development of our organization to prepare for market exploitation in Western Europe but with special emphasis on the United Kingdom.

We are particularly interested in the most cost-effective method of market entry and need to be fully appraised of the obstacles involved.

Yours sincerely,

Ali Harun,
Managing Director,
Hamid Foods Sdn Bhd

Questions

In your capacity as Colin Knight you have had time to prepare formal proposals for Ali Harun, managing director of Hamid Foods Sdn Bhd.

Your report should be confined to the UK market only and should meet the following specific requests from Ali Harun:

1. Specify the information requirements and means of data collection that are considered appropriate to assist with the UK market entry programme.
2. (i) Identify the options you consider open to enable Hamid Foods to secure UK market entry
   (ii) Propose criteria by which these options should be evaluated
   (iii) Select and justify one method for UK market entry in accordance with the selected criteria in part (b) above.
3. Explain the marketing and financial implications of the proposed method of UK market entry.

Glossary of Key Terms

A

Active exporting   A positive commitment of a company to its exporting activities.

Absolute advantage   The relative absolute cost differences between two countries which serve to explain the pattern of trade between these countries.

Administered vertical marketing   A channel where one member acts as leader and co-ordinator for two or more traditional levels of the marketing channel.

Adoption   The stages which a customer passes through en route to accepting and purchasing a new product.

AIDA model   An early model of how advertising works based on the notion that customers pass through four stages from awareness through interest and desire to action.

Always-a-share customers   Customers who have low switching costs and do not value long-term relationships with suppliers, making them more suited to transaction marketing.

ATR model   A 'weak advertising' model which suggests that customers pass through awareness, trial and reinforcement.

Automatic interaction detection (AID) A statistical technique whereby markets can be split successively for segmentation purposes.

B

BCG growth/share matrix   A portfolio planning model based on analysing the relative market share and market growth rates for a company's products and/or Strategic Business Units.

Below-the-line promotion   Any promotion which does not involve paid-for media channels.

Black box models   Relatively simple models of buyer behaviour which consider only inputs and outputs and do not purport to explain what goes on in the buyer's mind.

Brand barometers   A market research approach which provides quarterly information on brand performance and marketing in specified product categories.

Brand manager   A manager who is allocated responsibility for the overall marketing plan and results for a given brand or set of brands.

Break-even point   The point at which total revenue from the sale of a product exactly matches its total costs.

Break-even quantity   The quantity or volume of production of a product at which the break-even point is reached.

Buying centre   Another term for the decision making unit (see above).

Buy classes   The class or type of purchasing decision in organizational buying, there being three of these straight re-buys, modified re-buys and new task purchases

Buy phases   The different phases or stages which the organizational buyer may pass through during the purchasing process.

Business-to-business marketing Marketing which involves exchange relationships between two or more business customers and suppliers.

C

Call frequency   The number of times that any individual customer is visited by a sales person over a given period.

Casual exporting   A company exporting

in response to largely unsolicited foreign orders.

Category management   Organising marketing activities based on the different categories of products marketed by the company.

Category team   Group of people responsible for a particular category of products.

Closing   That point in the selling process where the sales person attempts to secure the order.

Cluster analysis   A range of statistical methods whereby data can be analysed to group customers into market segments.

Concentrated marketing   Targeting only one segment of the market.

Concept testing   The process of testing customer responses to a proposed new product concept.

Consumer panels   A group of consumers who provide continuous information for market research purposes.

Consumerism   A movement involved in trying to protect consumers from unscrupulous business practices.

Contribution   The amount contributed to covering fixed costs arrived at by deducting the variable costs from the price charged for a product.

Control parameters   Those elements which the control system is intended to measure and evaluate, for example profits, sales and market share.

Core competencies   The core skills and strengths which underpin a company's overall competitive advantage.

Corporate vertical marketing   A channel where one member owns two or more traditional levels of the marketing channel.

Cost-plus pricing   A pricing method based on adding a profit margin or mark-up to the average costs of a product.

Cross elasticity of demand   A measure for interpreting the price relationship between different products.

Customer tracking   The ongoing and systematic measurement and evaluation of customer feedback and attitudes.

D

Database   A store of information held by a company about its customers' markets and competitors.

Datacapture   The process of acquiring information to input to the database.

Datamining   The analysis of the database in an attempt to find important patterns of cause and effect and related variables.

Data warehousing   The transfer of data from different parts of the organization into one central database.

Decision making unit (DMU)   The group of people involved in the decision making process in organizational purchasing.

Decision Support System (DSS):   That part of the marketing information system which is concerned with translating data into information for decision making.

Decoding   Translating the signs and signals of a message from a sender so these signals make sense to the receiver.

Delphi forecasting   A technique of forecasting using a system of questionnaire based on structured semi-autonomous interaction.

Demand schedule   A summary relating different prices to the quantities demanded at each of these prices.

Depth interview   Structured or semi-structured interviews with individual respondents designed to uncover factors underpinning buyer behaviour and choice.

Derived demand   A situation where demand for a product is itself a function of demand for another product.

Differentiated marketing   Targeting several market segments using a different marketing mix for each.

Diffusion   The speed and extent of take-up of a new product through a market.

Diffusion index   An index based on a combination of key economic indicators to predict future movements in an economy.

Direct-response television (DRTV)   Television promotions designed to encourage the viewer to respond directly to the company promotion, e.g. by placing a telephone order.

Distinctive competence   Those strengths in an organization which enable it to perform marketing activities in certain areas particularly well compared to its competitors.

E

Early adopters   Those people in a market who purchase new products immediately after the innovators.

Econometric models   Complex models which seek to establish relationships between key economic variables.

Economic value pricing (EVC)   A technique of value-based pricing based on detailed assessments of the value in use of a product to a customer.

Efficiency control   The process of ensuring that the various elements and sub-elements of the marketing mix are being utilised as efficiently as possible.

Electronic data interchange (EDI) Computer-based systems for exchanging information electronically between customers and suppliers.

Encoding   Translating a message by the sender into a set of signs and signals which the receiver will understand.

Enhanced customer response (ECR)   The application of logistics management concepts such as JIT and supply chain management to the retail sector.

Environmental scanning   The process of identifying, monitoring and forecasting key environmental forces and factors which will affect marketing plans.

Ethnocentric orientation   A company which is characterized by concentrating primarily on its home markets.

Ex-11 technique   A development of spectral analysis which only separates out season and cyclical trends, fitting a time series to the remainder.

Exclusive distribution   A strategy for distribution based on stocking products through one or two specially selected distributors only.

Experience curve effect   The reduction in average unit costs as a result of increases in cumulative production.

Exponential smoothing   A group of techniques of sales forecasting which involves attaching greater weight to more recent information in the sales forecast.

Extranet   Computer-based systems for exchanging information electronically between all members of the supply chain.

F

Fixed costs   Costs which do not vary with the level of output.

Focus groups   A market research technique involving a trainer-moderator guiding a group of selected respondents through a semi-structured interview to investigate buyer behaviour and attitudes.

Franchises   A type of vertical marketing system based on one channel member licensing other channel members to market a product or service in a particular way.

Functional structure   Organizing marketing activities around the different functions of marketing, for example market research and advertising.

Futures research   A group of techniques designed to explore possible future needs and wants with a view to developing new or modified products and brands.

G

Gap analysis   A technique which compares future likely company performance against desired performance outcomes in order to identify any gaps.

Gatekeepers   Individuals and/or functions in an organization which control flows of information and/or access into and through the organization.

Geocentric orientation   A company which is characterized by a global approach to its marketing with high degrees of standardization.

Geodemographic segmentation   A variety of approaches to segmenting markets using a combination of geographic and demographic factors, such as ACORN and MOSAIC.

Going-rate pricing   An approach to pricing based on the prices set by competitors in the industry.

H

Hierarchy of effects model   An AIDA type model of how advertising works, which posits a similar sequence of stages but involving awareness, knowledge, liking, preference, conviction and purchase.

Historical analogy Forecasting future sales

patterns of a new product by comparing historical sales of similar past product.

Horizontal linkages   Linkages between primary and secondary activities in a company's value chain.

I

Innovator   A person in a market who is amongst the first to purchase a new product.

Input/output models   A system of forecasting based on analysing inputs and outputs of product materials through the different parts of an economy.

Interconglomerate structure   A type of structure for international marketing which emphasizes centralised control and planning of the financial but not marketing elements of the business.

Internal marketing   The application of marketing concepts and techniques to the internal staff of a company.

Intensive distribution   A strategy for distribution based on having products stocked in as many outlets as possible.

Internal marketing   The application of marketing concepts and techniques to internal customers within an organization.

Interstitial strategy   An innovation strategy based on developing new products to fit gaps in the market.

Intra-firm environment   The other functional areas within the organization with which the marketing department must interact and work with to develop and implement effective marketing strategies.

J

Just in time (JIT)   A purchasing and manufacturing system designed to deliver inputs to the production or distribution site only at the rate and time it is needed.

Just-In-Time (JIT)   An approach to purchasing and supply which is based on having raw materials and components delivered as near to the time of actual usage as possible.

Journey planning   The process of planning sales activities with regard to aspects such as travel time and customer call patterns so as to maximize the return from the salesperson's time.

K

Key account   A customer of strategic importance to a supplier.

Key factors for success   Those factors in a market which determine competitive success or failure in that market.

L

Law of diminishing Returns   The notion that increased expenditure in any given area will give rise to ever decreasing returns in terms of revenue.

Lean manufacturing   An approach to planning manufacturing processes such that minimum stocks of materials and work in progress are required.

Lifestyle segmentation   An approach to segmentation based on identifying characteristic modes and patterns of living affecting purchasing processes.

Lifecycle/stage segmentation   A variety of approaches to segmenting markets based on the notion of consumers passing through a series of distinct phases or stages in their lives.

Line depth   The number of products in a company's product line, the more products, the deeper the line.

Line width   The number of different product lines offered by a company.

Logistics   A systems approach to managing the whole of a distribution network, including channels and physical flows, so as to optimize the effectiveness of this.

Lost-for-good customers   Customers who have high switching costs and longer-term horizons making them suitable for relationship marketing.

M

Macro-environment   The broader environmental factors which lie outside the organizational boundaries and over which the marketer has little or no control, e.g. socio-cultural factors, political/legal factors.

Macropyramid structure   A type of structure for international marketing which is characterised by essentially central decision making and planning.

Management Information System (MIS): The overarching system of information gathering and analysis throughout an organisation of which the MkIS is a sub-system.

Marginal or direct-cost pricing The practice of pricing products such as to ensure that variable costs are covered and some contribution to fixed costs is made.

Marketing audit A systematic internal and external environmental review of a company's marketing performance for a given period of time.

Market challengers Companies which are actively seeking to become the market leader in the industry.

Market followers Companies in an industry which do not wish to challenge for market leadership and whose strategies are primarily shaped by the market leader.

Market leader The company in a market with the strongest competitive market position with regard to market share.

Market nichers Companies in an industry which focus their efforts on serving specialist parts/small segments of the overall market.

Market segments The breakdown of the total market for a product or service into sub-markets whereby each sub-market is distinguished by having its own particular needs and wants.

Marketing assets Company strengths which can be specifically used to advantage in the market place

Marketing audit A systematic critical and impartial review and appraisal of a company's total marketing operations, including objectives, strategies, organization, and activities.

Marketing Information System (MkIS): A system comprised of people, equipment and procedures to gather, sort, analyse, evaluate, and distribute information for marketing decision making.

Marketing management A management function designed to satisfy customer needs through the process of analysis, planning, implementation and control.

Marketing orientation A business orientation which focuses company efforts on the identifying and satisfying customer needs.

Materials management Those elements which facilitate the flow of goods and raw materials into and through an organization.

Matrix structures Organizing marketing activities using a combination of marketing organization structures, such as a combination of products and markets.

Maverick strategy An innovation strategy which reduces the size of the market for the existing technology.

Micro-environment Environmental factors which lie outside the organizational boundaries but over which the marketer may have some degree of control, e.g. competitors, suppliers, distributors.

Mission statement A general statement defining the nature of the business and its overall purpose.

Moving averages A statistical technique for forecasting sales based on of the arithmetic average of a number of previous consecutive points in a time series.

Multi-channel systems The use of a variety of different channel arrangements by a company in order to reach their target customers.

Multi-factor portfolio matrices Strategic planning tools which utilize multiple factors in order to assess the strategic position of Strategic Business Units and products.

Multi-national company Companies which do not distinguish between domestic and global marketing opportunities and have a single management strategy that guides their operating companies throughout the world.

Multivariate models Complex models of buyer behaviour which seek to model and explain how the different factors affecting buyer behaviour are interrelated.

Muting Turning the sound off on the television during the advertisement slots.

N

New task One of the categories of buy classes (see above) where the company is buying a product or service for the first time.

New-to-world products Innovations that

perform an entirely new function and therefore, potentially at least, create entirely new markets.

Noise Anything between the sender and the receiver of target messages which interferes and/or distorts message reception and interpretation.

O

Objective and task An approach to setting marketing budgets by determining the costs of the tasks required to be achieved in the marketing plan.

Off-the-peg research Normally syndicated research data which the marketer can purchase from a commercial marketing research company.

P

Panel consensus The use of panels of experts to forecast the future.

Physical distribution Elements of a logistics system which facilitate the flow of materials and products from the company to other members of the supply chain.

Physical evidence An additional marketing mix element for services encompassing the more tangible aspects of the service product offering, such as buildings, facilities, staff appearance.

Physical evidence An additional marketing mix element found in the marketing of service products which encompasses the more tangible aspects of a service product offering thereby enabling the customer to gauge the potential quality of the service.

Point of Sale (POS) Promotional and particularly merchandizing techniques which are designed to encourage sales at the point of purchase.

Price elasticity of demand A measure of the magnitude of the responsiveness or sensitivity of the quantity demanded of a product to a given change in some demand determinant, such as price, income, prices of other products, etc.

Primary activities Those value chain activities associated with the input, throughput and output of goods and services in the organization.

Primary data Data which is collected for the first time for the specific purpose of a particular market research study.

Process An additional marketing mix element found in the marketing of service products which encompasses the systems and procedures relating to how the service is provided to customers.

Process An additional marketing mix element for services encompassing the systems by which the service is provided.

Product-based structure Organizing marketing activities around the different product groups in the company.

Product item An individual product entity in the company's product portfolio which normally has a separate designation in the company's sales list.

Product lifecycle The concept which proposes that products pass through a series of stages in their lives: introduction, growth, maturity, and decline.

Product line A collection of products in a company that are closely related in some way to one another.

Product mix The sum total of individual product items and product lines which the company markets.

Product orientation A business orientation which focuses company efforts on product quality and engineering.

Production orientation A business orientation which focuses company efforts on the production of goods or services.

Profit control The evaluation of the profitability of different marketing entities, for example products, customer groups and territories.

Profit Impact of Marketing Strategies (PIMS) An empirical study conducted by the Strategic Planning Institute which seeks to identify and isolate the key factors underpinning profitability and strategic success in an industry.

Polycentric orientation A company which is characterized by planning its international marketing around each host country with little central control and standardization.

Promotional mix The collection of promotional tools which the marketer combines in any given promotional campaign.

Prospecting The process whereby the sales person identifies potential new customers and business.

Psychographics Another term for lifestyle segmentation (see above).

Q

Qualitative research Research which is aimed at uncovering qualitative aspects of consumer behaviour including, for example, perception, attitudes and motives.

Quality function deployment Systems for translating customer requirements into technical requirements at early stages of the product development process.

R

Regiocentric orientation A company which is characterized by planning on the basis of specific regions, for example geographical, political, economic.

Regression analysis A mathematical technique for assessing the degree of relationship between variables.

Relationship marketing An approach to marketing based upon creating and maintaining mutually satisfying exchange relationships between an organization and its customers.

Relationship marketing An approach to marketing based on developing long-term customer relationships through mutual exchange and trust.

Relevance trees A technique for systematically exploring all the possible alternative routes to achieving a given stated technological objective.

Research brief A document normally agreed between a company and its market research agency which outlines the objectives, scope, timescale, and costs of any proposed research.

S

Sales negotiation An attempt by two or more parties to vary selling terms in order to reach an agreement.

Sales orientation A business orientation which focuses company efforts on the disposal of stock through aggressive sales and promotion.

Sales promotion A collection of promotional techniques designed to encourage a short-term and immediate response by customers.

Sales quota The volume and/or value of sales which a sales person is required to achieve over a given period of time.

Sales response function An approach to setting marketing budgets by equating marginal sales return with marginal marketing expenditure.

Scenario writing A technique of helping to envisage likely possible future events.

Screening Those stages in the new product development process concerned to assess ideas with a view to dropping or retaining them.

Secondary data Data which already exists but was collected in the first instance for another purpose and by another party.

Selective distribution A strategy for distribution based on selecting a limited number of outlets in which products will be stocked.

Self-liquidating offer A promotional campaign which is designed to pay for itself through the sale of a special promotional product.

Self reference criterion The tendency to use one's own cultural experience and values when developing and implementing marketing plans in another country.

Service product An intangible product involving a deed, a performance or an effort that cannot be physically possessed

Silent languages Those aspects of communication in a culture other than written and oral language.

Spectral analyis A complex mathematical technique for decomposing sales patterns into their constituent sine wave forms.

SPIN model An approach to selling developed by the Huthwaite Research Group based on questioning and listening techniques.

Strategic business unit A part of a business which has its own customers and competitors and in theory can be operated as a separate individual business unit with its own resources, identifiable costs and revenues and management team.

Strategic control The evaluation and

control of the strategic marketing planning process.

Strategic fit   The matching of organizational strengths and weaknesses to environmental opportunities and threats.

Strategic group analysis   A method of identifying key competitors based on their degree of similarity with regard to key strategic characteristics.

Superordinate goals   The agreement and acceptance of an overriding common goal by the different members of a channel.

Supply chain management   The planning and management of the whole of a supply chain with a view to achieving the most effective and efficient system.

Support activities   Those value chain activities which facilitate primary activities

Switching costs   The costs to a customer associated with switching to another supplier.

T

Targeting   The selection of specific market segments by a company.

Target marketing   A three-step process involving identification of market segments, selection of target segments and development of positioning strategies.

Telesales   The selling part of telephone marketing.

Tide indicators   The use of observations in the sales of one product to forecast sales of another product which is closely related.

Total relationship marketing (TRM)   A term used to denote a company-wide approach to relationship management based on continuously improving all internal and external relationships in a company.

Transaction marketing   An approach to marketing based on the seller offering immediately attractive combinations of product, price and technical support in order to generate an individual sale.

Trend projection   A curve-fitting technique of sales forecasting which uses past trends to predict future sales.

U

Umbrella structure   A type of structure for international marketing which has centralized objectives but localised decision making.

Undifferentiated marketing   Often referred to as 'mass marketing', targeting the whole of the market using one marketing mix strategy.

Unique selling point (USP)   An aspect of a product, service or company which differentiates it from competitors and therefore may be used as a point of leverage in advertising and promotion.

Unique selling propositions (USP)   Those aspects of a company's product or service offerings that are unique amongst competing brands.

V

Value-based pricing   An approach to pricing based on assessing the perceived value of the product to a customer.

Value chain analysis   A technique for identifying potential competitive advantages by looking at the various value activities which the organization performs.

Variable costs   Costs which are more or less directly related to the volume of production or sales.

Variable mark up pricing   A variation of cost-plus pricing where the profit margin or mark up added to average costs is flexible.

Vertical linkages   Linkages in the value chain of an organization with its suppliers and distributors.

Vertical marketing systems   A marketing channel where the channel members acknowledge and desire interdependence.

Visionary forecasts   Subjective techniques of forecasting based on personal opinion and judgements.

Z

Zapping   Changing television channels using the remote control in order to avoid the advertising slots

Zero defects   Quality control and delivery systems designed to deliver supplies to customers which are totally free of defects.

Zipping   Fast-forwarding a video recording in order to bypass the advertising on the recording.

Index

535